GREAT BOOKS OF THE WESTERN WORLD

W9-AZI-357

GREAT BOOKS
OF THE WESTERN WORLD

ROBERT MAYNARD HUTCHINS, *EDITOR IN CHIEF*

31.

DESCARTES

SPINOZA

Rules for the Direction of the Mind
Discourse on the Method
Meditations on First Philosophy
Objections against the Meditations and Replies
The Geometry

BY RENÉ DESCARTES

Ethics

BY BENEDICT DE SPINOZA

WILLIAM BENTON, *Publisher*

ENCYCLOPÆDIA BRITANNICA, INC.

CHICAGO · LONDON · TORONTO · GENEVA · SYDNEY · TOKYO · MANILA

RULES FOR THE DIRECTION OF THE MIND, DISCOURSE ON THE METHOD, MEDITATIONS
ON FIRST PHILOSOPHY AND OBJECTIONS AGAINST THE MEDITATIONS AND REPLIES,
ARE REPRINTED FROM THE PHILOSOPHICAL WORKS OF DESCARTES,
RENDERED INTO ENGLISH BY ELIZABETH S. HALDANE AND G. R. T. ROSS,
BY ARRANGEMENT WITH CAMBRIDGE UNIVERSITY PRESS.

THE GEOMETRY OF RENÉ DESCARTES, TRANSLATED BY DAVID EUGENE SMITH AND
MARCIA L. LATHAM, IS REPRINTED BY ARRANGEMENT WITH THE OPEN COURT PUBLISHING
COMPANY. COPYRIGHT 1925 BY THE OPEN COURT PUBLISHING COMPANY.

THE ETHICS OF SPINOZA, TRANSLATED BY W. H. WHITE AND REVISED BY
A. H. STIRLING, IS REPRINTED BY ARRANGEMENT WITH OXFORD UNIVERSITY PRESS.

THE UNIVERSITY OF CHICAGO

The Great Books
is published with the editorial advice of the faculties
of The University of Chicago

GENERAL CONTENTS

DESCARTES

BIOGRAPHICAL NOTE
RENÉ DESCARTES, 1596–1650

DESCARTES by birth belonged to the lesser nobility; both of his parents came from high legal families. He was born at La Haye, in Touraine, on March 31, 1596. Although a younger son, he derived an income, sufficient to make him independent throughout his life, from the property left him by his mother.

While still a boy Descartes was sent to the Jesuit School at La Flèche, founded by Henry IV and "one of the most celebrated schools in Europe." He appears to have been at La Flèche from 1606 to 1615, following the Jesuit program of studies which aimed at reconciling the classical learning of the Renaissance with the scholastic philosophy of the Middle Ages. Suffering from poor health, he was entrusted to the special care of Father Dinet, afterwards the confessor to Louis XIII and Louis XIV. He was excused from morning duties and allowed to stay in bed, a habit he retained to the end of his life. After completing the full curriculum of languages and humane letters, logic, ethics, mathematics, physics, and metaphysics, Descartes later declared, "I found myself embarrassed with so many doubts and errors, that it seemed to me that the effort to instruct myself had no effect other than the increasing discovery of my own ignorance." Mathematics alone appeared to be an exception "because of the certainty of its demonstrations and the evidence of its reasoning." He completed his education at the University of Poitiers, where he took his degree in law, November 10, 1616.

Descartes spent the remainder of his youth in travelling, "resolved no longer to seek any other science than the knowledge of myself, or of the great book of the world." Like many young Frenchmen of the time, he enlisted as a gentleman volunteer in the army of Prince Maurice of Nassau in Holland. He was still interested in mathematics, and at Breda became a friend of Isaac Beeckman, mathematician and rector of the college at Dort. Beeckman, after their meeting, noted in his diary, "Mathematical physicists are scarce, and I myself had never had any conversation on that topic with anybody but him." Their discussions, according to Descartes, turned his mind to purely theoretical problems, and when he left Holland early in 1619 to seek more active military service in Germany, he had already completed an *Essay on Algebra* and a *Compendium on Music*, dedicated to his friend.

Descartes dated his life as a philosopher from 1619. Early in that year, after his study of algebra and geometry had yielded what he considered an "entirely new science," he wrote to his Dutch friend: "My project is unbelievably ambitious, but I cannot help feeling that I am sighting I know not what light in the chaos of present-day geometry, and I trust that it will help me in dispelling that most opaque darkness." In the fall, after the army had gone into winter quarters, he retired to a village near Ulm on the Danube to devote himself to study and speculation. "On November 10, 1619," he wrote, "when I was filled with enthusiasm, I discovered the foundations of the wonderful science." The discovery was followed by a series of three dreams which left Descartes the impression that "the Spirit of Truth had opened to him the treasures of all the sciences."

The experience of November 10 did not immediately alter his way of life. Some time previously he had remarked, "As comedians put on a mask to hide their timidity, so I go forward masked preparing to mount the stage of the world, which up to now I have known only as a spectator"; and for the next nine years he continued to live as a soldier and a "gentilhomme" while preparing to apply his newly discovered method to all knowledge. In 1622 he was back in France, frequenting the society of the leading scientists and philosophers. Through his friends and correspondence he was already known and esteemed for his scientific abilities, although he had not as yet published anything. He appears to have been reluctant to make his work public until his researches in physics promised to yield practical results, and he felt he could no longer "keep them concealed without greatly sinning against the law which obliges us to procure, as far as in us lies, the general good of all mankind." At the same time he had occasion to discuss his research with Cardinal Bérulle, who was so impressed that he declared

Descartes was morally obliged to make his thought known to the world. Feeling that he could not find in Paris the leisure and quiet he needed for writing, Descartes retired to Holland.

From 1629 until 1649 Descartes lived in Holland, leaving only for five short visits, three to France, one to England, and another to Denmark. He disliked dwelling for long in the same place and during that time changed his residence twenty-four times, concerned only, it would appear, to be in the neighborhood of a university and a Catholic church. Most of his more important works were written and published in Holland. He wrote the *Rules for the Direction of the Mind* during the first year, and by 1633 had all but completed his *Treatise on the World*, when the condemnation of Galileo caused him to abandon all thought of publishing it. In 1637 he brought out the *Discourse on Method* with the three "Essays" accompanying it, the *Dioptric, Meteors*, and *Geometry*. Through Mersenne, who acted as his personal secretary in Paris, he circulated a manuscript of his *Meditations* and obtained objections to its arguments; the work was published with his answers to the objections in 1641.

Descartes' philosophy became a source of controversy in Holland even before the appearance of his works, as a result of the teaching of his friends in the universities. Cartesianism was attacked as subversive of religion, and at one time Descartes was summoned before the magistrates of Utrecht, although the matter went no further because of the intervention of influential friends.

Among his friends and admirers was Princess Elizabeth, daughter of Emperor Frederick V, then in exile in Holland. Although she was only nineteen when the *Discourse* appeared, she was interested in philosophical discussion, and Descartes, in dedicating the *Principles of Philosophy* (1644) to her, declared that hers was "the only mind, as far as my experience goes, to which both metaphysics and mathematics are easy." Queen Christina of Sweden also became interested in the "new philosophy," and, through the French Ambassador, Descartes carried on a correspondence with her on ethical subjects, part of which was reworked and published as the *Treatise on the Passions of the Soul* (1649). Late in 1649 she persuaded Descartes to go to the Swedish court. He was charged with the task of drawing up a statute for a proposed academy of science and teaching philosophy to the Queen. The lessons in philosophy were scheduled to be given three times a week at five in the morning. Descartes contracted an inflammation of the lungs and died after a very brief illness, February 11, 1650.

CONTENTS

RULES
FOR THE DIRECTION OF
THE MIND

RULE I

The end of study should be to direct the mind towards the enunciation of sound and correct judgments on all matters that come before it.

WHENEVER men notice some similarity between two things, they are wont to ascribe to each, even in those respects in which the two differ, what they have found to be true of the other. Thus they erroneously compare the sciences, which entirely consist in the cognitive exercise of the mind, with the arts, which depend upon an exercise and disposition of the body. They see that not all the arts can be acquired by the same man, but that he who restricts himself to one, most readily becomes the best executant, since it is not so easy for the same hand to adapt itself both to agricultural operations and to harp-playing, or to the performance of several such tasks as to one alone. Hence they have held the same to be true of the sciences also, and distinguishing them from one another according to their subject matter, they have imagined that they ought to be studied separately, each in isolation from all the rest. But this is certainly wrong. For since the sciences taken all together are identical with human wisdom, which always remains one and the same, however applied to different subjects, and suffers no more differentiation proceeding from them than the light of the sun experiences from the variety of the things which it illumines, there is no need for minds to be confined at all within limits; for neither does the knowing of one truth have an effect like that of the acquisition of one art and prevent us from finding out another, it rather aids us to do so. Certainly it appears to me strange that so many people should investigate human customs with such care, the virtues of plants, the motions of the stars, the transmutations of metals, and the objects of similar sciences, while at the same time practically none bethink themselves about good understanding, or universal Wisdom, though nevertheless all other studies are to be esteemed not so much for their own value as because they contribute something to this. Consequently we are justified in bringing forward this as the first rule of all, since there is nothing more prone to turn us aside from the correct way of seeking out truth than this directing of our inquiries, not towards their general end, but towards certain special investigations. I do not here refer to perverse and censurable pursuits like empty glory or base gain; obviously counterfeit reasonings and quibbles suited to vulgar understanding open up a much more direct route to such a goal than does a sound apprehension of the truth. But I have in view even honourable and laudable pursuits, because these mislead us in a more subtle fashion. For example take our investigations of those sciences conducive to the conveniences of life or which yield that pleasure which is found in the contemplation of truth, practically the only joy in life that is complete and untroubled with any pain. There we may indeed expect to receive the legitimate fruits of scientific inquiry; but if, in the course of our study, we think of them, they frequently cause us to omit many facts which are necessary to the understanding of other matters, because they seem to be either of slight value or of little interest. Hence we must believe that all the sciences are so inter-connected, that it is much easier to study them all together than to isolate one from all the others. If, therefore, anyone wishes to search out the truth of things in serious earnest, he ought not to select one special science; for all the sciences are conjoined with each other and interdependent: he ought rather to think how to increase the natural light of reason, not for the purpose of resolving this or that difficulty of scholastic type, but in order that his understanding may light his will to its proper choice in all the contin-

1

gencies of life. In a short time he will see with amazement that he has made much more progress than those who are eager about particular ends, and that he has not only obtained all that they desire, but even higher results than fall within his expectation.

RULE II

Only those objects should engage our attention, to the sure and indubitable knowledge of which our mental powers seem to be adequate.

SCIENCE in its entirety is true and evident cognition. He is no more learned who has doubts on many matters than the man who has never thought of them; nay he appears to be less learned if he has formed wrong opinions on any particulars. Hence it were better not to study at all than to occupy one's self with objects of such difficulty, that, owing to our inability to distinguish true from false, we are forced to regard the doubtful as certain; for in those matters any hope of augmenting our knowledge is exceeded by the risk of diminishing it. Thus in accordance with the above maxim we reject all such merely probable knowledge and make it a rule to trust only what is completely known and incapable of being doubted. No doubt men of education may persuade themselves that there is but little of such certain knowledge, because, forsooth, a common failing of human nature has made them deem it too easy and open to everyone, and so led them to neglect to think upon such truths; but I nevertheless announce that there are more of these than they think—truths which suffice to give a rigorous demonstration of innumerable propositions, the discussion of which they have hitherto been unable to free from the element of probability. Further, because they have believed that it was unbecoming for a man of education to confess ignorance on any point, they have so accustomed themselves to trick out their fabricated explanations, that they have ended by gradually imposing on themselves and thus have issued them to the public as genuine.

But if we adhere closely to this rule we shall find left but few objects of legitimate study. For there is scarce any question occurring in the sciences about which talented men have not disagreed. But whenever two men come to opposite decisions about the same matter one of them at least must certainly be in the wrong, and apparently there is not even one of them who knows; for if the reasoning of the second was sound and clear he would be able so to lay it before the other as finally to succeed in convincing *his* understanding also. Hence apparently we cannot attain to a perfect knowledge in any such case of probable opinion, for it would be rashness to hope for more than others have attained to. Consequently if we reckon correctly, of the sciences already discovered, Arithmetic and Geometry alone are left, to which the observance of this rule reduces us.

Yet we do not therefore condemn that method of philosophizing which others have already discovered and those weapons of the schoolmen, probable syllogisms, which are so well suited for polemics. They indeed give practice to the wits of youths and, producing emulation among them, act as a stimulus: and it is much better for their minds to be moulded by opinions of this sort, uncertain though they appear, as being objects of controversy among the learned, than to be left entirely to their own devices. For thus through lack of guidance they might stray into some abyss; but as long as they follow in their masters' footsteps, though they may diverge at times from the truth, they will yet certainly find a path which is at least in this respect safer, that it has been approved of by more prudent people. We ourselves rejoice that we in earlier years experienced this scholastic training; but now, being released from that oath of allegiance which bound us to our old masters, and since, as becomes our riper years, we are no longer subject to the ferule, if we wish in earnest to establish for ourselves those rules which shall aid us in scaling the heights of human knowledge, we must admit assuredly among the primary members of our catalogue that maxim which forbids us to abuse our leisure as many do, who neglect all easy quests and take up their time only with difficult matters; for they, though certainly making all sorts of subtle conjectures and elaborating most plausible arguments with great ingenuity, frequently find too late that after all their labours they have only increased the multitude of their doubts, without acquiring any knowledge whatsoever.

But now let us proceed to explain more carefully our reasons for saying, as we did a little while ago, that of all the sciences known as yet, Arithmetic and Geometry alone are free from any taint of falsity or uncertainty. We must note then that there are two ways by which we arrive at the knowledge of facts, viz. by experience and by deduction. We must further observe that while our inferences from experience are frequently fallacious, deduction, or the pure illation of one thing from another, though it may be passed over, if it is not seen through, cannot be erroneous when performed by an understanding that is in the least degree rational. And it seems to me that the operation is profited but little by those constraining bonds by means of which the Dialecticians claim to control human reason, though I do not deny that that discipline may be serviceable for other purposes. My reason for saying so is that none of the mistakes which men can make (men, I say, not beasts) are due to faulty inference; they are caused merely by the fact that we found upon a basis of poorly comprehended experiences, or that propositions are posited which are hasty and groundless.

This furnishes us with an evident explanation of the great superiority in certitude of Arithmetic and Geometry to other sciences. The former alone deal with an object so pure and uncomplicated, that they need make no assumptions at all which experience renders uncertain, but wholly consist in the rational deduction of consequences. They are on that account much the easiest and clearest of all, and possess an object such as we require, for in them it is scarce humanly possible for anyone to err except by inadvertence. And yet we should not be surprised to find that plenty of people of their own accord prefer to apply their intelligence to other studies, or to Philosophy. The reason for this is that every person permits himself the liberty of making guesses in the matter of an obscure subject with more confidence than in one which is clear, and that it is much easier to have some vague notion about any subject, no matter what, than to arrive at the real truth about a single question however simple that may be.

But one conclusion now emerges out of these considerations, viz. not, indeed, that Arithmetic and Geometry are the sole sciences to be studied, but only that in our search for the direct road towards truth we should busy ourselves with no object about which we cannot attain a certitude equal to that of the demonstrations of Arithmetic and Geometry.

RULE III

In the subjects we propose to investigate, our inquiries should be directed, not to what others have thought, nor to what we ourselves conjecture, but to what we can clearly and perspicuously behold and with certainty deduce; for knowledge is not won in any other way.

To STUDY the writings of the ancients is right, because it is a great boon for us to be able to make use of the labours of so many men; and we should do so, both in order to discover what they have correctly made out in previous ages, and also that we may inform ourselves as to what in the various sciences is still left for investigation. But yet there is a great danger lest in a too absorbed study of these works we should become infected with their errors, guard against them as we may. For it is the way of writers, whenever they have allowed themselves rashly and credulously to take up a position in any controverted matter, to try with the subtlest of arguments to compel us to go along with them. But when, on the contrary, they have happily come upon something certain and evident, in displaying it they never fail to surround it with ambiguities, fearing, it would seem, lest the simplicity of their explanation should make us respect their discovery less, or because they grudge us an open vision of the truth.

Further, supposing now that all were wholly open and candid, and never thrust upon us doubtful opinions as true, but expounded every matter in good faith, yet since scarce anything has been asserted by any one man the contrary of which has not been alleged by another, we should be eternally uncertain which of the two to believe. It would be no use to total up the testimonies in favour of each, meaning to follow that opinion which was supported by the greater number of authors: for if it is a question of difficulty that is in dispute, it is more likely that the truth would have been discovered by few than by many. But even though all these men agreed among themselves, what they teach us would not suffice for us. For we shall not, e.g. all turn out to be mathematicians though we know by heart all the proofs that others have elaborated, unless we have an intellectual talent that fits us to resolve difficulties of any kind. Neither, though we have mastered all the arguments of Plato and Aristotle, if yet we have not the capacity for passing a solid judgment on these matters, shall we become Philosophers; we should have acquired the knowledge not of a science, but of history.

I lay down the rule also, that we must wholly refrain from ever mixing up conjectures with our pronouncements on the truth of things. This warning is of no little importance. There is no stronger reason for our finding nothing in the current Philosophy which is so evident and certain as not to be capable of being controverted, than the fact that the learned, not con tent with the recognition of what is clear and certain, in the first instance hazard the assertion of obscure and ill-comprehended theories, at which they have arrived merely by probable conjecture. Then afterwards they gradually attach complete credence to them, and mingling them promiscuously with what is true and evident, they finish by being unable to deduce any conclusion which does not appear to depend upon some proposition of the doubtful sort, and hence is not uncertain.

But lest we in turn should slip into the same error, we shall here take note of all those mental operations by which we are able, wholly without fear of illusion, to arrive at the knowledge of things. Now I admit only two, viz. intuition and induction.[1]

By *intuition* I understand, not the fluctuating testimony of the senses, nor the misleading judgment that proceeds from the blundering constructions of imagination, but the conception which an unclouded and attentive mind gives us so readily and distinctly that we are wholly freed from doubt about that which we understand. Or, what comes to the same thing, *intuition* is the undoubting conception of an unclouded and attentive mind, and springs from the light of reason alone; it is more certain than deduction itself, in that it is simpler, though deduction, as we have noted above, cannot by us be erroneously conducted. Thus each individual can mentally have intuition of the fact that he exists, and that he thinks; that the triangle is bounded by three lines only, the sphere by a single superficies, and so on. Facts of such a kind are far more numerous than many people think, disdaining as they do to direct their attention upon such simple matters.

But in case anyone may be put out by this new use of the term *intuition* and of other terms which in the following pages I am similarly compelled to dissever from their current meaning, I here make the general announcement that I pay no attention to the way in which particular terms have of late been employed in the schools, because it would have been difficult to employ the same terminology while my theory was wholly different. All that I take note of is the meaning of the Latin of each word, when, in cases where an appropriate term is lacking, I wish to transfer to the vocabulary that expresses my own meaning those that I deem most suitable.

This evidence and certitude, however, which belongs to intuition, is required not only in the

[1]Sense here seems to require "deduction."

enunciation of propositions, but also in discursive reasoning of whatever sort. For example consider this consequence: 2 and 2 amount to the same as 3 and 1. Now we need to see intuitively not only that 2 and 2 make 4, and that likewise 3 and 1 make 4, but further that the third of the above statements is a necessary conclusion from these two.

Hence now we are in a position to raise the question as to why we have, besides intuition, given this supplementary method of knowing, viz. knowing by *deduction*, by which we understand all necessary inference from other facts that are known with certainty. This, however, we could not avoid, because many things are known with certainty, though not by themselves evident, but only deduced from true and known principles by the continuous and uninterrupted action of a mind that has a clear vision of each step in the process. It is in a similar way that we know that the last link in a long chain is connected with the first, even though we do not take in by means of one and the same act of vision all the intermediate links on which that connection depends, but only remember that we have taken them successively under review and that each single one is united to its neighbour, from the first even to the last. Hence we distinguish this mental intuition from deduction by the fact that into the conception of the latter there enters a certain movement or succession, into that of the former there does not. Further deduction does not require an immediately presented evidence such as intuition possesses; its certitude is rather conferred upon it in some way by memory. The upshot of the matter is that it is possible to say that those propositions indeed which are immediately deduced from first principles are known now by intuition, now by deduction, i.e. in a way that differs according to our point of view. But the first principles themselves are given by intuition alone, while, on the contrary, the remote conclusions are furnished only by deduction.

These two methods are the most certain routes to knowledge, and the mind should admit no others. All the rest should be rejected as suspect of error and dangerous. But this does not prevent us from believing matters that have been divinely revealed as being more certain than our surest knowledge, since belief in these things, as all faith in obscure matters, is an action not of our intelligence, but of our will. They should be heeded also since, if they have any basis in our understanding, they can and ought to be, more than all things else, discovered by one or other of the ways abovementioned, as we hope perhaps to show at greater length on some future opportunity.

RULE IV

There is need of a method for finding out the truth.

So BLIND is the curiosity by which mortals are possessed, that they often conduct their minds along unexplored routes, having no reason to hope for success, but merely being willing to risk the experiment of finding whether the truth they seek lies there. As well might a man burning with an unintelligent desire to find treasure, continuously roam the streets, seeking to find something that a passer by might have chanced to drop. This is the way in which most Chemists, many Geometricians, and Philosophers not a few prosecute their studies. I do not deny that sometimes in these wanderings they are lucky enough to find something true. But I do not allow that this argues greater industry on their part, but only better luck. But however that may be, it were far better never to think of investigating truth at all, than to do so without a method. For it is very certain that unregulated inquiries and confused reflections of this kind only confound the natural light and blind our mental powers. Those who so become accustomed to walk in darkness weaken their eye-sight so much that afterwards they cannot bear the light of day. This is confirmed by experience; for how often do we not see that those who have never taken to letters, give a sounder and clearer decision about obvious matters than those who have spent all their time in the schools? Moreover by a method I mean certain and simple rules, such that, if a man observe them accurately, he shall never assume what is false as true, and will never spend his mental efforts to no purpose, but will always gradually increase his knowledge and so arrive at a true understanding of all that does not surpass his powers.

These two points must be carefully noted, viz. never to assume what is false as true, and to arrive at a knowledge which takes in all things. For, if we are without the knowledge of any of the things which we are capable of understanding, that is only because we have never perceived any way to bring us to this knowledge, or because we have fallen into the contrary error. But if our method rightly explains how our mental vision should be used, so as not to fall into the contrary error, and

how deduction should be discovered in order that we may arrive at the knowledge of all things, I do not see what else is needed to make it complete; for I have already said that no science is acquired except by mental intuition or deduction. There is besides no question of extending it further in order to show how these said operations ought to be effected, because they are the most simple and primary of all. Consequently, unless our understanding were already able to employ them, it could comprehend none of the precepts of that very method, not even the simplest. But as for the other mental operations, which Dialectic does its best to direct by making use of these prior ones, they are quite useless here; rather they are to be accounted impediments, because nothing can be added to the pure light of reason which does not in some way obscure it.

Since then the usefulness of this method is so great that without it study seems to be harmful rather than profitable, I am quite ready to believe that the greater minds of former ages had some knowledge of it, nature even conducting them to it. For the human mind has in it something that we may call divine, wherein are scattered the first germs of useful modes of thought. Consequently it often happens that however much neglected and choked by interfering studies they bear fruit of their own accord. Arithmetic and Geometry, the simplest sciences, give us an instance of this; for we have sufficient evidence that the ancient Geometricians made use of a certain analysis which they extended to the resolution of all problems, though they grudged the secret to posterity. At the present day also there flourishes a certain kind of Arithmetic, called Algebra, which designs to effect, when dealing with numbers, what the ancients achieved in the matter of figures. These two methods are nothing else than the spontaneous fruit sprung from the inborn principles of the discipline here in question; and I do not wonder that these sciences with their very simple subject matter should have yielded results so much more satisfactory than others in which greater obstructions choke all growth. But even in the latter case, if only we take care to cultivate them assiduously, fruits will certainly be able to come to full maturity.

This is the chief result which I have had in view in writing this treatise. For I should not think much of these rules, if they had no utility save for the solution of the empty problems with which Logicians and Geometers have been wont to beguile their leisure; my only achievement thus would have seemed to be an ability to argue about trifles more subtly than others. Further, though much mention is here made of numbers and figures, because no other sciences furnish us with illustrations of such self-evidence and certainty, the reader who follows my drift with sufficient attention will easily see that nothing is less in my mind than ordinary Mathematics, and that I am expounding quite another science, of which these illustrations are rather the outer husk than the constituents. Such a science should contain the primary rudiments of human reason, and its province ought to extend to the eliciting of true results in every subject. To speak freely, I am convinced that it is a more powerful instrument of knowledge than any other that has been bequeathed to us by human agency, as being the source of all others. But as for the outer covering I mentioned, I mean not to employ it to cover up and conceal my method for the purpose of warding off the vulgar; rather I hope so to clothe and embellish it that I may make it more suitable for presentation to the human mind.

When first I applied my mind to Mathematics I read straight away most of what is usually given by the mathematical writers, and I paid special attention to Arithmetic and Geometry, because they were said to be the simplest and so to speak the way to all the rest. But in neither case did I then meet with authors who fully satisfied me. I did indeed learn in their works many propositions about numbers which I found on calculation to be true. As to figures, they in a sense exhibited to my eyes a great number of truths and drew conclusions from certain consequences. But they did not seem to make it sufficiently plain to the mind itself why those things are so, and how they discovered them. Consequently I was not surprised that many people, even of talent and scholarship, should, after glancing at these sciences, have either given them up as being empty and childish or, taking them to be very difficult and intricate, been deterred at the very outset from learning them. For really there is nothing more futile than to busy one's self with bare numbers and imaginary figures in such a way as to appear to rest content with such trifles, and so to resort to those superficial demonstrations, which are discovered more frequently by chance than by skill, and are a matter more of the eyes and the imagination than of the understanding, that in a sense

one ceases to make use of one's reason. I might add that there is no more intricate task than that of solving by this method of proof new difficulties that arise, involved as they are with numerical confusions. But when I afterwards bethought myself how it could be that the earliest pioneers of Philosophy in bygone ages refused to admit to the study of wisdom any one who was not versed in Mathematics, evidently believing that this was the easiest and most indispensable mental exercise and preparation for laying hold of other more important sciences, I was confirmed in my suspicion that they had knowledge of a species of Mathematics very different from that which passes current in our time. I do not indeed imagine that they had a perfect knowledge of it, for they plainly show how little advanced they were by the insensate rejoicings they display and the pompous thanksgivings they offer for the most trifling discoveries. I am not shaken in my opinion by the fact that historians make a great deal of certain machines of theirs. Possibly these machines were quite simple, and yet the ignorant and wonder-loving multitude might easily have lauded them as miraculous. But I am convinced that certain primary germs of truth implanted by nature in human minds—though in our case the daily reading and hearing of innumerable diverse errors stifle them—had a very great vitality in that rude and unsophisticated age of the ancient world. Thus the same mental illumination which let them see that virtue was to be preferred to pleasure, and honour to utility, although they knew not why this was so, made them recognize true notions in Philosophy and Mathematics, although they were not yet able thoroughly to grasp these sciences. Indeed I seem to recognize certain traces of this true Mathematics in Pappus and Diophantus, who though not belonging to the earliest age, yet lived many centuries before our own times. But my opinion is that these writers then with a sort of low cunning, deplorable indeed, suppressed this knowledge. Possibly they acted just as many inventors are known to have done in the case of their discoveries, i.e. they feared that their method being so easy and simple would become cheapened on being divulged, and they preferred to exhibit in its place certain barren truths, deductively demonstrated with show enough of ingenuity, as the results of their art, in order to win from us our admiration for these achievements, rather than to disclose to us that method itself which would have wholly annulled the admiration accorded. Finally, there have been certain men of talent who in the present age have tried to revive this same art. For it seems to be precisely that science known by the barbarous name Algebra if only we could extricate it from that vast array of numbers and inexplicable figures by which it is overwhelmed, so that it might display the clearness and simplicity which, we imagine, ought to exist in a genuine Mathematics.

It was these reflections that recalled me from the particular studies of Arithmetic and Geometry to a general investigation of Mathematics, and thereupon I sought to determine what precisely was universally meant by that term, and why not only the above mentioned sciences, but also Astronomy, Music, Optics, Mechanics and several others are styled parts of Mathematics. Here indeed it is not enough to look at the origin of the word; for since the name "Mathematics" means exactly the same thing as "scientific study," these other branches could, with as much right as Geometry itself, be called Mathematics. Yet we see that almost anyone who has had the slightest schooling, can easily distinguish what relates to Mathematics in any question from that which belongs to the other sciences. But as I considered the matter carefully it gradually came to light that all those matters only were referred to Mathematics in which order and measurement are investigated, and that it makes no difference whether it be in numbers, figures, stars, sounds or any other object that the question of measurement arises. I saw consequently that there must be some general science to explain that element as a whole which gives rise to problems about order and measurement, restricted as these are to no special subject matter. This, I perceived, was called "Universal Mathematics," not a far fetched designation, but one of long standing which has passed into current use, because in this science is contained everything on account of which the others are called parts of Mathematics. We can see how much it excels in utility and simplicity the sciences subordinate to it, by the fact that it can deal with all the objects of which they have cognizance and many more besides, and that any difficulties it contains are found in them as well, added to the fact that in them fresh difficulties arise due to their special subject matter which in it do not exist. But now how comes it that though everyone knows the name of this science and understands what is its prov-

ince even without studying it attentively, so many people laboriously pursue the other dependent sciences, and no one cares to master this one? I should marvel indeed were I not aware that everyone thinks it to be so very easy, and had I not long since observed that the human mind passes over what it thinks it can easily accomplish, and hastens straight away to new and more imposing occupations.

I, however, conscious as I am of my inadequacy, have resolved that in my investigation into truth I shall follow obstinately such an order as will require me first to start with what is simplest and easiest, and never permit me to proceed farther until in the first sphere there seems to be nothing further to be done. This is why up to the present time to the best of my ability I have made a study of this universal Mathematics; consequently, I believe that when I go on to deal in their turn with more profound sciences, as I hope to do soon, my efforts will not be premature. But before I make this transition I shall try to bring together and arrange in an orderly manner, the facts which in my previous studies I have noted as being more worthy of attention. Thus I hope both that at a future date, when through advancing years my memory is enfeebled, I shall, if need be, conveniently be able to recall them by looking in this little book, and that having now disburdened my memory of them I may be free to concentrate my mind on my future studies.

RULE V

Method consists entirely in the order and disposition of the objects towards which our mental vision must be directed if we would find out any truth. We shall comply with it exactly if we reduce involved and obscure propositions step by step to those that are simpler, and then starting with the intuitive apprehension of all those that are absolutely simple, attempt to ascend to the knowledge of all others by precisely similar steps.

IN THIS alone lies the sum of all human endeavour, and he who would approach the investigation of truth must hold to this rule as closely as he who enters the labyrinth must follow the thread which guided Theseus. But many people either do not reflect on the precept at all, or ignore it altogether, or presume not to need it. Consequently, they often investigate the most difficult questions with so little regard to order, that, to my mind, they act like a man who should attempt to leap with one bound from the base to the summit of a house, either making no account of the ladders provided for his ascent or not noticing them. It is thus that all Astrologers behave, who, though in ignorance of the nature of the heavens, and even without having made proper observations of the movements of the heavenly bodies, expect to be able to indicate their effects. This is also what many do who study Mechanics apart from Physics, and rashly set about devising new instruments for producing motion. Along with them go also those Philosophers who, neglecting experience, imagine that truth will spring from their brain like Pallas from the head of Zeus.

Now it is obvious that all such people violate the present rule. But since the order here required is often so obscure and intricate that not everyone can make it out, they can scarcely avoid error unless they diligently observe what is laid down in the following proposition.

RULE VI

In order to separate out what is quite simple from what is complex, and to arrange these matters methodically, we ought, in the case of every series in which we have deduced certain facts the one from the other, to notice which fact is simple, and to mark the interval, greater, less, or equal, which separates all the others from this.

ALTHOUGH this proposition seems to teach nothing very new, it contains, nevertheless, the chief secret of method, and none in the whole of this treatise is of greater utility. For it tells us that all facts can be arranged in certain series, not indeed in the sense of being referred to some ontological genus such as the categories employed by Philosophers in their classification, but in so far as certain truths can be known from others; and thus, whenever a difficulty occurs we are able at once to perceive whether it will be profitable to examine certain others first, and which, and in what order.

Further, in order to do that correctly, we must note first that for the purpose of our procedure, which does not regard things as isolated realities, but compares them with one another in order to discover the dependence in knowledge of one upon the other, all things can be said to be either absolute or relative.

I call that absolute which contains within itself the pure and simple essence of which we are in quest. Thus the term will be applicable to whatever is considered as being independent, or a cause, or simple, universal, one, equal, like, straight, and so forth; and the absolute I call the simplest and the easiest of all, so that we can make use of it in the solution of questions.

But the relative is that which, while participating in the same nature, or at least sharing in it to some degree which enables us to relate it to the absolute and to deduce it from that by a chain of operations, involves in addition something else in its concept which I call relativity. Examples of this are found in whatever is said to be dependent, or an effect, composite, particular, many, unequal, unlike, oblique, etc. These relatives are the further removed from the absolute, in proportion as they contain more elements of relativity subordinate the one to the other. We state in this rule that these should all be distinguished and their correlative connection and natural order so observed, that we may be able by traversing all the intermediate steps to proceed from the most remote to that which is in the highest degree absolute.

Herein lies the secret of this whole method, that in all things we should diligently mark that which is most absolute. For some things are from one point of view more absolute than others, but from a different standpoint are more relative. Thus though the universal is more absolute than the particular because its essence is simpler, yet it can be held to be more relative than the latter, because it depends upon individuals for its existence, and so on. Certain things likewise are truly more absolute than others, but yet are not the most absolute of all. Thus relatively to individuals, species is something absolute, but contrasted with genus it is relative. So too, among things that can be measured, extension is something absolute, but among the various aspects of extension it is length that is absolute, and so on. Finally also, in order to bring out more clearly that we are considering here not the nature of each thing taken in isolation, but the series involved in knowing them, we have purposely enumerated cause and equality among our absolutes, though the nature of these terms is really relative. For though Philosophers make cause and effect correlative, we find that here even, if we ask what the effect is, we must first know the cause and not conversely. Equals too mutually imply one another, but we can know unequals only by comparing them with equals and not *per contra*.

Secondly, we must note that there are but few pure and simple essences, which either our experiences or some sort of light innate in us enable us to behold as primary and existing *per se*, not as depending on any others. These we say should be carefully noticed, for they are just those facts which we have called the simplest in any single series. All the others can only be perceived as deductions from these, either immediate and proximate, or not to be attained save by two or three or more acts of inference. The number of these acts should be noted in order that we may perceive whether the facts are separated from the primary and simplest proposition by a greater or smaller number of steps. And so pronounced is everywhere the inter-connection of ground and consequence, which gives rise, in the objects to be examined, to those series to which every inquiry must be reduced, that it can be investigated by a sure method. But because it is not easy to make a review of them all, and besides, since they have not so much to be kept in the memory as to be detected by a sort of mental penetration, we must seek for something which will so mould our intelligence as to let it perceive these connected sequences immediately whenever it needs to do so. For this purpose I have found nothing so effectual as to accustom ourselves to turn our attention with a sort of penetrative insight on the very minutest of the facts which we have already discovered.

Finally, we must in the third place note that our inquiry ought not to start with the investigation of difficult matters. Rather, before setting out to attack any definite problem, it behoves us first, without making any selection, to assemble those truths that are obvious as they present themselves to us, and afterwards, proceeding step by step, to inquire whether any others can be deduced from these, and again any others from these conclusions and so on, in order. This done, we should attentively think over the truths we have discovered and mark with diligence the reasons why we have been able to detect some more easily than others, and which these are. Thus, when we come to attack some definite problem we shall be able to judge what previous questions it were best to settle first. For example, if it comes into my thought that the number 6 is twice 3, I may then ask what is twice 6, viz. 12; again, perhaps I seek for the double of this, viz. 24, and again of this, viz. 48. Thus I may easily deduce that there is the same proportion between 3 and 6, as between 6 and 12, and likewise 12 and 24, and so on, and hence that the numbers 3, 6, 12, 24, 48, etc. are in continued proportion. But though these facts are all so clear as to seem almost childish, I am now able by attentive reflection to understand what is the form involved by all questions that can be propounded about the proportions or relations of things, and the order in which they should be investigated; and this discovery embraces the sum of the entire science of Pure Mathematics.

For first I perceive that it was not more difficult to discover the double of six than that of three; and that equally in all cases, when we have found a proportion between any two magnitudes, we can find innumerable others which have the same proportion between them. So, too, there is no increase of difficulty, if three, or four, or more of such magnitudes are sought for, because each has to be found separately and without any relation to the others. But next I notice that though, when the magnitudes 3 and 6 are given, one can easily find a third in continued proportion, viz. 12, it is yet not equally easy, when the two extremes, 3 and 12, are given, to find the mean proportional, viz. 6. When we look into the reason for this, it is clear that here we have a type of difficulty quite different from the former; for, in order to find the mean proportional, we must at the same time attend to the two extremes and to the proportion which exists between these two in order to discover a new ratio by dividing the previous one; and this is a very different thing from finding a third term in continued proportion with two given numbers. I go forward likewise and examine whether, when the numbers 3 and 24 were given, it would have been equally easy to determine one of the two intermediate proportionals, viz. 6 and 12. But here still another sort of difficulty arises more involved than the previous ones, for on this occasion we have to attend not to one or two things only but to three, in order to discover the fourth. We may go still further and inquire whether if only 3 and 48 had been given it would have been still more difficult to discover one of the three mean proportionals, viz. 6, 12, and 24. At the first blush this indeed appears to be so; but immediately afterwards it comes to mind that this difficulty can be split up and lessened, if first of all we ask only for the mean proportional between 3 and 48, viz. 12, and then seek for the other mean proportional between 3 and 12, viz. 6, and the other between 12 and 48, viz. 24. Thus, we have reduced the problem to the difficulty of the second type shown above.

These illustrations further lead me to note

that the quest for knowledge about the same thing can traverse different routes, the one much more difficult and obscure than the other. Thus, to find these four continued proportionals, 3, 6, 12, and 24, if two consecutive numbers be assumed, e.g. 3 and 6, or 6 and 12, or 12 and 24, in order that we may discover the others, our task will be easy. In this case we shall say that the proposition to be discovered is directly examined. But if the two numbers given are alternates, like 3 and 12, or 6 and 24, which are to lead us to the discovery of the others, then we shall call this an indirect investigation of the first mode. Likewise, if we are given two extremes like 3 and 24, in order to find out from these the intermediates 6 and 12, the investigation will be indirect and of the second mode. Thus I should be able to proceed further and deduce many other results from this example; but these will be sufficient, if the reader follows my meaning when I say that a proposition is directly deduced, or indirectly, and will reflect that from a knowledge of each of these matters that are simplest and primary, much may be discovered in other sciences by those who bring to them attentive thought and a power of sagacious analysis.

RULE VII

If we wish our science to be complete, those matters which promote the end we have in view must one and all be scrutinized by a movement of thought which is continuous and nowhere interrupted; they must also be included in an enumeration which is both adequate and methodical.

IT IS necessary to obey the injunctions of this rule if we hope to gain admission among the certain truths for those which, we have declared above, are not immediate deductions from primary and self-evident principles. For this deduction frequently involves such a long series of transitions from ground to consequent that when we come to the conclusion we have difficulty in recalling the whole of the route by which we have arrived at it. This is why I say that there must be a continuous movement of thought to make good this weakness of the memory. Thus, e.g. if I have first found out by separate mental operations what the relation is between the magnitudes A and B, then what between B and C, between C and D, and finally between D and E, that does not entail my seeing what the relation is between A and E, nor can the truths previously learnt give me a precise knowledge of it unless I recall them all. To remedy this I would run them over from time to time, keeping the imagination moving continuously in such a way that while it is intuitively perceiving each fact it simultaneously passes on to the next; and this I would do until I had learned to pass from the first to the last so quickly, that no stage in the process was left to the care of the memory, but I seemed to have the whole in intuition before me at the same time. This method will both relieve the memory, diminish the sluggishness of our thinking, and definitely enlarge our mental capacity.

But we must add that this movement should nowhere be interrupted. Often people who attempt to deduce a conclusion too quickly and from remote principles do not trace the whole chain of intermediate conclusions with sufficient accuracy to prevent them from passing over many steps without due consideration. But it is certain that wherever the smallest link is left out the chain is broken and the whole of the certainty of the conclusion falls to the ground.

Here we maintain that an enumeration [of the steps in a proof] is required as well, if we wish to make our science complete. For resolving most problems other precepts are profitable, but enumeration alone will secure our always passing a true and certain judgment on whatsoever engages our attention; by means of it nothing at all will escape us, but we shall evidently have some knowledge of every step.

This enumeration or induction is thus a review or inventory of all those matters that have a bearing on the problem raised, which is so thorough and accurate that by its means we can clearly and with confidence conclude that we have omitted nothing by mistake. Consequently as often as we have employed it, if the problem defies us, we shall at least be wiser in this respect, viz. that we are quite certain that we know of no way of resolving it. If it chances, as often it does, that we have been able to scan all the routes leading to it which lie open to the human intelligence, we shall be entitled boldly to assert that the solution of the problem lies outside the reach of human knowledge.

Furthermore, we must note that by adequate enumeration or induction is only meant that method by which we may attain surer conclusions than by any other type of proof, with the exception of simple intuition. But when the knowledge of some matter cannot be reduced to this, we must cast aside all syllogistic fetters and employ induction, the only method left us, but one in which all confidence should be reposed. For whenever single facts have been immediately deduced the one from the other, they have been already reduced, if the inference was evident, to a true intuition. But if we infer any single thing from various and disconnected facts, often our intellectual capacity is not so great as to be able to embrace them all in a single intuition; in which case our mind should be content with the certitude attaching to this operation. It is in precisely similar fashion that though we cannot with one single gaze distinguish all the links of a lengthy chain, yet if we have seen the connection of each with its neighbour, we shall be entitled to say that we have seen how the first is connected with the last.

I have declared that this operation ought to be adequate because it is often in danger of being defective and consequently exposed to error. For sometimes, even though in our enumeration we scrutinize many facts which are highly evident, yet if we omit the smallest step the chain is broken and the whole of the certitude of the conclusion falls to the ground. Sometimes also, even though all the facts are included in an accurate enumeration, the single steps are not distinguished from one another, and our knowledge of them all is thus only confused.

Further, while now the enumeration ought to be complete, now distinct, there are times when it need have neither of these characters; it was for this reason that I said only that it should be adequate. For if I want to prove by enumeration how many genera there are of corporeal things, or of those that in any way fall under the senses, I shall not assert that they are just so many and no more, unless I previously have become aware that I have included them all in my enumeration, and have distinguished them each separately from all the others. But if in the same way I wish to prove that the rational soul is not corporeal, I do not need a complete enumeration; it will be sufficient to include all bodies in certain collections in such a way as to be able to demonstrate that the rational soul has nothing to do with any of these. If, finally, I wish to show by enumeration that the area of a circle is greater than the area of all other figures whose perimeter is equal, there is no need for me to call in review all other figures; it is enough to demonstrate this of certain others in particular, in order to get thence by induction the same conclusion about all the others.

I added also that the enumeration ought to be methodical. This is both because we have no more serviceable remedy for the defects already instanced, than to scan all things in an orderly manner; and also because it often happens that if each single matter which concerns the quest in hand were to be investigated separately, no man's life would be long enough for the purpose, whether because they are far too many, or because it would chance that the same things had to be repeated too often. But if all these facts are arranged in the best order, they will for the most part be reduced to determinate classes, out of which it will be sufficient to take one example for exact inspection, or some one feature in a single case, or certain things rather than others, or at least we shall never have to waste our time in traversing the same ground twice. The advantage of this course is so great that often many particulars can, owing to a well devised arrangement, be gone over in a short space of time and with little trouble, though at first view the matter looked immense.

But this order which we employ in our enumerations can for the most part be varied and depends upon each man's judgment. For this reason, if we would elaborate it in our thought with greater penetration, we must remember what was said in our fifth proposition. There are also many of the trivial things of man's devising, in the discovery of which the whole method lies in the disposal of this order. Thus if you wish to construct a perfect anagram by the transposition of the letters of a name, there is no need to pass from the easy to the difficult, nor to distinguish absolute from relative. Here there is no place for these operations; it will be sufficient to adopt an order to be followed in the transpositions of the letters which we are to examine, such that the same arrangements are never handled twice over. The total number of transpositions should, e.g. be split up into definite classes, so that it may immediately appear in which there is the best hope of finding what is sought. In this way the task is often not tedious but merely child's play.

However, these three propositions should not be separated, because for the most part we have to think of them together, and all equally tend towards the perfecting of our method. There was no great reason for treating one before the other, and we have expounded them but briefly here. The reason for this is that in the rest of the treatise we have practically nothing else left for consideration. Therefore, we shall then exhibit in detail what here we have brought together in a general way.

RULE VIII

If in the matters to be examined we come to a step in the series of which our understanding is not sufficiently well able to have an intuitive cognition, we must stop short there. We must make no attempt to examine what follows; thus we shall spare ourselves superfluous labour.

THE THREE preceding rules prescribe and explain the order to be followed. The present rule, on the other hand, shows when it is wholly necessary and when it is merely useful. Thus it is necessary to examine whatever constitutes a single step in that series, by which we pass from relative to absolute, or conversely, before discussing what follows from it. But if, as often happens, many things pertain to the same step, though it is indeed always profitable to review them in order, in this case we are not forced to apply our method of observation so strictly and rigidly. Frequently it is permissible to proceed farther, even though we have not clear knowledge of all the facts it involves, but know only a few or a single one of them.

This rule is a necessary consequence of the reasons brought forward in support of the second. But it must not be thought that the present rule contributes nothing fresh towards the advancement of learning, though it seems only to bid us refrain from further discussion, and apparently does not unfold any truth. For beginners, indeed, it has no further value than to teach them how not to waste time, and it employs nearly the same arguments in doing so as Rule II. But it shows those who have perfectly mastered the seven preceding maxims, how in the pursuit of any science so to satisfy themselves as not to desire anything further. For the man who faithfully complies with the former rules in the solution of any difficulty, and yet by the present rule is bidden desist at a certain point, will then know for certainty that no amount of application will enable him to attain to the knowledge desired, and that not owing to a defect in his intelligence, but because the nature of the problem itself, or the fact that he is human, prevents him. But this knowledge is not the less science than that which reveals the nature of the thing itself; in fact he would seem to have some mental defect who should extend his curiosity farther.

But what we have been saying must be illustrated by one or two examples. If, for example, one who studies only Mathematics were

to seek to find that curve which in dioptrics is called the anaclastic, that from which parallel rays are so refracted that after the refraction they all meet in one point,—it will be easy to see, by applying Rules V and VI, that the determination of this line depends upon the relation which the angles of refraction bear to the angles of incidence. But because he is unable to discover this, since it is a matter not of Mathematics but of Physics, he is here forced to pause at the threshold. Nor will it avail him to try and learn this from the Philosophers or to gather it from experience; for this would be to break Rule III. Furthermore, this proposition is both composite and relative; but in the proper place we shall show that experience is unambiguous only when dealing with the wholly simple and absolute. Again, it will be vain for him to assume some relation or other as being that which prevails between such angles, and conjecture that this is the truest to fact; for in that case he would be on the track not of the anaclastic, but merely of that curve which could be deduced from his assumption.

If, however, a man who does not confine his studies to Mathematics, but, in accordance with the first rule, tries to discover the truth on all points, meets with the same difficulty, he will find in addition that this ratio between the angles of incidence and of refraction depends upon changes in their relation produced by varying the medium. Again these changes depend upon the manner in which the ray of light traverses the whole transparent body; while the knowledge of the way in which the light thus passes through presupposes a knowledge of the nature of the action of light, to understand which finally we must know what a natural potency is in general, this last being the most absolute term in the whole series in question. When, therefore, by a mental intuition he has clearly comprehended the nature of this, he will, in compliance with Rule V, proceed backwards by the same steps. And if when he comes to the second step he is unable straightway to determine the nature of light, he will, in accordance with the seventh rule enumerate all the other natural potencies, in order that the knowledge of some other of them may help him, at least by analogy (of which more anon), to understand this. This done, he will ask how the ray traverses the whole of the transparent body, and will so follow out the other points methodically, that at last he will arrive at the anaclastic itself. Though this has long defied the efforts of many inquirers, I see no reason why a man who fully carried out our method should fail to arrive at convincing knowledge of the matter.

But let us give the most splendid example of all. If a man proposes to himself the problem of examining all the truths for the knowledge of which human reason suffices—and I think that this is a task which should be undertaken once at least in his life by every person who seriously endeavours to attain equilibrium of thought—, he will, by the rules given above, certainly discover that nothing can be known prior to the understanding, since the knowledge of all things else depends upon this and not conversely. Then, when he has clearly grasped all those things which follow proximately on the knowledge of the naked understanding, he will enumerate among other things whatever instruments of thought we have other than the understanding; and these are only two, viz. imagination and sense. He will therefore devote all his energies to the distinguishing and examining of these three modes of cognition, and seeing that in the strict sense truth and falsity can be a matter of the understanding alone, though often it derives its origin from the other two faculties, he will attend carefully to every source of deception in order that he may be on his guard. He will also enumerate exactly all the ways leading to truth which lie open to us, in order that he may follow the right way. They are not so many that they cannot all be easily discovered and embraced in an adequate enumeration. And though this will seem marvellous and incredible to the inexpert, as soon as in each matter he has distinguished those cognitions which only fill and embellish the memory, from those which cause one to be deemed really more instructed, which it will be easy for him to do . . . ; he will feel assured that any absence of further knowledge is not due to lack of intelligence or of skill, and that nothing at all can be known by anyone else which he is not capable of knowing, provided only that he gives to it his utmost mental application. And though many problems may present themselves, from the solution of which this rule prohibits him, yet because he will clearly perceive that they pass the limits of human intelligence, he will deem that he is not the more ignorant on that account; rather, if he is reasonable, this very knowledge, that the solution can be discovered by no one, will abundantly satisfy his curiosity.

But lest we should always be uncertain as to the powers of the mind, and in order that we may not labour wrongly and at random before we set ourselves to think out things in detail, we ought once in our life to inquire diligently what the thoughts are of which the human mind is capable. In order the better to attain this end we ought, when two sets of inquiries are equally simple, to choose the more useful.

This method of ours resembles indeed those devices employed by the mechanical crafts, which do not need the aid of anything outside of them, but themselves supply the directions for making their own instruments. Thus if a man wished to practise any one of them, e.g. the craft of a smith, and were destitute of all instruments, he would be forced to use at first a hard stone or a rough lump of iron as an anvil, take a piece of rock in place of a hammer, make pieces of wood serve as tongs, and provide himself with other such tools as necessity required. Thus equipped, he would not then at once attempt to forge swords or helmets or any manufactured article of iron for others to use. He would first of all fashion hammer, anvil, tongs, and the other tools useful for himself. This example teaches us that, since thus at the outset we have been able to discover only some rough precepts, apparently the innate possession of our mind, rather than the product of technical skill, we should not forthwith attempt to settle the controversies of Philosophers, or solve the puzzles of the Mathematicians, by their help. We must first employ them for searching out with our utmost attention all the other things that are more urgently required in the investigation of truth. And this since there is no reason why it should appear more difficult to discover these than any of the answers which the problems propounded by Geometry or Physics or the other sciences are wont to demand.

Now no more useful inquiry can be proposed than that which seeks to determine the nature and the scope of human knowledge. This is why we state this very problem succinctly in the single question, which we deem should be answered at the very outset with the aid of the rules which we have already laid down. This investigation should be undertaken once at least in his life by anyone who has the slightest regard for truth, since in pursuing it the true instruments of knowledge and the whole method of inquiry come to light. But nothing seems to me more futile than the conduct of those who boldly dispute about the secrets of nature, the influence of the heavens on these lower regions, the predicting of future events and similar matters, as many do, without yet having ever asked even whether human reason is adequate to the solution of these problems. Neither ought it to seem such a toilsome and difficult matter to define the limits of that understanding of which we are directly aware as being with us, when we often have no hesitation in passing judgment even on things that are without us and quite foreign to us. Neither is it such an immense task to attempt to grasp in thought all the objects comprised within this whole of things, in order to discover how they singly fall under our mental scrutiny. For nothing can prove to be so complex or so vague as to defeat the efforts of the method of enumeration above described, directed towards restraining it within certain limits or arranging it under certain categories. But to put this to the test in the matter of the question above propounded, we first of all divide the whole problem relative to it into two parts; for it ought either to relate to us who are capable of knowledge, or to the things themselves which can be known: and these two factors we discuss separately.

In ourselves we notice that while it is the understanding alone which is capable of knowing, it yet is either helped or hindered by three other faculties, namely imagination, sense and memory. We must therefore examine these faculties in order, with a view to finding out where each may prove to be an impediment, so that we may be on our guard; or where it may profit us, so that we may use to the full the resources of these powers. This first part of our problem will accordingly be discussed with the aid of a sufficient enumeration, as will be shown in the succeeding proposition.

We come secondly to the things themselves which must be considered only in so far as they are the objects of the understanding. From this point of view we divide them into the class (1) of those whose nature is of the extremest simplicity and (2) of the complex and composite. Simple natures must be either spiritual or corporeal or at once spiritual and corporeal. Finally, among the composites there are some which the understanding realises to be complex before it judges that it can determine anything about them; but there are also others which it itself puts together. All these matters will be expounded at greater length in the twelfth proposition, where it will be shown that there can be no falsity save in the last class—that of the compounds made by the un-

derstanding itself. This is why we further subdivide these into the class of those which are deducible from natures which are of the maximum simplicity and are known *per se*, of which we shall treat in the whole of the succeeding book[1]; and into those which presuppose the existence of others which the facts themselves show us to be composite. To the exposition of these we destine the whole of the third[2] book.

But we shall indeed attempt in the whole of this treatise to follow so accurately the paths which conduct men to the knowledge of the truth, and to make them so easy, that anyone who has perfectly learned the whole of this method, however moderate may be his talent, may see that no avenue to the truth is closed to him from which everyone else is not also excluded, and that his ignorance is due neither to a deficiency in his capacity nor to his method of procedure. But as often as he applies his mind to the understanding of some matter, he will either be entirely successful, or he will realise that success depends upon a certain experiment which he is unable to perform, and in that case he will not blame his mental capacity although he is compelled to stop short there. Or finally, he may show that the knowledge desired wholly exceeds the limits of the human intelligence; and consequently he will believe that he is none the more ignorant on that account. For to have discovered this is knowledge in no less degree than the knowledge of anything else.

RULE IX

We ought to give the whole of our attention to the most insignificant and most easily mastered facts, and remain a long time in contemplation of them until we are accustomed to behold the truth clearly and distinctly.

WE HAVE now indicated the two operations of our understanding, intuition and deduction, on which alone we have said we must rely in the acquisition of knowledge. Let us therefore in this and in the following proposition proceed to explain how we can render ourselves more skilful in employing them, and at the same time cultivate the two principal faculties of the mind, to wit perspicacity, by viewing single objects distinctly, and sagacity, by the skilful deduction of certain facts from others.

[1]This begins at Prop. XIII. Of the later propositions we have the titles only in the case of XIX—XXI, while the last three are entirely lacking

[2]Apparently not even begun.

Truly we shall learn how to employ our mental intuition from comparing it with the way in which we employ our eyes. For he who attempts to view a multitude of objects with one and the same glance, sees none of them distinctly; and similarly the man who is wont to attend to many things at the same time by means of a single act of thought is confused in mind. But just as workmen, who are employed in very fine and delicate operations and are accustomed to direct their eyesight attentively to separate points, by practice have acquired a capacity for distinguishing objects of extreme minuteness and subtlety; so likewise people, who do not allow their thought to be distracted by various objects at the same time, but always concentrate it in attending to the simplest and easiest particulars, are clear-headed.

But it is a common failing of mortals to deem the more difficult the fairer; and they often think that they have learned nothing when they see a very clear and simple cause for a fact, while at the same time they are lost in admiration of certain sublime and profound philosophical explanations, even though these for the most part are based upon foundations which no one had adequately surveyed—a mental disorder which prizes the darkness higher than the light. But it is notable that those who have real knowledge discern the truth with equal facility whether they evolve it from matter that is simple or that is obscure; they grasp each fact by an act of thought that is similar, single, and distinct, after they have once arrived at the point in question. The whole of the difference between the apprehension of the simple and of the obscure lies in the route taken, which certainly ought to be longer if it conducts us from our initial and most absolute principles to a truth that is somewhat remote.

Everyone ought therefore to accustom himself to grasp in his thought at the same time facts that are at once so few and so simple, that he shall never believe that he has knowledge of anything which he does not mentally behold with a distinctness equal to that of the objects which he knows most distinctly of all. It is true that some men are born with a much greater aptitude for such discernment than others, but the mind can be made much more expert at such work by art and exercise. But there is one fact which I should here emphasize above all others; and that is that everyone should firmly persuade himself that none of the sciences, however abstruse, is to be deduced from lofty and obscure matters, but that they all proceed only from what is easy and more readily understood.

For example if I wish to examine whether it is possible for a natural force to pass at one and the same moment to a spot at a distance and yet to traverse the whole space in between, I shall not begin to study the force of magnetism or the influence of the stars, not even the speed of light, in order to discover whether actions such as these occur instantaneously; for the solution of this question would be more difficult than the problem proposed. I should rather bethink myself of the spatial motions of bodies, because nothing in the sphere of motion can be found more obvious to sense than this. I shall observe that while a stone cannot pass to another place in one and the same moment, because it is a body, yet a force similar to that which moves the stone is communicated exactly instantaneously if it passes unencumbered from one object to another. For instance, if I move one end of a stick of whatever length, I easily understand that the power by which that part of the stick is moved necessarily moves also all its other parts at the same moment, because then the force passes unencumbered and is not imprisoned in any body, e.g. a stone, which bears it along.

In the same way if I wish to understand how one and the same simple cause can produce contrary effects at the same time, I shall not cite the drugs of the doctors which expel certain humours and retain others; nor shall I romance about the moon's power of warming with its light and chilling by means of some occult power. I shall rather cast my eyes upon the balance in which the same weight raises one arm at the same time as it depresses the other, or take some other familiar instance.

RULE X

In order that it may acquire sagacity the mind should be exercised in pursuing just those inquiries of which the solution has already been found by others; and it ought to traverse in a systematic way even the most trifling of men's inventions though those ought to be preferred in which order is explained or implied.

I confess that my natural disposition is such that I have always found, not the following of the arguments of others, but the discovery of reasons by my own proper efforts, to yield me the highest intellectual satisfaction. It was this alone that attracted me, when I was still a young man, to the study of science. And whenever any book by its title promised some new discovery, before I read further I tried whether I could achieve something similar by means of some inborn faculty of invention, and I was careful lest a premature perusal of the book might deprive me of this harmless pleasure. So often was I successful that at length I perceived that I no longer came upon the truth by proceeding as others commonly do, viz. by pursuing vague and blind inquiries and relying more on good fortune than on skill. I saw that by long experience I had discovered certain rules which are of no little help in this inquiry, and which I used afterwards in devising further rules. Thus it was that I diligently elaborated the whole of this method and came to the conclusion that I had followed that plan of study which was the most fruitful of all.

But because not all minds are so much inclined to puzzle things out unaided, this proposition announces that we ought not immediately to occupy ourselves with the more difficult and arduous problems, but first should discuss those disciplines which are easiest and simplest, and those above all in which order most prevails. Such are the arts of the craftsmen who weave webs and tapestry, or of women who embroider or use in the same work threads with infinite modification of texture. With these are ranked all play with numbers and everything that belongs to Arithmetic, and the like. It is wonderful how all these studies discipline our mental powers, provided that we do not know the solutions from others, but invent them ourselves. For since nothing in these arts remains hidden, and they are wholly adjusted to the capacity of human cognition, they reveal to us with the greatest distinctness innumerable orderly systems, all different from each other, but none the less conforming to rule, in the proper observance of which systems of order consists the whole of human sagacity.

It was for this reason that we insisted that method must be employed in studying these matters; and this in those arts of less importance consists wholly in the close observation of the order which is found in the object studied, whether that be an order existing in the thing itself, or due to subtle human devising. Thus if we wish to make out some writing in which the meaning is disguised by the use of a cypher, though the order here fails to present itself, we yet make up an imaginary one, for the purpose both of testing all the conjectures we may make about single letters, words or sentences, and in order to arrange them so that when we sum them up we shall be able to tell all the inferences that we can deduce from them. We must principally beware of wasting our time in such cases by proceeding at random and unmethodically; for even though the solution can often be found without method, and by lucky people sometimes quicker, yet such procedure is likely to enfeeble the faculties and to make people accustomed to the trifling and the childish, so that for the future their minds will stick on the surface of things, incapable of penetrating beyond it. But meanwhile we must not fall into the error of those who, having devoted themselves solely to what is lofty and serious, find that after many years of toil they have acquired, not the profound knowledge they hoped for, but only mental confusion. Hence we must give ourselves practice first in those easier disciplines, but methodically, so that by open and familiar ways we may ceaselessly accustom ourselves to penetrate as easily as though we were at play into the very heart of these subjects. For by this means we shall afterwards gradually feel (and in a space of time shorter than we could at all hope for) that we are in a position with equal facility to deduce from evident first principles many propositions which at first sight are highly intricate and difficult.

It may perhaps strike some with surprise that here, where we are discussing how to improve our power of deducing one truth from another, we have omitted all the precepts of the dialecticians, by which they think to control the human reason. They prescribe certain formulae of argument, which lead to a conclusion with such necessity that, if the reason commits itself to their trust, even though it slackens its interest and no longer pays a heedful and close attention to the very proposition inferred, it can nevertheless at the same time come to a sure conclusion by virtue of the form of the argument alone. Exactly so; the fact is that frequently we notice that often the truth escapes away out of these imprisoning bonds, while the people themselves who have used them in order to capture it remain entangled in them. Other people are not so frequently entrapped; and it is a matter of experience that the most ingenious sophisms hardly ever impose on anyone who uses his unaided reason, while they are wont to deceive the sophists themselves.

Wherefore as we wish here to be particularly careful lest our reason should go on holiday while we are examining the truth of any matter, we reject those formulae as being opposed to our project, and look out rather for all the aids by which our thought may be kept attentive, as will be shown in the sequel. But, to say a few words more, that it may appear still more evident that this style of argument conributes nothing at all to the discovery of the truth, we must note that the Dialecticians are unable to devise any syllogism which has a true conclusion, unless they have first secured the material out of which to construct it, i.e. unless they have already ascertained the very truth which is deduced in that syllogism. Whence it is clear that from a formula of this kind they can gather nothing that is new, and hence the ordinary Dialectic is quite valueless for those who desire to investigate the truth of things. Its only possible use is to serve to explain at times more easily to others the truths we have already ascertained; hence it should be transferred from Philosophy to Rhetoric.

RULE XI

If, after we have recognized intuitively a number of simple truths, we wish to draw any inference from them, it is useful to run them over in a continuous and uninterrupted act of thought, to reflect upon their relations to one another, and to grasp together distinctly a number of these propositions so far as is possible at the same time. For this is a way of making our knowledge much more certain, and of greatly increasing the power of the mind.

HERE we have an opportunity of expounding more clearly what has been already said of mental intuition in the third and seventh rules. In one passage[1] we opposed it to deduction, while in the other we distinguished it from enumeration only, which we defined as an inference drawn from many and diverse things[2]. But the simple deduction of one thing from another, we said in the same passage[3], was effected by intuition.

It was necessary to do this, because two things are requisite for mental intuition. Firstly, the proposition intuited must be clear and distinct; secondly, it must be grasped in its totality at the same time and not successively. As for deduction, if we are thinking of how the process works, as we were in Rule III,

[1]Cf. p. 4.
[2]Cf. p. 10.
[3]Cf. p. 4.

it appears not to occur all at the same time, but involves a sort of movement on the part of our mind when it infers one thing from another. We were justified therefore in distinguishing deduction in that rule from intuition. But if we wish to consider deduction as an accomplished fact, as we did in what we said relatively to the seventh rule, then it no longer designates a movement, but rather the completion of a movement, and therefore we suppose that it is presented to us by intuition when it is simple and clear, but not when it is complex and involved. When this is the case we give it the name of enumeration or induction, because it cannot then be grasped as a whole at the same time by the mind, and its certainty depends to some extent on the memory, in which our judgments about the various matters enumerated must be retained, if from their assemblage a single fact is to be inferred.

All these distinctions had to be made if we were to elucidate this rule. We treated of mental intuition solely in Rule IX; the tenth dealt with enumeration alone; but now the present rule explains how these two operations aid and complete each other. In doing so they seem to grow into a single process by virtue of a sort of motion of thought which has an attentive and vision-like knowledge of one fact and yet can pass at the very same moment to another.

Now to this co-operation we assign a two-fold advantage. Firstly, it promotes a more certain knowledge of the conclusion with which we are concerned, and secondly, it makes the mind readier to discover fresh truths. In fact the memory, on which we have said depends the certainty of the conclusions which embrace more than we can grasp in a single act of intuition, though weak and liable to fail us, can be renewed and made stronger by this continuous and constantly repeated process of thought. Thus if diverse mental acts have led me to know what is the relation between a first and a second magnitude, next between the second and a third, then between the third and a fourth, and finally the fourth and a fifth, that need not lead me to see what is the relation between the first and the fifth, nor can I deduce it from what I already know, unless I remember all the other relations. Hence what I have to do is to run over them all repeatedly in my mind, until I pass so quickly from the first to the last that practically no step is left to the memory, and I seem to view the whole all at the same time.

Everyone must see that this plan does much

to counteract the slowness of the mind and to enlarge its capacity. But in addition we must note that the greatest advantage of this rule consists in the fact that, by reflecting on the mutual dependence of two propositions, we acquire the habit of distinguishing at a glance what is more or less relative, and what the steps are by which a relative fact is related to something absolute. For example, if I run over a number of magnitudes that are in continued proportion, I shall reflect upon all the following facts: viz. that the mental act is entirely similar—and not easier in the one case, more difficult in another—by which I grasp the relation between the first and the second, the second and third, third and fourth, and so on; while yet it is more difficult for me to conceive what the relation of the second is to the first and to the third at the same time, and much more difficult still to tell its relation to the first and fourth, and so on. These considerations then lead me to see why, if the first and second alone are given, I can easily find the third and fourth, and all the others; the reason being that this process requires only single and distinct acts of thought. But if only the first and the third are given, it is not so easy to recognize the mean, because this can only be accomplished by means of a mental operation in which two of the previous acts are involved. If the first and the fourth magnitudes alone are given, it is still more difficult to present to ourselves the two means, because here three acts of thought come in simultaneously. It would seem likely as a consequence that it would be even more difficult to discover the three means between the first and the fifth. The reason why this is not so is due to a fresh fact; viz. even though here four mental acts come together they can yet be disjoined, since four can be divided by another number. Thus I can discover the third by itself from the first and fifth, then the second from the first and third, and so on. If one accustoms one's self to reflect on these and similar problems, as often as a new question arises, at once one recognizes what produces its special difficulty, and what is the simplest method of dealing with all cases; and to be able to do so is a valuable aid to the discovery of the truth.

RULE XII

Finally wé ought to employ all the aids of understanding, imagination, sense and memory, first for the purpose of having a distinct intuition of simple propositions; partly also in order to compare the propositions to be proved with those we know already, so that we may be able to recognize their truth; partly also in order to discover the truths, which should be compared with each other so that nothing may be left lacking on which human industry may exercise itself.

THIS rule states the conclusion of all that we said before, and shows in general outline what had to be explained in detail, in this wise.

In the matter of cognition of facts two things alone have to be considered, ourselves who know and the objects themselves which are to be known. Within us there are four faculties only which we can use for this purpose, viz. understanding, imagination, sense and memory. The understanding is indeed alone capable of perceiving the truth, but yet it ought to be aided by imagination, sense and memory, lest perchance we omit any expedient that lies within our power. On the side of the facts to be known it is enough to examine three things; first, that which presents itself spontaneously, secondly, how we learn one thing by means of another, and thirdly, what (truths) are deduced from what. This enumeration appears to me to be complete, and to omit nothing to which our human powers can apply.

I should have liked therefore to have turned to the first point and to have explained in this passage, what the human mind is, what body, and how it is "informed" by mind; what the faculties in the complex whole are which serve the attainment of knowledge, and what the agency of each is. But this place seems hardly to give me sufficient room to take in all the matters which must be premised before the truth in this subject can become clear to all. For my desire is in all that I write to assert nothing controversial unless I have already stated the very reasons which have brought me to that conclusion, and by which I think that others also may be convinced.

But because at present I am prevented from doing this, it will suffice me to explain as briefly as possible that mode of viewing everything within us which is directed towards the discovery of truth, which most promotes my purpose. You need not believe that the facts are so unless you like. But what prevents us following these suppositions, if it appears that they do no harm to the truth, but only render it all much clearer? In Geometry you do precisely the same thing when you make certain assumptions about a quantity which do not in any way weaken the force of your arguments, though often our experience of its nature in

Physics makes us judge of it quite otherwise. Let us then conceive of the matter as follows:—all our external senses, in so far as they are part of the body, and despite the fact that we direct them towards objects, so manifesting activity, viz. a movement in space, nevertheless properly speaking perceive in virtue of passivity alone, just in the way that wax receives an impression from a seal. And it should not be thought that all we mean to assert is an analogy between the two. We ought to believe that the way is entirely the same in which the exterior figure of the sentient body is really modified by the object, as that in which the shape of the surface of the wax is altered by the seal. This has to be admitted not only in the case of the figure, hardness, roughness, etc. of a body which we perceive by touch, but even when we are aware of heat, cold, and the like qualities. It is likewise with the other senses. The first opaque structure in the eye receives the figure impressed upon it by the light with its various colours; and the first membrane in the ears, the nose, and the tongue that resists the further passage of the object, thus also acquires a new figure from the sound, the odour, and the savour, as the case may be.

It is exceedingly helpful to conceive all those matters thus, for nothing falls more readily under sense than figure, which can be touched and seen. Moreover that nothing false issues from this supposition more than from any other, is proved by the fact that the concept of figure is so common and simple that it is involved in every object of sense. Thus whatever you suppose colour to be, you cannot deny that it is extended and in consequence possessed of figure. Is there then any disadvantage, if, while taking care not to admit any new entity uselessly, or rashly to imagine that it exists, and not denying indeed the beliefs of others concerning colour, but merely abstracting from every other feature except that it possesses the nature of figure, we conceive the diversity existing between white, blue, and red, etc., as being like the difference between the following similar figures? The same argument applies to all cases; for it is certain that the infinitude of figures suffices to express all the differences in sensible things.

Secondly, we must believe that while the external sense is stimulated by the object, the figure which is conveyed to it is carried off to some other part of the body, that part called the common sense, in the very same instant and without the passage of any real entity from one to the other. It is in exactly the same manner that now when I write I recognize that at the very moment when the separate characters are being written down on the paper, not only is the lower end of the pen moved, but every motion in that part is simultaneously shared by the whole pen. All these diverse motions are traced by the upper end of the pen likewise in the air, although I do not conceive of anything real passing from the one extremity to the other. Now who imagines that the connection between the different parts of the human body is slighter than that between the ends of a pen, and what simpler way of expressing this could be found?

Thirdly, we must believe that the common sense has a function like that of a seal, and impresses on the fancy or imagination, as though on wax, those very figures and ideas which come uncontaminated and without bodily admixture from the external senses. But this fancy is a genuine part of the body, of sufficient size to allow its different parts to assume various figures in distinctness from each other and to let those parts acquire the practice of retaining the impressions for some time. In the latter case we give the faculty the name of memory.

In the fourth place, we must conceive that the motor force or the nerves themselves derive their origin from the brain, in which the fancy is located, and that the fancy moves them in various ways, just as the external senses act on the common sense, or the lower extremity of the pen moves the whole pen. This example also shows how the fancy can be the cause of many motions in the nerves, motions of which, however, it does not have the images stamped upon it, possessing only certain other images from which these latter follow. Just so the whole pen does not move exactly in the way in which its lower end does; nay the greater part seems

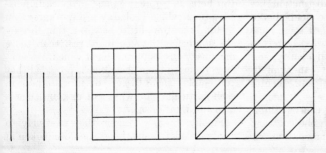

to have a motion that is quite different from and contrary to that of the other. This lets us understand how all the motions of the other animals can come about, though we can ascribe to them no knowledge at all, but only fancy of a purely corporeal kind. We can explain also how in ourselves all those operations occur which we perform without any aid from the reason.

Finally and in the fifth place, we must think that that power by which we are properly said to know things, is purely spiritual, and not less distinct from every part of the body than blood from bone, or hand from eye. It is a single agency, whether it receives impressions from the common sense simultaneously with the fancy, or applies itself to those that are preserved in the memory, or forms new ones. Often the imagination is so beset by these impressions that it is unable at the same time to receive ideas from the common sense, or to transfer them to the motor mechanism in the way befitting its purely corporeal character. In all these operations this cognitive power is at one time passive, at another active, and resembles now the seal and now the wax. But the resemblance on this occasion is only one of analogy, for among corporeal things there is nothing wholly similar to this faculty. It is one and the same agency which, when applying itself along with the imagination to the common sense, is said to see, touch, etc.; if applying itself to the imagination alone in so far as that is endowed with diverse impressions, it is said to remember; if it turn to the imagination in order to create fresh impressions, it is said to imagine or conceive; finally if it act alone it is said to understand. How this latter function takes place I shall explain at greater length in the proper place. Now it is the same faculty that in correspondence with those various functions is called either pure understanding, or imagination, or memory, or sense. It is properly called mind when it either forms new ideas in the fancy, or attends to those already formed. We consider it as capable of the above various operations, and this distinction between those terms must in the sequel be borne in mind. But after having grasped these facts the attentive reader will gather what help is to be expected from each particular faculty, and discover how far human effort can avail to supplement the deficiencies of our mental powers.

For, since the understanding can be stimulated by the imagination, or on the contrary act on it; and seeing that the imagination can act on the senses by means of the motor power applying them to objects, while they on the contrary can act on it, depicting on it the images of bodies; considering on the other hand that the memory, at least that which is corporeal and similar to that of the brutes, is in no respect distinct from the imagination; we come to the sure conclusion that, if the understanding deal with matters in which there is nothing corporeal or similar to the corporeal, it cannot be helped by those faculties, but that, on the contrary, to prevent their hampering it, the senses must be banished and the imagination as far as possible divested of every distinct impression. But if the understanding proposes to examine something that can be referred to the body, we must form the idea of that thing as distinctly as possible in the imagination; and in order to effect this with greater ease, the thing itself which this idea is to represent must be exhibited to the external senses. Now when the understanding wishes to have a distinct intuition of particular facts a multitude of objects is of no use to it. But if it wishes to deduce one thing from a number of objects, as often has to be done, we must banish from the ideas of the objects presented whatsoever does not require present attention, in order that the remainder may be the more readily retained in memory. In the same way it is not on those occasions that the objects themselves ought to be presented to the external senses, but rather certain compendious abbreviations which, provided they guard the memory against lapse, are the handier the shorter they are. Whosoever observes all these recommendations, will, in my opinion, omit nothing that relates to the first part of our rule.

Now we must approach the second part of our task. That was to distinguish accurately the notions of simple things from those which are built up out of them; to see in both cases where falsity might come in, so that we might be on our guard and give our attention to those matters only in which certainty was possible. But here, as before, we must make certain assumptions which probably are not agreed on by all. It matters little, however, though they are not believed to be more real than those imaginary circles by means of which Astronomers describe their phenomena, provided that you employ them to aid you in discerning in each particular case what sort of knowledge is true and what false.

Finally, then, we assert that relatively to our knowledge single things should be taken in in order different from that in which we should regard them when considered in their more real nature. Thus, for example, if we consider a body as having extension and figure, we shall indeed admit that from the point of view of the thing itself it is one and simple. For we cannot from that point of view regard it as compounded of corporeal nature, extension and figure, since these elements have never existed in isolation from each other. But relatively to our understanding we call it a compound constructed out of these three natures, because we have thought of them separately before we were able to judge that all three were found in one and the same subject. Hence here we shall treat of things only in relation to our understanding's awareness of them, and shall call those only simple, the cognition of which is so clear and so distinct that they cannot be analysed by the mind into others more distinctly known. Such are figure, extension, motion, etc.; all others we conceive to be in some way compounded out of these. This principle must be taken so universally as not even to leave out those objects which we sometimes obtain by abstraction from the simple natures themselves. This we do, for example, when we say that figure is the limit of an extended thing, conceiving by the term limit something more universal than by the term figure, since we can talk of a limit of duration, a limit of motion, and so on. But our contention is right, for then, even though we find the meaning of limit by abstracting it from figure, nevertheless it should not for that reason seem simpler than figure. Rather, since it is predicated of other things, as for example of the extreme bounds of a space of time or of a motion, etc., things which are wholly different from figure, it must be abstracted from those natures also; consequently it is something compounded out of a number of natures wholly diverse, of which it can be only ambiguously predicated.

Our second assertion is that those things which relatively to our understanding are called simple, are either purely intellectual or purely material, or else common both to intellect and to matter. Those are purely intellectual which our understanding apprehends by means of a certain inborn light, and without the aid of any corporeal image. That a number of such things exist is certain; and it is impossible to construct any corporeal idea which shall represent to us what the act of knowing is, what doubt is, what ignorance, and likewise what the action of the will is which it is possi-

ble to term volition, and so with other things. Yet we have a genuine knowledge of all these things, and know them so easily that in order to recognize them it is enough to be endowed with reason. Those things are purely material which we discern only in bodies; e.g. figure, extension, motion, etc. Finally those must be styled common which are ascribed now to corporeal things, now to spirits, without distinction. Such are existence, unity, duration and the like. To this group also we must ascribe those common notions which are, as it were, bonds for connecting together the other simple natures, and on whose evidence all the inferences which we obtain by reasoning depend. The following are examples:—things that are the same as a third thing are the same as one another. So too:—things which do not bear the same relation to a third thing, have some diversity from each other, etc. As a matter of fact these common notions can be discerned by the understanding either unaided or when it is aware of the images of material things.

But among these simple natures we must rank the privative and negative terms corresponding to them in so far as our intelligence grasps them. For it is quite as genuinely an act of knowledge by which I am intuitively aware of what nothing is, or an instant, or rest, as that by which I know what existence is, or lapse of time, or motion. This way of viewing the matter will be helpful in enabling us henceforth to say that all the rest of what we know is formed by composition out of these simple natures. Thus, for example, if I pronounce the judgment that some figure is not moving, I shall say that in a certain sense my idea is a complex of figure and rest; and so in other cases.

Thirdly, we assert that all these simple natures are known *per se* and are wholly free from falsity. It will be easy to show this, provided we distinguish that faculty of our understanding by which it has intuitive awareness of things and knows them, from that by which it judges, making use of affirmation and denial. For we may imagine ourselves to be ignorant of things which we really know, for example on such occasions as when we believe that in such things, over and above what we have present to us or attain to by thinking, there is something else hidden from us, and when this belief of ours is false. Whence it is evident that we are in error if we judge that any one of these simple natures is not completely known by us. For if our mind attains to the least acquaintance with it, as must be the case, since we are assumed to pass some judgment on it, this fact alone makes us infer that we know it completely. For otherwise it could not be said to be simple. but must be complex—a compound of that which is present in our perception of it, and that of which we think we are ignorant.

In the fourth place, we point out that the union of these things one with another is either necessary or contingent. It is necessary when one is so implied in the concept of another in a confused sort of way that we cannot conceive either distinctly, if our thought assigns to them separateness from each other. Thus figure is conjoined with extension, motion with duration or time, and so on, because it is impossible to conceive of a figure that has no extension, nor of a motion that has no duration. Thus likewise if I say "four and three are seven," this union is necessary. For we do not conceive the number seven distinctly unless we include in it the numbers three and four in some confused way. In the same way whatever is demonstrated of figures or numbers is necessarily united with that of which it is affirmed. Further, this necessity is not restricted to the field of sensible matters alone. The conclusion is necessary also in such a case—If Socrates says he doubts everything, it follows necessarily that he knows this at least—that he doubts. Likewise he knows that something can be either true or false, and so on, for all those consequences necessarily attach to the nature of doubt. The union, however, is contingent in those cases where the things are conjoined by no inseparable bond. Thus when we say a body is animate, a man is clothed, etc. Likewise many things are often necessarily united with one another, though most people, not noticing what their true relation is, reckon them among those that are contingently connected. As example, I give the following propositions:—"I exist, therefore God exists": also "I know, therefore I have a mind distinct from my body,"etc. Finally, we must note that very many necessary propositions become contingent when converted. Thus, though from the fact that I exist I may infallibly conclude that God exists, it is not for that reason allowable to affirm that because God exists I also exist.

Fifthly, we remark that no knowledge is at any time possible of anything beyond those simple natures and what may be called their intermixture or combination with each other. Indeed it is often easier to be aware of several of them in union with each other, than to separate one of them from the others. For, to illustrate, I am able to know what a triangle is, though I have never thought that in that knowledge was contained the knowledge of an angle, a line, the number three, figure, extension, etc. But that does not prevent me from saying that the nature of the triangle is composed of all these natures, and that they are better known than the triangle since they are the elements which we comprehend in it. It is possible also that in the triangle many other features are involved which escape our notice, such as the magnitude of the angles, which are equal to two right angles, and the innumerable relations which exist between the sides and the angles, or the size of the area, etc.

Sixthly, we say that those natures which we call composite are known by us, either because experience shows us what they are, or because we ourselves are responsible for their composition. Matter of experience consists of what we perceive by sense, what we hear from the lips of others, and generally whatever reaches our understanding either from external sources or from that contemplation which our mind directs backwards on itself. Here it must be noted that no direct experience can ever deceive the understanding if it restrict its attention accurately to the object presented to it, just as it is given to it either at firsthand or by means of an image; and if it moreover refrain from judging that the imagination faithfully reports the objects of the senses, or that the senses take on the true forms of things, or in fine that external things always are as they appear to be; for in all these judgments we are exposed to error. This happens, for example, when we believe as fact what is merely a story that someone has told us; or when one who is ill with jaundice judges everything to be yellow because his eye is tinged with yellow. So finally, too, when the imagination is diseased, as in cases of melancholia, and a man thinks that his own disorderly fancies represent real things. But the understanding of a wise man will not be deceived by these fancies, since he will judge that whatever comes to him from his imagination is really depicted in it, but yet will never assert that the object has passed complete and without any alteration from the external world to his senses, and from his senses to his imagination, unless he has some previous ground for believing this. Moreover we ourselves are responsible for the composition of the things present to our understanding when we believe that there is something in them which our mind never experiences when exercising direct perception. Thus if a man suffering from jaundice persuades himself that the things he sees are yellow, this thought of his will be composite, consisting partly of what his imagination represents to him, and partly of what he assumes on his own account, namely that the colour looks yellow not owing to the defect in his eye, but because the things he sees really are yellow. Whence the conclusion comes that we can go wrong only when the things we believe are in some way compounded by ourselves.

Seventhly, this compounding can come about in other ways, namely by impulse, by conjecture, or by deduction. Impulse sways the formation of judgments about things on the part of those whom their own initiative constrains to believe something, though they can assign no reason for their belief, but are merely determined either by some higher Power, or by their own free will, or by their fanciful disposition. The first cause is never a source of error, the second rarely, the third almost always. But a consideration of the first does not concern us here because it does not fall within the province of human skill. The working of conjecture is shown, for example, in this: water which is at a greater distance from the centre of the globe than earth, is likewise less dense substance, and likewise the air which is above the water, is still rarer; hence we hazard the guess that above the air nothing exists but a very pure aether, which is much rarer than air itself. Moreover nothing that we construct in this way really deceives us, if we merely judge it to be probable and never affirm it to be true; in fact it makes us better instructed.

Deduction is thus left to us as the only means of putting things together so as to be sure of their truth. Yet in it, too, there may be many defects. Thus if, in this space which is full of air, there is nothing to be perceived either by sight, touch, or any other sense, we conclude that the space is empty, we are in error, and our synthesis of the nature of a vacuum with that of this space is wrong. This is the result as often as we judge that we can deduce anything universal and necessary from a particular or contingent fact. But it is within our power to avoid this error, if, for example, we never interconnect any objects unless we are directly aware that the conjunction of the one with the other is wholly necessary. Thus we are justified if we deduce that nothing can have figure which has not extension, from the fact that figure and extension are necessarily conjoined.

From all these considerations we conclude firstly—that we have shown distinctly and, as we judge, by an adequate enumeration, what we were originally able to express only confusedly and in a rough and ready way. This was that mankind has no road towards certain knowledge open to it, save those of self-evident intuition and necessary deduction; further, that we have shown what those simple natures are of which we spoke in the eighth proposition. It is also quite clear that this mental vision extends both to all those simple natures, and to the knowledge of the necessary connections between them, and finally to everything else which the understanding accurately experiences either at first hand or in the imagination. Deduction, however, will be further treated in what follows.

Our second conclusion is that in order to know these simple natures no pains need be taken, because they are of themselves sufficiently well known. Application comes in only in isolating them from each other and scrutinizing them separately with steadfast mental gaze. There is no one whose intelligence is so dull as not to perceive that when he is seated he in some way differs from what he is when standing. But not everyone separates with equal distinctness the nature of position from the other elements contained in the cognition in question, or is able to assert that in this case nothing alters save the position. Now it is not without reason that we call attention to the above doctrine; for the learned have a way of being so clever as to contrive to render themselves blind to things that are in their own nature evident, and known by the simplest peasant. This happens when they try to explain by something more evident those things that are self-evident. For what they do is either to explain something else, or nothing at all. Who, for instance, does not perfectly see what that is, whatsoever it may be, in respect of which alteration occurs when we change position? But is there anyone who would grasp that very thing when he was told that *place is the surface of the body surrounding us?*[1] This would be strange seeing that that surface can change though I stay still and do not change my place, or that, on the contrary, it can so move along with me that, although it continues to surround me, I am nevertheless no longer in the same place. Do not these people really seem to use magic words which have a hidden force that eludes the grasp of human apprehension?

[1]Cf. reply to Obj. VI. (7), p. 228.

They define *motion*, a fact with which everyone is quite familiar, as *the actualisation of what exists in potentiality, in so far as it is potential!* Now who understands these words? And who at the same time does not know what motion is? Will not everyone admit that those philosophers have been trying to find a knot in a bulrush? We must therefore maintain that no definitions are to be used in explaining things of this kind lest we should take what is complex in place of what is simple. We must be content to isolate them from each other, and to give them, each of us, our individual attention, studying them with that degree of mental illumination which each of us possesses.

Our third conclusion is that the whole of human knowledge consists in a distinct perception of the way in which those simple natures combine in order to build up other objects. It is important to note this; because whenever some difficulty is brought forward for examination, almost everyone is brought to a standstill at the very outset, being in doubt as to the nature of the notions he ought to call to mind, and believing that he has to search for some new kind of fact previously unknown to him. Thus, if the question is, "what is the nature of the magnet?" people like that at once prognosticate difficulty and toil in the inquiry, and dismissing from mind every well-known fact, fasten on whatsoever is most difficult, vaguely hoping that by ranging over the fruitless field where multifarious causes lie, they will find something fresh. But he who reflects that there can be nothing to know in the magnet which does not consist of certain simple natures evident in themselves, will have no doubt how to proceed. He will first collect all the observations with which experience can supply him about this stone, and from these he will next try to deduce the character of that intermixture of simple natures which is necessary to produce all those effects which he has seen to take place in connection with the magnet. This achieved, he can boldly assert that he has discovered the real nature of the magnet in so far as human intelligence and the given experimental observations can supply him with this knowledge.

Finally, it follows fourthly from what has been said that we must not fancy that one kind of knowledge is more obscure than another, since all knowledge is of the same nature throughout, and consists solely in combining what is self-evident. This is a fact recognized by very few. People have their minds already occupied by the contrary opinion, and the more bold among them, indeed, allow themselves to uphold their private conjectures as though they were sound demonstrations, and in matters of which they are wholly ignorant feel premonitions of the vision of truths which seem to present themselves through a cloud. These they have no hesitation in propounding, attaching to their concepts certain words by means of which they are wont to carry on long and reasoned out discussions, but which in reality neither they nor their audience understand. On the other hand more diffident people often refrain from many investigations that are quite easy and are in the first degree necessary to life, merely because they think themselves unequal to the task. They believe that these matters can be discovered by others who are endowed with better mental faculties, and embrace the opinion of those in whose authority they have most confidence.

We assert fifthly that by deduction we can get only things from words, cause from effect, or effect from cause, like from like, or parts or the whole itself from the parts. . . .

For the rest, in order that there may be no want of coherence in our series of precepts, we divide the whole matter of knowledge into simple propositions and "questions."[1] In connection with simple propositions the only precepts we give are those which prepare our cognitive faculties for fixing distinctly before them any objects, whatsoever they are, and scrutinizing them with keen intelligence, since propositions of this type do not arise as the result of inquiry, but present themselves to us spontaneously. This part of our task we have undertaken in the first twelve rules, in which, we believe, we have displayed everything which, in our opinion, can facilitate the exercise of our reason. But as to "questions" some of them can be perfectly well comprehended, even though we are ignorant of their solution; these we shall treat by themselves in the next twelve rules. Finally there are others, whose meaning is not quite clear, and these we reserve for the last twelve. This division has been made advisedly, both in order to avoid mentioning anything which presupposes an acquaintance with what follows, and also for the purpose of unfolding first what we feel to be most important first to inculcate in cultivating the mental powers. Among the "questions" whose

---

[1] *Quaestiones.* Quotation marks have been employed wherever it is important to remember Descartes' special technical use of this term.

meaning is quite plain, we must to begin with note that we place those only in which we perceive three things distinctly; to wit, the marks by which we can identify what we are looking for when it occurs; what precisely the fact is from which our answer ought to be deduced; and how it is to be proved that these (the ground and its consequence) so depend one on another that it is impossible for either to change while the other remains unchanged. In this way we shall have all the premisses we require, and the only thing remaining to be shown will be how to discover the conclusion. This will not be a matter of deducing some one fact from a single simple matter (we have already said that we can do this without the help of rules), but of disentangling so skilfully some one fact that is conditioned by a number of others which all involve one another, that in recognizing it there shall be no need to call upon a higher degree of mental power than in making the simplest inference. "Questions" of this kind, being highly abstract and occurring almost exclusively in Arithmetic and Geometry, seem to the inexperienced of little value. But I warn them that people ought to busy and exercise themselves a long time in learning this art, who desire to master the subsequent portions of this method, in which all the other types of "question" are treated

RULE XIII

Once a "question" is perfectly understood, we must free it of every conception superfluous to its meaning, state it in its simplest terms, and, having recourse to an enumeration, split it up into the various sections beyond which analysis cannot go in minuteness.

THIS is the only respect in which we imitate the Dialecticians; just as they, in teaching their doctrine of the forms of syllogism, assume that the terms or matter of their syllogisms are already known, so also we on this occasion lay it down as a prerequisite that the question to be solved should be perfectly understood. But we do not, as they, distinguish two extremes and a middle term. The following is the way in which we look at the whole matter. Firstly, in every "question" there must be something of which we are ignorant; otherwise there is no use asking the question. Secondly, this very matter must be disignated in some way or other; otherwise there would be nothing to determine us to investigate it rather than anything else. Thirdly, it can only be so designated by the aid of something else which is al-

ready known. All three conditions are realised even in questions that are not fully understood. Thus if the problem be the nature of the magnet, we already know what is meant by the two words "magnet" and "nature," and this knowledge determines us to seek one sort of answer rather than another, and so on. But over and above this, if the question is to be perfectly stated, we require that it should be wholly determinate, so that we shall have nothing more to seek for than what can be inferred from the data. For example, some one might set me the question, what is to be inferred about the nature of the magnet from that set of experiments precisely which Gilbert[1] asserts he has performed, be they trustworthy or not. So again the question may be, what my conclusion is as to the nature of sound, founding my judgment merely on the precise fact that the three strings A, B, and C give out an identical sound, when by hypothesis B, though twice as thick as A, but not longer, is kept in tension by a weight that is twice as heavy; while C, though no thicker than A, but merely twice as long, is nevertheless kept in tension by a weight four times as heavy. Other illustrations might be given; but they all make it quite clear how all imperfectly expressed "questions" may be reduced to others whose meaning is quite clear, as I shall show at greater length in the proper place. We see how it is possible to follow this rule in divesting any difficulty, where the problem is properly realised, of every superfluous conception, and in reducing it to a form in which we no longer deem that we are treating of this or that special matter, but are dealing only in a general way with certain magnitudes which have to be fitted together. Thus, to illustrate, after we have limited ourselves to the consideration of this or that set of experiments merely relative to the magnet, there is no difficulty in dismissing from view all other aspects of the case.

We add also that the problem ought to be reduced to its simplest statement in accordance with Rules V and VI, and resolved into parts in accordance with Rule VII. Thus if I employ a number of experiments in investigating the magnet, I shall run them over successively, taking each by itself. Again if my inquiry is about sound, as in the case above, I shall separately consider the relation between strings A and B, then that between A and C, and so on, so that afterwards my enumeration

[1]Presumably the English physicist W. Gilbert (1540–1603), author of *De Magneto* (1600).

of results may be sufficient, and may embrace every case. These three rules are the only ones which the pure understanding need observe in dealing with the terms of any proposition before approaching its ultimate solution, though that requires us to employ the following eleven rules. The third part of this Treatise will show us more clearly how to apply them. Further by a "question" we understand everything in which either truth or falsity is found; and we must enumerate the different types of "question" in order to determine what we are able to accomplish in each case.

We have already said that there can be no falsity in the mere intuition of things, whether they are simple or united together. So conceived these are not called "questions," but they acquire that designation so soon as we prepare to pass some determinate judgment about them. Neither do we limit the title to those questions which are set us by other people. His own ignorance, or more correctly his own doubt, presented a subject of inquiry to Socrates when first he began to study it and to inquire whether it was true that he doubted everything, and maintained that such was indeed the case.

Moreover in our "questions" we seek to derive either things from words, or causes from effects, or effects from causes, or the whole or other parts from parts, or to infer several of these simultaneously.

We are said to seek to derive things from words when the difficulty consists merely in the obscurity of the language employed. To this class we refer firstly all riddles, like that of the Sphinx about the animal which to begin with is four-footed, then two-footed, and finally three-footed. A similar instance is that of the fishers who, standing on the bank with rods and hooks ready for the capture of fish, said that they no longer possessed those creatures which they had caught, but on the other hand those which they had not yet been able to catch. So in other cases; but besides these, in the majority of matters on which the learned dispute, the question is almost always one of names. We ought not to judge so ill of our great thinkers as to imagine that they conceive the objects themselves wrongly, in cases where they do not employ fit words in explaining them. Thus when people call *place* the *surface of the surrounding body,* there is no real error in their conception; they merely employ wrongly the word *place,* which by common use signifies that simple and self-evident nature in virtue of which a thing is said to be here or there. This consists wholly in a certain relation of the thing said to be in the place towards the parts of the space external to it, and is a feature which certain writers, seeing that the name place was reserved for the surface of the surrounding body, have improperly called the thing's *intrinsic position.* So it is in other cases; indeed these verbal questions are of such frequent occurrence, that almost all controversy would be removed from among Philosophers, if they were always to agree as to the meaning of words.

We seek to derive causes from effects when we ask concerning anything, whether it exists or what it is. . . .

Since, however, when a "question" is propounded for solution we are frequently unable at once to discern its type, or to determine whether the problem is to derive things from words, or causes from effects, etc., for this reason it seems to be superfluous to say more here in detail about these matters. It will occupy less space and will be more convenient, if at the same time we go over in order all the steps which must be followed if we are to solve a problem of any sort. After that, when any "question" is set, we must strive to understand distinctly what the inquiry is about.

For frequently people are in such a hurry in their investigations, that they bring only a blank understanding to their solution, without having settled what the marks are by which they are to recognize the fact of which they are in search, if it chance to occur. This is a proceeding as foolish as that of a boy, who, sent on an errand by his master, should be so eager to obey as to run off without having received his orders or knowing where to go.

However, though in every "question" something must be unknown, otherwise there is no need to raise it, we should nevertheless so define this unknown element by means of specific conditions that we shall be determined towards the investigation of one thing rather than another. These conditions to which, we maintain, attention must be paid at the very outset. We shall succeed in this if we so direct our mental vision as to have a distinct and intuitive presentation of each by itself, and inquire diligently how far the unknown fact for which we are in search is limited by each. For the human mind is wont to fall into error in two ways here; it either assumes more than is really given in determining the question, or, on the other hand, leaves something out.

We must take care to assume neither more nor less than our data furnish us. This applies chiefly to riddles and other problems where the object of the skill employed is to try to puzzle people's wits. But frequently also we must bear it in mind in other "questions," when it appears as though we could assume as true for the purpose of their solution a certain matter which we have accepted, not because we had a good reason for doing so, but merely because we had always believed it. Thus, for example, in the riddle put by the Sphinx, it is not necessary to believe that the word "foot" refers merely to the real foot of an animal; we must inquire also whether the term cannot be transferred to other things, as it may be, as it happens, to the hands of an infant, or an old man's staff, because in either case these accessories are employed as feet are in walking. So too, in the fishermen's conundrum, we must beware of letting the thought of fish occupy our minds to the exclusion of those creatures which the poor so often carry about with them unwillingly, and fling away from them when caught. So again, we must be on our guard when inquiring into the construction of a vessel, such as we once saw, in the midst of which stood a column and upon that a figure of Tantalus in the attitude of a man who wants to drink. Water when poured into the vessel remained within without leaking as long as it was not high enough to enter the mouth of Tantalus; but as soon as it touched the unhappy man's lips the whole of it at once flowed out and escaped. Now at the first blush it seems as if the whole of the ingenuity consisted in the construction of this figure of Tantalus, whereas in reality this is a mere accompaniment of the fact requiring explanation, and in no way conditions it. For the whole difficulty consists solely in the problem of how the vessel was constructed so as to let out the whole of the water when that arrived at a certain height, whereas before none escaped. Finally, likewise, if we seek to extract from the recorded observations of the stars an answer to the question as to what we can assert about their motions, it is not to be gratuitously assumed that the earth is immoveable and established in the midst of the universe, as the Ancients would have it, because from our earliest years it appears to be so. We ought to regard this as dubious, in order afterwards to examine what certainty there is in this matter to which we are able to attain. So in other cases.

On the other hand we sin by omission when there is some condition requisite to the determination of the question either expressed in it or in some way to be understood, which we do not bear in mind. This may happen in an inquiry into the subject of perpetual motion, not as we meet with it in nature in the movements of the stars and the flowing of springs, but as a motion contrived by human industry. Numbers of people have believed this to be possible, their idea being that the earth is in perpetual motion in a circle round its own axis, while again the magnet retains all the properties of the earth. A man might then believe that he would discover a perpetual motion if he so contrived it that a magnet should revolve in a circle, or at least that it communicated its own motion along with its other properties to a piece of iron. Now although he were to succeed in this, it would not be a perpetual motion artificially contrived; all he did would be to utilize a natural motion, just as if he were to station a wheel in the current of a river so as to secure an unceasing motion on its part. Thus in his procedure he would have omitted a condition requisite for the resolution of his problem.

When we have once adequately grasped the meaning of a "question," we ought to try and see exactly wherein the difficulty consists, in order that, by separating it out from all complicating circumstances, we may solve it the more easily. But over and above this we must attend to the various separate problems involved in it, in order that if there are any which are easy to resolve we may omit them; when these are removed, only that will remain of which we are still in ignorance. Thus in that instance of the vessel which was described a short time ago, it is indeed quite easy to see how the vessel should be made; a column must be fixed in its centre, a bird[1] must be painted on it. But all these things will be set aside as not touching the essential point; thus we are left with the difficulty by itself, consisting in the fact that the whole of the water, which had previously remained in the vessel, after reaching a certain height, flows out. It is for this that we have to seek a reason.

Here therefore we maintain that what is worth while doing is simply this—to explore in an orderly way all the data furnished by the proposition, to set aside everything which we see is clearly immaterial, to retain what is necessarily bound up with the problem, and to reserve what is doubtful for a more careful examination.

[1] Translate "a valve must be fitted in it."

RULE XIV

The same rule is to be applied also to the real extension of bodies. It must be set before the imagination by means of mere figures, for this is the best way to make it clear to the understanding.

BUT in proposing to make use of the imagination as an aid to our thinking, we must note that whenever one unknown fact is deduced from another that is already known, that does not show that we discover any new kind of entity, but merely that this whole mass of knowledge is extended in such a way that we perceive that the matter sought for participates in one way or another in the nature of the data given in the proposition. For example if a man has been blind from his birth it is not to be expected that we shall be able by any train of reasoning to make him perceive the true ideas of the colours which we have derived from our senses. But if a man has indeed once perceived the primary colours, though he has never seen the intermediate or mixed tints, it is possible for him to construct the images of those which he has not seen from their likeness to the others, by a sort of deduction. Similarly if in the magnet there be any sort of nature the like of which our mind has never yet known, it is hopeless to expect that reasoning will ever make us grasp it; we should have to be furnished either with some new sense or with a divine intellect. But we shall believe ourselves to have attained whatever in this matter can be achieved by our human faculties, if we discern with all possible distinctness that mixture of entities or natures already known which produces just those effects which we notice in the magnet.

Indeed all these previously known entities, viz. extension, figure, motion and the like, the enumeration of which does not belong to this place, are recognized by means of an idea which is one and the same in the various subject matters. The figure of a silver crown which we imagine, is just the same as that of one that is golden. Further this common idea is transferred from one subject to another, merely by means of the simple comparison by which we affirm that the object sought for is in this or that respect like, or identical with, or equal to a particular datum. Consequently in every train of reasoning it is by comparison merely that we attain to a precise knowledge of the truth. Here is an example:—all *A* is *B*, all *B* is *C*, therefore all *A* is *C*. Here we compare with one another a *quaesitum* and a *datum*, viz. *A* and

C, in respect of the fact that each is *B*, and so on. But because, as we have often announced, the syllogistic forms are of no aid in perceiving the truth about objects, it will be for the reader's profit to reject them altogether and to conceive that all knowledge whatsoever, other than that which consists in the simple and naked intuition of single independent objects, is a matter of the comparison of two things or more, with each other. In fact practically the whole of the task set the human reason consists in preparing for this operation; for when it is open and simple, we need no aid from art, but are bound to rely upon the light of nature alone, in beholding the truth which comparison gives us.

We must further mark that comparison should be simple and open, only as often as *quaesitum* and *datum* participate equally in a certain nature. Note that the only reason why preparation is required for comparison that is not of this nature is the fact that the common nature we spoke of does not exist equally in both, but is complicated with certain other relations or ratios. The chief part of our human industry consists merely in so transmuting these ratios as to show clearly a uniformity between the matter sought for and something else already known.

Next we must mark that nothing can be reduced to this uniformity, save that which admits of a greater and a less, and that all such matter is included under the term magnitude. Consequently when, in conformity with the previous rule, we have freed the terms of the problem from any reference to a particular subject, we shall discover that all we have left to deal with consists of magnitudes in general.

We shall, however, even in this case make use of our imagination, employing not the naked understanding but the intellect as aided by images of particulars depicted on the fancy. Finally we must note that nothing can be asserted of magnitudes in general that cannot also be ascribed to any particular instance.

This lets us easily conclude that there will be no slight profit in transferring whatsoever we find asserted of magnitudes in general to that particular species of magnitude which is most easily and distinctly depicted in our imagination. But it follows from what we stated about the twelfth rule that this must be the real extension of body abstracted from everything else except the fact that it has figure; for in that place we represented the imagination itself along with the ideas it contains as nothing more than a really material body possessing extension and figure. This is also itself evident; for no other subject displays more distinctly differences in ratio of whatsoever kind. Though one thing can be said to be more or less white than another, or a sound sharper or flatter, and so on, it is yet impossible to determine exactly whether the greater exceeds the less in the proportion two to one, or three to one, etc., unless we treat the quantity as being in a certain way analogous to the extension of a body possessing figure. Let us then take it as fixed and certain that perfectly definite "questions" are almost free from difficulty other than that of transmuting ratios so that they may be stated as equations. Let us agree, too, that everything in which we discover precisely this difficulty, can be easily, and ought to be, disengaged from reference to every other subject, and immediately stated in terms of extension and figure. It is about these alone that we shall for this reason henceforth treat, up to and as far as the twenty-fifth rule, omitting the consideration of everything else.

My desire is that here I may find a reader who is an eager student of Arithmetic and Geometry, though indeed I should prefer him to have had no practice in these arts, rather than to be an adept after the ordinary standard. For the employment of the rules which I here unfold is much easier in the study of Arithmetic and Geometry (and it is all that is needed in learning them) than in inquiries of any other kind. Further, its usefulness as a means towards the attainment of a profounder knowledge is so great, that I have no hesitation in saying that it was not the case that this part of our method was invented for the purpose of dealing with mathematical problems, but rather that mathematics should be studied almost solely for the purpose of training us in this method. I shall presume no knowledge of anything in mathematics except perhaps such facts as are self-evident and obvious to everyone. But the way in which people ordinarily think about them, even though not vitiated by any glaring errors, yet obscures our knowledge with many ambiguous and ill-conceived principles, which we shall try incidentally to correct in the following pages.

By extension we understand whatever has length, breadth, and depth, not inquiring whether it be a real body or merely space; nor does it appear to require further explanation, since there is nothing more easily perceived by our imagination. Yet the learned frequently employ distinctions so subtle that the light of nature is dissipated in attending to them, and even those matters of which no peasant is ever in doubt become invested in obscurity. Hence we announce that by extension we do not here mean anything distinct and separate from the extended object itself; and we make it a rule not to recognize those metaphysical entities which really cannot be presented to the imagination. For even though someone could persuade himself, for example, that supposing every extended object in the universe were annihilated, that would not prevent extension in itself alone existing, this conception of his would not involve the use of any corporeal image, but would be based on a false judgment of the intellect working by itself. He will admit this himself, if he reflect attentively on this very image of extension when, as will then happen, he tries to construct it in his imagination. For he will notice that, as he perceives it, it is not divested of a reference to every object, but that his imagination of it is quite different from his judgment about it. Consequently, whatever our understanding may believe as to the truth of the matter, those abstract entities are never given to our imagination as separate from the objects in which they inhere.

But since henceforth we are to attempt nothing without the aid of the imagination, it will be worth our while to distinguish carefully the ideas which in each separate case are to convey to the understanding the meaning of the words we employ. To this end we submit for consideration these three forms of expression:—*extension occupies place, body possesses extension*, and *extension is not body*.

The first statement shows how extension may be substituted for that which is extended. My conception is entirely the same if I say *extension occupies place*, as when I say *that which is extended occupies place*. Yet that is no reason why, in order to avoid ambiguity, it should be better to use the term *that which is extended;* for that does not indicate so distinctly our precise meaning, which is, that a subject occupies place owing to the fact that it is extended. Someone might interpret the expression to mean merely *that which is extended is an object occupying place*, just in the same way as if I had said *that which is animate occupies place*. This explains why we announced that here we would treat of extension, preferring that to "the extended," although we believe that there is no difference in the conception of the two.

Let us now take up these words: *body possesses extension*. Here the meaning of *extension* is not identical with that of body, yet we do not construct two distinct ideas in our imagination, one of body, the other of extension, but merely a single image of extended body; and from the point of view of the thing it is exactly as if I had said: *body is extended*, or better, *the extended is extended*. This is a peculiarity of those entities which have their being merely in something else, and can never be conceived without the subject in which they exist. How different is it with those matters which are really distinct from the subjects of which they are predicated. If, for example, I say *Peter has wealth*, my idea of Peter is quite different from that of wealth. So if I say *Paul is wealthy*, my image is quite different from that which I should have if I said *the wealthy man is wealthy*. Failure to distinguish the diversity between these two cases is the cause of the error of those numerous people who believe that extension contains something distinct from that which is extended, in the same way as Paul's wealth is something different from Paul himself.

Finally, take the expression: *extension is not body*. Here the term extension is taken quite otherwise than as above. When we give it this meaning there is no special idea corresponding to it in the imagination. In fact this entire assertion is the work of the naked understanding, which alone has the power of separating out abstract entities of this type. But this is a stumbling-block for many, who, not perceiving that extension so taken, cannot be grasped by the imagination, represent it to themselves by means of a genuine image. Now such an idea necessarily involves the concept of body, and if they say that extension so conceived is not body, their heedlessness involves them in the contradiction of saying that *the same thing is at the same time body and not body*. It is likewise of great moment to distinguish the meaning of the enunciations in which such names as *extension, figure, number, superficies, line, point, unity*, etc. are used in so restricted a way as to exclude matters from which they are not really distinct. Thus when we say: *extension* or *figure is not body; number is not the thing that is counted; a superficies is the boundary of a body, the line the limit of a surface, the point of a line; unity is not a quantity*, etc.; all these and similar propositions must be taken altogether outside the bounds of the imagination, if they are to be true. Consequently we shall not discuss them in the sequel.

But we should carefully note that in all other propositions in which these terms, though retaining the same signification and employed in abstraction from their subject matter, do not exclude or deny anything from which they are not really distinct, it is both possible and necessary to use the imagination as an aid. The reason is that even though the understanding in the strict sense attends merely to what is signified by the name, the imagination nevertheless ought to fashion a correct image of the object, in order that the very understanding itself may be able to fix upon other features belonging to it that are not expressed by the name in question, whenever there is occasion to do so, and may never imprudently believe that they have been excluded. Thus, if number be the question, we imagine an object which we can measure by summing a plurality of units. Now though it is allowable for the understanding to confine its attention for the present solely to the multiplicity displayed by the object, we must be on our guard nevertheless not on that account afterwards to come to any conclusion which implies that the object which we have described numerically has been excluded from our concept. But this is what those people do who ascribe mysterious properties to number, empty inanities in which they certainly would not believe so strongly, unless they conceived that number was something distinct from the things we number. In the same way, if we are dealing with figure, let us remember that we are concerned with an extended subject, though we restrict ourselves to conceiving it merely as possessing figure. When body is the object let us reflect that we are dealing with the very same thing, taken as possessing length, breadth and depth. Where superficies comes in, our object will still be the same though we conceive it as having length and breadth, and we shall leave out the element of depth, without denying it. The line will be considered as having length merely, while in the case of the point the object, though still the same, will be divested in our thought of every characteristic save that of being something existent.

In spite of the way in which I have dwelt on this topic, I fear that men's minds are so dominated by prejudice that very few are free from the danger of losing their way here, and that, notwithstanding the length of my discourse, I shall be found to have explained myself too briefly. Those very disciplines Arithmetic and Geometry, though the most certain of all the sciences, nevertheless lead us astray here. For is there a single Arithmetician who does not believe that the numbers with which he deals are not merely held in abstraction from any subject matter by the understanding, but are really distinct objects of the imagination? Does not your Geometrician obscure the clearness of his subject by employing irreconcileable principles? He tells you that lines have no breadth, surfaces no depth; yet he subsequently wishes to generate the one out of the other, not noticing that a line, the movement of which is conceived to create a surface, is really a body; or that, on the other hand, the line which has no breadth, is merely a mode of body. But, not to take more time in going over these matters, it will be more expeditious for us to expound the way in which we assume our object should be taken, in order that we may most easily give a proof of whatsoever is true in Arithmetic and Geometry.

Here therefore we deal with an extended object, considering nothing at all involved in it save extension, and purposely refraining from using the word quantity, because there are certain Philosophers so subtle as to distinguish it also from extension. We assume such a simplification of our problems as to leave nothing else to be inquired about except the determination of a certain extension by comparing it with a certain other extension that is already determinately known. For here we do not look to discover any new sort of fact; we merely wish to make a simplification of ratios, be they ever so involved, such that we may discover some equation between what is unknown and something known. Since this is so, it is certain that whatsoever differences in ratio exist in these subjects can be found to prevail also between two or more extensions. Hence our purpose is sufficiently served if in extension itself we consider everything that can aid us in setting out differences in ratio; but there are only three such features, viz. dimension, unity and figure.

By dimension I understand nothing but the mode and aspect according to which a subject is considered to be measurable. Thus it is not merely the case that length, breadth and depth are dimensions; but weight also is a dimension in terms of which the heaviness of objects is estimated. So, too, speed is a dimension of motion, and there are an infinite number of similar instances. For that very division of the whole into a number of parts of identical nature, whether it exist in the real order of things

or be merely the work of the understanding, gives us exactly that dimension in terms of which we apply number to objects. Again that mode which constitutes number is properly said to be a species of dimension, though there is not an absolute identity between the meaning of the two terms. For if we proceed by taking part after part until we reach the whole, the operation is then said to be counting, whereas if conversely we look upon the whole as something split up into parts, it is an object which we measure. Thus we measure centuries by years, days, hours and moments, while if we count up moments, hours, days and years, we shall finish with a total of centuries.

It clearly follows that there may be an infinite number of dimensions in the same subject, which make no addition at all to the objects which possess them, but have the same meaning whether they are based on anything real in the objects themselves, or are the arbitrary inventions of our own mind. Weight is indeed something real existing in a body, and the speed of motion is a reality, and so with the division of a century into years and days. But it is otherwise with the division of the day into hours and moments, etc. Yet all these subdivisions are exactly similar if considered merely from the point of view of dimension, as we ought to regard them both here and in the science of Mathematics. It falls rather to Physics to inquire whether they are founded on anything real.

Recognition of this fact throws much light on Geometry, since in that science almost everyone goes wrong in conceiving that quantity has three species, the line, the superficies, and the solid. But we have already stated that the line and the superficies are not conceived as being really distinct from solid body, or from one another. Moreover if they are taken in their bare essence as abstractions of the understanding, they are no more diverse species of quantity than the "animal" and "living creature" in man are diverse species of substance. Incidentally also we have to note that the three dimensions of body, length, breadth and depth, are only in name distinct from one another. For there is nothing to prevent us, in any solid body with which we are dealing, from taking any of the extensions it presents as the length, or any other as its depth, and so on. And though these three dimensions have a real basis in every extended object quâ extended, we have nevertheless no special concern in this science with them more than with countless others, which are either mental creations or have some other ground in objects. For example in the case of the triangle, if we wish to measure it exactly, we must acquaint ourselves with three features of its existence, viz. either its three sides, or two sides and an angle, or two angles and its area, and so forth. Now these can all be styled dimensions. Similarly in a trapezium five facts have to be noted, in a tetrahedron six, and so on. But if we wish to choose here those dimensions which shall give most aid to our imagination, we shall never attend at the same time to more than one or two of those depicted in our imagination, even though we know that in the matter set before us with which we are dealing several others are involved. For the art of our method consists in distinguishing as many elements as possible, so that though we attend to only a few simultaneously, we shall yet cover them all in time, taking one after the other.

The unit is that common element in which, as above remarked, all the things compared with each other should equally participate. If this be not already settled in our problems, we can represent it by one of the magnitudes already presented to us, or by any other magnitude we like, and it will be the common measure of all the others. We shall understand that in it there exists every dimension found in those very widely sundered facts which are to be compared with each other, and we shall conceive it either (1) merely as something extended, omitting every other more precise determination—and then it will be identical with the point of Geometry, considered as generating a line by its movement; or (2) we shall conceive it as a line, or (3) as a square.

To come to figures, we have already shown above how it is they alone that give us a means of constructing the images of all objects whatsoever. It remains to give notice in this place, that of the innumerable diverse species of figure, we shall employ only those which most readily express differences of relation or proportion. Moreover there are two sorts of objects only which are compared with each other, viz. numerical assemblages and magnitudes. Now there are also two sorts of figures by means of which these may be presented to our conception. For example we have the points

which represent a triangular[1] number, or again the "tree" which illustrates genealogical relation as in such a case—

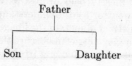

So in similar instances. Now these are figures designed to express numerical assemblages; but those which are continuous and undivided like the triangle, the square, etc.,

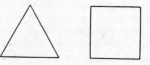

explain the nature of magnitudes.

But in order that we may point out which of all these figures we are going to use, it ought to be known that all the relations which can exist between things of this kind, must be referred to two heads, viz. either to order or to measurement.

We must further realise that while the discovery of an order is no light task, as may be seen throughout this treatise, which makes this practically its sole subject, yet once the order has been discovered there is no difficulty at all in knowing it. The seventh rule shows us how we may easily review in sequence mentally the separate elements which have been arranged in order, for the reason that in this class of relation the bond between the terms is a direct one involving nothing but the terms themselves, and not requiring mediation by means of a third term, as is the case in measurement. The unfolding of relations of measurement will therefore be all that we shall treat of here. For I recognize the order in which A and B stand, without considering anything except these two—the extreme terms of the relation. But I can recognize the ratio of the magnitude of two to that of three, only by considering some third thing, namely unity, which is the common measure of both.

We must likewise bear in mind that, by the help of the unit we have assumed, continuous

[1]"Triangular" numbers are the sums of the natural numbers, viz. 1, 3, 6, 10, etc., and thus can be constructed from any number n according to the formula $\dfrac{n(n+1)}{2}$.

magnitudes can sometimes be reduced in their entirety to numerical expressions, and that this can always be partly realised. Further it is possible to arrange our assemblage of units in such an order that the problem which previously was one requiring the solution of a question in measurement, is now a matter merely involving an inspection of order. Now our method helps us greatly in making the progress which this transformation effects.

Finally, remember that of the dimensions of continuous magnitude none are more distinctly conceived than length and breadth, and that we ought not to attend to more than these two simultaneously in the same figure, if we are to compare two diverse things with each other. The reason is, that when we have more than two diverse things to compare with each other, our method consists in reviewing them successively and attending only to two of them at the same time.

Observation of these facts leads us easily to our conclusion. This is that there is no less reason for abstracting our propositions from those figures of which Geometry treats, if the inquiry is one involving them, than from any other subject matter. Further, in doing so we need retain nothing but rectilinear and rectangular superficies, or else straight lines, which we also call figures, because they serve quite as well as surfaces in aiding us to imagine an object which actually has extension, as we have already said. Finally those same figures have to represent for us now continuous magnitudes, again a plurality of units or number also. Human ingenuity can devise nothing simpler for the complete expression of differences of relation.

RULE XV

It is likewise very often helpful to draw these figures and display them to the external senses, in order thus to facilitate the continued fixation of our attention.

THE way in which these figures should be depicted so that, in being displayed before our eyes, the images may be the more distinctly formed in our imagination is quite self-evident. To begin with we represent unity in three ways, viz. by a square, ☐, if we consider our unit as having length and breadth, or secondly by a line, ——, if we take it merely as having length, or lastly by a point, •, if we think only of the fact that it is that by aid of which we construct a numerical assemblage. But however it is depicted and conceived, we shall always remember that the unit is an object extended in every direction, and admitting of countless dimensions. So also the terms of our proposition, in cases where we have to attend at the same time to two different magnitudes belonging to them, will be represented by a rectangle whose two sides will be the two magnitudes in question. Where they are incommensurable with our unit we shall employ the following figure,

but where they are commensurable we shall use this

or this

and nothing more is needed save where it is a question of a numerical assemblage of units. Finally if we attend only to one of the magnitudes of the terms employed, we shall portray that either as a rectangle, of which one side is the magnitude considered and the other is unity, thus [＿＿＿＿] — and this will happen whenever the magnitude has to be compared with some surface. Or we shall employ a line alone, in this fashion, ——, if we take it as an incommensurable length; or thus, • • • • •, if it be a number.

RULE XVI

When we come across matters which do not require our present attention, it is better, even though they are necessary to our conclusion, to represent them by highly abbreviated symbols, rather than by complete figures. This guards against error due to defect of memory on the one hand, and, on the other, prevents that distraction of thought which an effort to keep those matters in mind while attending to other inferences would cause.

BUT because our maxim is that not more than two different dimensions out of the countless number that can be depicted in our imagination ought to be the object either of our bodily or of our mental vision, it is of importance so to retain all those outside the range of present attention that they may easily come up to mind as often as need requires.

Now memory seems to be a faculty created by nature for this very purpose. But since it is liable to fail us, and in order to obviate the need of expending any part of our attention in refreshing it, while we are engaged with other thoughts, art has most opportunely invented the device of writing. Relying on the help this gives us, we leave nothing whatsoever to memory, but keep our imagination wholly free to receive the ideas which are immediately occupying us, and set down on paper whatever ought to be preserved. In doing so we employ the very briefest symbols, in order that, after distinctly examining each point in accordance with Rule IX, we may be able, as Rule XI bids us do, to traverse them all with an extremely rapid motion of our thought and include as many as possible in a single intuitive glance.

Everything, therefore, which is to be looked upon as single from the point of view of the solution of our problem, will be represented by a single symbol which can be constructed in any way we please. But to make things easier we shall employ the characters a, b, c, etc. for expressing magnitudes already known, and A, B, C, etc. for symbolising those that are unknown. To these we shall often prefix the numerical symbols, 1, 2, 3, 4, etc., for the purpose of making clear their number, and again we shall append those symbols to the former when we want to indicate the number of the relations which are to be remarked in them. Thus if I employ the formula $2a^3$ that will be the equivalent of the words "the double of the magnitude which is symbolised by the letter a, and which contains three relations." By this device not only shall we economize our words, but, which is the chief thing, display the terms of our problem in such a detached and unencumbered way that, even though it is so full as to omit nothing, there will nevertheless be nothing superfluous to be discovered in our symbols, or anything to exercise our mental powers to no purpose, by requiring the mind to grasp a number of things at the same time.

In order that all this may be more clearly understood, we must note first, that while Arithmeticians have been wont to designate undivided magnitudes by groups of units, or else by some number, we on the other hand abstract at this point from numbers themselves no less than from Geometrical figures or anything else, as we did a little time ago. Our reason for doing this is partly to avoid the tedium of a long and superfluous calculation, but

chiefly that those portions of the matter considered which are relevant to the problem may always remain distinct, and may not be entangled with numbers that are of no help to us at all. Thus if we are trying to find the hypotenuse of the right-angled triangle whose sides are 9 and 12, the Arithmetician will tell us that it is $\sqrt{225}$, i.e. 15. But we shall write a and b in place of 9 and 12, and shall find the hypotenuse to be $\sqrt{a^2+b^2}$; and the two members of the expression a^2 and b^2 will remain distinct, whereas the number confuses them altogether.

Note further that by the number of relations attaching to a quantity I mean a sequence of ratios in continued proportion, such as the Algebra now in vogue attempts to express by sundry dimensions and figures. It calls the first of these the radix, the second the square, the third the cube, the fourth the biquadratic, and so on. I confess that for a long time I myself was imposed upon by these names. For, after the straight line and the square there was nothing which seemed to be capable of being placed more clearly before my imagination than the cube and the other figures of the same type; and with their aid I succeeded in solving not a few difficulties. But at last, after testing the matter well, I discovered that I had never found out anything by their means which I could not have recognized more easily and distinctly without employing their aid. I saw that this whole nomenclature must be abandoned, if our conceptions are not to become confused; for that very magnitude which goes by the name of the cube or the biquadratic, is nevertheless never to be presented to the imagination otherwise than as a line or a surface, in accordance with the previous rule. We must therefore be very clear about the fact that the radix, the square, the cube, etc., are merely magnitudes in continued proportion, which always imply the previous assumption of that arbitrarily chosen unit of which we spoke above. Now the first proportional is related to this unit directly and by a single ratio. But the second proportional requires the mediation of the first, and consequently is related to the unit by a pair of ratios. The third, being mediated by the first and second, has a triple relation to the standard unit, and so on. Therefore we shall henceforth call that magnitude, which in Algebra is styled the radix, the first proportional; that called the square we shall term the second proportional, and so in other cases.

Finally it must be noticed that even though here, in order to examine the nature of a difficulty, we abstract the terms involved from certain numerical complications, it yet often happens that a simpler solution will be found by employing the given numbers than if we abstract from them. This is due to the double function of numbers, already pointed out, which use the same symbols to express now order, and now measure. Hence, after seeking a solution in general terms for our problem, we ought to transform its terms by substituting for them the given numbers, in order to see whether these supply us with any simpler solution. Thus, to illustrate, after seeing that the hypotenuse of the right-angled triangle whose sides are a and b is $\sqrt{a^2+b^2}$, we should substitute 81 for a^2, and 144 for b^2. These added together give 225, the root of which, or mean proportional between unity and 225, is 15. This will let us see that a hypotenuse whose length is 15 is commensurable with sides whose lengths are 9 and 12, quite apart from the general law that it is the hypotenuse of a right-angled triangle whose sides are as 3 to 4. We, whose object is to discover a knowledge of things which shall be evident and distinct, insist on all those distinctions. It is quite otherwise with Arithmeticians, who, if the result required turns up, are quite content even though they do not perceive how it depends upon the data, though it is really in knowledge of this kind alone that science properly consists.

Moreover, it must be observed that, as a general rule, nothing that does not require to be continuously borne in mind ought to be committed to memory, if we can set it down on paper. This is to prevent that waste of our powers which occurs if some part of our attention is taken up with the presence of an object in our thought which it is superfluous to bear in mind. What we ought to do is to make a reference-table and set down in it the terms of the problem as they are first stated. Then we should state the way in which the abstract formulation is to be made and the symbols to be employed, in order that, when the solution has been obtained in terms of these symbols, we may easily apply it, without calling in the aid of memory at all, to the particular case we are considering: for it is only in passing from a lesser to a greater degree of generality that abstraction has any *raison d'être*. What I should write therefore would be something like this:—

In the right-angled triangle ABC to find the hypotenuse AC (stating the problem abstractly, in order that the derivation of the length of

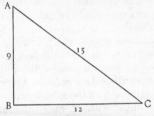

the hypotenuse from the lengths of the sides may be quite general). Then for AB, which is equal to 9, I shall substitute a; for BC, equal to 12, I put b, and similarly in other cases.

To conclude, we draw attention to the fact that these four rules will be further employed in the third part of this Treatise, though we shall conceive them somewhat more generally than we have been doing. But all this will be explained in its proper place.

RULE XVII

When a problem is proposed for discussion we should run it over, taking a direct course, and for this reason neglecting the fact that some of its terms are known, others unknown. To follow the true connection, when presenting to mind the dependence of separate items on one another, will also aid us to do this.

THE four previous rules showed us how, when the problems are determinate and fully comprehended, we may abstract them from their subject matter and so transform them that nothing remains to be investigated save how to discover certain magnitudes, from the fact that they bear such and such a relation to certain other magnitudes already given. But in the five following rules we shall now explain how these same problems are to be treated in such a way that though a single proposition contains ever so many unknown magnitudes they may all be subordinated to one another; the second will stand to the first, as the first to unity, and so too the third to the second, and the fourth to the third, and so in succession, making, however numerous, a total magnitude equal to a certain known magnitude. In doing this our method will be so sure that we may safely affirm that it passes the wit of man to reduce our terms to anything simpler.

For the present, however, I remark that in every inquiry that is to be solved by deduction there is one way that is plain and direct, by which we may more easily than by any other pass from one set of terms to another, while all other routes are more difficult and indirect. In order to understand this we must remember what was said relative to the eleventh rule, where we expounded the nature of that chain of propositions, a comparison of the neighbouring members of which enables us to see how the first is related to the last, even though it is not so easy to deduce the intermediate terms from the extremes. Now therefore if we fix our attention on the interdependence of the various links, without ever interrupting the order, so that we may thence infer how the last depends upon the first, we review the problem in a direct manner. But, on the other hand, if, from the fact that we know the first and the last to be connected with each other in a certain way, we should want to deduce the nature of the middle terms which connect them, we should then be following an order that was wholly indirect and upside down. But because here we are considering only involved inquiries, in which the problem is, given certain extremes, to find certain intermediates by the inverse process of reasoning, the whole of the device here disclosed will consist in treating the unknown as though they were known, and thus being able to adopt the easy and direct method of investigation even in problems involving any amount of intricacy. There is nothing to prevent us always achieving this result, since we have assumed from the commencement of this section of our work that we recognize the dependence of the unknown terms in the inquiry on those that are known to be such that the former are determined by the latter. This determination also is such that if, recognizing it, we consider the terms which first present themselves and reckon them even though unknown among the known, and thus deduce from them step by step and by a true connection all the other terms, even those which are known, treating them as though they were unknown, we shall fully realise the purpose of this rule. Illustrations of this doctrine, as of the most of what is immediately to follow, will be reserved until the twenty-fourth rule[1], since it will be more convenient to expound them there.

RULE XVIII

To this end only four operations are required, addition, subtraction, multiplication and division. Of these the two latter are often to be dis-

[1]No such rule has been found among Descartes' papers.

pensed with here, both in order to avoid any un foreseen complication, and because it will b easier to deal with them at a later stage.

IT is often from lack of experience on the part of the teacher that the multiplicity o rules proceeds; and matters that might have been reduced to one general rule are less clea if distributed among many particular statements. Wherefore we propose to reduce the whole of the operations which it is advisable to employ in going through our inquiry, i.e. in deducing certain magnitudes from others, to as few as four heads. It will become clear when we come to explain these how it is that they suffice for the purpose.

This is how we proceed. If we arrive at the knowledge of one magnitude owing to the fact that we already know the parts of which it is composed, the process is one of addition. If we discover the part because we already know the whole and the excess of the whole over this part, it is division. Further, it is impossible to derive a magnitude from others that are determinately fixed, and in which it is in any way contained, by any other methods. But if we have to derive a magnitude from others from which it is wholly diverse and in which it is in nowise contained, we must find some other way of relating it to them. Now if we trace out this connection or relation directly we must employ multiplication; if indirectly, division.

In explaining clearly these latter two operations the fact must be grasped that the unit of which we spoke before is here the basis and foundation of all the relations, and has the first place in the series of magnitudes in continued proportion. Further, remember that the given magnitudes occupy the second position, while those to be discovered stand at the third, the fourth and the remaining points in the series, if the proportion be direct. If, however, the proportion be indirect, the magnitude to be discovered occupies the second position or the other intermediate points, and that which is given, the last.

Thus if it is stated that as unity is to a, say to 5, which is given, so is b, i.e. 7, to the magnitude to be found[2], which is ab, i.e. 35, then a and b are at the second position, and ab, their product, at the third. So too if we are further told that as 1 is to c, say 9, so is ab, say 35, to the magnitude we are seeking, i.e. 315, then abc is in the fourth position, and is the product

[2]Note that here Descartes does not, and could not conveniently, adhere to his scheme of employing capital letters for the unknown quantities.

of two multiplications among the terms a, b and c, which are at the second position; so it is in other cases. Likewise as 1 is to a, say 5, so a, i.e. 5, is to a^2, i.e. 25. Again, as unity is to a, i.e. 5, so is a^2, i.e. 25, to a^3, i.e. 125; and finally as unity is to a, i.e. 5, so is a^3, i.e. 125, to a^4, i.e. 625, and so on. For the multiplication is performed in precisely the same way, whether the magnitude is multiplied by itself or by some other quite different number.

But if we now are told that, as unity is to a, say 5, the given divisor, so is B, say 7, *the quaesitum*, to ab, i.e. 35, the given dividend, we have on this occasion an example of the indirect or inverted order. For the only way to discover B, the *quaesitum*, is to divide the given ab by a, which is also given. The case is the same if the proposition is, "as unity is to A, say 5, the *quaesitum*, so is this A to a^2, i.e. 25, which is given"; or again, "as unity is to A, i.e. 5, the *quaesitum*, so is A^2, i.e. 25, which we also have to discover, to a^3, i.e. 125, which is given"; similarly in other cases. All these processes fall under the title "division," although we must note that these latter specimens of the process contain more difficulty than the former, because the magnitude to be found comes in a greater number of times in them, and consequently it involves a greater

number of relations in such problems. For on such occasions the meaning is the same as if the enunciation were, "extract the square root of a^2, i.e. 25," or "extract the cube root of a^3, i.e. 125," and so in other cases. This then is the way in which Arithmeticians commonly put the matter. But alternatively we may explain the problems in the terms employed by Geometricians: it comes to the same thing if we say, "find a mean proportional between that assumed magnitude, which we call unity, and that indicated by a^2," or "find two mean proportionals between unity and a^3," and so in other cases.

From these considerations it is easy to infer how these two operations suffice for the discovery of any magnitudes whatsoever which are to be deduced from others in virtue of some relation. And now that we have grasped them, the next thing to do is to show how these operations are to be brought before the scrutiny of the imagination and how presented to our actual vision, in order that we may explain how they may be used or practised.

In addition or subtraction we conceive our object under the aspect of a line, or of some extended magnitude in which length is alone to be considered. For if we are to add line a to line b,

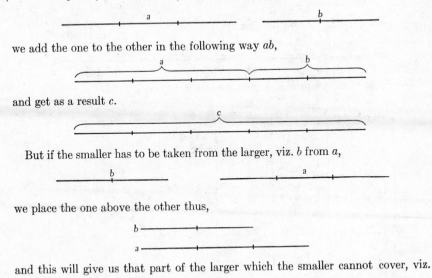

we add the one to the other in the following way ab,

and get as a result c.

But if the smaller has to be taken from the larger, viz. b from a,

we place the one above the other thus,

and this will give us that part of the larger which the smaller cannot cover, viz.

In multiplication we also conceive the given magnitudes as lines. But we imagine a rectangle to be constructed out of them; for, if we multiply a by b, we fit them together at right angles in the following way,

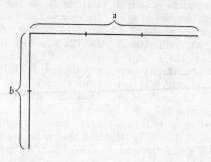

and so make the rectangle

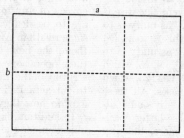

Again, if we wish to multiply *ab* by *c*,

we ought to conceive *ab* as a line, viz. *ab*,

in order that to represent *abc* we may obtain the following figure:

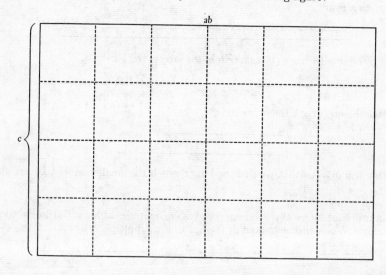

Finally, in a division in which the divisor is given, we imagine the magnitude to be divided to be a rectangle, one side of which is the divisor and the other the quotient. Thus if the rectangle ab is to be divided by a,

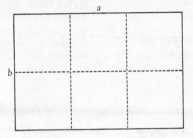

we take away from it the breadth a and are left with b for quotient:

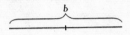

On the contrary, if this rectangle is divided by b, we take away the height b, and the quotient will be a,

But in those divisions in which the divisor is not given, but only indicated by some relation, as when we are bidden extract the square or cube root, then we must note that the term to be divided and all the others must be always conceived as lines in continued proportion, of which the first is unity, the last the magnitude to be divided. The way in which any number of mean proportionals between this and unity may be discovered will be disclosed in its proper place. At present it is sufficient to have pointed out that according to our hypothesis those operations have not yet been fully dealt with here, since to be carried out they require an indirect and reverse movement on the part of the imagination; and at present we are treating only of questions in which the movement of thought is to be direct.

As for the other[1] operations, they can be carried out with the greatest ease in the way in which we have stated they are to be conceived. Nevertheless it remains for us to show how the terms employed in them are to be constructed. For even though on our first taking up some problem we are free to conceive the terms involved as lines or as rectangles, without introducing any other figures, as was said in reference to the fourteenth rule, nevertheless it is frequently the case that, in the course of the solution, what was a rectangle, constructed by

[1] The direct operations.

the multiplication of two lines, must presently be conceived as a line, for the purpose of some further operation. Or it may be the case that the same rectangle, or a line formed by some addition or subtraction, has next to be conceived as some other rectangle drawn upon the line by which it is to be divided.

It is therefore worth our while here to expound how every rectangle may be transformed into a line, and conversely how a line or even a rectangle may be turned into another rectangle of which the side is indicated. This is the easiest thing in the world for Geometricians to do, provided they recognize that whenever we compare lines with some rectangle, as here, we always conceive those lines as rectangles, one side of which is the length that we took to represent our unit. For if we do so the whole matter resolves itself into the following proposition: Given a rectangle, to construct another rectangle equal to it upon a given side.

Now though this problem is one familiar to a mere beginner in Geometry, I wish to explain it, lest I should seem to have omitted something.

RULE XIX

Employing this method of reasoning we have to find out as many magnitudes as we have unknown terms, treated as though they were known, for the purpose of handling the problem in the direct way; and these must be expressed in the two different ways. For this will give us as many equations as there are unknowns.

RULE XX

Having got our equations, we must proceed to carry out such operations as we have neglected, taking care never to multiply where we can divide.

RULE XXI

If there are several equations of this kind, we should reduce them all to a single one, viz. that the terms of which do not occupy so many places in the series of magnitudes that are in continued proportion. The terms of the equation should then be themselves arranged in the order which this series follows.

CONTENTS

Discourse on the Method
of Rightly Conducting the Reason

DISCOURSE

ON THE METHOD OF RIGHTLY CONDUCTING THE REASON AND SEEKING FOR TRUTH IN THE SCIENCES

If this Discourse appears too long to be read all at once, it may be separated into six portions. And in the first there will be found various considerations respecting the sciences; in the second, the principal rules regarding the Method which the author has sought out; while in the third are some of the rules of morality which he has derived from this Method. In the fourth are the reasons by which he proves the existence of God and of the human soul, which form the foundation of his Metaphysic; In the fifth, the order of the questions regarding physics which he has investigated, and particularly the explanation of the movement of the heart, and of some other difficulties which pertain to medicine, as also the difference between the soul of man and that of the brutes. And in the last part the questions raised relate to those matters which the author believes to be requisite in order to advance further in the investigation of nature, in addition to the reasons that caused him to write.

PART I

GOOD SENSE is of all things in the world the most equally distributed, for everybody thinks himself so abundantly provided with it, that even those most difficult to please in all other matters do not commonly desire more of it than they already possess. It is unlikely that this is an error on their part; it seems rather to be evidence in support of the view that the power of forming a good judgment and of distinguishing the true from the false, which is properly speaking what is called Good Sense or Reason, is by nature equal in all men. Hence, too, it will show that the diversity of our opinions does not proceed from some men being more rational than others, but solely from the fact that our thoughts pass through diverse channels and the same objects are not considered by all. For to be possessed of good mental powers is not sufficient; the principal matter is to apply them well. The greatest minds are capable of the greatest vices as well as of the greatest virtues, and those who proceed very slowly may, provided they always follow the straight road, really advance much faster than those who, though they run, forsake it.

For myself I have never ventured to presume that my mind was in any way more perfect than that of the ordinary man; I have even longed to possess thought as quick, or an imagination as accurate and distinct, or a memory as comprehensive or ready, as some others. And besides these I do not know any other qualities that make for the perfection of the human mind. For as to reason or sense, inasmuch as it is the only thing that constitutes us men and distinguishes us from the brutes, I would fain believe that it is to be found complete in each individual, and in this I follow the common opinion of the philosophers, who say that the question of more or less occurs only in the sphere of the *accidents* and does not affect the *forms* or natures of the *individuals* in the same *species*.

But I shall not hesitate to say that I have had great good fortune from my youth up, in lighting upon and pursuing certain paths which have conducted me to considerations and maxims from which I have formed a Method, by whose assistance it appears to me I have the means of gradually increasing my knowledge and of little by little raising it to the highest possible point which the medioc-

41

rity of my talents and the brief duration of my life can permit me to reach. For I have already reaped from it fruits of such a nature that, even though I always try in the judgments I make on myself to lean to the side of self-depreciation rather than to that of arrogance, and though, looking with the eye of a philosopher on the diverse actions and enterprises of all mankind, I find scarcely any which do not seem to me vain and useless, I do not cease to receive extreme satisfaction in the progress which I seem to have already made in the search after truth, and to form such hopes for the future as to venture to believe that, if amongst the occupations of men, simply as men, there is some one in particular that is excellent and important, that is the one which I have selected.

It must always be recollected, however, that possibly I deceive myself, and that what I take to be gold and diamonds is perhaps no more than copper and glass. I know how subject we are to delusion in whatever touches ourselves, and also how much the judgments of our friends ought to be suspected when they are in our favour. But in this Discourse I shall be very happy to show the paths I have followed, and to set forth my life as in a picture, so that everyone may judge of it for himself; and thus in learning from the common talk what are the opinions which are held of it, a new means of obtaining self-instruction will be reached, which I shall add to those which I have been in the habit of using.

Thus my design is not here to teach the Method which everyone should follow in order to promote the good conduct of his Reason, but only to show in what manner I have endeavoured to conduct my own. Those who set about giving precepts must esteem themselves more skilful than those to whom they advance them, and if they fall short in the smallest matter they must of course take the blame for it. But regarding this Treatise simply as a history, or, if you prefer it, a fable in which, amongst certain things which may be imitated, there are possibly others also which it would not be right to follow, I hope that it will be of use to some without being hurtful to any, and that all will thank me for my frankness.

I have been nourished on letters since my childhood, and since I was given to believe that by their means a clear and certain knowledge could be obtained of all that is useful in life, I had an extreme desire to acquire instruction. But so soon as I had achieved the entire course of study at the close of which one is usually received into the ranks of the learned, I entirely changed my opinion. For I found myself embarrassed with so many doubts and errors that it seemed to me that the effort to instruct myself had no effect other than the increasing discovery of my own ignorance. And yet I was studying at one of the most celebrated Schools in Europe, where I thought that there must be men of learning if they were to be found anywhere in the world. I learned there all that others learned; and not being satisfied with the sciences that we were taught, I even read through all the books which fell into my hands, treating of what is considered most curious and rare. Along with this I knew the judgments that others had formed of me, and I did not feel that I was esteemed inferior to my fellow-students, although there were amongst them some destined to fill the places of our masters. And finally our century seemed to me as flourishing, and as fertile in great minds, as any which had preceded. And this made me take the liberty of judging all others by myself and of coming to the conclusion that there was no learning in the world such as I was formerly led to believe it to be.

I did not omit, however, always to hold in esteem those exercises which are the occupation of the Schools. I knew that the Languages which one learns there are essential for the understanding of all ancient literature; that fables with their charm stimulate the mind and histories of memorable deeds exalt it; and that, when read with discretion, these books assist in forming a sound judgment. I was aware that the reading of all good books is indeed like a conversation with the noblest men of past centuries who were the authors of them, nay a carefully studied conversation, in which they reveal to us none but the best of their thoughts. I deemed Eloquence to have a power and beauty beyond compare; that Poesy has most ravishing delicacy and sweetness; that in Mathematics there are the subtlest discoveries and inventions which may accomplish much, both in satisfying the curious, and in furthering all the arts, and in diminishing man's labour; that those writings that deal with Morals contain much that is instructive, and many exhortations to virtue which are most useful; that Theology points out the way to Heaven; that Philosophy teaches us to speak with an appearance of truth on all things, and causes us to be admired by the less learned; that Jurisprudence, Medicine and all other sciences bring onour and riches to those who cultivate them; nd finally that it is good to have examined all hings, even those most full of superstition and alsehood, in order that we may know their just value, and avoid being deceived by them.

But I considered that I had already given ufficient time to languages and likewise even o the reading of the literature of the ancients, ooth their histories and their fables. For to onverse with those of other centuries is almost he same thing as to travel. It is good to know omething of the customs of different peoples n order to judge more sanely of our own, and not to think that everything of a fashion not ours is absurd and contrary to reason, as do hose who have seen nothing. But when one employs too much time in travelling, one becomes a stranger in one's own country, and when one is too curious about things which were practised in past centuries, one is usually very ignorant about those which are practised in our own time. Besides, fables make one imagine many events possible which in reality are not so, and even the most accurate of histories, if they do not exactly misrepresent or exaggerate the value of things in order to render them more worthy of being read, at least omit in them all the circumstances which are basest and least notable; and from this fact it follows that what is retained is not portrayed as it really is, and that those who regulate their conduct by examples which they derive from such a source, are liable to fall into the extravagances of the knights-errant of Romance, and form projects beyond their power of performance.

I esteemed Eloquence most highly and I was enamoured of Poesy, but I thought that both were gifts of the mind rather than fruits of study. Those who have the strongest power of reasoning, and who most skilfully arrange their thoughts in order to render them clear and intelligible, have the best power of persuasion even if they can but speak the language of Lower Brittany and have never learned Rhetoric. And those who have the most delightful original ideas and who know how to express them with the maximum of style and suavity, would not fail to be the best poets even if the art of Poetry were unknown to them.

Most of all was I delighted with Mathematics because of the certainty of its demonstrations and the evidence of its reasoning; but I did not yet understand its true use, and, believing that it was of service only in the mechanical arts, I was astonished that, seeing how firm and solid was its basis, no loftier edifice had been reared thereupon. On the other hand I compared the works of the ancient pagans which deal with Morals to palaces most superb and magnificent, which are yet built on sand and mud alone. They praise the virtues most highly and show them to be more worthy of being prized than anything else in the world, but they do not sufficiently teach us to become acquainted with them, and often that which is called by a fine name is nothing but insensibility, or pride, or despair, or parricide.

I honoured our Theology and aspired as much as anyone to reach to heaven, but having learned to regard it as a most highly assured fact that the road is not less open to the most ignorant than to the most learned, and that the revealed truths which conduct thither are quite above our intelligence, I should not have dared to submit them to the feebleness of my reasonings; and I thought that, in order to undertake to examine them and succeed in so doing, it was necessary to have some extraordinary assistance from above and to be more than a mere man.

I shall not say anything about Philosophy, but that, seeing that it has been cultivated for many centuries by the best minds that have ever lived, and that nevertheless no single thing is to be found in it which is not subject of dispute, and in consequence which is not dubious, I had not enough presumption to hope to fare better there than other men had done. And also, considering how many conflicting opinions there may be regarding the self-same matter, all supported by learned people, while there can never be more than one which is true, I esteemed as well-nigh false all that only went as far as being probable.

Then as to the other sciences, inasmuch as they derive their principles from Philosophy, I judged that one could have built nothing solid on foundations so far from firm. And neither the honour nor the promised gain was sufficient to persuade me to cultivate them, for, thanks be to God, I did not find myself in a condition which obliged me to make a merchandise of science for the improvement of my fortune; and, although I did not pretend to scorn all glory like the Cynics, I yet had very small esteem for what I could not hope to acquire, excepting through fictitious titles. And, finally, as to false doctrines, I thought that I already knew well enough what they were worth to be subject to deception neither by the promises of an alchemist, the predictions of an astrologer, the impostures of a magician, the artifices or the empty boastings of any of those who make a profession of knowing that of which they are ignorant.

This is why, as soon as age permitted me to emerge from the control of my tutors, I entirely quitted the study of letters. And resolving to seek no other science than that which could be found in myself, or at least in the great book of the world, I employed the rest of my youth in travel, in seeing courts and armies, in intercourse with men of diverse temperaments and conditions, in collecting varied experiences, in proving myself in the various predicaments in which I was placed by fortune, and under all circumstances bringing my mind to bear on the things which came before it, so that I might derive some profit from my experience. For it seemed to me that I might meet with much more truth in the reasonings that each man makes on the matters that specially concern him, and the issue of which would very soon punish him if he made a wrong judgment, than in the case of those made by a man of letters in his study touching speculations which lead to no result, and which bring about no other consequences to himself excepting that he will be all the more vain the more they are removed from common sense, since in this case it proves him to have employed so much the more ingenuity and skill in trying to make them seem probable. And I always had an excessive desire to learn to distinguish the true from the false, in order to see clearly in my actions and to walk with confidence in this life.

It is true that while I only considered the manners of other men I found in them nothing to give me settled convictions; and I remarked in them almost as much diversity as I had formerly seen in the opinions of philosophers. So much was this the case that the greatest profit which I derived from their study was that, in seeing many things which, although they seem to us very extravagant and ridiculous, were yet commonly received and approved by other great nations, I learned to believe nothing too certainly of which I had only been convinced by example and custom. Thus little by little I was delivered from many errors which might have obscured our natural vision and rendered us less capable of listening to Reason. But after I had employed several years in thus studying the book of the world and trying to acquire some experience, I one day formed the resolution of also making myself an object of study and of employing all the strength of my mind in choosing the road I should follow. This succeeded much better, it appeared to me, than if I had never departed either from my country or my books.

PART II

I was then in Germany, to which country I had been attracted by the wars which are not yet at an end. And as I was returning from the coronation of the Emperor to join the army, the setting in of winter detained me in a quarter where, since I found no society to divert me, while fortunately I had also no cares or passions to trouble me, I remained the whole day shut up alone in a stove-heated room where I had complete leisure to occupy myself with my own thoughts. One of the first of the considerations that occurred to me was that there is very often less perfection in works composed of several portions, and carried out by the hands of various masters, than in those on which one individual alone has worked. Thus we see that buildings planned and carried out by one architect alone are usually more beautiful and better proportioned than those which many have tried to put in order and improve, making use of old walls which were built with other ends in view. In the same way also, those ancient cities which, originally mere villages, have become in the process of time great towns, are usually badly constructed in comparison with those which are regularly laid out on a plain by a surveyor who is free to follow his own ideas. Even though, considering their buildings each one apart, there is often as much or more display of skill in the one case than in the other, the former have large buildings and small buildings indiscriminately placed together, thus rendering the streets crooked and irregular, so that it might be said that it was chance rather than the will of men guided by reason that led to such an arrangement. And if we consider that this happens despite the fact that from all time there have been certain officials who have had the special duty of looking after the buildings of private individuals in order that they may be public ornaments, we shall understand how difficult it is to bring about much that is satisfactory in operating only upon the works of others. Thus I imagined that those people who were once half-savage, and who have become civilized only by slow degrees, merely forming their laws as the disagreeable necessities of their crimes and quarrels constrained them,

:ould not succeed in establishing so good a system of government as those who, from the time they first came together as communities, carried into effect the constitution laid down by some prudent legislator. Thus it is quite certain that the constitution of the true Religion whose ordinances are of God alone is incomparably better regulated than any other. And, to come down to human affairs, I believe that if Sparta was very flourishing in former times, this was not because of the excellence of each and every one of its laws, seeing that many were very strange and even contrary to good morals, but because, being drawn up by one individual, they all tended towards the same end. And similarly I thought that the sciences found in books—in those at least whose reasonings are only probable and which have no demonstrations, composed as they are of the gradually accumulated opinions of many different individuals—do not approach so near to the truth as the simple reasoning which a man of common sense can quite naturally carry out respecting the things which come immediately before him. Again I thought that since we have all been children before being men, and since it has for long fallen to us to be governed by our appetites and by our teachers (who often enough contradicted one another, and none of whom perhaps counselled us always for the best), it is almost impossible that our judgments should be so excellent or solid as they should have been had we had complete use of our reason since our birth, and had we been guided by its means alone.

It is true that we do not find that all the houses in a town are rased to the ground for the sole reason that the town is to be rebuilt in another fashion, with streets made more beautiful; but at the same time we see that many people cause their own houses to be knocked down in order to rebuild them, and that sometimes they are forced so to do where there is danger of the houses falling of themselves, and when the foundations are not secure. From such examples I argued to myself that there was no plausibility in the claim of any private individual to reform a state by altering everything, and by overturning it throughout, in order to set it right again. Nor is it likewise probable that the whole body of the Sciences, or the order of teaching established by the Schools, should be reformed. But as regards all the opinions which up to this time I had embraced, I thought I could not do better

than endeavour once for all to sweep them completely away, so that they might later on be replaced, either by others which were better, or by the same, when I had made them conform to the uniformity of a rational scheme. And I firmly believed that by this means I should succeed in directing my life much better than if I had only built on old foundations, and relied on principles of which I allowed myself to be in youth persuaded without having inquired into their truth. For although in so doing I recognised various difficulties, these were at the same time not unsurmountable, nor comparable to those which are found in reformation of the most insignificant kind in matters which concern the public. In the case of great bodies it is too difficult a task to raise them again when they are once thrown down, or even to keep them in their places when once thoroughly shaken; and their fall cannot be otherwise than very violent. Then as to any imperfections that they may possess (and the very diversity that is found between them is sufficient to tell us that these in many cases exist) custom has doubtless greatly mitigated them, while it has also helped us to avoid, or insensibly corrected a number against which mere foresight would have found it difficult to guard. And finally the imperfections are almost always more supportable than would be the process of removing them, just as the great roads which wind about amongst the mountains become, because of being frequented, little by little so well-beaten and easy that it is much better to follow them than to try to go more directly by climbing over rocks and descending to the foot of precipices.

This is the reason why I cannot in any way approve of those turbulent and unrestful spirits who, being called neither by birth nor fortune to the management of public affairs, never fail to have always in their minds some new reforms. And if I thought that in this treatise there was contained the smallest justification for this folly, I should be very sorry to allow it to be published. My design has never extended beyond trying to reform my own opinion and to build on a foundation which is entirely my own. If my work has given me a certain satisfaction, so that I here present to you a draft of it, I do not so do because I wish to advise anybody to imitate it. Those to whom God has been most beneficent in the bestowal of His graces will perhaps form designs which are more elevated; but I fear much that this particular one will seem too venturesome for many. The simple resolve to strip oneself of all opinions and beliefs formerly received is not to be regarded as an example that each man should follow, and the world may be said to be mainly composed of two classes of minds neither of which could prudently adopt it. There are those who, believing themselves to be cleverer than they are, cannot restrain themselves from being precipitate in judgment and have not sufficient patience to arrange their thoughts in proper order; hence, once a man of this description had taken the liberty of doubting the principles he formerly accepted, and had deviated from the beaten track, he would never be able to maintain the path which must be followed to reach the appointed end more quickly, and he would hence remain wandering astray all through his life. Secondly, there are those who having reason or modesty enough to judge that they are less capable of distinguishing truth from falsehood than some others from whom instruction might be obtained, are right in contenting themselves with following the opinions of these others rather than in searching better ones for themselves.

For myself I should doubtless have been of these last if I had never had more than a single master, or had I never known the diversities which have from all time existed between the opinions of men of the greatest learning. But I had been taught, even in my College days, that there is nothing imaginable so strange or so little credible that it has not been maintained by one philosopher or other, and I further recognised in the course of my travels that all those whose sentiments are very contrary to ours are yet not necessarily barbarians or savages, but may be possessed of reason in as great or even a greater degree than ourselves. I also considered how very different the self-same man, identical in mind and spirit, may become, according as he is brought up from childhood amongst the French or Germans, or has passed his whole life amongst Chinese or cannibals. I likewise noticed how even in the fashions of one's clothing the same thing that pleased us ten years ago, and which will perhaps please us once again before ten years are passed, seems at the present time extravagant and ridiculous. I thus concluded that it is much more custom and example that persuade us than any certain knowledge, and yet in spite of this the voice of the majority does not afford a proof of any value in truths a little difficult to discover, because such truths are

much more likely to have been discovered by one man than by a nation. I could not, however, put my finger on a single person whose opinions seemed preferable to those of others, and I found that I was, so to speak, constrained myself to undertake the direction of my procedure.

But like one who walks alone and in the twilight I resolved to go so slowly, and to use so much circumspection in all things, that if my advance was but very small, at least I guarded myself well from falling. I did not wish to set about the final rejection of any single opinion which might formerly have crept into my beliefs without having been introduced there by means of Reason, until I had first of all employed sufficient time in planning out the task which I had undertaken, and in seeking the true Method of arriving at a knowledge of all the things of which my mind was capable.

Among the different branches of Philosophy, I had in my younger days to a certain extent studied Logic; and in those of Mathematics, Geometrical Analysis and Algebra— three arts or sciences which seemed as though they ought to contribute something to the design I had in view. But in examining them I observed in respect to Logic that the syllogisms and the greater part of the other teaching served better in explaining to others those things that one knows (or like the art of Lully, in enabling one to speak without judgment of those things of which one is ignorant) than in learning what is new. And although in reality Logic contains many precepts which are very true and very good, there are at the same time mingled with them so many others which are hurtful or superfluous, that it is almost as difficult to separate the two as to draw a Diana or a Minerva out of a block of marble which is not yet roughly hewn. And as to the Analysis of the ancients and the Algebra of the moderns, besides the fact that they embrace only matters the most abstract, such as appear to have no actual use, the former is always so restricted to the consideration of symbols that it cannot exercise the Understanding without greatly fatiguing the Imagination; and in the latter one is so subjected to certain rules and formulas that the result is the construction of an art which is confused and obscure, and which embarrasses the mind, instead of a science which contributes to its cultivation. This made me feel that some other Method must be found, which, comprising the advantages of the three, is yet exempt from their aults. And as a multiplicity of laws often urnishes excuses for evil-doing, and as a State s hence much better ruled when, having but 'ery few laws, these are most strictly observed; o, instead of the great number of precepts of vhich Logic is composed, I believed that I hould find the four which I shall state quite ufficient, provided that I adhered to a firm md constant resolve never on any single occasion to fail in their observance.

The first of these was to accept nothing as rue which I did not clearly recognise to be so: hat is to say, carefully to avoid precipitation and prejudice in judgments, and to accept in hem nothing more than what was presented o my mind so clearly and distinctly that I ould have no occasion to doubt it.

The second was to divide up each of the difficulties which I examined into as many parts is possible, and as seemed requisite in order hat it might be resolved in the best manner possible.

The third was to carry on my reflections in lue order, commencing with objects that were he most simple and easy to understand, in order to rise little by little, or by degrees, to knowledge of the most complex, assuming an order, even if a fictitious one, among those which do not follow a natural sequence relatively to one another.

The last was in all cases to make enumerations so complete and reviews so general that I should be certain of having omitted nothing.

Those long chains of reasoning, simple and easy as they are, of which geometricians make use in order to arrive at the most difficult demonstrations, had caused me to imagine that all those things which fall under the cognizance of man might very likely be mutually related in the same fashion; and that, provided only that we abstain from receiving anything as true which is not so, and always retain the order which is necessary in order to deduce the one conclusion from the other, there can be nothing so remote that we cannot reach to it, nor so recondite that we cannot discover it. And I had not much trouble in discovering which objects it was necessary to begin with, for I already knew that it was with the most simple and those most easy to apprehend. Considering also that of all those who have hitherto sought for the truth in the Sciences, it has been the mathematicians alone who have been able to succeed in making any demonstrations, that is to say producing reasons which are evident and certain, I did not doubt

that it had been by means of a similar kind that they carried on their investigations. I did not at the same time hope for any practical result in so doing, except that my mind would become accustomed to the nourishment of truth and would not content itself with false reasoning. But for all that I had no intention of trying to master all those particular sciences that receive in common the name of Mathematics; but observing that, although their objects are different, they do not fail to agree in this, that they take nothing under consideration but the various relationships or proportions which are present in these objects, I thought that it would be better if I only examined these proportions in their general aspect, and without viewing them otherwise than in the objects which would serve most to facilitate a knowledge of them. Not that I should in any way restrict them to these objects, for I might later on all the more easily apply them to all other objects to which they were applicable. Then, having carefully noted that in order to comprehend the proportions I should sometimes require to consider each one in particular, and sometimes merely keep them in mind, or take them in groups, I thought that, in order the better to consider them in detail, I should picture them in the form of lines, because I could find no method more simple nor more capable of being distinctly represented to my imagination and senses. I considered, however, that in order to keep them in my memory or to embrace several at once, it would be essential that I should explain them by means of certain formulas, the shorter the better. And for this purpose it was requisite that I should borrow all that is best in Geometrical Analysis and Algebra, and correct the errors of the one by the other.

As a matter of fact, I can venture to say that the exact observation of the few precepts which I had chosen gave me so much facility in sifting out all the questions embraced in these two sciences, that in the two or three months which I employed in examining them —commencing with the most simple and general, and making each truth that I discovered a rule for helping me to find others—not only did I arrive at the solution of many questions which I had hitherto regarded as most difficult, but, towards the end, it seemed to me that I was able to determine in the case of those of which I was still ignorant, by what means, and in how far, it was possible to solve them. In this I might perhaps appear to you to be very vain if you did not remember that having but one truth to discover in respect to each matter, whoever succeeds in finding it knows in its regard as much as can be known. It is the same as with a child, for instance, who has been instructed in Arithmetic and has made an addition according to the rule prescribed; he may be sure of having found as regards the sum of figures given to him all that the human mind can know. For, in conclusion, the Method which teaches us to follow the true order and enumerate exactly every term in the matter under investigation contains everything which gives certainty to the rules of Arithmetic.

But what pleased me most in this Method was that I was certain by its means of exercising my reason in all things, if not perfectly, at least as well as was in my power. And besides this, I felt in making use of it that my mind gradually accustomed itself to conceive of its objects more accurately and distinctly; and not having restricted this Method to any particular matter, I promised myself to apply it as usefully to the difficulties of other sciences as I had done to those of Algebra. Not that on this account I dared undertake to examine just at once all those that might present themselves; for that would itself have been contrary to the order which the Method prescribes. But having noticed that the knowledge of these difficulties must be dependent on principles derived from Philosophy in which I yet found nothing to be certain, I thought that it was requisite above all to try to establish certainty in it. I considered also that since this endeavour is the most important in all the world, and that in which precipitation and prejudice were most to be feared, I should not try to grapple with it till I had attained to a much riper age than that of three and twenty, which was the age I had reached. I thought, too, that I should first of all employ much time in preparing myself for the work by eradicating from my mind all the wrong opinions which I had up to this time accepted, and accumulating a variety of experiences fitted later on to afford matter for my reasonings, and by ever exercising myself in the Method which I had prescribed, in order more and more to fortify myself in the power of using it.

PART III

And finally, as it is not sufficient, before commencing to rebuild the house which we inhabit, to pull it down and provide materials and an architect (or to act in this capacity ourselves, and make a careful drawing of its design), unless we have also provided ourselves with some other house where we can be comfortably lodged during the time of rebuilding, so in order that I should not remain irresolute in my actions while reason obliged me to be so in my judgments, and that I might not omit to carry on my life as happily as I could, I formed for myself a code of morals for the time being which did not consist of more than three or four maxims, which maxims I should like to enumerate to you.

The first was to obey the laws and customs of my country, adhering constantly to the religion in which by God's grace I had been instructed since my childhood, and in all other things directing my conduct by opinions the most moderate in nature, and the farthest removed from excess in all those which are commonly received and acted on by the most judicious of those with whom I might come in contact. For since I began to count my own opinions as nought, because I desired to place all under examination, I was convinced that I could not do better than follow those held by people on whose judgment reliance could be placed. And although such persons may possibly exist amongst the Persians and Chinese as well as amongst ourselves, it seemed to me that it was most expedient to bring my conduct into harmony with the ideas of those with whom I should have to live; and that, in order to ascertain that these were their real opinions, I should observe what they did rather than what they said, not only because in the corrupt state of our manners there are few people who desire to say all that they believe, but also because many are themselves ignorant of their beliefs. For since the act of thought by which we believe a thing is different from that by which we know that we believe it, the one often exists without the other. And amongst many opinions all equally received, I chose only the most moderate, both because these are always most suited for putting into practice, and probably the best (for all excess has a tendency to be bad), and also because I should have in a less degree turned aside from the right path, supposing that I was wrong, than if, having chosen an extreme course, I found that I had chosen amiss. I also made a point of counting as excess all the engagements by means of which we limit in some degree our liberty. Not that I hold in low esteem those laws which, in order to remedy the inconstancy of feeble souls, permit, when we have a good object in our view, that certain vows be taken, or contracts made, which oblige us to carry out that object. This sanction is even given for security in commerce where designs are wholly indifferent. But because I saw nothing in all the world remaining constant, and because for my own part I promised myself gradually to get my judgments to grow better and never to grow worse, I should have thought that I had committed a serious sin against commonsense if, because I approved of something at one time, I was obliged to regard it similarly at a later time, after it had possibly ceased to meet my approval, or after I had ceased to regard it in a favourable light.

My second maxim was that of being as firm and resolute in my actions as I could be, and not to follow less faithfully opinions the most dubious, when my mind was once made up regarding them, than if these had been beyond doubt. In this I should be following the example of travellers, who, finding themselves lost in a forest, know that they ought not to wander first to one side and then to the other, nor, still less, to stop in one place, but understand that they should continue to walk as straight as they can in one direction, not diverging for any slight reason, even though it was possibly chance alone that first determined them in their choice. By this means if they do not go exactly where they wish, they will at least arrive somewhere at the end, where probably they will be better off than in the middle of a forest. And thus since often enough in the actions of life no delay is permissible, it is very certain that, when it is beyond our power to discern the opinions which carry most truth, we should follow the most probable; and even although we notice no greater probability in the one opinion than in the other, we at least should make up our minds to follow a particular one and afterwards consider it as no longer doubtful in its relationship to practice, but as very true and very certain, inasmuch as the reason which caused us to determine upon it is known to be so. And henceforward this principle was sufficient to deliver me from all the penitence and remorse which usually affect the mind and agitate the conscience of those weak and vacillating creatures who allow themselves to keep changing their procedure, and practise as good, things which they afterwards judge to be evil.

My third maxim was to try always to conquer myself rather than fortune, and to alter my desires rather than change the order of the world, and generally to accustom myself to believe that there is nothing entirely within our power but our own thoughts: so that after we have done our best in regard to the things that are without us, our ill-success cannot possibly be failure on our part. And this alone seemed to me sufficient to prevent my desiring anything in the future beyond what I could actually obtain, hence rendering me content; for since our will does not naturally induce us to desire anything but what our understanding represents to it as in some way possible of attainment, it is certain that if we consider all good things which are outside of us as equally outside of our power, we should not have more regret in resigning those goods which appear to pertain to our birth, when we are deprived of them for no fault of our own, than we have in not possessing the kingdoms of China or Mexico. In the same way, making what is called a virtue out of a necessity, we should no more desire to be well if ill, or free, if in prison, than we now do to have our bodies formed of a substance as little corruptible as diamonds, or to have wings to fly with like birds. I allow, however, that to accustom oneself to regard all things from this point of view requires long exercise and meditation often repeated; and I believe that it is principally in this that is to be found the secret of those philosophers who, in ancient times, were able to free themselves from the empire of fortune, or, despite suffering or poverty, to rival their gods in their happiness. For, ceaselessly occupying themselves in considering the limits which were prescribed to them by nature, they persuaded themselves so completely that nothing was within their own power but their thoughts, that this conviction alone was sufficient to prevent their having any longing for other things. And they had so absolute a mastery over their thoughts that they had some reason for esteeming themselves as more rich and more powerful, and more free and more happy than other men, who, however favoured by nature or fortune they might be, if devoid of this philosophy, never could arrive at all at which they aim.

And last of all, to conclude this moral code, I felt it incumbent on me to make a review of the various occupations of men in this life in order to try to choose out the best; and without wishing to say anything of the employment of others I thought that I could not do better than continue in the one in which I found myself engaged, that is to say, in occupying my whole life in cultivating my Reason, and in advancing myself as much as possible in the knowledge of the truth in accordance with the method which I had prescribed myself. I had experienced so much satisfaction since beginning to use this method, that I did not believe that any sweeter or more innocent could in this life be found,—every day discovering by its means some truths which seemed to me sufficiently important, although commonly ignored by other men. The satisfaction which I had so filled my mind that all else seemed of no account. And, besides, the three preceding maxims were founded solely on the plan which I had formed of continuing to instruct myself. For since God has given to each of us some light with which to distinguish truth from error, I could not believe that I ought for a single moment to content myself with accepting the opinions held by others unless I had in view the employment of my own judgment in examining them at the proper time; and I could not have held myself free of scruple in following such opinions, if nevertheless I had not intended to lose no occasion of finding superior opinions, supposing them to exist; and finally, I should not have been able to restrain my desires nor to remain content, if I had not followed a road by which, thinking that I should be certain to be able to acquire all the knowledge of which I was capable, I also thought I should likewise be certain of obtaining all the best things which could ever come within my power. And inasmuch as our will impels us neither to follow after nor to flee from anything, excepting as our understanding represents it as good or evil, it is sufficient to judge wisely in order to act well, and the best judgment brings the best action—that is to say, the acquisition of all the virtues and all the other good things that it is possible to obtain. When one is certain that this point is reached, one cannot fail to be contented.

Having thus assured myself of these maxims, and having set them on one side along with the truths of religion which have always taken the first place in my creed, I judged that as far as the rest of my opinions were concerned, I could safely undertake to rid myself of them. And inasmuch as I hoped to be able to reach my end more successfully in converse with man than in living longer shut up in the warm room where these reflections had come to me, I hardly awaited the end of winter before I once more set myself to travel. And in all the nine following years I did nought but roam hither and thither, trying to be a spectator rather than an actor in all the comedies the world displays. More especially did I reflect in each matter that came before me as to anything which could make it subject to suspicion or doubt, and give occasion for mistake, and I rooted out of my mind all the errors which might have formerly crept in. Not that indeed I imitated the sceptics, who only doubt for the sake of doubting, and pretend to be always uncertain; for, on the contrary, my design was only to provide myself with good ground for assurance, and to reject the quicksand and mud in order to find the rock or clay. In this task, it seems to me, I succeeded pretty well, since in trying to discover the error or uncertainty of the propositions which I examined, not by feeble conjectures, but by clear and assured reasonings, I encountered nothing so dubious that I could not draw from it some conclusion that was tolerably secure, if this were no more than the inference that it contained in it nothing that was certain. And just as in pulling down an old house we usually preserve the debris to serve in building up another, so in destroying all those opinions which I considered to be ill-founded, I made various observations and acquired many experiences, which have since been of use to me in establishing those which are more certain. And more than this, I continued to exercise myself in the method which I had laid down for my use; for besides the fact that I was careful as a rule to conduct all my thoughts according to its maxims, I set aside some hours from time to time which I more especially employed in practising myself in the solution of mathematical problems according to the Method, or in the solution of other problems which though pertaining to other sciences, I was able to make almost similar to those of mathematics, by detaching them from all principles of other sciences which I found to be not sufficiently secure. You will see the result in many examples which are expounded in this volume.[1] And hence, without living to all appearance in any way differently from those who, having no occupation beyond spending their lives in ease and innocence, study to separate pleasure from vice, and who, in order to enjoy their leisure without weariness, make use of all distractions that are innocent and good, I did not cease to prosecute my design,

[1]The *Dioptrics*, *Meteors*, and *Geometry* were published originally in the same volume.

nd to profit perhaps even more in my study of Truth than if I had done nothing but read books or associate with literary people.

These nine years thus passed away before I had taken any definite part in regard to the difficulties as to which the learned are in the habit of disputing, or had commenced to seek the foundation of any philosophy more certain than the vulgar. And the example of many excellent men who had tried to do the same before me, but, as it appears to me, without success, made me imagine it to be so hard that possibly I should not have dared to undertake the task, had I not discovered that someone had spread abroad the report that I had already reached its conclusion. I cannot tell on what they based this opinion; if my conversation has contributed anything to it, this must have arisen from my confessing my ignorance more ingenuously than those who have studied a little usually do. And perhaps it was also due to my having shown forth my reasons for doubting many things which were held by others to be certain, rather than from having boasted of any special philosophic system. But being at heart honest enough not to desire to be esteemed as different from what I am, I thought that I must try by every means in my power to render myself worthy of the reputation which I had gained. And it is just eight years ago that this desire made me resolve to remove myself from all places where any acquaintances were possible, and to retire to a country such as this,[1] where the long-continued war has caused such order to be established that the armies which are maintained seem only to be of use in allowing the inhabitants to enjoy the fruits of peace with so much the more security; and where, in the crowded throng of a great and very active nation, which is more concerned with its own affairs than curious about those of others, without missing any of the conveniences of the most populous towns, I can live as solitary and retired as in deserts the most remote.

PART IV

I DO not know that I ought to tell you of the first meditations there made by me, for they are so metaphysical and so unusual that they may perhaps not be acceptable to everyone. And yet at the same time, in order that one may judge whether the foundations which I have laid are sufficiently secure, I find myself constrained in some measure to refer to them.

[1]Holland, where Descartes settled in 1629.

For a long time I had remarked that it is sometimes requisite in common life to follow opinions which one knows to be most uncertain, exactly as though they were indisputable, as has been said above. But because in this case I wished to give myself entirely to the search after Truth, I thought that it was necessary for me to take an apparently opposite course, and to reject as absolutely false everything as to which I could imagine the least ground of doubt, in order to see if afterwards there remained anything in my belief that was entirely certain. Thus, because our senses sometimes deceive us, I wished to suppose that nothing is just as they cause us to imagine it to be; and because there are men who deceive themselves in their reasoning and fall into paralogisms, even concerning the simplest matters of geometry, and judging that I was as subject to error as was any other, I rejected as false all the reasons formerly accepted by me as demonstrations. And since all the same thoughts and conceptions which we have while awake may also come to us in sleep, without any of them being at that time true, I resolved to assume that everything that ever entered into my mind was no more true than the illusions of my dreams. But immediately afterwards I noticed that whilst I thus wished to think all things false, it was absolutely essential that the "I" who thought this should be somewhat, and remarking that this truth "*I think, therefore I am*" was so certain and so assured that all the most extravagant suppositions brought forward by the sceptics were incapable of shaking it, I came to the conclusion that I could receive it without scruple as the first principle of the Philosophy for which I was seeking.

And then, examining attentively that which I was, I saw that I could conceive that I had no body, and that there was no world nor place where I might be; but yet that I could not for all that conceive that I was not. On the contrary, I saw from the very fact that I thought of doubting the truth of other things, it very evidently and certainly followed that I was; on the other hand if I had only ceased from thinking, even if all the rest of what I had ever imagined had really existed, I should have no reason for thinking that I had existed. From that I knew that I was a substance the whole essence or nature of which is to think, and that for its existence there is no need of any place, nor does it depend on any material thing; so that this "me," that is to say, the soul by which I am what I am, is entirely distinct from body, and is even more easy to know than is the latter; and even if body were not, the soul would not cease to be what it is.

After this I considered generally what in a proposition is requisite in order to be true and certain; for since I had just discovered one which I knew to be such, I thought that I ought also to know in what this certainty consisted. And having remarked that there was nothing at all in the statement *"I think, therefore I am"* which assures me of having thereby made a true assertion, excepting that I see very clearly that to think it is necessary to be, I came to the conclusion that I might assume, as a general rule, that the things which we conceive very clearly and distinctly are all true— remembering, however, that there is some difficulty in ascertaining which are those that we distinctly conceive.

Following upon this, and reflecting on the fact that I doubted, and that consequently my existence was not quite perfect (for I saw clearly that it was a greater perfection to know than to doubt), I resolved to inquire whence I had learnt to think of anything more perfect than I myself was; and I recognised very clearly that this conception must proceed from some nature which was really more perfect. As to the thoughts which I had of many other things outside of me, like the heavens, the earth, light, heat, and a thousand others, I had not so much difficulty in knowing whence they came, because, remarking nothing in them which seemed to render them superior to me, I could believe that, if they were true, they were dependencies upon my nature, in so far as it possessed some perfection; and if they were not true, that I held them from nought, that is to say, that they were in me because I had something lacking in my nature. But this could not apply to the idea of a Being more perfect than my own, for to hold it from nought would be manifestly impossible; and because it is no less contradictory to say of the more perfect that it is what results from and depends on the less perfect, than to say that there is something which proceeds from nothing, it was equally impossible that I should hold it from myself. In this way it could but follow that it had been placed in me by a Nature which was really more perfect than mine could be, and which even had within itself all the perfections of which I could form any idea—that is to say, to put it in a word, which was God. To which I added

that since I knew some perfections which I did not possess, I was not the only being in existence (I shall here use freely, if you will allow the terms of the School); but that there was necessarily some other more perfect Being on which I depended, or from which I acquired all that I had. For if I had existed alone and independent of any others, so that I should have had from myself all that perfection of being in which I participated to however small an extent, I should have been able for the same reason to have had all the remainder which I knew that I lacked; and thus I myself should have been infinite, eternal, immutable, omniscient, all-powerful, and, finally, I should have all the perfections which I could discern in God. For, in pursuance of the reasonings which I have just carried on, in order to know the nature of God as far as my nature is capable of knowing it, I had only to consider in reference to all these things of which I found some idea in myself, whether it was a perfection to possess them or not. And I was assured that none of those which indicated some imperfection were in Him, but that all else was present; and I saw that doubt, inconstancy, sadness, and such things, could not be in Him considering that I myself should have been glad to be without them. In addition to this I had ideas of many things which are sensible and corporeal, for, although I might suppose that I was dreaming, and that all that I saw or imagined was false, I could not at the same time deny that the ideas were really in my thoughts. But because I had already recognised very clearly in myself that the nature of the intelligence is distinct from that of the body, and observing that all composition gives evidence of dependency, and that dependency is manifestly an imperfection, I came to the conclusion that it could not be a perfection in God to be composed of these two natures, and that consequently He was not so composed. I judged, however, that if there were any bodies in the world, or even any intelligences or other natures which were not wholly perfect, their existence must depend on His power in such a way that they could not subsist without Him for a single moment.

After that I desired to seek for other truths, and having put before myself the object of the geometricians, which I conceived to be a continuous body, or a space indefinitely extended in length, breadth, height or depth, which was divisible into various parts, and which might have various figures and sizes, and might be moved or transposed in all sorts of ways (for all this the geometricians suppose to be in the object of their contemplation), I went through some of their simplest demonstrations, and having noticed that this great certainty which everyone attributes to these demonstrations is founded solely on the fact that they are conceived of with clearness, in accordance with the rule which I have just laid down, I also noticed that there was nothing at all in them to assure me of the existence of their object. For, to take an example, I saw very well that if we suppose a triangle to be given, the three angles must certainly be equal to two right angles; but for all that I saw no reason to be assured that there was any such triangle in existence, while on the contrary, on reverting to the examination of the idea which I had of a Perfect Being, I found that in this case existence was implied in it in the same manner in which the equality of its three angles to two right angles is implied in the idea of a triangle; or in the idea of a sphere, that all the points on its surface are equidistant from its centre, or even more evidently still. Consequently it is at least as certain that God, who is a Being so perfect, is, or exists, as any demonstration of geometry can possibly be.

What causes many, however, to persuade themselves that there is difficulty in knowing this truth, and even in knowing the nature of their soul, is the fact that they never raise their minds above the things of sense, or that they are so accustomed to consider nothing excepting by imagining it, which is a mode of thought specially adapted to material objects, that all that is not capable of being imagined appears to them not to be intelligible at all. This is manifest enough from the fact that even the philosophers in the Schools hold it as a maxim that there is nothing in the understanding which has not first of all been in the senses, in which there is certainly no doubt that the ideas of God and of the soul have never been. And it seems to me that those who desire to make use of their imagination in order to understand these ideas, act in the same way as if, to hear sounds or smell odours, they should wish to make use of their eyes: excepting that there is indeed this difference, that the sense of sight does not give us less assurance of the truth of its objects, than do those of scent or of hearing, while neither our imagination nor our senses can ever assure us of anything, if our understanding does not intervene.

If there are finally any persons who are not sufficiently persuaded of the existence of God and of their soul by the reasons which I have brought forward, I wish that they should know that all other things of which they perhaps think themselves more assured (such as possessing a body, and that there are stars and an earth and so on) are less certain. For, although we have a moral assurance of these things which is such that it seems that it would be extravagant in us to doubt them, at the same time no one, unless he is devoid of reason, can deny, when a metaphysical certainty is in question, that there is sufficient cause for our not having complete assurance, by observing the fact that when asleep we may similarly imagine that we have another body, and that we see other stars and another earth, without there being anything of the kind. For how do we know that the thoughts that come in dreams are more false than those that we have when we are awake, seeing that often enough the former are not less lively and vivid than the latter? And though the wisest minds may study the matter as much as they will, I do not believe that they will be able to give any sufficient reason for removing this doubt, unless they presuppose the existence of God. For to begin with, that which I have just taken as a rule, that is to say, that all the things that we very clearly and very distinctly conceive of are true, is certain only because God is or exists, and that He is a Perfect Being, and that all that is in us issues from Him. From this it follows that our ideas or notions, which to the extent of their being clear or distinct are ideas of real things issuing from God, cannot but to that extent be true. So that though we often enough have ideas which have an element of falsity, this can only be the case in regard to those which have in them somewhat that is confused or obscure, because in so far as they have this character they participate in negation—that is, they exist in us as confused only because we are not quite perfect. And it is evident that there is no less repugnance in the idea that error or imperfection, inasmuch as it is imperfection, proceeds from God, than there is in the idea of truth or perfection proceeding from nought. But if we did not know that all that is in us of reality and truth proceeds from a perfect and infinite Being, however clear and distinct were our ideas, we should not have any reason to assure ourselves that they had the perfection of being true.

But after the knowledge of God and of the

soul has thus rendered us certain of this rule, it is very easy to understand that the dreams which we imagine in our sleep should not make us in any way doubt the truth of the thoughts which we have when awake. For even if in sleep we had some very distinct idea such as a geometrician might have who discovered some new demonstration, the fact of being asleep would not militate against its truth. And as to the most ordinary error in our dreams, which consists in their representing to us various objects in the same way as do our external senses, it does not matter that this should give us occasion to suspect the truth of such ideas, because we may be likewise often enough deceived in them without our sleeping at all, just as when those who have the jaundice see everything as yellow, or when stars or other bodies which are very remote appear much smaller than they really are. For, finally, whether we are awake or asleep, we should never allow ourselves to be persuaded excepting by the evidence of our Reason. And it must be remarked that I speak of our Reason and not of our imagination nor of our senses; just as though we see the sun very clearly, we should not for that reason judge that it is of the size of which it appears to be; likewise we could quite well distinctly imagine the head of a lion on the body of a goat, without necessarily concluding that a chimera exists. For Reason does not insist that whatever we see or imagine thus is a truth, but it tells us clearly that all our ideas or notions must have some foundation of truth. For otherwise it could not be possible that God, who is all perfection and truth, should have placed them within us. And because our reasonings are never so evident nor so complete during sleep as during wakefulness, although sometimes our imaginations are then just as lively and acute, or even more so, Reason tells us that since our thoughts cannot possibly be all true, because we are not altogether perfect, that which they have of truth must infallibly be met with in our waking experience rather than in that of our dreams.

PART V

I should be very glad to proceed to show forth the complete chain of truths which I have deduced from these first, but because to do this it would have been necessary now to speak of many matters of dispute among the learned, with whom I have no desire to embroil myself, I think that it will be better to abstain. I shall only state generally what these truths are, so that it may be left to the decision of those best able to judge whether it would be of use for the public to be more particularly informed of them or not. I always remained firm in the resolution which I had made, not to assume any other principle than that of which I have just made use, in order to demonstrate the existence of God and of the Soul, and to accept nothing as true which did not appear to be more clear and more certain than the demonstrations of the geometricians had formerly seemed. And nevertheless I venture to say that not only have I found the means of satisfying myself in a short time as to the more important of those difficulties usually dealt with in philosophy, but I have also observed certain laws which God has so established in Nature, and of which He has imprinted such ideas on our minds, that, after having reflected sufficiently upon the matter, we cannot doubt their being accurately observed in all that exists or is done in the world. Further, in considering the sequence of these laws, it seems to me that I have discovered many truths more useful and more important than all that I had formerly learned or even hoped to learn.

But because I tried to explain the most important of these in a Treatise[1] which certain considerations prevented me from publishing, I cannot do better, in making them known, than here summarise briefly what that Treatise contains. I had planned to comprise in it all that I believed myself to know regarding the nature of material objects, before I set myself to write. However, just as the painters who cannot represent equally well on a plain surface all the various sides of a solid body, make selection of one of the most important, which alone is set in the light, while the others are put in shadow and made to appear only as they may be seen in looking at the former, so, fearing that I could not put in my Treatise all that I had in my mind, I undertook only to show very fully my conceptions of light. Later on, when occasion occurred, I resolved to add something about the sun and fixed stars, because light proceeds almost entirely from them; the heavens would be dealt with because they transmit light, the planets, the comets and the earth because they reflect it, and more particularly would all bodies which are on the earth, because they are either coloured or transparent, or else luminous; and finally I should deal

[1] *Le Monde*, suppressed on hearing of Galileo's condemnation.

with man because he is the spectator of all. For the very purpose of putting all these topics somewhat in shadow, and being able to express myself freely about them, without being obliged to adopt or to refute the opinions which are accepted by the learned, I resolved to leave all this world to their disputes, and to speak only of what would happen in a new world if God now created, somewhere in an imaginary space, matter sufficient wherewith to form it, and if He agitated in diverse ways, and without any order, the diverse portions of this matter, so that there resulted a chaos as confused as the poets ever feigned, and concluded His work by merely lending His concurrence to Nature in the usual way, leaving her to act in accordance with the laws which He had established. So, to begin with, I described this matter and tried to represent it in such a way, that it seems to me that nothing in the world could be more clear or intelligible, excepting what has just been said of God and the Soul. For I even went so far as expressly to assume that there was in it none of these forms or qualities which are so debated in the Schools, nor anything at all the knowledge of which is not so natural to our minds that none could even pretend to be ignorant of it. Further, I pointed out what are the laws of Nature, and, without resting my reasons on any other principle than the infinite perfections of God, I tried to demonstrate all those of which one could have any doubt, and to show that they are of such a nature that even if God had created other worlds, He could not have created any in which these laws would fail to be observed. After that, I showed how the greatest part of the matter of which this chaos is constituted, must in accordance with these laws, dispose and arrange itself in such a fashion as to render it similar to our heavens; and how meantime some of its parts must form an earth, some planets and comets, and some others a sun and fixed stars. And, enlarging on the subject of light, I here explained at length the nature of the light which would be found in the sun and stars, and how from these it crossed in an instant the immense space of the heavens, and how it was reflected from the planets and comets to the earth. To this I also added many things touching the substance, situation, movements, and all the different qualities of these heavens and stars, so that I thought I had said enough to make it clear that there is nothing to be seen in the heavens and stars pertaining to our system which must not, or at least may

not, appear exactly the same in those of the system which I described. From this point I came to speak more particularly of the earth, showing how, though I had expressly presupposed that God had not placed any weight in the matter of which it is composed, its parts did not fail all to gravitate exactly to its centre; and how, having water and air on its surface, the disposition of the heavens and of the stars, more particularly of the moon, must cause a flux or reflux, which in all its circumstances is similar to that which is observed in our seas, and besides that, a certain current both of water and air from east to west, such as may also be observed in the tropics. I also showed how the mountains, seas, fountains and rivers, could naturally be formed in it, how the metals came to be in the mines and the plants to grow in the fields; and generally how all bodies, called mixed or composite, might arise. And because I knew nothing but fire which could produce light, excepting the stars, I studied amongst other things to make very clear all that pertains to its nature, how it is formed, how nourished, how there is sometimes only heat without light, and sometimes light without heat; I showed, too, how different colours might by it be induced upon different bodies and qualities of diverse kinds, how some of these were liquefied and others solidified, how nearly all can be consumed or converted into ashes and smoke by its means, and finally how of these ashes, by the intensity of its action alone, it forms glass. Since this transformation of ashes into glass seemed to me as wonderful as any other process in nature, I took particular pleasure in describing it.

I did not at the same time wish to infer from all these facts that this world has been created in the manner which I described; for it is much more probable that at the beginning God made it such as it was to be. But it is certain, and it is an opinion commonly received by the theologians, that the action by which He now preserves it is just the same as that by which He at first created it. In this way, although He had not, to begin with, given this world any other form than that of chaos, provided that the laws of nature had once been established and that He had lent His aid in order that its action should be according to its wont, we may well believe, without doing outrage to the miracle of creation, that by this means alone all things which are purely material might in course of time have become such as we observe them to be at present; and their nature is much easier to understand when we see them coming to pass little by little in this manner, than were we to consider them as all complete to begin with.

From a description of inanimate bodies and plants I passed on to that of animals, and particularly to that of men. But since I had not yet sufficient knowledge to speak of them in the same style as of the rest, that is to say, demonstrating the effects from the causes, and showing from what beginnings and in what fashion Nature must produce them, I contented myself with supposing that God formed the body of man altogether like one of ours, in the outward figure of its members as well as in the interior conformation of its organs, without making use of any matter other than that which I had described, and without at the first placing in it a rational soul, or any other thing which might serve as a vegetative or as a sensitive soul; excepting that He kindled in the heart one of these fires without light, which I have already described, and which I did not conceive of as in any way different from that which makes the hay heat when shut up before it is dry, and which makes new wine grow frothy when it is left to ferment over the fruit. For, examining the functions which might in accordance with this supposition exist in this body, I found precisely all those which might exist in us without our having the power of thought, and consequently without our soul— that is to say, this part of us, distinct from the body, of which it has just been said that its nature is to think—contributing to it, functions which are identically the same as those in which animals lacking reason may be said to resemble us. For all that, I could not find in these functions any which, being dependent on thought, pertain to us alone, inasmuch as we are men; while I found all of them afterwards, when I assumed that God had created a rational soul and that He had united it to this body in a particular manner which I described.

But in order to show how I there treated of this matter, I wish here to set forth the explanation of the movement of heart and arteries which, being the first and most general movement that is observed in animals, will give us the means of easily judging as to what we ought to think about all the rest. And so that there may be less difficulty in understanding what I shall say on this matter, I should like that those not versed in anatomy should take the trouble, before reading this, of having cut up before their eyes the heart of some large animal which has lungs (for it is in all respects sufficiently similar to the heart of a man), and cause that there be demonstrated to them the two chambers or cavities which are within it. There is first of all that which is on the right side, with which two very large tubes or channels correspond, viz. the *vena cava*, which is the principal receptacle of the blood, and so to speak the trunk of a tree of which all the other veins of the body are the branches; and there is the arterial vein which has been badly named because it is nothing but an artery which, taking its origin from the heart, divides, after having issued from it, into many branches which proceed to disperse themselves all through the lungs. Then there is secondly the cavity on the left side with which there again correspond two tubes which are as large or larger than the preceding, viz. the venous artery, which has also been badly named, because it is nothing but a vein which comes from the lungs, where it is divided into many branches, interlaced with those of the arterial vein, and with those of the tube which is called the windpipe, through which enters the air which we breathe; and the great artery which, issuing from the heart, sends its branches throughout the body. I should also wish that the eleven little membranes, which, like so many doors, open and shut the four entrances which are in these two cavities, should be carefully shown. There are of these three at the entrance of the *vena cava*, where they are so arranged that they can in nowise prevent the blood which it contains from flowing into the right cavity of the heart and yet exactly prevent its issuing out; there are three at the entrance to the arterial vein, which, being arranged quite the other way, easily allow the blood which is in this cavity to pass into the lungs, but not that which is already in the lungs to return to this cavity. There are also two others at the entrance of the venous artery which allow the blood in the lungs to flow towards the left cavity of the heart, but do not permit its return; and three at the entrance of the great artery, which allow the blood to flow from the heart, but prevent its return. There is then no cause to seek for any other reason for the number of these membranes, except that the opening of the venous artery being oval, because of the situation where it is met with, may be conveniently closed with two membranes, while the others, being round, can be better closed with three. Further, I should have my readers consider that the grand artery nd the arterial vein are much harder and firm-r than are the venous artery and the *vena cava;* nd that these two last expand before entering he heart, and there form so to speak two pock-ts called auricles of the heart, which are com-osed of a tissue similar to its own; and also hat there is always more heat in the heart han in any other part of the body; and finally hat this heat is capable of causing any drop of lood that enters into its cavities promptly to xpand and dilate, as liquids usually do when hey are allowed to fall drop by drop into some ery hot vessel.

After this I do not need to say anything with view to explaining the movement of the eart, except that when its cavities are not full f blood there necessarily flows from the *vena ava* into the right cavity, and from the venous rtery into the left, enough blood to keep hese two vessels always full, and being full, hat their orifices, which are turned towards he heart, cannot then be closed. But as soon s two drops of blood have thus entered, one nto each of the cavities, these drops, which annot be otherwise than very large, because he openings by which they enter are very wide and the vessels from whence they come re very full of blood, rarefy and dilate because f the heat which they find there. By this neans, causing the whole heart to expand, hey force home and close the five little doors which are at the entrances of the two vessels whence they flow, thus preventing any more lood from coming down into the heart; and becoming more and more rarefied, they push pen the six doors which are in the entrances f the two other vessels through which they make their exit, by this means causing all the branches of the arterial vein and of the great artery to expand almost at the same instant s the heart. This last immediately afterward contracts as do also the arteries, because the blood which has entered them has cooled; and the six little doors close up again, and the five doors of the *vena cava* and of the venous artery re-open and make a way for two other drops of blood which cause the heart and the arteries once more to expand, just as we saw before. And because the blood which then enters the heart passes through these two pouches which are called auricles, it comes to pass that their movement is contrary to the movement of the heart, and that they contract when it expands. For the rest, in order that those who do not know the force of mathematical demonstra-tion and are unaccustomed to distinguish true

reasons from merely probable reasons, should not venture to deny what has been said with-out examination, I wish to acquaint them with the fact that this movement which I have just explained follows as necessarily from the very disposition of the organs, as can be seen by looking at the heart, and from the heat which can be felt with the fingers, and from the na-ture of the blood of which we can learn by ex-perience, as does that of a clock from the pow-er, the situation, and the form, of its counter-poise and of its wheels.

But if we ask how the blood in the veins does not exhaust itself in thus flowing continu-ally into the heart, and how the arteries do not become too full of blood, since all that passes through the heart flows into them, I need only reply by stating what has already been written by an English physician,[1] to whom the credit of having broken the ice in this matter must be ascribed, as also of being the first to teach that there are many little tubes at the extremities of the arteries whereby the blood that they re-ceive from the heart enters the little branches of the veins, whence it returns once more to the heart; in this way its course is just a per-petual circulation. He proves this very clearly by the common experience of surgeons, who, by binding the arm moderately firmly above the place where they open the vein, cause the blood to issue more abundantly than it would have done if they had not bound it at all; while quite a contrary result would occur if they bound it below, between the hand and the opening, or if they bound it very firmly above. For it is clear that when the bandage is moder-ately tight, though it may prevent the blood already in the arm from returning to the heart by the veins, it cannot for all that prevent more blood from coming anew by the arteries, because these are situated below the veins, and their walls, being stronger, are less easy to compress; and also that the blood which comes from the heart tends to pass by means of the arteries to the hand with greater force than it does to return from the hand to the heart by the veins. And because this blood escapes from the arm by the opening which is made in one of the veins, there must necessarily be some passages below the ligature, that is to say, towards the extremities of the arm, through which it can come thither from the arteries. This physician likewise proves very clearly the truth of that which he says of the course of the blood, by the existence of certain little mem-

[1]Harvey.

branes or valves which are so arranged in different places along the course of the veins, that they do not permit the blood to pass from the middle of the body towards the extremities, but only to return from the extremities to the heart; and further by the experiment which shows that all the blood which is in the body may issue from it in a very short time by means of one single artery that has been cut, and this is so even when it is very tightly bound very near the heart, and cut between it and the ligature, so that there could be no ground for supposing that the blood which flowed out of it could proceed from any other place but the heart.

But there are many other things which demonstrate that the true cause of this motion of the blood is that which I have stated. To begin with, the difference which is seen between the blood which issues from the veins, and that which issues from the arteries, can only proceed from the fact, that, being rarefied, and so to speak distilled by passing through the heart, it is more subtle and lively and warmer immediately after leaving the heart (that is to say, when in the arteries) than it is a little while before entering it (that is, when in the veins). And if attention be paid, we shall find that this difference does not appear clearly, excepting in the vicinity of the heart, and is not so clear in those parts which are further removed from it. Further, the consistency of the coverings of which the arterial vein and the great artery are composed, shows clearly enough that the blood beats against them with more force than it does in the case of the veins. And why should the left cavity of the heart and the great artery be larger and wider than the right cavity and the arterial vein, if it is not that the blood of the venous artery having only been in the lungs since it had passed through the heart, is more subtle and rarefies more effectively and easily than that which proceeds immediately from the *vena cava?* And what is it that the physicians can discover in feeling the pulse, unless they know that, according as the blood changes its nature, it may be rarefied by the warmth of the heart in a greater or less degree, and more or less quickly than before? And if we inquire how this heat is communicated to the other members, must it not be allowed that it is by means of the blood which, passing through the heart, is heated once again and thence is spread throughout all the body? From this it happens that if we take away the blood from any particular part, by

that same means we take away from it the heat; even if the heart were as ardent as a red hot iron it would not suffice to heat up the feet and hands as it actually does, unless it continually sent out to them new blood. We further understand from this that the true use of respiration is to carry sufficient fresh air into the lungs to cause the blood, which comes there from the right cavity of the heart, where it has been rarefied and so to speak transformed into vapours, to thicken, and become anew converted into blood before falling into the left cavity, without which process it would not be fit to serve as fuel for the fire which there exists. We are confirmed in this statement by seeing that the animals which have no lungs have also but one cavity in their hearts, and that in children, who cannot use them while still within their mother's wombs, there is an opening by which the blood flows from the *vena cava* into the left cavity of the heart, and a conduit through which it passes from the arterial vein into the great artery without passing through the lung. Again, how could digestion be carried on in the stomach if the heart did not send heat there by the arteries, and along with this some of the more fluid parts of the blood which aid in dissolving the foods which have been there placed? And is not the action which converts the juice of foods into blood easy to understand if we consider that it is distilled by passing and repassing through the heart possibly more than one or two hundred times in a day? What further need is there to explain the process of nutrition and the production of the different humours which are in the body, if we can say that the force with which the blood, in being rarefied, passes from the heart towards the extremities of the arteries, causes some of its parts to remain among those of the members where they are found and there to take the place of others which they oust; and that according to the situation or form or smallness of the little pores which they encounter, certain ones proceed to certain parts rather than others, just as a number of different sieves variously perforated, as everyone has probably seen, are capable of separating different species of grain? And finally what in all this is most remarkable of all, is the generation of the animal spirits, which resemble a very subtle wind, or rather a flame which is very pure and very vivid, and which, continually rising up in great abundance from the heart to the brain, thence proceeds through the nerves to the muscles, thereby giving the power of motion to all the members. And it is not necessary to suppose any other cause to explain how the particles of blood, which, being most agitated and most penetrating, are the most proper to constitute these spirits, proceed towards the brain rather than elsewhere, than that the arteries which carry them thither are those which proceed from the heart in the most direct lines, and that according to the laws of Mechanics, which are identical with those of Nature, when many objects tend to move together to the same point, where there is not room for all (as is the case with the particles of blood which issue from the left cavity of the heart and tend to go towards the brain), the weakest and least agitated parts must necessarily be turned aside by those that are stronger, which by this means are the only ones to reach it.

I had explained all these matters in some detail in the Treatise which I formerly intended to publish. And afterwards I had shown there, what must be the fabric of the nerves and muscles of the human body in order that the animal spirits therein contained should have the power to move the members, just as the heads of animals, a little while after decapitation, are still observed to move and bite the earth, notwithstanding that they are no longer animate; what changes are necessary in the brain to cause wakefulness, sleep and dreams; how light, sounds, smells, tastes, heat and all other qualities pertaining to external objects are able to imprint on it various ideas by the intervention of the senses; how hunger, thirst and other internal affections can also convey their impressions upon it; what should be regarded as the "common sense" by which these ideas are received, and what is meant by the memory which retains them, by the fancy which can change them in diverse ways and out of them constitute new ideas, and which, by the same means, distributing the animal spirits through the muscles, can cause the members of such a body to move in as many diverse ways, and in a manner as suitable to the objects which present themselves to its senses and to its internal passions, as can happen in our own case apart from the direction of our free will. And this will not seem strange to those, who, knowing how many different *automata* or moving machines can be made by the industry of man, without employing in so doing more than a very few parts in comparison with the great multitude of bones, muscles, nerves, arteries, veins, or other parts that are found in the body of each animal. From this aspect the body is regarded as a machine which, having been made by the hands of God, is incomparably better arranged, and possesses in itself movements which are much more admirable, than any of those which can be invented by man. Here I specially stopped to show that if there had been such machines, possessing the organs and outward form of a monkey or some other animal without reason, we should not have had any means of ascertaining that they were not of the same nature as those animals. On the other hand, if there were machines which bore a resemblance to our body and imitated our actions as far as it was morally possible to do so, we should always have two very certain tests by which to recognise that, for all that, they were not real men. The first is, that they could never use speech or other signs as we do when placing our thoughts on record for the benefit of others. For we can easily understand a machine's being constituted so that it can utter words, and even emit some responses to action on it of a corporeal kind, which brings about a change in its organs; for instance, if it is touched in a particular part it may ask what we wish to say to it; if in another part it may exclaim that it is being hurt, and so on. But it never happens that it arranges its speech in various ways, in order to reply appropriately to everything that may be said in its presence, as even the lowest type of man can do. And the second difference is, that although machines can perform certain things as well as or perhaps better than any of us can do, they infallibly fall short in others, by the which means we may discover that they did not act from knowledge, but only from the disposition of their organs. For while reason is a universal instrument which can serve for all contingencies, these organs have need of some special adaptation for every particular action. From this it follows that it is morally impossible that there should be sufficient diversity in any machine to allow it to act in all the events of life in the same way as our reason causes us to act.

By these two methods we may also recognise the difference that exists between men and brutes. For it is a very remarkable fact that there are none so depraved and stupid, without even excepting idiots, that they cannot arrange different words together, forming of them a statement by which they make known their thoughts; while, on the other hand, there is no other animal, however perfect and fortunately circumstanced it may be, which can do the same. It is not the want of organs that brings this to pass, for it is evident that magpies and parrots are able to utter words just like ourselves, and yet they cannot speak as we do, that is, so as to give evidence that they think of what they say. On the other hand, men who, being born deaf and dumb, are in the same degree, or even more than the brutes, destitute of the organs which serve the others for talking, are in the habit of themselves inventing certain signs by which they make themselves understood by those who, being usually in their company, have leisure to learn their language. And this does not merely show that the brutes have less reason than men, but that they have none at all, since it is clear that very little is required in order to be able to talk. And when we notice the inequality that exists between animals of the same species, as well as between men, and observe that some are more capable of receiving instruction than others, it is not credible that a monkey or a parrot, selected as the most perfect of its species, should not in these matters equal the stupidest child to be found, or at least a child whose mind is clouded, unless in the case of the brute the soul were of an entirely different nature from ours. And we ought not to confound speech with natural movements which betray passions and may be imitated by machines as well as be manifested by animals; nor must we think, as did some of the ancients, that brutes talk, although we do not understand their language. For if this were true, since they have many organs which are allied to our own, they could communicate their thoughts to us just as easily as to those of their own race. It is also a very remarkable fact that although there are many animals which exhibit more dexterity than we do in some of their actions, we at the same time observe that they do not manifest any dexterity at all in many others. Hence the fact that they do better than we do does not prove that they are endowed with mind, for in this case they would have more reason than any of us, and would surpass us in all other things. It rather shows that they have no reason at all, and that it is nature which acts in them according to the disposition of their organs, just as a clock which is only composed of wheels and weights is able to tell the hours and measure the time more correctly than we can do with all our wisdom.

I had described after this the rational soul and shown that it could not be in any way derived from the power of matter, like the other things of which I had spoken, but that it must be expressly created. I showed, too, that it is not sufficient that it should be lodged in the human body like a pilot in his ship, unless perhaps for the moving of its members, but that it is necessary that it should also be joined and united more closely to the body in order to have sensations and appetites similar to our own, and thus to form a true man. In conclusion, I have here enlarged a little on the subject of the soul, because it is one of the greatest importance. For next to the error of those who deny God, which I think I have already sufficiently refuted, there is none which is more effectual in leading feeble spirits from the straight path of virtue, than to imagine that the soul of the brute is of the same nature as our own, and that in consequence, after this life we have nothing to fear or to hope for, any more than the flies and ants. As a matter of fact, when one comes to know how greatly they differ, we understand much better the reasons which go to prove that our soul is in its nature entirely independent of body, and in consequence that it is not liable to die with it. And then, inasmuch as we observe no other causes capable of destroying it, we are naturally inclined to judge that it is immortal.

PART VI

IT IS three years since I arrived at the end of the Treatise which contained all these things; and I was commencing to revise it in order to place it in the hands of a printer, when I learned that certain persons, to whose opinions I defer, and whose authority cannot have less weight with my actions than my own reason has over my thoughts, had disapproved of a physical theory published a little while before by another person.[1] I will not say that I agreed with this opinion, but only that before their censure I observed in it nothing which I could possibly imagine to be prejudicial either to Religion or the State, or consequently which could have prevented me from giving expression to it in writing, if my reason had persuaded me to do so: and this made me fear that among my own opinions one might be found which should be misunderstood, notwithstanding the great care which I have always taken not to accept any new beliefs unless I had very certain proof of their truth, and not to give expression to what could tend to the disadvantage of any person. This sufficed to cause me to

[1]Galileo.

ter the resolution which I had made to pub-sh. For, although the reasons for my former esolution were very strong, my inclination, which always made me hate the profession of writing books, caused me immediately to find lenty of other reasons for excusing myself rom doing so. And these reasons, on the one ide and on the other, are of such a nature that ot only have I here some interest in giving xpression to them, but possibly the public nay also have some interest in knowing hem.

I have never made much of those things which proceed from my own mind, and so long s I culled no other fruits from the Method which I use, beyond that of satisfying myself especting certain difficulties which pertain to he speculative sciences, or trying to regulate my conduct by the reasons which it has taught me, I never believed myself to be obliged to write anything about it. For as regards that which concerns conduct, everyone is so con-ident of his own common sense, that there might be found as many reformers as heads, if t were permitted that others than those whom God has established as the sovereigns of his people, or at least to whom He has given suffi-cient grace and zeal to be prophets, should be allowed to make any changes in that. And, al-hough my speculations give me the greatest pleasure, I believed that others also had specu-ations which possibly pleased them even more. But so soon as I had acquired some general notions concerning Physics, and as, beginning to make use of them in various special difficul-ties, I observed to what point they might lead us, and how much they differ from the prin-ciples of which we have made use up to the present time, I believed that I could not keep them concealed without greatly sinning against the law which obliges us to procure, as much as in us lies, the general good of all mankind. For they caused me to see that it is possible to attain knowledge which is very useful in life, and that, instead of that speculative philoso-phy which is taught in the Schools, we may find a practical philosophy by means of which, knowing the force and the action of fire, water, air, the stars, heavens and all other bodies that environ us, as distinctly as we know the different crafts of our artisans, we can in the same way employ them in all those uses to which they are adapted, and thus render our-selves the masters and possessors of nature. This is not merely to be desired with a view to the invention of an infinity of arts and crafts

which enable us to enjoy without any trouble the fruits of the earth and all the good things which are to be found there, but also princi-pally because it brings about the preservation of health, which is without doubt the chief blessing and the foundation of all other bless-ings in this life. For the mind depends so much on the temperament and disposition of the bodily organs that, if it is possible to find a means of rendering men wiser and cleverer than they have hitherto been, I believe that it is in medicine that it must be sought. It is true that the medicine which is now in vogue con-tains little of which the utility is remarkable; but, without having any intention of decrying it, I am sure that there is no one, even among those who make its study a profession, who does not confess that all that men know is al-most nothing in comparison with what re-mains to be known; and that we could be free of an infinitude of maladies both of body and mind, and even also possibly of the infirmities of age, if we had sufficient knowledge of their causes, and of all the remedies with which na-ture has provided us. But, having the inten-tion of devoting all my life to the investigation of a knowledge which is so essential, and hav-ing discovered a path which appears to me to be of such a nature that we must by its means infallibly reach our end if we pursue it, unless, indeed, we are prevented by the shortness of life or by lack of experience, I judged that there was no better provision against these two im-pediments than faithfully to communicate to the public the little which I should myself have discovered, and to beg all well-inclined per-sons to proceed further by contributing, each one according to his own inclination and abil-ity, to the experiments which must be made, and then to communicate to the public all the things which they might discover, in order that the last should commence where the pre-ceding had left off; and thus, by joining to-gether the lives and labours of many, we should collectively proceed much further than any one in particular could succeed in doing.

I remarked also respecting experiments, that they become so much the more necessary the more one is advanced in knowledge, for to begin with it is better to make use simply of those which present themselves spontaneously to our senses, and of which we could not be ignorant provided that we reflected ever so little, rather than to seek out those which are more rare and recondite; the reason of this is that those which are more rare often mislead us so long as we do not know the causes of the more common, and the fact that the circumstances on which they depend are almost always so particular and so minute that it is very difficult to observe them. But in this the order which I have followed is as follows: I have first tried to discover generally the principles or first causes of everything that is or that can be in the world, without considering anything that might accomplish this end but God Himself who has created the world, or deriving them from any source excepting from certain germs of truths which are naturally existent in our souls. After that I considered which were the primary and most ordinary effects which might be deduced from these causes, and it seems to me that in this way I discovered the heavens, the stars, an earth, and even on the earth, water, air, fire, the minerals and some other such things, which are the most common and simple of any that exist, and consequently the easiest to know. Then, when I wished to descend to those which were more particular, so many objects of various kinds presented themselves to me, that I did not think it was possible for the human mind to distinguish the forms or species of bodies which are on the earth from an infinitude of others which might have been so if it had been the will of God to place them there, or consequently to apply them to our use, if it were not that we arrive at the causes by the effects, and avail ourselves of many particular experiments. In subsequently passing over in my mind all the objects which have ever been presented to my senses, I can truly venture to say that I have not there observed anything which I could not easily explain by the principles which I had discovered. But I must also confess that the power of nature is so ample and so vast, and these principles are so simple and general, that I observed hardly any particular effect as to which I could not at once recognise that it might be deduced from the principles in many different ways; and my greatest difficulty is usually to discover in which of these ways the effect does depend upon them. As to that, I do not know any other plan but again to try to find experiments of such a nature that their result is not the same if it has to be explained by one of the methods, as it would be if explained by the other. For the rest, I have now reached a position in which I discern, as it seems to me, sufficiently clearly what course must be adopted in order to make the majority of the experiments which may conduce to carry out this end. But I also perceive that they are of such a nature, and of so great a number, that neither my hands nor my income, though the latter were a thousand times larger than it is, could suffice for the whole; so that just in proportion as henceforth I shall have the power of carrying out more of them or less, shall make more or less progress in arriving at a knowledge of nature. This is what I had promised myself to make known by the Treatise which I had written, and to demonstrate in it so clearly the advantage which the public might receive from it, that I should induce all those who have the good of mankind at heart —that is to say, all those who are really virtuous in fact, and not only by a false semblance or by opinion—both to communicate to me those experiments that they have already carried out, and to help me in the investigation of those that still remain to be accomplished.

But I have since that time found other reasons which caused me to change my opinion, and consider that I should indeed continue to put in writing all the things which I judged to be of importance whenever I discovered them to be true, and that I should bestow on them the same care as I should have done had I wished to have them printed. I did this because it would give me so much the more occasion to examine them carefully (for there is no doubt that we always scrutinize more closely what we think will be seen by many, than what is done simply for ourselves, and often the things which have seemed true to me when I began to think about them, seemed false when I tried to place them on paper); and because I did not desire to lose any opportunity of benefiting the public if I were able to do so, and in order that if my works have any value, those into whose hands they will fall after my death, might have the power of making use of them as seems best to them. I, however, resolved that I should not consent to their being published during my lifetime, so that neither the contradictions and controversies to which they might possibly give rise, nor even the reputation, such as it might be, which they would bring to me, should give me any occasion to lose the time which I meant to set apart for my own instruction. For although it is true that each man is obliged to procure, as much as in him lies, the good of others, and that to be useful to nobody is popularly speaking to be worthless, it is at the same time true that our cares should extend further than the present time, and that it is good to set aside those things which may possibly be adapted to bring profit to the living, when we have in view the accomplishment of other ends which will bring much more advantage to our descendants. In the same way I should much like that men should know that the little which I have learned hitherto is almost nothing in comparison with that of which I am ignorant, and with the knowledge of which I do not despair of being able to attain. For it is much the same with those who little by little discover the truth in the Sciences, as with those who, commencing to become rich, have less trouble in obtaining great acquisitions than they formerly experienced, when poorer, in arriving at those much smaller in amount. Or we might compare them to the Generals of our armies, whose forces usually grow in proportion to their victories, and who require more leadership in order to hold together their troops after the loss of a battle, than is needed to take towns and provinces after having obtained a success. For he really gives battle who attempts to conquer all the difficulties and errors which prevent him from arriving at a knowledge of the truth, and it is to lose a battle to admit a false opinion touching a matter of any generality and importance. Much more skill is required in order to recover the position that one beforehand held, than is necessary to make great progress when one already possesses principles which are assured. For myself, if I have succeeded in discovering certain truths in the Sciences (and I hope that the matters contained in this volume will show that I have discovered some), I may say that they are resultant from, and dependent on, five or six principal difficulties which I have surmounted, and my encounter with these I look upon as so many battles in which I have had fortune on my side. I will not even hesitate to say that I think I shall have no need to win more than two or three other victories similar in kind in order to reach the accomplishment of my plans. And my age is not so advanced but that, in the ordinary course of nature, I may still have sufficient leisure for this end. But I believe myself to be so much the more bound to make the most of the time which remains, as I have the greater hope of being able to employ it well. And without doubt I should have many chances of being robbed of it, were I to publish the foundations of my Physics; for though these are nearly all so evident that it is only necessary to understand them in order to accept them, and although there are none of them as to which I do not believe myself capable of giving demonstration, yet because it is impossible that they should accord with all the various opinions of other men, I foresee that I should often be diverted from my main design by the opposition which they would bring to birth.

We may say that these contradictions might be useful both in making me aware of my errors, and, supposing that I had reached some satisfactory conclusion, in bringing others to a fuller understanding of my speculations; and, as many can see more than can a single man, they might help in leading others who from the present time may begin to avail themselves of my system, to assist me likewise with their discoveries. But though I recognise that I am extremely liable to err, and though I almost never trust the first reflections that I arrive at, the experience which I have had of the objections which may be made to my system prevents my having any hope of deriving profit from them. For I have often had experience of the judgments both of those whom I have esteemed as my friends, and of some others to whom I believed myself to be indifferent, and even, too, of some whose ill-feeling and envy would, I felt sure, make them endeavour to reveal what affection concealed from the eyes of my friends. But rarely has it happened that any objection has been made which I did not in some sort foresee, unless where it was something very far removed from my subject. In this way hardly ever have I encountered any censor of my opinions who did not appear to me to be either less rigorous or less judicial than myself. And I certainly never remarked that by means of disputations employed by the Schools any truth has been discovered of which we were formerly ignorant. And so long as each side attempts to vanquish his opponent, there is a much more serious attempt to establish probability than to weigh the reasons on either side; and those who have for long been excellent pleaders are not for that reason the best judges.

As to the advantage which others may receive from the communication of my reflections, it could not be very great, inasmuch as I have not yet carried them so far as that it is not necessary to add many things before they can be brought into practice. And I think I can without vanity say that if anyone is capable of doing this, it should be myself rather than another—not indeed that there may not be in the world many minds incomparably superior to my own, but because no one can so well understand a thing and make it his own when learnt from another as when it is discovered for himself. As regards the matter in hand there is so much truth in this, that although I have often explained some of my opinions to persons of very good intelligence, who, while I talked to them appeared to understand them very clearly, yet when they recounted them I remarked that they had almost always altered them in such a manner that I could no longer acknowledge them as mine. On this account I am very glad to have the opportunity here of begging my descendants never to believe that what is told to them proceeded from myself unless I have myself divulged it. And I do not in the least wonder at the extravagances attributed to all the ancient philosophers whose writings we do not possess, nor do I judge from these that their thoughts were very unreasonable, considering that theirs were the best minds of the time they lived in, but only that they have been imperfectly represented to us. We see, too, that it hardly ever happens that any of their disciples surpassed them, and I am sure that those who most passionately follow Aristotle now-a-days would think themselves happy if they had as much knowledge of nature as he had, even if this were on the condition that they should never attain to any more. They are like the ivy that never tries to mount above the trees which give it support, and which often even descends again after it has reached their summit; for it appears to me that such men also sink again—that is to say, somehow render themselves more ignorant than they would have been had they abstained from study altogether. For, not content with knowing all that is intelligibly explained in their author, they wish in addition to find in him the solution of many difficulties of which he says nothing, and in regard to which he possibly had no thought at all. At the same time their mode of philosophising is very convenient for those who have abilities of a very mediocre kind, for the obscurity of the distinctions and principles of which they make use, is the reason of their being able to talk of all things as boldly as though they really knew about them, and defend all that they say against the most subtle and acute, without any one having the means of convincing them to the contrary. In this they seem to me like a blind man who, in order to fight on equal terms with one who sees, would have the latter to come into the bottom of a very dark cave. I may say, too,

that it is in the interest of such people that I should abstain from publishing the principles of philosophy of which I make use, for, being so simple and evident as they are, I should, in publishing them, do the same as though I threw open the windows and caused daylight to enter the cave into which they have descended in order to fight. But even the best minds have no reason to desire to be acquainted with these principles, for if they wish to be able to talk of everything and acquire a reputation for learning, they will more readily attain their end by contenting themselves with the appearance of truth which may be found in all sorts of things without much trouble, than in seeking for truth which only reveals itself little by little in certain spheres, and which, when others come into question, obliges one to confess one's ignorance. If, however, they prefer the knowledge of some small amount of truth to the vanity of seeming to be ignorant of nothing, which knowledge is doubtless preferable, or they desire to follow a course similar to my own, it is not necessary that I should say any more than what I have already said in this Discourse. For if they are capable of passing beyond the point I have reached, they will also so much the more be able to find by themselves all that I believe myself to have discovered; since, not having examined anything but in its order, it is certain that what remains for me to discover is in itself more difficult and more recondite than anything that I have hitherto been able to meet with, and they would have much less pleasure in learning from me than from themselves. Besides, the habit which they will acquire of seeking first things that are simple and then little by little and by degrees passing to others more difficult, will be of more use than could be all my instructions. For, as regards myself, I am persuaded that if from my youth up I had been taught all the truths of which I have since sought the demonstrations, or if I had not had any difficulty in learning them, I should perhaps never have known any others, or at least I should never have acquired the habit or facility which I think I have obtained, of ever finding them anew, in proportion as I set myself to seek for them. And, in a word, if there is any work at all which cannot be so well achieved by another as by him who has begun it, it is that at which I labour.

It is true as regards the experiments which may conduce to this end, that one man could not possibly accomplish all of them. But yet

e could not, to good advantage, employ other
ands than his own, excepting those of arti-
ans or persons of that kind whom he could
ay, and whom the hope of gain—which is a
ery effectual incentive—might cause to per-
orm with exactitude all the things they were di-
ected to accomplish. As to those who, wheth-
r by curiosity or desire to learn, might pos-
ibly offer him their voluntary assistance, not
nly are they usually more ready with prom-
ses than with performance, planning out fine
ounding projects, none of which are ever real-
sed, but they will also infallibly demand pay-
nent for their trouble by requesting the ex-
olanation of certain difficulties, or at least by
mpty compliments and useless talk, which
ould not occupy any of the student's time
vithout causing it to be lost. And as to the
xperiments already made by others, even if
hey desired to communicate these to him—
vhich those who term them secrets would
never do—they are for the most part accom-
oanied by so many circumstances or superfluous matter, that it would be very difficult for
him to disentangle the truth. In addition to
this he would find nearly all so badly explained,
or even so false (because those who carried
them out were forced to make them appear to
be in conformity with their principles), that if
there had been some which might have been
of use to him, they would hardly be worth the
time that would be required in making the
selection. So true is this, that if there were
anywhere in the world a person whom one
knew to be assuredly capable of discovering
matters of the highest importance and those
of the greatest possible utility to the public,
and if for this reason all other men were eager
by every means in their power to help him in
reaching the end which he set before him, I do
not see that they could do anything for him
beyond contributing to defray the expenses of
the experiments which might be requisite, or,
for the rest, seeing that he was not deprived of
his leisure by the importunities of anyone.
But, in addition to the fact that I neither esteem myself so highly as to be willing to promise anything extraordinary, nor give scope to
an imagination so vain as to conceive that the
public should interest itself greatly in my designs, I do not yet own a soul so base as to be
willing to accept from anyone whatever a favour
which it might be supposed I did not merit.

All those considerations taken together were,
three years ago, the cause of my not desiring
to publish the Treatise which I had on hand,
and the reason why I even formed the resolution of not bringing to light during my life any
other of so general a kind, or one by which the
foundations of Physics could be understood.
But since then two other reasons came into
operation which compelled me to bring forward certain attempts, as I have done here,
and to render to the public some account of my
actions and designs. The first is that if I failed
to do so, many who knew the intention I formerly had of publishing certain writings, might
imagine that the causes for which I abstained
from so doing were more to my disadvantage
than they really were; for although I do not
care immoderately for glory, or, if I dare say
so, although I even hate it, inasmuch as I
judge it to be antagonistic to the repose which
I esteem above all other things, at the same
time I never tried to conceal my actions as
though they were crimes, nor have I used
many precautions against being known, partly
because I should have thought it damaging to
myself, and partly because it would have
given me a sort of disquietude which would
again have militated against the perfect repose
of spirit which I seek. And forasmuch as having in this way always held myself in a condition of indifference as regards whether I was
known or was not known, I have not yet been
able to prevent myself from acquiring some
sort of reputation, I thought that I should do
my best at least to prevent myself from acquiring an evil reputation. The other reason which
obliged me to put this in writing is that I am
becoming every day more and more alive to
the delay which is being suffered in the design
which I have of instructing myself, because of
the lack of an infinitude of experiments, which
it is impossible that I should perform without
the aid of others: and although I do not flatter
myself so much as to hope that the public
should to any large degree participate in my
interest, I yet do not wish to be found wanting,
both on my own account, and as one day giving occasion to those who will survive me of
reproaching me for the fact that I might have
left many matters in a much better condition
than I have done, had I not too much neglected to make them understand in what way they
could have contributed to the accomplishment of my designs.

And I thought that it was easy for me to
select certain matters which would not be the
occasion for many controversies, nor yet oblige
me to propound more of my principles than I
wish, and which yet would suffice to allow a

pretty clear manifestation of what I can do and what I cannot do in the sciences. In this I cannot say whether I have succeeded or have not succeeded, and I do not wish to anticipate the judgment of any one by myself speaking of my writings; but I shall be very glad if they will examine them. And in order that they may have the better opportunity of so doing, I beg all those who have any objections to offer to take the trouble of sending them to my publishers, so that, being made aware of them, I may try at the same time to subjoin my reply. By this means, the reader, seeing objections and reply at the same time, will the more easily judge of the truth; for I do not promise in any instance to make lengthy replies, but just to avow my errors very frankly if I am convinced of them; or, if I cannot perceive them, to say simply what I think requisite for the defence of the matters I have written, without adding the exposition of any new matter, so that I may not be endlessly engaged in passing from one side to the other.

If some of the matters of which I spoke in the beginning of the *Dioptrics* and *Meteors* should at first sight give offence because I call them hypotheses and do not appear to care about their proof, let them have the patience to read these in entirety, and I hope that they will find themselves satisfied. For it appears to me that the reasonings are so mutually interwoven, that as the later ones are demonstrated by the earlier, which are their causes, the earlier are reciprocally demonstrated by the later which are their effects. And it must not be imagined that in this I commit the fallacy which logicians name arguing in a circle, for, since experience renders the greater part of these effects very certain, the causes from which I deduce them do not so much serve to prove their existence as to explain them; on the other hand, the causes are explained by the effects. And I have not named them hypotheses with any other object than that it may be known that while I consider myself able to deduce them from the primary truths which I explained above, yet I particularly desired not to do so, in order that certain persons may not for this reason take occasion to build up some extravagant philosophic system on what they take to be my principles, and thus cause the blame to be put on me. I refer to those who imagine that in one day they may discover all that another has arrived at in twenty years of work, so soon as he has merely spoken to them two or three words on the subject; while they

are really all the more subject to err, and les capable of perceiving the truth as they are th more subtle and lively. For as regards the opin ions that are truly mine I do not apologise fo them as being new, inasmuch as if we conside the reasons of them well, I assure myself that they will be found to be so simple and so con formable to common sense, as to appear les extraordinary and less paradoxical than any others which may be held on similar subjects And I do not even boast of being the first dis coverer of any of them, but only state that I have adopted them, not because they have been held by others, nor because they have not been so held, but only because Reason has persuaded me of their truth.

Even if artisans are not at once able to carry out the invention[1] explained in the *Dioptrics*, I do not for that reason think that it can be said that it is to be condemned; for, inasmuch as great address and practice is required to make and adjust the mechanism which I have described without omitting any detail, I should not be less astonished at their succeeding at the first effort than I should be supposing some one were in one day to learn to play the guitar with skill, just because a good sheet of musical notation were set up before him. And if I write in French which is the language of my country, rather than in Latin which is that of my teachers, that is because I hope that those who avail themselves only of their natural reason in its purity may be better judges of my opinions than those who believe only in the writings of the ancients; and as to those who unite good sense with study, whom alone I crave for my judges, they will not, I feel sure, be so partial to Latin as to refuse to follow my reasoning because I expound it in a vulgar tongue.

For the rest, I do not desire to speak here more particularly of the progress which I hope in the future to make in the sciences, nor to bind myself as regards the public with any promise which I shall not with certainty be able to fulfil. But I will just say that I have resolved not to employ the time which remains to me in life in any other matter than in endeavouring to acquire some knowledge of nature, which shall be of such a kind that it will enable us to arrive at rules for Medicine more assured than those which have as yet been attained; and my inclination is so strongly opposed to any other kind of pursuit, more especially to those which can only be useful to

[1]Doubtless the machine for the purpose of cutting lenses which Descartes so minutely describes.

ome by being harmful to others, that if cerain circumstances had constrained me to emloy them, I do not think that I should have een capable of succeeding. In so saying I nake a declaration that I know very well cannot help me to make myself of consideration in the world, but to this end I have no desire to attain; and I shall always hold myself to be more indebted to those by whose favour I may enjoy my leisure without hindrance, than I shall be to any who may offer me the most honourable position in all the world.

CONTENTS

Meditations on First Philosophy

++++++++++++++++++

CONTENTS

Objections Against the Meditations, and Replies

MEDITATIONS
ON THE FIRST PHILOSOPHY

*TO THE MOST WISE AND ILLUSTRIOUS THE DEAN AND
DOCTORS OF THE SACRED FACULTY OF THEOLOGY
IN PARIS*

THE MOTIVE which induces me to present to you this Treatise is so excellent, and, when you become acquainted with its design, I am convinced that you will also have so excellent a motive for taking it under your protection, that I feel that I cannot do better, in order to render it in some sort acceptable to you, than in a few words to state what I have set myself to do.

I have always considered that the two questions respecting God and the Soul were the chief of those that ought to be demonstrated by philosophical rather than theological argument. For although it is quite enough for us faithful ones to accept by means of faith the fact that the human soul does not perish with the body, and that God exists, it certainly does not seem possible ever to persuade infidels of any religion, indeed, we may almost say, of any moral virtue, unless, to begin with, we prove these two facts by means of the natural reason. And inasmuch as often in this life greater rewards are offered for vice than for virtue, few people would prefer the right to the useful, were they restrained neither by the fear of God nor the expectation of another life; and although it is absolutely true that we must believe that there is a God, because we are so taught in the Holy Scriptures, and, on the other hand, that we must believe the Holy Scriptures because they come from God (the reason of this is, that, faith being a gift of God, He who gives the grace to cause us to believe other things can likewise give it to cause us to believe that He exists), we nevertheless could not place this argument before infidels, who might accuse us of reasoning in a circle. And, in truth, I have noticed that you, along with all the theologians, did not only affirm that the existence of God may be proved by the natural reason, but also that it may be inferred from the Holy Scriptures, that knowledge about Him is much clearer than that which we have of many created things, and, as a matter of fact, is so easy to acquire, that those who have it not are culpable in their ignorance. This indeed appears from the Wisdom of Solomon, chapter xiii., where it is said *"Howbeit they are not to be excused; for if their understanding was so great that they could discern the world and the creatures, why did they not rather find out the Lord thereof?"* and in Romans, chapter i., it is said that they are *"without excuse"*; and again in the same place, by these words *"that which may be known of God is manifest in them,"* it seems as though we were shown that all that which can be known of God may be made manifest by means which are not derived from anywhere but from ourselves, and from the simple consideration of the nature of our minds. Hence I thought it not beside my purpose to inquire how this is so, and how God may be more easily and certainly known than the things of the world.

And as regards the soul, although many have considered that it is not easy to know its nature, and some have even dared to say that human reasons have convinced us that it would perish with the body, and that faith alone could believe the contrary, nevertheless, inasmuch as the Lateran Council held under Leo X (in the eighth session) condemns these tenets, and as Leo expressly ordains Christian philosophers to refute their arguments and to employ all their powers in making known the truth, I have ventured in this treatise to undertake the same task.

More than that, I am aware that the principal reason which causes many impious persons not to desire to believe that there is a God, and that the human soul is distinct from the body, is that they declare that hitherto no one has been able to demonstrate these two facts; and although I am not of their opinion but, on the contrary, hold that the greater part of the reasons which have been brought forward concerning these two questions by so many great men are, when they are rightly understood, equal to so many demonstrations, and that it is almost impossible to invent new ones, it is yet in my opinion the case that nothing more useful can be accomplished in philosophy than once for all to seek with care for the best of these reasons, and to set them forth in so clear and exact a manner, that it will henceforth be evident to everybody that they are veritable demonstrations. And, finally, inasmuch as it was desired that I should undertake this task by many who were aware that I had cultivated a certain Method for the resolution of difficulties of every kind in the Sciences—a method which it is true is not novel, since there is nothing more ancient than the truth, but of which they were aware that I had made use successfully enough in other matters of difficulty—I have thought that it was my duty also to make trial of it in the present matter.

Now all that I could accomplish in the matter is contained in this Treatise. Not that I have here drawn together all the different reasons which might be brought forward to serve as proofs of this subject: for that never seemed to be necessary excepting when there was no one single proof that was certain. But I have treated the first and principal ones in such a manner that I can venture to bring them forward as very evident and very certain demonstrations. And more than that, I will say that these proofs are such that I do not think that there is any way open to the human mind by which it can ever succeed in discovering better. For the importance of the subject, and the glory of God to which all this relates, constrain me to speak here somewhat more freely of myself than is my habit. Nevertheless, whatever certainty and evidence I find in my reasons, I cannot persuade myself that all the world is capable of understanding them. Still, just as in Geometry there are many demonstrations that have been left to us by Archimedes, by Apollonius, by Pappus, and others, which are accepted by everyone as perfectly certain and evident (because they clearly contain nothing

which, considered by itself, is not very easy to understand, and as all through that which follows has an exact connection with, and dependence on that which precedes), nevertheless, because they are somewhat lengthy, and demand a mind wholly devoted to their consideration, they are only taken in and understood by a very limited number of persons. Similarly, although I judge that those of which I here make use are equal to, or even surpass in certainty and evidence, the demonstrations of Geometry, I yet apprehend that they cannot be adequately understood by many, both because they are also a little lengthy and dependent the one on the other, and principally because they demand a mind wholly free of prejudices, and one which can be easily detached from the affairs of the senses. And, truth to say, there are not so many in the world who are fitted for metaphysical speculations as there are for those of Geometry. And more than that; there is still this difference, that in Geometry, since each one is persuaded that nothing must be advanced of which there is not a certain demonstration, those who are not entirely adept more frequently err in approving what is false, in order to give the impression that they understand it, than in refuting the true. But the case is different in philosophy where everyone believes that all is problematical, and few give themselves to the search after truth; and the greater number, in their desire to acquire a reputation for boldness of thought, arrogantly combat the most important of truths.

That is why, whatever force there may be in my reasonings, seeing they belong to philosophy, I cannot hope that they will have much effect on the minds of men, unless you extend to them your protection. But the estimation in which your Company is universally held is so great, and the name of SORBONNE carries with it so much authority, that, next to the Sacred Councils, never has such deference been paid to the judgment of any Body, not only in what concerns the faith, but also in what regards human philosophy as well: everyone indeed believes that it is not possible to discover elsewhere more perspicacity and solidity, or more integrity and wisdom in pronouncing judgment. For this reason I have no doubt that if you deign to take the trouble in the first place of correcting this work (for being conscious not only of my infirmity, but also of my ignorance, I should not dare to state that it was free from errors), and then, after adding to it these things that are lacking to it, completing

hose which are imperfect, and yourselves tak-
ng the trouble to give a more ample explana-
ion of those things which have need of it, or
at least making me aware of the defects so that
I may apply myself to remedy them—when
his is done and when finally the reasonings by
which I prove that there is a God, and that the
human soul differs from the body, shall be
carried to that point of perspicuity to which I
am sure they can be carried in order that they
may be esteemed as perfectly exact demonstrations, if you deign to authorise your appro-
bation and to render public testimony to their
truth and certainty, I do not doubt, I say, that
henceforward all the errors and false opinions
which have ever existed regarding these two
questions will soon be effaced from the minds
of men. For the truth itself will easily cause all
men of mind and learning to subscribe to your
judgment; and your authority will cause the
atheists, who are usually more arrogant than

learned or judicious, to rid themselves of their
spirit of contradiction or lead them possibly
themselves to defend the reasonings which
they find being received as demonstrations by
all persons of consideration, lest they appear
not to understand them. And, finally, all
others will easily yield to such a mass of evidence, and there will be none who dares to
doubt the existence of God and the real and
true distinction between the human soul and
the body. It is for you now in your singular
wisdom to judge of the importance of the establishment of such beliefs [you who see the
disorders produced by the doubt of them].[1]
But it would not become me to say more in
consideration of the cause of God and religion
to those who have always been the most worthy supports of the Catholic Church.

[1]When it is thought desirable to insert additional readings from the French version, this will
be indicated by the use of square brackets.

PREFACE TO THE READER

I have already slightly touched on these two
questions of God and the human soul in the
Discourse on the Method of rightly conducting
the Reason and seeking truth in the Sciences,
published in French in the year 1637. Not that
I had the design of treating these with any
thoroughness, but only so to speak in passing,
and in order to ascertain by the judgment of
the readers how I should treat them later on.
For these questions have always appeared to
me to be of such importance that I judged it
suitable to speak of them more than once; and
the road which I follow in the explanation of
them is so little trodden, and so far removed
from the ordinary path, that I did not judge it
to be expedient to set it forth at length in
French and in a Discourse which might be
read by everyone, in case the feebler minds
should believe that it was permitted to them
to attempt to follow the same path.

But, having in this Discourse on Method
begged all those who have found in my writings somewhat deserving of censure to do me
the favour of acquainting me with the grounds
of it, nothing worthy of remark has been objected to in them beyond two matters: to these
two I wish here to reply in a few words before
undertaking their more detailed discussion.

The first objection is that it does not follow
from the fact that the human mind reflecting
on itself does not perceive itself to be other
than a thing that thinks, that its nature or its

essence consists only in its being a thing that
thinks, in the sense that this word *only* excludes all other things which might also be
supposed to pertain to the nature of the soul.
To this objection I reply that it was not my
intention in that place to exclude these in accordance with the order that looks to the truth
of the matter (as to which I was not then dealing), but only in accordance with the order of
my thought [perception]; thus my meaning
was that so far as I was aware, I knew nothing
clearly as belonging to my essence, excepting
that I was a thing that thinks, or a thing that
has in itself the faculty of thinking. But I shall
show hereafter how from the fact that I know
no other thing which pertains to my essence, it
follows that there is no other thing which really
does belong to it.

The second objection is that it does not follow from the fact that I have in myself the
idea of something more perfect than I am, that
this idea is more perfect than I, and much less
that what is represented by this idea exists.
But I reply that in this term *idea* there is here
something equivocal, for it may either be
taken materially, as an act of my understanding, and in this sense it cannot be said that it
is more perfect than I; or it may be taken objectively, as the thing which is represented by
this act, which, although we do not suppose it
to exist outside of my understanding, may,
none the less, be more perfect than I, because

of its essence. And in following out this Treatise I shall show more fully how, from the sole fact that I have in myself the idea of a thing more perfect than myself, it follows that this thing truly exists.

In addition to these two objections I have also seen two fairly lengthy works on this subject, which, however, did not so much impugn my reasonings as my conclusions, and this by arguments drawn from the ordinary atheistic sources. But, because such arguments cannot make any impression on the minds of those who really understand my reasonings, and as the judgments of many are so feeble and irrational that they very often allow themselves to be persuaded by the opinions which they have first formed, however false and far removed from reason they may be, rather than by a true and solid but subsequently received refutation of these opinions, I do not desire to reply here to their criticisms in case of being first of all obliged to state them. I shall only say in general that all that is said by the atheist against the existence of God, always depends either on the fact that we ascribe to God affections which are human, or that we attribute so much strength and wisdom to our minds that we even have the presumption to desire to determine and understand that which God can and ought to do. In this way all that they allege will cause us no difficulty, provided only we remember that we must consider our minds as things which are finite and limited, and God as a Being who is incomprehensible and infinite.

Now that I have once for all recognised and acknowledged the opinions of men, I at once begin to treat of God and the human soul, and at the same time to treat of the whole of the First Philosophy, without however expecting any praise from the vulgar and without the hope that my book will have many readers. On the contrary, I should never advise anyone to read it excepting those who desire to meditate seriously with me, and who can detach their minds from affairs of sense, and deliver themselves entirely from every sort of prejudice. I know too well that such men exist in a very small number. But for those who, without caring to comprehend the order and connections of my reasonings, form their criticisms on detached portions arbitrarily selected, as is the custom with many, these, I say, will not obtain much profit from reading this Treatise. And although they perhaps in several parts find occasion of cavilling, they can for all their pains make no objection which is urgent or deserving of reply.

And inasmuch as I make no promise to others to satisfy them at once, and as I do not presume so much on my own powers as to believe myself capable of foreseeing all that can cause difficulty to anyone, I shall first of all set forth in these Meditations the very considerations by which I persuade myself that I have reached a certain and evident knowledge of the truth, in order to see if, by the same reasons which persuaded me, I can also persuade others. And, after that, I shall reply to the objections which have been made to me by persons of genius and learning to whom I have sent my Meditations for examination, before submitting them to the press. For they have made so many objections and these so different, that I venture to promise that it will be difficult for anyone to bring to mind criticisms of any consequence which have not been already touched upon. This is why I beg those who read these Meditations to form no judgment upon them unless they have given themselves the trouble to read all the objections as well as the replies which I have made to them.

SYNOPSIS OF THE SIX FOLLOWING MEDITATIONS

In the first Meditation I set forth the reasons for which we may, generally speaking, doubt about all things and especially about material things, at least so long as we have no other foundations for the sciences than those which we have hitherto possessed. But although the utility of a Doubt which is so general does not at first appear, it is at the same time very great, inasmuch as it delivers us from every kind of prejudice, and sets out for us a very simple way by which the mind may detach itself from the senses; and finally it makes it impossible for us ever to doubt those things which we have once discovered to be true.

In the second Meditation, mind, which making use of the liberty which pertains to it, takes for granted that all those things of whose existence it has the least doubt, are non-existent, recognises that it is however absolutely impossible that it does not itself exist. This point is likewise of the greatest moment, inasmuch as by this means a distinction is easily drawn between the things which pertain to mind—that is to say to the intellectual nature—and those which pertain to body.

But because it may be that some expect from me in this place a statement of the reasons establishing the immortality of the soul, I feel that I should here make known to them that having aimed at writing nothing in all this Treatise of which I do not possess very exact demonstrations, I am obliged to follow a similar order to that made use of by the geometers, which is to begin by putting forward as premises all those things upon which the proposition that we seek depends, before coming to any conclusion regarding it. Now the first and principal matter which is requisite for thoroughly understanding the immortality of the soul is to form the clearest possible conception of it, and one which will be entirely distinct from all the conceptions which we may have of body; and in this Meditation this has been done. In addition to this it is requisite that we may be assured that all the things which we conceive clearly and distinctly are true in the very way in which we think them; and this could not be proved previously to the Fourth Meditation. Further we must have a distinct conception of corporeal nature, which is given partly in this Second, and partly in the Fifth and Sixth Meditations. And finally we should conclude from all this, that those things which we conceive clearly and distinctly as being diverse substances, as we regard mind and body to be, are really substances essentially distinct one from the other; and this is the conclusion of the Sixth Meditation. This is further confirmed in this same Meditation by the fact that we cannot conceive of body excepting in so far as it is divisible, while the mind cannot be conceived of excepting as indivisible. For we are not able to conceive of the half of a mind as we can do of the smallest of all bodies; so that we see that not only are their natures different but even in some respects contrary to one another. I have not however dealt further with this matter in this treatise, both because what I have said is sufficient to show clearly enough that the extinction of the mind does not follow from the corruption of the body, and also to give men the hope of another life after death, as also because the premises from which the immortality of the soul may be deduced depend on an elucidation of a complete system of Physics. This would mean to establish in the first place that all substances generally—that is to say all things which cannot exist without being created by God—are in their nature incorruptible, and that they can never cease to exist unless God, in denying to them his concurrence, reduce them to nought; and secondly that body, regarded generally, is a substance, which is the reason why it also cannot perish, but that the human body, inasmuch as it differs from other bodies, is composed only of a certain configuration of members and of other similar accidents, while the human mind is not similarly composed of any accidents, but is a pure substance. For although all the accidents of mind be changed, although, for instance, it think certain things, will others, perceive others, etc., despite all this it does not emerge from these changes another mind: the human body on the other hand becomes a different thing from the sole fact that the figure or form of any of its portions is found to be changed. From this it follows that the human body may indeed easily enough perish, but the mind [or soul of man (I make no distinction between them)] is owing to its nature immortal.

In the third Meditation it seems to me that I have explained at sufficient length the principal argument of which I make use in order to prove the existence of God. But none the less, because I did not wish in that place to make use of any comparisons derived from corporeal things, so as to withdraw as much as I could the minds of readers from the senses, there may perhaps have remained many obscurities which, however, will, I hope, be entirely removed by the Replies which I have made to the Objections which have been set before me. Amongst others there is, for example, this one, "How the idea in us of a being supremely perfect possesses so much objective reality [that is to say participates by representation in so many degrees of being and perfection] that it necessarily proceeds from a cause which is absolutely perfect." This is illustrated in these Replies by the comparison of a very perfect machine, the idea of which is found in the mind of some workman. For as the objective contrivance of this idea must have some cause, i.e. either the science of the workman or that of some other from whom he has received the idea, it is similarly impossible that the idea of God which is in us should not have God himself as its cause.

In the fourth Meditation it is shown that all these things which we very clearly and distinctly perceive are true, and at the same time it is explained in what the nature of error or falsity consists. This must of necessity be known both for the confirmation of the preceding truths and for the better comprehension of those that follow. (But it must meanwhile be remarked that I do not in any way there treat of sin—that is to say of the error which is committed in the pursuit of good and evil, but only of that which arises in the deciding between the true and the false. And I do not intend to speak of matters pertaining to the Faith or the conduct of life, but only of those which concern speculative truths, and which may be known by the sole aid of the light of nature.)

In the fifth Meditation corporeal nature generally is explained, and in addition to this the existence of God is demonstrated by a new proof in which there may possibly be certain difficulties also, but the solution of these will be seen in the Replies to the Objections. And further I show in what sense it is true to say that the certainty of geometrical demonstrations is itself dependent on the knowledge of God.

Finally, in the Sixth I distinguish the action of the understanding from that of the imagination; the marks by which this distinction is made are described. I here show that the mind of man is really distinct from the body, and at the same time that the two are so closely joined together that they form, so to speak, a single thing. All the errors which proceed from the senses are the surveyed, while the means of avoiding them ar demonstrated, and finally all the reasons from which we may deduce the existence of materia things are set forth. Not that I judge them to b very useful in establishing that which they prove to wit, that there is in truth a world, that me possess bodies, and other such things which neve have been doubted by anyone of sense; but be cause in considering these closely we come to se that they are neither so strong nor so evident a those arguments which lead us to the knowledge o our mind and of God; so that these last must b the most certain and most evident facts which ca fall within the cognizance of the human mind And this is the whole matter that I have tried t prove in these Meditations, for which reason here omit to speak of many other questions with which I dealt incidentally in this discussion.

MEDITATIONS

ON THE FIRST PHILOSOPHY IN WHICH THE EXISTENCE OF GOD AND THE DISTINCTION BETWEEN MIND AND BODY ARE DEMONSTRATED

MEDITATION I

Of the things which may be brought within the sphere of the doubtful.

It is now some years since I detected how many were the false beliefs that I had from my earliest youth admitted as true, and how doubtful was everything I had since constructed on this basis; and from that time I was convinced that I must once for all seriously undertake to rid myself of all the opinions which I had formerly accepted, and commence to build anew from the foundation, if I wanted to establish any firm and permanent structure in the sciences. But as this enterprise appeared to be a very great one, I waited until I had attained an age so mature that I could not hope that at any later date I should be better fitted to execute my design. This reason caused me to delay so long that I should feel that I was doing wrong were I to occupy in deliberation the time that yet remains to me for action. To-day, then, since very opportunely for the plan I have in view I have delivered my mind from every care [and am happily agitated by no passions] and since I have procured for myself an assured leisure in a peaceable retirement, I shall at last seriously and freely address myself to the general upheaval of all my former opinions.

Now for this object it is not necessary that I should show that all of these are false—I shall perhaps never arrive at this end. But inasmuch as reason already persuades me that I ought no less carefully to withhold my assent from matters which are not entirely certain and indubitable than from those which appear to me manifestly to be false, if I am able to find in each one some reason to doubt, this will suffice to justify my rejecting the whole. And for that end it will not be requisite that I should examine each in particular, which would be an endless undertaking; for owing to

the fact that the destruction of the foundations of necessity brings with it the downfall of the rest of the edifice, I shall only in the first place attack those principles upon which all my former opinions rested.

All that up to the present time I have accepted as most true and certain I have learned either from the senses or through the senses; but it is sometimes proved to me that these senses are deceptive, and it is wiser not to trust entirely to any thing by which we have once been deceived.

But it may be that although the senses sometimes deceive us concerning things which are hardly perceptible, or very far away, there are yet many others to be met with as to which we cannot reasonably have any doubt, although we recognise them by their means. For example, there is the fact that I am here, seated by the fire, attired in a dressing gown, having this paper in my hands and other similar matters. And how could I deny that these hands and this body are mine, were it not perhaps that I compare myself to certain persons, devoid of sense, whose cerebella are so troubled and clouded by the violent vapours of black bile, that they constantly assure us that they think they are kings when they are really quite poor, or that they are clothed in purple when they are really without covering, or who imagine that they have an earthenware head or are nothing but pumpkins or are made of glass. But they are mad, and I should not be any the less insane were I to follow examples so extravagant.

At the same time I must remember that I am a man, and that consequently I am in the habit of sleeping, and in my dreams representing to myself the same things or sometimes even less probable things, than do those who are insane in their waking moments. How often has it happened to me that in the night I dreamt that I found myself in this particular place, that I was dressed and seated near the fire, whilst in reality I was lying undressed in bed! At this moment it does indeed seem to me that it is with eyes awake that I am looking at this paper; that this head which I move is not asleep, that it is deliberately and of set purpose that I extend my hand and perceive it; what happens in sleep does not appear so clear nor so distinct as does all this. But in thinking over this I remind myself that on many occasions I have in sleep been deceived by similar illusions, and in dwelling carefully on this reflection I see so manifestly that there are no certain indications by which we may clearly distinguish wakefulness from sleep that I am lost in astonishment. And my astonishment is such that it is almost capable of persuading me that I now dream.

Now let us assume that we are asleep and that all these particulars, e.g. that we open our eyes, shake our head, extend our hands, and so on, are but false delusions; and let us reflect that possibly neither our hands nor our whole body are such as they appear to us to be. At the same time we must at least confess that the things which are represented to us in sleep are like painted representations which can only have been formed as the counterparts of something real and true, and that in this way those general things at least, i.e. eyes, a head, hands, and a whole body, are not imaginary things, but things really existent. For, as a matter of fact, painters, even when they study with the greatest skill to represent sirens and satyrs by forms the most strange and extraordinary, cannot give them natures which are entirely new, but merely make a certain medley of the members of different animals; or if their imagination is extravagant enough to invent something so novel that nothing similar has ever before been seen, and that then their work represents a thing purely fictitious and absolutely false, it is certain all the same that the colours of which this is composed are necessarily real. And for the same reason, although these general things, to wit, [a body], eyes, a head, hands, and such like, may be imaginary, we are bound at the same time to confess that there are at least some other objects yet more simple and more universal, which are real and true; and of these just in the same way as with certain real colours, all these images of things which dwell in our thoughts, whether true and real or false and fantastic, are formed.

To such a class of things pertains corporeal nature in general, and its extension, the figure of extended things, their quantity or magnitude and number, as also the place in which they are, the time which measures their duration, and so on.

That is possibly why our reasoning is not unjust when we conclude from this that Physics, Astronomy, Medicine and all other sciences which have as their end the consideration of composite things, are very dubious and uncertain; but that Arithmetic, Geometry and other sciences of that kind which only treat of things that are very simple and very general, without taking great trouble to ascertain whether they are actually existent or not, contain some measure of certainty and an element of the indubitable. For whether I am awake or asleep, two and three together always form five, and the square can never have more than four sides, and it does not seem possible that truths so clear and apparent can be suspected of any falsity [or uncertainty].

Nevertheless I have long had fixed in my mind the belief that an all-powerful God existed by whom I have been created such as I am. But how do I know that He has not brought it to pass that there is no earth, no heaven, no extended body, no magnitude, no place, and that nevertheless [I possess the perceptions of all these things and that] they seem to me to exist just exactly as I now see them? And, besides, as I sometimes imagine that others deceive themselves in the things which they think they know best, how do I know that I am not deceived every time that I add two and three, or count the sides of a square, or judge of things yet simpler, if anything simpler can be imagined? But possibly God has not desired that I should be thus deceived, for He is said to be supremely good. If, however, it is contrary to His goodness to have made me such that I constantly deceive myself, it would also appear to be contrary to His goodness to permit me to be sometimes deceived, and nevertheless I cannot doubt that He does permit this.

There may indeed be those who would prefer to deny the existence of a God so powerful rather than believe that all other things are uncertain. But let us not oppose them for the present, and grant that all that is here said of a God is a fable; nevertheless in whatever way they suppose that I have arrived at the state of being that I have reached—whether they attribute it to fate or to accident, or make out that it is by a continual succession of antecedents, or by some other method—since to

rr and deceive oneself is a defect, it is clear
hat the greater will be the probability of my
eing so imperfect as to deceive myself ever,
s is the Author to whom they assign my origin
he less powerful. To these reasons I have cer-
ainly nothing to reply, but at the end I feel
onstrained to confess that there is nothing in
ll that I formerly believed to be true, of which
 cannot in some measure doubt, and that not
nerely through want of thought or through
evity, but for reasons which are very powerful
nd maturely considered; so that henceforth I
ught not the less carefully to refrain from giv-
ng credence to these opinions than to that
vhich is manifestly false, if I desire to arrive
t any certainty [in the sciences].

But it is not sufficient to have made these
emarks, we must also be careful to keep them
n mind. For these ancient and commonly held
pinions still revert frequently to my mind,
ong and familiar custom having given them
he right to occupy my mind against my in-
lination and rendered them almost masters of
ny belief; nor will I ever lose the habit of de-
erring to them or of placing my confidence in
hem, so long as I consider them as they really
re, i.e. opinions in some measure doubtful, as
 have just shown, and at the same time highly
robable, so that there is much more reason to
elieve in than to deny them. That is why I
onsider that I shall not be acting amiss, if,
aking of set purpose a contrary belief, I allow
nyself to be deceived, and for a certain time
oretend that all these opinions are entirely
alse and imaginary, until at last, having thus
balanced my former prejudices with my latter
so that they cannot divert my opinions more
o one side than to the other], my judgment
vill no longer be dominated by bad usage or
urned away from the right knowledge of the
ruth. For I am assured that there can be nei-
her peril nor error in this course, and that I
annot at present yield too much to distrust,
ince I am not considering the question of ac-
ion, but only of knowledge.

I shall then suppose, not that God who is
supremely good and the fountain of truth, but
ome evil genius not less powerful than deceit-
ul, has employed his whole energies in deceiv-
ng me; I shall consider that the heavens, the
earth, colours, figures, sound, and all other ex-
ernal things are nought but the illusions and
dreams of which this genius has availed himself in order to lay traps for my credulity; I
shall consider myself as having no hands, no
eyes, no flesh, no blood, nor any senses, yet

falsely believing myself to possess all these
things; I shall remain obstinately attached to
this idea, and if by this means it is not in my
power to arrive at the knowledge of any truth,
I may at least do what is in my power [i.e.
suspend my judgment], and with firm purpose
avoid giving credence to any false thing, or
being imposed upon by this arch deceiver,
however powerful and deceptive he may be.
But this task is a laborious one, and insensibly
a certain lassitude leads me into the course of
my ordinary life. And just as a captive who in
sleep enjoys an imaginary liberty, when he begins to suspect that his liberty is but a dream,
fears to awaken, and conspires with these
agreeable illusions that the deception may be
prolonged, so insensibly of my own accord I
fall back into my former opinions, and I dread
awakening from this slumber, lest the laborious
wakefulness which would follow the tranquillity of this repose should have to be spent not
in daylight, but in the excessive darkness of
the difficulties which have just been discussed.

MEDITATION II

*Of the Nature of the Human Mind; and that it is
more easily known than the Body.*

The Meditation of yesterday filled my mind
with so many doubts that it is no longer in my
power to forget them. And yet I do not see in
what manner I can resolve them; and, just as
if I had all of a sudden fallen into very deep
water, I am so disconcerted that I can neither
make certain of setting my feet on the bottom,
nor can I swim and so support myself on the
surface. I shall nevertheless make an effort and
follow anew the same path as that on which I
yesterday entered, i.e. I shall proceed by setting aside all that in which the least doubt
could be supposed to exist, just as if I had discovered that it was absolutely false; and I shall
ever follow in this road until I have met with
something which is certain, or at least, if I can
do nothing else, until I have learned for certain that there is nothing in the world that is
certain. Archimedes, in order that he might
draw the terrestrial globe out of its place, and
transport it elsewhere, demanded only that
one point should be fixed and immoveable; in
the same way I shall have the right to conceive
high hopes if I am happy enough to discover
one thing only which is certain and indubitable.

I suppose, then, that all the things that I see
are false; I persuade myself that nothing has

ever existed of all that my fallacious memory represents to me. I consider that I possess no senses; I imagine that body, figure, extension, movement and place are but the fictions of my mind. What, then, can be esteemed as true? Perhaps nothing at all, unless that there is nothing in the world that is certain.

But how can I know there is not something different from those things that I have just considered, of which one cannot have the slightest doubt? Is there not some God, or some other being by whatever name we call it, who puts these reflections into my mind? That is not necessary, for is it not possible that I am capable of producing them myself? I myself, am I not at least something? But I have already denied that I had senses and body. Yet I hesitate, for what follows from that? Am I so dependent on body and senses that I cannot exist without these? But I was persuaded that there was nothing in all the world, that there was no heaven, no earth, that there were no minds, nor any bodies: was I not then likewise persuaded that I did not exist? Not at all; of a surety I myself did exist since I persuaded myself of something [or merely because I thought of something]. But there is some deceiver or other, very powerful and very cunning, who ever employs his ingenuity in deceiving me. Then without doubt I exist also if he deceives me, and let him deceive me as much as he will, he can never cause me to be nothing so long as I think that I am something. So that after having reflected well and carefully examined all things, we must come to the definite conclusion that this proposition: I am, I exist, is necessarily true each time that I pronounce it, or that I mentally conceive it.

But I do not yet know clearly enough what I am, I who am certain that I am; and hence I must be careful to see that I do not imprudently take some other object in place of myself, and thus that I do not go astray in respect of this knowledge that I hold to be the most certain and most evident of all that I have formerly learned. That is why I shall now consider anew what I believed myself to be before I embarked upon these last reflections; and of my former opinions I shall withdraw all that might even in a small degree be invalidated by the reasons which I have just brought forward, in order that there may be nothing at all left beyond what is absolutely certain and indubitable.

What then did I formerly believe myself to be? Undoubtedly I believed myself to be a man. But what is a man? Shall I say a reasonable animal? Certainly not; for then I should have to inquire what an animal is, and what is reasonable; and thus from a single question I should insensibly fall into an infinitude of others more difficult; and I should not wish to waste the little time and leisure remaining to me in trying to unravel subtleties like these. But I shall rather stop here to consider the thoughts which of themselves spring up in my mind, and which were not inspired by anything beyond my own nature alone when I applied myself to the consideration of my being. In the first place, then, I considered myself as having a face, hands, arms, and all that system of members composed of bones and flesh as seen in a corpse which I designated by the name of body. In addition to this I considered that I was nourished, that I walked, that I felt, and that I thought, and I referred all these actions to the soul: but I did not stop to consider what the soul was, or if I did stop I imagined that it was something extremely rare and subtle like a wind, a flame, or an ether which was spread throughout my grosser parts. As to body I had no manner of doubt about its nature, but thought I had a very clear knowledge of it; and if I had desired to explain it according to the notions that I had then formed of it, I should have described it thus: By the body I understand all that which can be defined by a certain figure: something which can be confined in a certain place, and which can fill a given space in such a way that every other body will be excluded from it; which can be perceived either by touch, or by sight, or by hearing, or by taste, or by smell: which can be moved in many ways not, in truth, by itself but by something which is foreign to it, by which it is touched [and from which it receives impressions]: for to have the power of self movement, as also of feeling or of thinking, I did not consider to appertain to the nature of body: on the contrary, I was rather astonished to find that faculties similar to them existed in some bodies.

But what am I, now that I suppose that there is a certain genius which is extremely powerful, and, if I may say so, malicious, who employs all his powers in deceiving me? Can I affirm that I possess the least of all those things which I have just said pertain to the nature of body? I pause to consider, I revolve all these things in my mind, and I find none of which I can say that it pertains to me. It would be tedious to stop to enumerate them. Let us pass to the attributes of soul and see if there is any one which is in me? What of nutrition or walking [the first mentioned]? But if it is so that I have no body it is also true that I can neither walk nor take nourishment. Another attribute is sensation. But one cannot feel without body, and besides I have thought I perceived many things during sleep that I recognised in my waking moments as not having been experienced at all. What of thinking? I find here that thought is an attribute that belongs to me; it alone cannot be separated from me. I am, I exist, that is certain. But how often? Just when I think; for it might possibly be the case if I ceased entirely to think, that I should likewise cease altogether to exist. I do not now admit anything which is not necessarily true: to speak accurately I am not more than a thing which thinks, that is to say a mind or a soul, or an understanding, or a reason, which are terms whose significance was formerly unknown to me. I am, however, a real thing and really exist; but what thing? I have answered: a thing which thinks.

And what more? I shall exercise my imagination [in order to see if I am not something more]. I am not a collection of members which we call the human body: I am not a subtle air distributed through these members, I am not a wind, a fire, a vapour, a breath, nor anything at all which I can imagine or conceive; because I have assumed that all these were nothing. Without changing that supposition I find that I only leave myself certain of the fact that I am somewhat. But perhaps it is true that these same things which I supposed were non-existent because they are unknown to me, are really not different from the self which I know. I am not sure about this, I shall not dispute about it now; I can only give judgment on things that are known to me. I know that I exist, and I inquire what I am, I whom I know to exist. But it is very certain that the knowledge of my existence taken in its precise significance does not depend on things whose existence is not yet known to me; consequently it does not depend on those which I can feign in imagination. And indeed the very term *feign* in imagination proves to me my error, for I really do this if I image myself a something, since to imagine is nothing else than to contemplate the figure or image of a corporeal thing. But I already know for certain that I am, and that it may be that all these images, and, speaking generally, all things that relate to the nature of body are nothing but dreams [and chimeras].

For this reason I see clearly that I have as little reason to say, "I shall stimulate my imagination in order to know more distinctly what I am," than if I were to say, "I am now awake, and I perceive somewhat that is real and true: but because I do not yet perceive it distinctly enough, I shall go to sleep of express purpose, so that my dreams may represent the perception with greatest truth and evidence." And, thus, I know for certain that nothing of all that I can understand by means of my imagination belongs to this knowledge which I have of myself, and that it is necessary to recall the mind from this mode of thought in order that it may be able to know its own nature with perfect distinctness.

But what then am I? A thing which thinks. What is a thing which thinks? It is a thing which doubts, understands, [conceives], affirms, denies, wills, refuses, which also imagines and feels.

Certainly it is no small matter if all these things pertain to my nature. But why should they not so pertain? Am I not that being who now doubts nearly everything, who nevertheless understands certain things, who affirms that one only is true, who denies all the others, who desires to know more, is averse from being deceived, who imagines many things, sometimes indeed despite his will, and who perceives many likewise, as by the intervention of the bodily organs? Is there nothing in all this which is as true as it is certain that I exist, even though I should always sleep and though he who has given me being employed all his ingenuity in deceiving me? Is there likewise any one of these attributes which can be distinguished from my thought, or which might be said to be separated from myself? For it is so evident of itself that it is I who doubts, who understands, and who desires, that there is no reason here to add anything to explain it. And I have certainly the power of imagining likewise; for although it may happen (as I formerly supposed) that none of the things which I imagine are true, nevertheless this power of imagining does not cease to be really in use, and it forms part of my thought. Finally, I am the same who feels, that is to say, who perceives certain things, as by the organs of sense, since in truth I see light, I hear noise, I feel heat. But it will be said that these phenomena are false and that I am dreaming. Let it be so; still it is at least quite certain that it seems to me that I see light, that I hear noise and that I feel heat. That cannot be false; properly speaking it is what is in me called feeling; and used in this precise sense that is no other thing than thinking.

From this time I begin to know what I am with a little more clearness and distinction than before; but nevertheless it still seems to me, and I cannot prevent myself from thinking, that corporeal things, whose images are framed by thought, which are tested by the senses, are much more distinctly known than that obscure part of me which does not come under the imagination. Although really it is very strange to say that I know and understand more distinctly these things whose existence seems to me dubious, which are unknown to me, and which do not belong to me, than others of the truth of which I am convinced, which are known to me and which pertain to my real nature, in a word, than myself. But I see clearly how the case stands: my mind loves to wander, and cannot yet suffer itself to be retained within the just limits of truth. Very good, let us once more give it the freest rein, so that, when afterwards we seize the proper occasion for pulling up, it may the more easily be regulated and controlled.

Let us begin by considering the commonest matters, those which we believe to be the most distinctly comprehended, to wit, the bodies which we touch and see; not indeed bodies in general, for these general ideas are usually a little more confused, but let us consider one body in particular. Let us take, for example, this piece of wax: it has been taken quite freshly from the hive, and it has not yet lost the sweetness of the honey which it contains; it still retains somewhat of the odour of the flowers from which it has been culled; its colour, its figure, its size are apparent; it is hard, cold, easily handled, and if you strike it with the finger, it will emit a sound. Finally all the things which are requisite to cause us distinctly to recognise a body, are met with in it. But notice that while I speak and approach the fire what remained of the taste is exhaled, the smell evaporates, the colour alters, the figure is destroyed, the size increases, it becomes liquid, it heats, scarcely can one handle it, and when one strikes it, no sound is emitted. Does the same wax remain after this change? We must confess that it remains; none would judge otherwise. What then did I know so distinctly in this piece of wax? It could certainly be nothing of all that the senses brought to my notice, since all these things which fall under taste, smell, sight, touch, and hearing, are found to be changed, and yet the same wax remains.

Perhaps it was what I now think, viz. that this wax was not that sweetness of honey, nor that agreeable scent of flowers, nor that particular whiteness, nor that figure, nor that sound, but simply a body which a little while before appeared to me as perceptible under these forms, and which is now perceptible under others. But what, precisely, is it that I imagine when I form such conceptions? Let us attentively consider this, and, abstracting from all that does not belong to the wax, let us see what remains. Certainly nothing remains excepting a certain extended thing which is flexible and movable. But what is the meaning of flexible and movable? Is it not that I imagine that this piece of wax being round is capable of becoming square and of passing from a square to a triangular figure? No, certainly it is not that, since I imagine it admits of an infinitude of similar changes, and I nevertheless do not know how to compass the infinitude by my imagination, and consequently this conception which I have of the wax is not brought about by the faculty of imagination. What now is this extension? Is it not also unknown? For it becomes greater when the wax is melted, greater when it is boiled, and greater still when the heat increases; and I should not conceive [clearly] according to truth what wax is, if I did not think that even this piece that we are considering is capable of receiving more variations in extension than I have ever imagined. We must then grant that I could not even understand through the imagination what this piece of wax is, and that it is my mind alone which perceives it. I say this piece of wax in particular, for as to wax in general it is yet clearer. But what is this piece of wax which cannot be understood excepting by the [understanding or] mind? It is certainly the same that I see, touch, imagine, and finally it is the same which I have always believed it to be from the beginning. But what must particularly be observed is that its perception is neither an act of vision, nor of touch, nor of imagination, and has never been such although it may have appeared formerly to be so, but only an intuition of the mind, which may be imperfect and confused as it was formerly, or clear and distinct as it is at present, according as my attention is more or less directed to the elements which are found in it, and of which it is composed.

Yet in the meantime I am greatly astonished when I consider [the great feebleness of mind] and its proneness to fall [insensibly] into error; for although without giving expression to my thoughts I consider all this in my own mind, words often impede me and I am almost deceived by the terms of ordinary language. For we say that we see the same wax, if it is present, and not that we simply judge that it is the same from its having the same colour and figure. From this I should conclude that I knew the wax by means of vision and not simply by the intuition of the mind; unless by chance I remember that, when looking from a window and saying I see men who pass in the street, I really do not see them, but infer that what I see is men, just as I say that I see wax. And yet what do I see from the window but hats and coats which may cover automatic machines? Yet I judge these to be men. And similarly solely by the faculty of judgment which rests in my mind, I comprehend that which I believed I saw with my eyes.

A man who makes it his aim to raise his knowledge above the common should be ashamed to derive the occasion for doubting from the forms of speech invented by the vulgar; I prefer to pass on and consider whether I had a more evident and perfect conception of what the wax was when I first perceived it, and when I believed I knew it by means of the external senses or at least by the common sense as it is called, that is to say by the imaginative faculty, or whether my present conception is clearer now that I have most carefully examined what it is, and in what way it can be known. It would certainly be absurd to doubt as to this. For what was there in this first perception which was distinct? What was there which might not as well have been perceived by any of the animals? But when I distinguish the wax from its external forms, and when, just as if I had taken from it its vestments, I consider it quite naked, it is certain that although some error may still be found in my judgment, I can nevertheless not perceive it thus without a human mind.

But finally what shall I say of this mind, that is, of myself, for up to this point I do not admit in myself anything but mind? What then, I who seem to perceive this piece of wax so distinctly, do I not know myself, not only with much more truth and certainty, but also with much more distinctness and clearness? For if I judge that the wax is or exists from the fact that I see it, it certainly follows much more clearly that I am or that I exist myself from the fact that I see it. For it may be that

what I see is not really wax, it may also be that I do not possess eyes with which to see anything; but it cannot be that when I see, or (for I no longer take account of the distinction) when I think I see, that I myself who think am nought. So if I judge that the wax exists from the fact that I touch it, the same thing will follow, to wit, that I am; and if I judge that my imagination, or some other cause, whatever it is, persuades me that the wax exists, I shall still conclude the same. And what I have here remarked of wax may be applied to all other things which are external to me [and which are met with outside of me]. And further, if the [notion or] perception of wax has seemed to me clearer and more distinct, not only after the sight or the touch, but also after many other causes have rendered it quite manifest to me, with how much more [evidence] and distinctness must it be said that I now know myself, since all the reasons which contribute to the knowledge of wax, or any other body whatever, are yet better proofs of the nature of my mind! And there are so many other things in the mind itself which may contribute to the elucidation of its nature, that those which depend on body such as these just mentioned, hardly merit being taken into account.

But finally here I am, having insensibly reverted to the point I desired, for, since it is now manifest to me that even bodies are not, properly speaking, known by the senses or by the faculty of imagination, but by the understanding only, and since they are not known from the fact that they are seen or touched, but only because they are understood, I see clearly that there is nothing which is easier for me to know than my mind. But because it is difficult to rid oneself so promptly of an opinion to which one was accustomed for so long, it will be well that I should halt a little at this point, so that by the length of my meditation I may more deeply imprint on my memory this new knowledge.

MEDITATION III

Of God: that He exists

I shall now close my eyes, I shall stop my ears, I shall call away all my senses, I shall efface even from my thoughts all the images of corporeal things, or at least (for that is hardly possible) I shall esteem them as vain and false; and thus holding converse only with myself and considering my own nature, I shall try little by little to reach a better knowledge of and a more familiar acquaintanceship with myself. I am a thing that thinks, that is to say, that doubts, affirms, denies, that knows a few things, that is ignorant of many [that loves, that hates], that wills, that desires, that also imagines and perceives; for as I remarked before, although the things which I perceive and imagine are perhaps nothing at all apart from me and in themselves, I am nevertheless assured that these modes of thought that I call perceptions and imaginations, inasmuch only as they are modes of thought, certainly reside [and are met with] in me.

And in the little that I have just said, I think I have summed up all that I really know, or at least all that hitherto I was aware that I knew. In order to try to extend my knowledge further, I shall now look around more carefully and see whether I cannot still discover in myself some other things which I have not hitherto perceived. I am certain that I am a thing which thinks; but do I not then likewise know what is requisite to render me certain of a truth? Certainly in this first knowledge there is nothing that assures me of its truth, excepting the clear and distinct perception of that which I state, which would not indeed suffice to assure me that what I say is true, if it could ever happen that a thing which I conceived so clearly and distinctly could be false; and accordingly it seems to me that already I can establish as a general rule that all things which I perceive very clearly and very distinctly are true.

At the same time I have before received and admitted many things to be very certain and manifest, which yet I afterwards recognised as being dubious. What then were these things? They were the earth, sky, stars and all other objects which I apprehended by means of the senses. But what did I clearly [and distinctly] perceive in them? Nothing more than that the ideas or thoughts of these things were presented to my mind. And not even now do I deny that these ideas are met with in me. But there was yet another thing which I affirmed, and which, owing to the habit which I had formed of believing it, I thought I perceived very clearly, although in truth I did not perceive it at all, to wit, that there were objects outside of me from which these ideas proceeded, and to which they were entirely similar. And it was in this that I erred, or, if perchance my judgment was correct, this was not due to any knowledge arising from my perception.

But when I took anything very simple and easy in the sphere of arithmetic or geometry into consideration, e.g. that two and three together made five, and other things of the sort, were not these present to my mind so clearly as to enable me to affirm that they were true? Certainly if I judged that since such matters could be doubted, this would not have been so for any other reason than that it came into my mind that perhaps a God might have endowed me with such a nature that I may have been deceived even concerning things which seemed to me most manifest. But every time that this preconceived opinion of the sovereign power of a God presents itself to my thought, I am constrained to confess that it is easy to Him, if He wishes it, to cause me to err, even in matters in which I believe myself to have the best evidence. And, on the other hand, always when I direct my attention to things which I believe myself to perceive very clearly, I am so persuaded of their truth that I let myself break out into words such as these: Let who will deceive me, He can never cause me to be nothing while I think that I am, or some day cause it to be true to say that I have never been, it being true now to say that I am, or that two and three make more or less than five, or any such thing in which I see a manifest contradiction. And, certainly, since I have no reason to believe that there is a God who is a deceiver, and as I have not yet satisfied myself that there is a God at all, the reason for doubt which depends on this opinion alone is very slight, and so to speak metaphysical. But in order to be able altogether to remove it, I must inquire whether there is a God as soon as the occasion presents itself; and if I find that there is a God, I must also inquire whether He may be a deceiver; for without a knowledge of these two truths I do not see that I can ever be certain of anything.

And in order that I may have an opportunity of inquiring into this in an orderly way [without interrupting the order of meditation which I have proposed to myself, and which is little by little to pass from the notions which I find first of all in my mind to those which I shall later on discover in it] it is requisite that I should here divide my thoughts into certain kinds, and that I should consider in which of these kinds there is, properly speaking, truth or error to be found. Of my thoughts some are, so to speak, images of the things, and to these alone is the title "idea" properly applied; examples are my thought of a man or of a chimera, of heaven, of an angel, or [even] of God. But other thoughts possess other forms as well.

For example in willing, fearing, approving, denying, though I always perceive something as the subject of the action of my mind, yet by this action I always add something else to the idea which I have of that thing; and of the thoughts of this kind some are called volitions or affections, and others judgments.

Now as to what concerns ideas, if we consider them only in themselves and do not relate them to anything else beyond themselves, they cannot properly speaking be false; for whether I imagine a goat or a chimera, it is not less true that I imagine the one than the other. We must not fear likewise that falsity can enter into will and into affections, for although I may desire evil things, or even things that never existed, it is not the less true that I desire them. Thus there remains no more than the judgments which we make, in which I must take the greatest care not to deceive myself. But the principal error and the commonest which we may meet with in them, consists in my judging that the ideas which are in me are similar or conformable to the things which are outside me; for without doubt if I considered the ideas only as certain modes of my thoughts, without trying to relate them to anything beyond, they could scarcely give me material for error.

But among these ideas, some appear to me to be innate, some adventitious, and others to be formed [or invented] by myself; for, as I have the power of understanding what is called a thing, or a truth, or a thought, it appears to me that I hold this power from no other source than my own nature. But if I now hear some sound, if I see the sun, or feel heat, I have hitherto judged that these sensations proceeded from certain things that exist outside of me; and finally it appears to me that sirens, hippogryphs, and the like, are formed out of my own mind. But again I may possibly persuade myself that all these ideas are of the nature of those which I term adventitious, or else that they are all innate, or all fictitious: for I have not yet clearly discovered their true origin.

And my principal task in this place is to consider, in respect to those ideas which appear to me to proceed from certain objects that are outside me, what are the reasons which cause me to think them similar to these objects. It seems indeed in the first place that I am taught this lesson by nature; and, secondly, I experience in myself that these ideas do not depend on my will nor therefore on myself—for they often present themselves to my mind in spite of my will. Just now, for instance, whether I will or whether I do not will, I feel heat, and thus I persuade myself that this feeling, or at least this idea of heat, is produced in me by something which is different from me, i.e. by the heat of the fire near which I sit. And nothing seems to me more obvious than to judge that this object imprints its likeness rather than anything else upon me.

Now I must discover whether these proofs are sufficiently strong and convincing. When I say that I am so instructed by nature, I merely mean a certain spontaneous inclination which impels me to believe in this connection, and not a natural light which makes me recognise that it is true. But these two things are very different; for I cannot doubt that which the natural light causes me to believe to be true, as, for example, it has shown me that I am from the fact that I doubt, or other facts of the same kind. And I possess no other faculty whereby to distinguish truth from falsehood, which can teach me that what this light shows me to be true is not really true, and no other faculty that is equally trustworthy. But as far as [apparently] natural impulses are concerned, I have frequently remarked, when I had to make active choice between virtue and vice, that they often enough led me to the part that was worse; and this is why I do not see any reason for following them in what regards truth and error.

And as to the other reason, which is that these ideas must proceed from objects outside me, since they do not depend on my will, I do not find it any the more convincing. For just as these impulses of which I have spoken are found in me, notwithstanding that they do not always concur with my will, so perhaps there is in me some faculty fitted to produce these ideas without the assistance of any external things, even though it is not yet known by me; just as, apparently, they have hitherto always been found in me during sleep without the aid of any external objects.

And finally, though they did proceed from objects different from myself, it is not a necessary consequence that they should resemble these. On the contrary, I have noticed that in many cases there was a great difference between the object and its idea. I find, for example, two completely diverse ideas of the sun in my mind; the one derives its origin from the senses, and should be placed in the category of adventitious ideas; according to this idea the sun seems to be extremely small; but the other is derived from astronomical reasonings, i.e. is elicited from certain notions that are innate in me, or else it is formed by me in some other manner; in accordance with it the sun appears to be several times greater than the earth. These two ideas cannot, indeed, both resemble the same sun, and reason makes me believe that the one which seems to have originated directly from the sun itself, is the one which is most dissimilar to it.

All this causes me to believe that until the present time it has not been by a judgment that was certain [or premeditated], but only by a sort of blind impulse that I believed that things existed outside of, and different from me, which, by the organs of my senses, or by some other method whatever it might be, conveyed these ideas or images to me [and imprinted on me their similitudes].

But there is yet another method of inquiring whether any of the objects of which I have ideas within me exist outside of me. If ideas are only taken as certain modes of thought, I recognise amongst them no difference or inequality, and all appear to proceed from me in the same manner; but when we consider them as images, one representing one thing and the other another, it is clear that they are very different one from the other. There is no doubt that those which represent to me substances are something more, and contain so to speak more objective reality within them [that is to say, by representation participate in a higher degree of being or perfection] than those that simply represent modes or accidents; and that idea again by which I understand a Supreme God, eternal, infinite, [immutable], omniscient, omnipotent, and Creator of all things which are outside of Himself, has certainly more objective reality in itself than those ideas by which finite substances are represented.

Now it is manifest by the natural light that there must at least be as much reality in the efficient and total cause as in its effect. For, pray, whence can the effect derive its reality, if not from its cause? And in what way can this cause communicate this reality to it, unless it possessed it in itself? And from this it follows, not only that something cannot proceed from nothing, but likewise that what is more perfect—that is to say, which has more reality within itself—cannot proceed from the less perfect. And this is not only evidently true of those effects which possess actual or formal reality, but also of the ideas in which we consider merely what is termed objective reality.

To take an example, the stone which has not yet existed not only cannot now commence to be unless it has been produced by something which possesses within itself, either formally or eminently, all that enters into the composition of the stone [i.e. it must possess the same things or other more excellent things than those which exist in the stone] and heat can only be produced in a subject in which it did not previously exist by a cause that is of an order [degree or kind] at least as perfect as heat, and so in all other cases. But further, the idea of heat, or of a stone, cannot exist in me unless it has been placed within me by some cause which possesses within it at least as much reality as that which I conceive to exist in the heat or the stone. For although this cause does not transmit anything of its actual or formal reality to my idea, we must not for that reason imagine that it is necessarily a less real cause; we must remember that [since every idea is a work of the mind] its nature is such that it demands of itself no other formal reality than that which it borrows from my thought, of which it is only a mode [i.e. a manner or way of thinking]. But in order that an idea should contain some one certain objective reality rather than another, it must without doubt derive it from some cause in which there is at least as much formal reality as this idea contains of objective reality. For if we imagine that something is found in an idea which is not found in the cause, it must then have been derived from nought; but however imperfect may be this mode of being by which a thing is objectively [or by representation] in the understanding by its idea, we cannot certainly say that this mode of being is nothing, nor, consequently, that the idea derives its origin from nothing.

Nor must I imagine that, since the reality that I consider in these ideas is only objective, it is not essential that this reality should be formally in the causes of my ideas, but that it is sufficient that it should be found objectively. For just as this mode of objective existence pertains to ideas by their proper nature, so does the mode of formal existence pertain to the causes of those ideas (this is at least true of the first and principal) by the nature peculiar to them. And although it may be the case that one idea gives birth to another idea, that cannot continue to be so indefinitely; for in the end we must reach an idea whose cause shall be, so to speak, an archetype, in which the whole reality [or perfection] which is, so to peak, objectively [or by representation] in these ideas is contained formally [and really]. Thus the light of nature causes me to know clearly that the ideas in me are like [pictures or] images which can, in truth, easily fall short of the perfection of the objects from which they have been derived, but which can never contain anything greater or more perfect.

And the longer and the more carefully that investigate these matters, the more clearly and distinctly do I recognise their truth. But what am I to conclude from it all in the end? It is this, that if the objective reality of any one of my ideas is of such a nature as clearly to make me recognise that it is not in me either formally or eminently, and that consequently cannot myself be the cause of it, it follows of necessity that I am not alone in the world, but that there is another being which exists, or which is the cause of this idea. On the other hand, had no such an idea existed in me, I should have had no sufficient argument to convince me of the existence of any being beyond myself; for I have made very careful investigation everywhere and up to the present time have been able to find no other ground.

But of my ideas, beyond that which represents me to myself, as to which there can here be no difficulty, there is another which represents a God, and there are others representing corporeal and inanimate things, others angels, others animals, and others again which represent to me men similar to myself.

As regards the ideas which represent to me other men, or animals, or angels, I can however easily conceive that they might be formed by an admixture of the other ideas which I have of myself, of corporeal things, and of God, even although there were apart from me neither men, nor animals, nor angels, in all the world.

And in regard to the ideas of corporeal objects, I do not recognise in them anything so great or so excellent that they might not have possibly proceeded from myself; for if I consider them more closely, and examine them individually, as I yesterday examined the idea of wax, I find that there is very little in them which I perceive clearly and distinctly. Magnitude or extension in length, breadth, or depth, I do so perceive; also figure which results from a termination of this extension, the situation which bodies of different figure preserve in relation to one another, and movement or change of situation; to which we may also add substance, duration and number. As to other things such as light, colours, sounds, scents, tastes, heat, cold and the other tactile qualities, they are thought by me with so much obscurity and confusion that I do not even know if they are true or false, i.e. whether the ideas which I form of these qualities are actually the ideas of real objects or not [or whether they only represent chimeras which cannot exist in fact]. For although I have before remarked that it is only in judgments that falsity, properly speaking, or formal falsity, can be met with, a certain material falsity may nevertheless be found in ideas, i.e. when these ideas represent what is nothing as though it were something. For example, the ideas which I have of cold and heat are so far from clear and distinct that by their means I cannot tell whether cold is merely a privation of heat, or heat a privation of cold, or whether both are real qualities, or are not such. And inasmuch as [since ideas resemble images] there cannot be any ideas which do not appear to represent some things, if it is correct to say that cold is merely a privation of heat, the idea which represents it to me as something real and positive will not be improperly termed false, and the same holds good of other similar ideas.

To these it is certainly not necessary that I should attribute any author other than myself. For if they are false, i.e. if they represent things which do not exist, the light of nature shows me that they issue from nought, that is to say, that they are only in me in so far as something is lacking to the perfection of my nature. But if they are true, nevertheless because they exhibit so little reality to me that I cannot even clearly distinguish the thing represented from non-being, I do not see any reason why they should not be produced by myself.

As to the clear and distinct idea which I have of corporeal things, some of them seem as though I might have derived them from the idea which I possess of myself, as those which I have of substance, duration, number, and such like. For [even] when I think that a stone is a substance, or at least a thing capable of existing of itself, and that I am a substance also, although I conceive that I am a thing that thinks and not one that is extended, and that the stone on the other hand is an extended thing which does not think, and that thus there is a notable difference between the two conceptions—they seem, nevertheless, to agree in this, that both represent substances. In the same way, when I perceive that I now exist and further recollect that I have in former times existed, and when I remember that I have various thoughts of which I can recognise the number, I acquire ideas of duration and number which I can afterwards transfer to any object that I please. But as to all the other qualities of which the ideas of corporeal things are composed, to wit, extension, figure, situation and motion, it is true that they are not formally in me, since I am only a thing that thinks; but because they are merely certain modes of substance [and so to speak the vestments under which corporeal substance appears to us] and because I myself am also a substance, it would seem that they might be contained in me eminently.

Hence there remains only the idea of God, concerning which we must consider whether it is something which cannot have proceeded from me myself. By the name God I understand a substance that is infinite [eternal, immutable], independent, all-knowing, all-powerful, and by which I myself and everything else, if anything else does exist, have been created. Now all these characteristics are such that the more diligently I attend to them, the less do they appear capable of proceeding from me alone; hence, from what has been already said, we must conclude that God necessarily exists.

For although the idea of substance is within me owing to the fact that I am substance, nevertheless I should not have the idea of an infinite substance—since I am finite—if it had not proceeded from some substance which was veritably infinite.

Nor should I imagine that I do not perceive the infinite by a true idea, but only by the negation of the finite, just as I perceive repose and darkness by the negation of movement and of light; for, on the contrary, I see that there is manifestly more reality in infinite substance than in finite, and therefore that in some way I have in me the notion of the infinite earlier than the finite—to wit, the notion of God before that of myself. For how would it be possible that I should know that I doubt and desire, that is to say, that something is lacking to me, and that I am not quite perfect, unless I had within me some idea of a Being more perfect than myself, in comparison with which I should recognise the deficiencies of my nature?

And we cannot say that this idea of God is perhaps materially false and that consequently I can derive it from nought [i.e. that possibly it exists in me because I am imperfect], as I have just said is the case with ideas of hea cold and other such things; for, on the co trary, as this idea is very clear and distinct an contains within it more objective reality tha any other, there can be none which is of itse more true, nor any in which there can be le suspicion of falsehood. The idea, I say, of th Being who is absolutely perfect and infinite, entirely true; for although, perhaps, we ca imagine that such a Being does not exist, w cannot nevertheless imagine that His idea re resents nothing real to me, as I have said of th idea of cold. This idea is also very clear an distinct; since all that I conceive clearly an distinctly of the real and the true, and of wha conveys some perfection, is in its entirety co tained in this idea. And this does not cease t be true although I do not comprehend the i finite, or though in God there is an infinitude things which I cannot comprehend, nor poss bly even reach in any way by thought; for it of the nature of the infinite that my natur which is finite and limited, should not compr hend it; and it is sufficient that I should under stand this, and that I should judge that a things which I clearly perceive and in which know that there is some perfection, and po sibly likewise an infinitude of properties which I am ignorant, are in God formally eminently, so that the idea which I have Him may become the most true, most clea and most distinct of all the ideas that are my mind.

But possibly I am something more than suppose myself to be, and perhaps all thos perfections which I attribute to God are some way potentially in me, although they d not yet disclose themselves, or issue in actio As a matter of fact I am already sensible tha my knowledge increases [and perfects itsel little by little, and I see nothing which ca prevent it from increasing more and more int infinitude; nor do I see, after it has thus bee increased [or perfected], anything to preven my being able to acquire by its means all th other perfections of the Divine nature; no finally why the power I have of acquiring thes perfections, if it really exists in me, shall no suffice to produce the ideas of them.

At the same time I recognise that this can not be. For, in the first place, although it wer true that every day my knowledge acquire new degrees of perfection, and that there wer in my nature many things potentially whic are not yet there actually, nevertheless thes excellences do not pertain to [or make th

nallest approach to] the idea which I have of
od in whom there is nothing merely potential
ut in whom all is present really and actual-
]; for it is an infallible token of imperfection
my knowledge that it increases little by
ttle. And further, although my knowledge
ows more and more, nevertheless I do not for
aat reason believe that it can ever be actually
finite, since it can never reach a point so high
aat it will be unable to attain to any greater
acrease. But I understand God to be actually
finite, so that He can add nothing to His
apreme perfection. And finally I perceive that
ae objective being of an idea cannot be pro-
uced by a being that exists potentially only,
hich properly speaking is nothing, but only
y a being which is formal or actual.

To speak the truth, I see nothing in all that
have just said which by the light of nature is
ot manifest to anyone who desires to think
ttentively on the subject; but when I slightly
elax my attention, my mind, finding its vision
omewhat obscured and, so to speak, blinded by
he images of sensible objects, I do not easily
ecollect the reason why the idea that I possess
f a being more perfect than I, must neces-
arily have been placed in me by a being which
s really more perfect; and this is why I wish
ere to go on to inquire whether I, who have
his idea, can exist if no such being exists.

And I ask, from whom do I then derive my
xistence? Perhaps from myself or from my
arents, or from some other source less perfect
han God; for we can imagine nothing more
perfect than God, or even as perfect as He is.

But [were I independent of every other and]
vere I myself the author of my being, I should
loubt nothing and I should desire nothing, and
inally no perfection would be lacking to me;
or I should have bestowed on myself every
perfection of which I possessed any idea and
hould thus be God. And it must not be imag-
ned that those things that are lacking to me
are perhaps more difficult of attainment than
hose which I already possess; for, on the contrary, it is quite evident that it was a matter of
much greater difficulty to bring to pass that
I, that is to say, a thing or a substance that
thinks, should emerge out of nothing, than it
would be to attain to the knowledge of many
things of which I am ignorant, and which are
only the accidents of this thinking substance.
But it is clear that if I had of myself possessed
this greater perfection of which I have just
spoken [that is to say, if I had been the author
of my own existence], I should not at least

have denied myself the things which are the
more easy to acquire [to wit, many branches of
knowledge of which my nature is destitute];
nor should I have deprived myself of any of
the things contained in the idea which I form
of God, because there are none of them which
seem to me especially difficult to acquire: and
if there were any that were more difficult to
acquire, they would certainly appear to me to
be such (supposing I myself were the origin of
the other things which I possess) since I should
discover in them that my powers were limited.

But though I assume that perhaps I have
always existed just as I am at present, neither
can I escape the force of this reasoning, and
imagine that the conclusion to be drawn from
this is, that I need not seek for any author of
my existence. For all the course of my life may
be divided into an infinite number of parts,
none of which is in any way dependent on the
other; and thus from the fact that I was in
existence a short time ago it does not follow
that I must be in existence now, unless some
cause at this instant, so to speak, produces me
anew, that is to say, conserves me. It is as a
matter of fact perfectly clear and evident to
all those who consider with attention the nature of time, that, in order to be conserved in
each moment in which it endures, a substance
has need of the same power and action as
would be necessary to produce and create it
anew, supposing it did not yet exist; so that
the light of nature shows us clearly that the
distinction between creation and conservation
is solely a distinction of the reason.

All that I thus require here is that I should
interrogate myself, if I wish to know whether
I possess a power which is capable of bringing
it to pass that I who now am shall still be in
the future; for since I am nothing but a thinking thing, or at least since thus far it is only
this portion of myself which is precisely in
question at present, if such a power did reside
in me, I should certainly be conscious of it.
But I am conscious of nothing of the kind, and
by this I know clearly that I depend on some
being different from myself.

Possibly, however, this being on which I depend is not that which I call God, and I am
created either by my parents or by some other
cause less perfect than God. This cannot be,
because, as I have just said, it is perfectly evident that there must be at least as much reality in the cause as in the effect; and thus since
I am a thinking thing, and possess an idea of
God within me, whatever in the end be the

cause assigned to my existence, it must be allowed that it is likewise a thinking thing and that it possesses in itself the idea of all the perfections which I attribute to God. We may again inquire whether this cause derives its origin from itself or from some other thing. For if from itself, it follows by the reasons before brought forward, that this cause must itself be God; for since it possesses the virtue of self-existence, it must also without doubt have the power of actually possessing all the perfections of which it has the idea, that is, all those which I conceive as existing in God. But if it derives its existence from some other cause than itself, we shall again ask, for the same reason, whether this second cause exists by itself or through another, until from one step to another, we finally arrive at an ultimate cause, which will be God.

And it is perfectly manifest that in this there can be no regression into infinity, since what is in question is not so much the cause which formerly created me, as that which conserves me at the present time.

Nor can we suppose that several causes may have concurred in my production, and that from one I have received the idea of one of the perfections which I attribute to God, and from another the idea of some other, so that all these perfections indeed exist somewhere in the universe, but not as complete in one unity which is God. On the contrary, the unity, the simplicity or the inseparability of all things which are in God is one of the principal perfections which I conceive to be in Him. And certainly the idea of this unity of all Divine perfections cannot have been placed in me by any cause from which I have not likewise received the ideas of all the other perfections; for this cause could not make me able to comprehend them as joined together in an inseparable unity without having at the same time caused me in some measure to know what they are [and in some way to recognise each one of them].

Finally, so far as my parents [from whom it appears I have sprung] are concerned, although all that I have ever been able to believe of them were true, that does not make it follow that it is they who conserve me, nor are they even the authors of my being in any sense, in so far as I am a thinking being; since what they did was merely to implant certain dispositions in that matter in which the self—i.e. the mind, which alone I at present identify with myself —is by me deemed to exist. And thus there can be no difficulty in their regard, but we must of necessity conclude from the fact alone that I exist, or that the idea of a Being supremely perfect—that is of God—is in me, that the proof of God's existence is grounded on the highest evidence.

It only remains to me to examine into the manner in which I have acquired this idea from God; for I have not received it through the senses, and it is never presented to me unexpectedly, as is usual with the ideas of sensible things when these things present themselves, or seem to present themselves, to the external organs of my senses; nor is it likewise a fiction of my mind, for it is not in my power to take from or to add anything to it; and consequently the only alternative is that it is innate in me, just as the idea of myself is innate in me.

And one certainly ought not to find it strange that God, in creating me, placed this idea within me to be like the mark of the workman imprinted on his work; and it is likewise not essential that the mark shall be something different from the work itself. For from the sole fact that God created me it is most probable that in some way he has placed his image and similitude upon me, and that I perceive this similitude (in which the idea of God is contained) by means of the same faculty by which I perceive myself—that is to say, when I reflect on myself I not only know that I am something [imperfect], incomplete and dependent on another, which incessantly aspires after something which is better and greater than myself, but I also know that He on whom I depend possesses in Himself all the great things towards which I aspire [and the ideas of which I find within myself], and that not indefinitely or potentially alone, but really, actually and infinitely; and that thus He is God. And the whole strength of the argument which I have here made use of to prove the existence of God consists in this, that I recognise that it is not possible that my nature should be what it is, and indeed that I should have in myself the idea of a God, if God did not veritably exist—a God, I say, whose idea is in me, i.e. who possesses all those supreme perfections of which our mind may indeed have some idea but without understanding them all, who is liable to no errors or defect [and who has none of all those marks which denote imperfection]. From this it is manifest that He cannot be a deceiver, since the light of nature teaches us that fraud and deception necessarily proceed from some defect.

But before I examine this matter with more

are, and pass on to the consideration of other ruths which may be derived from it, it seems o me right to pause for a while in order to ontemplate God Himself, to ponder at leisure Ilis marvellous attributes, to consider, and .dmire, and adore, the beauty of this light so esplendent, at least as far as the strength of ny mind, which is in some measure dazzled by he sight, will allow me to do so. For just as aith teaches us that the supreme felicity of the other life consists only in this contemplation of the Divine Majesty, so we continue to learn by experience that a similar meditation, though ncomparably less perfect, causes us to enjoy he greatest satisfaction of which we are capable in this life.

MEDITATION IV

Of the True and the False.

I have been well accustomed these past days to detach my mind from my senses, and I have accurately observed that there are very few things that one knows with certainty respecting corporeal objects, that there are many more which are known to us respecting the human mind, and yet more still regarding God Himself; so that I shall now without any difficulty abstract my thoughts from the consideration of [sensible or] imaginable objects, and carry them to those which, being withdrawn from all contact with matter, are purely intelligible. And certainly the idea which I possess of the human mind inasmuch as it is a thinking thing, and not extended in length, width and depth, nor participating in anything pertaining to body, is incomparably more distinct than is the idea of any corporeal thing. And when I consider that I doubt, that is to say, that I am an incomplete and dependent being, the idea of a being that is complete and independent, that is of God, presents itself to my mind with so much distinctness and clearness—and from the fact alone that this idea is found in me, or that I who possess this idea exist, I conclude so certainly that God exists, and that my existence depends entirely on Him in every moment of my life—that I do not think that the human mind is capable of knowing anything with more evidence and certitude. And it seems to me that I now have before me a road which will lead us from the contemplation of the true God (in whom all the treasures of science and wisdom are contained) to the knowledge of the other objects of the universe.

For, first of all, I recognise it to be impossible that He should ever deceive me; for in all fraud and deception some imperfection is to be found, and although it may appear that the power of deception is a mark of subtilty or power, yet the desire to deceive without doubt testifies to malice or feebleness, and accordingly cannot be found in God.

In the next place I experienced in myself a certain capacity for judging which I have doubtless received from God, like all the other things that I possess; and as He could not desire to deceive me, it is clear that He has not given me a faculty that will lead me to err if I use it aright.

And no doubt respecting this matter could remain, if it were not that the consequence would seem to follow that I can thus never be deceived; for if I hold all that I possess from God, and if He has not placed in me the capacity for error, it seems as though I could never fall into error. And it is true that when I think only of God [and direct my mind wholly to Him], I discover [in myself] no cause of error, or falsity; yet directly afterwards, when recurring to myself, experience shows me that I am nevertheless subject to an infinitude of errors, as to which, when we come to investigate them more closely, I notice that not only is there a real and positive idea of God or of a Being of supreme perfection present to my mind, but also, so to speak, a certain negative idea of nothing, that is, of that which is infinitely removed from any kind of perfection; and that I am in a sense something intermediate between God and nought, i.e. placed in such a manner between the Supreme Being and non-being, that there is in truth nothing in me that can lead to error in so far as a sovereign Being has formed me; but that, as I in some degree participate likewise in nought or in non-being, i.e. in so far as I am not myself the Supreme Being, and as I find myself subject to an infinitude of imperfections, I ought not to be astonished if I should fall into error. Thus do I recognise that error, in so far as it is such, is not a real thing depending on God, but simply a defect; and therefore, in order to fall into it, that I have no need to possess a special faculty given me by God for this very purpose, but that I fall into error from the fact that the power given me by God for the purpose of distinguishing truth from error is not infinite.

Nevertheless this does not quite satisfy me; for error is not a pure negation [i.e. is not the simple defect or want of some perfection which ought not to be mine], but it is a lack of some knowledge which it seems that I ought to possess. And on considering the nature of God it does not appear to me possible that He should have given me a faculty which is not perfect of its kind, that is, which is wanting in some perfection due to it. For if it is true that the more skilful the artizan, the more perfect is the work of his hands, what can have been produced by this supreme Creator of all things that is not in all its parts perfect? And certainly there is no doubt that God could have created me so that I could never have been subject to error; it is also certain that He ever wills what is best; is it then better that I should be subject to err than that I should not?

In considering this more attentively, it occurs to me, in the first place, that I should not be astonished if my intelligence is not capable of comprehending why God acts as He does; and that there is thus no reason to doubt of His existence from the fact that I may perhaps find many other things besides this as to which I am able to understand neither for what reason nor how God has produced them. For, in the first place, knowing that my nature is extremely feeble and limited, and that the nature of God is on the contrary immense, incomprehensible, and infinite, I have no further difficulty in recognising that there is an infinitude of matters in His power, the causes of which transcend my knowledge; and this reason suffices to convince me that the species of cause termed final, finds no useful employment in physical [or natural] things; for it does not appear to me that I can without temerity seek to investigate the [inscrutable] ends of God.

It further occurs to me that we should not consider one single creature separately, when we inquire as to whether the works of God are perfect, but should regard all his creations together. For the same thing which might possibly seem very imperfect with some semblance of reason if regarded by itself, is found to be very perfect if regarded as part of the whole universe; and although, since I resolved to doubt all things, I as yet have only known certainly my own existence and that of God, nevertheless since I have recognised the infinite power of God, I cannot deny that He may have produced many other things, or at least that He has the power of producing them, so that I may obtain a place as a part of a great universe.

Whereupon, regarding myself more closely, and considering what are my errors (for they alone testify to there being any imperfection in me), I answer that they depend on a combination of two causes, to wit, on the faculty of knowledge that rests in me, and on the power of choice or of free will—that is to say, of the understanding and at the same time of the will. For by the understanding alone I [neither assert nor deny anything, but] apprehend the ideas of things as to which I can form a judgment. But no error is properly speaking found in it, provided the word error is taken in its proper signification; and though there is possibly an infinitude of things in the world of which I have no idea in my understanding, we cannot for all that say that it is deprived of these ideas [as we might say of something which is required by its nature], but simply it does not possess these; because in truth there is no reason to prove that God should have given me a greater faculty of knowledge than He has given me; and however skilful a workman I represent Him to be, I should not for all that consider that He was bound to have placed in each of His works all the perfections which He may have been able to place in some. I likewise cannot complain that God has not given me a free choice or a will which is sufficient, ample and perfect, since as a matter of fact I am conscious of a will so extended as to be subject to no limits. And what seems to me very remarkable in this regard is that of all the qualities which I possess there is no one so perfect and so comprehensive that I do not very clearly recognise that it might be yet greater and more perfect. For, to take an example, if I consider the faculty of comprehension which I possess, I find that it is of very small extent and extremely limited, and at the same time I find the idea of another faculty much more ample and even infinite, and seeing that I can form the idea of it, I recognise from this very fact that it pertains to the nature of God. If in the same way I examine the memory, the imagination, or some other faculty, I do not find any which is not small and circumscribed, while in God it is immense [or infinite]. It is free-will alone or liberty of choice which I find to be so great in me that I can conceive no other idea to be more great; it is indeed the case that it is for the most part this will that causes me to know that in some manner I bear the image and similitude of God. For although the power of will is incomparably greater in God than in me, both by reason of the knowledge and the power which, conjoined with it, render it stronger and more efficacious, and by reason of its object, inasmuch as in God it extends to a great many things; it nevertheless does not seem to me greater if I consider it formally and precisely in itself: for the faculty of will consists alone in our having the power of choosing to do a thing or choosing not to do it (that is, to affirm or deny, to pursue or to shun it), or rather it consists alone in the fact that in order to affirm or deny, pursue or shun those things placed before us by the understanding, we act so that we are unconscious that any outside force constrains us in doing so. For in order that I should be free it is not necessary that I should be indifferent as to the choice of one or the other of two contraries; but contrariwise the more I lean to the one—whether I recognise clearly that the reasons of the good and true are to be found in it, or whether God so disposes my inward thought—the more freely do I choose and embrace it. And undoubtedly both divine grace and natural knowledge, far from diminishing my liberty, rather increase it and strengthen it. Hence this indifference which I feel, when I am not swayed to one side rather than to the other by lack of reason, is the lowest grade of liberty, and rather evinces a lack or negation in knowledge than a perfection of will: for if I always recognised clearly what was true and good, I should never have trouble in deliberating as to what judgment or choice I should make, and then I should be entirely free without ever being indifferent.

From all this I recognise that the power of will which I have received from God is not of itself the source of my errors—for it is very ample and very perfect of its kind—any more than is the power of understanding; for since I understand nothing but by the power which God has given me for understanding, there is no doubt that all that I understand, I understand as I ought, and it is not possible that I err in this. Whence then come my errors? They come from the sole fact that since the will is much wider in its range and compass than the understanding, I do not restrain it within the same bounds, but extend it also to things which I do not understand: and as the will is of itself indifferent to these, it easily falls into error and sin, and chooses the evil for the good, or the false for the true.

For example, when I lately examined whether anything existed in the world, and found that from the very fact that I considered this question it followed very clearly that I myself existed, I could not prevent myself from believing that a thing I so clearly conceived was true: not that I found myself compelled to do so by some external cause, but simply because from great clearness in my mind there followed a great inclination of my will; and I believed this with so much the greater freedom or spontaneity as I possessed the less indifference towards it. Now, on the contrary, I not only know that I exist, inasmuch as I am a thinking thing, but a certain representation of corporeal nature is also presented to my mind; and it comes to pass that I doubt whether this thinking nature which is in me, or rather by which I am what I am, differs from this corporeal nature, or whether both are not simply the same thing; and I here suppose that I do not yet know any reason to persuade me to adopt the one belief rather than the other. From this it follows that I am entirely indifferent as to which of the two I affirm or deny, or even whether I abstain from forming any judgment in the matter.

And this indifference does not only extend to matters as to which the understanding has no knowledge, but also in general to all those which are not apprehended with perfect clearness at the moment when the will is deliberating upon them; for, however probable are the conjectures which render me disposed to form a judgment respecting anything, the simple knowledge that I have that those are conjectures alone and not certain and indubitable reasons, suffices to occasion me to judge the contrary. Of this I have had great experience of late when I set aside as false all that I had formerly held to be absolutely true, for the sole reason that I remarked that it might in some measure be doubted.

But if I abstain from giving my judgment on any thing when I do not perceive it with sufficient clearness and distinctness, it is plain that I act rightly and am not deceived. But if I determine to deny or affirm, I no longer make use as I should of my free will, and if I affirm what is not true, it is evident that I deceive myself; even though I judge according to truth, this comes about only by chance, and I do not escape the blame of misusing my freedom; for the light of nature teaches us that the knowledge of the understanding should always precede the determination of the will. And it is in the misuse of the free will that the privation which constitutes the characteristic nature of error is met with. Privation, I say, is found in the act, in so far as it proceeds from me, but it is not found in the faculty which I have received from God, nor even in the act in so far as it depends on Him.

For I have certainly no cause to complain that God has not given me an intelligence which is more powerful, or a natural light which is stronger than that which I have received from Him, since it is proper to the finite understanding not to comprehend a multitude of things, and it is proper to a created understanding to be finite; on the contrary, I have every reason to render thanks to God who owes me nothing and who has given me all the perfections I possess, and I should be far from charging Him with injustice, and with having deprived me of, or wrongfully withheld from me, these perfections which He has not bestowed upon me.

I have further no reason to complain that He has given me a will more ample than my understanding, for since the will consists only of one single element, and is, so to speak, indivisible, it appears that its nature is such that nothing can be abstracted from it [without destroying it]; and certainly the more comprehensive it is found to be, the more reason I have to render gratitude to the giver.

And, finally, I must also not complain that God concurs with me in forming the acts of the will, that is the judgment in which I go astray, because these acts are entirely true and good, inasmuch as they depend on God; and in a certain sense more perfection accrues to my nature from the fact that I can form them, than if I could not do so. As to the privation in which alone the formal reason of error or sin consists, it has no need of any concurrence from God, since it is not a thing [or an existence], and since it is not related to God as to a cause, but should be termed merely a negation [according to the significance given to these words in the Schools]. For in fact it is not an imperfection in God that He has given me the liberty to give or withhold my assent from certain things as to which He has not placed a clear and distinct knowledge in my understanding; but it is without doubt an imperfection in me not to make a good use of my freedom, and to give my judgment readily on matters which I only understand obscurely. I nevertheless perceive that God could easily have created me so that I never should err, although I still remained free, and endowed with a limited knowledge, viz., by giving to my understanding a clear and distinct intelligence of all things as to which I should ever have to deliberate; or simply by His engraving deeply

in my memory the resolution never to form a judgment on anything without having a clear and distinct understanding of it, so that I could never forget it. And it is easy for me to understand that, in so far as I consider myself alone, and as if there were only myself in the world, I should have been much more perfect than I am, if God had created me so that I could never err. Nevertheless I cannot deny that in some sense it is a greater perfection in the whole universe that certain parts should not be exempt from error as others are than that all parts should be exactly similar. And I have no right to complain if God, having placed me in the world, has not called upon me to play a part that excels all others in distinction and perfection.

And further I have reason to be glad on the ground that if He has not given me the power of never going astray by the first means pointed out above, which depends on a clear and evident knowledge of all the things regarding which I can deliberate, He has at least left within my power the other means, which is firmly to adhere to the resolution never to give judgment on matters whose truth is not clearly known to me; for although I notice a certain weakness in my nature in that I cannot continually concentrate my mind on one single thought, I can yet, by attentive and frequently repeated meditation, impress it so forcibly on my memory that I shall never fail to recollect it whenever I have need of it, and thus acquire the habit of never going astray.

And inasmuch as it is in this that the greatest and principal perfection of man consists, it seems to me that I have not gained little by this day's Meditation, since I have discovered the source of falsity and error. And certainly there can be no other source than that which I have explained; for as often as I so restrain my will within the limits of my knowledge that it forms no judgment except on matters which are clearly and distinctly represented to it by the understanding, I can never be deceived; for every clear and distinct conception is without doubt something, and hence cannot derive its origin from what is nought, but must of necessity have God as its author—God, I say, who being supremely perfect, cannot be the cause of any error; and consequently we must conclude that such a conception [or such a judgment] is true. Nor have I only learned today what I should avoid in order that I may not err, but also how I should act in order to arrive at a knowledge of the truth; for without

oubt I shall arrive at this end if I devote my
ttention sufficiently to those things which I
erfectly understand; and if I separate from
hese that which I only understand confusedly
nd with obscurity. To these I shall henceforth
iligently give heed.

MEDITATION V

*Of the essence of material things, and, again, of
God, that He exists.*

Many other matters respecting the attributes of God and my own nature or mind remain for consideration; but I shall possibly on
another occasion resume the investigation of
these. Now (after first noting what must be
done or avoided, in order to arrive at a knowledge of the truth) my principal task is to endeavour to emerge from the state of doubt into
which I have these last days fallen, and to see
whether nothing certain can be known regard-
ng material things.

But before examining whether any such ob-
ects as I conceive exist outside of me, I must
consider the ideas of them in so far as they are
n my thought, and see which of them are distinct and which confused.

In the first place, I am able distinctly to
imagine that quantity which philosophers commonly call continuous, or the extension in
length, breadth, or depth, that is in this quantity, or rather in the object to which it is attributed. Further, I can number in it many different parts, and attribute to each of its parts
many sorts of size, figure, situation and local
movement, and, finally, I can assign to each of
these movements all degrees of duration.

And not only do I know these things with
distinctness when I consider them in general,
but, likewise [however little I apply my attention to the matter], I discover an infinitude of
particulars respecting numbers, figures, movements, and other such things, whose truth is so
manifest, and so well accords with my nature,
that when I begin to discover them, it seems
to me that I learn nothing new, or recollect
what I formerly knew—that is to say, that I
for the first time perceive things which were
already present to my mind, although I had
not as yet applied my mind to them.

And what I here find to be most important
is that I discover in myself an infinitude of
ideas of certain things which cannot be esteemed as pure negations, although they may
possibly have no existence outside of my
thought, and which are not framed by me,

although it is within my power either to think
or not to think them, but which possess natures which are true and immutable. For example, when I imagine a triangle, although
there may nowhere in the world be such a
figure outside my thought, or ever have been,
there is nevertheless in this figure a certain
determinate nature, form, or essence, which is
immutable and eternal, which I have not invented, and which in no wise depends on my
mind, as appears from the fact that diverse
properties of that triangle can be demonstrated, viz. that its three angles are equal to two
right angles, that the greatest side is subtended by the greatest angle, and the like, which
now, whether I wish it or do not wish it, I
recognise very clearly as pertaining to it, although I never thought of the matter at all
when I imagined a triangle for the first time,
and which therefore cannot be said to have
been invented by me.

Nor does the objection hold good that possibly this idea of a triangle has reached my mind
through the medium of my senses, since I have
sometimes seen bodies triangular in shape; because I can form in my mind an infinitude of
other figures regarding which we cannot have
the least conception of their ever having been
objects of sense, and I can nevertheless demonstrate various properties pertaining to their
nature as well as to that of the triangle, and
these must certainly all be true since I conceive them clearly. Hence they are something,
and not pure negation; for it is perfectly clear
that all that is true is something, and I have
already fully demonstrated that all that I
know clearly is true. And even although I had
not demonstrated this, the nature of my mind
is such that I could not prevent myself from
holding them to be true so long as I conceive
them clearly; and I recollect that even when I
was still strongly attached to the objects of
sense, I counted as the most certain those
truths which I conceived clearly as regards
figures, numbers, and the other matters which
pertain to arithmetic and geometry, and, in
general, to pure and abstract mathematics.

But now, if just because I can draw the idea
of something from my thought, it follows that
all which I know clearly and distinctly as pertaining to this object does really belong to
it, may I not derive from this an argument
demonstrating the existence of God? It is certain that I no less find the idea of God, that is
to say, the idea of a supremely perfect Being,
in me, than that of any figure or number what-

ever it is; and I do not know any less clearly and distinctly that an [actual and] external existence pertains to this nature than I know that all that which I am able to demonstrate of some figure or number truly pertains to the nature of this figure or number, and therefore, although all that I concluded in the preceding Meditations were found to be false, the existence of God would pass with me as at least as certain as I have ever held the truths of mathematics (which concern only numbers and figures) to be.

This indeed is not at first manifest, since it would seem to present some appearance of being a sophism. For being accustomed in all other things to make a distinction between existence and essence, I easily persuade myself that the existence can be separated from the essence of God, and that we can thus conceive God as not actually existing. But, nevertheless, when I think of it with more attention, I clearly see that existence can no more be separated from the essence of God than can its having its three angles equal to two right angles be separated from the essence of a [rectilinear] triangle, or the idea of a mountain from the idea of a valley; and so there is not any less repugnance to our conceiving a God (that is, a Being supremely perfect) to whom existence is lacking (that is to say, to whom a certain perfection is lacking), than to conceive of a mountain which has no valley.

But although I cannot really conceive of a God without existence any more than a mountain without a valley, still from the fact that I conceive of a mountain with a valley, it does not follow that there is such a mountain in the world; similarly, although I conceive of God as possessing existence, it would seem that it does not follow that there is a God which exists; for my thought does not impose any necessity upon such things, and just as I may imagine a winged horse, although no horse with wings exists, so I could perhaps attribute existence to God, although no God existed.

But a sophism is concealed in this objection; for from the fact that I cannot conceive a mountain without a valley, it does not follow that there is any mountain or any valley in existence, but only that the mountain and the valley, whether they exist or do not exist, cannot in any way be separated one from the other. While from the fact that I cannot conceive God without existence, it follows that existence is inseparable from Him, and hence that He really exists; not that my thought can bring this to pass, or impose any necessity on things, but, on the contrary, because the necessity which lies in the thing itself, i.e. the necessity of the existence of God determines me to think in this way. For it is not within my power to think of God without existence (that is of a supremely perfect Being devoid of a supreme perfection) though it is in my power to imagine a horse either with wings or without wings.

And we must not here object that it is in truth necessary for me to assert that God exists after having presupposed that He possesses every sort of perfection, since existence is one of these, but that as a matter of fact my original supposition was not necessary, just as it is not necessary to consider that all quadrilateral figures can be inscribed in the circle; for supposing I thought this, I should be constrained to admit that the rhombus might be inscribed in the circle since it is a quadrilateral figure, which, however, is manifestly false. [We must not, I say, make any such allegations because] although it is not necessary that I should at any time entertain the notion of God, nevertheless whenever it happens that I think of a first and a sovereign Being, and, so to speak, derive the idea of Him from the storehouse of my mind, it is necessary that I should attribute to Him every sort of perfection, although I do not get so far as to enumerate them all, or to apply my mind to each one in particular. And this necessity suffices to make me conclude (after having recognised that existence is a perfection) that this first and sovereign Being really exists; just as though it is not necessary for me ever to imagine any triangle, yet, whenever I wish to consider a rectilinear figure composed only of three angles, it is absolutely essential that I should attribute to it all those properties which serve to bring about the conclusion that its three angles are not greater than two right angles, even although I may not then be considering this point in particular. But when I consider which figures are capable of being inscribed in the circle, it is in no wise necessary that I should think that all quadrilateral figures are of this number; on the contrary, I cannot even pretend that this is the case, so long as I do not desire to accept anything which I cannot conceive clearly and distinctly. And in consequence there is a great difference between the false suppositions such as this, and the true ideas born within me, the first and principal of which is that of God. For really I discern in many ways that this idea is not something factitious, and depending solely on my thought, but that it is the image of a true and immutable nature; first of all, because I cannot conceive anything but God himself to whose essence existence [necessarily] pertains; in the second place because it is not possible for me to conceive two or more Gods in this same position; and, granted that there is one such God who now exists, I see clearly that it is necessary that He should have existed from all eternity, and that He must exist eternally; and finally, because I know an infinitude of other properties in God, none of which I can either diminish or change.

For the rest, whatever proof or argument I avail myself of, we must always return to the point that it is only those things which we conceive clearly and distinctly that have the power of persuading me entirely. And although amongst the matters which I conceive of in this way, some indeed are manifestly obvious to all, while others only manifest themselves to those who consider them closely and examine them attentively; still, after they have once been discovered, the latter are not esteemed as any less certain than the former. For example, in the case of every right-angled triangle, although it does not so manifestly appear that the square of the base is equal to the squares of the two other sides as that this base is opposite to the greatest angle; still, when this has once been apprehended, we are just as certain of its truth as of the truth of the other. And as regards God, if my mind were not preoccupied with prejudices, and if my thought did not find itself on all hands diverted by the continual pressure of sensible things, there would be nothing which I could know more immediately and more easily than Him. For is there anything more manifest than that there is a God, that is to say, a Supreme Being, to whose essence alone existence pertains?

And although for a firm grasp of this truth I have need of a strenuous application of mind, at present I not only feel myself to be as assured of it as of all that I hold as most certain, but I also remark that the certainty of all other things depends on it so absolutely, that without this knowledge it is impossible ever to know anything perfectly.

For although I am of such a nature that as long as I understand anything very clearly and distinctly, I am naturally impelled to believe it to be true, yet because I am also of such a nature that I cannot have my mind constantly fixed on the same object in order to perceive it

clearly, and as I often recollect having formed a past judgment without at the same time properly recollecting the reasons that led me to make it, it may happen meanwhile that other reasons present themselves to me, which would easily cause me to change my opinion, if I were ignorant of the facts of the existence of God, and thus I should have no true and certain knowledge, but only vague and vacillating opinions. Thus, for example, when I consider the nature of a [rectilinear] triangle, I who have some little knowledge of the principles of geometry recognise quite clearly that the three angles are equal to two right angles, and it is not possible for me not to believe this so long as I apply my mind to its demonstration; but so soon as I abstain from attending to the proof, although I still recollect having clearly comprehended it, it may easily occur that I come to doubt its truth, if I am ignorant of there being a God. For I can persuade myself of having been so constituted by nature that I can easily deceive myself even in those matters which I believe myself to apprehend with the greatest evidence and certainty, especially when I recollect that I have frequently judged matters to be true and certain which other reasons have afterwards impelled me to judge to be altogether false.

But after I have recognised that there is a God—because at the same time I have also recognised that all things depend upon Him, and that He is not a deceiver, and from that have inferred that what I perceive clearly and distinctly cannot fail to be true—although I no longer pay attention to the reasons for which I have judged this to be true, provided that I recollect having clearly and distinctly perceived it no contrary reason can be brought forward which could ever cause me to doubt of its truth; and thus I have a true and certain knowledge of it. And this same knowledge extends likewise to all other things which I recollect having formerly demonstrated, such as the truths of geometry and the like; for what can be alleged against them to cause me to place them in doubt? Will it be said that my nature is such as to cause me to be frequently deceived? But I already know that I cannot be deceived in the judgment whose grounds I know clearly. Will it be said that I formerly held many things to be true and certain which I have afterwards recognised to be false? But I had not any clear and distinct knowledge of these things, and not as yet knowing the rule whereby I assure myself of the truth, I had been impelled to give my assent from reasons which I have since recognised to be less strong than I had at the time imagined them to be. What further objection can then be raised? That possibly I am dreaming (an objection I myself made a little while ago), or that all the thoughts which I now have are no more true than the phantasies of my dreams? But even though I slept the case would be the same, for all that is clearly present to my mind is absolutely true.

And so I very clearly recognise that the certainty and truth of all knowledge depends alone on the knowledge of the true God, in so much that, before I knew Him, I could not have a perfect knowledge of any other thing. And now that I know Him I have the means of acquiring a perfect knowledge of an infinitude of things, not only of those which relate to God Himself and other intellectual matters, but also of those which pertain to corporeal nature in so far as it is the object of pure mathematics [which have no concern with whether it exists or not].

MEDITATION VI

Of the Existence of Material Things, and of the real distinction between the Soul and Body of Man.

Nothing further now remains but to inquire whether material things exist. And certainly I at least know that these may exist in so far as they are considered as the objects of pure mathematics, since in this aspect I perceive them clearly and distinctly. For there is no doubt that God possesses the power to produce everything that I am capable of perceiving with distinctness, and I have never deemed that anything was impossible for Him, unless I found a contradiction in attempting to conceive it clearly. Further, the faculty of imagination which I possess, and of which, experience tells me, I make use when I apply myself to the consideration of material things, is capable of persuading me of their existence; for when I attentively consider what imagination is, I find that it is nothing but a certain application of the faculty of knowledge to the body which is immediately present to it, and which therefore exists.

And to render this quite clear, I remark in the first place the difference that exists between the imagination and pure intellection [or conception]. For example, when I imagine a triangle, I do not conceive it only as a figure

comprehended by three lines, but I also apprehend these three lines as present by the power and inward vision of my mind, and this is what I call imagining. But if I desire to think of a chiliagon, I certainly conceive truly that it is a figure composed of a thousand sides, just as easily as I conceive of a triangle that it is a figure of three sides only; but I cannot in any way imagine the thousand sides of a chiliagon [as I do the three sides of a triangle], nor do I, so to speak, regard them as present [with the eyes of my mind]. And although in accordance with the habit I have formed of always employing the aid of my imagination when I think of corporeal things, it may happen that in imagining a chiliagon I confusedly represent to myself some figure, yet it is very evident that this figure is not a chiliagon, since it in no way differs from that which I represent to myself when I think of a myriagon or any other many-sided figure; nor does it serve my purpose in discovering the properties which go to form the distinction between a chiliagon and other polygons. But if the question turns upon a pentagon, it is quite true that I can conceive its figure as well as that of a chiliagon without the help of my imagination; but I can also imagine it by applying the attention of my mind to each of its five sides, and at the same time to the space which they enclose. And thus I clearly recognise that I have need of a particular effort of mind in order to effect the act of imagination, such as I do not require in order to understand, and this particular effort of mind clearly manifests the difference which exists between imagination and pure intellection.

I remark besides that this power of imagination which is in one, inasmuch as it differs from the power of understanding, is in no wise a necessary element in my nature, or in [my essence, that is to say, in] the essence of my mind; for although I did not possess it I should doubtless ever remain the same as I now am, from which it appears that we might conclude that it depends on something which differs from me. And I easily conceive that if some body exists with which my mind is conjoined and united in such a way that it can apply itself to consider it when it pleases, it may be that by this means it can imagine corporeal objects; so that this mode of thinking differs from pure intellection only inasmuch as mind in its intellectual activity in some manner turns on itself, and considers some of the ideas which it possesses in itself; while in imagining t turns towards the body, and there beholds n it something conformable to the idea which t has either conceived of itself or perceived by he senses. I easily understand, I say, that the magination could be thus constituted if it is rue that body exists; and because I can discover no other convenient mode of explaining t, I conjecture with probability that body does exist; but this is only with probability, nd although I examine all things with care, I nevertheless do not find that from this distinct dea of corporeal nature, which I have in my magination, I can derive any argument from which there will necessarily be deduced the existence of body.

But I am in the habit of imagining many other things besides this corporeal nature which s the object of pure mathematics, to wit, the colours, sounds, scents, pain, and other such things, although less distinctly. And inasmuch as I perceive these things much better through the senses, by the medium of which, and by the memory, they seem to have reached my imagination. I believe that, in order to examine them more conveniently, it is right that I should at the same time investigate the nature of sense perception, and that I should see if from the ideas which I apprehend by this mode of thought, which I call feeling, I cannot derive some certain proof of the existence of corporeal objects.

And first of all I shall recall to my memory those matters which I hitherto held to be true, as having perceived them through the senses, and the foundations on which my belief has rested; in the next place I shall examine the reasons which have since obliged me to place them in doubt; in the last place I shall consider which of them I must now believe.

First of all, then, I perceived that I had a head, hands, feet, and all other members of which this body—which I considered as a part, or possibly even as the whole, of myself —is composed. Further, I was sensible that this body was placed amidst many others, from which it was capable of being affected in many different ways, beneficial and hurtful, and I remarked that a certain feeling of pleasure accompanied those that were beneficial, and pain those which were harmful. And in addition to this pleasure and pain, I also experienced hunger, thirst, and other similar appetites, as also certain corporeal inclinations towards joy, sadness, anger, and other similar passions. And outside myself, in addition to extension, figure, and motions of bodies, I re-

marked in them hardness, heat, and all other tactile qualities, and, further, light and colour, and scents and sounds, the variety of which gave me the means of distinguishing the sky, the earth, the sea, and generally all the other bodies, one from the other. And certainly, considering the ideas of all these qualities which presented themselves to my mind, and which alone I perceived properly or immediately, it was not without reason that I believed myself to perceive objects quite different from my thought, to wit, bodies from which those ideas proceeded; for I found by experience that these ideas presented themselves to me without my consent being requisite, so that I could not perceive any object, however desirous I might be, unless it were present to the organs of sense; and it was not in my power not to perceive it, when it was present. And because the ideas which I received through the senses were much more lively, more clear, and even, in their own way, more distinct than any of those which I could of myself frame in meditation, or than those I found impressed on my memory, it appeared as though they could not have proceeded from my mind, so that they must necessarily have been produced in me by some other things. And having no knowledge of those objects excepting the knowledge which the ideas themselves gave me, nothing was more likely to occur to my mind than that the objects were similar to the ideas which were caused. And because I likewise remembered that I had formerly made use of my senses rather than my reason, and recognised that the ideas which I formed of myself were not so distinct as those which I perceived through the senses, and that they were most frequently even composed of portions of these last, I persuaded myself easily that I had no idea in my mind which had not formerly come to me through the senses. Nor was it without some reason that I believed that this body (which by a certain special right I call my own) belonged to me more properly and more strictly than any other; for in fact I could never be separated from it as from other bodies; I experienced in it and on account of it all my appetites and affections, and finally I was touched by the feeling of pain and the titillation of pleasure in its parts, and not in the parts of other bodies which were separated from it. But when I inquired, why, from some, I know not what, painful sensation, there follows sadness of mind, and from the pleasurable sensation there arises joy, or why this mysterious pinching of the stomach which I call hunger causes me to desire to eat, and dryness of throat causes a desire to drink, and so on, I could give no reason excepting that nature taught me so; for there is certainly no affinity (that I at least can understand) between the craving of the stomach and the desire to eat, any more than between the perception of whatever causes pain and the thought of sadness which arises from this perception. And in the same way it appeared to me that I had learned from nature all the other judgments which I formed regarding the objects of my senses, since I remarked that these judgments were formed in me before I had the leisure to weigh and consider any reasons which might oblige me to make them.

But afterwards many experiences little by little destroyed all the faith which I had rested in my senses; for I from time to time observed that those towers which from afar appeared to me to be round, more closely observed seemed square, and that colossal statues raised on the summit of these towers, appeared as quite tiny statues when viewed from the bottom; and so in an infinitude of other cases I found error in judgments founded on the external senses. And not only in those founded on the external senses, but even in those founded on the internal as well; for is there anything more intimate or more internal than pain? And yet I have learned from some persons whose arms or legs have been cut off, that they sometimes seemed to feel pain in the part which had been amputated, which made me think that I could not be quite certain that it was a certain member which pained me, even although I felt pain in it. And to those grounds of doubt I have lately added two others, which are very general; the first is that I never have believed myself to feel anything in waking moments which I cannot also sometimes believe myself to feel when I sleep, and as I do not think that these things which I seem to feel in sleep, proceed from objects outside of me, I do not see any reason why I should have this belief regarding objects which I seem to perceive while awake. The other was that being still ignorant, or rather supposing myself to be ignorant, of the author of my being, I saw nothing to prevent me from having been so constituted by nature that I might be deceived even in matters which seemed to me to be most certain. And as to the grounds on which I was formerly persuaded of the truth of sensible objects, I had not much trouble in replying to them. For since nature seemed to cause me to lean towards many things from which reason repelled me, I did not believe that I should trust much to the teachings of nature. And although the ideas which I receive by the senses do not depend on my will, I did not think that one should for that reason conclude that they proceeded from things different from myself, since possibly some faculty might be discovered in me—though hitherto unknown to me—which produced them.

But now that I begin to know myself better, and to discover more clearly the author of my being, I do not in truth think that I should rashly admit all the matters which the senses seem to teach us, but, on the other hand, I do not think that I should doubt them all universally.

And first of all, because I know that all things which I apprehend clearly and distinctly can be created by God as I apprehend them, it suffices that I am able to apprehend one thing apart from another clearly and distinctly in order to be certain that the one is different from the other, since they may be made to exist in separation at least by the omnipotence of God; and it does not signify by what power this separation is made in order to compel me to judge them to be different; and, therefore, just because I know certainly that I exist, and that meanwhile I do not remark that any other thing necessarily pertains to my nature or essence, excepting that I am a thinking thing, I rightly conclude that my essence consists solely in the fact that I am a thinking thing [or a substance whose whole essence or nature is to think]. And although possibly (or rather certainly, as I shall say in a moment) I possess a body with which I am very intimately conjoined, yet because, on the one side, I have a clear and distinct idea of myself inasmuch as I am only a thinking and unextended thing, and as, on the other, I possess a distinct idea of body, inasmuch as it is only an extended and unthinking thing, it is certain that this I [that is to say, my soul by which I am what I am], is entirely and absolutely distinct from my body, and can exist without it.

I further find in myself faculties employing modes of thinking peculiar to themselves, to wit, the faculties of imagination and feeling, without which I can easily conceive myself clearly and distinctly as a complete being; while, on the other hand, they cannot be so conceived apart from me, that is, without an intelligent substance in which they reside, for [in the notion we have of these faculties, or, to se the language of the Schools] in their formal concept, some kind of intellection is comprised, rom which I infer that they are distinct from me as its modes are from a thing. I observe also in me some other faculties such as that of change of position, the assumption of different figures and such like, which cannot be conceived, any more than can the preceding, apart from some substance to which they are attached, and consequently cannot exist without t; but it is very clear that these faculties, if it be true that they exist, must be attached to some corporeal or extended substance, and not to an intelligent substance, since in the clear and distinct conception of these there is some sort of extension found to be present, but no intellection at all. There is certainly further in me a certain passive faculty of perception, that is, of receiving and recognising the ideas of sensible things, but this would be useless to me [and I could in no way avail myself of it], if there were not either in me or in some other thing another active faculty capable of forming and producing these ideas. But this active faculty cannot exist in me [inasmuch as I am a thing that thinks] seeing that it does not presuppose thought, and also that those ideas are often produced in me without my contributing in any way to the same, and often even against my will; it is thus necessarily the case that the faculty resides in some substance different from me in which all the reality which is objectively in the ideas that are produced by this faculty is formally or eminently contained, as I remarked before. And this substance is either a body, that is, a corporeal nature in which there is contained formally [and really] all that which is objectively [and by representation] in those ideas, or it is God Himself, or some other creature more noble than body in which that same is contained eminently. But, since God is no deceiver, it is very manifest that He does not communicate to me these ideas immediately and by Himself, nor yet by the intervention of some creature in which their reality is not formally, but only eminently, contained. For since He has given me no faculty to recognise that this is the case, but, on the other hand, a very great inclination to believe [that they are sent to me or] that they are conveyed to me by corporeal objects, I do not see how He could be defended from the accusation of deceit if these ideas were produced by causes other than corporeal objects. Hence we must allow that corporeal things exist. However, they are perhaps not exactly what we perceive by the senses, since this comprehension by the senses is in many instances very obscure and confused; but we must at least admit that all things which I conceive in them clearly and distinctly, that is to say, all things which, speaking generally, are comprehended in the object of pure mathematics, are truly to be recognised as external objects.

As to other things, however, which are either particular only, as, for example, that the sun is of such and such a figure, etc., or which are less clearly and distinctly conceived, such as light, sound, pain and the like, it is certain that although they are very dubious and uncertain, yet on the sole ground that God is not a deceiver, and that consequently He has not permitted any falsity to exist in my opinion which He has not likewise given me the faculty of correcting, I may assuredly hope to conclude that I have within me the means of arriving at the truth even here. And first of all there is no doubt that in all things which nature teaches me there is some truth contained; for by nature, considered in general, I now understand no other thing than either God Himself or else the order and disposition which God has established in created things; and by my nature in particular I understand no other thing than the complexus of all the things which God has given me.

But there is nothing which this nature teaches me more expressly [nor more sensibly] than that I have a body which is adversely affected when I feel pain, which has need of food or drink when I experience the feelings of hunger and thirst, and so on; nor can I doubt there being some truth in all this.

Nature also teaches me by these sensations of pain, hunger, thirst, etc., that I am not only lodged in my body as a pilot in a vessel, but that I am very closely united to it, and so to speak so intermingled with it that I seem to compose with it one whole. For if that were not the case, when my body is hurt, I who am merely a thinking thing, should not feel pain, for I should perceive this wound by the understanding only, just as the sailor perceives by sight when something is damaged in his vessel; and when my body has need of drink or food, I should clearly understand the fact without being warned of it by confused feelings of hunger and thirst. For all these sensations of hunger, thirst, pain, etc. are in truth none other than certain confused modes of thought which are produced by the union and apparent intermingling of mind and body.

Moreover, nature teaches me that many other bodies exist around mine, of which some are to be avoided, and others sought after. And certainly from the fact that I am sensible of different sorts of colours, sounds, scents, tastes, heat, hardness, etc., I very easily conclude that there are in the bodies from which all these diverse sense-perceptions proceed certain variations which answer to them, although possibly these are not really at all similar to them. And also from the fact that amongst these different sense-perceptions some are very agreeable to me and others disagreeable, it is quite certain that my body (or rather myself in my entirety, inasmuch as I am formed of body and soul) may receive different impressions agreeable and disagreeable from the other bodies which surround it.

But there are many other things which nature seems to have taught me, but which at the same time I have never really received from her, but which have been brought about in my mind by a certain habit which I have of forming inconsiderate judgments on things; and thus it may easily happen that these judgments contain some error. Take, for example, the opinion which I hold that all space in which there is nothing that affects [or makes an impression on] my senses is void; that in a body which is warm there is something entirely similar to the idea of heat which is in me; that in a white or green body there is the same whiteness or greenness that I perceive; that in a bitter or sweet body there is the same taste, and so on in other instances; that the stars, the towers, and all other distant bodies are of the same figure and size as they appear from far off to our eyes, etc. But in order that in this there should be nothing which I do not conceive distinctly, I should define exactly what I really understand when I say that I am taught somewhat by nature. For here I take nature in a more limited signification than when I term it the sum of all the things given me by God, since in this sum many things are comprehended which only pertain to mind (and to these I do not refer in speaking of nature) such as the notion which I have of the fact that what has once been done cannot ever be undone and an infinitude of such things which I know by the light of nature [without the help of the body]; and seeing that it comprehends many other matters besides which only pertain to body, and are no longer here contained under the name of nature, such as the quality of weight which it possesses and the like, with

which I also do not deal; for in talking of nature I only treat of those things given by God to me as a being composed of mind and body. But the nature here described truly teaches me to flee from things which cause the sensation of pain, and seek after the things which communicate to me the sentiment of pleasure, and so forth; but I do not see that beyond this it teaches me that from those diverse sense-perceptions we should ever form any conclusion regarding things outside of us, without having [carefully and maturely] mentally examined them beforehand. For it seems to me that it is mind alone, and not mind and body in conjunction, that is requisite to a knowledge of the truth in regard to such things. Thus, although a star makes no larger an impression on my eye than the flame of a little candle there is yet in me no real or positive propensity impelling me to believe that it is not greater than that flame; but I have judged it to be so from my earliest years, without any rational foundation. And although in approaching fire I feel heat, and in approaching it a little too near I even feel pain, there is at the same time no reason in this which could persuade me that there is in the fire something resembling this heat any more than there is in it something resembling the pain; all that I have any reason to believe from this is, that there is something in it, whatever it may be, which excites in me these sensations of heat or of pain. So also, although there are spaces in which I find nothing which excites my senses, I must not from that conclude that these spaces contain no body; for I see in this, as in other similar things, that I have been in the habit of perverting the order of nature, because these perceptions of sense having been placed within me by nature merely for the purpose of signifying to my mind what things are beneficial or hurtful to the composite whole of which it forms a part, and being up to that point sufficiently clear and distinct, I yet avail myself of them as though they were absolute rules by which I might immediately determine the essence of the bodies which are outside me, as to which, in fact, they can teach me nothing but what is most obscure and confused.

But I have already sufficiently considered how, notwithstanding the supreme goodness of God, falsity enters into the judgments I make. Only here a new difficulty is presented—one respecting those things the pursuit or avoidance of which is taught me by nature, and also respecting the internal sensations which I possess, and in which I seem to have sometimes detected error [and thus to be directly deceived by my own nature]. To take an example, the agreeable taste of some food in which poison has been intermingled may induce me to partake of the poison, and thus deceive me. It is true, at the same time, that in this case nature may be excused, for it only induces me to desire food in which I find a pleasant taste, and not to desire the poison which is unknown to it; and thus I can infer nothing from this fact, except that my nature is not omniscient, at which there is certainly no reason to be astonished, since man, being finite in nature, can only have knowledge the perfectness of which is limited.

But we not unfrequently deceive ourselves even in those things to which we are directly impelled by nature, as perhaps with those who when they are sick desire to drink or eat things hurtful to them. It will perhaps be said here that the cause of their deceptiveness is that their nature is corrupt, but that does not remove the difficulty, because a sick man is none the less truly God's creature than he who is in health; and it is therefore as repugnant to God's goodness for the one to have a deceitful nature as it is for the other. And as a clock composed of wheels and counter-weights no less exactly observes the laws of nature when it is badly made, and does not show the time properly, than when it entirely satisfies the wishes of its maker, and as, if I consider the body of a man as being a sort of machine so built up and composed of nerves, muscles, veins, blood and skin, that though there were no mind in it at all, it would not cease to have the same motions as at present, exception being made of those movements which are due to the direction of the will, and in consequence depend upon the mind [as opposed to those which operate by the disposition of its organs], I easily recognise that it would be as natural to this body, supposing it to be, for example, dropsical, to suffer the parchedness of the throat which usually signifies to the mind the feeling of thirst, and to be disposed by this parched feeling to move the nerves and other parts in the way requisite for drinking, and thus to augment its malady and do harm to itself, as it is natural to it, when it has no indisposition, to be impelled to drink for its good by a similar cause. And although, considering the use to which the clock has been destined by its maker, I may say that it deflects from the order of its nature when it does not indicate the hours correctly; and as, in the same way, considering the machine of the human body as having been formed by God in order to have in itself all the movements usually manifested there, I have reason for thinking that it does not follow the order of nature when, if the throat is dry, drinking does harm to the conservation of health, nevertheless I recognise at the same time that this last mode of explaining nature is very different from the other. For this is but a purely verbal characterisation depending entirely on my thought, which compares a sick man and a badly constructed clock with the idea which I have of a healthy man and a well made clock, and it is hence extrinsic to the things to which it is applied; but according to the other interpretation of the term nature I understand something which is truly found in things and which is therefore not without some truth.

But certainly although in regard to the dropsical body it is only so to speak to apply an extrinsic term when we say that its nature is corrupted, inasmuch as apart from the need to drink, the throat is parched; yet in regard to the composite whole, that is to say, to the mind or soul united to this body, it is not a purely verbal predicate, but a real error of nature, for it to have thirst when drinking would be hurtful to it. And thus it still remains to inquire how the goodness of God does not prevent the nature of man so regarded from being fallacious.

In order to begin this examination, then, I here say, in the first place, that there is a great difference between mind and body, inasmuch as body is by nature always divisible, and the mind is entirely indivisible. For, as a matter of fact, when I consider the mind, that is to say, myself inasmuch as I am only a thinking thing, I cannot distinguish in myself any parts, but apprehend myself to be clearly one and entire; and although the whole mind seems to be united to the whole body, yet if a foot, or an arm, or some other part, is separated from my body, I am aware that nothing has been taken away from my mind. And the faculties of willing, feeling, conceiving, etc. cannot be properly said to be its parts, for it is one and the same mind which employs itself in willing and in feeling and understanding. But it is quite otherwise with corporeal or extended objects, for there is not one of these imaginable by me which my mind cannot easily divide into parts, and which consequently I do not recognise as being divisible; this would be sufficient to teach me that the mind or soul of man is entirely different from the body, if I had not already learned it from other sources.

I further notice that the mind does not receive the impressions from all parts of the body immediately, but only from the brain, or perhaps even from one of its smallest parts, to wit, from that in which the common sense is said to reside, which, whenever it is disposed in the same particular way, conveys the same thing to the mind, although meanwhile the other portions of the body may be differently disposed, as is testified by innumerable experiments which it is unnecessary here to recount.

I notice, also, that the nature of body is such that none of its parts can be moved by another part a little way off which cannot also be moved in the same way by each one of the parts which are between the two, although this more remote part does not act at all. As, for example, in the cord ABCD [which is in tension] if we pull the last part D, the first part A will not be moved in any way differently from what would be the case if one of the intervening parts B or C were pulled, and the last part D were to remain unmoved. And in the same way, when I feel pain in my foot, my knowledge of physics teaches me that this sensation is communicated by means of nerves dispersed through the foot, which, being extended like cords from there to the brain, when they are contracted in the foot, at the same time contract the inmost portions of the brain which is their extremity and place of origin, and then excite a certain movement which nature has established in order to cause the mind to be affected by a sensation of pain represented as existing in the foot. But because these nerves must pass through the tibia, the thigh, the loins, the back and the neck, in order to reach from the leg to the brain, it may happen that although their extremities which are in the foot are not affected, but only certain ones of their intervening parts [which pass by the loins or the neck], this action will excite the same movement in the brain that might have been excited there by a hurt received in the foot, in consequence of which the mind will necessarily feel in the foot the same pain as if it had received a hurt. And the same holds good of all the other perceptions of our senses.

I notice finally that since each of the movements which are in the portion of the brain by which the mind is immediately affected brings about one particular sensation only, we cannot under the circumstances imagine anything more likely than that this movement, amongst all the sensations which it is capable of impressing on it, causes mind to be affected by that one which is best fitted and most generally useful for the conservation of the human body when it is in health. But experience makes us aware that all the feelings with which nature inspires us are such as I have just spoken of; and there is therefore nothing in them which does not give testimony to the power and goodness of the God [who has produced them]. Thus, for example, when the nerves which are in the feet are violently or more than usually moved, their movement, passing through the medulla of the spine to the inmost parts of the brain, gives a sign to the mind which makes it feel somewhat, to wit, pain, as though in the foot, by which the mind is excited to do its utmost to remove the cause of the evil as dangerous and hurtful to the foot. It is true that God could have constituted the nature of man in such a way that this same movement in the brain would have conveyed something quite different to the mind; for example, it might have produced consciousness of itself either in so far as it is in the brain, or as it is in the foot, or as it is in some other place between the foot and the brain, or it might finally have produced consciousness of anything else whatsoever; but none of all this would have contributed so well to the conservation of the body. Similarly, when we desire to drink, a certain dryness of the throat is produced which moves its nerves, and by their means the internal portions of the brain; and this movement causes in the mind the sensation of thirst, because in this case there is nothing more useful to us than to become aware that we have need to drink for the conservation of our health; and the same holds good in other instances.

From this it is quite clear that, notwithstanding the supreme goodness of God, the nature of man, inasmuch as it is composed of mind and body, cannot be otherwise than sometimes a source of deception. For if there is any cause which excites, not in the foot but in some part of the nerves which are extended between the foot and the brain, or even in the brain itself, the same movement which usually is produced when the foot is detrimentally affected, pain will be experienced as though it were in the foot, and the sense will thus naturally be deceived; for since the same movement in the brain is capable of causing but one sensation in the mind, and this sensation is much more frequently excited by a cause which hurts the foot than by another existing in some other quarter, it is reasonable that it should convey to the mind pain in the foot rather than in any other part of the body. And although the parchedness of the throat does not always proceed, as it usually does, from the fact that drinking is necessary for the health of the body, but sometimes comes from quite a different cause, as is the case with dropsical patients, it is yet much better that it should mislead on this occasion than if, on the other hand, it were always to deceive us when the body is in good health; and so on in similar cases.

And certainly this consideration is of great service to me, not only in enabling me to recognise all the errors to which my nature is subject, but also in enabling me to avoid them or to correct them more easily. For knowing that all my senses more frequently indicate to me truth than falsehood respecting the things which concern that which is beneficial to the body, and being able almost always to avail myself of many of them in order to examine one particular thing, and, besides that, being able to make use of my memory in order to connect the present with the past, and of my understanding which already has discovered all the causes of my errors, I ought no longer to fear that falsity may be found in matters every day presented to me by my senses. And I ought to set aside all the doubts of these past days as hyperbolical and ridiculous, particularly that very common uncertainty respecting sleep, which I could not distinguish from the waking state; for at present I find a very notable difference between the two, inasmuch as our memory can never connect our dreams one with the other, or with the whole course of our lives, as it unites events which happen to us while we are awake. And, as a matter of fact, if someone, while I was awake, quite suddenly appeared to me and disappeared as fast as do the images which I see in sleep, so that I could not know from whence the form came nor whither it went, it would not be without reason that I should deem it a spectre or a phantom formed by my brain [and similar to those which I form in sleep], rather than a real man. But when I perceive things as to which I know distinctly both the place from which they proceed, and that in which they are, and the time at which they appeared to me; and when, without any interruption, I can connect the perceptions which I have of them with the whole course of my life, I am perfectly assured that these perceptions occur while I am waking and not during sleep. And I ought in no wise to doubt the truth of such matters, if, after having called up all my senses, my memory, and my understanding, to examine them, nothing is brought to evidence by any one of them which is repugnant to what is set forth by the others. For because God is in no wise a deceiver, it follows that I am not deceived in this. But because the exigencies of action often oblige us to make up our minds before having leisure to examine matters carefully, we must confess that the life of man is very frequently subject to error in respect to individual objects, and we must in the end acknowledge the infirmity of our nature.

OBJECTIONS
URGED BY CERTAIN MEN OF LEARNING AGAINST THE PRECEDING MEDITATIONS; WITH THE AUTHOR'S REPLIES

THE FIRST SET OF OBJECTIONS[1]

GENTLEMEN,

As soon as I recognized that you were so anxious that I should make a thorough examination of the writings of M. Descartes, it seemed impossible for me, in duty, to disoblige in this matter friends so dear to me. My reason in complying was both that you might witness the extent of my esteem for you, and also that I might reveal my lack of power and intellectual endowment; hence, I hoped, you might in future allow me the more indulgence, if I require it, or, if I came short, be less exacting.

In my estimation M. Descartes is in truth a man who combines the highest intellectual endowments with an extreme modesty—one of whom even Momus, had he come to life, would approve. "I think," he says, "hence I exist; nay, I am that very thinking, or the mind." True. "However, in thinking I have within me ideas of things, and firstly an idea of a being of extreme perfection and infinite." I grant this. "Moreover, I, not equalling the objective reality of this idea, am not its cause; hence it has some cause more perfect than I, and this immediately shows that there is something else besides me in existence, something more perfect than I am. This is a being who is an entity not in any indeterminate sense, but one which absolutely and without limitations embraces its whole reality wholly in itself, and is, as it were, an anticipatory cause, as Dionysius[2] says (de divin. nom. cap. 8)."

But here I am forced to stop a little, to avoid excessive exhaustion; for already my mind fluctuates like the Euripus with its changing tides.

Now I consent, now I deny; I approve and once more disapprove. To disagree with the champion of this theory I do not care, agree with him I cannot. But, pray, what sort of cause must an idea have? or, tell me, what is an idea? It is the thing thought of itself in so far as that is "objectively" in the understanding. But explain what "to be objectively in the understanding" is. As I was taught, it is the determination of an act of mind by a modification due to an object; but this is a merely external attribute of the thing and nothing belonging to its reality. For, as "being seen" is merely the direction of the act of vision towards the percipient so "being thought" or "being objectively in the understanding" is merely a standing still of our thought within itself and ending there, which can occur whether the thing is active or passive, indeed though it is even non-existent. Hence, why should I ask for a cause of that which is nothing actual, which is a mere name, a nonentity?

Nevertheless, says our great philosopher,— "because a certain idea has such and such an objective reality rather than another, it must owe this to some cause."[3] Nay it needs no cause, for its "objective reality" is a mere name and nothing actual. Further, a cause exerts some real and actual influence; but the objective existence which is nothing actual can be the recipient of nothing, and hence cannot be passively affected by the real activity of a cause, so far is it from requiring a cause. My conclusion is that, though I have ideas, there is no cause for their existence, so far from their being a cause for them greater than me and infinite.

"But, if you do not assign some cause for ideas, you must, at least, give some reason why this particular idea contains this particular objective reality rather than that." Quite right; it is

[1]The author of these objections of the first group is Caterus, a priest of Alkmaar, who sent them to Bannius and Bloemaert, two friends of Descartes.

[2]The reference is to the writings attributed in mediaeval times to Dionysius—Dionysius the Areopagite.

[3]Cf. Med. III, p. 84.

not my way to be niggardly with my friends but to be open-handed. I affirm universally of all ideas what M. Descartes says at other times of the triangle. He says:—"Though possibly no such figure exists anywhere outside my thought or has at any time existed, yet is its nature something unconditionally determinate, an essence, or form, that is immutable and eternal."[1] It is hence an eternal verity which requires no cause. A boat is a boat, as Davus is Davus and not Œdipus. If, however, you drive me to assign a reason, I shall say it is the imperfection of the mind, which is not infinite; for, not clasping in a single embrace the whole which exists simultaneously and all together, it parcels out and divides the omni-present good. Thus, because it cannot bring forth the whole, it conceives it in a series of acts, or, in technical language "inadequately."

M. Descartes further asserts, "Yet, however imperfect be the manner of the existence in which a thing is, by means of an idea, objectively in the understanding, nevertheless it is not merely nothing, nor consequently, can it proceed from nothing."

But this is equivocation; for, if "nothing" is the same as "an entity not actually existing," it is entirely non-existent, because it does not actually exist, and hence it proceeds from nothing, i.e. from no cause. But if by "nothing" something imaginary is meant, something vulgarly styled an "ens rationis," it is not "nothing" but something real which is distinctly conceived. But since it is merely conceived and is nothing actual, though it may be conceived, yet it cannot be caused [or banished from the mind].

But he proceeds, "Further, I should like to ask, whether "I" who have this idea could exist, if no such being existed,"[2] i.e. if none existed, "from which the idea of a being more perfect than I proceeds," as he says immediately before. "For," says he, "from what should I proceed? From myself, from my parents, or from some other beings? ... But, if I were self-originated, neither should I doubt, nor should I wish for anything, nor should I suffer lack of anything whatsoever, for I should have given myself all the perfections of which I have any idea, and should thus myself be God."[3] "But, if I am derived from something else, the end of the series of beings from which I come will ultimately be one which is self-originated, and hence what would have held good for myself (if self-

originated) will be true of this."[4] This is an argument that pursues the same path as that taken by St. Thomas,[5] and which he calls the proof from "the causality of an efficient cause." It is derived from Aristotle. But Aristotle and St. Thomas are not concerned with the causes of ideas. Perhaps they had no need to be, for might not the argument take a more direct and less devious course?—I think, hence I exist; nay I am that very thinking mind, that thinking. But that mind, that thought, springs either from itself or from something else. On the latter alternative, from what does that something else come? If it is self-derived, it must be God? for that which is self-originated will have no trouble in conferring all things on itself.

An entreaty I would press upon our author, is that he would not hide his meaning from this Reader, one eager to comprehend him, albeit perhaps lacking in acuteness. "Self-originated" has two senses, firstly a positive meaning equivalent to—derived from its own self as from a cause. Hence anything which was self-originated and conferred its own existence on itself, would, if giving itself what it desired by an act of choice involving premeditation, certainly give itself everything and would thus be God. Secondly, "self-originated" has a negative usage which equates it with "by itself" or "not derived from anything else"; so far as my memory serves me, it is universally employed in this sense.

But now, if anything is self-derived, i.e. not due to something else, how can I prove that it embraces all things and is infinite? I shall pay no heed to the reply that, if it is self-derived, it will have given itself everything, for it does not depend on itself as on a cause, nor did it anticipate its existence and so at a prior time choose what it should afterwards be. It is true I have heard this doctrine of Suarez "All limitations proceed from a cause, and the reason why anything is finite and limited is, either that its cause could not, or that it would not give it more being and perfection. Hence, if anything is self-derived and does not issue from a cause, it is necessarily unlimited and infinite."

But I do not wholly agree. For (be the thing ever so much self-originated, i.e. not due to something else), if the limitation be due to the thing's internal constitutional principles, i.e. to its very form and essence, which, however, you have not

[1] Cf. Med. v, p. 93.
[2] Cf. Med. iii, p. 87.
[3] Cf. Med. iii, p. 87.

[4] Cf. Med. iii, p. 87.
[5] Thomas Aquinas, *Summa Theologica*, Part I, Q 2, A 3 ("Whether God exists?") *Secunda via est ex ratione causae efficientis.* "The second way," etc.

yet proved to be infinite, what is your answer? It is certain that the hot, if you will concede that there is such a thing, is hot and not cold in virtue of its own internal constitutional principles, though you conceive that hot thing to derive its existence from nothing else. I doubt not that M. Descartes has no lack of reasons for substantiating that which others perhaps have not demonstrated with sufficient clearness.

At last I find a point of agreement with my adversary. He has erected as a general rule, "Whatever I know clearly and distinctly is something really true."[1] Nay "whatever I think is true; for almost from boyhood I have banished chimaeras and 'entities of reason' from my mind. No faculty can be deflected from its proper object: the will if it moves at all tends towards good: indeed not even the senses themselves err; sight sees what it sees, the ears hear what they hear: though what you see be tinsel there is nothing wrong with the vision; the error comes in when your judgment decides that it is gold you are beholding." Hence M. Descartes most properly assigns all error to the account of the will and judgment.

But now, from this cause infer what you wanted. "I apprehend clearly and distinctly an infinite being; hence it is something true and real." But will not someone ask, "Do you apprehend clearly and distinctly an infinite being?" But what then is the meaning of that well-worn maxim known to all?—The infinite quâ infinite is unknown. For if, when I think of a chiliagon and have a confused representation of some figure, I do not have a distinct image of the chiliagon or know it, because I do not have its thousand sides evident and distinct before my mind, shall I not be asked,—how can the infinite be thought of distinctly and not confusedly, if the infinite perfections of which it is composed cannot be perceived clearly, and, as it were, with true distinctness of vision?

Perhaps this is what St Thomas meant when he denied that the proposition "God is" is known "per se."[2] In objection to this he considers an argument drawn from Damascenus—"God exists: the knowledge of this truth nature has implanted in all; hence the truth that God exists is known "per se." His reply is the knowledge of the existence of God is, in a general sense, and, as he says, in a confused manner, to wit, in so far as He is man's highest existence, implanted by nature in all. But this is not an unqualified apprehension of the existence of

God, just as to know that someone is coming is not the same as to know Peter, though Pete[r] be the man who is coming,[3] etc. This is tantamount to saying that God is known in so far a[s] He falls under some general term or as fina[l] cause, or even as first and most perfect of beings or finally as something which contains all thing[s] in a confused and generic manner, but not in re[?]spect of the precise notion which expresses Hi[s] nature. I believe that M. Descartes will have n[o] difficulty in replying to anyone who raises [a] question here. Yet I am sure that owing to wha[t] I here bring forward, merely for discussion['s] sake, he will call to mind the doctrine of Boethius[.] That there are certain common mental conceptions which are only known "per se" by th[e] wise.[4] Hence no one should marvel if those wh[o] desire to know more (than others) ask man[y] questions, and for a long time linger over thos[e] topics which they know to have been laid down a[s] the first principles of the whole subject, and i[n] spite of this do not master it without strenuou[s] intellectual effort.

Let us then concede that someone has a clea[r] and distinct idea of a highest and most perfec[t] being; what further conclusion do you draw[?] That this infinite being exists, and that so cer[-] tainly that the existence of God should hav[e] certitude, at least for my mind, as great as tha[t] which mathematical truths have hitherto en[-] joyed.[5] Hence there is no less contradiction i[n] thinking of a God (that is of a being of th[e] highest perfection) who lacks existence (a par[-] ticular perfection) than in thinking of a hi[ll] which is not relative to a valley.[6] The whol[e] dispute hinges on this; he who gives way her[e] must admit defeat. Since my opponent is th[e] stronger combatant I should like for a little t[o] avoid engaging him at close quarters in orde[r] that, fated as I am to lose, I may yet postpon[e] what I cannot avoid.

Firstly then, though reason only and not au[-] thority is the arbiter in our discussion, yet, lest [I] be judged impertinent in gainsaying the conten[-] tions of such an illustrious philosopher, let m[e] quote you what St Thomas says; it is an objectio[n] he urges against his own doctrine:—As soon a[s] the intellect grasps the signification of th[e] name God, it knows that God exists; for the meaning of His name is an object nothin[g] greater than which can be conceived. Now tha[t] which exists in fact as well as in the mind i[s]

[1]Cf. Med. III, p. 86.
[2]Summa Theologica, Part I, Q 2, A 1.

[3]Summa Theologica, loc. cit.
[4]Quotation in Thomas Aquinas, loc. cit.
[5]Med. v, pp. 93–94.
[6]Cf. p. 94.

reater than what exists in the mind alone. Hence, since the name "God" being understood, God consequently exists in the mind, it follows that He really exists. *This argument formally expressed becomes—God is a being, a greater than which cannot be conceived; but that, a greater than which cannot be conceived, includes its existence; hence God by His very name or notion includes His existence, and as a direct consequence can neither be conceived as being, nor can be, devoid of existence. But now, kindly tell me is not this M. Descartes' own proof? St. Thomas defines God thus:—A being than which nothing greater can be conceived. M. Descartes calls Him a being of extreme perfection; certainly nothing greater than this can be conceived. St. Thomas goes on to argue—That than which nothing greater can be conceived includes its existence; otherwise a greater than it could be conceived, namely that which is conceived to contain its existence. Now does not M. Descartes bring up the same proposition as minor premise? "God is the most perfect being, the most perfect being comprises within itself its existence, for otherwise it would not have the highest perfection." St. Thomas's conclusion is:—Therefore since God, His name being understood, exists in the understanding, He exists in reality. That is to say, owing to the very fact that in the very concept of the essence of an entity, nothing greater than which can be conceived, existence is involved, it follows that that very entity exists. M. Descartes draws the same inference:—Yet, says he, owing to the fact that we cannot think of God as not existing, it follows that His existence is inseparable from Him, and hence that He in truth exists.*[1] *But now let St. Thomas reply both to himself and to M. Descartes.* Granted that everyone and anyone knows that by the name God is understood that which has been asserted, to wit, a being than which nothing greater can be thought, yet it does not follow that he understands that the thing signified by the name exists in reality, but only that it exists in the apprehension of the understanding. Nor can it be proved that it really exists, unless it be conceded that something really exists than which nothing greater can be thought— a proposition not granted by those who deny the existence of God. *This furnishes me with my reply, which will be brief—Though it be conceded that an entity of the highest perfection implies its existence by its very name, yet it does not follow that that very existence is anything actual in the real world, but merely that the concept of*

[1]Cf. Med. v, p. 94.

existence is inseparably united with the concept of highest being. Hence you cannot infer that the existence of God is anything actual, unless you assume that that highest being actually exists; for then it will actually contain all its perfections, together with this perfection of real existence.

Pardon me, gentlemen, if now I plead fatigue; but here is something in a lighter vein. This complex existent Lion *includes both lion and the mode existence; and includes them essentially, for if you take away either it will not be the same complex. But now, has not God from all eternity had clear and distinct knowledge of this composite object? Does not also the idea of this composite, in so far as it is composite, involve both its elements essentially? That is to say, does not its existence flow from the essence of this composite, existent Lion? Yet, I affirm, the distinct cognition of it which God possesses, that which he has from all eternity does not constrain either part of the complex to exist, unless you assume that the complex does exist; for then, indeed, it will imply all its essential perfections and hence also that of actual existence. Therefore, also, even though you have a distinct knowledge of a highest being, and granted that a being of supreme perfection includes existence in the concept of its essence, yet it does not follow that its existence is anything actual, unless on the hypothesis that that highest being does exist; for then indeed along with its other perfections it will in actuality include this, its existence, also. Hence the proof of the existence of this highest being must be drawn from some other source.*

I shall add but a few words about the essence of the soul and the distinction between soul and body; for I confess that the speculations of this wonderful genius have so exhausted me that I can add but little more. It appears that the distinction between soul and body, if real, is proved by the fact that they can be conceived as distinct and as isolated from each other. Here I leave my opponent to contend with (Duns) Scotus, who says that—In so far as one thing can be conceived as distinct and separate from another, the adequate distinction to draw between them is what he calls a formal and objective one, which is intermediate between a real distinction and a distinction of reason. It is thus that he distinguishes between the Divine justice and the Divine pity. They have, *he says,* concepts formally diverse prior to any operation of the understanding, so that, even then, the one is not the other: yet it does not follow that, because God's justice can be conceived apart from his pity, they can also exist apart.

But I see that I have far exceeded the bounds of

a letter. These are the criticisms for which, to my mind, the subject calls. I leave it to you, gentlemen, to pick out any that may seem to you to have merit. If you take my part, it will be easy to prevail upon M. Descartes kindly not to bear me ill

will in future for having in a few points contra dicted him. If you uphold him, I yield, and ow myself vanquished, the more eagerly from anxiet not to be overcome a second time. I send yo greetings.

A REPLY BY THE AUTHOR
TO THE FIRST SET OF OBJECTIONS

GENTLEMEN,

You have certainly stirred up a stout antagonist against me, one whose ability and learning might have caused me serious perplexity, unless like a pious and Christian theologian he had preferred to befriend the cause of God and of its unworthy champion, rather than to make a serious attack on it. But, though this insincerity redounds only to his credit, to act in collusion with it would tend to draw down censure on me; and thus I prefer to unmask his device for rendering me assistance, rather than to answer him as an opponent.

To begin with, he has put in brief compass my chief argument for proving the existence of God, so that it should the more readily abide in the reader's memory; having briefly indicated his assent to what he thinks clearly enough demonstrated, and having thus strengthened that with his authority, he finally comes to the crux of the difficulty, and raises a question only as to what is to be here understood by the term *idea*, and what sort of cause this aforesaid idea demands.

Now I have written somewhere *an idea is the thing thought of itself, in so far as it is objectively in the understanding.* But these words he evidently prefers to understand in a sense quite different from that in which I use them, meaning to furnish me with an opportunity of explaining them more clearly. *"Objective existence in the mind is,"* he says, *"the determination of the act of mind by a modification due to an object, which is merely an extrinsic appellation and nothing belonging to the object,"* etc.[1] Now, here it must be noticed firstly that he refers to the thing itself, which is as it were placed outside the understanding and respecting which it is certainly an extrinsic attribute to be objectively in the understanding, and secondly, that what I speak of is the idea, which at no time exists outside the mind, and in the case of

[1]Cf. Obj. I, p. 104.

which *"objective existence"* is indistinguishabl from being in the understanding in that way i which objects are wont to be there. Thus, fo example, if someone asks what feature in th sun's existence it is to exist in my mind, it wi be quite right to reply that this is a merel extrinsic attribute which affects it, and to wit one which determines an operation of the min in the mode due to the object. But if the ques tion be, what the idea of the sun is, and the re ply is given, that it is the object thought of in so far as that exists objectively in the under standing, he will not understand that it is th sun itself, in so far as that extrinsic attribut is in it; neither will *objective understandin* here signify that the mind's operation is her determined in the mode due to an object but that it is in the mind in the way i which objects are wont to exist there. Henc the idea of the sun will be the sun itself existin in the mind, not indeed formally, as it exists i the sky, but objectively, i.e. in the way i which objects are wont to exist in the mind and this mode of being is truly much less per fect than that in which things exist outside th mind, but it is not on that account mere noth ing, as I have already said.

When this learned theologian talks of *equivo cation,* I think that by this he means to war me, and prevent me from forgetting that whicl I have this moment mentioned. For, firstly, h says that a thing existing in the mind througl an idea, is not an *actual entity,* i.e. is nothing situated outside the intellect; and this is true Secondly he says that it is *not anything ficti tious or an entity of reason, but something rea which is distinctly conceived;* by which words h admits all I have assumed. Yet he adds, *be cause it is merely conceived and is nothing actua* (i.e. because it is merely an idea, and nothing situated outside the mind), *it may be indeec conceived, but by no means caused;*[2] i.e. it doe

[2]Cf. p. 105.

not require a cause in order to exist outside the mind. Agreed; but it does require a cause to make it be conceived, and it is of this cause alone that the question here is raised. Thus, if anyone has in his mind the idea of any machine showing high skill in its construction, it is certainly quite reasonable to ask what is the cause of that idea; and it is not sufficient to answer that the idea is nothing outside the mind, and hence can have no cause, but can merely be conceived; for here the whole question is— what is that which causes it to be conceived? Nor will it suffice to say that the mind itself is its cause, being the cause of its own acts; for this is not disputed, the question being the cause of the objective artifice which is in the idea. For there must be some definite cause of the fact that this idea of a machine displays this objective artifice rather than another, and its objective artifice bears to this cause the same relation that the objective reality of the idea of God bears to its cause. Various causes of such a contrivance might be assigned. It will be either a similar real machine already seen, the features of which are reproduced in the idea, or it will be great knowledge of mechanical science in the mind of him who thinks of it, or perchance a great intellectual acuteness, which has enabled the man to invent this device without previous scientific knowledge. We must note that every contrivance which in the idea has only objective existence, must necessarily exist in its cause, whatever that cause be, either formally or eminently. And we must apply the same rule to the objective reality which is in the idea of God. But in what will this exist unless in a God who really exists? My clear-sighted opponent, however, sees all this, and hence admits that we may ask *why this particular idea contains this particular objective reality rather than that*, and to this question he replies firstly: *that the same as what I have written about the idea of the triangle holds good of all ideas, viz. that though perchance the triangle nowhere exists, yet there does exist some determinate nature, or essence, or immutable and eternal form which belongs to it.*[1] Further he says *that this demands no cause.* But he sees well enough that this reply is nevertheless not satisfactory; for, although the nature of the triangle be immutable and eternal, that does not disallow the question why the idea exists in us. Hence he adds—*"If, however, you drive me to assign a reason, I shall say it is the imperfection of the mind,"* etc. But this reply seems to show merely that those who have desired to take exception to my views have no rejoinder to make that at all approaches the truth. For, sooth to say, there is no more probability that the imperfection of the human intellect is the cause of our possessing the idea of God, than that ignorance of mechanical science should be the cause of our imagining some machine showing highly intricate contrivance, rather than another less perfect one. On the contrary, clearly, if one possesses the idea of a machine which involves every contrivance that ingenuity can devise, it will be absolutely right to infer that it is the product of some cause, in which that extreme pitch of mechanical ingenuity was actually embodied, although in the idea it existed only objectively. By the same reasoning, when we have in us the idea of God, in which all thinkable perfection is contained, the evident conclusion is, that that idea depends upon some cause in which all that perfection also exists, to wit in the God who really exists. It is true that both cases would seem to be on the same footing, and that, just as all are not expert mechanicians, and hence cannot form the notion of a highly intricate machine, so all men might not have the same power of conceiving the idea of God; but since that idea is implanted in the same manner in the minds of all, and we perceive no source other than ourselves from which it comes, we suppose that it pertains to the nature of our mind. This indeed is not wrong, but we omit something else which principally merits its consideration and on which the whole force and evidence of this argument depends, namely, that this power of having in one's self the idea of God could not belong to our intellect, if this intellect were merely a finite entity, as in fact it is, and did it not have God as the cause of its existence. Hence I have undertaken the further enquiry—*whether I could exist if God did not exist*[2]—not for the purpose of adducing a proof distinct from the preceding one, but rather in order to give a more thoroughgoing explanation of it.

At this point my opponent, through excess of courtesy, has put me in an awkward position, for he compares my argument with another drawn from St. Thomas and from Aristotle, and thus he seems to compel me to explain why, having started with them on the same road, I have not kept to it at all points. But I beg him to excuse me from speaking of others, and to allow me to give an account only of what I have myself written.

[1] Cf. pp. 104–105.

[2] Cf. Med. III, p. 87.

Firstly then, I have not drawn my arguments from observing an order or succession of efficient causes in the realm of sensible things, partly because I deemed the existence of God to be much more evident than that of any sensible things, partly also because this succession of causes seemed to conduct merely to an acknowledgement of the imperfection of my intellect, because I could not understand how an infinity of such causes could have succeeded one another from all eternity in such a way that none of them has been absolutely first. For certainly, because I could not understand that, it does not follow that there *must* be a first cause, just as it does not follow that, because I cannot understand an infinity of divisions in a finite quantity, an ultimate atom can be arrived at, beyond which no further division is possible. The only consequence is that my intellect, which is finite, cannot comprehend the infinite. Therefore I prefer to use as the foundation of my proof my own existence, which is not dependent on any series of causes, and is so plain to my intelligence that nothing can be plainer; and about myself I do not so much ask, what was the original cause that produced me, as what it is that at present preserves me, the object of this being to disentangle myself from all question of the succession of causes.

Further, I have not asked what is the cause of my existence in so far as I consist of mind and body, but have limited myself definitely to my position in so far as I am merely a thing that thinks. And I think that this furthers my project in no small degree; for thus I have been able far better to free myself from prejudiced conclusions, to follow the dictates of the light of nature, to set questions to myself, and to affirm with certainty that there is nothing in me of which I am not in some way conscious. This clearly is quite different from judging that, because I was begotten by my father, he was the progeny of my grandfather, and, because in seeking out the parents of my parents I could not carry the process to infinity, deciding, in order to bring my quest to a conclusion, that hence there was some first cause of the series.

Moreover, I have not only asked what is the cause of my being in so far as I am a thinking thing, but chiefly in so far as I perceive that there exists in me, among other thoughts, the idea of a being of the highest perfection. For it is on this that the whole force of my demonstration depends; firstly because in that idea is contained the notion of what God is, at least i[n] so far as I can comprehend Him, and accordin[g] to the laws of true Logic, the question *"does [a] thing exist?"* must never be asked unless we a[l]ready understand *what the thing is;* secondly because it is this same idea that gives me th[e] opportunity of enquiring whether I procee[d] from myself or from something else, and [in] recognising my defects; finally it is that whic[h] shows me not only that there is some cause [of] my existence, but that further in this cause a[ll] perfections are contained, and that hence it i[s] God.

Finally, I have not said that it is impossibl[e] for anything to be its own efficient cause; fo[r] although that statement is manifestly tru[e] when the meaning of efficient cause is restrict[ed] to those causes that are prior in time t[o] their effects or different from them, yet it doe[s] not seem necessary to confine the term to thi[s] meaning in the present investigation. In th[e] first place the question would in such a case b[e] unmeaning, for who does not know that th[e] same thing can neither be prior to nor differen[t] from itself? Secondly, the light of nature doe[s] not require that the notion of an efficient caus[e] should compel it to be prior to its effect; on th[e] contrary, a thing does not properly conform t[o] the notion of cause except during the time tha[t] it produces its effect, and hence is not prior t[o] it. Moreover, the light of nature certainly tell[s] us that nothing exists about which the ques[-] tion, why it exists, cannot be asked, whethe[r] we enquire for its efficient cause, or, if it doe[s] not possess one, demand why it does not hav[e] one. Hence, if I did not believe that anythin[g] could in some way be related to itself exactl[y] as an efficient cause is related to its effect, s[o] far should I be from concluding that any firs[t] cause existed, that, on the contrary, I shoul[d] once more ask for the cause of that which ha[d] been called first, and so should never arrive a[t] the first of all. But I frankly allow that some[-] thing may exist in which there is such a grea[t] and inexhaustible power that it has needed n[o] assistance in order to exist, and requires non[e] for its preservation, and hence is in a certai[n] way the cause of its own existence; such [a] cause I understand God to be. For, even thoug[h] I had existed from all eternity and hence noth[-] ing had preceded my existence, none the les[s] seeing that I deem the various parts of time t[o] be separable from each other, and hence tha[t] it does not follow that, because I now exist, [I] shall in future do so, unless some cause were, s[o] to speak, to re-create me at each single moment[.]

should not hesitate to call that cause which reserves me an efficient cause. Thus, even though God has never been non-existent, yet because He is the very Being who actually reserves Himself in existence, it seems possible to call Him without undue impropriety the *cause of His own existence*. But it must be noted that here I do not mean a preservation which is effected by any positive operation of causal efficiency but one due merely to this fact, that the essential nature of God is such that He cannot be otherwise than always existent.

From these remarks it is easy for me to make my reply to the distinction in the use of the term "self-originated" or *per se*,[1] which, according to the counsel of my learned theological adversary, requires explanation. For, although those who, confining themselves to the peculiar and restricted meaning of efficient cause, think it impossible for a thing to be its own efficient cause, and do not discern here another species of cause analogous to an efficient cause, are accustomed to understand merely, when they say a thing exists *per se*, that it has no cause; yet, if those people would look to the facts rather than the words, they would easily see that the negative meaning of the term "self-originated" proceeds merely from the imperfection of the human intellect, and has no foundation in reality, and that there is a certain other positive signification which is drawn from the truth of things and from which alone my argument issues. For if, e.g. anyone should imagine that some body was something *per se*, he can only mean that it has no cause, and he affirms this for no positive reason, but merely in a negative manner, because he knows no cause for it. But this shows some imperfection in his judgment, as he will easily recognize if he remembers that the several parts of time are not derived from one another, and that hence, though that body be supposed to have existed up to the present time *per se*, i.e. without any cause, that will not suffice to make it exist in future, unless there be some power contained in it which continually, as it were, re-creates it; for then, when he sees that no such power is comprised in the idea of body, he will at once conclude that that body does not exist *per se*, taking the expression *per se* positively. Similarly when we say that God exists *per se*, we can indeed understand that negatively, our whole meaning being really that He has no cause. But, if we have previously enquired why He is or why He continues in being, and having regard to the immense and incomprehensible power which exists in the idea of Him we recognise that it is so exceedingly great that it is clearly the cause of His continuing to be, and that there can be nothing else besides it, we say that God exists *per se*, no longer negatively but in the highest positive sense. For, although we need not say that God is the efficient cause of His own self, lest, if we do so, we should be involved in a verbal dispute, yet, because we see that the fact of His existing *per se*, or having no cause other than Himself, issues, not from nothing, but from the real immensity of His power, it is quite permissible for us to think that in a certain sense He stands to Himself in the same way, as an efficient cause does to its effect, and that hence He exists *per se* in a positive sense. Each one may also ask himself whether he exists *per se* in the same sense, and, having found no power in himself sufficient to preserve him through even a moment of time, he will rightly conclude that he depends on something else, and indeed on something else which exists *per se*, because since the matter here concerns the present, not the past or the future, there is no room for an infinite regress. Nay, here I will add a statement I have not hitherto made in writing—that we cannot arrive merely at a secondary cause, but that the cause which has power sufficient to conserve a thing external to it must with all the more reason conserve itself by its own proper power, and so exist *per se*.

Moreover when it is said that all limitation is due to a cause,[2] while I hold that to be a real fact, I maintain that it is hardly expressed in proper terms, and that the difficulty is not solved; for, properly speaking, limitation is only the negation of a greater perfection, and this negation does not come from a cause but is the very thing so limited. But though it be true that every limited thing depends on a cause, yet that is not self-evident, but must be deduced from something else; for, as this subtle theologian well replies, a thing can be limited in two ways, either by that which produced it not having given it more perfection, or because its nature is such that it can only receive a certain amount, as e.g. in the case of the triangle, which by its nature can only have three sides. But it seems to me to be self-evident that everything that exists springs either from a cause or from itself considered as a cause; for, since we understand not only what existence is, but also what negation of existence is, we can-

[1] Cf. Obj. i, p. 105.   [2] Cf. p. 105.

not feign that anything exists *per se* as to which no reason can be given regarding why it exists rather than does not exist; hence there is no reason for not interpreting self-originated in the sense in which it implies causal power, that power, to wit, which passes all bounds, and which, as we can easily prove, can be found in God alone.

As to what my opponent finally grants[1] me, it is a principle which, though admitting no question, is yet commonly so little taken into consideration and is so effective in rescuing all Philosophy from the obscurity of darkness, that by confirming it by his authority the learned Doctor does much to further my endeavour.

But prudently he here enquires *whether I know the infinite distinctly and clearly;*[2] and although I have tried to anticipate this objection, yet it occurs so spontaneously to each one, that it is worth while to give it a detailed reply. Therefore here, to start with, I shall say that the infinite *quâ* infinite is in nowise comprehended, but that nevertheless it is understood, in so far as clearly and distinctly to understand a thing to be such that no limits can be found in it is to understand clearly that it is infinite.

Here indeed I distinguish between *the indefinite* and *the infinite*, and that alone do I, properly speaking, call infinite in which nowhere are limits to be found; in this sense God alone is infinite. That moreover in which only in a certain aspect do I recognize no limit, as e.g. the extension of imaginary space, the many in number, or the divisibility of the parts of quantity, and other similar things, I call indeed *indefinite* but not *infinite*, because such things are not limitless in every respect.

Besides that, I distinguish between the formal notion of the infinite or infinity and the thing which is infinite; for as for infinity, even though we understand it to have as much positive reality as may be, yet we understand it only in a certain negative fashion, from the fact, namely, that we perceive no limitation in the thing; but the thing itself which is infinite is indeed positively understood, though not adequately, i.e. we do not comprehend the whole of what is intelligible in it. But it is just as when gazing at the sea, we are said to behold it, though our sight does not cover it all nor measures its immensity; if indeed we view it from a distance in such a way as to take in the whole with a single glance, we see it only con-

fusedly, as we have a confused image of a chiliagon, when taking in all its sides at the same time; but if from near at hand we fix our glance on one portion of the sea, this act of vision can be clear and distinct, just as the image of a chiliagon may be, if it takes in only one or two of the figure's sides. By similar reasoning I admit along with all theologians that God cannot be comprehended by the human mind, and also that he cannot be distinctly known by those who try mentally to grasp Him at once in His entirety, and view Him, as it were, from a distance. This was the sense in which, in the words of St. Thomas in the passage quoted,[3] the knowledge of God was said to be found in us only in a certain confused way. But those who try to attend to His perfections singly, and intend not so much to comprehend them as to admire them and to employ all the power of their mind in contemplating them will assuredly find in Him a much ampler and readier supply of the material for clear and distinct cognition than in any created things.

Neither does St. Thomas here deny this contention, as is clear from his affirming in the following article that the existence of God is demonstrable. Moreover, wherever I have said that God can be clearly and distinctly known I have understood this to apply only to this finite cognition of ours, which is proportionate to the diminutive capacity of our minds. Besides, there was no reason for understanding otherwise in order to prove the truth of the propositions I have maintained, as will easily be noticed if people take heed that I have affirmed the doctrine in dispute only in two places, to wit where the question was asked whether, in the idea we form of God, there is anything real or only the negation of reality (as for example in the idea of cold nothing else is found than the negation of heat), a point which gives rise to no dispute [although we do not comprehend the infinite];[4] and again this doctrine appeared in the passage where I asserted that existence appertained to the notion of a being of the highest perfection, just as much as three sides to the notion of a triangle, a fact which can be understood without our having an adequate knowledge of God.

My opponent here compares one[5] of my arguments with another of St. Thomas's, so, as it were to force me to show which of the two has

[1] Cf. p. 106.
[2] Cf. p. 106.

[3] Cf. Objections 1, pp. 106–107.
[4] This clause occurs only in the French version. The round brackets above are also found only in it.
[5] Cf. p. 106.

he more force. This I seem to be able to do with a good enough grace, because neither did t. Thomas use that argument as his own, nor oes he draw the same conclusion from it; consequently there is nothing here in which I am t variance with the Angelic Doctor. He himelf asked whether the existence of God is in self known to man, i.e. whether it is obvious each single individual; he denies this, and I long with him. Now the argument to which e puts himself in opposition can be thus propounded. *When we understand what it is the ord God signifies, we understand that it is that, han which nothing greater can be conceived; but exist in reality as well as in the mind is greater han to exist in the mind alone; hence, when the eaning of the word God is understood, it is unerstood that God exists in fact as well as in the nderstanding.* Here there is a manifest error n the form of the argument; for the only conlusion to be drawn is—*hence, when we understand what the word God means, we understand hat it means that God exists in fact as well as in he mind:* but because a word implies something, that is no reason for this being true. My rgument, however, was of the following kind —That which we clearly and distinctly undertand to belong to the true and immutable nature of anything, its essence, or form, can be ruly affirmed of that thing; but, after we have vith sufficient accuracy investigated the nature of God, we clearly and distinctly undertand that to exist belongs to His true and imnutable nature; therefore we can with truth ffirm of God that He exists. This is at least a egitimate conclusion. But besides this the maor premise cannot be denied, because it was previously[1] conceded that *whatever we clearly nd distinctly perceive is true.* The minor alone emains, and in it there is, I confess, no little difficulty. This is firstly because we are so nuch accustomed to distinguish existence from ssence in the case of other things, that we do not with sufficient readiness notice how existnce belongs to the essence of God in a greater legree than in the case of other things. Furher, because we do not distinguish that which pelongs to the true and immutable nature of a thing from that which we by a mental fiction ssign to it, even if we do fairly clearly perceive that existence belongs to God's essence, we nevertheless do not conclude that God exists, because we do not know whether His essence is true and immutable or only a fiction we invent.

[1]Cf. Reply to Obj. i, p. 112.

But, in order to remove the first part of this difficulty we must distinguish between possible and necessary existence, and note that in the concept or idea of everything that is clearly and distinctly conceived, possible existence is contained, but necessary existence never, except in the idea of God alone. For I am sure that all who diligently attend to this diversity between the idea of God and that of all other things, will perceive that, even though other things are indeed conceived only as existing, yet it does not thence follow that they do exist, but only that they may exist, because we do not conceive that there is any necessity for actual existence being conjoined with their other properties; but, because we understand that actual existence is necessarily and at all times linked to God's other attributes, it follows certainly that God exists.

Further, to clear away the rest of the difficulty, we must observe that those ideas which do not contain a true and immutable nature, but only a fictitious one due to a mental synthesis, can be by that same mind analysed, not merely by abstraction (or restriction of the thought) but by a clear and distinct mental operation; hence it will be clear that those things which the understanding cannot so analyse have not been put together by it. For example, when I think of a winged horse, or of a lion actually existing, or of a triangle inscribed in a square, I easily understand that I can on the contrary think of a horse without wings, of a lion as not existing and of a triangle apart from a square, and so forth, and that hence these things have no true and immutable nature. But if I think of the triangle or the square (I pass by for the present the lion and the horse, because their natures are not wholly intelligible to us), then certainly whatever I recognise as being contained in the idea of the triangle, as that its angles are equal to right, etc., I shall truly affirm of the triangle; and similarly I shall affirm of the square whatsoever I find in the idea of it. For though I can think of the triangle, though stripping from it the equality of its angles to two right, yet I cannot deny that attribute of it by any clear and distinct mental operation, i.e. when I myself rightly understand what I say. Besides, if I think of a triangle inscribed in a square, not meaning to ascribe to the square that which belongs to the triangle alone, or to assign to the triangle the properties of the square, but for the purpose only of examining that which arises from the conjunction of the two, the nature of that composite will be not less true and immutable than that of the square or triangle alone; and hence it will be right to affirm that the square cannot be less than double the inscribed triangle, together with the similar properties which belong to the nature of this composite figure.

But if I think that existence is contained in the idea of a body of the highest perfection, because it is a greater perfection to exist in reality as well as in the mind than to exist in the intellect alone, I cannot then conclude that this utterly perfect body exists, but merely that it may exist; for I can well enough recognize that that idea has been put together by my mind uniting together all corporeal perfections, and that existence does not arise out of its other corporeal perfections, because it (existence) can be equally well affirmed and denied of them. Nay, because when I examine this idea of body I see in it no force by means of which it may produce or preserve itself, I rightly conclude that necessary existence, which alone is here in question, does not belong to the nature of a body, howsoever perfect it may be, any more than it belongs to the nature of a mountain not to have a valley, or any more than it pertains to the nature of a triangle to have its angles greater than two right angles. But now, if we ask not about a body but about a thing (of whatever sort this thing may turn out to be) which has all those perfections which can exist together, whether existence must be included in the number of these perfections we shall at first be in doubt, because our mind, being finite, and not accustomed to consider them unless separately, will perchance not at first see how necessary is the bond between them. But yet if we attentively consider whether existence is congruous with a being of the highest perfection, and what sort of existence is so, we shall be able clearly and distinctly to perceive in the first place that possible existence is at least predicable of it, as it is of all other things of which we have a distinct idea, even of those things which are composed by a fiction of the mind. Further, because we cannot think of God's existence as being possible, without at the same time, and by taking heed of His immeasurable power, acknowledging that He can exist by His own might, we hence conclude that He really exists and has existed from all eternity; for the light of nature makes it most plain that what can exist by its own power always exists. And thus we shall understand that necessary exist-

ence is comprised in the idea of a being of the highest power, not by any intellectual fiction but because it belongs to the true and immutable nature of that being to exist. We shall at the same time easily perceive that that all-powerful being must comprise in himself all the other perfections that are contained in the idea of God, and hence these by their own nature and without any mental fiction are conjoined together and exist in God.

All this is manifest to one who considers the matter attentively, and it differs from what I have already written only in the method of explanation adopted, which I have intentionally altered in order to suit a diversity of intelligences. But I shall not deny that this argument is such that those who do not bethink themselves of all those considerations that go to prove it, will very readily take it for a sophism; hence at the outset I had much doubt as to whether I should use it, fearing that those who did not attain to it might be given an opportunity of cavilling about the rest. But since there are two ways only of proving the existence of God, one by means of the effects due to him, the other by his essence or nature, and as I gave the former explanation in the third Meditation as well as I could, I considered that I should not afterwards omit the other proof.

In the matter of the formal distinction which the learned Theologian claims to draw from Scotus,[1] my reply is briefly to the effect that this distinction in no way differs from a modal one, and applies only to incomplete entities, which I have accurately demarcated from complete beings. This is sufficient to cause one thing to be conceived separately and as distinct from another by the abstracting action of a mind when it conceives the thing inadequately, without sufficing to cause two things to be thought of so distinctly and separately that we understand each to be an entity in itself and diverse from every other; in order that we may do this a real distinction is absolutely necessary. Thus, for example, there is a formal distinction between the motion and the figure of the same body, and I can quite well think of the motion without the figure and of the figure apart from the motion and of either apart from the body; but nevertheless I cannot think of the motion in a complete manner apart from the thing in which the motion exists nor of the figure in isolation from the object which has the figure; nor finally can I feign that anything incapable of having figure can possess motion,

[1]Cf. Obj. 1, p. 107.

r that what is incapable of movement has figure. So it is also that neither can I understand justice apart from a just being, or compassion apart from the compassionate; nor may I imagine that the same being as is just cannot be compassionate. But yet I understand in a complete manner what body is [that is to say I conceive of body as a complete thing], merely by thinking that it is extended, as figure, can move, etc., and by denying of it everything which belongs to the nature of mind. Conversely, also, I understand that mind is something complete which doubts, knows, wishes, etc., although I deny that anything belongs to it which is contained in the idea of body. But this could not be unless there were a real distinction between mind and body.

This is my answer, gentlemen, to your friend's subtle and most serviceable criticisms. If it still is defective, I ask to be informed about the omissions or the blunders it contains. To secure this from my critic through your good offices would be to have a great kindness conferred upon me.

THE SECOND SET OF OBJECTIONS[1]

SIR,

Your endeavour to maintain the cause of the Author of all things against a new race of rebellious giants has sped so well, that henceforth men of worth may hope that in future there will be none who, after attentive study of your Meditations, will not confess that an eternal divine Being does exist, on whom all things depend. Hence we have decided to draw your attention to certain passages noted beneath and to request you to shed such light upon them that nothing will remain in your work which, if at all demonstrable, is not clearly proved. For, since you have for so many years so exercised your mind by continual meditation, that matters which to others seem doubtful and obscure are to you most evident, and you perhaps know them by a simple intuitive act of mind, without noticing the indistinctness that the same facts have for others, it will be well to bring before your notice those things which need to be more clearly and fully explained and demonstrated. This done, there will scarce remain anyone to deny that those arguments of yours, entered upon for the purpose of promoting the greater glory of God and vast benefit to all mankind, have the force of demonstrations.

In the first place, *pray remember that it was not as an actual fact and in reality, but merely by a mental fiction, that you so stoutly resisted the claim of all bodies to be more than phantasms, in order that you might draw the conclusion that you were merely a thinking being; for otherwise there is perhaps a risk you might believe that you could draw the conclusion that you were in truth nothing other than mind, or thought, or a thinking being. This we find worthy of mention only in connection with the first two Meditations, in which you show clearly that it is at least certain that you, who think, exist. But let us pause a little here. Up to this point you know that you are a being that thinks; but you do not know what this thinking thing is. What if that were a body which by its various motions and encounters produces that which we call thought? For, granted that you rejected the claim of every sort of body, you may have been deceived in this, because you*

did *not rule out yourself, who are a body. For how will you prove that a body cannot think, or that its bodily motions are not thought itself? Possibly even, the whole bodily system, which you imagine you have rejected, or some of its parts, say the parts composing the brain, can unite to produce those motions which we call thoughts. "I am a thinking thing," you say; but who knows but you are a corporeal motion, or a body in motion?*

Secondly, *from the idea of a Supreme Being which, you contend, cannot be by you produced, you are bold enough to infer the necessary existence of the Supreme Being from which alone can come that idea that your mind perceives.[2] Yet we find in our own selves a sufficient basis on which alone to erect that said idea, even though that Supreme Being did not exist, or we were ignorant of its existence and did not even think of it though it did exist. Do I not see that I, in thinking, have some degree of perfection? And therefore I conclude that others besides me have a similar degree, and hence I have a basis on which to construct the thought of any number of degrees and so to add one degree of perfection to another to infinity, just as, given the existence of a single degree of light or heat, I can add and imagine fresh degrees up to infinity. Why, on similar reasoning, can I not add, to any degree of being that I perceive in myself, any other degree I please, and out of the whole number capable of addition construct the idea of a perfect being? "But," you say, "an effect can have no degree of perfection or reality which has not previously existed in its cause." In reply we urge (passing by the fact that experience shows us that flies and other animals, or even plants are produced by the sun, rain and the earth, in which life, a nobler thing than any merely corporeal grade of being, does not exist, and that hence an effect can derive from its cause some reality which yet is not found in the cause) that that idea is nothing but an entity of reason, which has no more nobility than your mind that thinks it. Besides this, how do you know that that idea would have come before your mind if you had not been nurtured among men of culture, but had passed all your life in some desert spot? Have you not derived it from reflections previously entertained, from books, from interchange of converse with your friends, etc., not from your*

[1] The title of the French translation is "The Second Objections Collected by the Rev. Father Mersenne from the Utterances of Divers Theologians and Philosophers."

[2] Cf. Med. III, p. 86.

wn mind alone or from a Supreme Being who xists? You must therefore prove more clearly hat that idea could not present itself to you unless Supreme Being did exist; though when you show his we shall all confess ourselves vanquished. But it seems to be shown clearly that that idea prings from previous notions by the fact that the atives of Canada, the Hurons, and other sav-ges, have no idea in their minds such as this, vhich is one that you can form from a previous urvey of corporeal things, in such a way that our idea refers only to this corporeal world, vhich embraces all the perfections that you can magine; hence you would have up to this point no rounds as yet for inferring more than an entirely erfect corporeal Entity, unless you were to add omething else conducting us to the [knowledge of he] incorporeal or spiritual. Let us add that you an construct the idea of an angel (just as you can orm the notion of a supremely perfect being) with-ut that idea being caused in you by a [really exist-ng] angel; though the angel has more perfection han you have. But you do not possess the idea of God any more than that of an infinite number or of in infinite line; and though you did possess this, yet there could be no such number. Put along with his the contention that the idea of the unity and simplicity of a sole perfection which embraces all other perfections, is merely the product of the rea-soning mind, and is formed in the same way as other universal unities, which do not exist in fact but merely in the understanding, as is illustrated by the cases of generic, transcendental and other unities.

Thirdly, since you are not yet certain of the aforesaid existence of God, and yet according to your statement, cannot be certain of anything or know anything clearly and distinctly unless pre-viously you know certainly and clearly that God exists, it follows that you cannot clearly and dis-tinctly know that you are a thinking thing, since, according to you, that knowledge depends on the clear knowledge of the existence of God, the proof of which you have not yet reached at that point where you draw the conclusion that you have a clear knowledge of what you are.

Take this also, that while an Atheist knows clearly and distinctly that the three angles of a triangle are equal to two right, yet he is far from believing in the existence of God; in fact he denies it, because if God existed there would be a su-preme existence, a highest good, i.e. an infinite Being. But the infinite in every type of perfection precludes the existence of anything else whatso-ever it be, e.g. of every variety of entity and good, nay even every sort of non-entity and evil; whereas there are in existence many entities, many good

things, as well as many non-entities and many evil things. We consider that you should give a solution of this objection, lest the impious should still have some case left them.

Fourthly, you deny that God lies or deceives; whereas some schoolmen may be found who af-firm this. Thus Gabriel,[1] Ariminensis,[2] and others think that in the absolute sense of the ex-pression God does utter falsehoods, i.e. what is the opposite of His intention and contrary to that which He has decreed; as when He uncondition-ally announced to the people of Nineveh through the Prophet, Yet forty days and Nineveh shall be destroyed; and when in many other cases He declared things that by no means came to pass, because His words were not meant to correspond with His intention or His decree. But, if God could harden the heart of Pharaoh and blind his eyes, if He communicated to His Prophets a spirit of lying, whence do you conclude that we cannot be deceived by Him? May not God so deal with men as a physician treats his patients, or as a father his children, dissimulation being employed in both cases, and that wisely and with profit? For if God showed to us His truth undimmed, what eyes, what mental vision could endure it?

Yet it is true that it is not necessary for God to contrive deception in order for you to be deceived in the things which you think you clearly and dis-tinctly perceive, if the cause of the illusion may re-side in you yourself, provided only that you are unaware of the fact. What if your nature be such as to be continually, or at least very frequently de-ceived? But what evidence is there that you are not deceived and cannot be deceived in those mat-ters whereof you have clear and distinct knowl-edge? How often have we not experienced the fact that a man has been deceived in those matters of which he believed that he had knowledge as plain as daylight? Hence we think that this prin-ciple of clear and distinct knowledge should be explained so clearly and distinctly that no one of sound mind may ever be deceived in matters that he believes himself to know clearly and distinctly; apart from this condition we cannot yet make out that there is a possibility of certitude in any de-gree attaching to your thinking or to the thoughts of the human race.

Fifthly, if the will never goes astray or errs, so long as it follows the clear and distinct knowledge of the mind that governs it, but exposes itself to danger if guided by a mental conception which is not clear and distinct, note that the following con-

[1]Gabriel Biel, fifteenth century, "the last of the Scholastics."

[2]Gregory of Rimini, fourteenth century.

sequences ensue:—a Turk or any other infidel does not only not err because he does not embrace the Christian [and Catholic] Religion, but in addition to this he does err if he does embrace it, since he does not apprehend its truth either clearly or distinctly. Nay, if this canon of yours is true, there will be practically nothing which the will may permissibly embrace, since there is hardly anything known to us with that clearness and distinctness that you want for a certitude that no doubt can shake. Beware then lest, in your desire to befriend the truth you do not prove too much, and, instead of establishing it, overthrow it.

Sixthly, in your reply to the preceding set of objections you appear to have gone astray in the drawing of your conclusion. This was how you propounded your argument—We may truly affirm of anything, that which we clearly and distinctively perceive to belong to its true and immutable nature; but (after we have investigated with sufficient accuracy what God is) we clearly and distinctly understand that to exist belongs to the nature of God.[1] The proper conclusion would have been:—therefore (after we have investigated with sufficient accuracy what God is) we can truly affirm that to exist belongs to God's nature. Whence it does not follow that God actually exists, but only that He ought to exist if His nature were anything possible or not contradictory; that is to say, that the nature or essence of God cannot be conceived apart from His existence and hence, as a consequence, if that essence is real, God exists as an actual fact. All this may be reduced to that argument which is stated by others in the following terms:—If it is not a contradiction that God exists, it is certain that He exists; but His existence is not a contradiction; hence, etc. But a difficulty occurs in the minor premise, which states that God's existence is not a contradiction, since our critics either profess to doubt the truth of this or deny it. Moreover that little clause in

[1]Cf. Reply to Obj. I, p. 112.

your argument ("after we have sufficiently investigated the nature of God") assumes as true something that all do not believe; and you know that you yourself confess that you can apprehend the infinite only inadequately. The same thing must be said in the case of each and any of God's attributes; for, since everything in God is utterly infinite, what mind can comprehend the smallest fragment of what exists in God except in a manner that is utterly inadequate? How then can you have "investigated with sufficient clearness and distinctness what God is"?

Seventhly, you say not one word [in your Meditations] about the immortality of the human soul, which nevertheless you should above all things have proved and demonstrated as against those men—themselves unworthy of immortality —who completely deny it and perchance have an enmity against it. But over and above this you do not seem to have sufficiently proved the distinctness of the soul from every species of body, as we have already said in our first criticism; to which we now add that it does not seem to follow from the distinction you draw between it and the body that it is incorruptible or immortal. What if its nature be limited by the duration of the life of the body, and God has granted it only such a supply of force and has so measured out its existence that, in the cessation of the corporeal life, it must come to an end?

These, Sir, are the difficulties on which we request you to shed light, in order that it may be profitable for each and all to read your Meditations, containing as they do so much subtlety and, in our opinion, so much truth. This is why it would be well worth the doing if, hard upon your solution of the difficulties, you advanced as premises certain definitions, postulates and axioms, and thence drew conclusions, conducting the whole proof by the geometrical method, in the use of which you are so highly expert. Thus would you cause each reader to have everything in his mind, as it were at a single glance, and to be penetrated throughout with a sense of the Divine being.

REPLY TO
THE SECOND SET OF OBJECTIONS

GENTLEMEN,

I had much pleasure in reading the criticisms you have passed on my little book dealing with First Philosophy; and I recognise the friendly disposition towards me that you dis-

play, united as it is with piety towards God and a zeal to promote His glory. I cannot be otherwise than glad not only that you should think my arguments worthy of your scrutiny, but also that you bring forward nothing in pposition to them to which I do not seem to e able quite easily to reply.

IRSTLY, you warn me *to remember that it was not actually but merely by a mental fiction hat I rejected the claim of bodies to be more than hantasms, in order to draw the conclusion that ' was merely a thinking being, so as to avoid hinking that it was a consequence of this that I was really nothing more than mind.*[1] But in the Second Meditation I have already shown that I bore this in mind sufficiently; here are the words:—*But perhaps it is the case that these very things, which I thus suppose to be non-existent because they are unknown to me, do not in very ruth differ from that self which I know. I cannot ell; this is not the subject I am now discussing, etc.*[2] By these words I meant expressly to warn the reader that in that passage I did not as yet ask whether the mind was distinct from the body, but was merely investigating these properties of mind of which I am able to attain to sure and evident knowledge. And, since I discovered many such properties, I can only in a qualified sense admit what you subjoin, namely, *That I am yet ignorant as to what a thinking thing is.*[3] For though I confess that as yet I have not discovered whether that thinking thing is the same as the body or something diverse from it, I do not, on that account, admit that I have no knowledge of the mind. Who has ever had such an acquaintance with anything as to know that there was absolutely nothing in it of which he was not aware? But in proportion as we perceive more in anything, the better do we say we know it; thus we have more knowledge of those men with whom we have lived a long time, than of those whose face merely we have seen or whose name we have heard, even though they too are not said to be absolutely unknown. It is in this sense that I think I have demonstrated that the mind, considered apart from what is customarily attributed to the body, is better known than the body viewed as separate from the mind; and this alone was what I intended to maintain.

But I see what you hint at, namely, that since I have written only six Meditations on First Philosophy my readers will marvel that in the first two no further conclusion is reached than that I have just now mentioned, and that hence they will think the Meditations to be too meagre, and unworthy of publication. To this I reply merely that I have no fear that anyone who reads with judgment what I have written should have occasion to suspect that my matter gave out; and moreover it appeared highly reasonable to confine to separate Meditations matters which demand a particular attention and must be considered apart from others.

Nothing conduces more to the obtaining of a secure knowledge of reality than a previous accustoming of ourselves to entertain doubts especially about corporeal things; and although I had long ago seen several books written by the Academics and Sceptics about this subject and felt some disgust in serving up again this stale dish, I could not for the above reasons refuse to allot to this subject one whole Meditation. I should be pleased also if my readers would expend not merely the little time which is required for reading it, in thinking over the matter of which the Meditation treats, but would give months, or at least weeks, to this, before going on further; for in this way the rest of the work will yield them a much richer harvest.

Further, since our previous ideas of what belongs to the mind have been wholly confused and mixed up with the ideas of sensible objects, and this was the first and chief reason why none of the propositions asserted of God and the soul could be understood with sufficient clearness, I thought I should perform something worth the doing if I showed how the properties or qualities of the soul are to be distinguished from those of the body. For although many have already maintained that, in order to understand the facts of metaphysics, the mind must be abstracted from the senses, no one hitherto, so far as I know, has shown how this is to be done. The true, and in my judgment, the only way to do this is found in my second Meditation, but such is its nature that it is not enough to have once seen how it goes; much time and many repetitions are required if we would, by forming the contrary habit of distinguishing intellectual from corporeal matters, for at least a few days, obliterate the life-long custom of confounding them. This appeared to me to be a very sound reason for treating of nothing further in the said Meditation.

But besides this you here ask *how I prove that a body cannot think.*[4] Pardon me if I reply that I have not yet given ground for the rais-

[1] Cf. Obj. II, p. 116.
[2] Cf. Med. II, p. 79.
[3] Cf. Obj. II, p. 116.
[4] Cf. p. 116.

ing of this question, for I first treat of it in the sixth Meditation. Here are the words:—*In order that I may be sure that one thing is diverse from another, it is sufficient that I should be able to conceive the one apart from the other, etc.*, and shortly afterwards I say: *Although I have a body very closely conjoined with me, yet since, on the one hand, I have a clear and distinct idea of myself, in so far as I am a thinking thing and not extended; and, on the other hand, I have a distinct idea of the body in so far as it is an extended, not a thinking thing, it is certain that I* (that is the mind [or soul, by which I am what I am]) *am really distinct from my body and can exist without it.*[1] It is easy from this to pass to the following:—*everything that can think is mind or is called mind, but, since mind and body are really distinct, no body is a mind; hence no body can think.*

I do not here see what you are able to deny. Do you deny that in order to recognise a real distinctness between objects it is sufficient for us to conceive one of them clearly apart from the other? If so, offer us some surer token of real distinction. I believe that none such can be found. What will you say? That those things are really distinct each of which can exist apart from the other. But once more I ask how you will know that one thing can be apart from the other; this, in order to be a sign of the distinctness, should be known. Perhaps you will say that it is given to you by the senses, since you can see, touch, etc., the one thing while the other is absent. But the trustworthiness of the senses is inferior to that of the intellect, and it is in many ways possible for one and the same thing to appear under various guises or in several places or in different manners, and so to be taken to be two things. And finally if you bear in mind what was said at the end of the second Meditation[2] about wax, you will see that, properly speaking, not even are bodies themselves perceived by sense, but that they are perceived by the intellect alone, so that there is no difference between perceiving by sense one thing apart from another, and having an idea of one thing and understanding that that idea is not the same as an idea of something else. Moreover, this knowledge can be drawn from no other source than the fact that the one thing is perceived apart from the other; nor can this be known with certainty unless the ideas in each case are clear and distinct. Hence that sign you offer of

real distinctness must be reduced to my criterion in order to be infallible.

But if any people deny that they have distinct ideas of mind and body, I can do nothing further than ask them to give sufficient attention to what is said in the second Meditation. I beg them to note that the opinion they perchance hold, namely, that the parts of the brain join their forces with the soul to form thoughts, has not arisen from any positive ground, but only from the fact that they have never had experience of separation from the body, and have not seldom been hindered by it in their operations, and that similarly if anyone had from infancy continually worn irons on his legs, he would think that those irons were part of his own body and that he needed them in order to walk.

SECONDLY, when you say that *in ourselves there is a sufficient foundation on which to construct the idea of God*, your assertion in no way conflicts with my opinion. I myself at the end of the third Meditation have expressly said that *this idea is innate in me*,[3] or alternatively that it comes to me from no other source than myself. I admit that *we could form this very idea, though we did not know that a supreme being existed*,[4] but not that we could do so *if it were in fact non-existent*, for on the contrary I have notified that *the whole force of my argument lies in the fact that the capacity for constructing such an idea could not exist in me, unless I were created by God*.[5]

Neither does what you say about flies, plants, etc., tend to prove that there can be any degree of perfection in the effect which has not antecedently existed in the cause. For it is certain that either there is no perfection in animals that lack reason, which does not exist also in inanimate bodies; or that, if such do exist, it comes to them from elsewhere, and that sun, rain and earth are not their adequate causes. It would also be highly irrational for anyone, simply because he did not notice any cause co-operating in the production of a fly, which had as many degrees of perfection as the fly, though meanwhile he was not sure that no cause beyond those he has noticed is at work, to make this an occasion for doubting a truth which, as I shall directly explain in greater detail, the light of Nature itself makes manifest.

To this I add that what you say by way of

[1]Cf. Med. vi, pp. 98–99.
[2]Cf. Med. ii, p. 80 Sqq.

[3]Cf. Med. iii, p. 88.
[4]Cf. Obj. ii, 116–117.
[5]Cf. Med. iii, p. 88.

objection about flies, being drawn from a consideration of material things, could not occur to people who, following my Meditations, withdraw their thoughts from the things of sense with a view to making a start with philosophical thinking.

There is also no more force in the objection you make in calling our idea of God an entity formed by thinking. For, firstly, it is not true that it is an *ens rationis* in the sense in which that means something non-existent, but only in the sense in which every mental operation is an *ens rationis*, meaning by this something that issues from thought; this entire world also could be called an entity formed by the divine thought, i.e. an entity created by a simple act of the divine mind. Secondly, I have already sufficiently insisted in various places that what I am concerned with is only the perfection of the idea or its objective reality which, not less than the objective artifice in the idea of a machine of highly ingenious device, requires a cause in which is actually contained everything that it, though only objectively, comprises.

I really do not see what can be added to make it clearer that that idea could not be present in my consciousness unless a supreme being existed, except that the reader might by attending more diligently to what I have written, free himself of the prejudices that perchance overwhelm his natural light, and might accustom his mind to put trust in ultimate principles, than which nothing can be more true or more evident, rather than in the obscure and false opinions which, however, long usage has fixed in his mind.

That *there is nothing in the effect, that has not existed in a similar or in some higher form in the cause*, is a first principle than which none clearer can be entertained. The common truth *"from nothing, nothing comes"* is identical with it. For, if we allow that there is something in the effect which did not exist in the cause, we must grant also that this something has been created by nothing; again the only reason why nothing cannot be the cause of a thing, is that in such a cause there would not be the same thing as existed in the effect.

It is a first principle that *the whole of the reality or perfection that exists only objectively in ideas must exist in them formally or in a superior manner in their causes*. It is on this alone we wholly rely, when believing that things situated outside the mind have real existence; for what should have led us to suspect their existence except the fact that the ideas of them were borne in on the mind by means of the senses?

But it will become clear to those who give sufficient attention to the matter and accompany me far in my reflections, that we possess the idea of a supreme and perfect being, and also that the objective reality of this idea exists in us neither formally nor eminently. A truth, however, which depends solely on being grasped by another's thought, cannot be forced on a listless mind.

Now, from these arguments we derive it as a most evident conclusion that God exists. But for the sake of those whose natural light is so exceeding small that they do not see this first principle, viz. *that every perfection existing objectively in an idea must exist actually in something that causes that idea,* I have demonstrated in a way more easily grasped an identical conclusion, from the fact that the mind possessing that idea cannot be self-derived; and I cannot in consequence see what more is wanted to secure your admission that I have prevailed.

Moreover, there is no force in your plea, that perchance the idea that conveys to me my knowledge of God has come *from notions previously entertained, from books, from conversations with friends, etc., not from my own mind alone.*[1] For the argument takes the same course as it follows in my own case, if I raise the question whether those from whom I am said to have acquired the idea have derived it from themselves or from anyone else; the conclusion will be always the same, that it is God from whom it first originated.

The objection you subjoin, *that the idea of God can be constructed out of a previous survey of corporeal things,*[2] seems to be no nearer the truth than if you should say that we have no faculty of hearing, but have attained to a knowledge of sound from seeing colours alone; you can imagine a greater analogy and parity between colours and sounds than between corporeal things and God. When you ask me *to add something conducting us to [the knowledge of] an incorporeal and spiritual entity,*[3] I can do nothing better than refer you back to my second Meditation, so that you may at least see that it is not wholly useless. For what could I achieve here in one or two paragraphs, if the longer discourse to be found there, designed as it were with this very matter in view, and one

[1] Cf. Obj. II, p. 116.
[2] Cf. Obj. II, p. 117.
[3] Cf. p. 117.

on which I think I have expended as much care as on anything that I have ever written, has been wholly unsuccessful?

There is no drawback in the fact that in that Meditation I dealt only with the human mind; most readily and gladly do I admit that the idea we have, e.g. of the Divine intellect, does not differ from that we have of our own, except merely as the idea of an infinite number differs from that of a number of the second or third power; and the same holds good of the various attributes of God, of which we find some trace in ourselves.

But, besides this, we have in the notion of God absolute immensity, simplicity, and a unity that embraces all other attributes; and of this idea we find no example in us: it is, as I have said before,[1] *like the mark of the workman imprinted on his work.* By means of this, too, we recognise that none of the particular attributes which we, owing to the limitations of our minds, assign piecemeal to God, just as we find them in ourselves, belong to Him and to us in precisely the same sense. Also we recognise that of various particular indefinite attributes of which we have ideas, as e.g. knowledge whether indefinite or infinite, likewise power, number, length, etc., and of various infinite attributes also, some are contained formally in the idea of God, e.g. knowledge and power, others only eminently, as number and length; and this would certainly not be so if that idea were nothing else than a figment in our minds.

If that were so it would not be so constantly conceived by all in the same way. It is most worthy of note that all metaphysicians are unanimous in their description of the attributes of God (those at least which can be grasped by the human mind unaided); and hence there is no physical or sensible object, nothing of which we have the most concrete and comprehensible idea, about the nature of which there is not more dispute among philosophers.

No man could go astray and fail to conceive that idea of God correctly if only he cared to attend to the nature of an all-perfect being. But those who confuse one thing with another, owing to this very fact utter contradictions; and constructing in their imagination a chimerical idea of God, not unreasonably afterwards deny that a God, who is represented by such an idea, exists. So here, when you talk of *a corporeal being of the highest perfection,* if you take the term "of the highest perfection" abso-

lutely, meaning that the corporeal thing is one in which all perfections are found, you utter a contradiction. For its very bodily nature involves many imperfections, as that a body is divisible into parts, that each of its parts is not the other, and other similar defects. For it is self-evident that it is a greater perfection not to be divided than to be divided, etc. But if you merely understand what is most perfect in the way of body, this will not be God.

I readily grant your further point, that *in the case of the idea of an angel, than which we are less perfect, there is certainly no need for that idea to be produced in us by an angel;* I myself have already in the third Meditation[2] said that *the idea can be constructed out of those that we possess of God and of man.* There is no point against me here.

Further, those who maintain that they do not possess the idea of God, but in place of it form some image, etc., while they refuse the name concede the fact. I certainly do not think that that idea is of a nature akin to the images of material things depicted in the imagination, but that it is something that we are aware of by an apprehension or judgment or inference of the understanding alone. And I maintain that there is a necessary conclusion from the fact alone that, howsoever it come about, by thought or understanding, I attain to the notion of a perfection that is higher than I; a result that may follow merely from the fact that in counting I cannot reach a highest of all numbers, and hence recognise that in enumeration there is something that exceeds my powers. And this conclusion is, not indeed to the effect that an infinite number does exist, nor yet that it implies a contradiction as you say,[3] but that I have received the power of conceiving that a number is thinkable, that is higher than any that can ever be thought by me, and have received it not from myself but from some other entity more perfect than I.

It is of no account whether or not one gives the name idea to this concept of an indefinitely great number. But in order to understand what is that entity more perfect than I am, and to discover whether it is this very infinite number as an actually existing fact, or whether it is something else, we must take into account all the other attributes that can exist in the being from which the idea originates, over and above the power of giving me that idea; and the result is that it is found to be God.

[1]Cf. Med. III, p. 88.

[2]Cf. Med. III, p. 85.
[3]Cf. Obj. II, p. 117.

Finally, when God is said to be *unthinkable*, that applies to the thought that grasps him adequately, and does not hold good of that inadequate thought which we possess and which suffices to let us know that he exists. It likewise does not matter though *the idea of the unity of all God's perfections is formed in the same way as "Porphyrian"[1] universals.* Though there is this important difference, that it designates a peculiar and positive perfection in God, while generic unity adds nothing real to the nature of the single individuals it unites.

THIRDLY, when I said that *we could know nothing with certainty unless we were first aware that God existed,* I announced in express terms that I referred only to the science apprehending such conclusions *as can recur in memory without attending further to the proofs which led me to make them.*[2] Further, knowledge of first principles is not usually called science by dialecticians. But when we become aware that we are thinking beings, this is a primitive act of knowledge derived from no syllogistic reasoning. He who says, *"I think, hence I am, or exist,"* does not deduce existence from thought by a syllogism, but, by a simple act of mental vision, recognises it as if it were a thing that is known *per se.* This is evident from the fact that if it were syllogistically deduced, the major premise, *that everything that thinks is, or exists,* would have to be known previously; but yet that has rather been learned from the experience of the individual—that unless he exists he cannot think. For our mind is so constituted by nature that general propositions are formed out of the knowledge of particulars.

That *an atheist can know clearly that the three angles of a triangle are equal to two right angles,* I do not deny, I merely affirm that, on the other hand, such knowledge on his part cannot constitute true science, because no knowledge that can be rendered doubtful should be called science. Since he is, as supposed, an Atheist, he cannot be sure that he is not deceived in the things that seem most evident to him, as has been sufficiently shown; and though perchance the doubt does not occur to him, nevertheless it may come up, if he examine the matter, or if another suggests it; he can never be safe from it unless he first recognises the existence of a God.

And it does not matter though he think he has demonstrations proving that there is no God. Since they are by no means true, the errors in them can always be pointed out to him, and when this takes place he will be driven from his opinion.

This would certainly not be difficult to do, if to represent all his proofs he were to bring into play only that principle you here append, viz. *that what is infinite in every kind of perfection excludes every other entity whatsoever, etc.*[3] For, in the first place, if he is asked whence comes his knowledge that that exclusion of all other entities is a characteristic of the infinite, there is nothing he can reasonably say in reply; for by the word *infinite* neither is he wont to understand that which excludes the existence of finite things, nor can he know anything of the characteristic of that which he deems to be nothing, and to have hence no characteristics at all, except what is contained merely in the meaning he has learned from others to attach to the word. Next, what could be the power of this imaginary infinite if it could never create anything? Finally, because we are aware of some power of thinking within us, we easily conceive that the power of thinking can reside in some other being, and that it is greater than in us. But though we think of it as increased to infinity, we do not on that account fear that the power we have should become less. And the same holds good of all the other attributes we ascribe to God, even that of His might, provided that we assume that no such power exists in us except as subject to the Divine will. Hence evidently He can be known as infinite without any prejudice to the existence of created things.

FOURTHLY,[4] *in denying that God lies, or is a deceiver,* I fancy that I am in agreement with all metaphysicians and theologians past and future. What you allege to the contrary refutes my position no more than, if I denied that anger existed in God, or that He was subject to other passions, you should bring forward in objection passages in Scripture where human attributes are ascribed to Him. Everyone knows the distinction between those modes of speaking of God that are suited to the vulgar understanding and do indeed contain some truth, a truth, however, relative to the human point of view,—modes of speaking which Holy Writ usually employs,—and those other expressions that give us the more bare and rigorous truth, though not that accommodated to

---

[1] E.g. generic unity; cf. Obj. ii, *loc. cit.*
[2] Cf. Med. v, pp. 95, 96.

[3] Cf. Obj. ii, p. 117.
[4] Cf. p. 117.

the human mind. It is these latter that everyone should employ in philosophy, and it was my duty to use them specially in my Meditations, since not even there did I assume that there were as yet any men known to me, neither did I consider myself as consisting of mind and body, but as mind only. Hence, it is clear that I did not then speak of the lie that is expressed in words, but only of the internal formal ill-will which is contained in deception.

Therefore, though the words of the Prophet you bring forward *"Yet forty days and Nineveh shall be destroyed,"* did not constitute even a verbal lie but only a threat, the fulfilment of which depended on a condition; and again though when it is said that *"God hardened Pharaoh's heart,"* or something to the same effect, it must not be thought that this was a positive act, but only a negative one, viz. in not granting Pharaoh the grace necessary to make him repent; I should be loath to censure those who say that God can utter verbal deceptions through His prophets (deceptions which, like those that doctors use for the benefit of their patients, are lies in which there is no evil intention).

Nay, over and above this, there is the fact that sometimes we are really misled by the very natural instinct which God has given us, as in the case of the thirst of the dropsical patient. A man is moved to drink by a natural disposition that is given him by God in order to preserve his body; but one afflicted with dropsy is deceived by this natural disposition, for drink is hurtful to him. But how this is compatible with the benevolence and truthfulness of God, I have explained in the sixth Meditation.

In cases, however, that cannot be thus explained, viz. in the case of our clearest and most accurate judgments which, if false, could not be corrected by any that are clearer, or by any other natural faculty, I clearly affirm that we cannot be deceived. For, since God is the highest being He cannot be otherwise than the highest good and highest truth, and hence it is contradictory that anything should proceed from Him that positively tends towards falsity. But yet since there is nothing real in us that is not given by God (as was proved along with His existence) and we have, as well, a real faculty of recognising truth, and distinguishing it from falsehood (as the mere existence in us of true and false ideas makes manifest), unless this faculty tended towards truth, at least when properly employed (i.e. when we give assent to none but clear and distinct perceptions, for no other correct use of this faculty can be imagined), God, who has given it to us must justly be held to be a deceiver.

Thus you see that, after becoming aware of the existence of God, it is incumbent on us to imagine that he is a deceiver if we wish to cast doubt upon our clear and distinct perceptions and since we cannot imagine that he is a deceiver, we must admit them all as true and certain.

But since I here perceive that you are still entangled in the difficulties which I brought forward in the first Meditation, and which I thought I had in the succeeding Meditations removed with sufficient care, I shall here a second time expound what seems to me the only basis on which human certitude can rest.

To begin with, directly we think that we rightly perceive something, we spontaneously persuade ourselves that it is true. Further, if this conviction is so strong that we have no reason to doubt concerning that of the truth of which we have persuaded ourselves, there is nothing more to enquire about; we have here all the certainty that can reasonably be desired. What is it to us, though perchance some one feigns that that, of the truth of which we are so firmly persuaded, appears false to God or to an Angel, and hence is, absolutely speaking, false? What heed do we pay to that absolute falsity, when we by no means believe that it exists or even suspect its existence? We have assumed a conviction so strong that nothing can remove it, and this persuasion is clearly the same as perfect certitude.

But it may be doubted whether there is any such certitude, whether such firm and immutable conviction exists.

It is indeed clear that no one possesses such certainty in those cases where there is the very least confusion and obscurity in our perception; for this obscurity, of whatsoever sort it be, is sufficient to make us doubt here. In matters perceived by sense alone, however clearly, certainty does not exist, because we have often noted that error can occur in sensation, as in the instance of the thirst of the dropsical man, or when one who is jaundiced sees snow as yellow; for he sees it thus with no less clearness and distinctness than we see it as white. If, then, any certitude does exist, it remains that it must be found only in the clear perceptions of the intellect.

But of these there are some so evident and

t the same time so simple, that in their case ve never doubt about believing them true: .g. that I, while I think, exist; that what is once done cannot be undone, and other similar truths, about which clearly we can possess this certainty. For we cannot doubt them unless ve think of them; but we cannot think of them without at the same time believing them to be true, the position taken up. Hence we can never doubt them without at the same time believing them to be true; i.e. we can never doubt them.

No difficulty is caused by the objection that *we have often found that others have been deceived in matters in which they believed they had knowledge as plain as daylight.*[1] For we have never noticed that this has occurred, nor could anyone find it to occur with these persons who have sought to draw the clearness of their vision from the intellect alone, but only with those who have made either the senses or some erroneous preconception the source from which they derived that evidence.

Again there is no difficulty though some one feign that the truth appear false to God or to an Angel, because the evidence of our perception does not allow us to pay any attention to such a fiction.

There are other matters that are indeed perceived very clearly by our intellect, when we attend sufficiently closely to the reasons on which our knowledge of them depends, and hence we cannot then be in doubt about them; but since we can forget those reasons, and yet remember the conclusions deduced from them, the question is raised whether we can entertain the same firm and immutable certainty as to these conclusions, during the time that we recollect that they have been deduced from first principles that are evident; for this remembrance must be assumed in order that they may be called conclusions. My answer is that those possess it who, in virtue of their knowledge of God, are aware that the faculty of understanding given by Him must tend towards truth; but that this certainty is not shared by others. But the subject has been so clearly explained at the end of the fifth Meditation that there seems to be nothing to add here.

FIFTHLY, I marvel that you deny that *the will runs into danger if guided by a mental conception that lacks clearness and distinctness.*[1] For what can give it certainty, if what guides it has not been clearly perceived? And who-

[1]Cf. Obj. ii, p. 117.

ever, whether philosopher, theologian or merely man employing reason, fails to admit that there is the less risk of error in our actions in proportion to the greater clearness with which we understand anything before giving our assent to it; while error occurs with those who pass judgment in ignorance of its grounds? Moreover no concept is said to be obscure or confused, except for the reason that it contains something of which we are in ignorance.

Consequently your objection about *the faith one should embrace*[2] affects me no more than it does any others who have at any time cultivated the human power of reason; and in truth it has no force against anyone. For although the things are dark of which our faith is said to treat, yet the grounds on which we embrace it are not obscure, but clearer than any natural light. Nay, we must distinguish between the matter or fact to which we assent, and the formal reason that constrains our will to assent to that. For it is in this reason alone that we require clearness. And as to the matter no one has ever denied that it may be obscure, indeed obscurity itself; for when I affirm that our concepts must be divested of obscurity in order that we may give credence to them without any danger of going astray, it is concerning this very obscurity that I form a clear judgment. Further, it should be noted that the clearness or evidence by which our will can be constrained to assent, is twofold, one sort proceeding from our natural light, the other from divine grace. But though the matters be obscure with which our faith is said to deal, nevertheless this is understood to hold only of the fact or matter of which it treats, and it is not meant that the formal reason on account of which we assent to matters of faith is obscure; for, on the other hand, this formal reason consists in a certain internal light, and it is when God supernaturally fills us with this illumination that we are confident that what is proposed for our belief has been revealed by Him, Himself, and that it is clearly impossible that He should lie: a fact more certain than any natural light and often indeed more evident than it on account of the light of grace.

But certainly the sin that Turks and other infidels commit in not embracing the Christian religion is not due to their refusal to assent to obscure doctrines as being obscure, but arises either because they strive against the divine grace that moves them internally, or because

[2]Cf. Obj. ii, p. 117–118.

by other sins they make themselves unworthy
of grace. I boldly affirm that an infidel who,
destitute of all supernatural grace, and plainly
ignoring all that we Christians believe to have
been revealed by God, embraces the faith to
him obscure, impelled thereto by certain fallacious reasonings, will not be a true believer, but
will the rather commit a sin in not using his
reason properly. I believe that no orthodox
Theologian has ever had any other opinion
than this, nor will those who read my works be
able to imagine that I have not recognised this
supernatural light, since in the fourth Meditation, in which I have investigated the cause of
falsity, I expressly said that *"it inclines our
inmost thought to will without yet diminishing
our liberty."*[1]

But I should like you to remember here that,
in matters that may be embraced by the will,
I made a very strict distinction between the
practical life and the contemplation of truth.
For to the extent to which the practical life is
involved, so far am I from thinking that assent
must be given only to what is clearly seen, that
on the contrary I believe that we need not always expect to find even probable truths there;
rather it is often the case that we must choose
one out of a number of alternatives about
which we are quite ignorant, and cleave to this
none the less firmly after we have decided for
it, as long as no arguments hostile to it can be
entertained, than if it had been selected for
reasons of the highest evidence, as I have explained on p. 49 of my Discourse on Method.[2]
But where only the contemplation of truth is
involved, who has ever denied that assent must
be refused when the matter is obscure and cannot be perceived with sufficient distinctness?
But that this latter question alone is the subject of discussion in my Meditations is proved
both by the very passages in debate, and by
the fact that at the end of the first Meditation
I made a statement in express terms to the
following effect *"that I could not at this point
yield too much to distrust, since my object was
not action, but knowledge."*[3]

SIXTHLY, at the point where you criticise
the conclusion of a syllogism constructed by
me, you yourselves seem to make a blunder in
the form of the argument. In order to derive
the conclusion you desire, you should have
worded the major premise thus: *that which we*

[1]Cf. Med. IV, pp. 90–91.
[2]Cf. *Discourse*, Part III, p. 49.
[3]Med. I, p. 77.

*clearly understand to belong to the nature of any
thing, can truthfully be asserted to belong to it.
nature;* and consequently nothing but an un
profitable tautology will be contained in it
But my major premise was as follows—*tha
which we clearly understand to belong to the na
ture of anything can truly be affirmed of tha
thing.* Thus, if to be an animal belongs to the
nature of man, it can be asserted that man is
animal: if to have its three angles equal to two
right angles belongs to the nature of the triangle, it can be asserted that the triangle has
its three angles equal to two right angles : i
existence belongs to the nature of God, it can
be affirmed that God exists, etc. But my minor
premise was *yet existence does belong to the nature of God.* Whence it is evident that the conclusion must be drawn as I drew it : *hence it can
be truly affirmed of God that He exists;* but not
as you wish: *hence we can truthfully affirm that
existence belongs to the nature of God.*

Thus, in order to make use of the exception
that you append, you should have denied the
major and said: *that which we clearly understand to belong to the nature of anything, cannot
on that account be ascribed to it, unless the nature of that thing be possible, or not contradictory.* But notice, kindly, how little value this
exception has. By *possible* either you mean, as
all commonly do, whatever does not disagree
with human thought; and in this sense it is
manifest that the nature of God, as I have described it, is possible because I have assigned
nothing to it that we did not clearly and distinctly perceive ought to belong to it, and consequently it cannot be in disagreement with
our thought. Or surely you imagine some other
kind of possibility, one proceeding from the object itself, but which, unless it agrees with the
preceding variety can never be known by the
human mind. But on this account it tells quite
as much against everything else that man may
know as against the nature or existence of God.
For that which entitles us to deny that God's
nature is possible though there is no impossibility on the part of its concept, (but on the
contrary all the things included in that concept of the divine nature are so connected that
there seems to be a contradiction in saying
that any one of them does not belong to God),
will permit us to deny that it is possible for the
three angles of a triangle to be equal to two
right angles, or that he, who actually thinks,
exists. Much more right will there be to deny
that anything we apprehend by our senses is
true, and thus the whole of human knowledge

ill be overturned, though for no good reason.

To take the argument you compare with mine: *if there is no contradiction in God's existence, it is certain that He exists; but there is no contradiction; therefore,* etc., it is true materially though formally a sophism. For in the major premise the expression *"there is contradiction"* stands in relation to the concept of the cause by virtue of which God's existence is possible; but in the minor it applies merely to the concept of the divine nature and existence itself. As is evident; for if the major be denied the proof will have to go thus: *if God has not yet existed, His existence is a contradiction, because no sufficient cause for bringing Him into existence can be assigned: but,* as was assumed, *His existence is not contradictory, hence,* etc. If, on the other hand, the minor be denied, the proof must thus be stated: *that is not contradictory in the formal concept of which there is nothing involving contradiction; but in the formal concept of the divine existence or nature there is nothing involving contradiction; therefore,* etc. Now these two proofs are very diverse. For it is possible that in a certain thing nothing may be conceived that prevents the existence of that thing, though meanwhile on the side of the cause there is known to be something that opposes its coming into being.

But though we conceive God only inadequately, or, if you prefer to put it thus, *in an utterly inadequate manner,*[1] this does not prevent its being certain that His nature is possible, or not contradictory; nor does it prevent our affirming truly that we have examined it with sufficient precision (i.e. with as much as is required in order to attain to this knowledge, and in order to know that necessary existence appertains to this same Divine nature). For all contradictoriness or impossibility is constituted by our thought, which cannot join together ideas that disagree with each other; it cannot reside in anything external to the mind, because by the very fact that a thing is outside the mind it is clear that it is not contradictory, but is possible. Moreover, contradictoriness in our concepts arises merely from their obscurity and confusion; there can be none in the case of clear and distinct ideas. Hence it suffices us to understand clearly and distinctly those few things that we perceive about God, though they form a quite inadequate knowledge, and to note that among the other constituents of this idea, however inadequate it be, necessary existence is found, in order to be able to affirm

[1] Cf. Obj. ii, p. 118.

that we have examined the nature of God with sufficient precision, and to maintain that it contains no contradiction.

SEVENTHLY, in the synopsis of my Meditations[2] I stated the reason why I have said nothing about the immortality of the soul. That I have sufficiently proved its distinctness from any body, I have shown above. But I admit that I cannot refute your further contention, viz. that *the immortality of the soul does not follow from its distinctness from the body, because that does not prevent its being said that God in creating it has given the soul a nature such that its period of existence must terminate simultaneously with that of the corporeal life.*[3] For I do not presume so far as to attempt to settle by the power of human reason any of the questions that depend upon the free-will of God. Natural knowledge shows that the mind is different from the body, and that it is likewise a substance; but that the human body, in so far as it differs from other bodies, is constituted entirely by the configuration of its parts and other similar accidents, and finally that the death of the body depends wholly on some division or change of figure. But we know no argument or example such as to convince us that the death or the annihilation of a substance such as the mind is, should follow from so light a cause as is a change in figure, which is no more than a mode, and indeed not a mode of mind, but of body that is really distinct from mind. Nor indeed is there any argument or example calculated to convince us that any substance can perish. But this is sufficient to let us conclude that the mind, so far as it can be known by aid of a natural philosophy, is immortal.

But if the question, which asks whether human souls cease to exist at the same time as the bodies which God has united to them are destroyed, is one affecting the Divine power, it is for God alone to reply. And since He has revealed to us that this will not happen, there should be not even the slightest doubt remaining.

It remains for me to thank you for your courtesy and candour in deigning to bring to my notice not only the difficulties that have occurred to you, but also those that can be brought forward by Atheists and people of hostile intent. I see nothing in what you have brought forward of which I have not already

[2] Cf. Synopsis to Meditations, p. 73.
[3] Cf. Obj. ii, p. 118.

in my Meditations given a solution and ruled out of court. (For those objections *about insects bred by the sun, about the natives of Canada, the people of Nineveh, the Turks, etc.*, cannot occur to those who follow the way I have pointed out, and abstract for a time from everything due to the senses, in order to pay heed to the dictates of the pure and uncorrupted reason, and consequently I thought that I had adequately barred them out.) But though this is so, I consider that these objections of yours will aid my purpose. For I scarce expect to have any readers who will care to attend so accurately to all that I have written as to bear in memory all that has gone before, when they have come to the end; and those who do not do so will easily fall into certain perplexities, which they will either find to be satisfactorily explained in this reply of mine, or which will occasion them to examine into the truth still further.

Further, in the matter of the counsel you give me about *propounding my arguments in geometrical fashion, in order that the reader may perceive them as it were with a single glance,*[1] it is worth while setting forth here the extent to which I have followed this method and that to which I intend in future to follow it. Now there are two things that I distinguish in the geometrical mode of writing, viz. the order and the method of proof.

The order consists merely in putting forward those things first that should be known without the aid of what comes subsequently, and arranging all other matters so that their proof depends solely on what precedes them. I certainly tried to follow this order as accurately as possible in my Meditations: and it was through keeping to this that I treated of the distinction between the mind and the body, not in the second Meditation, but finally in the sixth, and deliberately and consciously omitted much, because it required an explanation of much else besides.

Further, the method of proof is two-fold, one being analytic, the other synthetic.

Analysis shows the true way by which a thing was methodically discovered and derived, as it were effect from cause, so that, if the reader care to follow it and give sufficient attention to everything, he understands the matter no less perfectly and makes it as much his own as if he had himself discovered it. But it contains nothing to incite belief in an inattentive or hostile reader; for if the very least

[1] Cf. Obj. ii, *sub fin.*

thing brought forward escapes his notice, th necessity of the conclusions is lost; and o many matters which, nevertheless, should b specially noted, it often scarcely touches, be cause they are clear to anyone who gives suf cient attention to them.

Synthesis contrariwise employs an opposit procedure, one in which the search goes as were from effect to cause (though often her the proof itself is from cause to effect to greater extent than in the former case). It doe indeed clearly demonstrate its conclusions, an it employs a long series of definitions, postu lates, axioms, theorems and problems, so tha if one of the conclusions that follow is denie it may at once be shown to be contained i what has gone before. Thus the reader, how ever hostile and obstinate, is compelled to ren der his assent. Yet this method is not so satis factory as the other and does not equally we content the eager learner, because it does no show the way in which the matter taught wa discovered.

It was this synthesis alone that the ancien Geometers employed in their writings, not be cause they were wholly ignorant of the ana lytic method, but, in my opinion, because the set so high a value on it that they wishe to keep it to themselves as an importan secret.

But I have used in my Meditations only analysis, which is the best and truest metho of teaching. On the other hand, synthesis doubtless the method you here ask me to use though it very suitably finds a place after anal ysis in the domain of geometry, nevertheless cannot so conveniently be applied to these metaphysical matters we are discussing.

For there is this difference between the two cases, viz. that the primary notions that are the presuppositions of geometrical proofs har monize with the use of our senses, and are readily granted by all. Hence, no difficulty is involved in this case, except in the proper de duction of the consequences. But this may be performed by people of all sorts, even by the inattentive, if only they remember what has gone before; and the minute subdivisions of propositions is designed for the purpose of rendering citation easy and thus making peo ple recollect even against their will.

On the contrary, nothing in metaphysics causes more trouble than the making the per ception of its primary notions clear and dis tinct. For, though in their own nature they are as intelligible as, or even more intelligible than ose the geometricians study, yet being con- adicted by the many preconceptions of our nses to which we have since our earliest years een accustomed, they cannot be perfectly pprehended except by those who give strenu- us attention and study to them, and with- raw their minds as far as possible from mat- rs corporeal. Hence if they alone were brought orward it would be easy for anyone with a eal for contradiction to deny them.

This is why my writing took the form of Meditations rather than that of Philosophical Disputations or the theorems and problems of geometer; so that hence I might by this very act testify that I had no dealings except with hose who will not shrink from joining me in iving the matter attentive care and medita- ion. For from the very fact that anyone girds imself up for an attack upon the truth, he nakes himself less capable of perceiving the ruth itself, since he withdraws his mind from he consideration of those reasons that tend to onvince him of it, in order to discover others hat have the opposite effect.

But perhaps some one will here raise the objection, that, while indeed a man ought not o seek for hostile arguments when he knows hat it is the truth that is set before him, yet, o long as this is in doubt, it is right that he hould fully explore all the arguments on either ide, in order to find out which are the stronger. According to this objection it is unfair of me o want to have the truth of my contentions dmitted before they have been fully scruti- ised, while prohibiting any consideration of hose reasonings that oppose them.

This would certainly be a just criticism if any of the matters in which I desire attention and absence of hostility in my reader were capable of withdrawing him from the consider- ation of any others in which there was the least hope of finding greater truth than in mine. But consider that in what I bring forward you find the most extreme doubt about all matters, and that there is nothing I more strongly urge than that every single thing should be most care- fully examined and that nothing should be ad- mitted but what has been rendered so clear and distinct to our scrutiny that we cannot

withhold our assent from it. Consider, too, that, on the other hand, there is nothing else from which I wish to divert the minds of my readers, save beliefs which they have never properly examined and which are derived from no sound reasoning, but from the senses alone. There- fore I hardly think that anyone will believe that there is much risk in confining his atten- tion to my statement of the case; the danger will be no more than that of turning his gaze away from it towards other things which in some measure conflict with it and only darken counsel (i.e. to the prejudices of the senses).

Hence, in the first place, I rightly require singular attention on the part of my readers and have specially selected the style of writing which I thought would best secure it and which, I am convinced, will bring my readers more profit than they would acquire if I had used the synthetic method, one which would have made them appear to have learned more than they really had. But besides this I deem it quite fair to ignore wholly and to despise as of no account the criticisms of those who refuse to accompany me in my Meditations and cling to their preconceived opinions.

But I know how difficult it will be, even for one who does attend and seriously attempt to discover the truth, to have before his mind the entire bulk of what is contained in my Medita- tions, and at the same time to have distinct knowledge of each part of the argument; and yet, in my opinion, one who is to reap the full benefit from my work must know it both as a whole and in detail. Consequently, I append here something in the synthetic style that may I hope be somewhat to my readers' profit. I should, however, like them kindly to notice that I have not cared to include here so much as comes into my Meditations, for that would have caused me to be much more prolix than in the Meditations themselves, nor shall I ex- plain in such accurate detail that which I do include; this is partly for brevity and partly to prevent anyone, believing that what is here written is sufficient, examining without ade- quate care the actual Meditations, a work from which, I am convinced, much more profit will be derived.

ARGUMENTS
DEMONSTRATING THE EXISTENCE OF GOD AND THE DISTINCTION BETWEEN SOUL AND BODY, DRAWN UP IN GEOMETRICAL FASHION

DEFINITIONS

I. *Thought* is a word that covers everything that exists in us in such a way that we are immediately conscious of it. Thus all the operations of will, intellect, imagination, and of the senses are thoughts. But I have added *immediately*, for the purpose of excluding that which is a consequence of our thought; for example, voluntary movement, which, though indeed depending on thought as on a causal principle, is yet itself not thought.

II. *Idea* is a word by which I understand the form of any thought, that form by the immediate awareness of which I am conscious of that said thought; in such a way that, when understanding what I say, I can express nothing in words, without that very fact making it certain that I possess the idea of that which these words signify. And thus it is not only images depicted in the imagination that I call ideas; nay, to such images I here decidedly refuse the title of ideas, in so far as they are pictures in the corporeal imagination, i.e. in some part of the brain. They are ideas only in so far as they constitute the form of the mind itself that is directed towards that part of the brain.

III. By the *objective reality of an idea* I mean that in respect of which the thing represented in the idea is an entity, in so far as that exists in the idea; and in the same way we can talk of objective perfection, objective device, etc. For whatever we perceive as being as it were in the objects of our ideas, exists in the ideas themselves objectively.

IV. To exist *formally* is the term applied where the same thing exists in the object of an idea in such a manner that the way in which it exists in the object is exactly like what we know of it when aware of it; it exists *eminently* when, though not indeed of identical quality, it is yet of such amount as to be able to fulfil the function of an exact counterpart.

V. Everything in which there resides immediately, as in a subject, or by means of which there exists anything that we perceive, i.e. any property, quality, or attribute, of which we have a real idea, is called a *Substance*; neither do we have any other idea of substance itself, precisely taken, than that it is a thing in which this something that we perceive o which is present objectively in some of our ideas, exists formally or eminently. For b means of our natural light we know that a rea attribute cannot be an attribute of nothing.

VI. That substance in which thought im mediately resides, I call *Mind*. I use the term "mind" here rather than "spirit," as "spirit is equivocal and is frequently applied to wha is corporeal.

VII. That substance, which is the imme diate subject of extension in space and of th accidents that presuppose extension, e.g. fig ure, situation, movement in space etc., i called *Body*. But we must postpone till late on the inquiry as to whether it is one and th same substance or whether there are two di verse substances to which the names Min and Body apply.

VIII. That substance which we understan to be supremely perfect and in which we con ceive absolutely nothing involving defect o limitation of its perfection, is called *God*.

IX. When we say that any attribute is con tained in the nature or concept of anything that is precisely the same as saying that it i true of that thing or can be affirmed of it.

X. Two substances are said to be really dis tinct, when each of them can exist apart from the other.

POSTULATES

The *First* request I press upon my readers i a recognition of the weakness of the reasons o account of which they have hitherto truste their senses, and the insecurity of all the judg ments they have based upon them. I beg them to revolve this in their minds so long and s frequently that at length they will acquire the habit of no longer reposing too much trust in them. For I deem that this is necessary in order to attain to a perception of the certainty of metaphysical truths [not dependent on the senses].

Secondly, I ask them to make an object of study of their own mind and all the attributes attaching to it, of which they find they cannot doubt, notwithstanding it be supposed that whatever they have at any time derived from their senses is false; and I beg them not to desist from attending to it, until they have acquired the habit of perceiving it distinctly and of believing that it can be more readily known than any corporeal thing.

Thirdly, I bid them carefully rehearse those propositions, intelligible *per se*, which they find they possess, e.g. *that the same thing cannot at the same time both be and not be; that nothing cannot be the efficient cause of anything*, and so forth; and thus employ in its purity, and in freedom from the interference of the senses, that clarity of understanding that nature has implanted in them, but which sensuous objects are wont to disturb and obscure. For by this means the truth of the following Axioms will easily become evident to them.

Fourthly, I postulate an examination of the ideas of those natures in which there is a complex of many coexistent attributes, such as e.g. the nature of the triangle or of the square, or of any other figure; and so, too, the nature of Mind, the nature of Body, and above all the nature of God, or of a supremely perfect entity. My readers must also notice that everything which we perceive to be contained in these natures can be truly predicated of the things themselves. For example, because the equality of its three angles to two right angles is contained in the idea of the Triangle, and divisibility is contained in the nature of Body or of extended thing (for we can conceive nothing that is extended as being so small as not to be capable of being divided in thought at least), we constantly assert that in every Triangle the angles are equal to two right angles, and that every Body is divisible.

Fifthly, I require my readers to dwell long and much in contemplation of the nature of the supremely perfect Being. Among other things they must reflect that while possible existence indeed attaches to the ideas of all other natures, in the case of the idea of God that existence is not possible but wholly necessary. For from this alone and without any train of reasoning they will learn that God exists, and it will be not less self evident to them than the fact that number two is even and number three odd, and similar truths. For there are certain truths evident to some people, without proof, that can be made intelligible to others only by a train of reasoning.

Sixthly, I ask people to go carefully over all the examples of clear and distinct perception, and likewise those that illustrate that which is obscure and confused, mentioned in my Meditations, and so accustom themselves to distinguish what is clearly known from what is obscure. For examples teach us better than rules how to do this; and I think that I have there either explained, or at least to some extent touched upon, all the instances of this subject.

Seventhly and finally, I require them, in virtue of their consciousness that falsity has never been found in matters of clear perception, while, on the contrary, amidst what is only obscurely comprehended they have never come upon the truth, except accidentally, to consider it wholly irrational to regard as doubtful matters that are perceived clearly and distinctly by the understanding in its purity, on account of mere prejudices of the senses and hypotheses in which there is an element of the unknown. By doing so they will readily admit the truth and certainty of the following axioms. Yet I admit that several of them might have been much better explained and should have been brought forward as theorems if I had wished to be more exact.

AXIOMS OR COMMON PRINCIPLES

I. Nothing exists concerning which the question may not be raised—"what is the cause of its existence?" For this question may be asked even concerning God. Not that He requires any cause in order to exist, but because in the very immensity of His being lies the cause or reason why He needs no cause in order to exist.

II. The present time has no causal dependence on the time immediately preceding it. Hence, in order to secure the continued existence of a thing, no less a cause is required than that needed to produce it at the first.

III. A thing, and likewise an actually existing perfection belonging to anything, can never have *nothing*, or a non-existent thing, as the cause of its existence.

IV. Whatever reality or perfection exists in a thing, exists formally or else eminently in its first and adequate cause.

V. Whence it follows also that the objective reality of our ideas requires a cause in which the same reality is contained not indeed objectively, but formally or else eminently. We have to note that the admission of this axiom is highly necessary for the reason that we must account for our knowledge of all things, both of sensuous and of non-sensuous objects, and do so by means of it alone. For whence, e.g., comes our knowledge that there is a heaven? Because we behold it? But that vision does not reach the mind, except in so far as it is an idea, an idea, I say, inhering in the mind itself, and not an image depicted in the phantasy. But neither can we, in virtue of this idea, assert that there is a heaven, except because every idea needs to have some really existing cause of its objective reality; and this cause we judge to be the heaven itself, and so in other cases.

VI. There are diverse degrees of reality or (the quality of being an) entity. For substance has more reality than accident or mode; and infinite substance has more than finite substance. Hence there is more objective reality in the idea of substance than in that of accident; more in the idea of an infinite than in that of a finite substance.

VII. The will of a thinking being is borne, willingly indeed and freely (for that is of the essence of will), but none the less infallibly, towards the good that it clearly knows. Hence, if it knows certain perfections that it lacks, it will immediately give them to itself if they are in its power [for it will know that it is a greater good for it to possess them, than not to possess them].

VIII. That which can effect what is greater or more difficult, can also accomplish what is less.

IX. It is a greater thing to create or conserve substance than the attributes or properties of substance; it is not, moreover, a greater thing to create that than to conserve its existence, as I have already said.

X. Existence is contained in the idea or concept of everything, because we can conceive nothing except as existent, with this difference that possible or contingent existence is contained in the concept of a limited thing, but necessary and perfect existence in the concept of a supremely perfect being.

PROPOSITION I

The knowledge of the existence of God proceeds from the mere consideration of his nature.

Demonst. To say that something is contained in the nature or concept of anything is the same as to say that it is true of that thing (Def. IX). But necessary existence is contained in the concept of God (Ax. X). Hence it is true to affirm of God that necessary existence exists in Him, or that God Himself exists.

And this is the syllogism of which I mad use above, in replying to the sixth objection Its conclusion is self-evident to those who ar free from prejudices, as was said in the fift postulate. But, because it is not easy to arriv at such clearness of mind, we seek to establis it by other methods.

PROPOSITION II

A posteriori demonstration of God's existenc from the mere fact that the idea of God exists in u

Demonst. The objective reality of any o our ideas must have a cause, in which the ver same reality is contained, not merely objec tively but formally, or else eminently (Ax. v But we do possess the idea of God (Deff. and VIII), and the objective reality of this ide is contained in us neither formally nor emi nently (Ax. VI), nor can it be contained in any thing other than God Himself (Def. VIII) Hence this idea of God, which exists in us must have God as its cause, and hence Go exists (Ax. III).

PROPOSITION III

The existence of God is proved by the fact that we who possess this idea, ourselves exist.

Demonst. If I had the power of conservin my own existence, I should have had a pro portionately greater power of giving mysel the perfections that I lack (Axx. VIII and IX) for they are only attributes of substance whereas I am a substance. But I do not hav the power of giving myself these perfections otherwise I should already possess them (Ax VII). Therefore I do not have the power o conserving myself.

Further, I cannot exist without being con served, whilst I exist, either by myself, if have that power, or by some other one who ha that power (Axx. I and II); yet, though I d exist, I have not the power of conserving my self, as has just been proved. Consequently i is another being that conserves my existence

Besides, He to whom my conservation is du contains within Himself formally or eminentl everything that is in me (Ax. IV). But there exists in me the perception of many perfec tions that I do not possess, as well as of the idea of God (Deff. II and VIII). Therefore the perception of the same perfections exists in Him by whom I am conserved.

Finally, this same Being cannot possess the perception of any perfections of which He is lacking, or which He does not possess within

¹Cf. Reply to Obj. II, p. 126.

Iimself either formally or eminently (Ax. VII). For, since He has the power of conserving me, as has been already said, He would have the power of bestowing these upon Himself, if He lacked them (Axx. VIII and IX). But He possesses the perception of all those that I lack, and which I conceive can exist in God alone, as has been lately proved. Therefore He possesses those formally or eminently within Himself, and hence is God.

COROLLARY

God has created the heaven and the earth and all that in them is. Moreover He can bring to pass whatever we clearly conceive, exactly as we conceive it.

Demonst. This all follows clearly from the previous proposition. For in it we prove that God exists, from the fact that some one must exist in whom are formally or eminently all the perfections of which we have any idea. But we possess the idea of a power so great that by Him and Him alone, in whom this power is found, must heaven and earth be created, and a power such that likewise whatever else is apprehended by me as possible must be created by Him too. Hence concurrently with God's existence we have proved all this likewise about him.

PROPOSITION IV

There is a real distinction between mind and body.

Demonst. God can effect whatever we clearly perceive just as we perceive it (preceding Corollary). But we clearly perceive the mind, i.e. a thinking substance, apart from the body, i.e. apart from any extended substance (Post. II); and *vice versa* we can (as all admit) perceive body apart from mind. Hence, at least through the instrumentality of the Divine power, mind can exist apart from body, and body apart from mind.

But now, substances that can exist apart from each other, are really distinct (Def. x). But mind and body are substances (Deff. v, VI, and VII), that can exist apart from each other (just proved). Hence there is a real distinction between mind and body.

Here it must be noted that I employed the Divine power as a means, not because any extraordinary power was needed to effect the separation of mind and body, but because, treating as I did of God alone in what precedes, there was nothing else for me to use. But our knowledge of the real distinctness of two things is unaffected by any question as to the power that disunites them.

THE THIRD SET OF OBJECTIONS[1]
WITH THE AUTHOR'S REPLIES

OBJECTION I

[In reference to Meditation I, *Concerning those matters that may be brought within the sphere of the doubtful.*][2]

It is sufficiently obvious from what is said in this Meditation, that we have no criterion for distinguishing dreaming from waking and from what the senses truly tell us; and that hence the images present to us when we are awake and using our senses are not accidents inhering in external objects, and fail to prove that such external objects do as a fact exist. And therefore, if we follow our senses without using any train of reasoning, we shall be justified in doubting whether or not anything exists. Hence we acknowledge the truth of this Meditation. But, since Plato and other ancient Philosophers have talked about this want of certitude in the matters of sense, and since the difficulty in distinguishing the waking state from dreams is a matter of common observation, I should have been glad if our author, so distinguished in the handling of modern speculations, had refrained from publishing those matters of ancient lore.

REPLY

The reasons for doubt here admitted as true by this Philosopher were propounded by me only as possessing verisimilitude, and my reason for employing them was not that I might retail them as new, but partly that I might prepare my readers' minds for the study of intellectual matters and for distinguishing them from matters corporeal, a purpose for which such arguments seem wholly necessary; in part also because I intended to reply to these very arguments in the subsequent Meditations; and partly in order to show the strength of the truths I afterwards propound, by the fact that such metaphysical doubts cannot shake them. Hence, while I have sought no praise from their rehearsal, I believe that it

[1]The French version adds "urged by a Celebrated English Philosopher," i.e. Hobbes.
[2]What I have here enclosed within brackets is a marginal title in both the Latin and the French text of the standard French edition.

was impossible for me to omit them, as impossible as it would be for a medical writer to om the description of a disease when trying t teach the method of curing it.

OBJECTION II

[In opposition to the second Meditation, *Concerning the nature of the Human Mind.*]

I am a thing that thinks; *quite correct. Fro the fact that I think, or have an image, whethe sleeping or waking, it is inferred that I am exer cising thought; for* I think and I am exercisin thought *mean the same thing. From the fact tha I am exercising thought it follows that* I am since that which thinks is not nothing. But, whe it is added, this is the mind, the spirit, th understanding, the reason, *a doubt arises. Fo it does not seem to be good reasoning to say:* I an exercising thought, *hence* I am thought; *or* am using my intellect, *hence* I am intellect *For in the same way I might say,* I am walking *hence* I am the walking. *It is hence an assump tion on the part of M. Descartes that that which understands is the same as the exercise of under standing which is an act of that which under stands, or, at least, that that which understand is the same as the understanding, which is power possessed by that which thinks. Yet al Philosophers distinguish a subject from its fac ulties and activities, i.e. from its properties an essences; for the* entity *itself is one thing, it* essence *another. Hence it is possible for a thin that thinks to be the subject of the mind, reason or understanding, and hence to be something corporeal; and the opposite of this has been as sumed, not proved. Yet this inference is the basi of the conclusion that M. Descartes seems to wist to establish.*

In the same place he says, I know that I exist the question is, who am I—the being that I know? It is certain that the knowledge of thi being thus accurately determined does no depend on those things which I do not ye know to exist.[3]

It is quite certain that the knowledge of thi proposition, I exist, *depends upon that other one,* I think, *as he has himself correctly shown us*

[3]Cf. Med. II, p. 79.

134

ut whence comes our knowledge of this propo-
tion, I think? Certainly from that fact alone,
at we can conceive no activity whatsoever apart
om its subject, e.g. we cannot think of leaping
part from that which leaps, of knowing apart
om a knower, or of thinking without a thinker.

And hence it seems to follow that that which
inks is something corporeal; for, as it appears,
e subjects of all activities can be conceived only
fter a corporeal fashion, or as in material guise,
s M. Descartes himself afterwards shows, when
e illustrates by means of wax,[1] this wax was
nderstood to be always the same thing, i.e. the
lentical matter underlying the many successive
hanges, though its colour, consistency, figure
nd other activities were altered. Moreover it is
ot by another thought that I infer that I think;
or though anyone may think that he has thought
to think so is precisely the same as remember-
ng), yet we cannot think that we are thinking,
or similarly know that we know. For this would
ntail the repetition of the question an infinite
umber of times; whence do you know, that you
now, that you know, that you know?

Hence, since the knowledge of this proposition,
exist, depends upon the knowledge of that other,
think, and the knowledge of it upon the fact
hat we cannot separate thought from a matter
hat thinks, the proper inference seems to be that
hat which thinks is material rather than imma-
erial.

REPLY

Where I have said, this is the mind, the spirit,
he intellect, or the reason, I understood by
hese names not merely faculties, but rather
vhat is endowed with the faculty of thinking;
nd this sense the two former terms commonly,
he latter frequently bear. But I used them in
his sense so expressly and in so many places
hat I cannot see what occasion there was for
ny doubt about their meaning.

Further, there is here no parity between
valking and thinking; for walking is usually
eld to refer only to that action itself, while
hinking applies now to the action, now to the
aculty of thinking, and again to that in which
he faculty exists.

Again I do not assert that that which under-
tands and the activity of understanding are
he same thing, nor indeed do I mean that the
hing that understands and the understanding
re the same, if the term understanding be
aken to refer to the faculty of understanding;
hey are identical only when the understand-

[1] Cf. p. 80.

ing means the thing itself that understands. I
admit also quite gladly that, in order to designate that thing or substance, which I wished
to strip of everything that did not belong to it,
I employed the most highly abstract terms I
could; just as, on the contrary, this Philosopher
uses terms that are as concrete as possible, e.g.
subject, matter, body, to signify that which
thinks, fearing to let it be sundered from the
body.

But I have no fear of anyone thinking that
his method of coupling diverse things together
is better adapted to the discovery of the truth
than mine, that gives the greatest possible distinctness to every single thing. But, dropping
the verbal controversy, let us look to the facts
in dispute.

A thing that thinks, he says, may be something corporeal; and the opposite of this has been
assumed; not proved. But really I did not assume the opposite, neither did I use it as a
basis for my argument; I left it wholly undetermined until Meditation VI, in which its
proof is given.

Next he quite correctly says, that we cannot
conceive any activity apart from its subject, e.g.
thought apart from that which thinks, since
that which thinks is not nothing. But, wholly
without any reason, and in opposition to the
ordinary use of language and good Logic, he
adds, hence it seems to follow that that which
thinks is something corporeal; for the subjects of
all activities are indeed understood as falling
within the sphere of substance (or even, if you
care, as wearing the guise of matter, viz. metaphysical matter), but not on that account are
they to be defined as bodies.

On the other hand both logicians and as a
rule all men are wont to say that substances
are of two kinds, spiritual and corporeal. And
all that I proved, when I took wax as an example, was that its colour, hardness, and figure
did not belong to the formal nature of the wax
itself [i.e. that we can comprehend everything
that exists necessarily in the wax, without
thinking of these]. I did not there treat either
of the formal nature of the mind, or even of
the formal nature of body.

Again it is irrelevant to say, as this Philosopher here does, that one thought cannot be
the subject of another thought. Who, except
my antagonist himself, ever imagined that it
could? But now, for a brief explanation of the
matter,—it is certain that no thought can exist
apart from a thing that thinks; no activity, no
accident can be without a substance in which

to exist. Moreover, since we do not apprehend the substance itself immediately through itself, but by means only of the fact that it is the subject of certain activities, it is highly rational, and a requirement forced on us by custom, to give diverse names to those substances that we recognize to be the subjects of clearly diverse activities or accidents, and afterwards to inquire whether those diverse names refer to one and the same or to diverse things. But there are *certain* activities, which we call *corporeal*, e.g. magnitude, figure, motion, and all those that cannot be thought of apart from extension in space; and the substance in which they exist is called *body*. It cannot be pretended that the substance that is the subject of figure is different from that which is the subject of spatial motion, etc., since all these activities agree in presupposing extension. Further, there are other activities, which we call *thinking* activities, e.g. understanding, willing, imagining, feeling, etc., which agree in falling under the description of thought, perception, or consciousness. The substance in which they reside we call a *thinking thing* or *the mind*, or any other name we care, provided only we do not confound it with corporeal substance since thinking activities have no affinity with corporeal activities, and thought, which is the common nature in which the former agree, is totally different from extension, the common term[1] for describing the latter.

But after we have formed two distinct concepts of those two substances, it is easy, from what has been said in the sixth Meditation, to determine whether they are one and the same or distinct.

OBJECTION III

What then is there distinct from my thought? What can be said to be separate from me myself?

Perchance some one will answer the question thus—I, the very self that thinks, am held to be distinct from my own thought; and, though it is not really separate from me, my thought is held to be diverse from me, just in the way (as has been said before) that leaping is distinguished from the leaper. But if M. Descartes shows that he who understands and the understanding are identical we shall lapse back into the scholastic mode of speaking. The understanding understands, the vision sees, will wills, and by exact analogy, walking, or at least the faculty of walking, will walk. Now all this is obscure, incorrect,

[1]Quotation from Med. II, p. 79.

and quite unworthy of M. Descartes' wonte clearness.

REPLY

I do not deny that I, the thinker, am dis tinct from my own thought, in the way i which a thing is distinct from its mode. Bu when I ask, *what then is there distinct from m thought*, this is to be taken to refer to th various modes of thought there recounted, no to my substance; and when I add, *what can b said to be separate from me myself*, I mean onl that these modes of thinking exist entirely i me. I cannot see on what pretext the imputa tion here of doubt and obscurity rests.

OBJECTION IV

Hence it is left for me to concede that I do no even understand by the imagination what thi wax is, but conceive it by the mind alone.[2]

There is a great difference between imagining i.e. having some idea, and conceiving with th mind, i.e. inferring, as the result of a train o reasoning, that something is, or exists. But M Descartes has not explained to us the sense i which they differ. The ancient peripatetics als have taught clearly enough that substance is no perceived by the senses, but is known as a resul of reasoning.

But what shall we now say, if reasoning chanc to be nothing more than the uniting and stringin together of names or designations by the word is It will be a consequence of this that reason give us no conclusion about the nature of things, bu only about the terms that designate them, whether indeed, or not there is a convention (arbitraril made about their meanings) according to whic we join these names together. If this be so, as i possible, reasoning will depend on names, name on the imagination, and imagination, perchance as I think, on the motion of the corporeal organs Thus mind will be nothing but the motions i certain parts of an organic body.

REPLY

I have here explained the difference between imagination and a pure mental concept, a when in my illustration I enumerated the features in wax that were given by the imag ination and those solely due to a conception o the mind. But elsewhere also I have explained how it is that one and the same thing, e.g. pentagon, is in one way an object of the under standing, in another way of the imagination [for example how in order to imagine a penta

[2]Cf. Med. II, p. 80.

on a particular mental act is required which ves us this figure (i.e. its five sides and the ace they enclose) which we dispense with holly in our conception]. Moreover, in reaning we unite not names but the things signified by the names; and I marvel that the opposite can occur to anyone. For who doubts hether a Frenchman and a German are able reason in exactly the same way about the me things, though they yet conceive the ords in an entirely diverse way? And has not y opponent condemned himself in talking of nventions arbitrarily made about the meanings of words? For, if he admits that words gnify anything, why will he not allow our asonings to refer to this something that is gnified, rather than to the words alone? But, ally, it will be as correct to infer that earth heaven or anything else that is desired, as to nclude that mind is motion [for there are no ther two things in the world between which here is not as much agreement as there is beveen motion and spirit, which are of two enrely different natures].

OBJECTION V

n reference to the third Meditation—conrning God—some of these (thoughts of man) re, so to speak, images of things, and to these lone is the title "idea" properly applied; exmples are my thought of a man, or of a Chiera, of Heavens, of an Angel, or [even] of God.[1]

When I think of a man, I recognize an idea, r image, with figure and colour as its constitents; and concerning this I can raise the queson whether or not it is the likeness of a man. So is also when I think of the heavens. When I ink of the chimera, I recognize an idea or nage, being able at the same time to doubt hether or not it is the likeness of an animal, hich, though it does not exist, may yet exist or as at some other time existed.

But, when one thinks of an Angel, what is oticed in the mind is now the image of a flame, ow that of a fair winged child, and this, I may e sure, has no likeness to an Angel, and hence s not the idea of an Angel. But believing that reated beings exist that are the ministers of God, nvisible and immaterial, we give the name of ngel to this object of belief, this supposed being, hough the idea used in imagining an Angel is, evertheless, constructed out of the ideas of visible hings.

It is the same way with the most holy name of God; we have no image, no idea corresponding to

[1] Cf. Med. III, p. 82.

it. Hence we are forbidden to worship God in the form of an image, lest we should think we could conceive Him who is inconceivable.

Hence it appears that we have no idea of God. But just as one born blind who has frequently been brought close to a fire and has felt himself growing warm, recognizes that there is something which made him warm, and, if he hears it called fire, concludes that fire exists, though he has no acquaintance with its shape or colour, and has no idea of fire nor image that he can discover in his mind; so a man, recognizing that there must be some cause of his images and ideas, and another previous cause of this cause, and so on continuously, is finally carried on to a conclusion, or to the supposition of some eternal cause, which, never having begun to be, can have no cause prior to it: and hence he necessarily concludes that something eternal exists. But nevertheless he has no idea that he can assert to be that of this eternal being, and he merely gives a name to the object of his faith or reasoning and calls it God.

Since now it is from this position, viz. that there is an idea of God in our soul, that M. Descartes proceeds to prove the theorem that God (an all-powerful, all-wise Being, the creator of the world) exists, he should have explained this idea of God better, and he should have deduced from it not only God's existence, but also the creation of the world.

REPLY

Here the meaning assigned to the term idea is merely that of images depicted in the corporeal imagination; and, that being agreed on, it is easy for my critic to prove that there is no proper idea of Angel or of God. But I have, everywhere, from time to time, and principally in this place, shown that I take the term idea to stand for whatever the mind directly perceives; and so when I will or when I fear, since at the same time I perceive that I will and fear, that very volition and apprehension are ranked among my ideas. I employed this term because it was the term currently used by Philosophers for the forms of perception of the Divine mind, though we can discover no imagery in God; besides I had no other more suitable term. But I think I have sufficiently well explained what the idea of God is for those who care to follow my meaning; those who prefer to wrest my words from the sense I give them, I can never satisfy. The objection that here follows, relative to the creation of the world, is plainly irrelevant [for I proved that God exists, before asking whether there is a world created by him, and from the mere fact that God, i.e. a supremely perfect being exists, it follows that if there be a world it must have been created by him].

OBJECTION VI

But other (*thoughts*) possess other forms as well. For example, in willing, fearing, affirming, denying, though I always perceive something as the subject of my thought, yet in my thought I embrace something more than the similitude of that thing; and, of the thoughts of this kind, some are called volitions or affections, and others judgments.[1]

When a man wills or fears, he has indeed an image of the thing he fears or of the action he wills; but no explanation is given of what is further embraced in the thought of him who wills or fears. If indeed fearing be thinking, I fail to see how it can be anything other than the thought of the thing feared. In what respect does the fear produced by the onrush of a lion differ from the idea of the lion as it rushes on us, together with its effect (produced by such an idea in the heart), which impels the fearful man towards that animal motion we call flight? Now this motion of flight is not thought; whence we are left to infer that in fearing there is no thinking save that which consists in the representation of the thing feared. The same account holds true of volition.

Further you do not have affirmation and negation without words and names; consequently brute creatures cannot affirm or deny, not even in thought, and hence are likewise unable to judge. Yet a man and a beast may have similar thoughts. For, when we assert that a man runs, our thought does not differ from that which a dog has when it sees its master running. Hence neither affirmation nor negation add anything to the bare thought, unless that increment be our thinking that the names of which the affirmation consists are the names of the same thing in [the mind of] him who affirms. But this does not mean that anything more is contained in our thought than the representation of the thing, but merely that that representation is there twice over.

REPLY

It is self-evident that seeing a lion and fearing it at the same time is different from merely seeing it. So, too, it is one thing to see a man running, another thing to affirm to oneself that one sees it, an act that needs no language. I can see nothing here that needs an answer.

[1]Cf. p. 82.

OBJECTION VII

It remains for me to examine in what way have received that idea from God. I hav neither derived it from the senses; nor has ever come to me contrary to my expectatio as the ideas of sensible things are wont to d when these very things present themselves t the external organs of sense or seem to do s Neither also has it been constructed as a fi titious idea by me, for I can take nothin from it and am quite unable to add to i Hence the conclusion is left that it is innate i me, just as the idea of my own self is innat in me.[2]

If there is no idea of God (now it has not bee proved that it exists), as seems to be the case, th whole of this argument collapses. Further (if it my body that is being considered) the idea of m own self proceeds [principally] from sight; but (it is a question of the soul) there is no idea of th soul. We only infer by means of the reason th there is something internal in the human bod which imparts to it its animal motion, and b means of which it feels and moves; and thi whatever it be, we name the soul, without employ ing any idea.

REPLY

If there is an idea of God (as it is manifes there is), the whole of this objection collapse When it is said further that we have no idea the soul but that we arrive at it by an inferenc of reason, that is the same as saying that ther is no image of the soul depicted in the imagina tion, but that that which I have called its ide does, nevertheless, exist.

OBJECTION VIII

But the other idea of the sun is derived fron astronomical reasonings, i.e. is elicited fron certain notions that are innate in me.[3]

It seems that at one and the same time the ide of the sun must be single whether it is beheld b the eyes, or is given by our intelligence as man times larger than it appears. For this latte thought is not an idea of the sun, but an inferenc by argument that the idea of the sun would b many times larger if we viewed the sun from much nearer distance.

But at different times the ideas of the sun ma differ, e.g. when one looks at it with the naked ey and through a telescope. But astronomical rea sonings do not increase or decrease the idea o

[2]Cf. Med. III, p. 88.
[3]Cf. Med. III, pp. 83–84.

e sun; rather they show that the sensible idea misleading.

REPLY

Here, too, what is said not to be an idea of
ιe sun, but is, nevertheless, described, is ex-
tly what I call an idea. [But as long as my
itic refuses to come to terms with me about
ιe meaning of words, none of his objections
ιn be other than frivolous.]

OBJECTION IX

or without doubt those ideas, which reveal
ιbstance to me, are something greater, and,
ι to speak, contain within them more objec-
ve reality than those which represent only
ιodes or accidents. And again, that by means
ι which I apprehend a supreme God who
ι eternal, infinite, omniscient, all-powerful,
ιd the creator of all else there is besides,
ιssuredly possesses more objective reality
ιan those ideas that reveal to us finite
ιbstances.[1]

*I have frequently remarked above that there is
ι idea either of God or of the soul; I now add
ιat there is no idea of substance. For substance
ιhe substance that is a material, subject to acci-
ιnts and changes) is perceived and demon-
ιrated by the reason alone, without yet being con-
ιived by us, or furnishing us with any idea. If
ιat is true, how can it be maintained that the
ιeas which reveal substance to me are anything
ιeater or possess more objective reality than
ιose revealing accidents to us? Further I pray
ι. Descartes to investigate the meaning of more
ιality. Does reality admit of more and less? Or,
ι he thinks that one thing can be more a thing
ιan another, let him see how he is to explain it
ι our intelligence with the clearness called for in
ιemonstration, and such as he himself has at
ιher times employed.*

REPLY

I have frequently remarked that I give the
ιame idea to that with which reason makes us
ιcquainted just as I also do to anything else
ιhat is in any way perceived by us. I have like-
ιise explained how reality admits of more and
ιss: viz. in the way in which substance is
ιreater than mode; and if there be real qualities or incomplete substances, they are things
ι a greater extent than modes are, but less
ιhan complete substances. Finally, if there be
ι infinite and independent substance, it is
ιore a thing than a substance that is finite

[1]Cf. Med. III, p. 84.

and dependent. Now all this is quite self-evident [and so needs no further explanation].

OBJECTION X

Hence there remains alone the idea of God,
concerning which we must consider whether it
is not something that is capable of proceeding
from me myself. By the name God I understand a substance that is infinite [eternal, im-
mutable], independent, all-knowing, all-powerful, and by which both I myself and everything else, if anything else does exist, have been
created. Now all these characteristics are such
that, the more diligently I attend to them, the
less do they appear capable of proceeding from
me alone; hence, from what has been already
said, we must conclude that God necessarily
exists.[2]

*When I consider the attributes of God, in order
to gather thence the idea of God, and see whether
there is anything contained in it that cannot proceed from ourselves, I find, unless I am mistaken,
that what we assign in thought to the name of God
neither proceeds from ourselves nor needs to come
from any other source than external objects. For
by the word God I mean a substance, i.e. I understand that God exists (not by means of an idea
but by reasoning). This substance is infinite
(i.e. I can neither conceive nor imagine its
boundaries or extreme parts, without imagining
further parts beyond them): whence it follows
that corresponding to the term infinite there arises
an idea not of the Divine infinity, but of my own
bounds or limitations. It is also independent,
i.e. I have no conception of a cause from which
God originates; whence it is evident that I have
no idea corresponding to the term independent,
save the memory of my own ideas with their commencement at divers times and their consequent
dependence.*

*Wherefore to say that God is independent, is
merely to say that God is to be reckoned among
the number of those things, of the origin of which
we have no image. Similarly to say that God is
infinite, is identical with saying that He is among
those objects of the limits of which we have no
conception. Thus any idea of God is ruled out;
for what sort of idea is that which has neither
origin nor termination?*

*Take the term all-knowing. Here I ask: what
idea does M. Descartes employ in apprehending
the intellectual activity of God?*

*All-powerful. So too, what is the idea by which
we apprehend power, which is relative to that
which lies in the future, i.e. does not exist? I cer-*

[2]Cf. Med. III, p. 86.

tainly understand what power is by means of an image, or memory of past events, inferring it in this wise—Thus did He, hence thus was He able to do; therefore as long as the same agent exists He will be able to act so again, i.e. He has the power of acting. Now these are all ideas that can arise from external objects.

Creator of everything that exists. Of creation some image can be constructed by me out of the objects I behold, e.g. the birth of a human being or its growth from something small as a point to the size and figure it now possesses. We have no other idea than this corresponding to the term creator. But in order to prove creation it is not enough to be able to imagine the creation of the world. Hence, although it had been demonstrated that an infinite, independent, all-powerful, etc. *being exists, nevertheless it does not follow that a creator exists. Unless anyone thinks that it is correct to infer, from the fact that there is a being which we believe to have created everything, that hence the world was at some time created by him.*

Further, when M. Descartes says that the idea of God and that of the soul are innate in us, I should like to know whether the minds of those who are in a profound and dreamless sleep yet think. If not, they have at that time no ideas. Whence no idea is innate, for what is innate is always present.

REPLY

Nothing that we attribute to God can come from external objects as a copy proceeds from its exemplar, because in God there is nothing similar to what is found in external things, i.e. in corporeal objects. But whatever is unlike them in our thought [of God], must come manifestly not from them, but from the cause of that diversity existing in our thought [of God].

Further I ask how my critic derives the intellectual comprehension of God from external things. But I can easily explain the idea which I have of it, by saying that by idea I mean whatever is the form of any perception. For does anyone who understands something not perceive that he does so? and hence does he not possess that form or idea of mental action? It is by extending this indefinitely that we form the idea of the intellectual activity of God; similarly also with God's other attributes.

But, since we have employed the idea of God existing in us for the purpose of proving His existence, and such mighty power is comprised in this idea, that we comprehend that it

would be contradictory, if God exists, for any thing besides Him to exist, unless it were created by Him; it clearly follows, from the fac that His existence has been demonstrated that it has been also proved that the whol world, or whatever things other than God exis have been created by Him.

Finally when I say that an idea is innate i us [or imprinted in our souls by nature], I d not mean that it is always present to us. Th would make no idea innate. I mean merel that we possess the faculty of summoning u this idea.

OBJECTION XI

The whole force of the argument lies in this— that I know I could not exist, and possess th nature I have, that nature which puts me i possession of the idea of God, unless God di really exist, the God, I repeat, the idea whom is found in me.[1]

Since, then, it has not been proved that u possess an idea of God, and the Christian religio obliges us to believe that God is inconceivable which amounts, in my opinion, to saying that u have no idea of Him, it follows that no proof His existence has been effected, much less of H work of creation.

REPLY

When it is said that we cannot conceive God to conceive means to comprehend adequately For the rest, I am tired of repeating how it that we can have an idea of God. There nothing in these objections that invalidate my demonstrations.

OBJECTION XII

[Directed against the fourth Meditation, *Con cerning the true and the false.*]

And thus I am quite sure that error, in so fa as it is error, is nothing real, but merely defect Hence in order to go astray, it is not necessar for me to have a faculty specially assigned t me by God for this purpose.[2]

It is true that ignorance is merely a defect, an that we stand in need of no special positive fac ulty in order to be ignorant; but about error th case is not so clear. For it appears that stones an inanimate things are unable to err solely becaus they have no faculty of reasoning, or imagining Hence it is a very direct inference that, in order t err, a faculty of reasoning, or at least of imagina tion is required; now both of these are positiv

[1]Cf. Med. III, p. 88.
[2]Cf. Med. IV, p. 89.

culties with which all beings that err, and only
ings that err, have been endowed.

Further, M. Descartes says—I perceive that
ey (viz. my mistakes) depend upon the co-
eration of two causes, viz. my faculty of
gnition, and my faculty of choice, or the
eedom of my will.[1] *But this seems to be contra-
ctory to what went before. And we must note
re also that the freedom of the will has been
sumed without proof, and in opposition to the
inion of the Calvinists.*

REPLY

Although in order to err the faculty of reaning (or rather of judging, or affirming and
nying) is required, because error is a lack of
is power it does not hence follow that this
fect is anything real, just as it does not fol-
w that blindness is anything real, although
ones are not said to be blind merely because
ey are incapable of vision. I marvel that in
ese objections I have as yet found nothing
at is properly argued out. Further I made no
ssumption concerning freedom which is not a
atter of universal experience; our natural
ght makes this most evident and I cannot
ake out why it is said to be contradictory to
evious statements.

But though there are many who, looking to
e Divine foreordination, cannot conceive
w that is compatible with liberty on our
rt, nevertheless no one, when he considers
mself alone, fails to experience the fact that
will and to be free are the same thing [or
ther that there is no difference between what
voluntary and what is free]. But this is no
ace for examining other people's[2] opinions
out this matter.

OBJECTION XIII

or example, whilst I, during these days,
ught to discuss whether anything at all
isted, and noted that, from the very fact
at I raised this question, it was an evident
nsequence that I myself existed, I could not
deed refrain from judging that what I under-
ood so clearly was true; this was not owing
compulsion by some external force, but be-
use the consequence of the great mental
umination was a strong inclination of the
ill, and I believed the above truth the more
illingly and freely, the less indifferent I was
wards it.[3]

[1]Cf. Med. iv, p. 90.
[2]That is, Calvinists.
[3]Cf. Med. iv, p. 91.

This term, great mental illumination, *is met-
aphorical, and consequently is not adapted to the
purposes of argument. Moreover everyone who is
free from doubt claims to possess a similar illumination, and in his will there is the same inclination to believe that of which he does not doubt, as
in that of one who truly knows. Hence while this
illumination may be the cause that makes a man
obstinately defend or hold some opinion, it is not
the cause of his knowing it to be true.*

*Further, not only to know a thing to be true,
but also to believe it or give assent to it, have
nothing to do with the will. For, what is proved by
valid argument or is recounted as credible, is believed by us whether we will or no. It is true that
affirming and denying, maintaining or refuting
propositions, are acts of will; but it does not
follow on that account that internal assent depends upon the will.*

*Therefore the demonstration of the truth that
follows is not adequate*—and it is in this misuse
of our free-will, that this privation consists
that constitutes the form of error.[4]

REPLY

It does not at all matter whether or not the
term *great illumination* is proper to argument,
so long as it is serviceable for explanation, as
in fact it is. For no one can be unaware that by
mental illumination is meant clearness of cognition, which perhaps is not possessed by
everyone who thinks he possesses it. But
this does not prevent it from being very
different from a bigoted opinion, to the formation of which there goes no perceptual
evidence.

Moreover when it is here said that when a
thing is clearly perceived we give our assent
whether we will or no, that is the same as saying that we desire what we clearly know to be
good whether willing or unwilling; for the word
unwilling finds no entrance in such circumstances, implying as it does that we will and
do not will the same thing.

OBJECTION XIV

[To the fifth Meditation, *On the essence of material things.*]

As, for example, when I imagine a triangle,
though perhaps such a figure does not exist at
all outside my thought, or never has existed, it
has nevertheless a determinate nature, or
essence, or immutable and eternal form, which
is not a fiction of my construction, and does
not depend on my mind, as is evident from the

[4]Cf. Med. iv, pp. 91–92.

fact that various properties of that triangle may be demonstrated.[1]

If the triangle exists nowhere at all, I do not understand how it can have any nature; for that which exists nowhere does not exist. Hence it has no existence or nature. The triangle in the mind comes from the triangle we have seen, or from one imaginatively constructed out of triangles we have beheld. Now when we have once called the thing (from which we think that the idea of triangle originates) by the name triangle, although the triangle itself perishes, yet the name remains. In the same way if, in our thought, we have once conceived that the angles of a triangle are together all equal to two right angles, and have given this other name to the triangle—possessed of three angles equal to two right angles—although there were no angle at all in existence, yet the name would remain; and the truth of this proposition will be of eternal duration—a triangle is possessed of three angles equal to two right angles. But the nature of the triangle will not be of eternal duration, if it should chance that triangle perished.

In like manner the proposition, man is animal, *will be eternally true, because the names it employs are eternal, but if the human race were to perish there would no longer be a human nature.*

Whence it is evident that essence in so far as it is distinguished from existence is nothing else than a union of names by means of the verb is. *And thus essence without existence is a fiction of our mind. And it appears that as the image of a man in the mind is to the man, so is essence to existence; or that the essence of Socrates bears to his existence the relation that this proposition,* Socrates is a man, *to this other,* Socrates is or exists. *Now the proposition,* Socrates is a man, *means, when Socrates does not exist, merely the connection of its terms; and* is, *or* to be, *has underlying it the image of the unity of a thing designated by two names.*

REPLY

The distinction between essence and existence is known to all; and all that is here said about eternal names in place of concepts or ideas of an eternal truth, has been already satisfactorily refuted.

OBJECTION XV

[Directed against the sixth Meditation—*Concerning the existence of material things.*]

For since God has evidently given me no

[1]Cf. Med. v, p. 93.

faculty by which to know this (*whether or n our ideas proceed from bodies*), but on the co trary has given me a strong propensity towar the belief that they do proceed from corpore things, I fail to see how it could be made o that He is not a deceiver, if our ideas pr ceeded from some other source than corpore things. Consequently corporeal objects mu exist.[2]

It is the common belief that no fault is co mitted by medical men who deceive sick peop for their health's sake, nor by parents who mi lead their children for their good; and that the e in deception lies not in the falsity of what is sai but in the bad intent of those who practise it. M Descartes must therefore look to this propositio God can in no case deceive us, taken universall and see whether it is true; for if it is not true, th universally taken, the conclusion, hence co poreal things exist, does not follow.

REPLY

For the security of my conclusion we do n need to assume that we can never be deceive (for I have gladly admitted that we are ofte deceived), but that we are not deceived whe that error of ours would argue an intentio to deceive on the part of God, an intentio it is contradictory to impute to Him. On more this is bad reasoning on my critic part.

FINAL OBJECTION

For now I perceive how great the difference between the two (i.e. between waking an dreaming) from the fact that our dreams a never conjoined by our memory [with eac other and] with the whole of the rest of ou life's action [as happens with the things whic occur in waking moments].[3]

I ask whether it is really the case that one, wh dreams he doubts whether he dreams or no, unable to dream that his dream is connected wi the idea of a long series of past events. If he ca those things which to the dreamer appear to be th actions of his past life may be regarded as tr just as though he had been awake. Besides, sinc as M. Descartes himself asserts, all certitude an truth in knowledge depend alone upon our know ing the true God, either it will be impossible f an Atheist to infer from the memory of his pr vious life that he wakes, or it will be possible f a man to know that he is awake, apart fro knowledge of the true God.

[2]Cf. Med. VI, p. 99.
[3]Cf. Med. VI, p. 103.

REPLY

One who dreams cannot effect a real connection between what he dreams and the ideas of past events, though he can dream that he does connect them. For who denies that in his sleep a man may be deceived? But yet when he has awakened he will easily detect his error.

But an Atheist is able to infer from the memory of his past life that he is awake; still he cannot know that this sign is sufficient to give him the certainty that he is not in error, unless he knows that it has been created by a God who does not deceive.

THE FOURTH SET OF OBJECTIONS[1]

LETTER TO A MAN OF NOTE[2]

Sir,

The favour you have done me[3] I acknowledge, though I note that you expect a return for it. Kind though your action was, yet to let me share in the enjoyment of reading that most acute work only on condition I should disclose what I think of it, was to demand a requital, and surely a heavy one. Truly a hard condition, compliance with which the desire to acquaint myself with a fine piece of work has wrung from me, but one against which I should gladly protest if an exception could be claimed for one who "has committed a deed through the urgency of pleasure," and added to the concessions recognized by the Praetor of old, who excused acts "done under the influence of violence or fear."

What would you have? It is not my estimate of the author that you look for; you already know how much I appreciate the force of his genius and his distinguished learning. Likewise you are not unaware of the troublesome matters that at present take up my time and, if you have too exalted an opinion of me, it does not follow that I am unaware of my own inadequacy. And yet what you submit to me for examination demands both intellectual powers of no ordinary nature and above all a mind set free from care, in order that it may, by its disengagement from all external turmoil, have leisure for self-contemplation; and as you see, this is impossible without intent meditation and complete mental self-absorption. Nevertheless, if it is your bidding, I obey. The blame for my shortcomings will fall upon you, who compel me to take up my pen. But though Philosophy could arrogate to itself the whole of this work, yet since its author with great modesty of his own accord appears before the tribunal of the Theologians, I shall here play a double rôle. I shall first propound the chief objections that, in my opinion, philosophers can adduce in connection with the outstanding problems as to the nature of the human mind and [the existence] of God; secondly, I shall unfold certain

difficulties which a theologian can detect in th whole work.

The Nature of the Human Mind

The first thing that here occurs to me to b worthy of remark is that our distinguished autho should have taken as the foundation of the whol of his philosophy the doctrine laid down [befor him] by St. Augustine, a man of most penetratin intellect and of much note, not only in the spher of theology, but in that of philosophy as well. I "De Libero arbitrio," Book II, chap. 3., Alipiu when disputing with Euodius, setting about proof of the existence of God, says: Firstly, t start with the things that are most evident, ask you whether you yourself exist, or are yo apprehensive lest in [answering] this questio you are in error, when in any case, if you di not exist you could never be in error? Simila to this are the words of our author: But perhap there exists an all-powerful being, extremel cunning, who deceives me, who intentionall at all times deceives me. There is then n doubt that I exist, if he deceives me. But let u proceed, and, to pursue something more relevar to our purpose, let us discover how, from thi principle, we can demonstrate the fact that ou mind is [distinct and] separate from our body.

I am able to doubt whether I have a body, nay whether any body exists at all; yet I have no righ to doubt whether I am, or exist, so long as I doul or think.

Hence I, who doubt and think, am not a body otherwise in entertaining doubt concerning body I should doubt about myself.

Nay, even though I obstinately maintain tha no body at all exists, the position taken up is un shaken: I am something, hence I am not a body

This is really very acute, but someone coul bring up the objection which our author urge against himself; the fact that I doubt about bod or deny that body exists, does not bring it abou that no body exists. Hence perhaps it happen that these very things which I suppose to b nothing, because they are unknown to me, ye do not in truth differ from that self which I d know. I know nothing about it, he says, I d not dispute this matter; [I can judge onl

[1]By M. Arnauld, Doctor in Theology.
[2]Letter of the said M. Arnauld written to the Rev. Father Mersenne.
[3]In sending to him the *Meditations* of Descartes.

out things that are known to me.] I know
at I exist; I enquire who I, the known self,
n; it is quite certain that the knowledge of
is self thus precisely taken, does not depend
a those things of the existence of which I am
ot yet acquainted.[1]

But he admits in consonance with the argu-
ent laid down in the Method, that the proof has
roceeded only so far as to exclude from the na-
re of the human mind whatsoever is corporeal,
ot from the point of view of the ultimate
uth, but relatively only to his consciousness
he meaning being that nothing at all was
nown to him to belong to his essential nature,
yond the fact that he was a thinking being).[2]
ence it is evident from this reply that the argu-
ent is exactly where it was, and that therefore
e problem which he promises to solve remains
tirely untouched. The problem is: how it fol-
ws, from the fact that one is unaware that
nything else [(except the fact of being a think-
g thing)] belongs to one's essence, that
thing else really belongs to one's essence.
ut, not to conceal my dullness, I have been un-
le to discover in the whole of Meditation II
here he has shown this. Yet so far as I can con-
cture, he attempts this proof in Meditation VI,
cause he believes that it is dependent on the
ossession of the clear knowledge of God to which
. Meditation II he has not yet attained. Here is
s proof:

Because I know that all the things I clearly
nd distinctly understand can be created by
od just as I conceive them to exist, it is suf-
cient for me to be able to comprehend one
ing clearly and distinctly apart from an-
her, in order to be sure that the one is di-
rse from the other, because at least God can
olate them; and it does not matter by what
wer that isolation is effected, in order that I
ay be obliged to think them different from
e another. Hence because, on the one hand,
have a clear and distinct idea of myself in so
r as I am a thinking being, and not extended,
d on the other hand, a distinct idea of body,
so far as it is only an extended thing, not one
at thinks, it is certain that I am in reality
stinct from my body and can exist apart
om it.[3]

Here we must halt awhile; for on these few
ords the whole of the difficulty seems to hinge.
Firstly, in order to be true, the major premise
that syllogism must be held to refer to the ade-

quate notion of a thing [(i.e. the notion which
comprises everything which may be known of the
thing)], not to any notion, even a clear and distinct one. For M. Descartes in his reply to his
theological critic[4] admits that it is sufficient to
have a* formal *distinction and that a real one is
not required,* to cause one thing to be conceived
separately and as distinct from another by the
abstracting action of the mind when it conceives a thing inadequately.[5] *Whence in the same
passage he draws the conclusion which he adds:*
—But still I understand in a complete manner
what body is [(i.e. I conceive body as a complete thing)], merely by thinking that it is extended, has figure, can move, etc., and by denying of it everything which belongs to the
nature of mind. Conversely also, I understand
that mind is something complete, which
doubts, knows, wishes, etc., although I deny
that anything belongs to it which is contained
in the idea of body. Hence there is a real distinction between mind and body.[6]

*But, if anyone casts doubt on the (minor)
premise here assumed, and contends that it is
merely that your conception is inadequate when
you conceive yourself [(i.e. your mind)] as being
a thinking but not an extended thing, and similarly when you conceive yourself [(i.e. your body)]
as being an extended and not a thinking thing,
we must look to its proof in the previous part of
the argument. For I do not reckon a matter like
this to be so clear as to warrant us in assuming it
as an indemonstrable first principle and in dis-
pensing with proof.*

*Now as to the first part of the statement, name-
ly,* that you completely understand what body
is, merely by thinking that it is extended, has
figure, can move, etc., and by denying of it
everything which belongs to the nature of
mind, *this is of little value. For one who contends
that the human mind is corporeal does not on that
account believe that every body is a mind. Hence
body would be so related to mind as genus is to
species. But the genus can be conceived without
the species, even although one deny of it whatsoever is proper and peculiar to the species; whence
comes the common dictum of Logicians, "the
negation of the species does not negate the genus."
Thus, I can conceive figure without conceiving
any of the attributes proper to the circle. Therefore, we must prove over and above this that the
mind can be completely and adequately conceived
apart from the body.*

[1]Cf. Med. II, p. 79.
[2]Cf. Preface, pp. 71–72.
[3]Cf. Med. VI, pp. 98–99.

[4]Reply to Objections I.
[5]Reply to Obj. I, p. 114.
[6]Cf. p. 115.

I can discover no passage in the whole work capable of effecting this proof, save the proposition laid down at the outset:—I can deny that there is any body or that any extended thing exists, but yet it is certain that I exist, so long as I make this denial, or think; hence I am a thing that thinks and not a body, and the body does not pertain to the knowledge of myself.

But the only result that I can see this to give, is that a certain knowledge of myself be obtained without a knowledge of the body. But it is not yet quite clear to me that this knowledge is complete and adequate, so as to make me sure that I am not in error in excluding the body from my essence. I shall explain by means of an example:—

Let us assume that a certain man is quite sure that the angle in a semicircle is a right angle and that hence the triangle made by this angle and the diameter is right-angled; but suppose he questions and has not yet firmly apprehended, nay, let us imagine that, misled by some fallacy, he denies that the square on its base is equal to the squares on the sides of the right-angled triangle. Now, according to our author's reasoning, he will see himself confirmed in his false belief. For, he will argue, while I clearly and distinctly perceive that this triangle is right-angled, I yet doubt whether the square on its base is equal to the square on its sides. Hence the equality of the square on the base to those on the sides does not belong to its essence.

Further, even though I deny that the square on its base is equal to the squares on its sides, I yet remain certain that it is right-angled, and the knowledge that one of its angles is a right angle remains clear and distinct in my mind; and this remaining so, not God himself could cause it not to be right-angled.

Hence, that of which I doubt, or the removal of which leaves me with the idea still, cannot belong to its essence.

Besides, since I know that all things I clearly and distinctly understand can be created by God just as I conceive them to exist, it is sufficient for me, in order to be sure that one thing is distinct from another, to be able to comprehend the one clearly and distinctly apart from the other, because it can be isolated by God. *But I clearly and distinctly understand that this triangle is right-angled, without comprehending that the square on its base is equal to the squares on its sides. Hence God at least can create a right-angled triangle, the square on the base of which is not equal to the squares on its sides.*

I do not see what reply can here be made, except that the man in question does not perceive clearly that the triangle is right-angled. But whence do I obtain any perception of the nature of my mind clearer than that which he has of the nature of the triangle? He is as sure that the triangle in a semicircle has one right angle (which is the notion of a right-angled triangle) as I am in believing that I exist because I think.

Hence, just as a man errs in not believing the the equality of the square on its base to the square on its sides belongs to the nature of that triangle which he clearly and distinctly knows to be right angled, so why am I not perhaps in the wrong in thinking that nothing else belongs to my nature which I clearly and distinctly know to be something that thinks, except the fact that I am the thinking being? Perhaps it also belongs to my essence to be something extended.

And certainly, some one will say it is no marvel if, in deducing my existence from the fact that I think, the idea that I form of the self, which in this way an object of thought, represents me to my mind as merely a thinking being, since it has been derived from my thinking alone. And hence from this idea, no argument can be drawn to prove that nothing more belongs to my essence than what the idea contains.

In addition, it can be maintained that the argument proves too much and conducts us to the Platonic doctrine (refuted nevertheless by our author) that nothing corporeal belongs to the essence of man, who is hence entirely spirit while his body is merely the vehicle of spirit, whence follows the definition of man as a spirit that makes use of a body.

But if you reply that body is not absolutely excluded from my essence, but merely in so far precisely as I am a thinking being, the fear seems likely to arise that some one will entertain a suspicion that the knowledge of myself, in so far as I am a thinking being, is not the knowledge of any thing fully and adequately conceived, but known only inadequately and by a certain intellectual abstraction.

Hence, just as geometers conceive of a line as length without breadth, and of a surface as length and breadth together without depth, although there is no length apart from breadth, no breadth without depth, some one may perhaps doubt whether everything that thinks is not likewise something extended; a thing in which, nevertheless, over and above the attributes common to other extended things, e.g. the possession of figure, motion, etc., is found this unique faculty of thinking. Whence it follows that while by an intellectual abstraction, it can be apprehended by means of this character alone and unaided as a thing that thinks, it is quite possible that in reality corporeal attributes are compatible with a thinking being; just as quantity can be mentally conceived by means of length alone, while it is possible that in reality breadth and depth go along with length in every quantity.

The difficulty is increased by the fact that this power of thinking seems to be attached to corporeal organs, since we can believe it to be asleep in infants, extinguished in the case of lunatics; and this is an objection strongly urged by those impious men whose aim is the soul's slaughter.

Thus far I have dealt with the distinction between mind and body in real existence. But since M. Descartes has undertaken to prove the immortality of souls, it is right to ask whether that follows evidently from this separateness of existence. According to the principles of the vulgar philosophy that conclusion by no means can be drawn, for the common opinion is that the souls of animals are distinct from their bodies, but nevertheless perish with them.

I had carried my criticism to this point and was intending to show how, according to our author's principles, which I believed I had gathered from his method of philosophical enquiry, the immortality of the soul could be easily inferred from its distinctness from the body, when a new work,[1] a little treatise bearing the fruit of our author's reflections, came into my hands; and this work not only throws much light on the whole, but in connection with this passage brings forward exactly what I was to adduce with a view to the solution of the above problem.

For in the matter of the souls of animals, in other passages he lets us know sufficiently well that they have no soul, but merely a body disposed in a certain manner and so compounded of various organs that all the actions we see them perform can be effected in it and by its means.

But I fear that this belief will not carry persuasion into men's minds, unless supported by the strongest evidence. For at the first blush, it seems incredible that there is any way by which, without any intervention of the soul, it can come to pass that the light reflected from the body of a wolf into the eyes of a sheep should excite into motion the minute fibres of the optic nerves and by the penetration of this movement to the brain, discharge the animal spirits into the nerves in the manner requisite to make the sheep run off.

[1] The Synopsis of the *Meditations* (cf. pp. 72–74) sent by Descartes to Mersenne, Dec. 31, 1640, fifty days after the *Meditations*.

One thing which I here shall add is, that I wholly approve of M. Descartes' teaching, relative to the distinction between the imagination and thought or intelligence, and of the greater certainty attaching to that which we grasp by the reason than to what is perceived by the senses. For long ago, I learned from St. Augustine, De Animae Quantitate, ch. 15, *that we must give no countenance to those who would persuade us that what we discern by the intellect is less certain than what comes by the bodily eyes, vexed as they ever are with rheum. Whence also, in* Solil, bk. 1, ch. 4, *he says that he has found that in the matter of geometry the senses are like a ship. For, he says, when they had brought me to the destination I was making for, after I had quitted them and had begun on firm land to repeat all they had taught me, for a long time my footsteps tottered. Wherefore, I believe that one could more readily learn navigation on land than understand geometry by the use of the senses (alone) although they seem to give some help to us when first we begin to learn.*

Concerning God.

The first proof of the existence of God, that unfolded by our author in Meditation III, falls into two parts. The former is, that God exists, if the idea of Him exists in me; the second shows that I, in possessing this idea, can derive my existence only from God.

In the earlier part there is only one thing that does not secure my approval, and that is, that though M. Descartes had asserted that strictly speaking falsity was to be found in judgments only, he yet admits shortly afterwards that ideas may be false, not formally indeed, but materially. Now this seems to me to disagree with his first principles.

But I fear I may not be able to explain my thought with sufficient lucidity in a matter of such obscurity; an example will make it clearer. If, he says, cold is merely privation of heat, the idea of cold which represents it as though it were something positive, is false materially.[2]

Nay, if cold is merely the privation of heat, there can be no idea of cold which represents it as a positive thing, and our author here confuses idea with judgment.

For what is the idea of cold? It is cold itself in so far as it is objectively in the understanding. But if cold is a privation, it cannot exist objectively in the mind by the instrumentality of an idea, the objective existence of which is a positive entity. Hence, if cold is merely privation, there

[2] Cf. Med. III, p. 85.

can be no positive idea of it, and hence no idea materially false.

This is confirmed by the argument by which M. Descartes proves that the idea of an infinite being cannot be otherwise than true; for, although it can be pretended that such a being does not exist, it cannot be pretended that the idea of it displays nothing real to me.

Obviously, the same may be affirmed of every positive idea. For, although it can be imagined that the cold, which I believe to be represented by a positive idea, is not positive, yet I cannot pretend that a positive idea represents to me nothing real and positive; since a positive idea is not so styled by reason of the existence it has as a mode of thinking (in that sense all ideas would be positive), but from the objective existence which it contains and displays to our intellect. Hence, though that idea is possibly not the idea of cold, it cannot be a false idea.

But, you rejoin, its falsity consists in the very fact that it is not the idea of cold. Nay, it is your judgment that is false, if you deem it to be the idea of cold; but it, itself, is in itself most true. Similarly, the idea of God should not be called false, even materially, though some one transfer it to something which is not God, as idolaters have done.

Finally, what does that idea of cold, which you say is false materially, represent to your mind? Privation? In that case it is true. A positive entity? Then it is not the idea of cold. Further, what is the cause of that positive objective being, which makes you conclude that that idea is materially false? It is, *you reply*, myself, in so far as I participate in non-existence. *Therefore the positive objective existence of a certain idea may proceed from nothing, a conclusion which upsets the most important fundamental principles of M. Descartes.*

But let us proceed now to the second part of the argument where he asks, whether I myself, who possess the idea of an infinite being, can proceed from anything other than an infinite being, and especially whether I can be self-caused. *M. Descartes contends that I cannot be self-caused owing to the fact that,* if I myself had given myself existence, I should have given myself also all those perfections, the ideas of which I perceive in myself.[1] *But his theological critic acutely replies:*—"self-originated" should be taken not in a positive but in a negative sense which identifies it with "not derived from anything else."[2] But now, *he says,* if any-

thing is self-derived, i.e. not due to something else, how can I prove that it embraces all things and is infinite? *I shall pay no heed to the reply that, if it is self-derived it will have given itself everything; for it does not depend on itself as on a cause, nor did it anticipate its existence and so at a prior time choose what it should afterwards be.*[3]

To refute this argument, M. Descartes contends that existence per se should be taken not negatively but positively,[4] *especially in so far as it refers to God. So that God* in a certain sense stands to Himself in the same way as an efficient cause does to its effect. *Now this seems to me to be a strong assertion and to be untrue.*

Hence, while in part I agree with M. Descartes, I partly differ from him. I admit that I cannot be self-derived except in a positive sense, but I deny that the same should be said of God. Nay, I think that it is a manifest contradiction that anything should be positively self-derived in the sense of proceeding from itself as a cause. Hence I come to the same conclusion as our author, but by quite another route, as I shall here set forth:—

In order to be self-derived, I should have to proceed from myself positively and in the sense of coming from myself as a cause: hence I cannot be self-derived.

To prove the major premise of this syllogism, I rely on the grounds of my antagonist drawn from the doctrine that, since the various parts of time can all be dissevered from each other, from the fact that I exist it does not follow that I shall in future exist, unless some cause, as it were, re-creates me at every single moment.[5]

In the matter of the minor, [viz. that I cannot proceed from myself positively and as it were from a cause] I deem it to be so evident to the light of nature that its proof would be vain, a proving of the known by the less known. Indeed, our author seems to have acknowledged its truth, since he has not dared openly to deny it. Consider, I pray, those words in his reply to his theological opponent.

I have not, *so run his words,* said that it is impossible for anything to be its own efficient cause: for, although that statement is manifestly true when the meaning of efficient cause is restricted to those causes that are prior to their effects or different from them, yet it does not seem necessary to confine the term to this meaning in the present investigation, for the

---

[1]Cf. Med. III, pp. 86, 87.
[2]Obj. I, p. 105.

[3]Obj. I, p. 105.
[4]Reply to Obj. I, p. 111.
[5]Med. III, p. 87.

ght of nature does not require that the notion
an efficient cause should compel it to be
ior to its effect.[1]

*This is excellent so far as the first part goes,
t why has he omitted the second? Has he not
mitted to add that the same light of nature does
ot require that the notion of an efficient cause
ould compel it to be different from its effect,
ly because the light of nature does not permit
m to assert that?*

*Now surely, if every effect depends upon a
ause and receives its existence from a cause, is it
ot clear that the same thing cannot depend upon
self, cannot receive its existence from itself?*

*Further, every cause is the cause of an effect,
ery effect the effect of a cause; hence there is a
utual relation between cause and effect. But a
utual relation can be possessed only by two
ings.*

*Again, it is merely absurd to conceive of a
ing as receiving existence and yet possessing
at very existence before the time at which we
onceive that it received it; but that would be the
sult if we attributed the notions of cause and
fect to the same thing in respect of itself. What
the notion of cause? The conferring of exis-
nce. What is the notion of effect? The receiving
existence. Moreover, the notion of cause is
rior in nature to that of effect.*

*But we cannot conceive a thing by means of the
otion of cause as giving existence, unless we con-
ive it as possessing existence. Hence we should
ve to conceive that a thing possessed existence
fore conceiving it to receive existence; yet when
nything receives, the receiving precedes the pos-
ssing.*

*This reasoning may be otherwise couched thus:
—no one gives what he does not possess; hence no
ne can give himself existence unless he already
ossess it, but, if he already possess it, why
ould he give it to himself?*

Finally, M. Descartes asserts that the light of
ature lets us know that the distinction be-
ween creation and conservation is solely a
istinction of the reason.[2] *But this self-same
ght of nature lets us know that nothing can
reate itself, and that hence nothing can conserve
self.*

*But to pass down from the general thesis to the
articular one concerning God, it will now, in my
pinion, be more evident that God can be self-
erived not in the positive sense, but only neg-
tively, i.e., in the sense of not proceeding from
nything else.*

*And firstly, it clearly follows from the premise
that M. Descartes advances in order to prove that
if a body exists per se, it must be per se in the
positive sense. For, he says, the several parts
of time are not derived from one another, and
hence, though that body be supposed to have
existed up to the present time per se, i.e. without any cause, that will not suffice to make it
exist in future, unless there be some power
contained in it which, as it were, re-creates it
continually.[3]*

*But, far from this argument being applicable
to the case of a supremely perfect and infinite
being, the opposite rather can clearly be inferred,
and for opposite reasons. For the idea of an infinite being contains within it that of infinite
duration, i.e. a duration bounded by no limits,
and hence indivisible, unchanging, and existing
all at once; one in which it is only erroneously
and by reason of the imperfection of our intellect
that the conception of prior and posterior can be
applied.*

*Whence it manifestly follows that the infinite
Being cannot be thought to exist even for one moment without our conceiving at the same time
that it always has and always will exist (a fact
that our author himself elsewhere proves); hence
it is idle to ask why it continues in existence.*

*Nay, as Augustine frequently shows (an
author whom none since the time of the sacred
writers have surpassed in the worthiness and
sublimity of what they say concerning God), in
God there is no past or future, but always present
existence [which clearly shows that we cannot
without absurdity ask why God continues to
exist].*

*Further, God cannot be thought to be self-de-
rived in the positive sense, as if He originally
brought Himself into existence, for in that case
He would have existed before He existed. He is
said to be self-derived merely because, as our
author frequently declares, as a fact He maintains Himself in existence.*

*Yet, in the case of an infinite being, conserva-
tion must be denied no less than creation. For
what, pray, is conservation but the continual reproduction of some things? Hence, all conservation implies some initial production. Another
reason is that the very term continuation, just
like that of conservation, implies something of
potentiality. But an infinite being is pure actuality without any potentiality.*

*Hence, let us conclude that God cannot be con-
ceived to be self-originated in the positive sense,
except by reason of the imperfection of our in-*

[1]Cf. Reply to Obj. I, p. 110.
[2]Med. III, p. 87.
[3]Reply to Obj. I, p. 111.

tellect, that thinks of God as existing after the fashion of created things. This conclusion will be rendered more evident by the following argument.

We seek to discover the efficient cause of a thing only with respect to its existence, not with respect to its essence. For example, if I see a triangle, I may enquire about the efficient cause that brought this triangle into existence, but it will be absurd for me to ask what is the efficient cause by reason of which the triangle has its three angles equal to two right angles. The correct reply to such a question would not be to assign an efficient cause, but to say merely, "because such is the nature of the triangle." This is why the mathematicians, not concerning themselves with the existence of their objects, do not employ efficient and final causes in their proofs. But existence, nay, if you like, continuance in existence, is involved in the essence of an infinite being, no less than the equality of its three angles to two right angles is involved in that of a triangle. Therefore, just as the reply to the question why the triangle has its three angles equal to two right angles should not be in terms of an efficient cause, but the reason assigned should be the eternal and immutable nature of the triangle; so when we ask why God exists, or continues in existence, we must seek for no efficient cause, either within God or without Him, and for nothing similar to an efficient cause (for my contention touches the thing not the name for it): we should state as our reason this alone, "because such is the nature of a supremely perfect being."

Hence in opposition to what M. Descartes says: the light of nature tells us that nothing exists about which the question, why it exists, cannot be asked, whether we enquire for its efficient cause, or, if it does not possess one, demand why it does not have one,[1] I reply that the answer to the question why God exists should not be in terms of efficient causality, but merely "because He is God," i.e. an infinite Being. And when we are asked for the efficient cause of God, we must reply that He needs no efficient cause. And if our interrogator plies us with the question why no efficient cause is required, we must answer "because He is an infinite Being, and in such a case existence and essence are identical"; for only those things, the actual existence of which can be distinguished from their essence, require an efficient cause.

Therefore the doctrine collapses that is contained in the immediately subsequent passage, which here I quote:—Hence if I did not believe that anything could in some way be related to

[1]Cf; p. 110.

itself exactly as an efficient cause is related t its effect, so far should I be from concludin that any first cause existed, that, on the con trary, I should once more ask for the cause c that which had been called first, and so shoul never arrive at the first cause of all.

By no means; if I thought that I must enquir for the efficient cause of anything whatsoever, c for something analogous to the efficient cause, should seek for a cause of that given thing wha soever it was, different from it, because to me it i most manifest that nothing can in any way be s related to itself as is an efficient cause towards it effect.

I think I am right in bringing this to the notic of M. Descartes in order that he may give carefu and attentive consideration to these matters, be cause I am sure that theologians, almost withou exception, must take offence at the doctrine tha God is self-originated in a positive sense, an proceeds, as it were, from a cause.

The only remaining scruple I have is an un certainty as to how a circular reasoning is to b avoided in saying: the only secure reason w have for believing that what we clearly an distinctly perceive is true, is the fact that Go exists.[2]

But we can be sure that God exists, only be cause we clearly and evidently perceive tha therefore prior to being certain that God exists, u should be certain that whatever we clearly an evidently perceive is true.

Something which had escaped me I now ad viz., that I believe that M. Descartes is in erro though he affirms it as certain, when he makes th statement that nothing can exist in him, in s far as he is a thinking being, of which he is no conscious.[3] By the self in so far as it is a think ing being, nothing more is meant than the mind in so far as it is distinct from the body. But wh does not see that much may be in the mind, of th existence of which the mind is not conscious? Th mind of an infant in its mother's womb possesse the faculty of thought without being conscious c it. There are innumerable similar instances the I pass by in silence.

Matters Likely to Cause Difficulty to Theologian

Here, in order to curtail a discussion that ha already grown wearisome, I prefer to aim brevity and to indicate my points rather than debate them in detail.

First I am apprehensive lest offence may b caused by our author's free method of specula

[2]Med. v, p. 95.
[3]Med. III, p. 87 (paraphrased).

tion, which renders everything doubtful. He does, in fact, admit in the Method[1] that this style of thinking is dangerous for a mediocre intelligence; I confess, however, that in the Synopsis this cause of alarm is somewhat mitigated.

Nevertheless, this Meditation should appear equipped with a slight preface in which it is pointed out that the doubt entertained about these matters is not really serious, and that the intention is merely to set on one side for a little those matters which give rise to the very least and most hyperbolical[2] doubt, as our author in another place phrases it, in order to discover something so firm and steadfast that no one, however perverse in his opinions, can have any doubt about it. Consequently, when it comes to the place at which these words appear:—that since I was ignorant of the author of my being,[3] I deem that it would be better to write instead:—I feigned that I was ignorant.

In Meditation IV, which treats of the True and the False, I greatly desire, for reasons that it would be tedious to recount, that he would explain, and that, either in this Meditation itself or in the Synopsis, two particular matters.

The first is why in enquiring into the cause of error, while treating copiously of the mistakes made in distinguishing between the true and the false, he does not also treat of the error that occurs in the pursuit of good and evil.

For, since that former enquiry sufficiently promotes our author's design and object, and what is here said of the source of error may arouse the gravest objections, if it is extended to the pursuit of good and evil, prudence, to my mind, requires, nay, the correct order of exposition, about which our author is so careful, demands the omission of certain irrelevancies that may give rise to contention, lest the reader quarrel over inessentials and be prevented from perceiving what is important.

The second point I wish to bring to our author's notice is that he, when he maintains that we should assent only to what we clearly and distinctly know, deals only with such matters as pertain to the sciences and fall in within the province of theory, and not with those things that concern our faith, and the conduct of life; and this is why he censures the rashness of the opinionative [i.e. of those who think they understand matters of which they have no knowledge], but not the just persuasion of those who accept with caution what they believe.

For there are three things in the soul of man, as St. Augustine, in *De Utilit. Credendi, ch.* 15, with great sagacity reminds us, that seem to stand in close proximity to each other [and appear to be virtually the same thing], but which are well worthy of being distinguished: viz. knowing, believing, opining.

He knows, whose comprehension of anything is based on sure grounds. *He believes* who, influenced by some strong authority, thinks something to be true without having sure grounds on which to base his comprehension. *The opinionative man is* he who thinks he understands that of which he has no knowledge.

To be opinionative is moreover a grave fault, and that for two reasons: firstly, he who is convinced that he already knows is thereby debarred from being able to learn, if indeed the matter is one that can be comprehended: further, his presumption is in itself a sign of an ill-disposed mind.

Hence, what we know we owe to reason; what we believe, to *authority;* while our mere opinions are born of *error.* All this has been said in order that we may understand how, while clinging to our faith in matters we do not as yet comprehend, we are exempt from the charge of opinionative presumption.

For those who say that we should believe nothing that we do not know to be true, stand in dread only of the imputation of opinionativeness, for it is disgraceful and calamitous to fall into this error. But anyone who after serious consideration sees the great difference between one who fancies that he knows [what he does not know] and one who, understanding that he does not understand a certain matter, yet believes it owing to the influence of some authority, will at once feel himself freed from the peril of error, the charge of an inhuman lack of assurance and the imputation of arrogance.

A little later,[4] St. Augustine in ch. 12, adds: many arguments could be brought to show that nothing at all in human society will remain secure, if we make up our minds to believe nothing that we cannot regard as fully comprehended. *So far St. Augustine.*

M. Descartes can well enough judge how important it is to point out this distinction; but the many people who in these days are prone to impiety may make a bad use of his words, for the purpose of shattering the faith.

---

[1] Cf. *Method*, pp. 45, 46.
[2] Med. VI, p. 98.
[3] Cf. p. 103.

[4] This must be wrong, as the previous citation refers to ch. 15.

But the chief ground of offence to theologians that I anticipate is that, according to M. Descartes' doctrines, the teachings of the Church relative to the sacred mysteries of the Eucharist cannot remain unaffected and intact.

For it is an article of our faith that the substance of the bread passes out of the bread of the Eucharist, and that only its accidents remain. Now these are extension, figure, colour, odour, savour and the other sensible qualities.

But M. Descartes recognizes no sense-qualities, but only certain motions of the minute bodies that surround us, by means of which we perceive the different impressions to which we afterwards give the names of colour, savour, and odour. Hence there remain figure, extension and mobility. But M. Descartes denies that those powers can be comprehended apart from the substance in which they inhere and that hence they

cannot exist apart from it; and this is repeated in the reply to his theological critic.[1]

Likewise he acknowledges only a formal[2] distinction between these affections and substance, but a formal difference seems not to allow things so distinguished to be sundered from each other even by the Divine power.

I am confident that M. Descartes, whose piety is so well known to us, will weigh this with diligence and attention and will judge that he must take the greatest pains, lest, while meaning to maintain the cause of God against the attacks of the impious, he appears to have at all endangered that faith, which God's own authority has founded, and by the grace of which he hopes to obtain that eternal life, of which he has undertaken to convince the world.

[1]Cf. above, p. 114.
[2]Cf. above, p. 114.

REPLY TO
THE FOURTH SET OF OBJECTIONS

I COULD not possibly desire any one to examine my writings who could show more insight and courtesy than the opponent whose criticisms you have forwarded. The gentleness with which he has treated me lets me see that he is well-disposed both to me and to the cause I maintain. Yet so accurately has he reconnoitred the positions he attacks, so thoroughly has he scrutinized them, that I am confident that nothing in the rest of the field has escaped his keen gaze. Further, so acutely has he contested the points from which he has decided to withhold his approval, that I have no apprehension lest it be thought that complaisance has made him conceal anything. The result is, that instead of my being disturbed by his objections, my feeling is rather one of gratification at not meeting with opposition in a greater number of places.

REPLY TO THE FIRST PART

The Nature of the Human Mind

I shall not take up time here by thanking my distinguished critic for bringing to my aid the authority of St. Augustine, and for expounding my arguments in a way which betokened a fear that others might not deem them strong enough.

I come first of all to the passage where my

demonstration commences of how, *from the fact that I knew that nothing belongs to my essence (i.e. to the essence of the mind alone) beyond the fact that I am a thinking being, it follows that in actual truth nothing else does belong to it.*[1] That was, to be sure, the place where I proved that God exists, that God, to wit, who can accomplish whatever I clearly and distinctly know to be possible.

For although much exists in me of which I am not yet conscious (for example in that passage I did, as a fact, assume that I was not yet aware that my mind had the power of moving the body, and that it was substantially united with it), yet since that which I do perceive is adequate to allow of my existing with it as my sole possession, I am certain that God could have created me without putting me in possession of those other attributes of which I am unaware. Hence it was that those additional attributes were judged not to belong to the essence of the mind.

For in my opinion nothing without which a thing can still exist is comprised in its essence, and although mind belongs to the essence of man, to be united to a human body is in the proper sense no part of the essence of mind.

I must also explain what my meaning was

[1]Obj. IV, p. 145.

n saying *that a real distinction cannot be in-ferred from the fact that one thing is conceived apart from another by means of the abstracting action of the mind when it conceives a thing in-adequately, but only from the fact that each of them is comprehended apart from the other in a complete manner, or as a complete thing.*[1]

For I do not think that an adequate knowl-edge of the thing is, in this case, required, as M. Arnauld assumes; nay, we have here the difference that if any knowledge is to be *ade-quate*, it must embrace all the properties which exist in the thing known. Hence, there is none but God who knows that He has adequate cognition of all things.

But a created mind actually possessed of adequate knowledge in many cases can never know that this is in its possession unless God give it a private revelation of the fact. But in order to have adequate knowledge of anything, it requires merely to have in itself a power of knowing what is adequate for that thing. And this can easily occur. But in order to know that he has this knowledge, or that God has put nothing in the thing in question over and above what he has knowledge of, a man's power of knowing would need to equal the in-finite capacity of God—an obvious absurdity.

But now, in order to apprehend a real dis-tinction between two things, we do not need to have adequate knowledge of them, unless we can be aware that it is adequate; but this being unattainable, as has just been said, it follows that an adequate knowledge is not required.

Hence, when I said that *to apprehend one thing apart from another by means of an act of abstraction on the part of the intellect when its conceptions are inadequate, is not sufficient,* I did not think that it would be thence inferred that an *adequate* cognition was required for the purpose of inferring a real distinction, but merely a cognition which we had not, by an intellectual abstraction, rendered *inadequate*.

It is one thing for a cognition to be entirely adequate, of which fact we could never be sure unless it were revealed by God; it is quite another for our knowledge to have sufficient adequacy to let us see that we have not ren-dered it inadequate by an intellectual abstrac-tion.

Similarly, when I said that a thing must be comprehended in a *complete* manner, I meant not that the intellectual operation must be adequate, but merely that we must have a

[1]Cf. p. 145.

knowledge of the thing sufficient to let us know that it is *complete*.

I thought this had been sufficiently plain from previous and subsequent passages alike; for, shortly before I had distinguished *incom-plete* from *complete* entities and had said that *each single thing* that has a really distinct ex-istence, *must be understood to be an entity in itself and diverse from every other.*[2]

But afterwards, preserving the same mean-ing as when I said that *I understood in a com-plete manner what body is,* I immediately added that *I understood also that mind is something complete;*[3] I thus took "to understand in a complete manner" and "to understand that a thing is something complete" in one and the same sense.

But at this point a question may justly be raised as to what I understand by *a complete thing,* and how I prove that, *understanding two things to be complete in isolation from one an-other is sufficient to establish a real distinction between them.*

Therefore, to the first query I reply that by *a complete thing* I mean merely a substance en-dowed with those forms or attributes which suffice to let me recognise that it is a substance.

For we do not have immediate cognition of substances, as has been elsewhere noted; rather from the mere fact that we perceive certain forms or attributes which must inhere in some-thing in order to have existence, we name the thing in which they exist a *substance.*

But if, afterwards, we desired to strip that substance of those attributes by which we ap-prehend it, we should utterly destroy our knowledge of it; and thus, while we might in-deed apply words to it, they would not be words of the meaning of which we had a clear and distinct perception.

I do not ignore the fact that certain sub-stances are popularly called *incomplete sub-stances.* But if they are said to be incomplete, because they cannot exist by themselves [and unsupported by other things], I confess it seems to me to be a contradiction for them to be substances; i.e. for them to be things sub-sisting by themselves and at the same time incomplete, i.e. not capable of subsisting by themselves. But it is true that in another sense they can be called incomplete sub-stances; viz. in a sense which allows that, in so far as they are substances, they have no lack of completeness, and merely asserts that

[2]Cf. Reply to Objections i, p. 114.
[3]Cf. p. 115.

they are incomplete in so far as they are referred to some other substance, in unison with which they form a single self-subsistent thing [distinct from everything else].

Thus, the hand is an incomplete substance, when taken in relation with the body, of which it is a part; but, regarded alone, it is a complete substance. Quite in the same way mind and body are incomplete substances viewed in relation to the man who is the unity which together they form; but, taken alone, they are complete.

For, as to be extended, divisible, possessed of figure, etc. are the forms or attributes by which I recognise that substance called *body;* so, to be a knowing, willing, doubting being, etc. are the forms by which I recognize the substance called *mind;* and I know that thinking substance is a complete thing, no less than that which is extended.

But it can nowise be maintained that, in the words of M. Arnauld, *body is related to mind as genus is to species;*[1] for, although the genus can be apprehended apart from this or that specific difference, the species can by no means be thought apart from the genus.

For, to illustrate, we easily apprehend figure, without thinking at all of a circle (although that mental act is not distinct unless we refer to some specific figure, and it does not give us a complete thing, unless it embraces the nature of the body); but we are cognisant of no specific difference belonging to the circle, unless at the same time we think of figure.

But mind can be perceived clearly and distinctly, or sufficiently so to let it be considered to be a complete thing without any of those forms or attributes by which we recognize that body is a substance, as I think I have sufficiently shown in the Second Meditation; and body is understood distinctly and as a complete thing apart from the attributes attaching to the mind.

Nevertheless M. Arnauld here urges that *although a certain notion of myself can be obtained without a knowledge of the body, it yet does not thence result that this knowledge is complete and adequate, so as to make me sure that I am not in error in excluding the body from my essence.*[2] He elucidates his meaning by taking as an illustration the triangle inscribed in a semicircle, which we can clearly and distinctly know to be right-angled, though we do not know, or even deny, that the square on its

base is equal to the squares on its sides: and nevertheless we cannot thence infer that we can have a [right-angled] triangle, the square on the base of which is not equal to the squares on the sides.

But, as to this illustration, the example differs in many respects from the case in hand.

For firstly, although perhaps a triangle may be taken in the concrete as a substance possessing triangular shape, certainly the property of having the square on the base equal to the squares on the sides is not a substance; so too, neither can either of these two things be understood to be a complete thing in the sense in which *Mind and Body* are; indeed, they cannot be called *things* in the sense in which I used the word when I said *that I might comprehend one thing* (i.e. one complete thing) *apart from the other, etc.*[3] as is evident from the succeeding words—*Besides, I discover in myself faculties, etc.*[4] For I did not assert these faculties to be *things*, but distinguished them accurately from things or substances.

Secondly, although we can clearly and distinctly understand that the triangle in the semicircle is right-angled, without noting that the square on its base equals those on its sides, we yet cannot clearly apprehend a triangle in which the square on the base is equal to those on the sides, without at the same time perceiving that it is right-angled. But we do clearly and distinctly perceive mind without body and body without mind.

Thirdly, although our concept of the triangle inscribed in the semicircle may be such as not to comprise the equality between the square on its base and those on its sides, it cannot be such that no ratio between the square on the base and those on the sides is held to prevail in the triangle in question; and hence, so long as we remain ignorant of what the ratio is, nothing can be denied of the triangle other than what we clearly know not to belong to it: but to know this in the case of the equality of the ratio is entirely impossible. Now, on the other hand, there is nothing included in the concept of body that belongs to the mind; and nothing in that of mind that belongs to the body.

Therefore, though I said that *it was sufficient to be able to apprehend one thing clearly and distinctly apart from another, etc.*, we cannot go on to complete the argument thus:—*but I clearly*

[1] Obj. IV, p. 145.
[2] Cf. above, p. 146.

[3] Cf. Med. VI, p. 97.
[4] Cf. p. 97.

nd *distinctly apprehend this triangle*,[1] *etc.*
irstly, because the ratio between the square
n the base and those on the sides is not a
omplete thing. Secondly, because that ratio
s clearly understood only in the case of the
ight-angled triangle. Thirdly, because the
riangle itself cannot be distinctly appre-
ended if the ratio between the squares on the
ase and on the sides is denied.

But now I must explain how it is that, *from
he mere fact that I apprehend one substance
learly and distinctly apart from another, I am
ure that the one excludes the other*.[2]

Really the notion of *substance* is just this—
hat which can exist by itself, without the aid
f any other substance. No one who perceives
wo substances by means of two diverse
oncepts ever doubts that they are really
istinct.

Consequently, if I had not been in search of
a certitude greater than the vulgar, I should
ave been satisfied with showing in the Second
Meditation that *Mind* was apprehended as a
hing that subsists, although nothing belong-
ng to the body be ascribed to it, and conversely that *Body* was understood to be some-
hing subsistent without anything being attributed to it that pertains to the mind. And I
should have added nothing more in order to
prove that there was a real distinction between
mind and body: because commonly we judge
that all things stand to each other in respect to
their actual relations in the same way as they
are related in our consciousness. But, since one
of those hyperbolical doubts adduced in the
First Meditation went so far as to prevent me
from being sure of this very fact (viz. that
things are in their true nature exactly as we
perceive them to be), so long as I supposed
that I had no knowledge of the author of my
being, all that I have said about God and
about truth in the Third, Fourth and Fifth
Meditations serves to further the conclusion
as to the real distinction between *mind* and
body, which is finally completed in Meditation
VI.

My opponent, however, says, *I apprehend
the triangle inscribed in the semicircle without
knowing that the square on its base is equal to the
squares on the sides*.[3] True, that triangle may
indeed be apprehended although there is no
thought of the ratio prevailing between the
squares on the base and sides; but we can

never think that this ratio must be denied. It
is quite otherwise in the case of the mind
where, not only do we understand that it
exists apart from the body, but also that all
the attributes of body may be denied of it; for
reciprocal exclusion of one another belongs to
the nature of substances.

There is no conflict between my theory and
the point M. Arnauld next brings up, *that it is
no marvel if, in deducing my existence from the
fact that I think, the idea I thus form of myself
represents me merely as a thinking being*.[4] For,
similarly when I examine the nature of body
I find nothing at all in it that savours of
thought; and there is no better proof of the
distinctness of two things than if, when we
study each separately, we find nothing in the
one that does not differ from what we find in
the other.

Further, I fail to see how this argument
proves too much.[5] For, in order to prove that
one thing is really distinct from another,
nothing less can be said, than that the divine
power is able to separate one from the other.
I thought I took sufficient care to prevent anyone thence inferring that *man was* merely *a
spirit that makes use of a body;* for in this very
Sixth Meditation in which I have dealt with
the distinction between mind and body, I have
at the same time proved that mind was substantially united with body; and I employed
arguments, the efficacy of which in establishing this proof I cannot remember to have seen
in any other case surpassed. Likewise, just as
one who said that a man's arm was a substance
really distinct from the rest of his body, would
not therefore deny that it belonged to the
nature of the complete man, and as in saying
that the arm belongs to the nature of the complete man no suspicion is raised that it cannot
subsist by itself, so I think that I have neither
proved too much in showing that mind can
exist apart from body, nor yet too little in
saying that it is substantially united to the
body, because that substantial union does not
prevent the formation of a clear and distinct
concept of the mind alone as of a complete
thing. Hence this differs greatly from the concept of a superficies or of a line, which cannot
be apprehended as complete things unless, in
addition to length and breadth, depth be
ascribed to them.

Finally, the fact that *the power of thinking is
asleep in infants and in maniacs*—though not

[1]Cf.Obj. IV, p. 146.
[2]Cf. Med. VI, p. 97.
[3]Cf. Obj. IV, p. 146.

[4]Cf. p. 146.
[5]Cf. p. 146.

indeed *extinct*,[1] yet troubled—should not make us believe that it is conjoined with the corporeal organs in such a way as to be incapable of existing apart from them. The fact that our thought is often in our experience impeded by them, does not allow us to infer that it is produced by them; for this there is not even the slightest proof.

I do not, however, deny that the close conjunction between soul and body of which our senses constantly give us experience, is the cause of our not perceiving their real distinction without attentive reflection. But, in my judgment, those who frequently revolve in their thought what was said in the Second Meditation, will easily persuade themselves that mind is distinguished from body not by a mere fiction or intellectual abstraction, but is known as a distinct thing because it is really distinct.

I make no reply to M. Arnauld's additions[2] about the immortality of the soul, because they are not in conflict with my doctrine. As for the matter of the souls of brutes,[3] this is not the place to treat the subject, and I could not, without taking in the whole of Physics, say more about them than in the explanations given in the fifth part of the *Discourse on Method*.[4] Yet, not to pass over the matter altogether, I should point out that the chief thing to note appears to me to be that motion is impossible alike in our own bodies and in those of the brutes, unless all the organs or instruments are present, by means of which it can be effected in a machine. Hence in our very selves the mind [(or the soul)] by no means moves the external limbs immediately, but merely directs the subtle fluid styled the animal spirits, that passes from the heart through the brain towards the muscles, and determines this fluid to perform definite motions, these animal spirits being in their own nature capable of being utilized with equal facility for many distinct actions. But the greater part of our motions do not depend on the mind at all. Such are the beating of the heart, the digestion of our food, nutrition, respiration when we are asleep, and even walking, singing and similar acts when we are awake, if performed without the mind attending to them. When a man in falling thrusts out his hand to save his head he does that without his reason counselling him

so to act, but merely because the sight of the impending fall penetrating to his brain, drive the animal spirits into the nerves in the manner necessary for this motion, and for producing it without the mind's desiring it, an as though it were the working of a machine. Now, when we experience this as a fact in ourselves, why should we marvel so greatly *if the light reflected from the body of a wolf into the eyes of a sheep*[5] should be equally capable of exciting in it the motion of flight?

But if we wish by reasoning to determine whether any of the motions of brutes are similar to those which we accomplish with the aid of the mind, or whether they resemble those that depend along upon the *influxus* of the animal spirits and the disposition of the organs we must pay heed to the differences that prevail between the two classes: viz. those differences explained in the fifth part of the *Discourse on Method*, for I have been able to discover no others. Then it will be seen that all the actions of brutes resemble only those of ours that occur without the aid of the mind. Whence we are driven to conclude that we can recognize no principle of motion in them beyond the disposition of their organs and the continual discharge of the animal spirits that are produced by the beat of the heart as it rarefies the blood. At the same time we shall perceive that we have had no cause for ascribing anything more to them, beyond that, nor distinguishing these two principles of motion when previously we have noted that the principle depending solely on the animal spirits and organs exists in ourselves and in the brutes alike, we have inadvisedly believed that the other principle, that consisting wholly of mind and thought, also existed in them. And it is true that a persuasion held from our earliest years, though afterwards shown by argument to be false, is not easily and only by long and frequent attention to these arguments expelled from our belief.

Reply to the Second Part, concerning God

Up to this point I have attempted to refute M. Arnauld's arguments and to withstand his attack; for the rest, as they are wont who combat with a stronger antagonist, I shall not oppose myself directly to his onslaught, but rather avoid the blow.

In this section only three points are raised and these may be readily admitted in the sense in which he understands them. But I attached

[1] Obj. iv, p. 147.
[2] Cf. p. 147.
[3] Cf. p. 147.
[4] *Meth.* v, pp. 59 sqq.
[5] Obj. iv, p. 147.

different meaning to what I wrote, a meaning that appears to me to be also correct.

The first assertion is *that certain ideas are false materially.*[1] i.e. according to my interpretation, that they supply the judgment with material for error. But my critic, taking ideas in their formal aspect, contends that falsity never resides in them.

The second is, that God is self-originated *in a positive sense, the sense implying as it were derivation from a cause.*[2] Here I had in mind merely that the reason why God requires no efficient cause in order to exist, is based on something positive, to wit, the very immensity of God, than which nothing can be more positive. M. Arnauld, however, shows that God is neither self-produced nor conserved by Himself by any positive activity belonging to an efficient cause; and this I likewise clearly affirm.

The third controverted statement is *that nothing can exist in the mind of which we are not conscious;*[3] which I in affirming held to refer to the acts of the mind, while it is of the mental faculties that he denies it.

But, to trace things out one by one, when he says, *if cold be merely a privation, there can be no idea which represents that as something positive,* it is clear that he treats of this idea only in its *formal* aspect. For, since ideas themselves are forms, and are never composed of any matter, when we take them as representing something, we regard them not *in a material guise* but *formally;* but if we were to consider them not in so far as they represent this or that other thing, but in the respect in which they are operations of the intellect, it might be said that they were taken materially, but then they would have no reference to the truth or falsity of objects. Hence it seems to me that ideas cannot be said to be materially false in any other sense than that which I have just explained. Thus, whether cold be something positive or a privation, my idea of it does not differ; it remains in me exactly the same as I have always had it. And I say that it furnishes me with material for error, if as a fact cold is a privation and does not possess so much reality as heat, because in considering either of the ideas of heat and cold just as I received them both from my senses, I am unable to perceive that more reality is revealed to me by one than by the other.

[1]Obj. IV, p. 147.
[2]Cf. p. 148.
[3]Cf. p. 150.

But it is not the case that I have *confused judgment and idea;*[4] for I have stated that in the latter the falsity we find is *material,* while in the former it can only be *formal.*

Moreover, when my critic asserts that *the idea of cold is cold itself in so far as that is objectively present in the understanding;*[5] I think that his distinction is of value. For, in the case of obscure and confused ideas, among which those of heat and cold must be enumerated, it often happens that they are referred to something other than that of which they are in truth the ideas. Thus, if cold is really a privation, the idea of cold is not cold itself in so far as that is objectively present in the understanding, but something else which I wrongly take for that privation, to wit, some sensation that has no existence outside the understanding.

But the same does not hold of the idea of God, at least of the idea of Him that is clear and distinct, because it cannot be said that this refers to something with which it is not in conformity. Touching the confused ideas of the gods that idolaters fashion, I do not see why they cannot be said to be materially false, in so far as they furnish those who employ them with false judgments. Though indeed ideas that give the judgment little or no occasion for error cannot, it seems, be said with equal reason to be materially false as those that give it much opportunity; moreover, it is easy by example to show that some ideas do give much more occasion for error than others. For this does not exist to such an extent in the confused ideas fashioned by the caprice of the mind (such as those of false gods) as in those that the senses give us in a confused way, such as the ideas of heat and cold; if indeed, as I said, it is true that they reveal to us nothing real. But opportunity for error is greatest in ideas that come from the appetites of sense; e.g. does not the thirst of the dropsical patient give him much material for error, in occasioning him to judge that the drink, that really will be harmful to him, will do him good?

But M. Arnauld asks what that idea of cold reveals to me, that I said was materially false. *For,* he says, *if it reveals privation, it is thereby true; if it display to him some positive entity it is not the idea of cold.*[6] Quite right; but the only reason why I call that idea materially false is because, since it is obscure and confused, I

[4]Cf. above, p. 148.
[5]Cf. p. 148.
[6]Cf. p. 148.

cannot decide whether it displays to me something outside my sensation or not; and this is why I have an opportunity for judging that it is something positive, although perchance it is only a privation.

Hence it must not be asked, *what the cause is of that positive objective entity, from which I say it results that this idea is false materially;*[1] because I do not assert that its material falsity proceeds from any positive entity, but merely from its obscurity, which, to be sure, does have something positive as its underlying subject, viz. the sensation itself.

In very truth, that positive entity exists in me in so far as I am something real; but the obscurity which alone causes me to think that that idea of the sensation of cold represents an object external to me, called cold, has no real cause, but arises merely from the fact that my nature is not in every respect perfect.

My chief principles are in no way shaken by this objection. But I should have more dread lest, not having spent much time in reading the writings of philosophers, I might not have followed sufficiently their fashion of speaking, in calling ideas that give the judgment occasion for error *materially* false, unless in the first author on whom I have chanced, I had found the term *materially* used with the same meaning: viz. Fr. Suarez, *Metaphysical Disputations*, 9, section 2, no. 4.

Let us now turn to the chief charge my distinguished critic brings against me. To me, indeed, there seems to be nothing worthy of censure in the passage mentioned, viz. where I said that *it is quite permissible for us to think that God in a certain sense stands to Himself in the same way as an efficient cause does to its effect.*[2] For by this very statement I have denied that doctrine which M. Arnauld thinks *bold and untrue,* viz. that God is His own efficient cause. In saying that *in a certain sense God stood so to Himself,* I showed that I did not think the relation to be identical in both cases; and in introducing what I said with these words—*it is quite permissible for us to think,* I showed that the matter could only be explained by the imperfection of the human understanding. But in the rest of what I wrote I have confirmed this at every point; for at the very beginning, where I said that *nothing existed as to the efficient cause of which we might not inquire,* I added, *or, if it does not possess an efficient cause, demand why that is*

[1]Cf. Obj. IV, p. 148.
[2]Cf. above, p. 148.

awanting.[3] The words sufficiently show that I believed something did exist which does not require an efficient cause. Moreover, what else could that be than God? Shortly afterwards I said that *in God there is such a great and inexhaustible power, that He has needed no assistance in order to exist, and requires none for His preservation, and hence He is in a certain way the cause of His own existence.*[4] Here the expression *cause of His own existence* can by no means be understood as efficient cause; it merely means that the inexhaustible power of God is the cause or reason why He needs no cause. It was because that inexhaustible power or immensity of His essence, is as highly *positive* as is possible, that I said that the reason or cause why God does not require a cause was *a positive one.* This I could not have affirmed of any finite thing however perfect in its own kind; if it were alleged to be *self-derived,* this could be understood only *in a negative sense,* since no reason could be derived from its positive nature on account of which we could understand that it did not require an efficient cause.

In the same way I have at all points compared the formal cause or reason derived from God's essential nature, which explains why He Himself does not need any cause in order to exist, with the efficient cause, without which finite things cannot exist; consequently, the difference between the two may be learned from my very words. Nor have I anywhere said that God conserves Himself by any positive transeunt action, in the way in which created beings are preserved in existence by Him; I have said merely that the immensity of the power, or essence, on account of which He needs no one to preserve Him in existence, is something *positive.*

Therefore I can readily admit everything M. Arnauld brings forward in order to prove that God is not His own efficient cause, and that He does not conserve Himself by any transeunt action, or any continual reproduction of Himself; and this is the sole conclusion of his argument. But, as I hope, even he will not deny that that immensity of power, on account of which God needs no cause in order to exist, is in Him something *positive,* and that nothing *positive* of this type could be conceived in any other thing, on account of which it should require no cause in order to exist; and this alone was what I meant to express in say-

[3]Reply to Obj. I, p. 110.
[4]Cf. p. 110.

ng that nothing could be understood to be self-derived unless *in a negative sense*, except God alone. I had no need to assume more than this, in order to resolve the difficulty that had been brought forward.

But since my critic warns me with such seriousness that *Theologians, almost without exception, must take offence at the doctrine that God is self-originated in a positive sense, and proceeds, as it were, from a cause*, I shall explain in more detail why this fashion of speech is in this question exceedingly useful, and even necessary, and why it seems to me to be quite free from any suspicion of being likely to cause offence.

I am aware that the Theologians of the Latin church do not employ the word "cause" in matters of divinity, where they treat of the procession of persons in the Holy Trinity, and that where the Greeks used αἴτιον and ἀρχή indifferently, they have preferred to employ the word *principium* alone taken in its most general sense, lest from the usage anyone might infer that the Son was not so great as the Father. But where no such danger of error can come in, and the question relates to God not as a trinity but as a unity, I see no reason why the word *cause* should be so much shunned, especially when we have come to the point when it seems very useful and almost necessary to employ the term.

No term can have a higher utility than to prove the existence of God; and none can be more necessary than this if, without it, God's existence cannot be clearly demonstrated.

But I think that it is manifest to all, that to consider the efficient cause is the primary and principal, not to say the only means of proving the existence of God. We shall not be able to pursue this proof with accuracy, if we do not grant our mind the liberty of asking for an efficient cause in every case, even in that of God; for with what right should we exclude God, before we have proved that He exists? Hence in every single case we must inquire whether it is *derived from itself or from something else;* and indeed by this means the existence of God may be inferred, although it be not expressly explained what is the meaning of anything being *self-derived*. For those who follow the guidance of the light of nature alone, spontaneously form here a concept common to efficient and formal cause alike. Hence, when a thing is *derived from something else* it is derived from that as from an efficient cause; but what is *self-derived* comes as it were from a formal

cause; it results from having an essential nature which renders it independent of an efficient cause. On this account I did not explain that matter in my Meditations, assuming that it was self-evident.

But when those who are accustomed to judge in accordance with the notion that nothing can be its own efficient cause, and are familiar with the accurate distinction between formal and efficient cause, see the question raised whether anything is self-derived, it easily follows that, taking that to apply only to the efficient cause properly so styled, they think that the expression *self-derived* should not be held to mean derived from itself *as from a cause*, but merely in a negative sense and as *not having a cause;* and so consequently it results that the existence of something is implied, into the cause of the existence of which we ought not to inquire. But if this interpretation of *self-derived* were admitted, there would be no reason by which to prove God's existence from His effects, as was shown correctly by the author of the first Objections; hence we must on no account sanction it.

But in order to reply expressly to this, let me say that I think we must show that, intermediate between *efficient cause*, in the proper sense, and *no cause*, there is something else, viz. *the positive essence of a thing*, to which the concept of efficient cause can be extended in the way in which in Geometry we are wont to extend the concept of a circular line, that is as long as possible, to that of a straight line; or the concept of a rectilinear polygon with an indefinite number of sides to that of a circle. I see no better way of explaining this than in saying, as I did, *that the meaning of efficient cause was in the present investigation not to be confined to those causes which are prior in time to their effects, or different from them; in the first place because the question (whether a thing can be its own efficient cause) would be unmeaning, since no one is unaware that the same thing cannot be prior to or different from itself; secondly because the former of these two conditions can be omitted from the concept without impairing the integrity of the notion of efficient cause.*[1]

For the fact that the cause need not be prior in time is evident from its not having the character of a cause except while it produces its effect, as I have said.

But from the fact that the second condition cannot also be annulled, we may only infer that it is not an efficient cause in the proper

[1] Cf. above, pp. 110, 149.

sense of the term, which I admit. We cannot, however, conclude that it is in no sense a positive cause, which may be held to be analogous to an efficient cause; and this is all that my argument requires. For by the very light of nature by which I perceive that I should have given myself all the perfections of which I have any idea, if I had indeed given myself existence, I am aware also that nothing can give itself existence in that way which is implied by the meaning to which we restrict the term efficient cause, viz. in a way such that the same thing, in so far as it gives itself being, is different from itself in so far as it receives being; for to be the same thing and not the same thing, i.e. a different thing, is a contradiction.

Thus it comes that when the question is raised whether anything can give itself existence, this must be understood merely to mean whether anything has a nature or essence such that it does not need to have any efficient cause in order to exist.

When the statement is added *that if anything is such it will give itself all the perfections of which it has any idea, if indeed it does not as yet possess them*,[1] the meaning is that it cannot fail to have in actuality all the perfections that it knows, because by the light of nature we perceive that a thing, the essence of which is so limitless that it does not stand in need of an efficient cause in order that it may exist, does not require an efficient cause either, in order to possess all the perfections of which it is aware, and that its own essential nature gives to it eminently[2] whatever we can think that an efficient cause is able to bestow on anything else.

These words also, *it will give them to itself, if it does not as yet possess them*, are merely explanatory. For the same light of nature lets us know that the thing does not at the present moment have the power and desire to give itself anything new, but that its essential nature is such that from all eternity it is in possession of everything which we can imagine it would bestow on itself if it did not already possess it.

Nevertheless, all the above forms of expression which are derived from the analogy of efficient causation are highly necessary in order to guide the light of nature so as to give us a clear comprehension of those matters; they are exactly parallel to the way in which

Archimedes, by comparing the sphere an other curvilinear figures with rectilinear fi ures, demonstrates of the former properti that could hardly otherwise be understoo And, just as no exception is taken to suc proofs, though they make us regard the sphe as similar to a polyhedron, so, in my opinio I cannot here be blamed for using the analog of efficient causality in order to explain ma ters that appertain to the formal cause, i.e. t the very essence of God.

Nor can any danger of error be apprehende at this point, since that single feature peculi to an efficient cause and incapable of bein extended to the formal cause involves a man fest contradiction, and hence such a though can be entertained by no one, viz. that any thing should be different from itself, i.e. th same thing and not the same thing.

We must mark here, too, that my languag ascribes to God the dignity implied by th word cause in a way that does not require tha He should have the imperfection attached t being an effect. For, exactly as Theologian though styling the Father the *originating prin ciple* of the Son, do not on that account admi that the Son is something *originated*, s though admitting that God is, in a sense, *H own cause*, I have nevertheless nowhere calle him similarly *His own effect;* for, in truth effect is used chiefly when speaking of a efficient cause and is regarded as of inferio nature to it, though often higher than othe causes.

Moreover, in taking the entire essence of thing as its formal cause here, I merely follow the footsteps of Aristotle. For in *Post. Anal* Bk II ch. 11, after passing over the materia cause, he names as αἰτία[3] primarily τὸ τί ἦ εἶναι,[4] or, as it is rendered in philosophica Latin, *the formal cause;* and he extends this t all the essential natures of all things, since a that point he is not treating of the causes of physical compound (as neither do I in thi place), but generally of the causes from which knowledge of any kind may be derived.

But it can be shown that it was hardly possible for me to refrain in this inquiry from ascribing to God the character of a cause, from the fact that, though my distinguished critic has tried to perform in another way the same task as I undertook, he has quite failed in his attempt, at least, as it appears to me. For after taking many words to show that God is not

---

[1] Cf. Obj. IV, p. 148 (not quoted exactly).
[2] Eminenter.

[3] cause.
[4] a thing's essential nature.

His own efficient cause, because the concept of an efficient cause requires diversity between it and its effect, after showing that God is not self-originated in the positive sense (where positive is taken to imply the positive tranceunt action of a cause), after likewise maintaining that God does not conserve Himself in the sense in which conservation means the continuous production of a thing, all of which contentions I gladly admit; after all this he once more hastens to prove that God should not be called the efficient cause of Himself, *because we seek to discover the efficient cause of a thing only with respect to its existence and not at all with respect to its essence. But existence is involved in the essence of an infinite being, no less than the equality of its angles to two right angles is involved in that of a triangle. Therefore when we ask why God exists, we must not attempt to reply by assigning an efficient cause any more than we should do if asked why the triangle has its three angles equal to two right angles.*[1] But this syllogism can easily be manipulated so as to tell against its author; thus, although we do not enquire for an efficient cause with respect to a thing's essence, nevertheless we can do so with regard to its existence; but in God essence and existence are not distinguished; hence we may enquire about the efficient cause of God.

But in order to reconcile those two matters, we should reply to the question as to why God exists, not indeed by assigning an efficient cause in the proper sense, but only by giving the essence of the thing or formal cause, which, owing to the very fact that in God existence is not distinguished from essence, has a strong analogy with the efficient cause, and may on this ground be called similar to an efficient cause.

Finally, M. Arnauld adds that *when we are asked for the efficient cause of God, we must reply that He needs no efficient cause. And if our interrogator plies us with the question why no efficient cause is required, we must answer, "because He is an infinite Being, and in such a case existence and essence are identical,*[2] *for only those things, the existence of which can be distinguished from their essence require an efficient cause."* He thinks that this overthrows my contention that *if I did not believe that anything could in some way be related to itself exactly as an efficient cause is related towards its effect, in enquiring into the causes of things I should never arrive at a*

first cause of all.[3] But to me it seems that this reasoning is neither overthrown nor in any way shaken or enfeebled. The main force not only of my argument but of all demonstrations that may be brought up to prove the existence of God from the effects that flow from Him, depends on this. Moreover, there is no argument advanced by practically any theologian that is not based on the effects of God's causality.

Therefore, far from making intelligible the proof of God's existence, when he does not permit us to assign to the relation He has towards Himself the analogy of efficient causation, it is rather the case that M. Arnauld prevents his reader from understanding it, especially at the end, where he draws the conclusion:—*that if he thought he must enquire for the efficient cause of anything whatsoever, or for something analogous to the efficient cause, he would seek for as cause of that given thing, whatsoever it was, something that was different from it.* For how could those who have not as yet known God enquire into the efficient cause of other things, in order thus to arrive at the knowledge of God, unless they believed that it was possible to enquire for the efficient cause of everything whatsoever? And how could they make God, as being the first cause, the end of their investigation if they thought that things must in all cases have a cause distinct from themselves?

My opponent here seems to act as if (following Archimedes, who, in speaking about the properties he has demonstrated of the sphere, taking it as analogous to rectilinear figures inscribed within it, had said: "If I imagined that the sphere could not be taken for a rectilinear figure or as after the fashion of a rectilinear figure with an infinite number of sides, I should attach no force to this proof, because properly it holds not of the sphere as a curvilinear figure, but applies to it merely as a rectilinear figure with an infinite number of sides"); it seems, I repeat, as if, at once unwilling to take the sphere in this way, but at the same time desirous of retaining the proof of Archimedes, he said: "If I thought that the conclusion here drawn must be judged to be true of a rectilinear figure with an infinite number of sides, I should not admit that it holds good of the sphere, because I know quite certainly that the sphere is by no means a rectilinear figure." But so saying he could not arrive at the same result as Archimedes but, on the contrary,

[1] Cf. above, p. 150 (abridged).
[2] Cf. p. 150.
[3] Cf. p. 150 (abridged).

would quite prevent himself and others from properly understanding the proof.

I have pursued this topic at somewhat greater length than the subject demanded, in order to prove that it is a matter of great anxiety to me to prevent anything from appearing in my writings capable of giving just offence to theologians.

Finally, to prove that I have not argued in a circle in saying, *that the only secure reason we have for believing that what we clearly and distinctly perceive is true, is the fact that God exists; but that clearly we can be sure that God exists only because we perceive that,*[1] I may cite the explanations that I have already given at sufficient length in my reply to the second set of Objections, numbers 3 and 4. There I distinguished those matters that in actual truth we clearly perceive from those we remember to have formerly perceived. For first, we are sure that God exists because we have attended to the proofs that established this fact; but afterwards it is enough for us to remember that we have perceived something clearly, in order to be sure that it is true; but this would not suffice, unless we knew that God existed and that he did not deceive us.

The fact *that nothing can exist in the mind, in so far as it is a thinking thing, of which it is not conscious,*[2] seems to me self-evident, because we conceive nothing to exist in it, viewed in this light, that is not thought, and something dependent on thought; for otherwise it would not belong to the mind, in so far as it is a thinking thing. But there can exist in us no thought of which, at the very moment that it is present in us, we are not conscious. Wherefore I have no doubt that the mind begins to think at the same time as it is infused into the body of an infant, and is at the same time conscious of its own thought, though afterwards it does not remember that, because the specific forms of these thoughts do not live in the memory.

But it has to be noted that, while indeed we are always in actuality conscious of acts or operations of the mind, that is not the case with the faculties or powers of mind, except potentially. So that when we dispose ourselves to the exercise of any faculty, if the faculty reside in us, we are immediately actually conscious of it; and hence we can deny that it exists in the mind, if we can form no consciousness of it.

[1]Cf. p. 150.
[2]Cf. p. 150.

Reply Relative to Those Matters Likely to Caus‹ Difficulty to Theologians

Whilst I have combated M. Arnauld's firs‹ objections and have avoided any collision with his second, I am quite willing to agree to th‹ next set of criticisms, except in the case of th‹ final one; and here I hope without great diffi culty to get him himself to yield his assent t‹ me.

Hence I quite admit that what is found i‹ the first Meditation and even in the others i‹ not suited to the capacity of every under standing, and this I have avouched on ever‹ possible occasion and always shall proclaim This was why I did not discuss the sam‹ matters in the *Discourse on Method*, which wa‹ written in French, but reserved them for th‹ *Meditations*, which, I announced, should b‹ read only by intellectual and educated persons No one should say that I had better have re frained from penning matters, the reading o‹ which many people ought to avoid; for I be lieve these things to be necessary to such a‹ extent, that nothing stable or firm in philos ophy can, I am convinced, be ever established without them. And though fire and steel ma‹ not be handled without danger by children o‹ careless people, yet they are so important fo‹ life that no one thinks that we should for th‹ above reason do without them.

Now, as to the fact that in the fourth Medi tation I treated only *of the mistakes made i‹ distinguishing between the true and the false, bu‹ not of the error that occurs in the pursuit of goo‹ and evil,*[3] *and touching the fact that I always ex cluded those things that concern our faith and th‹ conduct of life, when I asserted that we shoul‹ assent only to what we clearly and distinctly know;* with these two facts the whole context of my works manifests agreement. I explained this also expressly in my reply to the second set of Objections, no. 5,[4] and I set it forth also in the Synopsis. I make this statement in order to show how much value I attach to M. Arnauld's judgment and how much I esteem his advice.

The remaining matter is the Sacrament of the Eucharist. M. Arnauld believes that my doctrines are in conflict with this, *because it is an article of our faith that the substance of the bread passes out of the bread of the Eucharist, and that only its accidents remain;*[5] *further he believes that I recognise no real accidents, but*

[3]Cf. above, p. 150.
[4]Cf. above, pp. 125, 126.
[5]Obj. IV, p. 152.

ly modes which cannot be comprehended apart
om the substance in which they inhere, and
ence cannot exist apart from it.[1]

But I have no difficulty in parrying this ob-
ction when I say that I have never as yet
enied the existence of real accidents. For,
hough in the *Dioptric* and the work on *Me-
ors* I did not employ them in explaining the
atters of which I treated, nevertheless, in
he *Meteors*, p. 164, I expressly said that I did
ot deny their reality. But in these *Medita-
ons*, while I assumed indeed that I was as yet
naware of their existence, I did not on that
ccount deny their reality. For the analytic
tyle of composition which I adopted allows us
ometimes to make certain assumptions with-
ut their being as yet sufficiently investigated,
s was evident in the first Meditation, in which
provisionally assumed many doctrines that
afterwards refuted. Further, it was not my
urpose at this point to formulate any doc-
rine about the nature of accidents; I simply
rought forward what seemed at a preliminary
urvey to be true of them. Finally, from the
act that I alleged that modes could not be
onceived apart from some substance in which
hey inhered, it should not be inferred that I
leny that they can be held apart from it by
he divine power, because I firmly hold and
elieve that God is able to accomplish many
hings that we are incapable of comprehending.

But I shall here express myself more frankly
nd shall not conceal the fact that I am convinced that the only thing by which our senses
re stimulated is that superficies which forms
he boundary of the dimensions of the per-
eived body. For contact takes place only at
he surface. Likewise, not I alone, but prac-
ically all philosophers along with Aristotle
imself, affirm that no sense is stimulated
therwise than by contact. Thus, for example,
bread or wine cannot be perceived except in so
far as its surface is in contact with the organ of
sense, either immediately or by the mediation
of air or other bodies, as I believe, or as many
philosophers allege, by the intervention of
"intentional forms."[2]

But we must note that we should not form
our idea of that surface merely from the external figure of bodies that is felt by the fingers;
we should take into account also those tiny

crevices that are found between the minute
grains of the flour of which the bread is composed, as well as between the particles of spirit,
water, vinegar and lees or tartar that combine
or constitute the wine, and so in the case of the
particles of other bodies also. For, as a fact,
these particles, possessing diverse figures and
motions are never so closely united with each
other as not to leave many interstices between
them, which are not vacant, but filled with air
or some other material. Thus in bread we can
see with the naked eye fairly large spaces,
which may be filled not merely with air, but
with water, wine and other liquids. But since
the bread remains always self-identical, although the air or other material contained in
its pores changes, it is clear that these things
do not belong to its substance; hence we see
that its surface is not that superficies that
traces the briefest outline round it, but that
which immediately envelopes its separate
particles.

We must likewise observe that not only does
the whole of this superficies move when the
whole piece of bread is transferred from one
place to another, but that it also has a partial
movement, as happens when some of the particles of bread are set in motion by the entrance
of air or other bodies into its pores. Hence, if
there are any bodies such that any or all of
their parts are in continual motion (which I
think holds of many of the constituent parts of
bread and in the case of all the particles in
wine), we must believe that the superficies of
these things are continually in some sort of
motion.

Finally, we must note that, by the superficies of bread or of wine or of any other body,
is meant not any part of their substance, nor
indeed any part of the quantity of the body,
nor even a part of the circumjacent bodies, but
merely *that limit which is conceived to lie between the single particles of a body and the bodies
that surround it, a boundary which has absolutely
none but a modal reality.*

But now, since contact is effected at this
boundary alone and nothing is perceived unless
by contact, it is clear that from the single
statement that the substance of the bread and
wine is changed into the substance of some
other body in such a way that this new substance is entirely contained within the same
limits as those within which the other substances previously were, or in precisely the
same place as that in which the bread and
wine previously existed, or rather (since these

[1]Cf; p. 152 (abridged).
[2]The theory that the "form" or sensible character of the object propagated copies of itself
through the medium and that those alone were
directly perceived.

boundaries are continually moving) in that in which they would exist if they were present, it necessarily follows that that new substance would act on our senses in entirely the same way as that in which the bread and wine would act, if no transubstantiation had occurred.

Moreover, it is the teaching of the Church in the Council of Trent, session 13, canons 2 and 4, *that the whole substance of the bread is changed into the substance of the body of Christ our Lord, while only the semblance of the bread remains unaltered.* Here I do not see what can be meant by the appearance of the bread, except that superficies which intervenes between its single particles and the bodies surrounding them.

For, as has already been said, it is at this superficies alone that contact occurs; and Aristotle himself supports us in saying that not only that sense which is in special called *touch*, but the other senses also perceive by touching:—*De Anima*, Book III. chap. 13: καὶ τὰ ἄλλα αἰσθητήρια ἀφῇ αἰσθάνεται.

Further, there is no one who thinks that here by species is meant anything else than exactly what is required for acting on the senses. There is no one, too, who believes in the conversion of the bread into the body of Christ, that does not at the same time believe that this body of Christ is accurately comprised within that superficies beneath which the bread, if it were present, would be found; and this even though it is not there in the proper sense of being in a place, *but sacramentally and with that form of existence which, though we have a difficulty in expressing it in words, yet when our thought is illumined by faith, we can still believe to be possible with God, and ought always firmly so to believe.* Now, all these matters are so conveniently and correctly explained by my principles that not only have I nothing here to fear in the way of giving the slightest cause of offence to orthodox theologians, but on the contrary I confidently anticipate reaping gratitude from them, because in my Physics I propound those doctrines which agree with Theology much better than the common opinions. As a matter of fact, never, to my knowledge at least, has the Church in any passage taught that the semblances of the wine and bread that remain in the Sacrament of the Eucharist are real accidents of any sort which, when the substance in which they inhered is removed, miraculously subsist by themselves.

But perhaps because the Theologians who first tried to explain this matter in a phil sophical way were so firmly convinced tha the accidents that stimulate our senses ar something real and distinct from substance that they did not even remark that doub might in conceivable circumstances be cast o their opinion; the semblances manifested b the bread were likewise believed by them with out any scrutiny or valid reason to be re accidents of this kind. Thenceforward, the were wholly taken up with explaining how th accidents could exist without their subjec But here they found such difficulty that (lik wayfarers who have arrived among thicket that seem to offer no clear thoroughfare) fro the difficulty of the situation alone they wer bound to infer that they had wandered fro the straight road.

For, firstly they seem to contradict them selves; at least those do who admit that a sense-perception is effected by contact, whe they suppose that in objects something othe than the various disposition of their super ficies is required for the purpose of stimulatin the senses; for it is self-evident that in orde to effect contact surface alone is necessary Those, on the other hand, who do not mak the above admission are unable to describ what happens with any appearance of ver similitude.

Further, the human mind is unable to thin that the accidents of bread are realities an yet exist apart from the substance of th bread, without thinking of them after th fashion of a substance. Hence there seems t be a contradiction in believing with the Churc that the whole substance of the bread i changed, and meanwhile thinking that some thing real remains, which previously was i the bread, for nothing real can be conceived t remain, except what subsists, and though it i called an accident, we nevertheless conceive i as a substance. Hence, in reality, it is the sam as to say that while indeed the whole of th substance of the bread is changed, there ye remains that part of its substance that is calle a real accident, and this, if not verbally, is a any rate in thought a contradiction.

And this seems to be the chief reason why certain people have at this point disagreed with the Roman Church. Does anyone no believe that when we are free to choose, and there is no reason, either theological or indeed philosophical, compelling us to embrace cer tain particular opinions, we should most read ily select those beliefs that can give others ne opportunity or pretext for turning aside from the truth of the faith? But I think I have here shown with sufficient clearness that the doctrine that assumes the existence of real accidents does not harmonize with theological reasoning; that it is wholly in conflict with philosophical thought I hope clearly to demonstrate in a treatise on the principles of philosophy on which I am now engaged. Then I shall show how colour, savour, weight and whatever else stimulates the sense, depend wholly upon the exterior surface of bodies.

Finally, if we assume the existence of real accidents, it follows that by the miracle of transubstantiation, which alone can be inferred from the words of consecration, something new and indeed incomprehensible is gratuitously added, something that permits those real accidents to exist apart from the substance of the bread, without themselves in the meantime being substances. But this not only conflicts with human reason, but also with the theological axiom that says that the words of consecration effect nothing beyond what they signify; the theologians refuse to assign to miraculous causes what can be explained by the natural reason. But my explanation of the matter removes all their difficulties. For, far from its postulating some miraculous agency in order to explain the conservation of the accidents after the substance is removed, it refuses to admit that without a new miracle (such as might alter the dimensions in question) could they be annulled. It has been related that such an event has happened and that at such times the priest has found in his hand flesh or a tiny child. But this confirms my contention, for it has never been believed that what happened was due to a cessation of the miracle; it has always been ascribed to a new miracle.

Besides this, there is nothing incomprehensible or difficult in the idea of God, the creator of all things, being able to change one substance into another, and the second substance remaining comprised within the same superficies as that which bounded the former. For nothing can be more consonant with reason, no statement better received in the general ranks of the philosophers, than the assertion that not only all sensation, but generally all action of body on body, is effected by contact, and that this contact can occur only at the surface. Whence it evidently follows that the same substance, whatever be the change in the substance that lies beneath it, must always act and be acted on in the same way.

Wherefore, if I here may speak the truth freely and without offence, I avow that I venture to hope that a time will some day come when the doctrine that postulates the existence of real accidents will be banished by theologians as being foreign to rational thought, incomprehensible, and causing uncertainty in the faith; and mine will be accepted in its place as being certain and indubitable. I have purposely made no concealment here, in order that I may combat to the best of my ability the calumnies of those who, wishing to be thought more learned than others, are never so much enraged as when some new scientific doctrine, of which they cannot pretend they previously had knowledge, is brought forward. Frequently, their opposition is more bitter in proportion as they believe that the doctrine is true and important, and when unable to refute it by argument, they maintain without a shadow of reason that it is contrary to Holy Scripture and the verities of the faith. This truly is impiety—to attempt to employ the authority of the Church in order to overthrow the truth. But I appeal from such people to the judgment of pious and orthodox theologians, to whose opinion and decision I willingly submit myself.

ANNOUNCEMENT BY THE AUTHOR RELATIVE
TO THE FIFTH SET OF OBJECTIONS

BEFORE the appearance of the first edition of these *Meditations* I wished to have them examined not only by the learned Doctors of the Sorbonne, but also by all other men of science who should care to take the trouble of reading them. I thus hoped that by causing these objections and my replies to be printed as a continuation of the Meditations, each in the order in which they were composed, I should thereby render the truth much more evident. And though the objections that were sent to me fifth in order did not appear to me to be the most important and are very lengthy, I did not fail to have them printed in their proper order, so as not to disoblige their author. I likewise caused him to be furnished with a proof of the impression lest anything should be set down as his, of which he did not approve. But as he has since composed a work of great size,[1] containing these same objections, together with several new counter-arguments or answers to my replies, and since he there complains of me for having published them, as if I had done so against his wishes, and says that he sent them to me only for my private instruction, I shall henceforth gladly comply with his desire and so relieve this volume of their presence. This was the reason why, on learning that M. Clerselier was taking the trouble to translate the other Objections, I begged him to omit these latter ones. And in order that he may have no cause to regret their absence, I have to inform the reader at this place that I have lately read them a second time, and that I have read also all the new counter-arguments in the huge volume containing them, with the purpose of extracting thence all the points I should judge to stand in need of a reply; but I have been unable to discover one, to which, in my opinion, those who have at all understood the meaning of my Meditations will not be able to reply without any aid from me. As to those who judge books only by their size or by their title, I have no ambition to secure praise from them.

[1] Petri Gassendi, *Disquisitio metaphysica*, Amsterdam, 1644.

LETTER TO M. CLERSELIER

TO SERVE AS A REPLY TO A SELECTION OF THE PRINCIPAL OBJECTIONS TAKEN BY M. GASSENDI TO THE PRECEDING REPLIES[1]

[*12th January*, 1646]

SIR,

I owe you a deep debt of gratitude for noticing that I have neglected to reply to the huge volume of hostile arguments which the Author of the fifth set of Objections has composed in answer to my Replies, and for having asked some of your friends to extract the strongest arguments from this book, as well as for sending me the selection[2] which they have made. In this you have shown more anxiety for my reputation than I myself possess; for I assure you that to me it is a matter of indifference whether I am esteemed or contemned by the people with whom such arguments have weight. Those of my friends who have read his book, and the best heads among them, have declared to me that they have found nothing in it to arrest their attention; now I am content to have satisfied them alone. I know that the greater part of mankind seize on appearance more readily than on the truth, judge wrongly more frequently than aright. This is why I hold that their approval is not worth the trouble I should incur in doing all that might be required in order to secure it. But none the less I am pleased with the selection you have sent me, and I feel obliged to reply to it, more

[1] To the Replies to Objections V.
[2] This selection is not extant.

order to express my gratitude to your friends or their trouble, than because I need to defend myself. For I believe that those who have taken the trouble to make it must now believe, as I do, that all the objections that this book contains are founded solely on the misunderstanding of certain terms or on certain false suppositions. But though all the objections they have remarked on are of that sort, yet they have been so diligent as even to have added certain ones which I do not remember to have previously read.

They notice three criticisms directed against the first Meditation: 1. *That I demand an impossibility in desiring the abandonment of every kind of prejudice.* 2. *That in thinking one has given up every prejudice one acquires other beliefs of a still more prejudiced kind.* 3. *That the method I have proposed of doubting everything does not promote the discovery of any single truth.*

The first of these criticisms is due to the author of this book not having reflected that the word prejudice does not apply to all the notions in our mind, of which it is impossible for us to divest ourselves, but only to all those opinions our belief in which is a result of previous judgments. And since judging or refraining from judgment is an act of the will, as I have explained in the appropriate place, it is evident that it is under our control; for in order to rid one's self of all prejudice, nothing needs to be done except to resolve to affirm or deny none of the matters we have previously affirmed or denied, unless after a fresh examination. But yet we do not on that account cease to retain all these same notions in the memory. Nevertheless I have said that there was a difficulty in expelling from our belief everything that had been put there previously, partly because we need to have some reason for doubting before determining to do so: it was for this cause that I propounded the chief reasons for doubting in my first Meditation. Another source also of the difficulty is that whatever be the resolution we have formed of denying or affirming nothing, it is easy to forget, if we have not impressed it firmly on the memory; and this was why I recommended that this should be thought of earnestly.

The second objection is nothing but a manifest falsity: for though I said that we must even compel ourselves to deny the things we had previously affirmed with too great assurance, I expressly limited the period during which we should so behave to the time in which we bend our thought to the discovery of something more certain than what we had been able thus to deny: and during this time it is evident that we could not entertain any belief of a prejudicial character.

The third criticism is mere cavilling. True, mere doubt alone does not suffice to establish any truth; but that does not prevent it from being useful in preparing the mind for the subsequent establishment of truth. This is the sole purpose for which I have employed it.

Your friends mark six objections to Meditation II. The first is that in the statement, *I think, hence I exist,* the author of these criticisms will have it that I imply the assumption of this major premiss, *he who thinks, exists,* and I have thus already espoused a prejudice. Here he once more mishandles the word *prejudice:* for though we may apply this term to that proposition when it is brought forward without scrutiny, and we believe it merely because we remember we have made this same judgment previously, we cannot maintain on every occasion that it is a prejudice, i.e. when we subject it to examination, the cause being that it appears to be so evident to the understanding that we should fail to disbelieve it even on the first occasion in our life on which it occurred to us, on which occasion it would not be a prejudice. But the greater error here is our critic's assumption that the knowledge of particular truths is always deduced from universal propositions in consonance with the order of the sequence observed in the syllogism of dialectic. This shows that he is but little acquainted with the method by which truth should be investigated. For it is certain that in order to discover the truth we should always start with particular notions, in order to arrive at general conceptions subsequently, though we may also in the reverse way, after having discovered the universals, deduce other particulars from them. Thus in teaching a child the elements of geometry we shall certainly not make him understand the general truth that *"when equals are taken from equals the remainders are equal,"* or that *"the whole is greater than its parts,"* unless by showing him examples in particular cases. For want of guarding against this error our author has been led astray into the many fallacious reasonings which have gone to swell his book. He has merely constructed false major premises according to his whim, as though I had deduced from these the truths I have explained.

The second objection which your friends remark is: *that, in order to know that I think, I must know what thought is; which I certainly do not know*, they say, *because I have denied everything*. But I have denied nothing but prejudices, and by no means notions like these, which are known without any affirmation or denial.

Thirdly: *Thought cannot lack an object, for example the body*. Here we must keep clear of the ambiguity in the word thought; it can be taken either for the thing that thinks or for that thing's activity. Now I deny that the thing that thinks needs any object other than itself in order to exercise its activity, though it can also reach out to material things when it examines them.

Fourthly: *Even though I have a thought of myself, I do not know whether that thought is a corporeal action or a self-moved atom, rather than an immaterial substance*. Here we have once more the ambiguity in the word thought, and, apart from this, I see nothing but a baseless question somewhat of this kind—you esteem that you are a man, because you perceive in yourself all the things on account of which you bestow the name of men on all who possess them; but how do you know that you are not an elephant rather than a man, owing to some other causes which you cannot perceive? After the substance which thinks has judged that it is an intelligence because it has remarked in itself all the properties of thinking substances, and has been unable to recognise any of those belonging to body, once more it is asked how it knows that it is not a body, rather than an immaterial substance.

Similar to this is the fifth objection: *That though I find nothing extended in my thought, it does not follow that it is really not extended, because my thought is not the rule of the truth of things*. Likewise the sixth: *That possibly the distinction drawn by my thought between thought and body, is false*. But here we must particularly notice the equivocation in the words:—*my thought is not the rule of the truth of things*. For, if anyone care to allege that my thought ought not to be the rule for others, so as to make them believe something because I think it true, I entirely agree. But that is not at all to the point here. For I have never wished to force anyone to follow my authority; on the contrary I have announced in divers places that one should never let one's self be persuaded except by received proofs. Further, if the word thought be taken indifferently for every psychical operation, it is certain that we can have many thoughts, from which we can infer nothing relative to the truth of matters outside of us. But that also is not to the point here, where the question concerns only those thoughts that form clear and distinct perceptions, and the judgments which everyone can make on his own account in the train of these perceptions. This is why, in the sense in which these words should be here understood, I say that each individual's thought, i.e. the perception or knowledge which he has of a thing ought to be for him the rule for the truth of that thing; that is to say, that all the judgments he makes should be conformable with that perception in order to be correct. Even in the matter of the truths of the faith, we should perceive some reason persuading us that they have been revealed by God, before determining ourselves to believe them; and though those who are ignorant do well to follow the judgment of the more capable, touching those matters that are difficult of apprehension, it must nevertheless be their own perception that tells them that they are ignorant and that those whose judgments they wish to follow are less ignorant, otherwise they would do ill to follow them, and would act as automata or as mere animals rather than as men. Hence it is the most absurd and extravagant error that a philosopher can commit, to wish to make judgments which have no relation to his perception of things. Yet I fail to see how my critic can avoid the censure of having fallen into this error, in the greater part of his objections; for he does not wish each individual to stand firmly by his own perceptions, but claims that we should rather believe the opinions or fancies he pleases to set before us, though we wholly fail to grasp them as perceptions.

In opposition to the third Meditation your friends have remarked:—1. *That not everyone has experience of the presence of the idea of God within him. 2. That if I had this idea I should comprehend it. 3. That several people have read my arguments, whom they have failed to persuade. 4. That it does not follow from the fact that I know myself to be imperfect, that God exists*. But, if we take the word idea in the way in which I expressly said I took it, without getting out of the difficulty by the equivocation practised by those who restrict it to the images of material things, likenesses formed in the imagination, we shall be unable to deny that we have some idea of God, except by saying that we do not understand the words—*that thing which is the most perfect that we can con-*

ive; for that is what all men call God. But
go so far as to assert that they do not under-
and the words which are the commonest in
e mouths of men, is to have recourse to
range extremes in order to find objections.
esides, it is the most impious confession one
an make, to say of one's own accord, in the
nse in which I have taken the word idea, that
ne has no idea of God: for this is not merely
say that one does not know it by means of
e natural reason, but also that neither by
ith nor by any other means could one have
ny knowledge of it, because if one has no
ea, i.e. no perception corresponding to the
gnification of the word God, it is vain to say
ne believes that God exists; it would be the
me as saying that one believes that nothing
xists, and thus one would remain plunged in
e abyss of impiety and the extremity of
norance.

What they add—that if I had this idea I should
omprehend it—is alleged without grounds. For,
ecause the word comprehend conveys a sense
f limitation, a finite spirit cannot comprehend
od, who is infinite. But that does not prevent
im from apprehending Him, just as one can
ouch a mountain without being able to em-
race it.

Their statement about my arguments—that
everal people have read them without being per-
uaded by them—can easily be refuted; for
here are others who have understood them
nd have been satisfied with them. For more
redence should be attached to what one man
who does not mean to lie) says, if he alleges
hat he has seen or learned something, than
ne should give to a thousand others who deny
, for the mere reason that it was impossible
or them to see it or become aware of it. Thus
t the discovery of the Antipodes the report of
few sailors who had circumnavigated the
arth was believed rather than the thousands
f philosophers who had not believed the earth
o be round. Further, though they here cite as
onfirmation the Elements of Euclid, saying
hat everyone finds them easy to apprehend, I
eg my critics to consider that among those
nen who are counted the most learned in the
Philosophy of the Schools, there is not one in a
undred who understands them, and that
here is not one in ten thousand who under-
tands all the demonstrations of Apollonius or
Archimedes, though they are as evident and as
ertain as those of Euclid.

Finally, when they say that it does not follow
rom the fact that I recognise some imperfections

in myself that God exists, they prove nothing.
For I do not deduce this conclusion from that
premiss alone, without adding something else;
they merely remind me of the artifice of my
critic who has the habit of mutilating my arguments and reporting only parts of them, in order to make them appear to be imperfect.

I see nothing in these remarks touching the
three other meditations to which I have not
elsewhere given an ample reply, e.g. to their
objection:—1. That I have reasoned in a circle
in drawing my proofs of the existence of God from
certain notions that exist in us, and afterwards
saying that we can be certain of nothing unless
we already know that God exists. 2. That the
knowledge of God's existence contributes nothing
to the acquisition of a knowledge of the truths of
mathematics. 3. That God may deceive us. On
this subject consult my reply to the second set
of objections, numbers 3 and 4, and the end of
part 2 of the reply to the fourth set of objections.[1]

But at the end my critics add a reflection
which is not, to my knowledge, to be found in
the book of counter arguments written by this
Author, though it is very similar to his criticisms. Many people of great acumen, they say,
believe that they clearly see that the mathematical
extension, which I take as the basal principle of
my Physics, is nothing but my thought, and that
it has and can have no subsistence outside of my
mind, being merely an abstraction that I form
from a physical body; that consequently the whole
of my Physics is but imaginary and fictitious, as
is likewise all pure mathematics: and that the
physical nature of the real things that God has
created requires a matter that is real, solid, and
not imaginary. Here we have the objection of
objections, and the sum of the whole doctrine
of these men of great acumen who are here
brought into evidence. Everything that we are
able to understand and conceive, is, according
to their story, but imagination—the fictitious
creation of our mind, and can have no real subsistence: whence it follows that nothing exists
which we can comprehend, conceive, or imagine, or admit as true, and that we must close
the door against reason, and content ourselves
with being monkeys or parrots, and no longer
be men, if we wish to place ourselves on a level
with these acute intelligences. For, if the
things which we conceive must be esteemed to
be false merely because we can conceive them,
what is there left for us but to accept as true
the things we do not conceive, and to make

[1]Cf. pp. 123-125 and p. 162.

our system of belief out of them, imitating others without knowing why we do so, like the monkeys, and uttering only those words which we do not understand, like parrots? But I have something substantial wherewith to console myself, inasmuch as my critics here conjoin my Physics with pure Mathematics, which it is my deepest wish my Physics should resemble.

As for the two questions added at the end, viz.—*how the soul moves the body if it is not material? and how it can receive the specific forms of corporeal objects?* these give me here merely the opportunity of declaring that our Author had no right, under pretext of criticising me, to propound a mass of questions like this, the solution of which was not necessary for the proof of what I have written, questions of which the most ignorant man might raise more in a quarter of an hour than the wisest could solve in a lifetime. Thus I do not feel called upon to answer any of them. Likewise these objections, among other things, presuppose an explanation of the nature of the union between soul and body, a matter of which I have not yet treated. But to you, for your own benefit, I declare that the whole of the perplexity involved in these questions arises entirely from a false supposition that can by no manner of means be proved, viz. that if the soul and the body are two substances of diverse nature, that prevents them from being capable of acting on one another; for, on the contrary, those who admit the existence of real accidents, like heat, weight, and so forth, do not doubt that these accidents have the power of acting on the body, and nevertheless there is more difference between them and it, i.e. between accidents and a substance, than there is between two substances.

For the rest, since I have my pen in my hand, I may call attention here to two of the ambiguities which I have found in this book of counter-arguments, because they are such as to my mind, might most easily entrap an inattentive reader, and I desire in this way to testify to you that if I had found anything else worthy of a reply I should not have passed it over.

The first is on page 79, where because I have said in one place,[1] that while the soul is in

[1]Med. II, p. 79.

doubt of the existence of all material things i knows itself precisely, *in the strict sense, only* as an immaterial substance; and seven or eigh lines lower down, in order to show that, b using the words *in the strict sense, only*, I do no mean an entire exclusion or negation, but onl an abstraction from material things, I sai that, in spite of that, I was not sure that ther was nothing corporeal in the soul, althoug nothing of such a nature was known to exis in it; my opponents are so unjust to me as t wish to persuade the reader that in saying *i the strict sense, only*, I wished to exclude th body, and have thus contradicted myself after wards in saying that I did not wish to exclud it. I make no reply to the subsequent accusa tion of having assumed something in the Sixt Meditation that I had not previously proved and of having thus committed a fallacy. It i easy to detect the falsity of this charge, which i only too common in the whole of this book, an might make me suspect that its Author ha not acted in good faith, if I had not know his character and did not believe he has bee the first to be entrapped by so false a belief.

The other ambiguity is on p. 84, where h wishes to make *to abstract* and *to distinguis* have the same meaning, though all the tim there is a great difference between them: for i distinguishing a substance from its accidents we must consider both one and the other, an this helps greatly in becoming acquainted wit substance; whereas if instead one only sepa rates by abstraction this substance from thes accidents, i.e. if one considers it quite alon without thinking of them, that prevents on from knowing it well, because it is by its acci dents that substance is manifested.

Here, my dear Sir, is the whole of the repl for which this great book of counter-argu ments calls; for, though perhaps I should bet ter content my critic's friends if I reporte every hostile argument one after the other, believe I should not please my own friends who would have cause to reprove me for hav ing occupied time with a task for which ther was little need, and of thus putting my leisur at the disposal of all those who might care t squander theirs in plying me with useless ques tions. But I give you my thanks for your kin attentions. Adieu.

THE FIFTH SET OF OBJECTIONS[1]

LETTER FROM P. GASSENDI TO M. DESCARTES

SIR,

Our friend Mersenne did me a great kindness in communicating to me your magnificent work—your *Meditations on First Philosophy.* The excellence of your arguments, the perspicuity of your intellect, and the brilliance of your expression have caused me extraordinary delight. It gives me great pleasure to compliment you on the sublimity and felicity with which your mind assails the task of extending the boundaries of the sciences and bringing to light those matters that preceding ages have found most difficult to drag from their obscurity. To me it has proved hard to comply, as friendship obliged me to do, with the request M. Mersenne also made, and let you know if I took any exception to your doctrine and had any scruple unsatisfied. Especially I foresaw that, if I did not agree with your arguments, I should merely display my own lack of acuteness or rather should merely manifest rashness, if I dared to utter my dissent in the smallest matter, and appear to oppose you. Nevertheless I have yielded to my friend, thinking besides that you would approve of his plan rather than of mine; since indeed your candour will easily let you see that my intention is solely to display to you without disguise the reasons I have for doubting. I testify that this will be amply confirmed if you have patience to scrutinize them thoroughly; or as to any influence they may have in causing you the slightest sense of insecurity in your reasonings, or in causing you to consume, in replying, any time destined for more valuable studies, I declare myself not responsible for this. Nay, I cannot without shame-facedness expose my difficulties to your gaze, sure as I am that there is none of them that has not often suggested itself to you in your reflections, and which you have not with full consciousness dismissed as of no account, or determined to keep out of sight. Consequently, though I bring forward certain hypotheses, I bring them forward merely as hypotheses, and they are hypotheses that affect not the truths themselves of which you have undertaken the proof, but the method and cogency of your proof. I unaffectedly acknowledge the existence of Almighty God and the immortality of our souls; my doubts concern merely the validity of the reasoning by which you prove those matters, as well as other things involved in the scheme of Metaphysical science.

RELATIVE TO MEDITATION I

Of the Things Which May Be Brought Within the Sphere of the Doubtful

In the matter of the first Meditation, there is really little for me to linger over; I agree with your plan of freeing your mind from every prejudice. On one point only I am not clear; that is, why you should not have preferred to indicate simply and with few words that what you previously knew was uncertain, in order subsequently to choose what might be found to be true, rather than by regarding everything as false, not so much to dismiss an old prejudice, as to take up with a new one. Thus, for example, it became necessary to feign that God was a deceiver, or some evil spirit that mocks us, in order to convince yourself; whereas it would have seemed to be sufficient to ascribe that to the obscurity of the human mind and the weakness of its nature alone. Further, you feign that you are dreaming in order to cast doubt on everything, and consider that everything that happens is done to make sport of us. But will that compel you to believe that you are not awake and to deem uncertain and false the events that occur before your eyes? Say what you will, no one will be convinced that you have convinced yourself that none of the things you have learned are true, and that your senses, or a dream, or God, or an evil spirit have 'imposed on you. Would it not have been better and more consonant with philosophic candour and the love of the truth to state the actual facts in a straightforward and simple manner, rather than to incur the possible objection of having recourse to an artifice, of eagerness for verbal trickery and seeking evasions? Yet, since you have been pleased to take this way, I shall make no further criticism on it.

RELATIVE TO MEDITATION II

Of the Nature of the Human Mind; and That it is More Easily Known than the Body

1. When it comes to the second Meditation, I see that you still persist in keeping up the game

---

[1]The French translation by Clerselier was published contrary to the advice of Descartes in the edition sanctioned by him.

of pretence, and yet that you recognize at least that you exist; *which thus establishes the* conclusion that this proposition:—I am, I exist, is true each time that you pronounce it, or that you mentally conceive it.[1] *But I don't see that you needed all this mechanism, when you had other grounds for being sure, and it was true, that you existed. You might have inferred that from any other activity, since our natural light informs us that whatever acts also exists.*

You add that this does not yet let you know clearly enough what you are.[2] *But this is admitted, and in quite a serious spirit; we grant it quite willingly: to know this requires toil and exertion. But surely this knowledge might have been sought for without all the circumlocution and all those suppositions.*

You next wish to contemplate yourself as what you have believed yourself to be, in such a way that, when every doubtful element is withdrawn, nothing may be left beyond what is absolutely certain and indubitable.[3] *But you will do this with the approval of everyone. You tackle the matter; and believing that you are a man, you ask,* what is man? *Purposely dismissing the common definition you select those characteristics* which at the first glance presented themselves to you, e.g. that you had a face, hands, and other members which you designated by the name body; and likewise that you were nourished, that you walked, that you felt, that you thought, features which you referred to the soul.[4] *So far, so good, only what becomes of the distinction you draw between the soul and the body? You say* that you did not then perceive what the soul was, but imagined merely that it was like a wind, a flame, or an ether, which was spread throughout your grosser parts.[5] *That is worth noting.* But body you did not doubt to have a nature identical with whatever can be defined by figure, or can be confined in a certain place, can fill a space from which it can exclude every other body, can be perceived by touch, sight, hearing, smell or taste, and can be moved in many ways.[6] *But these things you can even at present attribute to bodies, provided you do not attribute all of them to every corporeal thing; inasmuch as wind is a body, and yet is not perceived by sight. And you cannot exclude the other attributes which you mention next in order, for wind, fire, also move*

many things. Moreover, what you subjoin, viz that you denied to body the power of moving itself cannot, so far as it appears, be successfully maintained; for this implies that every body must by its own nature be without motion, and that all its motions must proceed from an incorporeal principle; and it must be thought that neither can water flow nor an animal move, unless through the agency of some incorporeal mover.

2. *Next you investigate whether,* the existence of a deceiving agent being up to this point supposed, you can affirm that any of the things which you judged to belong to the nature of body exist in you. You say that after the most careful scrutiny nothing of such a sort can be found in you.[7] *Already at this point you consider yourself not as a complete human being, but as that inner and more hidden part, such as you deemed the soul to be. Wherefore I ask thee, O soul, or whatever the name be by which you choose to be addressed, have you by this time corrected that notion in virtue of which you previously imagined that you were something similar to wind, or a like substance, diffused throughout the members of the body? You certainly have not. Why then, cannot you be a wind, or rather a very subtle spirit, which, by means of the heat of the heart, is distilled from the purest of the blood or from some other source; or may there not be some other cause by which you are evoked and preserved; and may you not, being diffused throughout the members, attribute life to them, and see with the eye, hear with the ear, think by means of the brain and discharge the other functions which by common consent are ascribed to you? If that be so, why may you not have the same figure as the whole of this body has, just as the air takes the shape of the vessel which contains it? Why may you not believe that you are bounded too by the same circumambient medium as surrounds the body, or by the bodily epidermis? May you not occupy space, or those parts of space which the solid body or its parts do not completely fill? In truth, the solid body possesses pores through which you yourself may be diffused, in such a way that, where the parts of which you consist are found none of its parts exist; just as in a mixture of wine and water, where the particles of the former are, the parts of the second are not found, howsoever much sight be unable to distinguish between the two. Why will it be impossible for you to exclude another body from the same space as you occupy, when the parts composing the solid body are incapable of existing in the same tiny portions of space in which you are found? Why*

[1] Cf. Med. II, p. 78.
[2] Cf. p. 78.
[3] Cf. p. 78.
[4] Cf. p. 78.
[5] Cf. p. 78.
[6] Cf. p. 78.

[7] Cf. pp. 78–79.

nnot you participate in many motions? For
.en you assign many motions to the members
.emselves, how can you move them unless you
.urself are moved? Certainly you must not be
.moved if you are to cause movement, where ex-
.ion is called for; nor can you rest immoveable
.en the body itself is moved. If this be so, why
. you say that none of those things exist in
.u which are relative to the nature of the
.dy?

3. You proceed to say that, of the things
.cribed to soul, neither nourishment nor walk-
.g belong to you.[1] But, in the first place, a
.ing may be a body and yet not be nourished.
.condly, if you are such a body as we have de-
.ribed breath to be, why, if your more solid mem-
.rs are nourished by more solid substance, may
.u—a more rarefied one—not be also nourished
. a rarer substance? Further, are you not young
.d vigorous when that body, of which these are
.e parts, is in the vigour of youth? And when it is
.eak, are you not yourself weak? In the matter of
.oving, when it is owing to you that your mem-
.rs move and never pass into any position ex-
.pt you move and transport them thither, how
.n that be possible without movement on your
.rt? But, you say, if now I do not possess a
.dy, these are nothing but figments.[1] But
.hether you are making game of us or playing
.ith yourself, there is no reason for our delaying
.re. If, however, you are speaking seriously,
.u must prove that you neither have any body
.hich you inform, nor are of such a nature as to
. nourished and to move along with it.

You proceed, saying that you are without
.nsation.[1] But yourself assuredly are such as to
.e colour, hear sounds, etc. This, you say, can-
.ot occur apart from the body. I grant you
.at; but, in the first place, a body is present to
.u and you yourself reside within the eye, which
.rtainly does not see without you; and secondly
.u may be a rarefied body operating by means of
.e sense-organs. You say I have thought I per-
.ived many things during sleep that subse-
.uently I recognised as not having been ex-
.erienced at all. But though you go wrong if,
.ithout using the eye, you seemed to have experi-
.ces which do not occur without the eye coming
.to play, nevertheless so to err is not your uni-
.rsal experience, nor have you not employed
.ur eye, by which you perceive and by which you
.ke in the images, which now you can use with-
.t employing the eye.

At length you come to the conclusion that
.ought belongs to you. True, that is not to be

denied; but you still have to prove that the power
of thinking is so much superior to the nature of
body, that neither breath nor any other mobile
pure, and rarefied body, can by any means be so
adapted as to be capable of exercising thought.
You will have to prove at the same time that the
souls of the brutes are incorporeal inasmuch as
they think, or, over and above the functioning of
the external senses, are aware of something internal, not only while awake, but when dreaming.
Again, you must prove that this solid body contributes absolutely nothing to your thinking
(though you have never existed without it nor
have ever hitherto had any thought in isolation
from it), and that your thinking is hence independent of it; so that you can neither be impeded
nor disturbed by the foul and dense vapours or
fumes, which sometimes so afflict the brain.

4. Your conclusion is: I am, to speak accurately, a Thing which thinks, that is to say, a
mind or a soul, or an understanding, or a reason.[2] Here I confess that I have been suffering
from a deception. For I believed that I was addressing the human soul, or that internal principle, by which a man lives, feels, moves from
place to place and understands, and after all I
was only speaking to a mind, which has divested
itself not only of the body but of the soul itself.
Have you, my worthy sir, in attaining to this result, followed the example of those ancients, who,
though they thought that the soul was diffused
throughout the whole body, believed that its principal part—the dominating part—was located in
a determinate region of the body, e.g. in the brain,
or in the heart? Not that they judged that the soul
was not also to be found there, but that they believed that the mind was, as it were, added to the
soul existing there, was linked to it, and along
with it informed that region. I ought really to
have remembered that from the discussion in
your Discourse on Method. There you appeared
to decide that all those offices, ascribed both to the
vegetative and to the sensitive soul, do not depend
on the rational soul and can be exercised without
it before it is introduced into the body, as does
happen in the case of the brutes, in whom your
contention is that no reason is found. I do not
know how I managed to forget this, except for the
reason that I remained in doubt as to whether
that principle by means of which we and the
brutes alike exercise the vegetative function and
feel, was not according to your nomenclature to
be styled soul, soul being exclusively reserved for
the human mind. Yet since it is that principle
that is properly said to animate us, mind is ca-

[1]Med. II, pp. 78–79.

[2]Cf. pp. 78–79.

pable of no other function than to make us think, as you indeed assert. And, since this is so, call it now Mind, *and let it be, taken precisely,* a Thing which thinks.

You add that it is thought alone which cannot be separated from you. *Truly it is impossible to deny this of you, if you are primarily Mind alone and refuse to allow that your substance can be distinguished from the substance of the soul except in thought; though here I pause and ask whether, when you say* that thought cannot be separated from you, *you mean that you, as long as you exist, think to an indefinite extent. This is indeed in conformity with the pronouncement of those celebrated philosophers who, in order to prove your immortality, assumed that you were in perpetual motion, or, as I interpret it, thought continuously. But this will not gain the adhesion of those who cannot comprehend how you can think during a lethargic sleep, or while in the womb. Besides, I have a difficulty here as to whether you think that you have been infused into the body or one of its parts during the uterine stage of existence or at birth. But I should be loth to be troublesome with my enquiries, or to reflect whether you remember what your thoughts were when in the womb, or in the days, months, and years succeeding your birth; or, if you replied that you had forgotten, to ask why this was so. Yet I suggest that you should remember how obscure, how meagre, how nearly nonexistent your thought must have been during those periods of life.*

Proceeding, you maintain that you are not the complex of members which we call the human body.[1] *But that must be admitted because you are considering yourself solely as a thing which thinks, as a part of the concrete human whole, distinct from this exterior and more solid part.* "I am not," *you say,* "a subtle air distributed through these members, I am not a wind, a fire, a vapour, nor a breath, nor anything which I can construct in imagination. For I have assumed that all these were nothing; and let that supposition be unchanged." *But halt here, O Mind, and let those suppositions, or rather those fictions, take themselves off. You say,* "I am not air or anything of such a nature." *But, if the total soul be something of the kind, wherefore may not you who are thought to be the noblest part of the soul, be deemed to be, as it were, the flower, or the subtlest, purest, and most active part of it. You say* "perhaps those same things which I supposed were non-existent, are real things and are not different from

[1]Cf. p. 79.

the self which I know? I do not know abou this, I shall not dispute about it now." *But you do not know, if you do not dispute the ma ter, why do you assume that you are none of thes things?* "I know," *you say,* "that I exist; bu the knowledge of my existence taken in its pre cise significance cannot depend on that whic I do not know." *Granted, but remember that yo have not proved that you are not air, or a vapou or many other things.*

5. *In sequence to this you describe that whic you call the imagination. You say that to im agine is nothing else than to contemplate th figure or image of a corporeal thing, obviousl for the purpose of inferring that you are aware your own nature by means of some other specie of thought than imagination. But, though it permissible for you to define imagination in a cordance with your own opinions, I ask you wh if you are corporeal (the contradictory of whic you have not proved), you cannot contempla yourself in the guise of some corporeal figure image? And I ask you, when you so regard you self, if you are conscious of or observe anythin other than a pure, transparent, and rarefied su stance like wind, which pervades the whole boo or at least the brain or a part of it, animatin you, and discharging your vital functions throug the body.* "I know," *you say,* "that nothing all that I can understand by means of the im agination belongs to this knowledge which have of myself." *But you do not state how yo know this; and since a short time ago you had d cided that you did not know whether or not thes things belonged to you, I ask you whence you no derive your conclusion?*

6. *Your next point is:* that it is necessary t recall the mind from these modes of though with the utmost diligence, in order that it ma be able to know its own nature with perfe distinctness.[2] *Very sound advice; but, after ha ing thus with the utmost diligence recalled you self, report, I pray you, how distinctly you ha perceived your own nature. For all that you r cord is that you are a Thing which thinks, truth we all previously believed; but you do n reveal to us what the nature of this operative su stance is, how it coheres, and how it adapts itse for discharging such various functions in suc various ways, and many other such things abo which we have hitherto been in ignorance.*

You allege that intellect can perceive tha which imagination is incapable of discernin (the imagination which you identify with th "common sense"). But, my worthy Mind, ca

[2]Cf. p. 79.

ou prove that there are many internal faculties nd not a single, simple faculty by means of vhich we are conscious of everything whatsoever t be? When I behold the sun with open eyes, sen-ation most manifestly occurs. When, subse-uently, I bethink myself of the sun, keeping my yes closed, internal cognition manifestly occurs. But how, in fine, shall I be able to discern that I verceive the sun with the common sense, or facul-y of imagination, and not really with the mind, r understanding, and so at pleasure apprehend he sun, now by the activity of the understanding, vhich is other than the imagination, now by the ct of the imagination which is different from hat of the understanding? True, if it were pos-ible for an understanding to exist after cerebral rouble had set in, and injury to the imagination, n understanding which discharged all its pecul-ar and incommunicable functions, then under-tanding could be said to be as easily distinguish-ble from imagination as imagination from ex-ernal sense. But since the reverse of this is true, ve have certainly no ready means of setting up his distinction.

When it is said, as you will have it, that im-gination occurs when we contemplate the im-ge of a corporeal object, you see that, since here is no other way of contemplating corporeal hings, bodies must be apprehended by the im-gination alone, or, at least that no other faculty f knowing can be discerned.

You mention that you still cannot prevent vourself thinking that corporeal things, the mages of which are framed by thought, which re made known by the activity of the senses, re more distinctly known than that obscure nd unknown part of you which does not come nder the imagination: so that it seems strange o you that you should know and understand nore distinctly things the existence of which is ubious and which seem foreign to you.[1] To begin with, that is an excellent saying "that nknown part of you." For in truth you do not know what it is nor what is its nature; nor hence can you come to know that it is of such a sort as to be incapable of entering the imagination. Further, all our knowledge seems to find its source in the senses; and although you deny that whatever is in the understanding must have existed previously in the sense, my contention seems to be none the less true, since unless knowledge enters by a sort of invasion alone,—at a stroke, as it were, it must yet be elaborated and perfected by analogy, by composi-ion, by division, by amplification, by attenu-

[1]P. 80, sub fin.

ation (of the things of sense)[2] and other similar devices which it is unnecessary to recount. Hence it is by no means strange that those things which of themselves rush in and excite the sense make a more lively impression on the mind than that made by objects which the mind itself constructs out of the material that chances to meet its senses and which it grasps, being receptive in so far only as it is given the opportunity of so acting. Also you indeed call material things doubtful; but if you cared to confess the truth, you would ac-knowledge that you are not less certain of the exist-ence of the body which you inhabit, and of all the things that surround you, than of your own ex-istence. And if you manifest yourself to yourself by that operation alone which is called thought, how does that compare with the manifestations of things of this sort? They indeed are made mani-fest not only by various operations, but also by many other highly convincing circumstances, by their magnitude, figure, solidity, colour, savour, etc., so that, though they are external to you, it is by no means strange that you should know and comprehend them more distinctly than yourself. But you ask how it is possible to understand something foreign to you better than yourself. I reply that the case of the eye, which sees other things but does not see itself, illustrates how this is possible.

7. "But," you ask, "what then am I? A thing which thinks. What is a thing which thinks? It is a thing which doubts, under-stands, affirms, denies, wills, refuses, which also imagines and feels." You mention many things here which in themselves cause me no diffi-culty. This alone makes me pause, your saying that you are a thing which feels. It is indeed strange, for you had previously maintained the opposite; or perchance did you mean that in addi-tion to yourself there is a corporeal faculty resid-ing in the eye, in the ear, and in the other organs, which receiving the semblance of things, gives rise to the act of sensation in a way that allows you thereupon to complete it, and brings it to pass that you are really the very self which sees, hears and perceives other things? It is for this reason, in my opinion, that you make sensation as well as imagination a species of thought. So be it; but look to it, nevertheless, that that sensation which exists in the brutes, since it is not dissimilar to your sensation, be not capable of earning the title of thought also, and that thus the brutes themselves may have a mind not dissimilar to your own.

You will say, I, holding the citadel in the brain, receive whatsoever is sent me by the

[2]Tr.

(animal)[1] spirits which permeate the nerves, and thus the act of sense which is said to be effected by the whole body is transacted in my presence. Good; *but in the brutes there are nerves, (animal) spirits, a brain, and a conscious principle residing therein, which in a similar manner receives the messages sent by the animal spirits and accomplishes the act of sensation. You will say that that principle in the brain of brutes is nothing other than the Fancy or faculty of imagination. But kindly show that the principle in the human brain is other than the Fancy or imaginative faculty. I asked you a little while back for a criterion by means of which you could prove that it was different, a criterion which, in my opinion, you are not likely to offer me. True, you assert that the operations of the human principle far surpass those which are to be obtained in brutes. But, in the same way as man may be the most outstanding of all the animals, yet without being detached from his place in the number of the animals, so, though you are for the above reasons proved to be the most excellent of imaginative faculties or Fancies, you do not lose your place in the ranks of such faculties. For even that self which you specially style the mind, though it may very well imply a higher nature, cannot be anything of a diverse type. Indeed, in order to prove that you are of a diverse (i.e. as you contend of an incorporeal) nature, you ought to display some operation in a way different from that in which the brutes act, and to carry this on, if not without the brain, at least in independence of it; but this is not complied with. (Indeed the reverse happens),[2] if, as a matter of fact, you are troubled when the brain is troubled, are overwhelmed when it is overcome, and if you yourself are unable to retain any trace of the semblances of things which it has lost. You say* that in the brutes everything takes place through a blind impulse of the (animal) spirits and the other organs, just in the same way as motion is achieved in a clock or any other machine. *But however true this be in the case of the other functions, like nutrition, the pulsation of the arteries, and so forth, which very functions take place in man in precisely the same way as in brutes, can it be said that either the operations of sense, or what are called the emotions of the soul are effected in brutes by means of a blind impulse, and not in our case also? A morsel of food discharges a semblance of itself into the eye of the dog, and this being transferred to the brain, attaches itself to the soul, as it were, by means of hooks; and the* soul itself thenceforth and the whole body, whic coheres with it, is haled to that food, as it were, b chains of the most delicate contriving. The stor also which someone picks up threateningly send forth a semblance of itself, which, acting like lever, gives a propulsion to the soul and reverse the course of the body and compels it to tak flight. But does not the very same thing happen i man? Perhaps you know of some other way i which this can take place; if so, I should be muc indebted if you would explain it to me.

You say "I (the soul)"[3] am free and there i a power within me by means of which I ca turn a man equally from fleeing and from go ing forward." *But the imaginative princip does as much in a brute; a dog may for the tim disregard blows and threats and rush at the foo it sees (and man often does much the same thing! You say that the dog barks by mere impulsio and not owing to resolve, as in the case of me speaking. But in the case of man there are cause at work too, and hence we might deem that h speaking was due to impulsion; for that als which we attribute to choice is due to the stronge impulse, and the brute also exercises his ow choice when one impulse is greater than th others. I have indeed witnessed a dog attuning i barks to the sound of a trumpet in such a way a to imitate all the changes in its notes, sharp flat, slow and quick, however much more fre quent and prolonged the sounds were made, ca priciously and suddenly. You say brutes lac reason. But while doubtless they are withou human reason, they do have a reason of their ow Hence evidently they cannot be called irration except in comparison with us, or relatively to ou species of reason, since in any case λόγος ratio seems to be as general in its significance and can be as easily ascribed to them, as the ter cognitive faculty or internal sense. You say tha they do not reason to conclusions. But thoug they do not reason so perfectly and about so man things as man, they still do reason; and the differ ence seems to be merely one of more or less. Yo say that they do not speak. But though they d not utter human expressions (as is natural seein they are not man) yet they emit their own peculia cries, and employ them just as we do our voca sounds. You say that a man in delirium ca weave together a number of cries in order to sig nify something; while the cleverest of the animal cannot do so. But consider whether it is fair o you to demand human sounds in the brute, and no to attend to its own proper cries. But this discus sion would take too much time if pursued further*

[1]Tr.
[2]Tr.

[3]Tr.

8. *Next you adduce* the instance of a piece of wax, *and concerning it you have much to say, in order to show* that what are called the accidents of the wax are one thing, the wax itself or the substance of the wax another, and that we require only the mind or understanding, but not sense or imagination in order to perceive distinctly the wax itself, and its substance.[1] *But firstly that itself is what everyone commonly allows, namely, that the concept of wax or of its substance can be abstracted from the concept of its accidents. But is it the case that this secures a distinct perception of the substance or nature of the wax? We indeed conceive that besides the colour, the figure, the capacity for being liquefied, etc., there is something which is the subject of the accidents and the observed changes of the wax; but as to what that is or what is its nature, we are ignorant. Nay, it always eludes our apprehension and it is only by conjecture that we think that there must be some substratum. Hence I marvel how you can maintain that, after you have finished stripping off those forms, as it were the vestures, of the wax, you perceive perfectly and very clearly what the wax is. For you do indeed perceive that the wax or its substance is something over and above such forms; but what that is you do not perceive, unless you are deceiving us. It is not revealed to you, as a man can be revealed to sight whose clothing and hat alone we have previously beheld, if we strip him of these in order to discover who and what he is. Further, when you think you perceive that in some way or other, how, I pray, do you perceive it? Is it not as something continuous and extended? For you do not conceive it as a point, though it is of such a nature as to be now more widely, now less extended. And since extension of this kind is not infinite, but has a limit, do you not conceive it as in some way possessing figure? Further, when you seem as it were to see it, do you not attach some colour to it, albeit confused? You certainly take it to be something more of a bodily nature, and so equally more visible than the mere void. Whence even the activity of your understanding is imagination of a kind. Tell us in good faith whether you maintain that you conceive it apart from any extension, figure and colour? If so, then what is it?*

What you have to say about seeing men, or perceiving them by the mind, men, however, whose hats and cloaks we alone behold[2] *does not prove that the mind is anything more than a faculty of imagination which is capable of passing judgment. For certainly the dog, in which you do not admit the presence of a mind similar to yours, judges in a similar manner, when it sees, not its master, but his hat or clothes [and yet recognises him]. Nay more. Although his master stand or sit, lie down, recline, draw himself together or stretch himself out, it yet recognises him always as its master, who can exist under all these forms, though nevertheless he does not [preserve the same proportions and] exist under one form rather than another, as wax does. And when it chases the hare that runs from it, do you not believe it thinks that it is throughout the same hare which it sees both intact and dead, and subsequently skinned and chopped into pieces? Your next point, that the perception of colour, hardness, and so forth, is not an act of vision or of touch, but only an intuition of the mind, may be granted, as long as mind is not taken to be something different from the imaginative faculty itself. But when you add, that that act of intuition may be imperfect and confused, or perfect and distinct in proportion as we attend more or less closely to the elements of which the wax is composed; this certainly shows, not that the mental intuition of this we know not what over and above all the forms of the wax, is a clear and distinct knowledge of the wax, but that it is a survey effected by the senses, of all, so far as that is possible, the accidents and mutations which the wax can sustain. From these we shall assuredly be able to conceive and explain what it is we mean by the term wax; but we shall not be able either to conceive by itself or explain to others that naked, or rather that inscrutable substance.*

9. *You next add:* But what should I say of this mind, that is of myself, for up to this point I do not admit in myself anything but mind? What then am I who seem to perceive this wax so distinctly, do I not know myself not only with much more truth, and certainty, but also with much more distinctness and clearness? For, if I judged that the wax is or exists from the fact that I see it, how much more clearly does it follow that I exist? For it may be that what I see is not really wax. It may also happen that I do not even possess eyes with which to see anything. But it cannot be that when I see, or (for I do not now take account of the distinction), when I think I see, that I myself who think am nought. So if I judge that wax exists from the fact that I touch it, the same thing will follow, to wit, that I am; and so if I judge from the fact that I imagine it, or from any other cause, the same result will follow. But what I have here remarked of wax may be

[1] Cf. Med. II, pp. 80, 81.
[2] Cf. p. 81.

applied to all other things which are external to me.[1] *These are your own words; and I here repeat them in order to let you see that while they indeed prove that you distinctly perceive that you exist, from the fact that you distinctly see and are aware of the existence of wax and those accidents of it, they yet do not prove that you for this reason know what or of what nature you are, either distinctly or indistinctly. Yet to do so had been worth your while, for of your existence there is no doubt. Notice meanwhile, though I do not mean to dwell on the point, that neither have I previously raised the objection that, since you do not admit the existence in you of anything beyond mind alone, and therefore rule out eyes, hands and the rest of the organs, it is vain to talk of wax and its accidents, which you see, touch, etc.; you certainly cannot see them without using your eyes, touch them without employing the hands (or, to adopt your mode of expression, think that you see and touch them).*

You proceed: If the perception of wax has seemed to me clearer and more distinct not only after the sight and touch, but also after many other causes have rendered it quite manifest to me, with how much more distinctness must it be said that I now know myself, since all the reasons which contribute to the knowledge of wax, or to any other body whatever, are yet better proof of the nature of my mind?[2] *But, just as your conclusions about wax prove only the perception of the existence of mind, and fail to reveal its nature, so will all other examples fail to prove anything more. But, if you wish to deduce something more from the perception of the substance of wax and other things, the only conclusion you can arrive at will be that just as we conceive that substance confusedly only and as an unknown somewhat, so we must also conceive of the mind. Hence you may well repeat that phrase of yours—that obscure and unknown part of me.*

Your conclusion is: And finally, behold I have without premeditation reverted to the point I desired. For, since it is now manifest that the mind itself and bodies are not, properly speaking, known by the senses or by the faculty of imagination, but by the understanding only; and since they are not known owing to the fact that they are seen and touched, I see clearly that there is nothing which is easier for me to know than my mind. *So you have it; but I do not see how you deduce or are clearly aware, that anything else can be known of your*

[1]Med. III, p. 82.
[2]Med. II, p. 80.

Mind than that it exists. Whence that also whic was promised by the very title of the Meditatio viz. that the human mind considered by itse would be shown to be better known than the bod; cannot in my estimation be complied with. For was not your project to prove that the human min existed and that its existence was better know than that of the body, when really no one dispute its existence; rather you doubtless wished to mal its nature better known than that of the body an that is what you, however, have not achieve Truly, O Mind, you have recounted of corpore nature the very things, the list of which we kno viz. extension, figure, occupation of space, et But what about yourself? You are not a materi complex, not air, not wind, not a fire, or one many other things. To grant you these resul (though some of them you yourself refuted), the are not however what we expected. They are fo sooth negatives and we want to know, not wh you are not, but what you really are. Hence, yo refer us to your main conclusion, viz. that yo are a Thing which thinks, i.e. doubts, affirm etc. But first, to say that you are a Thing is say nothing which is known. For "thing" is general term, undifferentiated and vague and n applying to you more than to anything else in t entire world, to anything which is not whol non-existent. You are a Thing? That is to sa you are not nothing; or, what is precisely t same, you are something. But a stone is not not ing, i.e. is something; and so is a fly, and so o with everything else. Next, in saying that you a a Thinking being, though you do assign a pred cate known to us, yet it was not previously u known and was not the object of your enquir Who doubts your thinking? That which baffles u that which we seek to discover is that inner su stance belonging to you, the property of which to think. Wherefore, your conclusion should co respond with your quest, and that is to discove not that you are a Thinking thing, but of wh nature you, the thing which thinks, are. Is it n the case that it will not be sufficient for you to sa when a knowledge of wine superior to the vulge is sought for: wine is a thing which is liquid, e tracted from grapes, is white or red, is sweet, in toxicating and so on? Rather you will try to di cover and to declare how that internal substanc in accordance with what you have observed of fabrication, has been compounded out of a mi ture of spirits, humour, tartar and other element in some or other particular quantity and propo tion. Hence, similarly, since a knowledge of you self superior to the vulgar, i.e. to what you pr viously possessed, is called for, you see qui early that it is not enough to inform us that you *e* a thing which thinks, doubts, understands, *c.*, but that you ought to scrutinise yourself, as were, by a chemical method of procedure in *der* to be able to reveal and demonstrate to us *our* internal substance. If you accomplish this, *e* shall certainly ourselves discover by investi- *ation* whether you are better known than the *body* itself, of which anatomy, chemistry and *any* other sciences, many senses and numbers *experiments* of all kinds tell us so much.

RELATIVE TO MEDITATION III

Of God: That He Exists

1. *In your Third Meditation, from the fact at your clear and distinct knowledge of the roposition,* I am a thing which thinks, *was cognized by you to be the cause of your certainty* its truth, you infer that you are able to set up *is* general Rule: that all things which I per- *eive very clearly and very distinctly are true.*[1] *ut though amid the obscurity that surrounds us, ere may very well be no better Rule obtainable, et when we see that many minds of the first rank, hich seem to have perceived many things so learly and distinctly, have judged that the truth f things is hidden either in God or in a well, may not be open to us to suspect that the Rule is per- aps fallacious? And really, since you are not gnorant of the argument of the Sceptics, tell me hat else can we infer to be true as being clearly nd distinctly perceived, except that that which ppears to anyone does appear? Thus it is true at the taste of a melon appears to me to be of is precise kind. But how shall I persuade my- elf that therefore it is true that such a savour ex- sts in the melon? When as a boy and in enjoy- ent of good health, I thought otherwise, indeed, receiving clearly and distinctly that the melon ad another taste. Likewise, I see that many men hink otherwise also, as well as many animals hat are well equipped in respect of the sense f taste and are quite healthy. Does then one truth onflict with another? Or is it rather the case that t is not because a thing is clearly and distinctly erceived that it is of itself true, but that that only s true which is clearly and distinctly perceived to e so. Practically the same account must be given f those things that are relative to the mind. I ould have sworn at other times that we cannot ass from a lesser to a greater quantity without assing through the stage of equality (to a fixed uantity):*[2] *that two lines which continually ap- roach one another cannot fail to meet if pro-*

duced to infinity. I seemed to myself to perceive those truths so clearly and distinctly that I took them for the truest and most indubitable of axi- oms: nevertheless arguments subsequently pre- sented themselves which convinced me of the oppo- site, seeming to make me perceive that more clearly and more distinctly. But when I now again consider the nature of Mathematical assump- tions I once more waver. Whence it may indeed be said that it is true that I acknowledge the truth of such and such propositions, in so far as I assume or conceive that quantity, lines and so forth are constituted in this way; but that they are for this reason of themselves true, cannot be safely advanced. But whatever may be the case in mathe- matical matters, I ask you, as regards the other matters which we are now investigating, what is the reason that men's opinions about them are so many and so various? Each person thinks that he clearly and distinctly perceives that proposition which he defends. To prevent you from saying that many people either imitate or feign belief, I direct your attention to those people who face even death for the sake of the opinions they hold, even though they see others facing it for the sake of the opposite cause: surely, you do not believe that at that point the cries they utter are not au- thentic. You yourself indeed experience this diffi- culty, because previously you admitted many things to be altogether certain and manifest, which you afterwards discovered to be dubi- ous.[3] *In this passage, however, you neither refute nor confirm your Rule, but merely snatch the opportunity of expatiating about the Ideas by which you may be deceived, in so far as they represent something as being external to you, which is, nevertheless, perhaps not external to you; and once more you treat of a God who may deceive, and by whom you may be led into error respecting these propositions:*—"two and three are five," "the square has not more than four sides."[4] *Evidently you thus suggest that the proof of the rule is to be expected, waiting until you have shown that a God exists who cannot be a de- ceiver. Yet to throw out this warning hint, you ought not so much to take pains to substantiate this Rule, following which we so readily mistake the false for the true, as to propound a method which will direct us and show us when we are in error and when not, so often as we think that we clearly and distinctly perceive anything.*

2. *You next distinguish* Ideas (by which you mean thoughts in so far as they resemble images) *as innate, adventitious and factitious. In the*

[1]Med. III, p. 82.
[2]Tr.

[3]Med. III, p. 82.
[4]Cf. p. 82.

first class you put, your understanding of what a thing, what truth, what thought is; *in the second,* your hearing of a noise, seeing the sun, feeling (the heat of)[1] the fire; *in the third,* the Sirens and Hippogryphs you construct imaginatively. *You add also* that perhaps these may be all adventitious or all innate or all made by yourself, inasmuch as you have not yet clearly grasped their origin. *Further, lest meanwhile, before you have grasped this, some fallacy creep in, it is well to note that all Ideas seem to be adventitious, and proceed from things existing outside the mind and falling under some sense faculty. Thus the mind has a power (or rather is itself the power) not only of perceiving the adventitious Ideas themselves or of perceiving those which things convey to it by means of the senses, I repeat, bare and distinct, and wholly such as it receives them within itself; but also of uniting, dividing, diminishing, enlarging, arranging, and of performing other operations of this description.*

Hence the third class of Ideas at least is not distinct from the second; for the Idea of a chimaera is nothing else than the idea of the head of a lion, the belly of a goat and the tail of a serpent, out of which the mind forms a single Idea, though apart or singly they are adventitious. So the Idea of a Giant or a man conceived as being like a mountain or the whole world, is merely adventitious. It is the idea of a man of the common stature, amplified at pleasure by the mind, though presented with greater confusedness in proportion as it is amplified in thought. So, too, the Idea of a Pyramid, of a city, or of anything else which one has not seen, is merely the Idea of a Pyramid, city or another thing previously seen, somewhat altered in form and consequently multiplied and arranged in some confused way.

As for the forms which you say are innate, they certainly seem to be non-existent, and any that are said to be of such character appear also to have an adventitious origin. You say, my nature is the source of my power of understanding what a thing is.[2] *But I do not think that you mean to speak of the power of understanding itself, which is not in doubt, and is not the subject of investigation here; but rather of the Idea of a Thing. Neither do you mean the Idea of any particular Thing; for the Sun, this stone and all single things are Things, the Ideas of which you say are not innate. Hence you speak of the Idea of Thing taken universally and as practically synonymous with "entity" and extending as*

widely as it. *But I ask you, how can this Idea in the mind, without all the single things bei~ there also, together with their genera, from whi~ it abstracts and forms a conception which~ proper to none of the particulars and yet agre~ with them all? If the Idea of Thing is innate, t~ Idea of animal, of plant, stone, of all universe will have to be innate also. There will be no ne~ for us to give ourselves the labour of discrimin~ ing from each other the many particulars, whi~ enables us, after again making a number of d~ tinctions, to retain that alone which is common all, or, what amounts to the same thing, frame t~ Idea of a genus.*

You say also that it is your nature which e~ ables you to understand what truth is, *or, as* interpret, *gives you the Idea of truth. But truth is merely the conformity of a judgme~ with the thing about which the judgment is passe~ truth is a certain relation, and hence not to distinguished from that very thing and that Id~ as related to each other, or what is the same thin~ from the very Idea of the thing; for the Idea repr~ sents both itself and the thing in so far as it h~ such and such a character. Whence the Idea~ Truth is merely the Idea of a thing in so far as is conformable to that thing, or represents it~ having the nature it possesses. The consequence~ that if the Idea of the thing is not innate but a~ ventitious, the Idea of truth is also adventitiou~ and not innate. If this holds of each particul~ truth, it must also hold of truth universally, t~ notion of which, or Idea (as has already bee~ maintained in the case of the idea of thing) constructed out of particular notions or Ideas.*

You allege that it is to your nature you ow~ your comprehension of what thought is (*I co~ tinue to interpret once more* the Idea of thought~ *But, just as the mind can, out of the Idea of on~ city, construct in imagination the Idea of a~ other, so can it, out of the Idea of one operatio~ say, seeing or tasting, construct the Idea of a~ other, e.g. of thought. Surely, there is a recognise~ analogy between the cognitive faculties, and eac~ readily conduces to a knowledge of the othe~ Though there is no need for much expenditure~ labour in connection with the Idea of thought; should rather be reserved for that of mind, and~ the same extent for that of the soul; for if that~ acknowledged to be innate, there will be no har~ in admitting that the Idea of thought is also i~ nate. Hence we must wait until you have prove~ your thesis in the case of the mind or the soul.*

3. *You seem* afterwards to make it doubtf~ not only whether any Ideas proceed from e~ ternal things, but also whether there are an~

[1]Tr.
[2]Med. iii, p. 83.

xternal objects at all. *And you seem thence to infer that although there exist in you the Ideas f things said to be external, those Ideas nevertheless do not prove that the things exist, since hey do not necessarily proceed from them, ut may be due to yourself or to some other ause, I know not what. It was for this reason I incy, that you previously continued to say:* That ou had not previously perceived earth, sky, r stars, but the Ideas of earth, sky and stars, vhich might possibly be a source of delusion. *Therefore, if you are not yet convinced of the existence of earth, sky, stars, and other objects, why, ray, do you walk about on the earth or alter the osition of your body in order to behold the sun? Vhy do you approach the fire in order to feel its eat? Why sit down at a table to a meal, in order o satisfy your hunger? Why move your tongue in rder to speak, or your hand in order to send this vriting to us? Certainly the doubts you express nay be asserted or subtly derived from our thought, ut they do not advance the matter in hand, and ince you are not really in doubt about the existnce of things external to you, let us act seriously nd in good faith and talk about things just as hey really are. But if, assuming the existence of xternal objects, you think that it has been propery proved that the Ideas we have of them cannot be lerived from them themselves, you will have to disose not only of the objections you yourself bring, ut of additional difficulties which can be raised.*

Thus you do recognise that ideas appear admittedly to proceed from objects, because we eem to be taught this lesson by nature and beause we are sensible that those ideas do not lepend on us, or on our will.[1] *But, not to menion either these arguments or their solution, you ught also among other things to have brought up nd solved the objection in which it is asked:— vhy one born blind has no idea of colour or one orn deaf of sound, if it is not because external hings have not been able to convey from themelves any semblance of themselves into the mind f the afflicted individual? For the inlets have een closed since birth, and obstacles placed there or all time, which prevent anything from passing hrough them.*

Afterwards you press the example of the Sun, of which you have two ideas, one derived from he senses, viz. that in accordance with which he sun seems to be extremely small; while the other is derived from astronomical reasonings, nd represents the sun to be of great size. That dea is true and more similar (to its object)[2]

[1]Cf. p. 83.
[2]Tr.

which is not drawn from the senses, but is elicited from your innate notions, or achieved by some other means. *But each of that pair of ideas of the Sun is true, similar to, and in conformity with the Sun; only one is less, the other more so. In precisely the same way the two ideas we have of a man, the one proceeding from him at ten yards' distance, the other at a hundred or a thousand, are similar to him, true, and in conformity with him. But the one has these qualities in a greater degree than the others, in respect that the idea which we have when the man is near is to a slight degree impaired, while that which proceeds from a distance suffers to a greater extent. All this might be explained in a few words if it were permitted, or if you did not grasp it sufficiently yourself.*

Moreover, though it is by the mind alone that we are aware of that vast idea of the sun, the idea is not on that account elicited from any innate notion. Rather what occurs is, that in so far as experience proves and reason, supporting it, confirms the belief that things at a distance appear smaller than when they are near, the idea which finds entrance by the channels of sense is merely amplified by the mind's own power, and so much the more in proportion to what is known to be the sun's distance from us and the precise number of semi-diameters of the earth to which its diameter is equal.

Do you wish to infer that no part of this idea is implanted in us by nature? Ask what it is in one born blind. You will find in the first place that in his mind it has neither colour nor brilliance; secondly, that neither is it round, unless someone has told him that it is round and he himself has previously handled round bodies. Finally you will discover that it is not of such great magnitude unless the blind person has either by reasoning or owing to the influence of authority amplified his previously received notion.

Yet—allow me to interpose this reflection—I ask you: have we ourselves, we who have seen the Sun so often, who have so many times beheld its apparent diameter, and have as frequently reasoned as to its true diameter, have we, I say, any other than the common image of the sun? It is true that by reason we infer that the sun exceeds the earth in size more than a hundred and sixty times; but do we on that account possess the idea of a body of such a vast extent? It is true we amplify this idea which we receive from the senses as much as possible, we exert our mind as much as we can; yet we manage to present ourselves with nothing but mere obscurity, and as often as we wish to have a distinct thought of the Sun, the

mind must return to that sensible appearance
which it has received through the medium of the
eye. It is sufficient for the mind not to deny that
the Sun is really greater than it appears, and that
if the eye approached nearer to it, it would have
an idea of greater extent; but meanwhile it is to
the idea in its presented magnitude that the mind
attends.

4. Next, recognising the inequality and diversity between ideas, you say: There is no doubt
that those which represent to me substances are
something more, and contain, so to speak,
more objective reality within them, than those
that simply represent modes or accidents; and
that idea again by which I understand a Supreme God, eternal, infinite, omnipotent, the
Creator of all things which are outside of Himself, has certainly more objective reality in itself than those by which finite substances are
represented.[1] Here you go at such a great pace
that we must arrest your course for a little. I do
not indeed have any difficulty about that which
you call objective reality. It is enough if you in
conformity with the common expression, according to which external things exist subjectively and
formally in themselves, but objectively or ideally
in the understanding, mean (as is evident) merely
that an idea should agree with the thing of which
it is the idea; and that it hence contains nothing of
a representative nature which is not really in the
thing itself, and represents more reality in proportion as the thing it represents contains more
reality in itself. True, you immediately afterwards distinguish objective from formal reality
which, as I interpret, is the idea itself, not as
representative, but as an actual entity. But it is
agreed that whether it be the idea or the objective
reality of the idea, it must not be measured by the
total formal reality of the thing, or that which the
thing has in itself, but merely by that part (of the
thing)[2] of which the understanding has acquired
knowledge, or (what is the very same) according
to the acquaintance with the thing which the understanding possesses. Thus, for example, you
will be said to possess a perfect idea of a man, if
you have surveyed him attentively and frequently
and in many aspects; while the idea of him whom
you have but seen in passing and on one occasion,
and partially only, will certainly be imperfect.
But if you have beheld not the man himself but a
mask covering his face and his garments clothing
his body completely, we must say either that you
have no idea of him, or that if you do possess one
it is extremely imperfect and confused.

[1]Med. III, p. 84.
[2]Tr.

These are my grounds for maintaining tha
though we have indeed a distinct idea of acciden
and one that is true of them, that of the substanc
which underlies them is only confused and qui
fictitious. Hence, though you say that there
more objective reality in the idea of substanc
than in the idea of accidents, it must first b
denied that there is a true idea or representatio
of substance, and hence that it possesses any o
jective reality. Secondly, even though it shoul
have been admitted that it does possess some, w
must deny that it has more than the ideas of acc
dents possess, since everything that owns a reali
of this sort, holds it from the ideas of those acc
dents, under which, or after the fashion of whic
we have said substance is conceived, when we de
clare that it could be conceived only as somethin
extended and possessing figure and colour.

Concerning what you add about the idea o
God, I ask you how, when you are not yet su
whether a God exists, you know that God is repr
sented by the idea of Him, as supreme, eterna
infinite, omnipotent and as creator of a
things? Do you not take this from your previousl
received knowledge of God, in so far as you ha
heard these attributes ascribed to him? If you ha
not heard so much before, would you descri
God so? You will reply that this is brought for
ward merely as an example and without implyin
any definition as yet. So be it: but take care le
afterwards you take it as a matter already decide

You allege that there is more objective realit
in the idea of an infinite God than in the ide
of a finite thing. But, firstly, since the huma
understanding is not capable of conceiving in
finity, neither, consequently, does it possess o
have cognisance of an idea which is representa
tive of an infinite thing. Wherefore also he wh
says that a thing is infinite, attributes to a thin
which he does not comprehend a name which h
does not understand, since, just as the thing ex
tends beyond his widest grasp, so the negation o
limit ascribed to its extension is not understoo
by him, whose comprehension is always confine
within some bounds.

Next, though every highest perfection is won
to be ascribed to God, all such seem to be derive
from the things which we customarily admire i
ourselves, e.g. length of existence, power, knowl
edge, kindness, blessedness, etc.; we amplif
these as much as possible, and then pronounc
God to be everlasting, all-powerful, all-knowing
most excellent, most blessed, etc., but the ide
which represents all these attributes does not con
tain more objective reality on that account tha
the finite things taken together have, out of th

leas of which that idea is compounded, afterwards being magnified in the aforesaid way. For
either does he who says eternal, thereby embrace
in his mind the total extent of the duration of that
which has never begun to be and never will cease
to exist; nor does he who says omnipotent en-
visage the whole multitude of possible effects; and
so in the case of the others.

Lastly, can anyone affirm that he possesses an
idea of God which is true, or which represents
God as He is? How slight a thing would God be,
unless He were other and had other attributes
than this feeble idea of ours contains! Must we
not believe that man relatively to God has a smaller proportion of perfection than that which the
tiniest creature, a tick, burrowing in its skin,
possesses relatively to an elephant? Hence, if the
man who from observation of the perfections of
the tick should construct in his mind an idea
which he maintained was that of an elephant,
would be held to be very silly, how can he be satisfied with himself, who out of human perfections
that he beholds shapes an idea which is, he contends, that of God, and resembles Him? Tell me
also how we recognise in God those perfections
which in ourselves we find to be so tiny? And when
we have detected them, what sort of essence must
we therefore imagine is that of God? God is most
certainly infinitely beyond the widest grasp, and
when our mind addresses itself to the contemplation of God, it not only gets befogged but comes to
a standstill. Hence it follows both that we have no
reason to assert that we possess any cognate idea
which represents God, and it is enough if, on the
analogy of our human qualities, we derive and
construct an idea of some sort or other for our use
—an idea which does not transcend human comprehension, and contains no reality which we do
not perceive in other things or by means of other
things.

5. You assume, next, that it is manifest by
the natural light that there must be at least as
much reality in the efficient and total cause as
in its effect.[1] You do so in order that you may
infer that there must be at least as much formal
reality in the cause of the idea as this idea contains of objective reality.[2] But this is a huge
stride forward and we must arrest your progress
for a little.

First, that common saying—there is nothing
in the effect which is not in the cause—seems
to be understood of the material, rather than of
efficient causality. For the efficient cause is something external and frequently of a diverse nature

from the effect. And although the effect may be
said to hold its reality from the efficient cause, yet
it does not acquire that which the efficient cause
has necessarily in itself, but that which can be
communicated from another source. The thing is
quite clear in effects due to art. For although the
house owes all its reality to the builder, the latter
transfers to it a reality which he has derived not
from himself but from some other source. So, likewise the sun acts, in variously transforming a
lower material and generating animals of various
kinds. Nay, even the parent from whom, we
grant, his offspring derives something material,
acquires that, not from an efficient, but from a
material principle. Your objection, that the effect must be contained in its cause either formally or eminently, proves nothing more than
that the form which the effect possesses is sometimes similar to the form of its cause, sometimes
indeed dissimilar and less perfect, to such an extent that the form of its cause towers high above it.
But it does not follow that for this reason even an
eminent cause gives any of its being or, in respect
of what it contains formally, shares its form with
its effect. For although that seems to be the case
in the generation of living creatures, nevertheless
you will not say that a father, in begetting a son,
divides up and gives to him part of his rational
soul. In a single word, an efficient cause contains
its effect only in the sense that it is able to form it
out of a given material and bring it into actual
existence.

Further, touching what you infer about objective reality, I employ the example of my own
image, which I can behold either in a mirror
which I hold up in front of me, or in a painting.
For, as I myself am the cause of my image in the
mirror in so far as I dispatch from myself and
convey into the mirror some semblance of myself,
and as the painter is the cause of the image which
appears in the picture; so, when the idea or image of me exists in you or in any other mind, it
may be asked whether I myself am its cause, in so
far as I transmit the semblance of myself into the
eye, and by the medium of the eye into the mind
itself. Or is there some other cause which de-
lineates it in the mind as with a stile or pencil?
But evidently no cause beyond myself is required;
for although afterwards my understanding may
amplify, diminish, compound, and handle it in
other ways, I nevertheless am myself the primary
cause of the whole of the reality which it contains
within it. What is here said of me is to be understood also of all external objects.

Now the reality attaching to an idea is distinguished as two-fold by you. Its formal reality

[1]Med. III, p. 84.
[2]Cf. p. 84.

cannot indeed be anything other than the fine substance which has issued out of me, and has been received into the understanding and has been fashioned into an idea. (But if you will not allow that the semblance proceeding from an object is a substantial effluence, adopt whatever theory you will, you decrease the image's reality.) But its objective reality can only be the representation of or likeness to me which the idea carries, or indeed only that proportion in the disposition of its parts in virtue of which they recall me. Whichever way you take it, there seems to be nothing real there; since all that exists is the mere relation of the parts of the idea to each other and to me, i.e. a mode of its formal existence, in respect of which it is constructed in this particular way. But this is no matter; call it, if you like, the objective reality of an idea.

Arguing from this position, it seems that you ought to compare the formal reality of an idea with my formal reality or with my substance, and the objective reality of an idea with the proportion prevailing between my members or my external figure and form. You, however, prefer to compare the objective reality of an idea with my formal reality.

Further, whatever be the explanation of the axiom discussed above, it is clear not only that as much formal reality must exist in me as there is of objective reality in the idea of me, but that even the formal reality of my idea is, as nearly as possible, nothing when compared with my formal reality and my entire substance. Hence we must indeed concede to you that there must be as much formal reality in the cause of an idea as there is of objective reality in its idea, when the whole of the reality in the idea is practically nothing as compared with that of its cause.

6. You add: that if you possessed an idea the objective reality of which was so great that you could contain it neither eminently nor formally, and thus could not yourself be the cause of it then, at length, it followed of necessity that some other being besides yourself existed in the world. For, otherwise, you would have had no sufficient argument to convince you of the existence of anything else.[1] True, according to what you have already maintained, you are not the cause of the reality of your ideas; rather the things themselves represented by the ideas are the cause, in so far as they convey into you as into a mirror the images of themselves, even though you can derive from those ideas the opportunity at times of manufacturing the notion of chimaeras. But whether you are their cause or not, is

[1]Cf. p. 85.

it because of this that you are uncertain about th existence of anything else besides yourself in th world? Answer sincerely, I pray, for there is n need for us, whatever the truth turn out to be abou ideas, to search for arguments to decide this mat ter.

Next you run over the list of the ideas yo possess, and besides the idea of yourself yo enumerate the ideas of God, of corporeal an inanimate things, of angels, animals and men this is in order that, since you say there is n difficulty about the idea of yourself, you ma infer that the ideas of men, of animals and o angels are composed of those which you hav of yourself and of God, and that the ideas o corporeal things might have proceeded from you also.[2] But here it occurs to me to wonder ho you can be said to have an idea of yourself (an one so fertile as to furnish you with such a suppl of other ideas) and how it can be maintained tha the matter presents no difficulties; when, never theless, you have really either no idea of yourself or one which is very confused and imperfect, as w have already observed in passing judgment on th previous Meditation. In it you even inferred tha nothing could be more easily and more clearl perceived by you than yourself. What if it be th case that, as you do not and cannot possess a idea of yourself, it may be said that anything els is more capable of being easily and clearly per ceived by you than yourself?

In my reflections as to the reason why it is th case that neither does sight see itself, nor th understanding understand itself, the thought pre sents itself to me that nothing acts on itself. Thu neither does the hand (or the tip of the finger strike itself nor does the foot kick itself. But sinc in other cases, in order for us to acquire knowl edge of a thing, that thing must act on the facult that discerns it and must convey into it the sem blance of itself, or inform it with its sensible ap pearance; it is quite clear that the faculty itself since it is not outside itself, cannot convey a sim ilar semblance of itself into itself, and cannot con sequently acquire knowledge of itself, or, what i the same thing, perceive itself. And why, do yo think, does the eye, though incapable of seein itself in itself, yet see itself in the mirror? Why because there is a space between the eye and th mirror, and the eye so acts on the mirror, convey ing thither its sensible appearance, that the mir ror re-acts on it again, conveying back to the ey that sensible appearance's own appearance. Giv me then a mirror in which you yourself may i similar fashion act; I promise you that the resul

[2]Cf. p. 85.

*ill be that this will reflect back your semblance
·to yourself, and that you then will at length per-
·ive yourself, not indeed by a direct, but a re-
·ected cognition. But, if you do not give this,
·ere is no hope of your knowing yourself.*

*I could here also press the point: how can you
· said to have an idea of God, except one such as,
·nd acquired in the way that, we have said?
·hence comes your idea of the Angels? Unless
·u had been told of them you would never have
·ought of them. Of the animals? and of other
·ings? I am practically certain that of these you
·uld have had no idea unless they had entered
·ur senses; just as you have no idea of many
·her things, of which neither the appearance nor
·e report has reached you. But, dismissing this,
· do admit that the ideas existing in the mind of
·iverse things can be so compounded, as to give
·se to many of the forms of other things, although
·ose which you enumerate do not seem to account
·fficiently for the great diversity of form you
·ention, and indeed do not suffice for the distinct
·nd determinate idea of any definite thing.*

*Moreover, I have doubt only about the ideas of
·orporeal things, and this is due to the fact that
·ere is no small difficulty in seeing how you are
·ble to deduce them from yourself, and out of
·he idea of yourself alone,[1] as long as you pose
·s incorporeal and consider yourself as such. For,
· you have known only incorporeal substance,
·ow can you grasp the notion of corporeal sub-
·ance as well? Is there any analogy between the
·tter and the former? You say that they both
·gree in this,—in being capable of existing; but
·at agreement cannot be comprehended unless
·rst both the two things which agree are com-
·rehended. What you do is to make a common no-
·ion which implies an understanding of the par-
·iculars before it is formed. Certainly if the mind
·an, out of that incorporeal substance, form the
·dea of corporeal substance, there is no reason
·hy we should doubt that a blind man, even one
·ho has been completely enshrouded in darkness
·rom his birth, can form in his own mind the
·deas of light and of the colours. You say that
·onsequently the ideas of extension, figure and
·notion, and of other common sensibles can be
·erived; but doubtless it is easy for you to say
·his. What I marvel at is, why you do not deduce
·ight, colour and other similar things with a like
·acility. But we must not linger over these matters.*

7. *You conclude:* Hence there remains alone
the idea of God, concerning which we must
discover whether it is not something that is
capable of proceeding from me myself. By the

name God I understand a substance that is infinite, independent, all-knowing, all-powerful,
and by which I myself and everything else, if
anything else does exist, have been created.
Now all these characteristics are such that the
more diligently I attend to them, the less do
they appear capable of proceeding from me
alone; hence, from what has been already said,
we must conclude that God necessarily exists.[2]
*This is, of course, the conclusion for which you
were making. But, as I grasp the inference, I do
not see how you get this result. You say that those
characteristics which you understand to exist in
God are of such a nature as to be incapable of
proceeding from you alone: your intention in so
doing is to show that they must proceed from
God. But, firstly, nothing is more true than that
they have not proceeded from you alone, so that
you have had no knowledge of them derived from
yourself and merely by means of your own efforts; for they have proceeded and are derived
from objects, from parents, from masters, from
teachers, and from the society in which you have
moved. But you will say: "I am mind alone: I
admit nothing outside of myself, not even the
ears by which I hear nor the people who converse
with me." You may assert this: but would you
assert it, unless you heard us with your ears, and
there were men from whom you learned words.
Let us talk in earnest, and tell me sincerely: do
you not derive those sound-words which you utter
in speaking of God, from the society in which you
have lived? And since the sounds you use are due
to intercourse with other men, is it not from the
same source that you derive the notions underlying and designated by those sounds? Hence
though not due to you alone, they do not seem on
that account to proceed from God, but to come
from some other quarter. Further, what is there
in those things which, on the opportunity first
being furnished by the objects, you could not
henceforth derive from yourself? Do you, for that
reason, apprehend something which is beyond
human grasp? It is true that if you comprehended
the nature of God there would be reason for your
thinking that it was from God you derived this
knowledge. But all those terms which you apply
to God are merely certain perfections observed to
exist in human beings and other things, which
the human mind is able to understand, collect and
amplify, as has already been said several times.*

You say: that although the idea of substance
might come from yourself, because you are a
substance, the idea of an infinite substance
could not be so derived, because you are not

[1]Cf pp. 85–86.　　　　[2]Cf. p. 86.

infinite.[1] *But you do not possess for that reason any idea of an infinite substance, except in a verbal sense, and in the way in which men are said to comprehend (which is really not to comprehend) the infinite. Hence there is no necessity in this, for such an idea to proceed from an infinite substance; for it can be made, in the way already specified, by composition and amplification. Unless, when the early Philosophers, from the comprehension of the visible space, the single world, and limited principles which they understood, derived the ideas of those very things, and held them in such a way that by enlarging them they formed the idea of an infinite universe, of infinite worlds and of infinite principles; you would say that those ideas had not been formed by the exertions of their own minds but had issued into the mind from the infinite universe, the infinite worlds, and infinite principles. Moreover, consider your defences:*—that you perceive the infinite by a true idea:[2] *surely if that idea were true it would reveal the nature of the infinite and consequently you would apprehend what is its leading feature, i.e. infinity. But your thought always stops short at something finite, and you talk of the infinite only because you do not perceive what is beyond your perceptions; consequently there is not much error in saying that you perceive the infinite by negation of the finite. Nor does it suffice to say* that you perceive more reality in an infinite substance[3] *than in a finite. For you ought to perceive an infinite reality, which, nevertheless you do not do. Nay also, you do not really perceive more when you merely amplify the finite and thereupon imagine that there is more reality in that which has been enlarged than exists in it, the very same thing, while it remains within narrow bounds. Unless you also mean that those Philosophers, who conceived many worlds to exist, perceived a greater actually existing reality when doing so, than while they entertained the thought of a single world. Incidentally this suggests to me that the reason why the human mind becomes more confused in proportion to the extent to which it amplifies some form and Idea, seems to lie in the fact that the mind wrests such a form from its setting, annuls the distinctness of its parts, and so attenuates the whole, that at length it vanishes away. I might remember also that mental confusion will result from the opposite cause, as e.g. when an Idea is too much condensed.*

You say: that there is no obstacle in the fact

that you do not comprehend the infinite or a[...] that is in it, and that it is sufficient for you [...] understand a few particulars in order to [...] said to have a true idea of it, and one that h[...] the maximum clearness and distinctness.[4] *B[...] nay, you do not have a true idea of the infini[...] your idea is only of the finite, if you do not com[...] prehend the infinite, but merely the finite. Y[...] can at most be said to know part of the infinit[...] but not, on that account, the infinite itself; just [...] a man who had never gone outside an unde[...] ground cave, might indeed be said to know part [...] the world but not, for that reason, the world itsel[...] Hence, because of this, he will turn out to be foo[...] ish if he thinks that the idea of such a limite[...] portion of the world is the true and genuine ide[...] of the whole. But, you say, it is of the nature [...] the infinite not to be comprehended by yo[...] who are finite. I believe you; but neither is it [...] the nature of a true idea of an infinite thing [...] represent merely a tiny part of it; or what [...] rather no part of it, on account of its bearing n[...] proportion to the whole. You say, that it is suf[...] cient for you to have knowledge of those fe[...] things, things you perceive clearly. This fo[...] sooth, is as though it were sufficient to percei[...] the tip of a hair belonging to the man of whom yo[...] want to have an idea which resembles the realit[...] Would it not be a fine likeness of me if the painte[...] were to depict a single hair of mine or the tip of [...] merely? But what we may know of an infini[...] God is in proportion less not only by much, or b[...] very much, but is even infinitely less than one [...] my hairs, or the tip of it, relatively to my who[...] self. In one word, these known facts prove nothin[...] of God which they do not likewise prove of th[...] infinite series of worlds mentioned before; an[...] this is all the more true in proportion as thes[...] could be more clearly understood from our clea[...] knowledge of this one world,—than God, or an in[...] finite entity can be derived in thought from you[...] substance, as to the nature of which you are n[...] yet agreed.*

8. Elsewhere you argue thus: For how woul[...] it be possible that I should know that I doub[...] and desire, that is to say, that something i[...] lacking to me, and that I am not wholly per[...] fect, unless I had within me some idea of a Be[...] ing more perfect than myself, in comparing my[...] self with which I recognized my deficiencies? [...] *But if you are in doubt about any matter, if yo[...] desire something and recognize that something i[...] lacking to you, what is there wonderful in tha[...] when you do not know everything, are not every[...]*

[1]Cf. p. 86.
[2]Cf. p. 86.
[3]Cf. p. 86.

[4]Cf. p. 86.
[5]Cf. p. 86.

thing, do not have everything? Do you acknowledge that hence you are not wholly perfect? Even this is certainly quite true and can be said without disparagement. Is it hence you gather that something more perfect than you exists? What? As if whatever you desire were not in some way or other more perfect than you. Thus when you desire bread the bread is not in every sense more perfect than you or than your body; it is more perfect only than that emptiness which exists in your stomach. How then do you gather that there is something more perfect than you? It is viz. in so far as you behold the totality of things which embrace both you and the bread and the rest of things; and in so doing, noticing that the separate parts of the whole have some perfection and are serviceable to one another and are able to reinforce each other, you easily come to understand that there is more perfection in the whole than in the part; and that, since you are only a part, you must acknowledge that there is something more perfect than you. It is, then, in this way that you can have the idea of a being that is more perfect than you, by comparing yourself with which you recognize your defects. I pass by the fact that other parts also may be more perfect, that you may desire what they possess and, by comparing yourself with them, acknowledge your defects. Thus you might know a man who was healthier, stronger, more handsome, more learned, calmer, and hence more perfect than yourself; and it would not be difficult for you to conceive the idea of him, and by comparing yourself with that, learn that you did not possess that degree of health, strength, and of the other perfections which existed in him.

Shortly afterwards you propose to yourself the objection: But possibly I am something more than I suppose myself to be, and perhaps all those perfections which I attribute to God are in some way potentially in me, although they do not yet issue in action; as may be the case, if my knowledge tends more and more to grow to infinity.[1] *But you reply:* that though it were true that my knowledge gradually increased and that there were in me potentially many things which were not yet there actually, nevertheless none of these excellencies pertain to the idea of God, in which there is nothing potential, for the fact that it increases little by little is an absolutely certain token of the imperfection of my knowledge. *But though it is indeed true that what you perceive in the idea is actually in the idea, yet that is not a reason why it should exist in the thing of which you have the*

[1]Cf. p. 86.

idea. Thus the architect constructs for himself the idea of a house, which idea is actually a complex of the walls, floors, roof, and windows, etc., he has traced; nevertheless that house and its component parts do not yet exist in actuality, but only potentially. Thus the above idea of the Philosophers contains in actuality an infinity of worlds; yet you cannot say that therefore there is actually an infinity of worlds. Hence, whether something exist in you, or whether it do not exist in you potentially, it is sufficient that your idea or knowledge be capable of being gradually increased and expanded; and it cannot be thence inferred that what is represented and apprehended by means of the idea does actually exist. I gladly accept what you next recognize, viz. that your knowledge never will become infinite. But you ought to acknowledge that you will never possess a true and faithful idea of God; for there is always more, nay infinitely more to know about God, than about that man, the tip of whose hair merely you have seen. As a matter of fact even if you have not seen the whole of that man, you have yet seen another, by comparison with whom you are able to make some conjecture about him. But nothing is ever presented to our knowledge similar to God and His immensity.

You say that you understand God to be actually infinite, so that He can add nothing to His perfection. *But this judgment is about a matter of which you are in ignorance and is drawn merely from a presumption, in the way that our Philosophers derived their opinion about an infinity of worlds, infinite principles, and an infinite universe, to the immensity of which nothing could be added. But how can there be any truth in what you subjoin, viz.:* that the objective being of an idea cannot be due to a potential but only to an actual being, *if what we have just said about the Architect's idea or that of the ancient Philosophers be correct? I ask you especially how this can be so, when, as you remember, ideas of this sort are composed of others which the mind has previously acquired, having derived them from actually existing causes.*

9. *You next ask,* whether, possessing now as you do the idea of a being more perfect than yourself, you yourself could exist, if no such being existed? *Your reply is:* "From whom then could I derive my existence? Perhaps from myself or from my parents, or from some other source less perfect than God?"[2] *Then you go on to prove* that you do not derive your existence from yourself. *But this is not at all necessary. You also state the reason why you*

[2]Cf. p. 87.

have not always existed. *But that also is super-fluous, except in so far as you wish at the same time to infer that you depend upon a cause which not only produces you, but also conserves you. Thus from the fact that your lifetime falls into many parts, you infer that you must be created in each one of them, on account of the mutual independence that exists among them.*[1] *But consider if this can be so understood. There are indeed certain effects which, in order to continue in existence and never at any moment to fail, require the continuous and efficient presence of the cause which started them. An example of such an effect is the light of the sun (though effects of this kind are not so much actually identical, but rather equivalent, as in the case of a river its water is said to be). But there are other things which we see continue, not merely when the cause which they acknowledge is no longer active, but, if you care, even when it is destroyed and reduced to nothing. Of such a sort are things which are pro-created or manufactured, so many in number as to make it distasteful to recount them; but it suf-fices that you are one of these, whatsoever the cause of your existence turn out to be. But, you maintain, the different parts of the time in which you exist do not depend on one another. Here we may object and ask, what thing there is of which we can think, the parts of which are more inseparable from one another? What thing has parts, the order and connection of which is more inviolable? Is there anything in which there is less power of detaching the prior from the pos-terior of its parts, in which they cohere more closely and depend more on one another? But not to press this point, I ask what difference this de-pendence or independence of the parts of time, which are external, successive and non-active, makes to your production or reproduction? Cer-tainly nothing more than the flow or passage by of the particles of water makes to the production and reproduction of a rock past which the river flows. But, you say, from the fact that you ex-isted a little while ago it does not follow that you must now exist. I quite agree: but this is not because a cause is required to create you anew, but owing to the fact that the cause is not held to be absent which might destroy you, or because you ought not to have within you that weakness owing to which you will finally cease to exist.*

You allege that it is hence manifest by means of the light of nature, that the distinction be-tween creation and conservation is solely a dis-tinction of the reason.[2] *But how is it manifest,* except perhaps in the case of light itself and simi-lar effects? *You add that you do not possess a power which is capable of bringing it to pass that you shall exist shortly afterwards, be-cause you are not conscious of it, and are yet a thinking thing.*[3] *But you do possess a power by means of which you may judge that you will in future exist: though this does not follow neces-sarily or indubitably, because that power of yours, or natural constitution, does not go so far as to guard against every destructive cause whether internal or external. Hence also you will exist because you have a power, not of producing yourself anew, but one which suffices to enable you to continue to exist, unless some destructive cause supervenes. Moreover your conclusion, that you depend upon a being distinct from yourself, is correct; but not in the sense of your being produced anew by it, but in the sense of your being originally produced by it. You go on to say that such a being cannot be your parents or any other cause whatsoever. But why not your parents, by whom you seem so manifestly produced, along with your body? Not to speak of the sun and the other co-operative causes.* "Ah," you say, "I am a thing which thinks, and have within me the idea of God." *But were not your parents or their minds also thinking things, also possessing the idea of God? Hence you should not here urge that dictum of which we have already talked, viz.* that there must be at least as much reality in the cause as in the effect. *You say, if there be another cause besides God, we may again enquire whether this cause derives its origin from God or from some other thing. For, if from itself, it will be God; if from some other cause, we can ask the question over and over again, until we arrive at that which is self-derived, and is God, since an infinite regress is not permitted.*[4] *But if your parents were the cause of your existence, that cause might have been not self-derived, but dependent on something else; and that again might have been due to some-thing else and so on to infinity. Nor can you prove that that regress to infinity is absurd, un-less you at the same time show that the world has a definite beginning in time, and that hence there was a first parent, who had no parent. An infinite regress seems certainly to be absurd only in the case of causes which are so connected and sub-ordinated to one another, that no action on the part of the lower is possible without the activity of the higher; e.g. in the case where something is moved by a stone, itself impelled by a stick, which*

[1]Cf. p. 87.
[2]Cf. p. 87.

[3]Cf. p. 87.
[4]Cf. pp. 87–88.

the hand moves, or when the last link in a chain lifts a weight, while this link itself is moved by the one above it and that by another; for in these circumstances we must go on until we come to one thing in motion which a first moves. But in those causes which are so arranged that, though the former is taken away, that which depends upon it survives and may continue to act, it does not seem equally absurd. Hence when you say: that it is sufficiently manifest that here there can be no infinite regress,[1] see if it was so manifest to Aristotle, who was so strongly persuaded that there had never been a first parent. You proceed: nor can several partial causes have concurred in your production, from which you have received the idea of the various perfections attributed to God, since they can only be found in a God who is one and single, whose unity or simplicity is a perfection of a very high order.[2] But whether the cause of your existence is to be found in one thing or in many, it is not, therefore, necessary that such things should impress in you the idea of their perfections, which you have been able to unite. Meanwhile, however, you give us the opportunity of asking why, if there are not many causes of your existence it has been possible at least for many things to exist, by admiring the perfections of which you have concluded that the Being must be a blessed one in which they all exist together. You know how the poets describe Pandora. Nay, have not you, admiring in various men some outstanding knowledge, wisdom, justice, constancy, power, health, beauty, blessedness, length of existence, etc., been able to unite all these and consider how sublime he would be who possessed them all at the same time? Why can you not then increase all these perfections in various degrees until he would be all the more to be admired were it so that nothing was lacking to his knowledge, power, duration, etc., or could be added to it; for in these circumstances he would be all-powerful, all-knowing, eternal and so on? And when you found that such perfections could not coincide with human nature, might you not think that that would be a blissful nature, in which such a conjunction of attributes was possible? Might it not be worthy of your investigation to discover whether there is such a being in existence or no? Why might it not be possible for various arguments to induce you to believe that it was more reasonable that such a being should exist rather than not exist? Would it not be possible next to divest this of corporeity, limitation, and all the remaining qualities, which imply a certain imperfec-

tion? Most people seem certainly to have proceeded in this way; although, as there are nevertheless various modes and degrees of reasoning, some have let God remain corporeal, some have allowed Him human members, and others have made Him not one but many, not to speak of other and too popular descriptions. In connection with that perfection of unity there is no contradiction in the conception of all the perfections ascribed to God as being intimately joined together and inseparable. But yet the idea by which you embrace them has not been placed in you by Him, but has been drawn by you from the things which you have seen, and has been amplified in the manner described. Thus certainly do we have the description, not only of Pandora, the goddess dowered with all gifts and perfections, but also of the perfect State, the perfect Orator, etc. Finally, from the fact that you exist and possess the idea of a supremely perfect being, you conclude, that you have a highly evident demonstration of the existence of God. But though your conclusion, viz. that God exists is true, it is not clear from what you have said, that you have demonstrated it in the most evident manner.

10. You say, "it remains for me to examine into the manner in which I have acquired this idea from God; for neither have I derived it from the senses, nor is it a fictitious idea made by me (for it is not in my power to take from or add anything to it); and consequently the only alternative left is that it is innate in me, just as the idea of myself is."[3] But I have frequently already said that you may have partly derived it from the senses, partly made it up. Moreover, as to your contention that you can add nothing to and take away nothing from it, consider that, to begin with, it was not equally perfect. Reflect that there may be men, or Angels, or other natures more instructed than your own, from whom you may receive some information about God, which you have not yet known. Reflect that God at least could so instruct you and give you finally such a degree of illumination, whether in this life or in another, that you would esteem as nought anything which you now know of Him. Whatever that knowledge finally be, consider that as the ascent can be made from the perfections of created things to the knowledge of the perfections of God, and that as they are not all known at a single moment, but can be discovered in increasing numbers from day to day, so it will be possible for the idea of God not to be possessed in its perfection at a single moment, but to be-

[1]Cf. p. 88.
[2]Cf. p. 88.

[3]Cf. p. 88.

come more perfect from day to day. You proceed: And one certainly ought not to find it strange that God, in creating me, placed this idea within me, to serve as the mark of the workman imprinted on his work. It is likewise not essential that this mark should be something different from the work itself. For, from the sole fact that God created me, it is most probable that in some way he has placed His image and similitude upon me, and that I perceive this similitude (in which the idea of God is contained) by means of the same faculty by which I perceive myself: that is to say, when I reflect on myself, I not only know that I am something incomplete and dependent on another, something also which incessantly aspires after what is greater and better than myself; but I also know that He on whom I depend possesses in Himself all the great things to which I aspire, and that not indefinitely or potentially alone; but really, actually, and infinitely, and that thus He is God.[1] There is indeed much appearance of truth in all this, and my objection is not that it is not true. But, I ask you, where do you get your proof? Passing by what has been already said let us ask: If the idea of God exists in you like the mark of the workman imprinted on his work, what is the mode in which it is impressed? What is the form of that mark? How do you detect it? If it is not other than the work or thing itself, are you then an idea? Are you yourself nothing else than a mode of thought? Are you both the mark impressed and the subject on which it is impressed? You say that it is to be believed that you have been fashioned after the image and similitude of God. To religious faith this is indeed credible, but how can it be understood by the natural reason, unless you make God to have a human form? And in what can this similitude to this Eternal Being consist? Can you, who are dust and ashes, presume to be similar to Him, who is of an incorporeal, boundless, entirely perfect, most glorious and, what is the principal matter, an entirely invisible and incomprehensible nature? Have you known that face to face, so as to be able, by comparing yourself with it, to affirm that you resemble it? You say that it is to be believed owing to the fact that He created you. On the contrary, that fact makes it incredible; inasmuch as the work does not resemble the workman, unless when it is generated by him by a communication of his nature. But you have not been begotten by God in this way; nor are you His offspring or a participator in His nature. You have merely

[1]Cf. p. 88.

been created by Him, i.e. made by Him according to an idea; and hence you cannot say that you resemble Him more than the house resembles the workman who builds its walls. And this is true even though we grant, what you have not yet proved, your creation by God. You say that you perceive a likeness, while at the same time you understand that you are a thing which is incomplete, dependent, and aspiring towards what is better. But is not this rather a proof of God's dissimilitude, since He on the contrary is most complete, most independent and entirely self-sufficient, being greatest and best of all? I pass by the fact that when you know yourself to be dependent, you do not therefore immediately understand that that on which you depend is other than your parents; while if you do understand it to be something else, no reason offers why you should think that you resemble it. I pass by the fact also that it is strange that the rest of mankind or of minds do not understand the same thing as you do; and especially since there is no reason why we should refuse to think that God has impressed the idea of Himself on them as on you. Assuredly this one thing especially proves that there is no such idea which has been impressed on us by God; since if there had been, it would have been imprinted on all and, likewise, as one and the same, and all men would conceive God by means of a similar form and semblance, would ascribe the same qualities to him, and think the same thing about Him. And the opposite is most notorious. These discussions, however, have now taken up too much time.

RELATIVE TO MEDITATION IV

Of the True and the False

1. In the fourth Meditation you recount at the beginning what you think you have proved in the previous ones, and by means of which you presume you have opened a way for further progress. Not to interpose delay I shall cease from continually insisting that you ought to have demonstrated your results more cogently; it will be sufficient if you bear in mind what has been conceded and what has not; in order that our argument may avoid being affected with prejudice.

You reason consequently that it is impossible that God should deceive you;[2] and, in order to free from blame that faculty which misleads you and is exposed to error, and which you have received from Him, you conjecture that the fault resides in non-being, of which you say you have some idea, and in which according to your account you participate, and between which and

[2]Med. IV, p. 89.

God you are, *according to your belief*, a mean.[1] *This is indeed a capital argument. But to pass by the contention that it cannot be explained how one can have, or what is the idea of, non-being; how we can participate in non-being, etc., I merely observe that by this distinction we do not obviate the fact that God might have given man a faculty of judgment immune from error. For without giving him an infinite capacity, He might have given him one of such a kind as not to assent to error, so that man would have had a clear perception of what he knew; and in regard to what he did not know he would not have committed himself in one direction rather than in another.*

On your presenting to yourself this objection, you pronounce the opinion that you ought not to be astonished if certain things are done by God, the reason of which you do not understand.[2] *That is indeed quite correct; but still it is surprising that you possess a true idea which represents God as all-knowing, all-powerful and wholly good, while you nevertheless see that certain of his works are not absolutely perfect and complete. So that since He at least might have made them more perfect, but yet did not do so, that seems to argue that He either did not know how, or could not, or did not wish to do so. At least it would be an imperfection in Him, if, possessing both the knowledge and the power to do so, He had refused, and had preferred imperfection to perfection.*

In refusing to employ final causes in an investigation into Physical things,[3] *you act in a way which perhaps in another situation would have been quite correct. But in treating of God, it is really to be feared that you have rejected the principal argument whereby the Divine wisdom, foreknowledge, power and existence as well, may be established by our natural light. Thus, to omit the world as a whole, the heavens, and other outstanding parts of it, whence or how will you derive better arguments than from the function of the parts in plants, in animals, in men, and in your own self (or in your body) who bear the similitude of God? It is a fact we can witness that many great men not only rise to a knowledge of God from the anatomical study of the human body, but also hymn His praises in that He has given such a conformation to all the members, and assigned to them their employment, so that He is to be extolled on account of His incomparable care and foresight.*

You will say that there are physical causes of such a form and arrangement which ought to be

investigated, and that those people are foolish who have recourse to the end, rather than to the active cause or the material. But no mortal can comprehend, much less explain, what agent it is which forms and disposes in the way we observe, those valves which are constituted to serve as the orifices of the vessels in the cavities of the heart. Nor can we tell of what conformation the matter is out of which it elaborates them, or whence that matter is derived; nor how the cause applies itself to its work, what instrument it employs, nor how it secures them; nor what it stands in need of in order to render these valves of the proper temper, consistency, coherence, flexibility, size, figure and disposition in space. Since, then, I say, no Physical scientist is able to comprehend and declare them and other matters, what prevents him from at least admiring that most excellent contrivance and the marvellous providence which has given us valves accurately adapted to that design? Why should we not praise him, if he thereupon acknowledge that some First Cause must necessarily be admitted, which has disposed those and other matters in the wisest possible manner, and in a way most consonant with His own purposes?

You say that it is rash to investigate God's purposes. But though this may be true, if those purposes are meant which God Himself wished hidden or of which He has prohibited the investigation, it is, nevertheless, certainly not so, in the case of those which he has, as it were, placed publicly before us, which with little labour come to light, and are besides such as to procure great praise for God Himself, as for their author.

You will say perhaps that the idea of God existing in everyone, suffices to give a true and genuine knowledge of God and of His providence, and apart from any reference either to the purposes of things or to anything else whatsoever. But not every one is so happily situated as you, so as to have that idea in all its perfection from birth upwards, and to behold it so clearly when offered to them. Wherefore you should not grudge those, to whom God has not granted such a degree of insight, permission to acknowledge and glorify the Doer of those works from the inspection of His works. I need not recall the fact that there is no objection to using that idea which also seems to be so constructed out of our consciousness of things, that you, if you were to speak frankly, would admit you owe not indeed little but practically everything to this consciousness, for tell me, I pray, how much progress do you suppose you would have made, if from the time at which you were infused into the body, you had dwelled in it up till now with closed eyes and sealed ears, and in short had had no perception by external sense of anything outside us or of this whole universe of objects? What if meanwhile you—the whole of you—had passed the whole time in inward meditation and in revolving thoughts round and round? Tell me in good faith, and describe the ideas of God and of yourself which you think you would have acquired.

2. *The solution you next offer is,* that the creature, recognised as imperfect, should be considered not as a whole, but rather as a part of the universe, from which point of view it will be perfect.[1] *Your distinction is certainly to be commended, but at the present point we are not treating of the imperfection of a part in so far as it is a part and is compared with the integrity of the whole, but in so far as it is something complete in itself and performs a special function. And when you relate this again to the universe the difficulty always remains, whether in truth the universe would have been more perfect, if all its parts had been perfect, than as the case actually holds, when many of its parts are imperfect. Thus that State will be more perfect in which all the citizens are good, than in another in which many or some are bad.*

Whence, also, when a little later you say: that the perfection of the universe is in some sense greater, in that certain of its parts are not exempt from error, than if they all had been alike,[2] *it is exactly as if you were to say that the perfection of a state is greater in that some of its citizens are evil than in the case when they are all good. This lets us see that just as it ought evidently to be the desire of a good prince that all his subjects should be good, so it seems it should have been the resolution of the Author of the universe to create and keep all its parts free from defect. And though you are able to allege that the perfection of those parts which are free from defect, appears greater when contrasted with those which are not exempt from it, that nevertheless is merely accidental; just as the virtue of good men, if more striking owing to the contrast between the good and the evil, is so only by accident. Consequently, just as we should not want any of the citizens to be evil, in order that the good might thereby become more distinguished, so, it seems, it ought never to have come to pass that any part of the universe should be subject to error, in order that the parts that were free from it might thus be rendered more conspicuous.*

You say: that you have no right to complain, if God has not called upon you to play a part

in the world that excels all others in distinction and perfection.[3] *But this does not remove the question why it has not been sufficient for Him to give you the smallest of perfect parts to play, and not to have given you one that was imperfect. For though, likewise, it would not be considered culpable on the part of a prince to refuse to assign offices of the highest dignity to the whole of his subjects, but to call some people to the discharge of duties of intermediate importance, others to the fulfilling of the humblest functions, nevertheless he would be blamed if over and above destining some to the execution of the most insignificant offices, he had also assigned to some a function that was base.*

You declare: that you can bring no reason to show why God ought to have given you a greater faculty of knowledge than He has given you; and however skilful a workman you represent Him to be, you should not, for all that, consider that He was bound to have placed in each and all of his works the perfections which He has been able to place in some.[4] *But the objection I only now stated remains undiminished. You must see that the difficulty is not so much, why God has not given you a greater faculty of knowing, as why He has given you one that falls into error; no controversy is raised as to why the supreme artificer has willed not to give every thing every perfection, but why He has chosen to allot some things imperfections as well.*

You allege: that though you cannot be free from error by means of possessing a clear knowledge of all things, you may yet avoid it by express resolve, the resolve by which you firmly make up your mind to assent to nothing which you do not clearly perceive.[5] *But however much you may be able to bear this in mind attentively, it is not an imperfection not to have clear perception of that which we need to distinguish and appraise, and to be perpetually exposed to the risk of error.*

You maintain: that error resides in the act itself, in so far as it proceeds from you and is a sort of privation, not in the faculty which you have received from God, nor even in the act in so far as it depends on Him.[6] *But, though the error does not attach directly to the faculty received from God, nevertheless it does attach to it indirectly, inasmuch as in its creation there is that imperfection which makes error possible. Wherefore, though, as you say, you have cer-*

[1] Cf. p. 90.
[2] Cf. p. 92.

[3] Cf. p. 92.
[4] Cf. p. 90.
[5] Cf. p. 92.
[6] Cf. p. 92.

inly no cause to complain of God, who in uth owes you nothing, and yet has conferred ose boons upon you, for which you should nder thanks to Him, *we must yet continue to onder why He has not given us more perfect culties, if He really knew, if He had the power, d if not inspired with malice.*

You add: that neither must you complain at God concurs with you in the act of erring; cause all these acts are true and good in so r as they depend upon God, and in a certain nse more perfection accrues to you from the ct that you can form such acts than if you uld not do so: while the privation in which one the formal reason of falsity or error con- sts, does not require any concurrence on the art of God, since it is not a real thing nor is lated to Him.[1] *But subtle though that distinc- on be, it is nevertheless not quite satisfactory. indeed God does not concur in the privation hich is present in the act and is its falsity and rror, He yet concurs in the act; and unless He oncurred with it there would be no privation. esides, He Himself is the Author of that power hich is deceived or falls into error, and conse- uently is the source of a power which, so to peak, lacks power. Thus the defect in the act is, seems, to be referred not so much to that power hich lacks power as to its Author who created it ith this lack of power and, though he was able to o so, declined to make it effective, or more effec- ive than it is. It is certainly counted no fault in a orkman if he does not take the trouble of making very large key to open a little casket, but if, fter making it so small, he shapes it so that it ails to open the box, or does so with difficulty. hus also, though God is indeed not to be blamed or giving to a mannikin a faculty of judging not o great as he thought would be necessary for either ll or most or the greatest of creatures, it is still trange why he has assigned to us a faculty which s so uncertain, so confused, and so unequal to he task of deciding those few things on which He has willed that man should pass judgment.*

3. *You next ask:* what is the cause of the ex- stence of falsity or error in you.[2] *In the first place I do not question your right of calling* understanding *only the faculty of being aware of ideas, or of apprehending things themselves* simply and without any affirmation or denial, *while you make* the will *and the power of free choice the faculty of judgment, to which it be- longs to affirm or deny, to assent or dissent. The sole question I propound is why the will and lib-*

erty *of choice is circumscribed by no limits in your account, while the range of the understand- ing is circumscribed. The truth is that these two faculties seem to have domains of equal extent and that the understanding has at least no nar- rower a range than the will, since will is never directed towards anything of which the under- standing has not previously had cognizance.*

I said "at least no narrower a range"; for really the understanding seems to extend even fur- ther than the will. This is so if, as a fact, will or decision, and judgment, never arise, and conse- quently neither do the choice of, the striving after, and aversion from a thing which we have not ap- prehended, nor unless the idea of that thing is perceived and set before us by the understanding. But besides this we understand in a confused fashion many things which lead to no judgment, no striving after or avoidance of them. Likewise, the faculty of judgment is often uncertain, so that, when reasons of equal weight are present, or when no reason exists, no judgment follows, while meanwhile the understanding apprehends the matters that still continue unaffected by judgment.

Your statement, that you can always under- stand more and more; to take an example, you can more and more comprehend the faculty of understanding itself, of which you can form even an infinite idea,[3] *of its own self proves that your understanding is not more limited than your will, when it is able to extend even to an in- finite object. But when you take into account the fact that you acknowledge* that your will equals the Divine will, not indeed in actual extent but formally, *consider whether the same may not be asserted of the understanding also, since you have defined the formal notion of the understand- ing in just the same way as you have that of the will. But tell us briefly to what the will may ex- tend which escapes the understanding? Hence it seems that the cause of error is not, as you say,* due to the will extending more widely than the understanding, and going on to judge of mat- ters of which the understanding is not aware.[4] *It is rather due to the fact that, both ranging as they do over an equally wide domain, the under- standing fails to discern something well, and the will fails to judge correctly.*

Wherefore there is no reason for extending the will beyond the bounds of the intellect, since it is not the case that it judges of things which the understanding does not perceive, and judges ill for the sole reason that the understanding per- ceives badly.

[1] Med. IV, pp. 92–93.
[2] Cf. p. 91.

[3] Cf. p. 90.
[4] Cf. p. 90.

In the example about your non-existence,[1] *when you bring up the argument you have constructed relative to the existence of objects, you proceed correctly in so far as the reasoning refers to your own existence. But, in so far as it concerns other things, you seem to have proceeded on a false assumption; for, whatever you say, or rather pretend to say, your doubt is not genuine, and your judgment entirely allows that something else exists beyond yourself, distinct from you: it is a matter of which you are already aware that something else distinct from yourself exists. It is possible for you to suppose as you do that there is no reason to persuade you to adopt the one belief rather than the other. But at the same time you ought to suppose that no judgment will follow, and that your will will always be indifferent, and will not determine itself to come to a decision, until the time that a greater probability on the one side rather than the other presents itself to the understanding.*

Your next statement: that this indifference extends to those matters which are not apprehended with perfect clearness, in such a way that, however probable be the conjectures which render you disposed to form a judgment on one particular side, the simple knowledge you possess, that they are conjectures, may occasion you to judge the contrary:[2] *seems to be in no way true. For that knowledge which tells you that they are merely conjectures will indeed cause you to pass judgment in favour of that conclusion to which they point, with a certain amount of insecurity and hesitation; but it will never make you decide for the opposite belief, unless conjectures subsequently present themselves, which are not equally but even more probable than the others.*

Though you add, that you had experience of this lately, when setting aside as false what you had formerly supposed to be absolutely true, *remember that this has not been conceded to you. For you cannot really have felt persuaded yourself that you have not seen the sun, the earth, men, and other objects, that you have not heard sounds, have not walked, eaten, or written, have not spoken (have not, i.e. used your body or its organs), and so forth.*

Finally, therefore, the form of error does not seem to consist in the incorrect use of the free will,[3] *as you maintain, so much as in the dissonance between the judgment and the thing whereof we judge; it seems to arise indeed from the fact that the understanding apprehends that*

thing otherwise than as it is. Whence it seems *be not so much the blame of the free will, whic judges wrong, as of the understanding whic does not give the correct reason. Thus the de pendence of the power of choice upon the under standing seems to be such that, if the intellect in deed perceives something clearly or seems to do so the will passes a judgment which is agreed on an determinate, whether that be really true, or wheth er it be thought to be true; if, on the other hand the perception on the part of the understanding b obscure, then our will passes a judgment which doubtful and hesitating, though taken for th time to be more true than its opposite, and th whether the matter is really true or false. The re sult is that it is not so much in our power t guard against error, as to refrain from persistin in error, and that the appropriate exercise o judgment is not so much the reinforcing of the strength of the will, as the application of the under standing to the discovery of clearer knowledge tha that which our judgment is always likely to follow*

4. *In your conclusion you exaggerate the prof to be derived from this Meditation; you also pre scribe how you should act in order to arrive a a knowledge of the truth; for, you say, you wi arrive at this if you only devote your attentio sufficiently to those things which you perfectl understand, and if you separate them from that which you apprehend more confusedl and obscurely.[4]*

Now this is not only true but it is a truth whic could be grasped altogether apart from the pre vious Meditation, which thus seems to have bee superfluous. Nevertheless, my good Sir, note tha the difficulty appears not to affect the question whether, in order to avoid error, we ought to un derstand a thing clearly and distinctly, but con cerns the art or method by which it is possible t discern that our knowledge is so clear and dis tinct that it must be true and cannot possibly mis lead us. Nay, at the outset I made the objection tha not infrequently we are deceived even though we seem to have a knowledge of the matter which nothing car excel in respect of clearness and distinctness. You yourself also brought up this objection agains yourself, and nevertheless we still await the reve lation of that art or method, to the exposition o which your energies should be chiefly directed.

RELATIVE TO MEDITATION V

Of the Essence of Material Things; and, Again, of God, That He Exists

1. *In the Fifth Meditation you first say that you distinctly imagine quantity, i.e. extension*

[1]Cf. p. 91.
[2]Cf. p. 91.
[3]Cf. p. 91.
[4]Cf. p. 92–93.

length, breadth and depth; *likewise* number, gure, situation, motion and duration.[1] *Out of ll these, the ideas of which you say you possess, ou select figure and, from among the figures, the riangle, of which you write as follows:* although here may nowhere in the world be such a fig- re outside my thought, or ever have been, here is nevertheless in this figure a determi- ate nature, which I have not invented, and hich does not depend upon my mind, as ap- ears from the fact that divers properties can e demonstrated of that triangle, viz. that its hree angles are equal to two right angles, that he greatest side is subtended by the greatest ngle, and the like, which now, whether I wish ; or do not wish it, I recognise very clearly, ven though I have never thought of them at ll before when I imagined a triangle, and hich therefore have not been invented by ne.[2] *So much only do you have respecting the ssence of material things; for the few remarks ou add refer to the same matter. I have, indeed, o desire to raise difficulties here; I suggest only hat it seems to be a serious matter to set up some mmutable and eternal nature in addition to }od the all-powerful.*

You will say that you merely bring forward a roposition of the schools, which states that the atures or essences of things are eternal, and that ropositions can be asserted about them which ave an eternal truth. But this is equally difficult, nd besides, we cannot conceive how the nature of nan can exist, when there is no human being, or ow it can be said that the rose is a flower when ot a single rose exists.

They say that it is one thing to talk of the es- ence, another thing to talk of the existence of hings, and that though indeed things do not exist rom all eternity, their essence is still eternal. But ince the chief thing in objects is their essence, loes God do anything of much moment when He roduces existence on their part? It is clear that o Him it is no more than for a tailor to try a coat n his customer. Yet how can people maintain hat the essence of man in Plato is eternal and ndependent of God? In virtue of being a univer- al, do they say? But in Plato nothing but what is ndividual has real existence. Though the mind, rom seeing Plato, Socrates, and the resembling natures of other men, is wont to form a certain ommon concept in which they all agree, and which can hence be reckoned the universal nature or essence of man, in so far as it is understood to be applicable to every man; yet it can by no means

[1]Med. v, p. 93.
[2]Cf. p. 93.

be shown that the universal existed before Plato and the others existed and the mind performed the abstraction.

You will reply; is not that proposition, man is animal, *true even before man exists, and hence from all eternity? I say no, it seems not to be true, except in the sense that whensoever man comes into existence he will be animal. This is so, even though we allow the seeming distinction between those two statements:* man exists *and* man is ani- mal, *owing to the fact that existence is more ex- pressly signified by the former, essence by the lat- ter. Nevertheless, from the former, essence is not excluded, nor existence from the latter. When we say* man exists, *we mean the man that is ani- mal; when we assert that* man is an animal, *we mean man while he exists. But besides, since this proposition,* man is animal, *is not of greater necessity than that other;* Plato is a man, *it will therefore possess an eternal truth, and the indi- vidual essence of Plato will not be less independ- ent of God than the universal essence of man is; so likewise other similar results will ensue, which it would be tedious to pursue. Yet I add that since man is said to be of such a nature that he cannot exist without being animal, we must not therefore imagine that such a nature is anything or exists anywhere outside the mind; but that the meaning is merely this, that if anything is a human being it must itself resemble these other objects, to which, on account of their mutual resemblance, the same appellation "man" is given. This is a resem- blance, I repeat, between individual natures, from which the understanding derives the oppor- tunity of forming a concept or the idea or form of a common nature, from which anything that will be human ought not to deviate.*

Hence, I say the same of that triangle of yours and its nature. For the triangle is indeed a sort of mental rule which you employ in discovering whether something deserves to be called a triangle. But there is no necessity for us on that account to say that such a triangle is something real and a true nature over and above the understanding, which alone, from beholding material triangles, has formed it and has elaborated it as a common notion exactly in the way we have described in the case of the nature of man.

Hence, also, we ought not to think that the prop- erties demonstrated of material triangles, agree with them because they derive those properties from the ideal triangle; they rather contain those properties themselves, and the ideal triangle does not possess them except in so far as the under- standing, after observing the material ones, as- signs them to it, with a view to restoring them

*again in the process of demonstration. This is in
the same way as the properties of human nature
do not exist in Plato and Socrates in the sense
that they receive them from the universal nature
of man, the facts being rather that the mind ascribes those properties to it after discerning them
in Plato, Socrates and others, with the intention
of restoring them to those individual cases, when
reasoning is called for.*

*It is known that the understanding, after see-
ing Plato, Socrates and others, all of whom are
rational beings, has put together this universal
proposition:* every man is rational; *and then
when it wishes to prove that Plato is rational, it
uses that as a premise in its syllogism. Likewise,
O Mind, you indeed say* that you have the idea
of a triangle, and would have possessed it,
even though you had never seen any triangular
shape among bodies, just as you have ideas of
many other figures which have never presented
themselves to your senses.[1]

*But, if, as I have said above, you had been de-
prived of all sense-functions in such a way that
you had never either seen or touched the various
surfaces or extremities of bodies, do you think
you would have been able to possess or elaborate
within you the idea of a triangle or of any other
figure?* You have many ideas which have not
entered into you by way of the senses. *So you
say; but it is easy for you to have them, because
you construct them out of those which have so
entered and you elaborate them into various
others, in the ways I above expounded.*

*Besides this we should have spoken here of that
false nature of the triangle, which is supposed to
consist of lines which are devoid of breadth, to
contain an area which has no depth, and to terminate at three points which are wholly without
parts. But this would involve too wide a digres-
sion.*

2. *You next attempt the proof of God's existence and the vital part of your argument lies in
these words:* When I think attentively I clearly
see that the existence can no more be separated
from the essence of God than can there be separated from the essence of a triangle the equality in magnitude of its three angles to two right
angles, or the idea of a mountain from the idea
of a valley; so that there is no less incongruity
in our conceiving a God (i.e. a Being who is
supremely perfect) to Whom existence is lacking (i.e. in Whom a certain perfection is missing), than to think of a mountain which is not
accompanied by a valley.[2] *But we must note*

that a comparison of this kind is not sufficiently
accurate.

For though you properly enough compare essence with essence, in your next step it is neither
existence with essence, nor property with property that you compare, but existence with property. Hence it seems that you either ought to have
said that God's omnipotence can no more be separated from His essence than can that equality in
magnitude of the angles of a triangle from its essence; or at least, that God's existence can no
more be separated from His essence than the existence from the essence of a triangle. Thus taken
each comparison would have proceeded on correct
lines, and the truth would have been conceded
not only of the former but of the latter, although
this would not be evidence that you had established your conclusion that God necessarily exists, because neither does the triangle necessarily
exist, although its essence and its existence cannot in reality be severed, howsoever much the
mind separates them or thinks of them apart, in
the same way as the Divine essence and existence
may be thought of separately.

Next we must note that you place existence
among the Divine perfections, without, however,
putting it among the perfections of a triangle or
of a mountain, though in exactly similar fashion,
and in its own way, it may be said to be a perfection of each. But, sooth to say, existence is a perfection neither in God nor in anything else; it is
rather that in the absence of which there is no
perfection.

This must be so if, indeed, that which does not
exist has neither perfection nor imperfection, and
that which exists and has various perfections,
does not have its existence as a particular perfection and as one of the number of its perfections,
but as that by means of which the thing itself
equally with its perfections is in existence, and
without which neither can it be said to possess
perfections, nor can perfections be said to be possessed by it. Hence neither is existence held to exist in a thing in the way that perfections do, nor
if the thing lacks existence is it said to be imperfect (or deprived of a perfection), so much as to
be nothing.

Wherefore, as in enumerating the perfections
of a triangle you do not mention existence, nor
hence conclude that the triangle exists, so, in
enumerating the perfections of God, you ought
not to have put existence among them, in order to
draw the conclusion that God exists, unless you
wanted to beg the question.

You say: in everything else I have distinguished existence from essence but not in God.

---

[1] Cf. p. 93.
[2] Med. v, p. 94.

ut how, I pray, is the existence of Plato distin-
iished from the essence of Plato, unless by
ought? For, supposing now that Plato no longer
:ists, where is his essence? Is it not in the same
ay that essence and existence are distinguished
j thought in God?

You yourself raise the objection: Perhaps,
1st as from my thinking of a mountain with
valley, or of a winged horse, it does not fol-
w that therefore either the mountain or such
horse exists; so from the fact that I think of
od as existing it does not follow that He ex-
ts: but you go on to argue that a sophism is la-
nt here. But it would not be difficult to expose
e fallacy which you have yourself constructed,
specially by assuming something that is so man-
est a contradiction as that an existing God does
ot exist, and not assuming the same thing
bout man, or horse.

But if you had drawn a parallel between the
ountain with its valley, or the horse with its
ings, and God as possessing knowledge, power
nd other attributes, then the difficulty would have
een carried forward and you would have had to
xplain how it is possible for a sloping mountain
r a winged horse to be thought of without their
xisting, while a God who has knowledge and
ower cannot be conceived of without His existnce being involved.

You say: that it is not in your power to
hink of God without existence (that is of a
upremely perfect Being devoid of a supreme
erfection) as it is within your power to im-
gine a horse either with wings or without
ings.[1] But nothing is to be added to this, except
hat, as you are free to think of a horse that does
ot have wings without thinking of its existence,
hat existence which, if added, will be a perfec-
ion in it due to you; so you are free to think of a
iod that has knowledge, power and the other per-
ections, without thinking of His existence, which,
f possessed by Him would render His perfection
omplete. Whence, just as from the fact that a
orse is thought of as possessing the perfection of
eing winged, it is not therefore inferred that it
as existence, the chief of perfections, through
our instrumentality; so neither from the fact
hat God is considered as possessing knowledge
nd other perfections is His existence deduced
rom that: rather it finally remains to be proved.
Although you say: that existence quite as much
is other perfections is included in the idea of a
Being of the highest perfection, you affirm
what has to be proved, and assume your conclusion as a premise. For I might also, on the other

[1]Cf. p. 94.

part, say that in the idea of a perfect Pegasus,
there was contained not only the perfection of having wings, but also that of existing. For as God is
thought to be perfect in every kind of perfection,
so is Pegasus thought to be perfect in its own kind,
and you can bring forward in criticism nothing
which cannot, if the parallel between the two be
duly observed, be taken to hold of both alike.

You say: as in thinking of a triangle it is not
necessary for me to think that its three angles
are equal to two right angles, though that is
none the less true, as is afterwards clear when
we attend to the matter; so we may indeed
think of the other perfections of God without
thinking of His existence, though that is none
the less true when we note that it is a perfection. But you see what may be said, viz. that as
that property is discovered afterwards to exist in
the triangle, because a demonstration proves it,
so we must employ a demonstration in order to
discover existence in God. Otherwise it will certainly be easy for me to show that anything is in
anything.

You say: that when you attribute all perfections to God, you do not act as if you imagined
that all quadrilateral figures were inscribed in
the circle; since, as herein you would err,—
and this is borne out by your knowledge that
the rhombus cannot be inscribed in it, you do
not in the other case go astray, because you
afterwards find that existence is congruent
with God.[2] But this apparently, is inevitably to
act in the same way; or, if that is not so, you
must show that existence is not incompatible
with God, in the same way as you prove that being
inscribed in a circle is incompatible with the
rhombus. I pass by your remaining assertions,
which are either unexplained or unproved by you,
or are solved by considerations you have already
adduced as, for example: that nothing can be
conceived, to the essence of which existence
belongs, save God alone; that we cannot frame
the thought of two or more such Gods; that
such a God has from all eternity existed and
will continue to all eternity; that you perceive
many other things in God, which can suffer
neither diminution nor change.[3] To this is
added the necessity for inspecting these matters
more nearly and investigating them more diligently, in order that their truth may be revealed
and that they may be acknowledged as certain,
etc.

You declare, finally, that the certainty and
truth of all knowledge so depends upon our

[2]Cf. p. 94.
[3]Cf. p. 94.

apprehension of the true God alone, that, if we do not possess this, we can have no true certainty or knowledge.[1] *You bring forward the following example, saying:* When I consider the nature of a triangle, I who have some little knowledge of the principles of geometry, recognise quite clearly that the three angles are equal to two right angles; and it is not possible for me not to believe this so long as I apply my mind to its demonstration. But as soon as I divert my attention from its proof, howsoever well I recollect having clearly comprehended it, I may easily come to doubt about its truth, if I am ignorant of there being a God. For I might persuade myself of having been so constituted by nature as sometimes to be deceived in those matters which I believe myself to apprehend with the greatest evidence: especially when I recollect that I have frequently judged matters to be true and certain which other reasons have afterwards impelled me to judge to be altogether false. But after I have recognised that there is a God because at the same time I have recognised that all things depend upon Him and that He is not a deceiver, and from that I have inferred, that what I clearly and distinctly perceive cannot fail to be true: even though I no longer pay attention to the reason for which I believe that thing to be true: provided that I recollect having clearly and distinctly perceived it, no contrary reason can be brought forward which could cause me to doubt of its truth. On the contrary I have a true and certain knowledge of it. And this same knowledge extends likewise to all other things which I recollect having formerly demonstrated, such as the truths of geometry and the like.[2]

In reply to this, my good Sir, since I admit that you are speaking seriously, there is nothing to say, but that it seems that you will have difficulty in getting anyone to believe that you were less certain of those geometrical proofs before the time when you established by reasoning the above conclusion about God, than after you had done so. For really those demonstrations seem to have an evidence and certainty of such a kind as by themselves to extort our assent to them, and when once recognised they do not allow the mind to have any further doubt. So true is this that the mind will as likely as not bid that evil Genius go to perdition; just as you might have done when you (although the existence of God was not yet known) asserted with much emphasis that you could not be im-

posed on about that proposition and inference: think, hence I exist. Nay, even, however true be, as nothing can be truer, that God exists, th He is the Author of everything, and that He is n a deceiver, since, nevertheless, these facts seem t be less evident than those geometrical proofs (c which the only proof required is that many con trovert God's existence, His creation of the worl and many other truths), while no one denies th demonstrations of Geometry, is there anyon whom you can persuade that the evidence and cer tainty of the latter is communicated to them fron the former? Likewise who fancies that Diagoras Theodorus, or any similar atheist cannot be ren dered certain of the truth of those mathematica demonstrations? Again, how often among be lievers do you come across one who, if asked wh he is sure that in a (right-angled) triangle th square on its base is equal to the square on it sides, will reply: "because I know that God ex ists, and that God cannot deceive, and that He i the cause of this fact as likewise as of all others.' Will he not rather reply: "because I know it, an it has been shown to me by an indubitable demon stration"? How much the more likely is this to b the reply of Pythagoras, Plato, Archimedes, Eu clid, and other mathematicians, none of whom seems to bring up the thought of God in order t be quite certain of his demonstrations! Yet, be cause you do not pledge your word for others but only for yourself, and your attitude is als pious, there is really no reason for my objectin to it.*

RELATIVE TO MEDITATION VI

Of the Existence of Material Things, and of th Real Distinction Between the Soul and the Bod of Man.

1. *In the Sixth Meditation I do not object t what you say at the beginning:* that materia things may exist in so far as they are the objec of pure mathematics;[3] *since, nevertheless, ma terial things are the object of mixed, not of pur mathematics; and the objects of pure mathemat ics, e.g. the point, the line, the superficies, an the indivisible things consisting of these an functioning as indivisible, are incapable of ac tual existence. I have difficulty only because her a second time you distinguish* imagination from intellection. *Nay, O Mind, these two appear t be the action of one and the same faculty, as w have indicated above; and, if there is any dis tinction between them, it does not seem to be mor than one of greater and less. Consider how thes conclusions may thence be now proved.*

[1] Med. V, p. 95.
[2] Cf. pp. 95–96.
[3] Med. VI, p. 96.

You said above: to imagine is merely to con-emplate the figure or image of something cor-poreal. *But here you do not deny that* to under-tand is to contemplate the triangle, the pen-agon, the chiliagon, the myriagon, *and the ther things of this kind, which are the figures of orporeal things. You now indeed set up the dis-inction that* the imagination involves a certain pplication of the cognitive faculty to a body, vhile intellection does not involve any such pplication or effort. *So that,* when you simply nd without trouble perceive the triangle as a igure consisting of three angles, *you say that* hat is an act of understanding. But when, not vithout some effort on your part, you have hat figure, as it were, present, and investigate t, examine it, and recognise and discern its hree angles distinctly and severally, then, *you ay,* you imagine. *And hence,* since you indeed erceive without any trouble that the chilia-;on is a figure with a thousand angles, but yet :annot by application or an effort of attention, liscover it, and have it, as it were, present be-ore you and discern all its angles individually,[1] out are as confused about it as about the myri-agon, or any other figure of this description, ou therefore deem that you employ Intellec-ion in the case of the chiliagon or the myria-;on, and not Imagination.

But, nevertheless,[1] there is no reason why you hould not extend your imagination, as well as our intellection, to the chiliagon, as you do to he triangle. For you do try to some extent to im-igine that figure with its host of angles in some 'ashion, though the number of its angles is so great that you cannot conceive it clearly. Besides, hough you do perceive that a figure of a thousand ingles is signified by the word chiliagon, *that is merely the force of the name; for this will not :ause you to understand a thousand angles bet-'er than you imagine them.*

But we must note that the loss of distinctness ind increase of confusedness is gradual. For you vill perceive and imagine (or understand) the quadrilateral more confusedly than the triangle, yet more distinctly than the pentagon. Again this is more confused than the quadrilateral, but more distinct than the hexagon, and so on in order, un-til you have nothing explicit to put before your-self; and because you now are not able to have an explicit conception, you make an effort in order to omit as much as possible.

Wherefore, if you indeed wish to call it imagi-nation and intellection at the same time, when you ire aware of the figure distinctly and with some

[1]Cf. p. 96.

sensible effort, but intellection alone, when you view it confusedly merely and without or with but slight effort, you have my consent. But that will furnish no reason why you should set up more than one type of internal cognition, since it is accidental only whether you contemplate a figure in ways that differ in terms of more and less, dis-tinct or confused, attentiveness or carelessness. Assuredly, when we wish to run over the hepta-gon, the octagon, and the other figures up to the chiliagon, or the myriagon, and continuously and all through attend to the greater or less degree of distinctness or remissness of attention, shall we be able to say where or in what figure imagina-tion ceases and intellection alone remains? Does it not rather turn out to be the case that there is a continuous scale and progression in one sort of knowledge, the distinctness and toil of which de-creases continuously and insensibly, while its confusedness and effortlessness increases? Inde-pendently of this, note that you depreciate intel-lection, while lauding imagination. For do you not merely heap scorn on the former in allotting to it remissness and confusion, but commend the latter, in ascribing to it diligent care and per-spicuity?

Afterwards you assert: that the power of im-agination in so far as it is distinguished from the power of understanding is not a necessary part of your essence.[2] *But how can that be, if they are one and the same power, the functions of which differ merely in respect of greater and less?*

You add: that the mind, in imagining, turns towards the body, but, in its intellectual ac-tivity, turns towards itself or the idea it pos-sesses. *But what if the mind is unable to turn towards itself or towards any idea without at the same time turning itself towards something cor-poreal, or represented by a corporeal idea? For indeed the triangle, the pentagon, the chiliagon, the myriagon and the other figures or their ideas are altogether corporeal, and the mind cannot in its intellectual activity attend to them except as to something corporeal or similar to the corporeal. In so far as the ideas of things reputed to be im-material are concerned, such as the idea of God, of an Angel, or of the human soul or mind, it is certain also that the ideas we do possess about these things are either corporeal or after the fash-ion of the corporeal, and drawn from the human form and, at other times, from the most subtle, the simplest and most imperceptible objects such as air or ether, as we mentioned above. Moreover your statement,* that it is only with the prob-ability that you conjecture that any body ex-

[2]Cf. p. 96.

ists, *cannot be uttered by you seriously, and hence need cause us no delay.*

2. *Next you have a discussion about Sense, and first you very rightly make an enumeration of those matters which had become known to you by means of the senses and had been believed by you to be true, taking nature alone as your judge and guide. Immediately afterwards you relate the experiences, which so shook the beliefs you had derived from your senses, as to drive you to that position at which we found you in the First Meditation.*

At this point I have no desire to begin a controversy about the trustworthiness of the senses; for, if there is deception or falsity, it is not in sense, which is merely passive and has to do only with things that appear and must appear in the way they do owing to their own appropriate causes; it resides in the judgment or in the mind, which does not act with sufficient circumspection, and does not notice that things at a distance, owing to this and that cause appear more confused and smaller than they really are when they are near at hand, and so in other cases. Nevertheless, wherever deception does occur, we must not deny that some error exists; only the difficulty is, whether the error is always such that we can never be sure of the truth in the case of anything perceived by the senses.

But there is really no need to search for obvious examples. To take only the instances which you adduce, or rather cite as objections, I maintain that in these cases the truth of our belief seems to be amply confirmed; when we behold a tower close at hand and touch it we are sure that it is square, though, when further off, we had occasion to pronounce it to be round, or at least were able to doubt whether it was round or square or of some other figure.

Similarly, that feeling of pain, which appears still to exist in the foot or in the hand after these members have been cut off, may on occasion cause deception in those indeed who have had these limbs cut off; and that is because the sensorial spirits have been accustomed to pass downwards into them and express sensation in them. Nevertheless those who are whole are so certain that they feel the pain in the foot or in the hand which they see pricked, that they cannot doubt about it.

Similarly also, since we wake and dream alternately as long as we are alive, deception may occur owing to a dream, because things appear in the dream to be present which are not present. Nevertheless, neither do we always dream, nor, when we are really awake, can we doubt whether we are awake or dreaming.

So, too, since we can think that we are of a na̅ ture exposed to deceptions, even in things th̅ seem most sure, we none the less think that we a̅ naturally capable of apprehending truth. An̅ just as we sometimes err, as when we do not d̅ tect a sophism, or when we look at a stick plunge̅ to half its length in water, so also we sometim̅ apprehend the truth, as in a geometrical demo̅ stration, or when the stick is taken out of th̅ water, the circumstances being such that in ne̅ ther of these cases can we doubt at all about th̅ truth. And just as in other cases we may be i̅ doubt, so at least in this case no doubt is pe̅ mitted, namely that these things appear as the̅ do; indeed it cannot be other than absolutely tr̅ that such things appear.

Moreover, as to the fact that reason counsels u̅ not to believe much to which we are impelled b̅ nature, it cannot at least remove the truth of the̅ which appears—of the phenomenon. Yet ther̅ is no need for us here to discuss the questio̅ whether reason conflicts with sensuous impulsio̅ and opposes it merely as the right hand oppose̅ the left when holding it up as it droops fro̅ weariness, or whether their opposition is of an̅ other sort.

3. *You next address yourself to your purpose̅ but in a light and, as it were, skirmishing fashio̅ For you proceed to say:* But now that I begin t̅ be better acquainted with myself and with th̅ author of my being, I do not in truth thin̅ that I should rashly admit all the matter̅ which my senses seem to teach me; neither, o̅ the other hand, do I think that I should doub̅ them all.[1] *Quite right: though doubtless you ha̅ thought the very same thing already.*

The next passage is: And first of all, becaus̅ I know that all the things which I apprehen̅ clearly and distinctly can be created by Go̅ as I apprehend them, it suffices that I am abl̅ to apprehend one thing apart from anothe̅ clearly and distinctly in order to be certai̅ that the one is different from the other, sinc̅ they may be made to exist in isolation by Go̅ at least; and it does not matter by what powe̅ their separation is made, in order to compel m̅ to judge them to be different.[2] *In reply to thi̅ there is nothing to be said, save that you emplo̅ what is obscure to demonstrate something that i̅ clear, not that I allege that there is any obscurit̅ in the inference. I do not raise a difficulty indee̅ about the fact that you should previously hav̅ proved that God exists, nor, as to the matters t̅ which His power extends, about the proof that H̅*

[1]Cf. p. 98.
[2]Cf. p. 98.

in effect what even you are able to comprehend. should ask merely whether you clearly and disnctly apprehend in a triangle that property, hat the greater side subtends the greater ngle, *separately from that other, according to* which the three angles taken together are held to be equal to two right angles. *Do you admit* that God can therefore separate and isolate the latter property from the former, so that the triangle possesses the one and not the other, or that the latter also may be disjoined from the triangle?

But, not to delay you here, inasmuch as this separation is but little to the point, you add: And hence from this very thing, because I know that I exist, and that meanwhile I do not remark that any other thing pertains to my nature or essence, excepting this alone, that I am thinking thing, *I rightly conclude that my* ssence consists solely in the fact that I am a thinking thing. *Here I should arrest your progress; but either it is enough to repeat what I said* in connection with the second Meditation, or we must await your inference.

For finally you say: And although possibly or rather certainly, as I shall say in a moment) possess a body with which I am very intimately conjoined, yet because on the one side have a clear and distinct idea of myself, insmuch as I am only a thinking and not an extended thing, and on the other I possess a distinct idea of body, inasmuch as it is only an xtended and not a thinking thing; it is certain hat I am really distinct from my body, and can exist without it.

So this was your objective, was it? Hence, since the whole of the difficulty hinges on this, we must halt awhile, in order to see how you manage to make this position good. The principal matter here in question is the distinction between you and body. But what body do you here mean? Plainly this solid body composed of members, the body to which, without doubt, the following words refer: I possess a body connected with myself and it is certain that I am distinct from my body, etc.

But now, O Mind, there is no difficulty about this body. There would be a difficulty, if with the greater part of philosophers I were to object that you were the realisation, the perfection, the activity, the form, the appearance, or, to use, a popular fashion of speech, a mode of the body. They, forsooth, do not acknowledge that you are more distinct and separable from your body than figure, or any other mode. This, too, they maintain, whether you are the entire soul, or are besides also νοῦς δυνάμει, νοῦς παθητικός, the po-

tential intellect, or passive intellect, as they style it. But it pleases me to deal somewhat liberally with you and consider you as though you were the νοῦς ποιητικός, the active intellect, nay, even as χωριστός, i.e. capable of separate existence, though separable in another sense than they imagined.

For since those philosophers assigned it to all men (if not rather to all things) as something common to them and as being the source of intellectual activity on the part of the potential intellect, exactly in the same way and with the same necessity as light supplies the eye with the opportunity of seeing (whence they were wont to compare it to the light of the sun, and hence to regard it as coming from without), I myself rather consider you (as you also are quite willing I should) as a certain special intellect exercising domination in the body.

Moreover, I repeat that the difficulty is not as to whether you are separable or not from this body (whence, shortly before, I hinted that it was not necessary to recur to the power of God in order to secure the separability of those things which you apprehend as separate), but from the body which you yourself are: seeing that possibly you really are a subtle body diffused within that solid one, or occupying some seat within it. But you have not yet convinced us that you are anything absolutely incorporeal. Likewise, though in the second Meditation you proclaimed that you are not a wind, nor a fire, nor a vapour, nor a breath, do be advised of the warning I give you, that the statement thus announced has not been proved.

You said that you did not at that point dispute about those matters; *but you have not subsequently discussed them, nor have you in any way proved that you are not a body of this kind. I had hoped that here you would make the matter good; but if you do discuss anything, if you do prove anything, your discussion and proof merely show that you are not the solid body, about which, as I have already said, there is no difficulty.*

4. But, *you say,* I have on the one hand a clear and distinct idea of myself, in so far as I am merely a thinking thing and not extended, and on the other a distinct idea of body, in so far as it is an extended thing, but not one that thinks. *Firstly, however, in so far as the idea of body is concerned, there appears to be no need for spending much pains over it. For, if you indeed make this pronouncement about the idea of body universally, we must repeat our previous objection, namely that you have to prove that it is incompatible with the nature of body to be capable*

of thinking. Thus it would be a begging of the question when the problem was raised by you as to whether you are a subtle body or not, *in a way that implied that thought is incompatible with body.*

But since you make that assertion and certainly treat only of that solid body, from which you maintain that you are separable and distinct, I do not on that account so much deny that you have an idea of yourself, as maintain that you could not possess it if you were really an unextended thing. For, I ask you, how do you think that you, an unextended subject, could receive into yourself the semblance or idea of a body which is extended? For, if such a semblance proceeds from the body, it is certainly corporeal and has parts outside of other parts, and consequently is corporeal. Or alternatively, whether or not its impression is due to some other source, since necessarily it always represents an extended body, it must still have parts and, consequently, be extended. Otherwise, if it has no parts, how will it represent parts? If it has no extension how will it represent extension? If devoid of figure, how represent an object possessing figure? If it has no position, how can it represent a thing which has upper and lower, right and left, and intermediate parts? If without variation, how represent the various colours, etc.? Therefore an idea appears not to lack extension utterly. But unless it is devoid of extension how can you, if unextended, be its subject? How will you unite it to you? How lay hold of it? How will you be able to feel it gradually fade and finally vanish away?

Next, relatively to your idea of yourself nothing is to be added to what has been already said, and especially in the second Meditation. For thence it is proved that, far from having a clear and distinct idea of yourself, you seem to be wholly without one. This is because, even though you recognise that you think, you do not know of what nature you, who think, are. Hence, since this operation alone is known to you, the chief matter is, nevertheless, hidden from you, namely, the substance which so operates. This brings up the comparison in which you may be likened to a blind man, who, on feeling heat, and being told that it proceeds from the sun, should think that he has a clear and distinct idea of the sun, inasmuch as, if anyone ask him what the sun is, he can reply: it is something which produces heat.

But, you will say, I here add not only that I am a thinking thing, *but that I am* a thing which is not extended. *But not to mention that this is asserted without proof, since it is still in question, I ask firstly: for all that, have you a clear and dis-*

tinct idea of yourself? You say that you are no extended; *but in so doing you say what you ar* not, *not what you are. In order to have a clear an distinct idea, or, what is the same thing, a tru and genuine idea of anything, is it not necessar to know the thing itself positively, and so to spea affirmatively, or does it suffice to know that it i not any other thing? Would it not then be a clea and distinct idea of Bucephalus, if one knew o him that he was not a fly?*

But, not to urge this, my question is rather are you not an extended thing, or are you not dif fused throughout the body? I cannot tell what yo will reply; for, though from the outset I recog nised that you existed only in the brain, I forme that belief rather by conjecture than by directl follow. ing your opinion. I derived my conjectur from the statement which ensues, in which yo assert, that you are not affected by all parts o the body, but only by the brain, or even b one of its smallest parts.[1] But I was not quit certain whether you were found therefore only i the brain or in a part of it, since you might b found in the whole body, but be acted on at onl one part. Thus it would be according to the pop ular belief, which takes the soul to be diffuse throughout the entire body, while yet it is in th eye alone that it has vision.

Similarly, the following words moved one t doubt: "and, although the whole mind seems t be united to the whole body,"[2] etc. *You indee do not there assert that you are united with th whole of the body, but you do not deny it. How soever it be, with your leave let me consider yo firstly as diffused throughout the whole body Whether you are the same as the soul, or some thing diverse from it, I ask you, O unextended thing, what you are that are spread from head t heel, or that are coextensive with the body, tha have a like number of parts corresponding to it parts? Will you say that you are therefore unex tended, because you are a whole in a whole, an are wholly in every part? I pray you tell me, i you maintain this, how you conceive it. Can single thing thus be at the same time wholly i several parts? Faith assures us of this in the cas of the sacred mystery (of the Eucharist).[3] But th question here is relative to you, a natural object and is indeed one relative to our natural light Can we grasp how there can be a plurality o places without there being a plurality of object located in them? Is not a hundred more than one Likewise, if a thing is wholly in one place, can i*

[1]Med. VI, p. 102.
[2]Cf. p. 102.
[3]Tr.

in others, unless it is itself outside itself, as
ace is outside place? Say what you will, it will
least be obscure and uncertain whether you are
holly in any part and not rather in the various
rts of the body by means of your several parts.
nd since it is much more evident that nothing
n exist as a whole in different places, it will
rn out to be still more clear that you are not
holly in the single parts of your body but merely
the whole as a whole, and that you are so by
eans of your parts diffused through the whole,
d consequently that you have extension.

Secondly, let us suppose that you are in the
ain alone, or merely in some minute part of it.
ou perceive that the same thing is clearly an ob-
ction, since, however small that part be, it is
vertheless extended, and you are coextensive
ith it, and consequently are extended and have
rticular parts corresponding to its particular
rts. Will you say that you take that part of the
ain to be a point? That is surely incredible, but
ppose it is a point. If it is indeed something
hysical, the same difficulty remains, because
ch a point is extended and is certainly not de-
id of parts. If it is a Mathematical point you
ow that it is given only by the imagination.
ut let it be given or let rather us feign that in the
ain there is given a Mathematical point, to
hich you are united, and in which you exist.
ow, see how useless a fiction this will turn out
be. For, if it is to be assumed, we must feign it
exist in such a way that you are at the meeting
lace of the nerves by which all the regions in-
rmed by the soul transmit to the brain the ideas
semblances of the things perceived by the
nses. But firstly, the nerves do not all meet at
ne point, whether for the reason that, as the
rain is continued into the spinal marrow, many
erves all over the back pass into that, or because
ose which extend to the middle of the head are
ot found to terminate in the same part of the
rain. But let us assume that they all do meet;
one the less they cannot all unite in a mathe-
atical point, since they are bodies, not mathe-
atical lines, and so able to meet in a mathe-
atical point. And supposing we grant that they
o so unite, it will be impossible for the spirits[1]
hich pass through these to pass out of the nerves
r to enter them, as being bodies; since body can-
ot be in or pass through what is not a place, as
e mathematical point is. But though we should
llow that the animal spirits do exist in or pass
rough what is not a place, nevertheless you, ex-
sting as you do in a point, in which there are

[1]The "animal spirits" correspond to the "ner-
ous impulses" of modern psychology.

neither right hand parts nor left hand, neither
higher nor lower, nor anything similar, cannot
judge as to whence they come nor what they report.

Moreover, I say the same thing of those spirits
which you must transmit in order to have feeling
or to report tidings, and in order to move. I omit
that we cannot grasp how you impress a motion
upon them, you who are yourself in a point, unless you are really a body, or unless you have a
body by which you are in contact with them and
at the same time propel them. For, if you say that
they are moved by themselves, and that you only
direct their motion, remember that you somewhere else denied that the body is moved by
itself;[2] so that we must thence infer that you are
the cause of that movement. Next, explain to us
how such a direction can take place without some
effort and so some motion on your part? How can
there be effort directed towards anything, and motion on its part, without mutual contact of what
moves and what is moved? How can there be contact apart from body, when (as is so clear to the
natural light)

Apart from body, naught touches
or is touched?[3]

Yet why do I delay here when it is on you that
the onus rests of proving that you are unextended
and hence incorporeal? But neither do I think
that you will find an argument in the fact that
man is popularly said to consist of soul and body,
inferring that if one part is said to be body, the
other must be declared not to be body. For, if you
did so, you would give us an opportunity of
drawing the distinction in such a way that man
should be held to consist of a double body, viz. the
solid one and the subtle one; and according to
this scheme while the former retained the name
body, the common term, the other would be given
the name soul. I pass by the fact that the same
thing would be said about the other animals, to
which you have not granted a mind similar to
your own; lucky they, if by your sanction they
possess even a soul! Hence, therefore, when you
conclude that you are certain that you are
really distinct from your body, you see that that
would be admitted, but that it would not therefore
be conceded that you were incorporeal, and not
rather a species of very subtle body distinct from
your grosser body.

You add that hence you can exist apart from
it.[4] But after being conceded the point that you

[2]Med. II, p. 78.
[3]A misquotation of Lucretius (De Rerum natura,
I, 305).
[4]Med. VI, p. 98.

can exist apart from that grosser body in the same way as an odoriferous vapour does while passing out of an apple and dispersing into the air, what do you think you have gained? Something more certainly than the above mentioned Philosophers[1] wish to prove, who believe that you wholly perish at death itself; being as it were like a figure which on the alteration of the superficies so disappears, that it may be said to be non-existent or wholly nothing. Indeed, since you were something corporeal as well, or a fine substance, you will not be said to vanish wholly at death, or wholly to pass into nothing, but to exist by means of your dispersed parts, howsoever much, on account of being thus drawn asunder, you are not likely to think any more, and will be said to be neither a thinking thing, nor a mind, nor a soul. Yet, all these objections I bring, not in order to cast doubt on the conclusion you intend to prove, but merely by way of expressing my disagreement as to the cogency of the argument set forth by you.

5. In connection with this, you interpose several things tending to the same conclusion, on all of which we need not insist. One thing I note, and that is that you say that nature teaches you by the sensation of pain, hunger, thirst, etc., that you are not lodged in the body as a sailor in a ship, but that you are very closely united with it and, so to speak, intermingled with it so as to compose one whole along with it. For if that were not the case, you say, "when my body is hurt, I who am merely a thinking thing would not feel pain, but should perceive the wound with the mere understanding, just as the sailor perceives by sight when something is damaged in his vessel, and when my body has need of food or drink, I should clearly understand this fact, and not have the confused feelings of hunger and thirst. For all these sensations of hunger, thirst, pain, etc. are in truth none other than certain confused modes of thought which are produced by the union and apparent intermingling of mind and body."[2]

This is indeed quite right; but it still remains to be explained, how that union and apparent intermingling, or confusion, can be found in you, if you are incorporeal, unextended and indivisible. For if you are not greater than a point, how can you be united with the entire body, which is of such great magnitude? How, at least, can you be united with the brain, or some minute part in it, which (as has been said) must yet have some magnitude or extension, however small it be? If you are wholly without parts, how can you mix or

appear to mix with its minute subdivisions? F[or] there is no mixture unless each of the things to [be] mixed has parts that can mix with one anothe[r]. Further, if you are discrete, how could you be i[n]volved with and form one thing along with matt[er] itself? Again since conjunction or union exis[ts] between certain parts, ought there not to be a rela[tion] of similarity between parts of this sort? B[ut] what must the union of the corporeal with the i[n]corporeal be thought to be? Do we conceive ho[w] stone and air are fused together, as in pumi[ce] stone, so as to become a fusion of uniform chara[c]ter? Yet the similarity between stone and a[ir] which itself is also a body, is greater than that b[e]tween body and soul, or a wholly incorpore[al] mind. Further, ought not that union to take pla[ce] by means of the closest contact? But how, as [I] said before, can that take place, apart from bod[y]? How will that which is corporeal seize upon th[at] which is incorporeal, so to hold it conjoined wi[th] itself, or how will the incorporeal grasp the co[r]poreal, so as reciprocally to keep it bound to i[t]self, if in it, the incorporeal, there is nothi[ng] which it can use to grasp the other, or by which [it] can be grasped.

Hence, since you admit that you feel pain, [I] ask you how you think that you, if you are inco[r]poreal and unextended, are capable of experienc[c]ing the sensation of pain. Thus the affection pa[in] can only be understood as arising from some pul[l]ing asunder of bodily parts when something i[n]terferes and annuls their continuity. For exampl[e] a state of pain is an unnatural state, but how ca[n] that be in an unnatural state or be affected co[n]trary to nature, which by nature is of one sor[t] simple, indivisible and immutable? Again, sin[ce] pain is either alteration, or cannot occur witho[ut] it, how can that be altered, which, being more d[e]void of parts than a point, cannot be altered n[or] can cease to be just as it is, unless it turns in[to] nothing? I add also: since pain comes from th[e] foot, the arm, and from other regions at the sam[e] time, ought there not to be in you various parts, [in] which you receive it in various ways, in order n[ot] to be confused and to regard it as being the pai[n] of merely one part. But, in a word, the gener[al] difficulty always remains, viz. how the corpore[al] can have anything in common with the inco[r]poreal, or what relationship may be establishe[d] between the one and the other.

6. I pass by the other passages in which, in [a] very copious and neat argument, you strive [to] show that something else is in existence beside[s] yourself and God. For you deduce the conclusio[n] that your body and its corporeal faculties exis[t] and likewise other bodies which despatch in[to]

[1] Cf. above, Obj. v, p. 198.
[2] Med. vi, p. 99.

ur senses and into yourself the semblances of
emselves, and produce the experiences of pleas-
e and pain, which beget in you desire and
ersion.

And from this you at length derive the follow-
g conclusion, which is, as it were, the fruit of
ur reasoning, in order that since all the sen-
tions relative to the things which have to do
ith the welfare of the body more frequently
dicate to you truth than falsehood, you may
ence infer that you ought no longer to fear
at falsity may be found in matters every day
presented to you by the senses.[1] You say the
me, consequently, about dreams, for since they
e not connected with the whole of our ac-
ons and course of life in the same way as
hat we experience when awake, you thence
tablish the conclusion that real things are pre-
nted to you, not in sleep, but when you are
vake.[2] Hence, you say next, since God is not a
ceiver, it follows that you are not deceived
such matters. This is an extremely pious
atement; and so, too, you are assuredly quite in
e right when you finally conclude: that the life
man is subject to error, and that we must
knowledge the infirmity of our nature.

These, my good Sir, are the observations that

[1]Med. vi, p. 103.
[2]Cf. p. 103.

occurred to me in connection with your Meditations. I repeat that you ought not to give yourself
any thought about them, since my judgment is not
of such moment as to deserve to have any weight
with you. For as, when some food is pleasant to
my palate, I do not defend my taste, which I see
is offensive to others, as being more perfect than
anyone else's; so, when my mind welcomes an
opinion which does not please others, I am far
from holding that I have hit upon the truer theory.
I think that the truth is rather this—that each enjoys his own opinion; and I hold that it is almost
as unjust to wish everyone to have the same belief,
as to want all people to be alike in the sense of
taste: I say so, in order that you may hold yourself free to dismiss everything that I have said as
not worth a straw, and to omit it altogether. It
will be enough if you acknowledge my strong
affection for you, and do not esteem as nought my
admiration for your personal worth. Perhaps
some matter has been advanced somewhat incon-
siderately, as is only too likely to happen when
one is expressing dissent. Any such passage
which may occur I wholly disavow and sacrifice;
pray blot it out, and be assured, that I have desired nothing more than to deserve well of you and
to keep my friendship with you quite intact.

With kind regards,

Paris, 16th May, 1641.

REPLY TO
THE FIFTH SET OF OBJECTIONS

R,

The essay in which you criticize my medi-
tions is exceedingly well-written and care-
lly executed, and to me it appears that it will
o much to set them in a clear light. Conse-
uently I consider that I am greatly beholden
) you for writing it, as well as to the Rev.
ather Mersenne for inciting you to do so.
ur friend, who is such an eager enquirer into
ll things, and who more especially promotes
nweariedly everything that tends to the glory
f God, knows that the best way of determin-
g whether my arguments are to be treated as
ccurate demonstrations, is that some men of
utstanding eminence in scholarship and abili-
y, should subject them to a rigorous criticism,
) as finally to make trial of my powers of giv-
g a satisfactory answer to their objections.
his is why he has challenged so many to at-

tempt the task, and has prevailed upon some
to do so, among whom I am glad to see you.
For, though in order to refute my opinions you
have not so much employed philosophical reasoning as made use of certain oratorical devices so as to elude my argument, this is in itself a matter of gratification to me, since I shall
for this reason infer that it will not be easy to
bring up in opposition to me arguments which
differ from those which you have read in the
preceding criticisms urged by other people.
Further, if such had existed, they would not
have escaped your penetration and industry,
and I hold that here your only purpose has
been to bring to my notice those conceptions
which might be used to avoid the force of my
arguments by those whose minds are so im-
mersed in matters of sense as to shrink from all
metaphysical reflections, and that you thus

gave me an opportunity for meeting these. Wherefore here I shall reply to you not as a keen-eyed philosopher, but as to one of these fleshly individuals whom you impersonate.

OF THE OBJECTIONS URGED AGAINST THE FIRST MEDITATION

You say that *you approve of my determination to rid my mind of prejudices*, especially since no one can pretend that there is any fault to find with this; but you would prefer me to proceed *simply and with few words*,[1] i.e. to carry out my resolve only in a perfunctory manner. This is forsooth to assume that it is very easy for all to free themselves from the errors in which, since infancy, they have been steeped, and that too much care may be employed in carrying this out, a contention which no one maintains. I suppose you wished to show that many men, though verbally admitting that prejudices should be avoided, nevertheless completely fail to avoid them, because they expend no toil and pains upon the attempt, and never think that anything which they have once admitted to be true should be regarded as a prejudice. You certainly play the rôle of such people excellently here, and omit none of their possible arguments, but there is nothing in this action which seems to suggest the Philosopher. For when you say that there is no need *to imagine that God is a deceiver* or *that we are dreaming*, or anything of the kind, a Philosopher would have considered that there was some necessity for showing the reason why such matters could not be considered as doubtful, or if he had no reason, as in truth there is none, he would not have made the said assertion. Neither would he have added that in this place *it was sufficient to plead the obscurity of the human mind* or *the feebleness of our nature*. The elimination of our errors is in no way furthered by alleging that we err owing to the dimness of our thought or the feebleness of our nature; for that is the same as merely saying that we err because we are exposed to errors, and clearly it is more useful to attend, as I have done, to all those cases in which error may chance to arise, lest we readily give the error our assent. Likewise a Philosopher would not have said *that I, in considering everything doubtful as false, did not so much dismiss an old prejudice as take up with a new one;* or he would first have tried to show that out of this supposition there arose some danger of deception. But you, on the contrary, shortly afterwards affirm *that I can-*

[1]Cf. above Objections v, p. 171.

not force myself to treat as doubtful or false t *things that I supposed to be false*, i.e. that I cann adopt the prejudice which you feared I mig adopt. This would cause no more surprise to Philosopher than that at some time a sti which has been straightened out should I similarly bent back again into the opposit i.e. crooked, shape. For he knows that falsiti are often assumed instead of truths for th purpose of throwing light on the truth: for e ample, Astronomers imagine the existence the equator, the zodiac, and other circles in t heaven, while Geometricians attach new lin to given figures, and Philosophers frequent act in similar fashion. But the man who d scribes this as *having recourse to an artific eagerness for verbal trickery, and seeking ev sions*, and declares *that it is unworthy of phil sophical candour and the love of truth*, manifes that he at least has no desire to make use philosophical candour or to employ any arg ment other than rhetorical humbug.

CONCERNING THE OBJECTIONS TO THE SECOND MEDITATION

1. Here you proceed to employ rhetoric wiles in place of reasoning; for you preten that I speak in jest when I am quite seriou and take as serious, and as uttered and assert as true, what I propounded only as a questic and as arising out of common opinion for th purpose of enquiring further into it. My stat ment *that the entire testimony of the senses mu be considered to be uncertain, nay, even false*, quite serious and so necessary for the con prehension of my meditations, that he who w not or cannot admit that, is unfit to urge an objection to them that merits a reply. But w must note the distinction emphasized by me various passages, between the practical activ ties of our life and an enquiry into truth; fo when it is a case of regulating our life, it woul assuredly be stupid not to trust the senses, an those sceptics were quite ridiculous who neglected human affairs that they had to preserved by their friends from tumbling dow precipices. It was for this reason that som where I announced *that no one in his soun mind seriously doubted about such matters*:[2] b when we raise an enquiry into what is th surest knowledge which the human mind ca obtain, it is clearly unreasonable to refuse treat them as doubtful, nay even to reje them as false, so as to allow us to become awa that certain other things, which cannot be th

[2]*Meditations*, Synopsis, p. 74.

jected, are for this very reason more certain, and in actual truth better known by us.

Moreover, you do not accept in good faith and as seriously meant, my statement that I did not yet sufficiently understand who the thinker was, though I had explained that very assertion. You also fail to allow my statement that I did not doubt about that in which the nature of the body consisted, and had assigned no power of self-movement to it, and had imagined myself to be a soul after the fashion of wind or flame or something of the kind, assertions that I then made, deriving them from common opinion, only in order that I might show them to be false in their appropriate place. What warrant have you for saying that *nutrition, motion, feeling etc. are referred by me to the soul*, in order that you may immediately add: *I grant this, but what becomes of the distinction you draw between the soul and the body?*[1] The fact is, that shortly before, I, in express terms, referred nutrition to the body alone, while motion and sensibility I refer for the most part also to the body, and ascribe nothing that belongs to them to the soul, save only as much as consists in thinking.

Next, what grounds have you for saying *that there was no need of such an elaborate mechanism in order to prove that I exist?*[2] Really these very words of yours give me the best grounds for believing that my labours have not yet been sufficiently great, since I have as yet failed to make you understand the matter rightly. When you say that *I could have inferred the same conclusion from any of my other actions*, you wander far from the truth, because there is none of my activities of which I am wholly certain (in the sense of having metaphysical certitude, which alone is here involved), save thinking alone. For example you have no right to make the inference: *I walk, hence I exist*, except in so far as our awareness of walking is a thought; it is of this alone that the inference holds good, not of the motion of the body, which sometimes does not exist, as in dreams, when nevertheless I appear to walk. Hence from the fact that I think that I walk I can very well infer the existence of the mind which so thinks, but not that of the body which walks. So it is also in all other cases.

2. Next, with a not infelicitous comedy, you proceed to question me, no longer as a complete man, but as a soul in separation from the body; and in so doing you seem to remind me

that these objections proceed not from the mind of an acute philosopher but from the flesh alone. I ask you therefore, O flesh, or whatever the name be by which you prefer to be known, have you so little intercourse with the mind, that you have not been able to note when I corrected that popular notion, by which it is imagined that that which thinks is like wind or some similar body? I corrected it then, surely, when I showed that it could be supposed that no wind or other body existed, and that nevertheless everything by means of which I recognize myself as a thinking being remains. Hence your subsequent questions as to *why I cannot therefore be still a wind, and why I cannot occupy space, and why I cannot be subject to many motions*,[3] etc., are so devoid of sense as to require no reply.

3. The next objections have no more force: *—if I am a sort of attenuated body, why can I not be nourished*,[4] and the rest. I deny that I am a body. Also, once and for all, to bring the matter to completeness, since you almost always employ the same style, and do not attack my arguments but disingenuously suppress them, as if they were of no account, or quote them only imperfectly and in a mutilated form, and thus bring together a number of difficulties which would in a popular way and by unskilled persons be urged against my conclusions, or others akin to them or even unlike them, difficulties which either are irrelevant, or have been refuted or solved by me in their appropriate places; since this is, so I declare that it is not worth while replying to each single question, for I should have to repeat a hundred times what I have already written. I shall only deal shortly with those which seem likely to cause difficulty to readers not wholly incompetent. As for those who look not so much to the force of the argument as to the multitude of the words employed, I do not value their approval so highly as to wish to become more wordy for the sake of meriting it.

Therefore I will first note, that I do not accept your statement *that the mind grows and waxes faint along* with the body, and you have no argument to prove it; for from the fact that it does not work with equal perfection in the body of an infant and in that of an adult, and that its activities are frequently impeded by wine and other corporeal bodies, this alone follows, that as long as it is united with the body, it uses it as its instrument in those operations

[1]Cf. above, Obj. v, p. 172.
[2]Cf. above, p. 172.

[3]Cf. above, pp. 172–173.
[4]Cf. above, p. 173.

in which it is principally engaged, but not that it is rendered more or less perfect by the body; your contention will have no more force than were we to argue from the fact that a workman does not get good results as long as he uses a bad instrument, that he had acquired his skill in his art from the excellence of his instrument.

It is to be noticed also that you seem wholly to fail to understand, O flesh, what it is to employ reason, when in your argument to show that the trustworthiness of the senses ought not to be impugned by me, you say that *although at times, when not using the eye, I appeared to have experiences that do not occur without the eye coming into play, yet so to err was not my universal experience.*[1] You seem to imagine that we have not a sufficient cause for doubt if at any one time we detect an error; and again you seem to think that we might always note the error each time that we fall into it, when, on the contrary, the error consists in the very fact that it is not recognized by us as an error.

Finally, since you often demand an argument from me, when you, O flesh, possess none yourself, and since the "onus" of the proof presses on you, we must note that, in philosophizing correctly, there is no need for us to prove the falsity of all those things which we do not admit because we do not know whether they are true. We have merely to take the greatest care not to admit as true what we cannot prove to be true. Thus when I find that I am a thinking substance, and form a clear and distinct concept of that substance, in which there is none of those attributes which belong to the concept of corporeal substance, this is quite sufficient to let me affirm that I, in so far as I know myself, am nothing but a thing which thinks, which statement alone I have affirmed in the second Meditation—that with which we are at present occupied. Neither was I bound to admit that this thinking substance was some mobile, simple, and rarified body, and when I had found no reason inducing me to believe that. But it is for you, it is your duty, to expound the reason, if you have one; you have no right to demand that I shall prove that false which I refused to entertain only for the reason that I had no knowledge about it. You act as if, when I asserted that I now lived in Holland, you were to deny that that was to be believed, unless I proved that I was neither in China nor in any other part of the world, because it is perchance possible that the same body should, owing to the action of the divine power, exist

in two different places. But when you add *the I must also prove that the souls of brutes are in corporeal, and that solid matter contributes noth ing to thinking,*[2] you not only show that you d not know on whom the onus of proof lies, bu also of what should be proved by each person for neither do I think that the souls of brute are incorporeal, nor do I believe that solid mat ter contributes nothing to their thinking: merely say that this is by no means the plac for the consideration of those matters.

4. You here pursue the question of the ob scurity arising out of the ambiguity of th word *soul*, an obscurity which I took suc pains to remove that it is wearisome to repea here what I have said. Therefore, I shall de clare only, that names have been conferred o things for the most part by the inexpert, an that for this reason they do not always fit th things with sufficient accuracy; that it is no our part to change them after custom has ac cepted them, but only to permit the emenda tion of their meanings, when we perceive tha others do not understand them aright. Thu because probably men in the earliest times di not distinguish in us that principle in virtue o which we are nourished, grow, and perform a those operations which are common to us wit the brutes apart from any thought, from tha by which we think they called both by th single name *soul;* then, perceiving the distinc tion between nutrition and thinking, they calle that which thinks *mind*, believing also tha this was the chief part of the soul. But I, per ceiving that the principle by which we ar nourished is wholly distinct from that b means of which we think, have declared tha the name *soul* when used for both is equivoca and I say that, when soul is taken to mean *th primary actuality* or *chief essence of man*, i must be understood to apply only to the prin ciple by which we think, and I have called i by the name *mind* as often as possible in orde to avoid ambiguity; for I consider the min not as part of the soul but as the whole of tha soul which thinks.

You have a difficulty, however, you say, *as t whether I think that the soul always thinks.*[3] Bu why should it not always think, when it is thinking substance? Why is it strange that w do not remember the thoughts it has had whe in the womb or in a stupor, when we do no even remember the most of those we know w have had when grown up, in good health, an

[1]Cf. above, p. 173.

[2]Cf. above, p. 173.
[3]Cf. above, p. 174.

awake? For the recollection of the thoughts which the mind has had during the period of its union with the body, it is necessary for certain traces of them to be impressed on the brain; and turning and applying itself to these the mind remembers. Is it remarkable if the brain of an infant or of one in a stupor is unfit to receive these residual impressions?

Finally, when I said *perhaps it is the case that what I have not yet known* (to wit, my body) *is not diverse from that which I do know* (my mind), *I do not know, I do not discuss this matter,* etc.; you object; *if you are ignorant, if you do not dispute the matter, why do you assume that you are none of those things?*[1] But here it is false that I have assumed something of which I was ignorant; for plainly, on the contrary, because I did not know whether body was the same as mind or not, I made no assumption about the matter, but treated of the mind alone, until afterwards in the sixth Meditation, not assuming but demonstrating the matter, I showed that mind was really distinct from the body. But you, O flesh, are to the highest degree involved in error, since though you have no reason or the very slightest by which to show that mind is not distinct from body, you none the less assume it.

5. To one who gives close attention to my words what I have said of the imagination is sufficiently clear; but there is no reason for wonder if to the unreflective it is quite obscure. Moreover, I warn those people that my statements as to what I have asserted to be no part of the knowledge which I have of myself do not conflict with what I said before about those matters, as to which I was ignorant whether or not they appertained to me; for it is plainly one thing to appertain to me, another to belong to the knowledge which I have of myself.

6. What you say here, my admired flesh, seems to me not to consist of objections so much as of carpings that require no answer.

7. Here also you find much to carp at, but your complaints seem to require a reply no more than the preceding ones. For your queries about the brutes are not relevant here, since the mind when communing with itself can experience the fact that it thinks, but has no evidence of this kind as to whether or not the brutes think; it can only come to a conclusion afterwards about this matter by reasoning *a posteriori* from their actions. I have no difficulty in disowning those inept statements which you put into my mouth, for it is enough

[1]Cf. above, p. 174.

for me to have pointed out once that you do not reproduce faithfully everything I have said. But I have often adduced the criterion by which the difference between mind and body is detected; viz. that the whole nature of the mind consists in thinking, while the whole nature of the body consists in being an extended thing, and that there is nothing at all common to thought and extension. I have often also shown distinctly that mind can act independently of the brain; for certainly the brain can be of no use in pure thought: its only use is for imagining and perceiving. And although, when imagination or sensation is intense (as occurs when the brain is troubled or disturbed), the mind does not readily find room for thinking of other matters, yet we experience the fact that, when imagination is not so strong, we often understand something entirely diverse from it: for example, when we sleep we perceive that we are dreaming, while in having the dream we must employ the imagination; yet our awareness of the fact that we are dreaming is an act of the intellect alone.

8. Here, as frequently elsewhere, you merely show that you do not properly understand what you attempt to criticize. For, neither have I abstracted the concept of wax from that of its accidents; rather have I tried to show how its substance was manifested by means of accidents, and how the reflective and distinct perception of it, one such as you, O flesh, seem never to have had, differs from the vulgar and confused idea. Nor can I see what argument you rely on to prove your confident affirmation that a dog can discriminate in the same way as we do, unless that, since you see that it is made of flesh, you believe that everything which exists in you is also in it. But I, failing to detect mind in it, think that nothing similar to that which I recognize in mind is found in it.

9. I am surprised that while here you confess that all those matters which I am aware of in wax, *show indeed that I distinctly know that I exist,* you maintain *that they do not demonstrate what I am,*[2] since the one thing cannot be proved without the other. Nor do I see what else you expect the matter to yield, unless it be some revelation about the colour, odour, or taste of the human mind, or the nature of the salt, sulphur, or mercury that go to its composition; for you wish us to examine it, as though it were a wine, *by a sort of chemical analysis.*[3]

[2]Cf. above, pp. 177–178.
[3]Cf. above, 179.

That is really worthy of you, O flesh, and of all those who, conceiving nothing except what is wholly confused, are ignorant of the proper object of investigation in each inquiry. As for me, my belief has always been that nothing else is required in order to manifest the nature of substance except its various attributes, so that our comprehension of its nature is more perfect in proportion to the number of its attributes which we discern. Just as in wax we are able to distinguish many attributes, one that it is white, another that it is hard, a third that it can be liquefied, etc., so also in mind we can recognize as many—one that it has the power of being aware of the whiteness of wax, another that it possess the power of recognizing its hardness, a third of knowing that it can be liquefied, i.e. that it can lose its hardness, etc.; for he can perceive its hardness who is not aware of its whiteness, viz. a man born blind; and so in the other cases. Whence it can be clearly inferred that nothing yields the knowledge of so many attributes as our mind, because as many can be enumerated in its case as there are attributes in everything else, owing to the fact that it knows these; and hence its nature is best known of all. Finally, you here incidentally urge the objection that, *while not admitting the existence in myself of anything save mind, I none the less speak of the wax that I see and touch, which I could not do except by using my hands and eyes.*[1] But you ought to have noticed that I had carefully pointed out that I did not then deal with the sight and touch which are effected by means of organs, but solely with the thought of seeing and touching; and that this does not imply the use of these organs is testified to us every recurring night in dreams. True you have not really failed to note this; you have only wished to show how absurd and unjust are the cavillings of those whose design is not so much to understand as to raise objections.

CONCERNING THE OBJECTIONS TO THE THIRD MEDITATION

1. Splendid! Here at length you do bring up an argument against me, a feat which, so far as I can make out, you have hitherto failed to accomplish. In order to prove *that it is not a sure rule that what we very clearly and distinctly perceive is true*, you allege that to great intellects, which it appears ought to have had the most numerous clear and distinct perceptions, it has seemed nevertheless that the truth of

[1]Cf. above, p. 178.

things was hidden either in God or at the bottom of a well. Here I admit that your argument as drawn from authority is quite right. But, O flesh, you should have remembered that you here were addressing a mind so far withdrawn from corporeal things that it does not even know that anyone has existed before it, and hence cannot be influence by the authority of others. Your passage referring to the sceptics is a good enough commonplace, but proves nothing, as neither does your point about people facing death on behalf of false opinions, because it can never be proved that they clearly and distinctly perceive what they pertinaciously affirm. I do not question what you next say, viz. that it is not so much a question of taking pains to establish the truth of the rule, as of finding a method for deciding whether we err or not when we think that we perceive something clearly. But I contend that this has been carefully attended to in its proper place where I first laid aside all prejudices, and afterwards enumerated all the chief ideas, distinguishing the clear from the obscure and confused.

2. I marvel indeed at the train of reasoning by which you try to prove that all our ideas are adventitious and none of them constructed by us, saying—*because the mind has the power not only of perceiving these very adventitious ideas, but, besides this, of bringing together, dividing, reducing, enlarging, arranging, and everything similar to this:*[2] whence you conclude that the ideas of chimaeras which the mind makes by uniting, dividing, etc., are not made by it itself but are adventitious. In the same way you will be able to prove that Praxiteles never made any statues, because he did not produce from himself the marble used in their sculpture; and again that you cannot have made these objections, because to their composition have gone words which have not been invented by you but have been communicated to you from others. But, as a matter of fact, the form of a chimaera does not reside in the parts of goat or lion, nor does the form of your objections lie in the single words which you have used but consists solely in the putting of them together.

I am also surprised that you maintain the thesis that the idea of *Thing* cannot exist in the mind *unless at the same time the ideas of animal plant, stone, and of all universals are found there.*[3] This is as though, in order to acknowl-

[2]Above, p. 180.
[3]Above, p. 180.

lge that I am a thinking thing, I ought to cknowledge that I am a thinking thing, I ught to acknowledge animals and plants, nce I ought to acknowledge *Thing,* i.e. what *hing* is. You have nothing truer than this to rge here when dealing with *the truth;* and nally, since you attack only matters about *h*ich I have made no assertion, you merely rage warfare with the winds.

3. Here, in order to break down the reasons n account of which I thought that we must oubt the existence of material things, you ask *hy I walk about on the earth etc.*[1] But this man- *f*estly involves a begging of the question; for ou assume what has to be proved, viz. that it s so certain that I walk on the earth that I can ave no doubt on the matter.

In adding to my own objections—those I rged against myself and myself refuted—the ollowing one, viz. *why one born blind has no dea of colour, or one born deaf, of sound,*[2] you uite clearly show that you have not a single riticism of moment to make. How do you now that one born blind has no idea of colour, *v*hen often enough in our case even when the yes are closed the sense of light and colour is timulated? And, though your contention be onceded, has not the man who denies the ex- stence of material things as much ground for aying that one congenitally blind is destitute *f* ideas of colour because his mind lacks the aculty of forming them, as you have for assert- ng that their absence is due to his being with- ut eyes to see?

Your next point regarding the twofold idea *f* the sun proves nothing; but, in taking both deas as one because they refer to the single hing, the sun, your action amounts to saying hat the true and the false do not differ when *f*firmed of the same subject. Further, in deny- ng that the notion derived from astronomical easoning is an idea, you restrict the term idea o the images alone which are depicted in the magination, contrary to my express assump- ion.

4. You do exactly the same thing when you leny that substance is a true idea, because, orsooth, substance is perceived not by the im- gination but by the intellect alone. Yet you know that long ago, O flesh, I protested that I nad nothing to do with those whose wish it is o employ their imagination only and not the ntellect.

Really when you say that the *idea of sub- stance has no more reality than it holds from the ideas of those accidents under which, or after the fashion of which, it is conceived,*[3] you show that you have in truth no distinct idea of it at all; for substance can never be conceived after the fashion of accidents, nor can it derive its reali- ty from them. On the contrary accidents are commonly conceived by Philosophers after the fashion of substance, viz. as often as they are said to be real accidents; for no reality (i.e. no kind of being other than modal) can be as- cribed to them, which is not taken from the idea of substance.

Nay, when you say that the idea of God pos- sesses reality only *owing to the fact that we have heard certain attributes predicated of Him,*[4] I should like you to tell us whence men at the beginning, the men from whom we have learned them, drew this very idea of God. If it was from themselves, why may we not derive this same idea from ourselves? If from a revelation by God, this proves that God exists.

Moreover, in your next statement, *that he who says that anything is infinite attributes to a thing which he does not comprehend a name which he does not understand,*[5] you fail to dis- tinguish an exercise of intellect conformable to the scale of our understanding, such as each one of us experiences himself to employ in thinking about the infinite, with a concept ade- quate to the things, such as no one possesses not only in the matter of the infinite but per- haps not even in connection with any thing else however small. Neither is it true that the in- finite is apprehended by a negation of boundary or limitation, since on the contrary all limita- tion contains a negation of the infinite.

Further, it is not the case that *the idea which represents all those perfections which we ascribe to God contains no more objective reality than finite things have.*[6] You yourself confess that these perfections are amplified by our under- standing in order to be ascribed to God. Do you, then, not think that the things which are so augmented are not greater than those that have not been so dealt with? Again, what can account for the power of amplifying all created perfections, i.e. of conceiving something great- er or more ample than they, unless the fact that the idea of something greater, viz. of God, exists in us? Finally, neither is it true that *God will mean something very little, unless He be*

[1]Cf. above, p. 181.
[2]Cf. above, p. 181.

[3]Cf. above, p. 182.
[4]Cf. above, p. 182.
[5]p. 182.
[6]Above, pp. 182–183.

greater than as conceived by us; for He is conceived as infinite and nothing can be greater than the infinite. You, however, confuse intellectual activity with imagination, and feign that we imagine God after the fashion of some huge man, in the same way as if one who had never seen an elephant were to imagine that it was like a very huge insect, e.g. a tick; which, I agree with you, would be excessively foolish.

5. Here, though you make a great display so as to appear to contradict me, yet you do not conflict with me at all, since clearly you come to the same conclusion as I do. Nevertheless you intersperse a number of statements drawn from here and there, from which I strongly dissent, as e.g. that the axiom, *nothing exists in the effect which has not previously existed in the cause,* is to be understood of the material rather than of the efficient cause;[1] for the perfection of the form can never be understood to pre-exist in the material but only in the efficient cause. So, too, with your doctrine *that the formal reality of an idea is a substance,* and so forth.

6. If you had anything to say in proof of the existence of material things, without doubt you would have advanced it here. But when you only ask *whether my mind is uncertain as to whether anything else besides itself exists in the world,*[2] and feign that there is no need to search for arguments to decide this, thus making an appeal merely to prejudiced beliefs, you show much more clearly that you can give no reason for what you affirm, than if you had refrained from saying anything.

No point that you raise here in disputing about ideas requires any reply, since you restrict the term idea solely to the images depicted in the fancy, while I extend it to whatever is thought.

But, by the way, I should like to ask what the argument is by which you prove *that nothing acts on itself.*[3] It is, forsooth, not your wont to employ argument. But here you have used as an illustration the finger which does not strike itself and the eye which does not see itself in itself but in a mirror, to prove your case. To this we have an easy reply; it is not the eye which sees the mirror rather than itself, but the mind which alone recognizes both mirror, and eye, and itself as well. Likewise, other examples can be given in the domain of corporeal things: e.g. when a top draws itself round in a

circle, is not that rotation an action which i[t] exerts on itself?

Finally, it must be noted that I did not as[sert] that *I deduced the ideas of material thing[s] from the mind,*[4] as you rather insincerely her[e] pretend I do. For afterwards I showed in ex[-] press terms that they often come from bodies and that it was owing to this that the existenc[e] of corporeal things was demonstrated. But i[n] this passage I only explained that no suc[h] reality was found in them as to make us con[-] clude, from the fact that nothing exists in th[e] effect which has not formally or eminently pre[-] existed in the cause, that they cannot hav[e] originated solely from the mind; and this con[-] tention you do not attack at all.

7. In this passage you have nothing to sa[y] which you have not mentioned already an[d] which has not been refuted by me. I shall mak[e] one observation about the idea of the infinit[e] *which,* you say, *cannot be true, unless I compre[-] hend the infinite;* your opinion is *that at most [I] could be said to know part of the infinite, but in[-] deed a very small part of it, which bears no mor[e] proportion to the infinite than the representatio[n] of a tiny hair does to the entirety of the man t[o] whom the hair belongs.*[5] I announce, I say, tha[t] it is a manifest contradiction that, when [I] comprehend anything, that thing should b[e] infinite; for the idea of the infinite, in order t[o] be true, cannot by any means be compre[-] hended, since this very incomprehensibility i[s] comprised within the formal concept of the in[-] finite. Likewise it is none the less manifest tha[t] the idea we possess of the infinite does not rep[-] resent merely a part of it, but really the whol[e] infinite, in that fashion in which it has to b[e] represented through the instrumentality of [a] human idea, although doubtless another muc[h] more perfect, i.e. more accurate and more dis[-] tinct idea, can be framed by God, or by an[y] other intelligent nature more perfect than [a] human being. This is parallel to the case of on[e] ignorant of geometry who, we do not doub[t,] has the idea of a complete triangle when h[e] understands that it is a figure comprised with[-] in three lines, although Geometricians ca[n] learn many other things about the said tri[-] angle and discover them in its idea, of whic[h] the beginner is unaware. Thus, just as it suf[-] fices to understand a figure bounded by thre[e] lines in order to have an idea of a complete tri[-] angle, so also it is enough to understand [a] thing bounded by no limits in order to have [a]

---

[1] Above, p. 183.
[2] Above, p. 184.
[3] Above, p. 184.

[4] Above, p. 185.
[5] Cf. above, p. 186.

rue and complete idea of the whole of infinity.

8. Here you repeat the same error when you eny that we can have a true idea of God. For, lthough we are not aware of everything which s in God, yet everything we do cognize in Him s truly there. The remarks you interpose here nd there, such as, *that bread is not more per-ect than him who desires it;*[1] *that though I per-eive something actually to exist in idea, that is o reason why it should exist actually in the hing of which it is the idea;*[2] *that I pass judg-nent on matters of which I am ignorant,*[3] and the ike, show only that you, O flesh, wish rashly o attack matters which in many cases you ave failed to understand. For it is not *to be nferred from the fact that a man desires bread, hat the bread is more perfect than the man,* but nly that he who is in want of bread is less per-ect than he himself is when he has no lack. \gain *from the fact that something exists in idea, do not infer that it exists in the actual world,* xcept when no other cause for that idea can e given but the thing which it represents as ctually existing; and this I have shown to be rue not of many worlds, nor of any other hing, save God alone. Nor, once more, do I ass judgment on matters of which I am igno-ant, for I have adduced reasons for my judg-nent, reasons so convincing that none of them as been at all impugned by you.

9. When you deny *that we continually require he activity of the primal cause in order that we nay continue to exist,* you dispute a matter vhich all Metaphysicians affirm to be mani-est, but one about which the unlearned often lo not reflect, attending as they do only to auses *of coming* into being, but not to those f being. Thus an architect is the cause of a ouse and a father of his son *in respect of com-ng into being* merely, and for this reason, when t is an absolute production, an effect can re-nain in existence without any cause of this ind; but the sun is the cause of the light pro-eeding from it, and God is the cause of cre-ted things, not only *in respect of their coming nto existence,* but also *in respect of their con-inuing to exist,* and must always expend His ctivity on the effect in the same way in order o make it stay the same thing.

This can be plainly demonstrated from what explained about the independence of the arts of time, which you in vain attempt to lude by propounding *the necessary character of*

the connection between the parts of time con-sidered in the abstract.[4] Here it is not a ques-tion of abstract time, but of the time or dura-tion of something which endures; and you will not deny that the single moments of this time can be separated from their neighbours, i.e. that a thing which endures through individual moments may cease to exist.

When you allege *that we possess a power which suffices to guarantee our preservation, un-less some destructive cause supervene,*[5] you do not notice that you ascribe to the creature a perfection of the Creator, if the creature is to be able to continue in existence in independ-ence of anything else; while you assign to the Creator the imperfection of a creature, be-cause He must aim at non-existence by means of a positive act, whenever he wishes to cause a cessation of our existence.

Your subsequent statement—that *the pos-sibility of a regress to the infinite is not absurd,* is invalidated by what you yourself afterwards say. For you allow *that it is absurd in the case of causes which are so connected with one another that no action on the part of the lower is possible without the higher;*[6] now it is with such a cause alone that we are concerned here, viz. with causes *in being,* not with causes *in bringing into existence,* like parents. Hence I am not in conflict with the authority of Aristotle; nor does your argument about Pandora bear against me. You allow that all the perfections I see in man can be in varying degrees so aug-mented that afterwards I behold them to be such as cannot fall within human nature; but this is all I want in order to prove the existence of God. For it is that very power of amplifying all human perfections to such an extent that they are apprehended as more than human; and this, I maintain, could not have come about unless we had been created by God. Yet I am by no means surprised that the evidence of my demonstration of this position is not clear to you, for I have not up to this point noticed that you have correctly grasped any of my arguments.

10. In attacking my statement, *that nothing can be added, nothing taken away from the idea of God,*[7] you appear not to have attended to that common saying among Philosophers— that the essences of things are indivisible. For the idea represents the essence of the thing,

---

[1]Above, p. 187.
[2]Above, p. 187.
[3]Above, p. 187.

[4]Cf. above, p. 188.
[5]Cf. above, p. 188.
[6]Above, pp. 188–189.
[7]Above, p. 189.

and if something is added to it or subtracted from it, it is forthwith the idea of something else: it is thus that Pandora, thus that all false gods are portrayed by people who do not conceive the true God aright. But after the idea of the true God is once conceived, although new perfections can be detected in it which had not previously been noticed, this does not cause any increase in that idea, but merely renders it more distinct and explicit, because they must all have been contained in the very same idea, since it is assumed to have been true. The idea of the triangle is similarly not increased when we have remarked in it certain properties previously ignored. Further, I should inform you that *the idea of God is not formed by us seriatim by amplifying the perfections of created beings*, but is constituted as a whole at one time by the fact that mentally we apprehend an infinite being that is incapable of any amplification.

When you ask *whence I get my proof that the idea of God is, as it were, the mark of a workman imprinted on his work, and what is the mode in which it is impressed, what is the form of that mark,*[1] it is very much as if I, coming across a picture which showed a technique that pointed to Apelles alone as the painter, were to say that that inimitable technique was, so to speak, a mark impressed by Apelles on all his pictures in order to distinguish them from others, but you replied with the questions: "what is the form of that mark?" and "what is its mode of impression?" Such an enquiry would seem to merit laughter rather than any reply.

What answer do you deserve when you go on to say: *if it is not other than the work or thing itself, you yourself then are an idea, you are nothing but a mode of thought, you are yourself both the mark impressed and the subject on which it is impressed?*[2] Would it not be an equally clever thing to urge, when I said that the technique of Apelles was that by which his pictures were distinguished from others, that it was nothing other than the pictures themselves: that therefore those pictures were nothing but the technique, and did not consist of matter at all, and that hence they were merely a mode of painting, etc.?

When, in order to disprove *that we are made after the image of God*, you state its consequence, that *God will therefore have a human form*, and go on to recount all the particulars in which human nature differs from the divine, is there anything cleverer in this than if, in order to show that certain pictures by Apelles were not made after the likeness of Alexander you were to allege that this implied that Alexander was like a picture, whereas pictures were composed of wood and paint, not of bones and flesh as Alexander is? Now the nature of an image is not such that it is identical with that of which it is an image in all particulars, but only that it copies it in certain respects; and it is clear that that perfect power of thought which we understand to be in God, is represented by that less perfect faculty which we possess.

In preferring to compare God's act of creation to the operation of a workman rather than to generation by a parent, your action has no warrant. For, although these three modes of action are wholly distinct, yet there is less distance to traverse in arguing from natural production to the divine, than in proceeding from artificial production. But, neither did I say that there was as much resemblance between us and God as prevails between children and parent; nor likewise is there never any likeness between the work of a workman and himself: take for example the sculptor who chisels a likeness of himself.

With how bad faith do you report my words when you pretend that I said that *I perceived a likeness to God in the fact that I am an incomplete and dependent being*, when on the contrary I brought that into the argument to prove our dissimilarity from God, lest it should be thought that I wished to make men equal with God. For I said that not only did I perceive that I was inferior to God in these very matters, though nevertheless I aspired to greater things, but that also those very qualities were greater in God—those qualities to which, though they were so great, I found something comparable in myself; and this was shown by the fact that I dared to aspire to them.

Finally, when you say how strange it is that *other men do not think about God in the same way as I do, when He has impressed the idea of Himself on them exactly as on me*, it is precisely as if you were to marvel that since all are acquainted with the idea of a triangle, they do not all perceive an equal number of truths about it, and some probably reason about this very figure incorrectly.

CONCERNING THE OBJECTIONS TO THE FOURTH MEDITATION

I have sufficiently explained our idea of *nothing*, and the way in which we participate

[1] Above, p. 190.
[2] Above, p. 190.

n *non-existence*, by calling it a negative idea ind saying that it means merely that we are iot the Supreme Being, and that we lack many hings. But you are always discovering imginary difficulties.

When you say *that I see that certain of God's vorks are not absolutely perfect and complete*[1] you openly invent something which I have ieither stated there nor thought; all that I said oeing that if certain things were considered iot in the light of being but part of the world, is they really are, but as complete wholes, ːhen they might seem to be imperfect.

The arguments you adduce on behalf of final ːausality are to be referred to the efficient ːause; thus it is open to us, from beholding the ises of the various parts in plants and animals to regard with admiration the God who brings these into existence, and from a survey of His works to learn to know and glorify the author of these works, but that does not imply that we can divine the purpose for which He made each thing. And although in Ethics, where it is often allowable to employ conjecture, it is at times pious to consider the end which we may conjecture God set before Himself in ruling the universe, certainly in Physics, where everything should rest upon the securest arguments, it is futile to do so. We cannot pretend that certain of God's purposes rather than others are openly displayed; all seems to be equally hidden in the abyss of His inscrutable wisdom. Likewise, you ought not to pretend that mortals can understand no other sort of cause; for there is nothing else which is not much easier to comprehend than one of God's purposes, while, as to those which you have brought forward in illustrating the difficulty in question, there is no one who does not think that he is acquainted with them.

Finally, as you here ask me in such a straightforward manner, *what sort of an idea I think my mind would have possessed either of God or of myself, if, from the time at which it was infused into the body, it had remained there with closed eyes and without employing any of the other senses,*[2] I shall give you my answer ingenuously and candidly. I do not doubt that the mind under such circumstances (provided only that we suppose that it is not impeded by the body in its thinking, as equally at the same time that it is not aided by it) would have exactly the same idea of God and of itself as it now possesses, save only that these ideas would be

much purer and clearer. For the senses hamper the mind in many things and in nowise aid the perception of these ideas, and there is nothing to prevent all men noticing equally well that they have these ideas, except the fact that they are too much occupied with the perception of the images of corporeal things.

2. Here you are everywhere guilty of a false assumption in taking as a positive imperfection *the fact that we are liable to err*, since this is really (except with respect to God) the negation of a greater perfection. Again the comparison between the citizens of a State and the parts of the universe is not strictly accurate; for a bad disposition on the part of citizens is, relatively to the State, something positive, but this does not apply to a man's being liable to err, or not possessing all perfections, when that is taken relatively to the good of the universe. A better comparison could be drawn between the man who would like to have the whole of the human body covered with eyes, in order that it might appear more beautiful, because no bodily part is more beautiful than the eye, and him who thinks that no existing creatures ought to be liable to err, i.e. should not be wholly perfect.

It is plainly a false supposition on your part *that God has assigned to some a function which is base,*[3] *and has allotted imperfections to us,* and so forth. Plainly, likewise, it is false *that God has assigned to man a faculty of judgment which is so uncertain, so confused, and so unequal to the task of deciding those few things on which He has willed that man should pass judgment.*[4]

3. You desire me here *briefly to state to what the will may extend, which escapes the understanding.*[5] Precisely to everything in which we happen to err. Thus when you judge that the mind is a certain attenuated body, you are indeed able to understand that the mind is itself, i.e. a thinking thing, and likewise that an attenuated body is an extended thing; but assuredly you do not understand that the thing which thinks and the extended thing are one and the same thing, you only wish to believe it because you have already believed it and do not willingly change your mind. Thus when you judge that an apple which has been poisoned will suit you as food, you indeed understand that its odour, colour, and similar qualities are pleasant, but not that the apple is therefore good for you as food; it is because

[1]Above, p. 191.
[2]Above, pp. 191–192.

[3]Above, p. 192.
[4]Above, p. 192.
[5]Above, p. 193.

you wish to believe it that you pass that judgment. So while I confess that there is nothing that we wish about which we do not understand something, I deny that what we understand equals what we will; for we may wish many things about the same matter of which we understand very little. Moreover, when we judge wrongly, we do not therefore will wrongly, but perchance something wrong; neither do we understand anything wrongly; we are only said to understand awrong when we judge that we understand something better than we really understand it.

You next deny certain truths about the indeterminateness of the will; and although they are in themselves quite evident, I refuse to undertake to prove them before your eyes. For these matters are such that anyone ought to experience them in himself, rather than be convinced of them by ratiocination; but you, O flesh, appear not to pay heed to what the mind transacts within itself. Refuse then to be free, if freedom does not please you; I at least shall rejoice in my liberty, since I experience it in myself, and you have assailed it not with proof but with bare negations merely. Perchance I shall receive more credence from others, because I affirm that which I have experienced and anyone may experience in himself, than you who make your denial merely because you chance not to have experienced it.

Yet it can be shown conclusively from your words that you yourself have had that experience. For in denying *that we can guard against error*, because you will not have it that the will can be borne towards anything to which it is not determined by the understanding, you at the same time allow that *we can refrain from persisting in error*.[1] But to do so is wholly impossible unless the will has the power of directing itself towards one side or the other apart from any determination by the understanding, the fact which you denied. For, if the understanding has once determined the will to propound some false judgment, I ask you: when first it (the will) begins to take heed lest it continue in error, what is it that determines it to do so? If that determination is due to itself then it can be moved in a certain direction without impulsion by the understanding, which you denied, and about which alone the dispute has been raised. If, on the other hand, it is the understanding which is responsible, it is not the will itself which takes heed; and what happens is merely that, just as it was for-

[1]Above, p. 194.

merly impelled towards the falsity which th[e] understanding set before it, so now it acci dentally happens to be directed towards th[e] truth, because the understanding has set th[e] truth before it. But besides this I should like t[o] know what conception you have of the natur[e] of falsity, and how you think that it can be a[n] object of the understanding. I, who by falsit[y] understand only the privation of truth, a[m] convinced that it is an absolute contradictio[n] that the understanding should apprehend th[e] false under the guise of the truth; but thi[s] would be a necessary consequence if under standing could determine the will to embrac[e] the false.

4. As to the profit to be derived from thes[e] Meditations I have given sufficient warning i[n] the brief preface, which I think you have read that those will not gain much *who, not takin[g] care to comprehend the sequence and connectio[n] of my arguments, devote themselves only to con troverting isolated passages.*[2] Further, as to th[e] method by which we are able to distinguis[h] those things which we really perceive clearly from that which we only think we so perceive although I believe that I have expounded i[t] with sufficient care, as has been already said I nevertheless am by no means confident tha[t] people who make too little effort to dives[t] themselves of their prejudices, and so com plain that I have not spoken of these *simpl[y] and in few words*, will easily grasp thi[s] method.

CONCERNING THE OBJECTIONS TO THE FIFTH MEDITATION

1. Here, after quoting one or two of my words, you add that *they are all that I have t[o] say about the question in hand;*[3] and this com pels me to warn you that you have not paid enough attention to the mutual connection between my statements. For I believe it to be such that, to the proof of any one matter, everything which has gone before contributes as well as much of what follows. Hence it is impossible for you in good faith to report what I have to say about any one topic, unless you take into account the whole of what I have said about the others.

You say *that it seems to you to be a serious matter to set up some immutable and eternal being in addition to God;* and you would be quite right if it were a question of existence, or merely if I had set up something with an immuta-

[2]*Meditations*, Preface, p. 72.
[3]Above, p. 195.

bility not dependent on God. But in the same way as the poets feign that, while the fates were indeed established by Jove, yet once established, he was restricted in his action by his maintenance of them; similarly I do not think that the essence of things, and those mathematical truths which may be known about them, are independent of God; yet I think that because God so wished it and brought it to pass, they *are* immutable and eternal. Now whether you think this to have serious consequences or the reverse, to me it is sufficient if it is true.

Your attack upon the universals of the dialecticians, which you next undertake, does not touch me, since I do not conceive of universals in the same way as they do. But as to the essences which are clearly and distinctly conceived, such as that of the triangle or of any other geometrical figure, I shall easily compel you to acknowledge that the ideas existing in us of those things, are not derived from particulars; for here you say that they are false, evidently because they do not agree with your preconceived notions about the nature of things.

Shortly afterwards, also, you say *that the objects of pure mathematics, e.g. the point, the line, the superficies, and the indivisible things consisting of these, and functioning as indivisibles, are incapable of actual existence:*[1] whence it follows that no triangle and none at all of the things which are understood to belong to the essence of the triangle or any of the other geometrical figures, has existed at any time; hence it follows that these essences are not derived from any existing things. But, say you, they are false. That is forsooth in your opinion, because you suppose the nature of things to be such that these essences cannot be conformable to it. But, unless you also maintain that the whole of geometry is a fiction, you cannot deny that many truths are demonstrated of them, which, being always the same, are rightly styled immutable and eternal. But though they happen not to be conformable to the nature of things as it exists in your conception, as they likewise fail to agree with the atomic theory constructed by Democritus and Epicurus, this is merely an external attribute relatively to them and makes no difference to them; they are, nevertheless, conformable certainly with the real nature of things which has been established by the true God. But this does not imply that there are substances in ex-

[1]Cf. above, p. 198.

istence which possess length without breadth, or breadth without depth, but merely that the figures of geometry are considered not as substances but as the boundaries within which substance is contained.

Meanwhile, moreover, I do not admit *that the ideas of these figures have at any time entered our minds through the senses,*[2] as is the common persuasion. For though, doubtless, figures such as the Geometers consider can exist in reality, I deny that any can be presented to us except such minute ones that they fail altogether to affect our senses. For, let us suppose that these figures consist as far as possible of straight lines; yet it will be quite impossible for any really straight part of the line to affect our senses, because when we examine with a magnifying glass those lines that appear to us to be most straight, we find them to be irregular and bending everywhere in an undulating manner. Hence when first in infancy we see a triangular figure depicted on paper, this figure cannot show us how a real triangle ought to be conceived, in the way in which Geometricians consider it, because the true triangle is contained in this figure, just as the statue of Mercury is contained in a rough block of wood. But because we already possess within us the idea of a true triangle, and it can be more easily conceived by our mind than the more complex figure of the triangle drawn on paper, we, therefore, when we see that composite figure, apprehend not it itself, but rather the authentic triangle. This is exactly the same as when we look at a piece of paper on which little strokes have been drawn with ink to represent a man's face; for the idea produced in us in this way is not so much that of the lines of the sketch as of the man. But this could not have happened unless the human face had been known to us by other means, and we had been more accustomed to think of it than of those minute lines, which indeed we often fail to distinguish from each other when they are moved to a slightly greater distance away from us. So certainly we should not be able to recognize the geometrical triangle by looking at that which is drawn on paper, unless our mind possessed an idea of it derived from other sources.

2. Here I do not see to what class of reality you wish to assign existence, nor do I see why it may not be said to be a property as well as omnipotence, taking the word property as equivalent to any attribute or anything which can be predicated of a thing, as in the present

[2]Cf. above, p. 196.

case it should be by all means regarded. Nay, necessary existence in the case of God is also a true property in the strictest sense of the word, because it belongs to Him and forms part of His essence alone. Hence the existence of a triangle cannot be compared with the existence of God, because existence manifestly has a different relation to essence in the case of God and in the case of a triangle.

Nor is it more a begging of the question,[1] *to enumerate existence among the things belonging to the essence of God,* than to reckon the equality of the three angles of a triangle to two right angles among the properties of the triangle.

Nor is it true *that essence and existence can be thought, the one apart from the other in God,*[2] as in a triangle, because God *is* His existence, while a triangle is not its own existence. I do not, nevertheless, deny that existence is a possible perfection in the idea of a triangle, as it is a necessary one in the idea of God; for this fact makes the idea of the triangle one of higher rank than the ideas of those chimerical things whose existence can never be supposed. Hence you have not diminished the force of this argument of mine in the slightest, and you still remain deluded *by that fallacy, which you say I could have exposed so easily.*[3]

I have elsewhere given a sufficient answer to your next objections. You are plainly in error when you say *that existence is not demonstrated of God, as it is demonstrated of the triangle that its three angles are equal to two right angles;*[4] for the way in which both are proved is alike, except that the demonstration proving existence in God is much simpler and clearer. I pass over the rest, because, though saying *that I explain nothing*, you yourself explain nothing and prove nothing, save only that you are able to prove nothing.

3. Against these criticisms in which you point to Diogenes, Theodorus, Pythagoras and others, and adduce the case of the Sceptics, who had doubts about these very geometrical demonstrations, I affirm that they would not have done so, if, as they might have done, they had known God. Further, one thing is not proved to be better known than another, because it appears to be true to more people, but only because to those who know both, as they may, it appears to be prior in knowledge, and more evident and certain.

CONCERNING THE OBJECTIONS TO THE SIXTH MEDITATION

1. I have already dealt with the objection *that material things as the objects of pure mathematics do not exist.*

Moreover, it is false that the thinking of a Chiliagon is confused; for many deductions can be drawn from it most clearly and distinctly, which would not occur if it were perceived only in a confused manner or, as you say, merely *in respect of the force of the name.* But as a matter of fact we perceive the whole figure at the same time clearly although we are not able to imagine it as a whole at the same time; which proves that the two powers of understanding and imagining differ, not so much in respect of more and less, but as two wholly diverse modes of operation. Thus, in thinking, the mind employs itself alone, but in imagining it contemplates a corporeal form. And though geometrical figures are wholly corporeal, nevertheless the ideas by which they are understood, when they do not fall under the imagination, are not on that account to be reckoned corporeal.

Finally, it is worthy of you alone, O flesh, to think *that the idea of God, of an Angel, and of the human mind, are corporeal, or after the fashion of the corporeal, derived forsooth from the human form, and from other very subtle, simple, and imperceptible objects, such as air or aether.*[5] For whosoever thus represents God or the mind to himself, tries to imagine a thing which is not imageable, and constructs nothing but a corporeal idea to which he falsely assigns the name God or mind. For, in the true idea of mind, nothing is contained but thought and its attributes, of which none is corporeal.

2. In this passage you show very clearly that you rely on prejudices merely and never divest yourself of them, when you wish to make out that we suspect no falsity in matters in which we have never detected falsity; it is thus that, *when we behold a tower close at hand and touch it, we are sure that it is square,*[6] if it appear to be square; so, too, when we are really awake *we cannot doubt whether we are awake or dreaming;*[7] and so forth. Now you have no reason to think that all the things in which error can reside have been noticed by you, and it could easily be proved that you sometimes are wrong about those things which you accept as certain. But

[1] Cf. above, p. 196.
[2] Cf. above, pp. 196–197.
[3] Cf. above, p. 197.
[4] Cf. above, p. 197.

[5] Cf. above, p. 199.
[6] Cf. above, p. 200.
[7] Cf. above, p. 200.

when you come round to the position at which you state, *that at least we cannot doubt that things appear as they do*,[1] you have returned to the true path; your statement is one that I have myself made in the second Meditation. But here the question raised concerned the reality of external objects, and in what you have contributed to this there is nothing correct.

3. I shall not here delay to notice your tedious and frequent repetitions of such statements as, e.g. *that I have failed to prove certain matters*, which nevertheless I have demonstrated; *that I have treated only of the solid body*, though I have dealt with every kind of matter, even of the subtlest; etc. What opposition other than a plain denial is merited by affirmations of this kind, which are not supported by reasons? Yet, incidentally, I should like to discover what argument you use to prove that I have treated of solid matter rather than of that which is subtle. Have I not said: "*I possess (a body) united with myself, and it is certain that I am distinct from my body*"? And I cannot see why these words are not equally applicable to an impalpable and to a solid body; nor do I think that anyone but you could fail to see this. Apart from this, in the second Meditation I made it evident that mind could be understood as an existing substance, though we did not understand anything to exist that was wind, or fire, or vapour, or breath, or anything else of a bodily nature however impalpable and refined. I said, however, that at that point[2] I did not discuss whether it was in truth distinct from every kind of body; but in the present passage[3] I did discuss the matter and proved my assertion. But you show that you have wholly failed to comprehend the controversy by your confusion of the issue as to what may be known of the soul with the question as to that which the soul really is.

4. Here you ask, *how I think that I, an unextended subject, can receive into myself the resemblance or idea of a thing which is extended.*[4] I reply that no corporeal resemblance can be received in the mind, but that what occurs there is the pure thinking of a thing, whether it be corporeal or equally whether it be one that is incorporeal and lacking any corporeal semblance. But as to imagination, which can only be exercised in reference to corporeal things,

my opinion is that it requires the presence of a semblance which is truly corporeal, and to which the mind applies itself, without, however, its being received in the mind.

Your statement *about the idea of the sun, which a blind man can derive merely from the sun's warmth*,[5] is easily refuted. For the blind man can have a clear and distinct idea of the sun as a source of heat, although he does not possess the idea of it as a source of light. Nor is your comparison of me to that blind man just: firstly, because the act of knowledge which apprehends a thing that thinks is much more extensive than our apprehension of a thing which warms, as it is much more than that of anything else, as was shown in its proper place; secondly, because no one can prove that idea of the sun which the blind man forms, does not contain everything which can be learned of the sun, save those who, being endowed with sight, are aware in addition of its light and figure. You, however, not only know nothing more than I do of mind, but do not even have knowledge of the very thing I recognize in it; so that in this comparison it is rather you who play the part of blind man, while I, along with the whole human race, could at most be said to be one-eyed.

In adding that *the mind is not extended*,[6] my intention was not thereby to explain what mind is, but merely to proclaim that those people are wrong who think that it is extended. In the same way if any people affirmed *that Bucephalus was Music*,[7] it would not be idle of others to deny the statement. In good truth your subsequent attempts to prove that mind is extended because it makes use of a body which is extended, seem to employ no better reasoning than if you were to argue that because Bucephalus neighs and whinnies, and so utters sounds that are comparable with Music, it followed that Bucephalus is Music. For, though mind is united with the whole body, it does not follow that it itself is extended throughout the body, because it is not part of its notion to be extended, but merely to think. Neither does it apprehend extension by means of an extended semblance existing in it, although it images it by applying itself to a corporeal semblance which is extended, as has already been said. Finally, there is no necessity

---

[1]Cf. above, p. 200.
[2]Med. II, p. 79.
[3]Med. VI, pp. 98–99.
[4]Objections v, p. 202.

[5]Cf. above, p. 202.
[6]Above, p. 202.
[7]Descartes misread Gassendi's *musca* (fly) as *musica*. Cf. above, p. 202. The mistake must have occurred when he saw Gassendi's work in MS.

for it itself to be a body although it has the power of moving body.

5. What you say at this point *relatively to the union of mind and body*[1] is similar to what precedes. At no place do you bring an objection to my arguments; you only set forth the doubts which you think follow from my conclusions, though they arise merely from your wishing to subject to the scrutiny of the imagination matters which, by their own nature, do not fall under it. Thus when you wish to compare the union of mind and body with the mixture of two bodies, it is enough for me to reply that no such comparison ought to be set up, because the two things are wholly diverse, and we must not imagine that there are parts in mind because it is aware of parts in body. Whence do you derive the conclusion that everything which mind knows must exist in mind? If that were so, then, when it was aware of the magnitude of the earth, it would be obliged to have that object within it, and consequently would not only be extended but greater in extent than the whole world.

[1] Cf. above, p. 204.

6. Here, though you do not contradict me at all, you have nevertheless much to say; and hence the reader may discover that the number of your arguments is not to be inferred from any proportion between them and the prolixity of your words.

Up to this point we have had a discussion between mind and flesh, and, as was but natural, in many things they disagreed. But now, at the end, I catch sight of the real Gassendi, and look up to him as a man of great philosophical eminence. I salute him as a man noted for his intellectual candour and integrity of life, and shall endeavour, by employing all the courtesies which I can muster, to merit his friendship at all times. I therefore ask him not to take it amiss if, in replying to his objections, I have used a Philosophical freedom, since their entire contents caused me very great pleasure. Among other things I rejoiced that such a long and carefully composed dissertation contained nothing in opposition to my reasoning, nothing opposed even to my conclusions, to which I was not able very easily to reply.

THE SIXTH SET OF OBJECTIONS[1]

Though we have read through your Meditations with very great attention, as well as your previous replies to objections, there are still some slight difficulties left, which it is right you should remove.

The first is that it does not appear altogether certain that we exist, from the fact that we think.[2] For in order to be sure that you think, you ought to know what to think, or what thinking, is, and what your existence is; but since you do not yet know what these things are, how can you know that you think or exist? Since, then, in saying I think, *you do not know what you are saying, and since in adding* therefore I exist, *you are equally ignorant of the meaning of what you say, and indeed do not know that you are saying or thinking anything, since in order to do so it seems to be necessary for you to know that you know what you are saying, and once more to know that you know that you know what you say, and so on to infinity, it is clear that you cannot know whether you exist, or even whether you think.*

But to point out a second difficulty, when you say that you think *and* exist,[3] *someone will maintain that you deceive yourself, and that you do not think, but are only moved, and that you are nothing other than a corporeal motion, since no one meanwhile has been able to grasp the demonstration by means of which you think that you have proved that no corporeal motion can be what you call thought. Have you, then, by means of that Analysis which you employ, so subdivided all the motions of your subtle matter, that you are sure that you can show us, who give our utmost attention and are, we think, sufficiently clear sighted, that the reduction of our thoughts to those corporeal motions is self-contradictory?*

Our third difficulty is very much of the same kind. For though some of the Church Fathers have, along with the Platonists, believed that the Angels are corporeal (which led to the Lateran Council's conclusion that they could be depicted), and entertained the same belief with regard to the rational soul, which some of them indeed thought was conveyed to each man from his progenitor; they nevertheless maintained that Angels and the soul alike thought; hence they seem to have be-

lieved that this could be effected by corporeal motions, or even was identical with those very corporeal motions, from which they in no way distinguished thinking. The thinking of monkeys, dogs, and other animals seems to confirm this; for dogs bark in their sleep, as if they were chasing hares or rushing at robbers; and they are aware when awake that they run, and when dreaming, that they bark: though, with you, we recognize that there is nothing in them distinct from their bodies. But if you deny that the dog knows that it is running or thinking, besides the fact that this is an unproved assertion, the dog himself might perhaps pass a similar judgment with respect to us, that we forsooth are unaware that we run and think, when we run or when we think. For firstly you do not behold the dog's internal mode of operation, just as he is not directly aware of yours, and secondly there is no lack of men of great attainments who at the present day concede reason to the animals or have in previous ages done so. So far are we from believing that all these operations can be satisfactorily explained by mechanism, without imputing to them sensation, life, and soul, that we are ready to stake anything in proving that that is both an impossibility and an absurdity. Finally, there are not lacking those who are likely to assert that man himself also is without sensation and understanding, and that all his actions can be effected by means of dynamical mechanisms and do not imply mind at all, if apes, dogs, and elephants can discharge all their functions in virtue of this mechanism; since, if the limited reasoning power of the brutes differs from human reason, it does so only in degree, and this implies no difference in essence.

Our fourth difficulty tenders the knowledge of the Atheist,[4] which he asserts to be absolutely certain and, judged according to your canon, most evident, when he makes the statements: if equals be taken from equals, the remainders are equal; the three angles of a rectilinear triangle are equal to two right angles, and thousands similar; for he cannot frame those statements mentally without believing them to be absolutely certain. The Atheist contends that this is so true that even if God does not exist and is not even possible, as he believes, he is no less certain of these matters than if God did really exist. He

[1]By Divers Theologians and Philosophers.
[2]Cf. Med. II, p. 78.
[3]Cf. Med. VI, pp. 98–99.

[4]Cf. Reply to Obj. II, above p. 123.

denies that any reason for doubting can be advanced, to disturb him in the slightest or make him hesitate. For, what will you advance? That God, if He exists, can deceive him? The Atheist will reply that he could not be deceived in these matters even though God were to put forth all the force of His omnipotence in the attempt.

Hence arises the fifth difficulty whose root is found in that deception which you wholly deny of God Himself.[1] For, since many Theologians believe that the damned, both angels and men, are continuously deceived by God's having implanted in them the idea of a fire that is torturing them, so that they firmly believe and think that they clearly see and perceive that they are really being tortured by the fire, though no such fire exists, is it not possible that God deceives us with similar ideas and continually makes sport of us by despatching similar phantasms or ideas into our minds? Hence we should imagine that we clearly saw, and perceived by each of our senses things that nevertheless are not outside us, so that sky and earth are not real, and we do not really possess arms and feet and eyes etc. This can happen without any wrongfulness or injustice, since the Lord is supreme over everything and has the absolute power of disposing what belongs to him; especially since such action avails to repress the pride of men, and punish their sins, whether the punishment inflicted be on account of original sin or of other causes obscure to us. These contentions seem to be confirmed by those passages of Scripture which show that we can know nothing, e.g. the words of Paul in 1st Corinthians, chapter 8, verse 2: If any man thinketh, he says, that he knoweth anything, he knows not yet as he ought to know; and the passage in Ecclesiastes, c. 8, v. 17: I beheld that of all the works of God man can find out no reason of those that are done under the sun; and so much the more as a man labours to seek it out, the less shall he discover; nay even though a wise man says that he knows, he shall not be able to find it out. And that the wise man in saying this, has employed deliberate reason, and not spoken in haste, or thoughtlessly and violently, the whole of his book makes clear, especially when the question of the mind comes up, which, you contend, is immortal. For in verse 19, c. 3, he says that the death of man is as the death of beasts. And lest you should reply that this is to be understood of the body alone, he adds that man has no preeminence over the beasts. Further, speaking of the spirit of man itself, he denies that there is anyone who knoweth whether it goeth upward,

i.e. whether it is immortal, or whether it goeth downwards with the spirits of the beasts, i.e. perishes. Neither may you allege that these words are said in the character of an unbeliever; in such a case the writer ought to have made that quite clear and provided a refutation of these statements. Again you must not contend that no reply on your part is called for, since Scripture is a matter for the Theologians; for since you are a Christian it is proper for you to be ready to reply to everything that can be objected to the faith, especially against the positions you desire to establish, and to use all your powers to make your results satisfactory.

The sixth difficulty arises from the indifference of the judgment[2] or liberty which you refuse to allow to the perfection of choice, but ascribe to an imperfect will alone, thus removing the indifference as often as the mind clearly perceives what ought to be believed, or performed, or left undone. But do you not see that by positing this you destroy the liberty of God, from Whom you remove that indifference as to whether He will create this world rather than another, or any world at all? Though yet it belongs to the faith to believe that God has from eternity been indifferent as to whether He would create one, or many, worlds, or no world. But who doubts that God has at all times had the clearest vision of all things that were to be done or left undone? Therefore the clearest vision and perception of things does not annul the indifference of choice; and if it cannot harmonize with human liberty, neither will it be compatible with the divine, since the essences of things are, like numbers, indivisible and unchanging. Wherefore indifference is included no less in the divine than in human freedom of choice.

The seventh difficulty will affect the superficies[3] in which or by means of which you say that all sensations take place. For we do not understand how it can happen that it is neither part of the sentient bodies, nor part of the air itself and its vapours, of which you say that it is no part, not even the exterior. Nor at the same time do we comprehend that no body whatsoever nor substance, as you assert, possesses real accidents which by the divine power may exist apart from any subject and, as a matter of fact, do exist, in the Sacrament of the Altar. There is however no reason for our Doctors to be perturbed until they have seen whether you are going to prove that in your Physics, for which you make us hope, and which they scarcely believe will propound the

[1] Cf. Med. III, p. 88, and Med. IV, p. 89.

[2] Cf. Med. IV, pp. 90–91.
[3] Cf. Reply to Obj. IV, above, p. 164.

matter so clearly that your conclusions will be capable of acceptance, or will merit acceptance, to the exclusion of the former doctrine.

The eighth difficulty arises out of your reply to the fifth set of objections. How can the truths of Geometry or Metaphysics such as you mention be immutable and eternal, and yet not be independent of God?[1] What is the species of causality by which they are related to Him or dependent on Him? What possible action of God's could annul the nature of the triangle? And how could He from all eternity bring it to pass that it was untrue that twice four was eight? or that a triangle had not three angles? Hence either these truths depend upon the understanding alone while it thinks them, or upon existing things, or they are independent, since God evidently could not have brought it to pass that any of these essences or verities was not from all eternity.

Finally, the ninth difficulty seems to us very important, when you say that we ought to distrust the operation of the senses, and that the certitude of the understanding far exceeds that of the senses.[2] But what if the understanding can enjoy no certitude, which it has not first received from a good disposition of the senses? Or again if it cannot correct the error of any sense, unless another sense first correct the said error? Refraction makes a stick thrust into the water appear broken, though nevertheless it is straight; what corrects the error? The understanding? Not at all; it is the sense of touch. So, too, in other cases. Hence if you bring in all the senses properly disposed, which always give the same report, you will obtain the greatest possible certainty of which man is capable; but this certitude will often escape you if you trust to the operations of your mind, which often goes astray in matters about which it believed there was no possibility of doubt.

These are the principal matters which caused us trouble. And we pray you to add some sure rule and certain infallible tokens by which we may be quite sure, when we apprehend one thing

[1]Cf. Reply to Obj. v, above, pp. 216–217.
[2]Cf. Med. I, p. 75 and Med. VI, p. 98.

thus perfectly apart from another, that it is certain that the one is so distinct from the other, that the two can, by the divine power at least, exist apart; i.e. we wish to know surely, clearly, and distinctly that that distinction of the understanding is not due to the understanding itself but proceeds from the very things distinguished. For when we contemplate the immensity of God, not thinking of His justice; or when we view His immensity, not thinking of the Son or of the Holy Spirit; do we have a complete perception of that immensity, or of God as existing, apart from those other Persons, whose existence an infidel could deny with as much right as you deny mind or thought of the body? Therefore just as it will be a false conclusion for anyone to argue that the Son and the Holy Spirit are in essence distinct from God the Father, or can be separated from Him, so neither will anyone grant that thought or the human mind can be distinguished from the body, though you may conceive the one apart from the other, and deny the one of the other; nor may you think that this can be proved by means of any mental abstraction on your part. If you can manage to reply to these objections, there seems to be certainly nothing at all left to which our Theologians can take exception.

APPENDIX

A few questions derived from other people will here be added in order that your reply to them may be conjoined to your answer to the previous objections, since they belong to the same argument. Certain very learned and clear-sighted men wish to have a careful explanation of the three following points.

1. How I know with certainty that I have a clear idea of my soul.
2. How I know with certainty that that idea is wholly diverse from anything else.
3. How I know with certainty that that contains no element of corporeity.

Certain others have propounded the following argument.

CERTAIN PHILOSOPHERS AND GEOMETRICIANS TO MONSIEUR DESCARTES

With howsoever great an effort we bethink ourselves as to whether the idea of our mind or that of a human being, i.e. our knowledge and perception of it, contains anything corporeal, we do not venture to assert that what we call thought can in

no wise attach to any body, whatsoever be the motions which characterize it. For since we discern that while there are certain bodies which do not think, there are others, e.g. human bodies and perchance those of the brutes which do think, will *you not regard us as being guilty of sophistry and undue boldness, if we therefore conclude that there are no bodies which think? We can scarce refrain from believing that we would deserve to be for all time derided by you, if we had first forged that argument derived from ideas on behalf of the mind as well as of God, and you had then by your analytical method condemned it. But you seem to be so much preoccupied and prepossessed by this method that you have apparently now so obscured your mental vision that you are no longer free to see that the several mental properties or operations which you discover within you depend upon corporeal motions.*

If not, unloose the bond which, you say, confines us with adamantine chains and prevents our minds from raising their flight above the body. The bond consists in this—We perceive very well *that two and three make five, that if equals be taken from equals the remainders are equal; we are convinced of the truth of these and a thousand other propositions, just as you find you also are. Why are we not similarly convinced by your ideas or our own, that the human soul is distinct from the body and that God exists? You will say that you are not able to put this truth into our minds unless we think along with you. But lo! we have read what you have written seven times and have, so far as in us lay, given an attention to it equal to that of the Angels, and have nevertheless not yet been convinced. We do not, however, think that you will prefer to say* that our minds are all steeped in brutish ignorance and wholly unfit for Metaphysical investigation, though for thirty years accustomed to deal with that science; we believe that you will not rather do this than confess that your arguments derived from the idea of the mind and that of God are not of such weight and power as to be able to master and in due right bring into subjection the intelligence of men of learning who have tried with all their power to detach themselves from solid matter. On the contrary, we think that you will make that confession if you re-read your Meditations in the spirit of critical analysis with which you would treat them if they had been brought forward by an opponent.

Finally, as long as we do not know what can be achieved by bodies and their motions, and since you admit that no one can know everything which God has implanted in any body and can implant, apart from a revelation by God Himself, how can you be sure that God has not implanted in certain bodies a power and property of such a kind that they can doubt, think, etc.?

These are our arguments or, if you so prefer it, our prejudices. If you can cure us of them, we call God to witness that great will be the thanks with which all of us will reward you for freeing us from the tangle of thorns which is suffocating in us the truth you have sown. May the all-good God bring this to pass, the God towards whose glory alone we know all your efforts have been directed.

REPLY TO
THE SIXTH SET OF OBJECTIONS

1. It is indeed true that *no one can be sure that he knows or that he exists, unless he knows what thought is and what existence.*[1] Not that this requires a cognition formed by reflection or one acquired by demonstration; much less does it require a cognition of a reflective cognition, by which we know that we know, and again know that we know that we know, and so *ad infinitum.* Such knowledge could never be obtained about anything. It is altogether enough for one to know it by means of that internal cognition which always precedes reflective knowledge, and which, when the object is thought and existence, is innate in all men; so that, however overwhelmed by prejudice and

[1] Objections vi, p. 221.

attentive to the words rather than their signification, though we may feign that we do not possess that knowledge, we cannot nevertheless really be without it. When, therefore, anyone perceives that he thinks and that it thence follows that he exists, although he chance never previously to have asked what thought is, nor what existence, he cannot nevertheless fail to have a knowledge of each sufficient to give him assurance on this score.

2. Nor can it occur that, when one perceives that he thinks, understanding at the same time what it is to move, he should think *that he is deceived, and that he does not think but only moves.*[2] For since plainly the idea or notion he

[2] Cf. above, p. 221.

as of thought is quite different from that of corporeal movement, he must necessarily understand the one as quite different from the other. Yet on account of his habit of ascribing many diverse properties, between which he discerns no connection, to one and the same subject, he may doubt, he may even affirm that he is one and the same thing which thinks and moves in space. But it must be noted that there are two ways in which things of which we have diverse ideas can be taken to be one and the same thing; to wit, either in respect of unity and identity of nature, or merely by unity of composition. Thus, for example, our ideas of figure and motion are not the same, neither those of understanding and willing, nor of bones and flesh, nor of thought and of an extended thing. Nevertheless, we clearly perceive that to the same substance to which the possibility of having figure belongs, the possibility of moving also belongs, so that what is figured and mobile is one by unity of nature; similarly, we see that a thing which is intelligent and wills is one and the same by unity of nature. But we do not perceive the same in the case of the thing which we regard under the form of bone, and of that which we view as flesh; hence we cannot take these to be one and the same thing by unity of nature, but only by unity of composition, viz. in so far as the animal possessing bone and flesh is one and the same. But now the question is, whether we perceive a thinking thing and an extended thing to be one and the same by unity of nature, a unity such that we find that between thought and extension there is the same affinity and connection as we notice to prevail between figure and motion, or between understanding and willing. Or whether shall we rather say that they are one and the same only by unity of composition, in so far as they are found in the same man, in the way in which bones and flesh exist in the same animal. Now this latter alternative is that which I affirm, because I find a total diversity between the nature of an extended and that of a thinking thing, a diversity not less than that between bones and flesh.

But since at this point an appeal to authority enters into the dispute, I am compelled, lest this should imperil the truth, to reply to what you add, viz. *that no one hitherto has been able mentally to grasp my demonstration*, by saying that though not many people have as yet examined my argument, quite a number affirm that they understand it. And just as the witness of one man who, having made a voyage to America, declares that he has seen the Antipodes, merits more credence than that of a thousand others who deny their existence merely because they have no knowledge of them; so likewise in the case of those who properly examine the validity of arguments, greater weight attaches to the authority of one man who says that he understands a certain argument aright, than of a thousand others who, without appending any reason, maintain that it cannot be understood. For though they do not understand it, that does not prevent its being understood by others; and, since, in inferring this conclusion, they show that they do not have an accurate apprehension of what it is to reason, very little faith should be reposed in them.

Lastly to the question:—*whether by my Analysis I have subdivided all the motions of my subtle matter so as to be sure that I can show men who have given their best attention and are, as they think, sufficiently clear-sighted, that the reduction of our thoughts to corporeal motions,* i.e. as I interpret, that thoughts and corporeal motions are one and the same, *is self-contradictory*, I reply that, though to me it is very certain, I do not promise that others can be convinced of the same truth however attentive they are and, in their own judgment, clear-sighted. At least I cannot promise it so long as they fasten their attention not on the objects of pure intelligence but on those of the imagination, as apparently those have done, who have pretended that the dissection of some subtle matter will give us the distinction between thought and motion. For the distinction can only be grasped by observing that the motions of a thing that thinks and that of a thing that is extended or mobile are wholly diverse and mutually independent of each other, and that it is self-contradictory that those things which are clearly understood by us to be diverse and independent, cannot be sundered, at least by God. So that however often we find them in one and the same subject as, e.g., thought and corporeal motions in the same man, we ought not on that account to believe that they are one and the same thing by unity of nature but only in virtue of unity of composition.

3. What is here advanced about the Platonists and their partisans, has now been rejected by the whole Catholic Church and commonly by all Philosophers. Moreover the Lateran Council, though concluding that Angels could

be depicted, did not at the same time agree that they were corporeal. But even though they were in truth believed to be corporeal, we should certainly not even in their case have reason to believe that their minds are more inseparable from their bodies than men's are; neither also, though it were imagined that the human soul were derived from the procreator, could it be concluded that the soul is corporeal, but only that as the body arises from the body of the parents so the soul itself proceeded from the parents' soul. As for dogs and apes, even though I were to grant that thought existed in them, it would in nowise follow that the human mind was not to be distinguished from the body, but, on the contrary, rather that in other animals also there was a mind distinct from their body. This is a doctrine that these very Platonists, whose authority you lately lauded, held, following the Pythagoreans in this, as is clear from their belief in Metempsychosis. However, not only have I asserted that plainly the brutes do not possess thought, as is here assumed, but I have given a most stringent proof of this, a proof which no one has hitherto refuted. Yet the people who affirm that *dogs when awake know that they run, and even when dreaming, that they are barking,*[1] as if they could take up their station in the animals' hearts, really assert this merely and do not prove it. For although they add *that they do not believe that the operations of the beasts can be explained by mechanism, apart from sensation, life, and soul* (i.e. as I interpret, without thought; for I have neither denied to the brutes what is vulgarly called life, nor a corporeal soul, nor organic sense), *and that they are ready to stake anything in proving that that is both an impossibility and an absurdity,* this should not be taken to be a reason. The like can be asserted about any other proposition however true; nay people are not wont to offer pledges, except where their proof lacks reasons; and since once upon a time men scouted the existence of the Antipodes in almost exactly the same way, I fancy that a matter should not be straightway held to be false because certain people scout it.

You conclude by adding that *those are not lacking who are likely to assert that man himself also is without sensation and understanding, and that all his actions can be effected by means of dynamical mechanisms and do not imply mind at all, if apes, dogs, and elephants can discharge all their functions in virtue of this mechanism.*

[1]Cf. above, p. 221.

But this argument surely proves nothing at a except that there are some men who conceiv all things so confusedly, and who stick so ter aciously to the opinions that they have take up in a prejudiced manner and understan only in a verbal way, that, rather than chang them, they deny of themselves facts that the can at no moment fail to experience withi them. For surely we cannot help at every mo ment experiencing within us that we think nor can anyone infer from the fact that it ha been shown that the animate brutes can dis charge all these operations entirely withou thought, that he therefore does not think; un less it be that having previously persuade himself that his actions are entirely like thos of the brutes, just because he has ascribe thought to them, he were to adhere so perti naciously to these very words, *'men and brute operate in the same way,'* that when it wa shown to him that the brutes did not think, h preferred to divest himself of that thought o his of which he could not fail to have an inne consciousness, rather than to alter his opinio that he acted in the same way as the brutes But I cannot easily persuade myself that ther are many people of this kind. Far more will b found who, if it is conceded *that thought is no to be distinguished from bodily motion,* will wit much better reason conclude that it is th same thing in us and in them, since they notic in them all corporeal movements as in us: the will add *that a difference merely of greater an less makes no difference to the essence,* and wil infer that, though perchance they think tha there is less reason in the beasts than in us our minds are exactly of the same species; an such a conclusion will be justly drawn.

4. As to the Atheist's knowledge, it is eas to prove that it is not immutable and certain For, as I have already in a former place said in proportion to the impotence assigned to th author of his being, the greater will be hi reason for doubting whether he may not be o such an imperfect nature as to be deceived i matters which appear most evident to him and he cannot be set free from that doubt un less he first acknowledges that he has bee created by the true God, a God who has n intention to deceive.

5. Moreover, that it is self-contradictory that men should be deceived by God is clearly demonstrated from the fact that the form o deception is non-existence, towards which th supreme existent cannot incline. In this al Theologians are agreed, and all the certainty

of the Christian faith depends upon this doctrine. For why should we trust God's revelations, if we thought that we were sometimes deceived by Him? And though Theologians commonly affirm that the damned are tortured by hell fire, they do not therefore believe that they *are deceived by a false idea of a tormenting fire which God has implanted in them*, but rather that they are tortured by real fire, for the reason that, *just as the incorporeal spirit of the living man is naturally confined in the body, so by the divine power it is easily after death confined in corporeal fire.* Cf. *The Master of the Sentences*, Book IV, Distinction 44.

As to the passages of Scripture, I do not think that it is my part to reply to them, unless when they appear to contradict some opinion that is peculiar to me. For when my doctrine merely contains things that are common to all Christians, such as are the object of attack here, e.g. that something can be known and that human souls are not like those of animals, I should stand in dread of the charge of arrogance, if I did not prefer to content myself with the replies that have already been discovered by others, rather than devise new arguments; for I have never intermeddled with theological studies, except in so far as they contributed to my private instruction, nor do I find within me so much of the divine grace as to feel called to this sacred occupation. But I shall not on the present occasion avail myself of this resource, for fear that I may give some people an opportunity of thinking that I keep silence because I cannot give a satisfactory explanation of the passages adduced.

Firstly, therefore, I maintain that the passage from St. Paul, I Corinth. chap. 8. ver. 2,[1] ought only to be understood of the knowledge which is not conjoined with love, i.e. of the knowledge of the Atheists, because whoever knows God as he ought, cannot avoid loving Him or fail to have love. And this is confirmed by the preceding words: *"Knowledge puffeth up, but love edifieth,"* and those which immediately follow: *"Moreover if anyone love God, He (i.e. God) is known by him."* Thus the Apostle does not mean that we can possess no knowledge at all, because he admits that those who love God know him, i.e. have knowledge about him. He says merely that those who have not love and hence do not know God sufficiently, although they imagine that in other matters they know something, nevertheless do not

know as they ought to know, just because they ought to begin with the knowledge of God, and subsequently range the knowledge of all other things under this single cognition, as I have explained in my Meditations. Thus this very passage, which was adduced against me, so openly confirms my opinion about this matter, that I disbelieve that it can be properly explained by those who differ from me. But if anyone contends that the pronoun *"He"* does not refer to God but to the man who is known of God and approved by Him, another Apostle, to wit St. John in his first Epistle, chap. 2, wholly favours my explanation. For in verse 2[2] he says as follows: *and hereby we know that we know Him, if we keep His commandments;* in chap. 4. verse 7, *everyone that loveth is begotten of God and knoweth God.*

The same conclusion must be derived from the passages in Ecclesiastes. For it has to be noted that Solomon in that book, while indeed not acting the part of an unbeliever but in his own character, in so far as he was previously a sinner and had turned away from God, there repenting of his sins says that, in so far as he employed human wisdom and did not relate that wisdom to God, he could find nothing which wholly satisfied or in which there was not vanity. Hence on this account he says in many places that we ought to turn towards God, as expressly in chap. 11. verse 9: *And know thou that for all these things God will call thee into judgment,* and in what follows up to the end of the book. Especially also those words in chap. 8. verse 17:—*"And I understood that of all the works of God man can find out no reason of those that are done under the sun"* etc. —should not be understood to hold good of any man, but of him whom he has described in the previous verse: *There is that neither by day nor night seeth sleep with his eyes.* It appears that thus the Prophet meant to announce there that those who are too assiduous in their studies are not fitted to lay hold of the truth; and certainly those who know me will not readily say that this saying applies to me. But we should attend especially to those words: *"the things which are done under the sun."* For the words recur frequently in the book, and always refer to natural things to the exclusion of their subordination to God, just because God, being above all things cannot be comprised among those which are under the sun. Hence the sense of the words cited is, that man cannot know natural objects properly, so long

[1] Above, p. 222.

[2] Verse 3 in the Authorized Version.

as he does not know God, which is just my own contention. Finally, in chap. 3 verse 19, it is clearly not said that *"the death of man is as the death of beasts"* nor that *"man has no pre-eminence over the beasts,"* except in so far as this refers to the body, for in the passage there is mention only of those things that pertain to the body. Immediately afterwards also he adds something separately about the soul: *who knoweth if the spirit of the sons of Adam ascends upwards and if the spirit of the beasts descends downwards?* That means, if human spirits are to enjoy celestial bliss, what man knows this by human reasonings and as long as he does not turn himself toward God? Certainly I have tried to prove by natural reason that the soul is not corporeal: but I admit that it can only be known through faith whether it is to ascend above.

6. As to the freedom of the will, a very different account must be given of it as it exists in God and as it exists in us. For it is self-contradictory that the will of God should not have been from eternity indifferent to all that has come to pass or that ever will occur, because we can form no conception of anything good or true, of anything to be believed or to be performed or to be omitted, the idea of which existed in the divine understanding before God's will determined Him so to act as to bring it to pass. Nor do I here speak of priority of time; I mean that it was not even prior in order, or in nature, or in reasoned relation, as they say [in the schools], so that that idea of good impelled God to choose one thing rather than another. Thus, to illustrate, God did not will to create the world in time because he saw that it would be better thus than if he created it from all eternity; nor did he will the three angles of a triangle to be equal to two right angles because he knew that they could not be otherwise. On the contrary, because he worked to create the world in time it is for that reason better than if he had created it from all eternity; and it is because he willed the three angles of a triangle to be necessarily equal to two right angles that this is true and cannot be otherwise; and so in other cases. And though it may be said that it is the merit of the saints which is the cause of their obtaining eternal life, this causes no difficulty; for their merits are not causes of their obtaining this in the sense that they determine God to will anything; they are merely the cause of an effect of which God wished them from all eternity to be the cause. Thus that supreme indifference

in God is the supreme proof of his omnipotence. But as to man, since he finds the nature of all goodness and truth already determined by God, and his will cannot bear upon anything else, it is evident that he embraces the true and the good the more willingly and hence the more freely in proportion as he sees the true and the good the more clearly, and that he is never indifferent save when he does not know what is the more true or the better, or at least when he does not see clearly enough to prevent him from doubting about it. Thus the indifference which attaches to human liberty is very different from that which belongs to the divine. Neither does it here matter that the essences of things are said to be indivisible: for firstly no essence can belong in a univocal sense both to God and His creature; and finally indifference does not belong to the essence of human liberty, since we are free not only when our ignorance of the right renders us indifferent, but also, and chiefly, when a clear perception impels us to prosecute some definite course.

7. My conception of the superficies by which I believe our senses are affected, is not different from that employed (or which ought to be employed) by all mathematicians and philosophers; they distinguish it from body and assume it to be wholly devoid of depth. But the term superficies is taken in two ways by mathematicians: viz. in the sense of a body, to the length and breadth of which they attend and which is viewed altogether apart from its depth, although depth be not denied of it; or only as a mode of body, when straightway all depth is denied of it. Consequently for the sake of avoiding ambiguity I said that I spoke of that superficies which, being only a mode, can be no part of body; for a body is a substance, and a mode cannot be a part of substance. Yet I did not deny that it was the extremity of a body; nay, on the contrary, I said that it could with the greatest propriety be called the extremity of the contained body as much as of the containing, in the sense in which one says that bodies are contiguous when their extremities are together. For certainly when two bodies touch each other, the extremity of each is one and the same, and this is part of neither but the same mode of both, and can even remain although these bodies are removed, provided only that others of accurately the same size and figure succeed to their place. Nay that space which the Aristotelains call the superficies of the surrounding body can be understood to be no other superficies than that which

no substance but a mode. For neither is the place of a town changed, although the surrounding air be changed or some other substance be substituted for it, nor consequently does the superficies which is here taken for a place form any part of the surrounding air or of the town.

In order to refute the doctrine of the reality of accidents it seems to me that there is no need to produce other arguments than those which I have already employed. For firstly, since all sensation is effected through contact, it is of a corporeal superficies alone that we can have sensation; and yet if there are real accidents they must be different from that superficies, which is merely a mode; therefore if there are any such, we cannot have sensation of them. But who ever believed that they existed unless he thought he experienced them by sensation? Secondly it is contradictory that real accidents should exist, because whatever is real can exist separately apart from any other subject; but whatever can exist separately is substance, not accident. And it makes no difference whether it be said that real accidents can be disjoined from their subject, not naturally, but merely by the divine power; for coming to pass naturally is nowise different from coming to pass by the ordinary power of God, which does not differ at all from his extraordinary power, and does not make any further contribution to things, so that if everything which can exist naturally apart from a subject is substance, so whatever by the power of God, however extraordinary it may be, is capable of existing without a subject, must likewise be termed substance. I do indeed admit that one substance can be the accident of another: but yet when this happens it is not the substance itself which has the form of an accident, but only the mode in which it is accidental. For example, when his clothing is an accident of a man, it is not the clothing itself but merely his *being clothed* which is an accident. But because the principal reason which moved Philosophers to posit real accidents was that they thought that the perceptions of the senses could not be explained without assuming them, I have promised that I will explain these facts minutely with reference to each sense in my Physics. Not that I wish that any of my opinions should be taken on trust, but that I thought that those who have judged correctly in the matter of those accidents which I have already explained in the case of vision in my Dioptrics, will easily guess what I am able to make good in the case of the others.

8. To one who pays attention to God's immensity, it is clear that nothing at all can exist which does not depend on Him. This is true not only of everything that subsists, but of all order, of every law, and of every reason of truth and goodness; for otherwise God, as has been said just before, would not have been wholly indifferent to the creation of what he has created. For if any reason for what is good had preceded His preordination, it would have determined Him towards that which it was best to bring about; but on the contrary because He determined Himself towards those things which ought to be accomplished, for that reason, as it stands in Genesis, *they are very good;* that is to say, the reason for their goodness is the fact that He wished to create them so. Nor is it worth while asking in what class of cause fall that goodness or those other truths, mathematical as well as metaphysical, which depend upon God; for since those who enumerated the classes of cause did not pay sufficient attention to causality of this type, it would have been by no means strange if they had given it no name. Nevertheless they did give it a name; for it can be styled efficient causality in the same sense as the king is the efficient cause of the laws, although a law is not a thing which exists physically, but is merely as they say [in the Schools] a moral entity. Again it is useless to inquire how God could from all eternity bring it about that it should be untrue that twice four is eight, etc.; for I admit that that cannot be understood by us. Yet, since on the other hand I correctly understand that nothing in any category of causation can exist which does not depend upon God, and that it would have been easy for Him so to appoint that we human beings should not understand how these very things could be otherwise than they are, it would be irrational to doubt concerning that which we correctly understand, because of that which we do not understand and perceive no need to understand. Hence neither should we think *that eternal truths depend upon the human understanding or on other existing things;* they must depend on God alone, who, as the supreme legislator, ordained them from all eternity.

9. In order rightly to see what amount of certainty belongs to sense we must distinguish three grades as falling within it. To the first belongs the immediate affection of the bodily organ by external objects; and this can be

nothing else than the motion of the particles of the sensory organs and the change of figure and position due to that motion. The second comprises the immediate mental result, due to the mind's union with the corporeal organ affected; such are the perceptions of pain, of pleasurable stimulation, of thirst, of hunger, of colours, of sound, savour, odour, cold, heat, and the like, which in the sixth Meditation are stated to arise from the union and, as it were, the intermixture of mind and body. Finally, the third contains all those judgments which, on the occasion of motions occurring in the corporeal organ, we have from our earliest years been accustomed to pass about things external to us.

For example, when I see a staff, it is not to be thought that *intentional species* fly off from it and reach the eye, but merely that rays of light reflected from the staff excite certain motions in the optic nerve and, by its mediation, in the brain as well, as I have explained at sufficient length in the Dioptrics. It is in this cerebral motion, which is common to us and to the brutes, that the first grade of perception consists. But from this the second grade of perception results; and that merely extends to the perception of the colour or light reflected from the stick, and is due to the fact that the mind is so intimately conjoined with the brain as to be affected by the motions arising in it. Nothing more than this should be assigned to sense, if we wish to distinguish it accurately from the intellect. For though my judgment that there is a staff situated without me, which judgment results from the sensation of colour by which I am affected, and likewise my reasoning from the extension of that colour, its boundaries, and its position relatively to the parts of my brain, to the size, the shape, and the distance of the said staff, are vulgarly assigned to sense, and are consequently here referred to the third grade of sensation, they clearly depend upon the understanding alone. That magnitude, distance and figure can be perceived by reasoning alone, which deduces them one from another, I have proved in the Dioptrics. The difference lies in this alone, that those judgments which now for the first time arise on account of some new apprehension, are assigned to the understanding; but those which have been made from our earliest years in exactly the same manner as at present, about the things that have been wont to affect our senses, as similarly the conclusions of our reasonings, are referred by us to sense. And

the reason for this is just that in these matte custom makes us reason and judge so quickl or rather we recall the judgments previousl made about similar things; and thus we fail t distinguish the difference between these ope ations and a simple sense preception.

From this it is clear that when we say tha *the certitude obtainable by the understanding much greater than that attaching to the senses* th meaning of those words is, that those judg ments which when we are in full maturity ne observations have led us to make, are sure than those we have formed in early infanc and apart from all reflection; and this is ce tainly true. For it is clear that here there is n question of the first or second grade of sense perception, because in them no falsity can re side. When, therefore, it is alleged that refrac tion makes a staff appear broken in the wate it is the same as if it were said that it appear to us in the same way as it would to an infan who judged that it was broken, and as it doe even to us who, owing to the prejudices t which we from our earliest years have grow accustomed, judge in the same way. But cannot grant what you here add, viz. that tha error is corrected *not by the understanding bu by the touch*. For, although it is owing to touc that we judge that the staff is straight, an that by the mode of judging to which from in fancy we are accustomed, and which is henc called *sense*, this, nevertheless, does not suffic to correct the error. Over and above this w need to have some reason to show us why i this matter we ought to believe the tactua judgment rather than that derived from vision and this reason, not having been possessed by us from the times of infancy, must be attrib uted not to sense but to the understanding Hence, in this instance, it is the understanding solely which corrects the error of sense; and no case can ever be adduced in which erro results from our trusting the operation of th mind more than sense.

10. Since the remainder of what you bring forward consists of doubts rather than of ob jections, I do not take so much upon me as t dare to promise that I shall be able to give a satisfactory account of matters concerning which I see that so many learned and cleve men have hitherto had difficulties. Neverthe less, in order to do my best and not prove wanting in my cause, I shall relate in good faith the means by which I had the fortune to free myself wholly from these same doubts For thus, if they chance to be of use to others,

shall be highly pleased; if not, I shall feel
uilty of no rashness.

When first the reasons expounded in these
editations had led me to infer that the
uman mind was really distinct from the body
nd was more easily known than it, and so on,
hat compelled me to assent to this was that I
und nothing in these arguments which was
ot coherent nor derived from highly evident
rinciples according to the rules of Logic. But
confess that I was not thereby wholly per-
uaded, and that I had almost the same expe-
ence as the Astronomers, who, after many
oofs had convinced them that the Sun was
.any times larger than the Earth, could not
evail upon themselves to forego judging that
. was smaller than the Earth when they
ewed it with their eyes. But when I pro-
eded farther, and, relying on the same fun-
.mental principles, paused in the considera-
on of Physical things, first of all by attending
, the ideas or notions of each separate thing
hich I found within me, and by distinguishing
.e one carefully from the other, in order that
.l my judgments might harmonize with them,
observed that nothing at all belonged to the
ature or essence of body, except that it was
. thing with length, breadth, and depth, ad-
.itting of various shapes and various motions.
found also that its shapes and motions were
nly modes, which no power could make to
xist apart from it; and on the other hand that
olours, odours, savours, and the rest of such
.ings, were merely sensations existing in my
nought, and differing no less from bodies than
ain differs from the shape and motion of the
.strument which inflicts it. Finally, I saw that
ravity, hardness, the power of heating, of at-
racting, and of purging, and all other qualities
hich we experience in bodies, consisted solely
. motion or its absence, and in the configura-
on and situation of their parts.

But since these opinions differed very great-
y from the beliefs which I had previously pos-
essed respecting the same things, I began to
eflect as to what had caused me to believe
therwise before; and the chief reason I no-
iced to be that from infancy I had passed
arious judgments about physical things, for
xample, judgments which contributed much
o the preservation of the life which I was then
ntering; and I had afterwards retained the
ame opinions which I had before conceived
ouching these things. But since at that age
he mind did not employ the corporeal organs
roperly and, remaining firmly attached to

these, had no thoughts apart from them, it
perceived things only confusedly; and although it was conscious of its own proper nature, and possessed an idea of thought as well
as of extension, nevertheless, having no intellectual knowledge, though at the same time it
had an imagination of something, it took them
both to be one and the same, and referred all
its notions of intellectual matters to the body.
Finally, since during the rest of my life I had
never freed myself from these prejudices, there
was nothing which I knew with sufficient distinctness, and nothing which I did not assume
to be corporeal; even though the ideas of those
things which I supposed to be corporeal were
formed and conceived in such a way as to refer
to minds rather than to bodies.

For since I conceived gravity, for example,
in the fashion of a real quality of a certain
order, which inhered in solid bodies, although
I called it a quality, in so far as I referred it to
the bodies in which it inhered, yet because I
added the epithet real, I thought in truth that
it was a substance; just as clothing regarded
by itself is a substance, although when referred
to the man whom it clothes it is quality. Similarly, the mind, though as a matter of fact a
substance, can be styled the quality of the
body to which it is conjoined. And although I
imagined that gravity was diffused throughout
the whole of the body possessing weight, nevertheless I did not ascribe to it that very extension which constituted the nature of the body;
for true bodily extension is of such a nature as
to prevent any interpenetration of parts. At
the same time I believed that there was as
much gravity in a man of gold or of some other
metal a foot long, as in a piece of wood ten feet
long; nay I believed that it was all contracted
within a mathematical point. In fact I also saw
that while it remained coextensive with the
heavy body, it could exercise its force at any
point of the body, because whatever the part
might be to which a rope was attached, it
pulled the rope with all its weight, exactly as if
the gravity resided in the part alone which the
rope touched and was not diffused through the
others. Indeed it is in no other way that I now
understand mind to be coextensive with the
body, the whole in the whole, and the whole in
any of its parts. But the chief sign that my
idea of gravity was derived from that which I
had of the mind, is that I thought that gravity
carried bodies toward the centre of the earth
as if it contained some knowledge of this centre
within it. For it could not act as it did without

knowledge, nor can there be any knowledge except in the mind. At the same time I attributed also to gravity certain things which cannot be understood to apply to mind in the same sense; as e.g. that it was divisible, measurable, etc.

But after I had noted these things with sufficient care, and had accurately distinguished the idea of mind from the ideas of body and corporeal movement, and had discovered that all my previous ideas of real qualities or substantial forms had been composed or manufactured by me out of the former set of ideas, I easily released myself from all the doubts that are here advanced. For firstly I had no doubt that I possessed *a clear idea of my own mind,*[1] of which naturally I had the most intimate knowledge, nor could I doubt that *that idea was wholly diverse from the idea of other things, and contained within it no element of corporeity.* For since I had sought to find out the true ideas of all other things as well, and seemed to have a general acquaintance with all of them, I found nothing in them which was not wholly different from the idea of the mind. And I saw that there was a much greater distinction between those which, though I thought of each attentively, appeared none the less distinct on that account, such as mind and body, than between those, in the case of which, though we can understand the one without thinking of the other, we do not see that the one can exist without the other, when we think of each. Thus certainly God's immensity can be understood, though we do not attend to His justice; but it is wholly contradictory that when we attend to either we should think that God is great without being just. It is possible also rightly to apprehend God's existence, without having knowledge of the persons of the holy Trinity, which indeed a mind illumined by faith can alone perceive; yet when they are once recognized, I deny that there can be discerned between them a real distinction in respect of the divine essence, whatever be admitted to prevail in respect of their relation to one another.

Finally, I had no fear lest, preoccupied with my Analysis, I might perhaps have been led astray when, seeing that *there are certain bodies which do not think,*[2] or rather clearly understanding that certain bodies can exist without thought, I preferred to conclude that thought did not belong to the nature of the body, rather than to infer from my observing that

certain other bodies, e.g. human bodies, do thin. that thought was a mode of body. For, i truth, I have never seen or perceived tha human bodies think, but only that they a the same men who possess both thought and body. And I clearly saw that this fact must b due to the compounding of a thinking with corporeal thing, because when I examined th thinking thing separately I found nothing in belonging to the body, just as neither could discover anything of the nature of thought i corporeal nature separately considered. Bu on the other hand, when I examined all th modes of body and of mind alike, I perceive none at all the concept of which did not de pend on the concept of the thing of which was a mode. Likewise, from the fact that w often perceive two things conjoined, it is no permissible to conclude that they are one an the same thing; but from the fact that w sometimes notice one of them apart from th other, it is highly proper to infer that they ar diverse. Neither should the power of God dete us from drawing this conclusion, because it not less conceptually repugnant that thos things which we clearly perceive to be twai and diverse should be intrinsically and apar from all composition one and the same, tha that those which are in no way distinct shoul be dissevered. Consequently, if God has im planted in certain bodies the power of thinkin (as He really has in the case of human bodies' this very power can be separated from them, an thus it is none the less really distinct from them

Neither do I marvel that formerly, before had liberated myself from the prejudices of th senses, I rightly perceived *that two and thre make five, that if equals be taken from equals th remainders are equal,*[3] and many similar thing when nevertheless I did not think *that the sou of man was distinct from his body.* For it is eas to see that the reason why, when a mere infan I made no mistake respecting these proposi tions which all equally admit, was that I, lik all other children, was not accustomed t count two and three, before the capacity fo judging that they make five had developed On the other hand from my earliest years conceived mind and body as a sort of unit (noticing in a confused way that I was com pounded out of them); and this occurs prac tically in all imperfect knowledge, viz. tha many things are apprehended as a unity which afterwards a more careful scrutiny show to be distinct.

[1]Obj. vi, Appendix (1), p. 223.
[2]Cf. above, p. 223.

[3]Obj. vi, p. 224.

But I do marvel greatly that learned men, *accustomed to the study of Metaphysics for thirty years*,[1] after reading my Meditations *seven times over, should think that if I re-read them in the same spirit of critical analysis with which I would treat them if they had been brought forward by an opponent, I should not believe that the arguments therein contained were of such weight and power, as to compel assent on the part of all*, though meanwhile they themselves can point to no flaw in my reasonings. Indeed they do me more honour than I deserve, or than would be paid to any man, in thinking that I employ an Analysis by the aid of which either true demonstrations are overthrown, or false ones so cloaked and embellished as to be incapable of refutation by anyone. On the contrary I announce that I have only sought to discover a method for detecting the certitude of true and the error of false arguments. Hence, it is not the fact that men of learning do not yet assent to my conclusions which moves me, so much as that after attentive and frequent reading of my arguments, they can point to nothing in them that is either wrongly assumed or incorrectly reasoned. For their difficulty in admitting the conclusions can be ascribed to

[1] Cf. above, p. 224.

their inveterate habit of thinking otherwise about these matters; thus their case would be similar to that of the Astronomers above mentioned, who had a difficulty in imagining that the Sun was greater than the Earth, although that fact was proved by the strictest reasoning. But I do not see that there can be any reason why neither they nor any others, to my knowledge, have up to this time found no error in my reasonings, except that these are wholly true and certain; especially since they are derived from no obscure or unknown principles, but are deduced step by step from, to begin with, a complete doubt as to all things, and next from those truths which, to a mind set free from prejudice, seem most evident and most certain of all. For hence it follows that no flaws at all can exist in them that would not be easily noticed by anyone of average ability. Hence, I think that I have a right to conclude not so much that my doctrines are invalidated by the authority of these men of great learning, though after a repeated perusal of my writings they have not yet succeeded in gaining their assent, as that, on the contrary, their authority strengthens my position, since after so much accurate scrutiny they have noted no errors or fallacies in my proofs.

THE SEVENTH SET

OF OBJECTIONS WITH THE AUTHOR'S ANNOTATIONS THEREON, OTHERWISE A DISSERTATION CONCERNING THE FIRST PHILOSOPHY

MY DEAR SIR,

You set me many questions concerning the new method of investigating the truth, and you not only require me to answer but insistently urge me to reply. Nevertheless I shall keep my own counsel and decline to do you this favour, unless you first concede me something. In this dissertation let me wholly leave out of sight those who have written or said aught about this subject. To this I join the request that you would so construct your interrogations as not to seem to ask about what others have thought and with what mind and what issue they conceived their opinions, or whether these were true or not. Let us imagine that no one has had anything to say, write, or think about those matters, and investigate only the things that your meditations and inquiry into a new method of philosophizing, will show you to be subjects of difficulty. This will enable us both to discuss the truth and to discuss it in a way that will allow us to observe the laws of that friendship and respect which ought to be shown towards learned men. Since you consent and promise to observe this, I also shall respond to your compliance. Therefore

ANNOTATIONS

You set me many questions. Since I received this dissertation from its author after I had imperatively demanded that the comments I heard he had written on my Meditations concerning First Philosophy "should either be openly published or at least sent to me, in order that I might put them along with the remaining objections to the same Meditations that others had made," I could not do otherwise than put it along with them here. Nor also could I doubt that I am the person whom he here addresses, though really I do not remember of ever having asked him what he thought *of my method of investigating the truth.* On the contrary, having a year and a half ago seen a certain Attack of his upon me, wherein I judged there was no attempt to discover the truth, while things which I had neither written nor thought were fathered upon me, I made no concealment of the fact that in future I shoul[d] regard anything that came from him alone [as] unworthy of a reply. But because this writer [is] a member of a Society[1] famous on account [of] its learning and piety, and all who belong to [it] are in such close union with one another tha[t] it is unusual for one member to do anything [of] which all the others do not approve, I adm[itted] that I not only demanded but urgently i[n]sisted, that some members of that Societ[y] should examine my writings and should thin[k] fit to point out to me whatever in them wa[s] alien to the truth. I appended many reason[s] on account of which I hoped that they woul[d] not refuse me this request. I said that, hopin[g] for this, "I should value very highly anythin[g] written in future either by this author or b[y] any other member of the same Society, con[c]erning my opinions. I likewise should n[o] doubt that, whatsoever was the name of th[e] man credited with its composition, this wor[k] would come from the hands not of that on[e] man alone, but of several of the most learne[d] and most sagacious members of the Society, and that consequently it would contain n[o] cavilling, no sophistry, no abuse, and no empt[y] verbiage, but only the strongest and most i[r]refutable reasoning. I doubted not that n[o] argument which could legitimately be brough[t] against me would be omitted; so that th[r]u their efforts alone would, I trusted, free m[e] from all my errors, and if anything I had pub[l]ished was not refuted in their reply, I shoul[d] believe that it was incapable of being refute[d] by anyone, but was wholly true and certain." Therefore, I should hold the above opinion about the present dissertation, and should be[l]ieve that it was written by order of the whol[e] Society, if I was sure that it contained no cav[i]lling, no sophistry, no abuse, and no empt[y] verbiage. But if the opposite is the case, I cer[t]ainly believe it to be a crime to attribute it t[o] men of such sanctity. And since I do not trus[t] my own judgment in this matter I shall stat[e]

[1]The Jesuits.

my opinion here with frankness and candour, not expecting the reader by any means to believe what I say, but merely to give him an opportunity of investigating the truth.

Nevertheless I shall keep my own counsel etc. Here my critic declares that he will assail no one's writing, but will merely reply to my questions. But the truth is that I have never asked him any question; indeed I have never spoken to the man nor even seen him. The questions which he pretends I asked, he has constructed for the most part out of expressions which occur in my Meditations; and thus it is quite evident that it is precisely those Meditations which he attacks. Now it is possible that he has reputable and pious motives for pretending that the opposite is the case; but if that is not so I cannot help suspecting that he hopes by this means to be freer to impute things to me, because nothing in what I have written can convict him of falsehood if he professes that it is not these he attacks. Besides, it looks as if he wishes to avoid giving his readers an opportunity of reading my work; for to talk of my book would be to put them in the way of reading it. Again, it appears that he wishes to describe me as being so futile and ignorant that the reader will turn away from anything which at any time comes from my pen. He thus tries to make a mask for me clumsily pieced together out of fragments of my Meditations, not for the purpose of hiding my features but of rendering them uncomely. I, however, now strip it off and cast it from me, both because I am not accustomed to dramatic acting with its masks, and because the methods of the play-house are hardly in keeping here, where I am engaged on discussing a very serious question with a man who follows the religious life.

FIRST QUESTION

WHETHER AND HOW DOUBTFUL MATTERS ARE TO BE TREATED AS THOUGH THEY WERE FALSE

You ask me first whether that law for investigating the truth is valid; that everything in which here is the minimum of dubiety is to be treated as though it were false.

If I am to reply, I must first put several questions to you:

1. *What is that* minimum of dubiety *you mention?*

2. *What is* to treat a thing as though it were false?

3. *In what respect is it* to be treated as though it were false?

1. WHAT IS THE MINIMUM OF DOUBT?

In respect of doubt, what is that Minimum *you mention? You say, "I will not detain you long. That is to some extent doubtful, about which I may doubt whether it is so or otherwise, not rashly indeed, but for valid reasons. Besides that is to some extent doubtful, concerning which, in spite of its seeming clear to me, I may be deceived by some evil Spirit, who wishes to make sport of me, employing his devices and sleight of hand to make that which is really false appear to be true and clear. The degree of doubtfulness in the first class of dubious matters is not slight; while the second does contain some dubiety, and though it is the minimum of doubt, it is enough not only to allow us to call the matter doubtful but to make it really so. Do you wish for an illustration? That earth, sky, and colour exist; that you have head, or eyes, or body, or mind, are matters of dubiety falling within the first class of the doubtful. To the second belong such statements as: 2 and 3 make 5; the whole is greater than its part; and the like."*

All very well. But if this is the case, tell me, pray, what there is wholly exempt from doubt? What is immune from the fear with which that subtle rascally Spirit threatens us? "Nothing," you say, *"absolutely nothing, until we have proved with certainty and from the most impregnable metaphysical principles that God exists and cannot deceive us. Consequently we get this unique law: if I do not know whether God exists, and, if he exists, whether he may be a deceiver, I clearly am incapable of ever being sure about anything else. But, to show you thoroughly what I mean, I should point out that unless I have first known that God exists, and is a veracious God who will restrain that evil spirit, I shall have occasion and indeed will be bound always to fear that it is making sport of me and is imposing the false upon me, in the guise of the truth, as clear and certain. But when I thoroughly understand that God exists and can neither be deceived nor deceive, and so must of necessity prevent that Spirit imposing on me in matters that I understand clearly and distinctly, then if there are any such, if I perceive anything clearly and distinctly, I shall say that these are true, are certain, so that then the following will be the law of truth and certainty: Everything is true which I perceive very clearly and distinctly."* I have no further question to ask here, but pass to the second point, viz.

2. WHAT IS MEANT BY TREATING A THING AS THOUGH IT WERE FALSE?

Now since it is doubtful whether you possess eyes, head, or body, and consequently must treat those beliefs as though they were false, I should like to know what you mean by that. Does it consist in saying and believing "it is false that I have eyes, head, or body," or in believing and with a general reversal of all my opinions, *saying, "I do not have either eyes or head or body"? To be succinct, does it consist in believing, saying, and affirming the opposite of what is doubtful?* "Exactly so" *you reply. All very well. But kindly reply further. It is not certain that 2 and 3 make 5. Shall I then believe and affirm "2 and 3 do not make 5"?* "Believe it and affirm it," *you reply. I go further. It is not certain that while I speak I am waking and not dreaming. Shall I then believe and affirm: "thus while I speak I am not awake but am dreaming"?* "Believe it and say it," *is your response. Not to weary you, I shall conclude by bringing up the following question. It is not certain that what appears clear and certain to the man who doubts whether he is waking or dreaming, is really clear and certain. Shall I therefore believe and say: "that which appears clear and certain to a man who doubts whether he is waking or dreaming, is not clear and certain but obscure and false"? Why do you hesitate?* You cannot indulge your diffidence more than is fair. *Have you never had the experience which many have had, viz. of seeming to see many things while asleep that appeared clear and certain, but which afterwards are discovered to be doubtful, nay false?* It is indeed prudent never at all to trust those who have even once deceived you. *But you say, "it is altogether different with matters of the highest certainty. They are such that they cannot appear doubtful either to one who dreams or to a madman."* But, my dear sir, are you speaking seriously when you give out that matters of the highest certainty cannot appear doubtful even to dreamers or to madmen? What sort of things can they be? If people when asleep, or the insane, sometimes think things to be certain which are ridiculous and extravagant, may they not believe matters of certainty, even of the highest certainty, to be false and doubtful? I knew a man who once, when falling asleep, heard the clock strike four, and counted the strokes thus—one, one, one, one. Then because he fancied in his mind that this was absurd he shouted out "Ho! Ho! the clock is going mad. It has struck one o'clock four times!" Really is there anything too absurd and irrational to come

into the mind of one who is dreaming or in a delirium? What will a dreamer not believe? Of what will he not approve, and plume himself about it as though it were a magnificent discovery of his own? But not to carry our conflict into other matters, let us take your statement: What appears certain to a man who is in doubt whether he is dreaming or awake, is certain, and so certain that it can be laid down as the basis of a science and a metaphysic of the highest certainty and accuracy. Now you have certainly failed to persuade me that this dictum is as certain as that other: "2 and 3 make 5," and at least not so certain that no one can doubt it at all, nor can be deceived in it by some evil Spirit; nor do I fear that if I persist in thinking so, anyone will think my conduct obstinate. Therefore, one of two alternative conclusions results. Either in accordance with your principle it is not certain that what appears to be certain to a man who doubts whether he is awake or dreaming is certain; and consequently what appears to be certain to a man who doubts whether he is awake or dreaming may and ought to be considered as false and as wholly false. Or else, if you have any other principle peculiar to yourself you will communicate it to me. I now come to my third question, and

3. TO WHAT EXTENT IS A THING TO BE TREATED AS FALSE?

I ask, since it seems not to be certain that 2 and 3 make 5, and since the principle previously quoted obliges us to believe and say 2 and 3 do not make 5, ought I to believe this continuously to the extent of persuading myself that it cannot be otherwise than so, and that that is certain? You are astonished at my question. *It does not seem strange to me, since I myself am astonished. Yet reply you must, if you are to get an answer from me. Do you wish to have it a certainty that 2 and 3 do not make 5? Nay do you wish that to be, and to seem to all, so certain as to be safe from the wiles of an evil spirit?*

You laugh, and say: *"How did that ever come into a sane man's head?"*

What then? Is it to be doubtful and uncertain, just in the same way as the statement—2 and 3 make 5? If this is so, and the statement—2 and 3 do not make 5, is doubtful, I shall believe, and in accordance with your principle assert, that it is false. Consequently, I shall affirm the opposite and assert:—2 and 3 do make 5. I shall accord the same treatment to the remaining objects of doubt and, since it does not seem to be certain that any body exists, I shall say: no body exists. Then because that statement, no body exists, i not certain, I shall state, my attitude being completely reversed, some body does exist. *Thus body will at the same time exist and not exist.*

That is so, you say. This is what it is to doubt, viz. to move in a circle, to advance and retire, to affirm a thing and to deny it, to screw up and unscrew the peg.

That is quite splendid. But what am I to do in the matter of using those statements that are dubious? Take the case, 2 and 3 make 5; or that other, some body exists. *Shall I affirm them or deny them?*

You say you will neither affirm them nor deny them. You will employ neither, and will regard both their affirmation and their denial as false; you will look for nothing from those who so assent, except an assent to this also as a matter of doubt and uncertainty.

Since there is nothing more for me to ask, I shall reply in my turn, employing however a short epitome of your doctrine, which is as follows.

1. *It is possible for us to be in doubt about all things, and especially about material things, so long as we have no other foundation for the sciences than those on which we have hitherto relied.*

2. *To treat anything as false is to withhold your assent from it as though it were openly false and, altering our attitude to its direct opposite, to assume an opinion which represents it as false and imaginary.*

3. *That which is doubtful is to be treated as though it were false in such a way that its opposite also is doubtful, and we have to consider it, too, as false.*

ANNOTATIONS

I should be ashamed to be too diligent and spend many words in commenting on all the things which, though here expressed in words almost identical with mine, I nevertheless do not recognize as mine. I merely ask my readers to recall what I said in Meditation I, and at the beginning of II and III, and in the synopsis of these *Meditations*. For they will acknowledge that almost everything here set down, though drawn from these sources, is so perverted, distorted, and wrongly interpreted that, although in their right place they contain nothing that is not highly rational, here, nevertheless, they seem to be extremely absurd.

For valid reasons.[1] I said at the end of Mediation I that everything which I had not yet comprehended with sufficient clearness could be doubted by us, provided we did so for reasons that were very powerful and mature-

[1]Cf. above, p. 235.

ly considered." But I did so because there the question was about only that supreme kind of doubt which, I have insisted, is metaphysical, hyperbolical, and not to be transferred to the sphere of the practical needs of life by any means. It was of this doubt also that I said the very least ground of suspicion was a sufficient reason for causing it. But my critic in his friendly and frank way brings forward as an example of the things of which I said we might doubt "for valid reasons" the questions whether the earth exists, or whether I have a body, in order that the readers, who know nothing of this metaphysical doubt, referring it to the practical life, may think that I am out of my mind.

Nothing, you say, absolutely nothing.[2] I have sufficiently explained in various places the sense in which that *nothing* ought to be understood. So, for example, that as long as we attend to some truth which we perceive very clearly, we cannot indeed doubt it. But when, as often happens, we do not attend to any truth in this way, although we remember that we have often known such truths quite well, there is none, nevertheless, of which we may not rightly doubt if we are unaware of the fact that everything we perceive clearly is true. Here, however, my friend with great accuracy interprets my *nothing* in such a way that, from the fact that once, to wit in Meditation I, I said there was nothing of which we might not doubt, assuming there that I was not attending to anything which I clearly perceived, he infers that in the following Meditations also I can be sure of nothing. This is to imply that the arguments which for a time cause us to doubt any matter, have no legitimacy or validity unless they prove that the matter must always be in doubt.

To believe, to say, to affirm the opposite of what is doubtful.[3] When I said that doubtful matters should sometimes be treated as though they were false, or rejected as if they were false, I clearly explained that I merely meant that, for the purpose of investigating the truths that are metaphysically certain, we should pay no more credence to doubtful matters than to what is plainly false. Thus surely no sane man can interpret my words otherwise, or attribute to me the opinion of wishing to believe the opposite of what is doubtful, especially, as the matter is subsequently put, *of believing it to the extent of persuading myself that it cannot be*

[2]Cf. above, p. 235.
[3]Cf. above, p. 236.

otherwise than thus, and that that is certain.[1] At least only a man who is not ashamed of being a caviller could do such a thing. And although my critic does not actually affirm this interpretation of my words, but merely puts it forward tentatively, I am surprised that a man of his holiness should in this respect copy the basest detractors, who often take this method of giving utterance to the opinion which they wish to be entertained about others, adding that they themselves do not believe it, so that, having stated the calumny, they may get off scot free.

It is altogether different with matters of the highest certainty. They are such that they cannot appear doubtful either to one who dreams or to a madman.[2] I cannot tell by what Analysis my subtlest of critics is able to extract this from my words. It would indeed have been possible to infer from what I have said that everything which anyone clearly and distinctly perceives is true, although that person in the meantime may doubt whether he is dreaming or awake, nay, if you want it so, even though he is really dreaming or is delirious. This is for the reason that nothing whatsoever can be clearly and distinctly perceived, whoever be the person perceiving it, that it is not perceived to be such as it is, i.e. which is not true. But because it is the wise alone who know how to distinguish rightly between what is so perceived, and what merely seems or appears to be clear and distinct, I am not surprised that our good friend mistakes the one for the other.

This is what it is to doubt, viz. to move in a circle etc.[3] I said that we ought to pay no more credence to things that are doubtful than if they were false, in order that we may wholly dismiss them from mind and not in order to affirm now one thing, now its opposite. My critic, however, leaves no opportunity for cavilling untried. But meanwhile it is worth noting that he himself at the end, where he says he makes a brief epitome of my doctrine, attributes to me none of those opinions which either previously or in the sequel he attacks and holds up to scorn. Doubtless this is to let us know that he was only jesting when he concocted them and ascribed them to me, and did not seriously believe that I entertained them.

REPLY

Reply 1. Assume the meaning of the law, "in the investigation of the truth that which is to the

[1]Cf. p. 236.
[2]Cf. p. 236.
[3]Cf. p. 237.

slightest extent doubtful is to be treated as though it were false," to be: "when we are investigating matters that are certain, we ought not to rely on anything which is not certain or is to the slightest extent doubtful." In this case your law is quite sound, is of established usage, and one of the best known truths common to all Philosophers.

Reply 2. If the said law is understood to mean the following: "when we investigate matters that are certain, we ought to reject everything that is not certain, or is in any way doubtful, and make no use of such matters at all, to the extent of treating them as though they were non-existent, or rather not taking them into account at all, but rather dismissing them wholly from mind": in this case again your law is quite sound, valid, and a commonplace with beginners. It is, in fact, so like the preceding version of it as to be hardly distinguishable from it.

Reply 3. Suppose the law next to be taken in the following way: "when we investigate matters that are certain, we ought to reject everything that is doubtful and affirm that the asserted fact does not exist, but that its opposite really holds; and we ought to take this latter statement as a secure foundation for our argument, or to put it otherwise, make use of the assumption that the matters doubted do not exist, or base our argument upon their non-existence." Now in this case the law is invalid, fallacious, and in conflict with sound Philosophy. For it assumes something doubtful and uncertain for the purpose of investigating what is true and certain. To express the matter differently, it assumes as certain something that may be wholly otherwise than as we suppose it to be; to wit, we treat doubtful things as though they did not exist, whereas it is quite possible that they do exist.

Reply 4. If a man were to understand that law as last expressed and employ it in his investigation of matters that are true and certain, he would expend all his toil and trouble and labour to no profit since, like anyone else who did so, he would achieve the opposite of his quest quite as much as his object itself. Do you want an illustration? Suppose a man were to enquire whether he were a body or were corporeal, and to that intent made use of the following statements:—"it is not certain that any body exists; therefore in accordance with the law just approved, I shall affirm and say—no body exists." Then he will resume: "no body exists; but I am and exist, as I have quite properly ascertained from other sources: therefore I cannot be a body." Very fine indeed; but look and see how the same beginning will lead to the opposite conclusion. "It is not certain," he says "that any body exists; therefore, in accordance with

e law, I shall affirm and assert that no body ex-
ts." But what sort of a statement is that? No
·dy exists? That is certainly doubtful and un-
·rtain. Who can make it good? Whence will he
·aw his proof? His proof is merely fictitious.
No body exists" is really a doubtful statement;
·erefore in accordance with your law I shall say:
some body does exist." But I am and exist;
·erefore possibly I am a body, if there is no
·ason for believing otherwise. Look at our result:
·-possibly I am body and it is impossible for me
· be a body. Is that enough for you? But I fear
·at I have done quite as much as I obtain in the
·llowing questions. Therefore,[1]

ANNOTATIONS

Here in his first two replies my critic has ap-
·roved of everything which I laid down con-
·rning the subject under discussion, or that
·n be elicited from my writings. But he adds
·at it is quite common property, a common-
·ace of philosophers. Yet in his two latter re-
·lies he censures the opinion which he wishes
·eople to believe held, though that is so ab-
·rd as to be incapable of entering the mind of
· sane man. But it is very astute of him to do
·, meaning as he does to influence by his
·uthority those who have not read my Medi-
·ations or have not read them attentively
·nough to understand properly what is in
·em. Thus they will think that my opinions
·re ridiculous, while others who do not believe
·is will at least be persuaded that I have ad-
·uced nothing that is not quite common prop-
·ty and a commonplace of beginners. True, I do
·ot dispute this last statement. I have never
·ught to derive any praise from the novelty
·f my opinions. For, on the contrary, I believe
·em to be the most ancient of all beliefs, as
·eing the truest. Further, it is my habit to
·tudy nothing so much as the scrutiny of cer-
·in very simple truths, which, being innate in
·ur minds, are such that, when they are laid
·efore anyone else, he believes that he has
·ever been ignorant of them. But certainly it
·ay easily be understood that my critic im-
·ugns my theories merely because he thinks
·em good and new. For if he believed them
·o be so absurd as he makes them out to be, he
·ould surely judge them worthy of contempt
·nd silence, rather than of a long and factitious
·efutation.

Therefore, in accordance with the law just ap-
·roved, I shall affirm and say the opposite.[2] I

should like to know where he has ever found
this law promulgated. He has already laid
quite enough stress upon it, but in the same
passage I have already given a sufficient denial to my authorship of it, viz. in my annotations on the words: To believe, say, and affirm
the opposite of what is doubtful. Nor do I believe
that he will go on maintaining that it is mine
if he is questioned about the matter. He introduced me above in paragraph 3, as speaking
about doubtful matters in the following terms:
You will neither affirm nor deny them, you will employ neither, and will regard both their affirmation and denial as false. Shortly afterwards in
his epitome of my doctrine his version is that
we ought to withhold our assent from the doubtful as though it were openly false, and, altering
our attitude to its direct opposite, assume an
opinion which represents it as being false and
imaginary.[3] Now this is plainly something
quite different from affirming and saying the
opposite, in such a way as to treat that opposite as true in the way he here supposes I do.
Further when I, in Meditation I, said that I
sometimes tried to convince myself of the opposite of the belief that I had formerly rashly
held, I immediately added that I wished to do
so in order to balance the weight of my prejudices equally on both sides and not be inclined
towards one rather than the other. But I made
it clear that it was not my intention to regard
either as true or to set that up as the foundation of our most certain knowledge, as is unfairly represented elsewhere by my critic.
Therefore, I should like to know what his intention was in bringing up this law of his
framing. If it is for the purpose of ascribing it
fictitiously to me, I mark a lack of candour on
his part; for it is clear from what he has said
that he knows well enough that it is not any
law of mine, because no one could believe that
both alternatives ought to be considered false,
as he said was my opinion, and at the same
time affirm and allege that the opposite of one
of them was true, as his version of the law has
it. But if he adduced this law merely to show
animus, in order that he might have some
means of attacking me, I nevertheless wonder
at the acumen of his intellect, that has been
able to excogitate nothing more plausible or
subtle. I marvel that he has had leisure to expend so many words in refuting an opinion of
an absurdity that would hardly impose even
on a child of seven years of age. For we must
observe that up to the present time he has at-

[1]Cf. Second Question, p. 240.
[2]Cf. p. 237.

[3]Cf. p. 237.

tacked nothing at all but this perfectly inept law of his own framing. Finally, I marvel at the strength of his imagination, seeing that, waging war as he does merely upon that most unreal of chimaeras which he has evolved from his own brain, he has nevertheless adopted the same attitude and employed the same words, as if he had really had me as his opponent, and been face to face with me in the conflict.

SECOND QUESTION

WHETHER IT IS A GOOD METHOD OF PHILOSOPHIZING TO SET ASIDE EVERYTHING THAT IS DOUBTFUL

You ask, 2: whether it is a good method of philosophizing to set aside all matters that involve any doubt. Unless you disclose this method in some detail you need not expect an answer from me. However, you do this.

"In order to philosophize," you say, "in order to discover whether there be anything certain, and of the highest certainty, and what that is, this is my procedure. Since all is doubtful and uncertain, I treat everything which I have ever believed, or which I have previously known, as false, and I set all such things aside completely, and convince myself that neither earth nor sky nor any of the things I previously believed to be in the world exist; nay, not even the world itself, nor my body, nor mind, in a word nothing, I affirm, exists. Then having made this general renunciation, and having protested that nothing exists, I plunge into my own philosophy and, led by its counsels I track out the true and certain cautiously and prudently, just as if there existed some very powerful and cunning Spirit who wanted to lead me into error. Wherefore, not to be deceived, I look around attentively and have quite determined on the plan of admitting nothing that is not of such a nature that, however much that scoundrelly Spirit strives to deceive me, he is quite unable to do so in this case, and even I myself cannot compel myself to conceal my knowledge of the fact or deny it. I reflect therefore, I revolve and revolve things in my thought until something of the kind sought may arrive, and when I have struck upon it, I use it (as Archimedes used his fulcrum) for eliciting other facts, and in this wise I derive one fact from another in a way that shows them to be wholly certain and well attested."

That is very fine indeed, and so far as appearances go, I should have no difficulty in replying that this method appears to me to be both brilliant and distinguished. But because you expect a careful reply, and I cannot give you that witho[ut] first employing and practising your method a[nd] so testing it, let us enter that well beaten and sa[fe] road, and ourselves find out where it really lea[ds] to; and knowing as you do its meanderings, [its] defiles, and detours, and having long exercise[d] yourself in tracing them, I beg you to conduct [me] through them yourself. Come, express your min[d]: you have either a comrade or a pupil with you [to] whom to show the way. What do you bid me d[o?] Though it is new to me and, since I am not a[c-] customed to its obscurity, to be dreaded, I a[m] quite willing to enter that route, such a powerf[ul] attraction does the appearance of the truth exe[r-] cise over me. I hear your reply; you bid me [do] what I see you do, plant my steps where you p[ut] yours. That is certainly an excellent way of com[-] manding and leading me! How well you let m[e] think of you! I am ready.

1. THE DISCLOSING OF THE ENTRY INTO THE METHOD

"Firstly," you say, *"as I revolved previo[us] truths in my mind,* I feel constrained to confe[ss] that there is nothing in all that I formerly b[e-] lieved to be true of which I cannot in som[e] measure doubt, and that, not just throug[h] want of thought or through levity, but fo[r] reasons which are very powerful and mature[ly] considered; so that henceforth I ought not th[e] less carefully to refrain from giving creden[ce] to these opinions than to that which is man[i-] festly false, if I desire to arrive at any ce[r-] tainty.[1] Wherefore, I shall not be acting amis[s] if, taking of set purpose a contrary belief, [I] outwit my own self and pretend for a time tha[t] all those old opinions are entirely false an[d] imaginary, until at last, having thus balance[d] my former prejudices with my latter, my judg[-] ment will no longer be dominated by ba[d] usage or turned away from the right know[l-] edge of the truth.[2] Therefore, let me suppos[e] that some evil genius not less powerful tha[n] deceitful has employed his whole energies i[n] deceiving me. I shall consider that the heaven[s] the earth, colours, figures, sounds, and all othe[r] material things are nothing but the illusion[s] and dreams of which this genius has availe[d] himself in order to lay traps for my credulity[.] I shall persuade myself that nothing at all exist[s] in the world, that there is no sky, no earth, tho[se] there are no minds, no bodies; (remember I sa[y] no minds, no bodies). This is the goal, and th[e]

[1]Cf. Med. I, pp. 76–77.
[2]Cf. Med. I, p. 77.
[3]Cf. Med. I, p. 77.

rincipal goal. I shall consider myself as having
o hands, no eyes, no flesh, no blood, nor any
nse, yet as falsely believing myself to possess
l these things. I shall remain obstinately at-
ched to this idea."[1]

Here kindly pause a little, in order that we
ay collect a fresh supply of energy. The novelty
 your proposal has not failed to move me some-
hat. Do you bid me renounce every old belief?

You say, "I bid you set aside everything."

Everything? He who says "everything," leaves
o room for exceptions.

You repeat, "everything."

Really I can with difficulty bring myself to do
, yet I shall obey. But it is exceedingly hard
nd, to speak frankly, I have a scruple in com-
lying, a scruple which, if you do not relieve me
om it, will I fear prevent our entry into the
ethod from being so successful as we wish. You
nfess that you doubt all your old beliefs and, as
ou say, you are compelled to confess this. Why
ot permit the same force to bear on me that I also
ay be forced to admit it? Tell me what it is that
mpels you. True, you have just now said that
e reasons influencing you were valid and well
onsidered. But what are they then? If they are
alid, why set them aside? Why not retain them?
 they are doubtful and replete with suspicion
ow can they have brought any force to bear upon
ou?

But you say, "they are a mere preliminary;
ok and see. It is my wont to send them in front,
ke slingers, to begin the battle. For example, our
nses sometimes deceive us; we sometimes dream;
ometimes people go delirious and believe they see
ings which they do not see, and which exist
owhere."

Have you finished speaking? When you prom-
sed me valid and well-considered reasons, I
xpected them to be certain and free from all
oubt, such as are demanded by your tract which
e are now employing, and rising to such a pitch
 accuracy as to dispel the least suspicion of
ubiety. But are the reasons you allege of this
ature? Not mere doubts and nought but sus-
icious surmises? "Our senses sometimes deceive
s." "We sometimes dream." "People sometimes
o delirious." But whence do you derive all that
ith certainty and complete infallibility, and in
ccordance with that rule of yours which you have
lways in evidence?—"We must take the ut-
ost pains not to admit anything as true which
e cannot prove to be true?" Has there been
ny time when you said to yourself with certain-
: "Now without doubt my senses are deceiving

[1]Cf. Med. I, p. **77.**

me, and of this I am quite aware"; "Now I am
dreaming"; "I was dreaming a little time ago";
"This man is suffering from a frenzy, and believes he sees things which he does not see, but yet
is not lying"? If you say there ever was such a
time, be sure you prove that; nay, satisfy yourself lest that evil Spirit you spoke of may perhaps
have given you an illusion. It is greatly to be
feared that when you now make the statement as
something valid and well-considered, that rascal
is making a mock of you, and is winking at the
man he has hoodwinked. But, if you say that
there was no such time, why so confidently assert:
"Sometimes we dream"? Why not in accordance
with your first law determine to say: "It is not
quite certain that our senses sometimes deceive
us, that we have sometimes dreamed, that men
have sometimes gone delirious; therefore, I shall
assert and resolve upon the following: 'Our
senses never deceive us, we never dream, people
never go delirious'"?

But, you say, "I suspect it." Now this is my
scruple. So far as I have proceeded I have found
your arguments to be feeble, and like fleeting suspicions. Consequently, I fear to press on. It is I
now who am suspicious.

You reply: "Suspect away. It is enough if you
are suspicious. It is enough if you say: 'I don't
know whether I am awake or dreaming. I don't
know whether my senses deceive me, or do not.'"

I beg your pardon, but for me it is not enough.
Nor do I at all see how you make the following inference: "I don't know whether I am awake or
dreaming": "therefore I sometimes dream."
What if I never do? What if always? What if you
cannot even dream, and that Spirit is convulsed
with laughter because he has at length persuaded
you that you sometimes dream and are deceived,
while that is far from being the case? Trust me,
from the time when you brought that Spirit on the
stage, from the time when you subjected your
valid and well-considered reasons to that "perhaps," you have raised an evil that has brought
you no advantage. What if the sly fellow presents
all these matters as doubtful and unstable, when
they really are quite reliable, meaning thereby,
after you have turned aside from them all, to lead
you into the abyss? Would it not be more prudent,
before you turn aside from them all, to propound
some reliable law which will enable you to set
aside what you do set aside without fear of error?
The matter is certainly important, nay of the
highest moment, that general renunciation of our
old opinions which you propose; and if you comply
with my suggestions, you will call your thoughts
into council and seriously deliberate them.

Nay, you say, "I cannot yield too much to distrust," and "I know that there can be neither peril nor error in this course."[1]

What? "I know"? Is that certain and beyond all doubt? And has our great shipwreck of truth left at least this driftwood floating? Or is it the case that because you are opening a new Philosophy and are thinking of the whole school, this has to be written in golden letters on your portal: "I cannot indulge my incredulity too much." Is it the consequence that the entrants into your temple are bidden to lay aside their ancient belief that "2 and 3 make 5," but to retain this, "I cannot indulge my incredulity too much"? But what will you say if a disciple chance to murmur at this; if he cannot swallow the fact that he is bidden abandon the old belief which everyone accepts, that "2 and 3 make 5" because an evil Spirit may deceive him, while he is instructed to retain that doubtful principle, full of flaws—"I cannot indulge my incredulity too much"—as if in this case the evil Spirit could not impose upon him? But will you substantiate this for me, so that I shall not be in fear, shall have no apprehensions about that evil Spirit? Certainly, though you may try to strengthen my confidence in any way you please, it is not without extreme fear of too great incredulity that I renounce all my ancient and practically innate beliefs, and forswear as false—"an argument in Barbara *has a valid conclusion." And to judge by your demeanour, not even you who offer yourself as a guide to others are free from fear. Be frank and ingenuous as is your wont; do you feel no scruple in giving up that ancient belief—"I have a clear and distinct idea of God"? Do you readily renounce— "Everything which I perceive very clearly and distinctly is true"—or—"To think, to grow, to feel, do not appertain at all to the body but to the mind"? But why should I go through the whole series of such statements? My question regarding them is serious and I ask you kindly to reply. Can you in thus parting with the old Philosophy and entering the new, reject, divest yourself of, forswear these as false. I mean from the heart? Do you assert and affirm the opposite: "now I do not have a clear and distinct idea of God"; "up to the present I have been mistaken in believing that growth, thought and sensation did not appertain to the body at all, but to the mind"? But what have I done? I have been forgetful of what I promised to do. I had committed myself entirely to you at the beginning, had vowed myself your ally and disciple, and here I am hesitating at the very outset, timid and obstinate. Pray forgive me! I have*

[1]Cf. Med. I, p. 77.

sinned greatly and have merely shown the small ness of my intellectual capacity. It was my du to have laid aside all fear and to plunge bold into the fog of renunciation; but I have been u willing and have resisted. If you spare me I sho make amends and quite wipe out my ill-deeds b a full and generous enfranchisement and remi sion of all my old beliefs. I renounce, I forswee everything which I once held true. Do not min though I do not protest my belief in that sky earth which you wish to do away with. Nothir exists, absolutely nothing. Go on and lead t way; I shall follow. You are certainly easy follow! So don't refuse to lead on.

ANNOTATIONS

And it is all doubtful, everything I have pr viously known.[2] Here my critic has writte *known* for *thought I knew.* For there is an o position between the words *I knew* and *doubtful* which doubtless he has nevertheles failed to perceive. Nor must we set his actio down as malicious. If that were so he woul not have treated the matter so cursorily bu would have pretended that the contradictio was one of my creating and would have mad a long story of it.

Remember I say no minds, no bodies.[3] This advanced in order to give an opportunity fo much pettifogging argument afterwards, be cause at the outset, since I assumed that I di not yet fully comprehend the nature of th mind, I put it in the list of dubious matter But afterwards perceiving that the thing whic thinks cannot fail to exist, and applying to tha thinking thing the term mind, I said that min exists. Now this looks as though I had for gotten that I had first denied the same, whe I took the mind to be something unknown t me. It looks, too, as if I had thought that w must always deny the things which I the denied because they seemed to me doubtfu and that it was impossible I should ever com pass the restoration of their certainty and ev dence. We must note too that throughout h treats doubtfulness and certainty not as re lations of our thought to objects, but as prop erties of the objects and as inhering in the eternally. The consequence is that nothing w have once learned to be doubtful can ever b rendered certain. But this must be attribute merely to his goodness of heart, not to spite.

Everything?[4] Here he is making play wit

[2]Cf. Second Question, p. 240.
[3]Cf. above, p. 240.
[4]Cf. above, p. 241.

e meaning of the word *everything* just as
ove he did with the word *nothing*. The argu-
ent is quite futile.

You are compelled to confess this.[1] Here again
an empty trifling with the word *compelled*.
r we may well enough be compelled to doubt
arguments that are in themselves doubtful,
d not to be afterwards retained, as we above
ted. They are indeed valid so long as we do
t possess any others to remove our doubt
d introduce certainty. It was because I found
ne such during the course of Meditation I,
wever much I looked around and reflected,
at I therefore said that my reasons for doubt-
g were valid and well considered. But this
ceeds my critic's comprehension. For he
lds: *When you promised valid reasons I ex-
cted them to be certain and free from all doubt,
ch as are demanded by your tract,*[2] as if the
naginary brochure which he has invented
ould be referred to the statements of the first
Ieditation. Shortly afterwards he says: *Has
ere been any time when you said to yourself
ith certainty: "Now without doubt my senses
e deceiving me, and of this I am quite aware,"
c.?*[3] But he does not see that here again there
a contradiction, because something is held
be true without doubt, and at the same time
ae very same thing is doubted. What a man
e is!

*Why so confidently assert, "sometimes we
ream"?* Here again he errs, but without evil
atent. For I asserted nothing at all confident-
in the first Meditation, which is full of
oubt, and from which alone all these state-
ents are drawn. He could in it find equally
ell: "we never dream," and "we sometimes
ream." When shortly afterwards he adds:
or do I at all see how you make the following
nference. "I don't know whether I am awake or
reaming; therefore I sometimes dream";*[4] he
scribes to me a style of reasoning worthy only
f himself, because he is so good-natured.

What if that sly fellow (the evil Spirit) *pre-
ents all these matters as doubtful and unstable
hen they really are quite reliable?*[5] Here it is
lear, as I pointed out above, that he treats
oubt and certainty as though they existed in
he objects, not in our thought. Otherwise how
ould he pretend that I propounded something
s dubious which was not dubious but certain?

Seeing that the only cause that makes a thing
dubious is that it is propounded as dubious.
But perhaps it was the evil Spirit that prevented him from seeing the contradiction in
his words. It is to be regretted that this Spirit
so often causes difficulties in our critic's thinking.

*The matter is certainly important, nay of the
highest moment, that general renunciation of our
old opinions which you propose.*[6] I pointed this
out with quite enough emphasis at the end of
my reply to the fourth set of objections, and in
my preface to these Meditations, which I
therefore presented only to those of robuster
mental powers to read.[7] I already pointed the
same thing out also in very express terms in
my discourse on Method which appeared in
French in 1637, pp. 16 and 17. Since I there
described two kinds of mind, by both of which
such a renunciation is to be strenuously avoided, my critic ought not to father his own errors
on me if he chance to be included in either of
these two classes.

What? "I know" etc.[8] When I said that I
knew that I ran no risk in making that renunciation, I added: *because then, on that occasion,
I was not considering the question of action, but
only of knowledge.*[9] From this it is clearly evident that when I said "I know" I spoke only of
the moral mode of knowing, which suffices for
the regulation of life, and which I have often
insisted is so vastly different from that Metaphysical mode of knowing which is here in
question, that apparently no one but our critic
could fail to recognize that.

*That doubtful principle, full of flaws—I can-
not indulge my incredulity too far.*[10] Here again
there is a contradiction in his words. For no
one fails to recognize that a person who is in-
credulous and hence neither affirms nor denies
anything, cannot be led into error even by any
evil Spirit. But the example my critic adduces
above, about the man who counted one o'clock
four times, shows that a person adding 2 and 3
together can be deceived.

*But it is not without extreme fear of too great
incredulity that I renounce these old beliefs.*[11]
Though he is at great pains to prove that we
ought not to distrust ourselves too much, it is
nevertheless worthy of note that he does not
bring the least scrap of argument to prove that,

[1]Cf. above, p. 241.
[2]Cf. p. 241.
[3]Cf. p. 241.
[4]Cf. p. 241.
[5]Cf. p. 241.

[6]Cf. p. 241.
[7]Med., *Preface*, p. 72.
[8]Cf. above, p. 242.
[9]Cf. Med. II, pp. 77–78.
[10]Cf. above, p. 242.
[11]Cf. p. 242.

except that he fears or distrusts our need of distrusting ourselves. Here again then is a contradiction. For because he is fearful, but does not know for certainty that he ought not to distrust himself, it follows that he ought to distrust himself.

Do you feel no scruple in giving up that ancient belief, "I have a clear and distinct idea of God"? Do you readily renounce, "Everything which I very clearly perceive is true"?[1] He calls these ancient beliefs because he fears lest they may be regarded as new and as first perceived by me. But so far as I am concerned he may do so. He also wishes to suggest a scruple concerning God, though he does so only casually; perchance lest those who know how studiously I have excepted everything which pertains to piety and generally to morals from this renunciation, may think he is calumniating me. Finally, he does not see that the renunciation affects only those who do not yet perceive anything clearly and distinctly. Thus, for example, the Sceptics with whom he is familiar, have never, in so far as they are Sceptics, perceived any thing clearly. For owing to the mere fact of having perceived anything clearly they would have ceased to doubt and to be Sceptics. Further, because before making this renunciation scarcely any others perceive anything clearly, at least with that clearness required for metaphysical certainty, the renunciation is therefore very advantageous for those who are capable of such clear knowledge and who do not yet possess that. But as things show, it would not be thus beneficial to our author; indeed I believe that he ought carefully to refrain from it.

Whether "To think, to grow, to feel do not belong to the body but to the mind[2] *is not to be set aside without hesitation"?* My critic reports these words as though they were mine, and at the same time as though they were so certain as to be incapable of being doubted by anyone. But nothing is more noteworthy than that in my Meditations I ascribe nutrition wholly to the body, not to the mind or that part of man which thinks. Thus it is proved by this fact alone, firstly that he wholly fails to understand my Meditations, though he has undertaken to refute them, and that he falsifies matters, because it was when I was quoting popular opinion that I referred growth and nutrition to the soul. Next he shows that he himself holds many beliefs as indubitable which are not to

[1]Cf. p. 242.
[2]Cf. p. 242.

be admitted without examination. But final he comes to the complete truth of the matte when he concludes that in these things *he h merely shown the smallness of his intellectu capacity.*[3]

THE ACTUAL ENTRY INTO THE METHOD

You say, "after setting aside everything old I b gin to philosophize thus. I am, I think; I am, long as I think. This assertion, 'I exist,' necessarily true each time that I pronounce or that I mentally conceive it."[4]

Splendid, my good friend! You have found t point which Archimedes wanted to discove there is no doubt that, if you so please, you will able to move the world; look, now it all begins sway and tremble. But I beg you (for I have doubt you wish to prune things down, so th there shall be nothing in your Method which not apt, coherent and necessary) say why y have mentioned the mind, when you say it mentally conceived?[5] *Did you not order t banishment of mind and body? But perhaps was by chance that you let this pass: it is so dif cult even for an expert to forget altogether t things to which we have been accustomed sin childhood, that it may be easily thought that slip on the part of a raw hand like me, if it chan to occur, is hardly likely to be thought ill of. B go on, I entreat you.*

You say, "I shall consider what I am, an what I formerly believed myself to be, befo I embarked upon these last reflections. I sha withdraw all that might even in the slighte extent be invalidated by the reasons which have just brought forward, in order that the may be nothing at all left beyond what is a solutely certain and indubitable.[6]

Shall I dare, before you push onwards, to a why you, the man who has abandoned with suc solemn declarations all your old beliefs as dub ous and false, want to inspect them again, as you hoped to get something good out of these ra and tatters. What if once you thought ill of you self? Nay, since everything you forswore a lit time ago was dubious and uncertain (otherwi why did you set it aside?), how does it come abo that the same things are now not dubious and u certain? Unless, perchance, that renunciatio you made was like Circe's drug, to call a potion

[3]Cf. p. 242.
[4]Cf. Med. ii, p. 77.
[5]Cf. Med. ii, p. 77.
[6]Cf. Med. ii, pp. 77–78.

forgetfulness by another name. Yet, it is an evil thing both to suspect your counsel and to regard it as sound. It is often the case that people who bring their friends into palaces and public halls to show them the sights enter by a private side-door not by the official and public entrance. I shall follow even by subterranean passages if I have hopes of arriving some time at the truth.

You say, "What then did I formerly believe myself to be? A man undoubtedly."[1]

Here again suffer me to admire the devices you employ, you who, in order to investigate the certain, employ the doubtful; who in order to bring us into that light bid us plunge into darkness. Do you want me to take heed of what I formerly believed myself to be? Do you wish me to pick up again that clouted coat, old and worn as it is and long since set aside, "I am a man"? Suppose that we were to have among us here Pythagoras or one of his disciples. He might tell you that he had been a barn-door fowl. I don't need to accentuate this objection by instancing madmen, fanatics, or delirious and frenzied people. But you are experienced, an expert guide. You know all the twists and turnings of the argument and I shall keep up heart.

Your next words are, "What is man?"

If you want me to reply, permit me first to ask: which man is it about whom you are enquiring? What do you enquire about when you ask what is man? Do you mean that man which once I falsely fancied I was, which I believed myself to be, and whom, ever since, thanks to you, I made my renunciation, I have affirmed I am not? If it is this man, the man of whom I formed such an erroneous conception, he is a certain compound of soul and body. Have I done enough? I believe so, because you continue as follows.

ANNOTATIONS

I thus begin philosophizing: I am, I think. I am, so long as I think. Note that my critic here admits that the beginning of philosophizing or of the firm establishment of any proposition has been based by me on my knowledge of my own existence. This lets us see that, when in other places he has pretended that I based it on the positive or affirmative renunciation of all doubtful beliefs, he has asserted the contrary of what he really believed. I need not mention further how subtly he introduces me at the commencement of my philosophical labours, with "I am, I think" etc. For even though I say nothing his candour will be in all cases quite apparent.

[1]Cf. Med. II, p. 78.

Why did you mention the mind, when saying "is mentally conceived"? Did you not order the banishment of mind and body? I have already said that it is the word *mind* which supplies him with this puzzle. But *is mentally conceived* means merely *is thought;* hence he is quite wrong in assuming that *mind* is mentioned in so far as it is part of man. Besides, though I had already rejected body and mind with all other things, as being doubtful or not yet clearly perceived by me, this does not prevent me from picking them up again, if I chance to perceive them clearly. But of course my critic cannot grasp this because he thinks that doubt is something inseparable from the objects doubted. For shortly afterwards he asks: *How does it come about that the same things are now not dubious and uncertain?* (meaning the things which formerly were doubtful). He wants me likewise to forswear them with every solemnity, and wonders at my devices, saying I employ the doubtful in order to investigate what is certain; as if I had taken as the foundation of my Philosophy the principle that everything doubtful must be taken to be falsehood.

Do you want me to take heed of what I formerly believed myself to be? Do you wish me to pick up again that clouted coat etc.?[2] Here I shall make use of a very homely example for the purpose of explaining to him the rationale of my procedure, in order that in future he may not misunderstand it or dare to pretend that he does not understand it. Supposing he had a basket of apples and, fearing that some of them were rotten, wanted to take those out lest they might make the rest go wrong, how could he do that? Would he not first turn the whole of the apples out of the basket and look them over one by one, and then having selected those which he saw not to be rotten, place them again in the basket and leave out the others? It is therefore just in the same way that those who have never rightly philosophized have in their mind a variety of opinions some of which they justly fear not to be true, seeing that it was in their earliest years that they began to amass those beliefs. They then try to separate the false from the true lest the presence of the former should produce a general uncertainty about all. Now there is no better way of doing this than to reject all at once together as uncertain or false, and then having inspected each singly and in order, to reinstate only those which they know to be true and indubitable. Thus it

[2]Cf. above, p. 245.

was no bad course to reject everything at the outset, and then, noticing that I knew nothing more certainly and evidently than that in virtue of my thinking I existed, it was not wrong to assert this first. Finally, it was not wrong for me afterwards to ask, who was the person I formerly believed myself to be, not meaning now to adopt exactly the same beliefs, but in order to reinstate any among them that were true, and reject those that were false and reserve such as were doubtful for examination at a future time. Whence it is evident that it is quite silly of our critic to call this the *art of eliciting certainties out of uncertainties* or, as below, *a method of dreaming*.[1] Again all his trivialities here about Pythagoras's barn-door fowls, and what follows in the next two paragraphs about the opinion of others is quite irrelevant. For there was no need, nor was it my wish to recount all the opinions that others have held, but merely to set forth what had naturally and spontaneously occurred to myself or what the popular opinion had been, whether that were true or false, since my purpose in repeating those beliefs was not directed towards securing belief in them but merely concerned their examination.

3. WHAT IS BODY?

You say, "what is body?" "what did I formerly understand by body?"

Do not be vexed if I keep a sharp look-out, if everywhere I am fearful of falling into a snare. Wherefore pray tell me, what body is it about which you ask? That which I once represented in my mind, consisting of definite properties, but of which, I am forced by the law of renunciation to suppose, my conception was erroneous? Or do you have some other sort of body in view, supposing that any other such can exist? How do I know? I am in doubt as to which it is. But if you mean the former kind it is easy for me to reply: By body I understood all that which can be defined by a certain figure, something which can be confined in a certain place, which can fill a given space in such a way that every other body will be excluded from it; which can be perceived by sense, and moved by any other body that comes in contact with it.[2] *This was my belief about body of the former kind. Consequently, I gave the name of body to everything possessing the properties I have recounted in this list. Nevertheless, I did not go on to believe that*

nothing different from that could either be or be called body, especially since it is one thing to say, "I understood by body, this or that," and quite another "I understood nothing but this or that to be body." If it is the second kind of body about which you are enquiring, I shall quote in my reply the opinion of more recent philosophers (since it is not so much my individual opinion you seek to discover as what anyone may chance to believe). By body I understand everything admitting of being circumscribed by a place like a stone. Another property is the capacity of being defined by its place in such a way that the whole of it is in the whole of the place, and the whole is in every part, as is the case of the indivisible parts of quantity, or of a stone, or of similar things, which some of our more recent writers introduce and portray as being indivisible after the fashion of the Angels or of indivisible souls, securing in this a certain amount of applause at least among themselves, as we may see in Oviedo.[3] A further quality is to be extended actually, like a stone, or virtually like the above-mentioned indivisibles. Another is to be divisible into a number of parts, like the stone, or to be incapable of such partition, like the said indivisibles. Yet, again, a body may be moved by another, as a stone that is forced upwards, or by itself, like a stone falling downwards. Once more it can feel, as a dog does, think, as monkeys can, or imagine, like a mule. Anything that I have formerly come across, which was moved either by something else or by itself, which felt, imagined, or thought, I have called a body, unless there was some reason for not doing so, and such things I even now call body.

But this, you say, was wrong and quite erroneous. For I judged that to have the power of self-movement, as also of feeling or thinking, by no means pertained to the nature of body.[4]

You judged? Since you say so, I believe it; thought is free. But while you so thought, you allowed each individual to retain his own opinion freely; and I shall not believe you to be, as you would like, the arbiter of all thoughts, rejecting some and approving others, unless you possess some canon that is certain and handy. But since you have made no mention of this, when you bade us renounce all our former beliefs, I shall take advantage of the liberty that nature has granted us. You formerly judged, and I formerly judged. I judged one thing, you another, and perhaps both of us were wrong. Certainly our judging was not free from doubt, if both of us had at the very

[1]Cf. above, p. 246, below p. 247, and also p. 251.

[2]Cf. Med. II, pp. 78–79.

[3]A Catholic writer on philosophy who published his works in France.

[4]Cf. Med. II. p. 78–79.

outset to divest ourselves of those previous opinions. Wherefore, not to prolong the strife too far, if you wish to define body in your own peculiar way, as in the way first given, I have no objections. I go so far as to admit, as long as I remember your definition, that you have defined not body universally but a certain kind of body which you have grasped in a single conception. But I contend that you have omitted the rest of the things known as body, which according to the opinion of the learned are subject to dispute, or about which nothing certain, at least nothing so certain as you require has been determined, so as to enable us to say whether they are bodies or not. Thus it is doubtful and uncertain whether up to the present we have secured a correct definition of all body. I ask you therefore kindly to proceed and I shall follow with a gladness that is gladness itself; such a power over me does the new and unwonted hope of deriving the certain from the uncertain exercise.

ANNOTATIONS

Feel as a dog does; think as monkeys can; or imagine like a mule. This is designed to introduce a verbal dispute. Desiring to be able to show that I have been wrong in assigning as the differentia between mind and body the fact that the former thought, while the other did not, but is extended, he says that everything which feels, imagines, and thinks receives from him the title body. Well, let him call such objects mules or monkeys if he likes. If he ever succeeds in establishing their acceptation in this sense I shall not refuse to employ the terms. But meanwhile he has no reason for blaming me for using the recognized expressions.

4. WHAT SOUL IS

You say, "What is soul?" "What did I understand by the soul?" And here is your reply. Either I did not perceive what this was or I imagined it to be something extremely rare like a wind, a flame, or an ether, which was spread through my grosser parts. To it, however, I referred nutrition, locomotion, feeling and thought.[1]

That is quite enough. But you will surely allow me to put a question here. When you enquire about the soul, do you ask us to produce our old opinions, the beliefs we formerly held?

You say, "Yes."

But do you think that our opinions were correct, so that this would render your method of no

[1] Cf. Med. II, p. 78.

use? Do you think that no one has wandered so very far in the dark? The truth is that the beliefs of Philosophers about the soul have been so various and so discordant, that I cannot sufficiently admire the skill by which you hope so confidently to extract a wholesome drug of assured use out of such a worthless sediment. Yet we know that the poison of adders will yield us a medicine. Do you then wish me to add to your beliefs about the mind the opinions actual or possible that certain other people may have? You don't want to enquire of me whether these opinions are right or wrong; it is enough if an opinion is such as to entail the holders' thinking that it can be driven out of their mind by no force of reasoning. Now certain of them will say that the soul is a certain kind of body so-called. Why be astonished? This is their opinion and, as they believe, it does not lack some colour of truth. Thus they call it body; but that consists in whatever is extended, has three dimensions, is divisible into determinate parts. Again, to take a particular illustration, they find in, say, a horse, something extended, and divisible, such as flesh, bones, and all that external bodily structure that invades our senses: they therefore conclude, constrained to do so by weight of reasoning, that besides that external structure there is something internal, and that that is indeed of a fine texture, dissolved and extended throughout the bodily frame, tri-dimensional and divisible, so that when the foot is cut off some part of that internal thing also is lost. They believe that the horse is a compound of two extended things, which are tri-dimensional, and divisible. Thus it is a union of two bodies which, as differing from one another, receive distinct names, the one—the external structure—retaining the name of Body, while the other—the internal—is called Soul. Further, as regarding sense, imagination, and thought, they think that the capacity for exercising these functions resides in the soul, or internal body, though they involve a certain relation to the external frame, apart from which there is no sensation. The account varies from writer to writer; so why should I go over them one by one? Among them will be found some who think that all souls are as we have just described them.

You reply—"what impiety! no more of that!"

Yes, it is impious. But why do you ask about it? What do you make of atheists? Of fleshly minded men whose thoughts are always riveted on the dregs of creation, so that they are aware of nothing but body and flesh? Nay, since you wish by your method to establish and demonstrate the incorporeal and spiritual nature of man's soul, you should by no means take that as granted, but

*rather persuade yourself that you will have op-
ponents who will deny this, or who at least for
purposes of disputation will maintain the opinions which I have expounded to you. Wherefore,
pretend that one of these people is present, ready
to reply to your question "what is the soul?" as
you yourself replied before: The soul is something
corporeal, of a fine structure and subtle, spread
throughout the external body, and the principle of
all sensation, imagination, and thought. Thus
there are three grades of being, Body, the Corporeal or soul, and Mind or spirit, as to the nature of which we are enquiring. Wherefore let us
henceforth express these three grades by the three
terms Body, Soul, and Mind. I repeat, let there
be some one to make this reply to your question.
Has he given a sufficient answer? However, I
don't want to anticipate anything belonging to
your method; I shall rather follow. Then you go
on to say—*

ANNOTATIONS

You say, "yes."[1] Here and almost everywhere else my opponent introduces me as
making replies which are quite different from
my real beliefs. But it would be too tedious to
recount all his fabrications.

*Nay, since you wish by your method to estab-
lish and demonstrate the incorporeal and spiritual nature of man's soul, you should by no
means take that as granted.*[2] This is false—to
pretend that I took for granted what I ought
to have proved. To such fabrications, which
are so freely spread abroad and have absolutely nothing to rest on, there is nothing to be replied save that they are false. Nothing at all
about what is to be called body, or soul, or
mind appeared in my discussion. What I did
on the other hand was to explain two things,
viz. that which thinks and that which is extended, to which two I proved that everything
else could be referred. I established also by
reasoning the fact that these two things are
substances really distinct from one another.
One of these substances I called mind, the other
body; and if my critic doesn't like these names
he can invent others, and I shall not mind.

5. A TEST APPLIED TO OUR ENTRY
INTO THE METHOD

*You say, "all is well; the foundations have
been auspiciously laid; I am, so long as I think.
This is certain, this is unshaken. But next I must
erect something upon this and take great care lest*

[1]Cf. p. 247.
[2]Cf. p. 247.

*the evil Spirit impose upon me. I am. But what
am I? Doubtless some one of the opinions I previously held about myself is true. I believed myself to be a man, and that man possesses body and
soul. Am I then a body? Or am I a mind? Body
is extended, bounded in place, impenetrable and
capable of being seen. Have I any of these qualities? Extension? How could it exist in me, seeing there is no such thing to be found? I dismissed
it at the outset. Shall I ascribe to myself the capacity for being touched or being seen? But the
facts are that though I believe I am visible or can
be touched by myself, I am not really seen, not
really touched. This was fixed for me from the
time when I made my renunciation. What then?
I attend, I think, I turn my thoughts round and
round, but nothing turns up. I am tired of going
over the same old round. I find within myself
none of the attributes that attach to body. I am not
a body. I am, nevertheless, and know that I am;
and, while I know that I am, I know nothing belonging to the body. Am I then a mind? What did
I formerly believe to belong to the mind? Is any
attribute of that kind to be found in me? I
thought that it belonged to the mind to think. But
after all, after all I think. Eureka! Eureka! I
have found it. I am, I think. I am, so long as I
think; I am a thinking thing; I am mind, understanding, reason. This is my method, which has
enabled me happily to proceed. Follow comrade!"*

*O lucky man! to emerge from such darkness
practically at one bound into the light. But, I beg
you, give me your hand and steady my tottering
steps, while I stumble along in your footprints.
I should like to follow them exactly but, in proportion to my capacity, rather more slowly. I am,
I think. But what am I? Any of the things that I
formerly believed myself to be? But were my opinions true? That is not certain. I have abandoned
all my old beliefs and treat them as false. I was
wrong to trust them.*

*"Nay, but," you exclaim, "plant yourself
firmly here!" Plant myself firmly? Everything
totters! What if I am something else? "You are
too captious," you say; "you are either a body or
a mind."*

*Be it so, thus! Though, as a fact, I waver.
Kindly take my hand, I scarcely dare to go on.
What, pray, if I am a soul? What if something
else? I cannot tell.*

But, you reply, "exactly; either body or mind."

*Be it so, then. I am either a body or a mind.
Am I not rather a body? Certainly I must be a
body, if I find anything in myself which I formerly believed to belong to body. Yet I fear I was
wrong to hold that belief.*

"Come on," you reply, *"fear nothing!"*

I shall venture, therefore, since you so raise my spirits. I had formerly believed that to think was something pertaining to body. But after all, after all, I think. Eureka! Eureka! I have found it! I am, I think, I am a thinking thing, I am something corporeal, I am extension, something divisible, terms previously devoid of meaning for me. What! do you get angry and let me go on ahead and spurn me with your hand? I have gained the bank and stand on the same shore as you, thanks to you and the renunciation you made.

"But you have no business to be here," you reply.

Why? what have I done wrong?

"It is quite wrong of you to bring up the assertion that you had formerly believed yourself to be something corporeal. What you ought to have believed was that you were something mental."

But why had you not given me warning about this principle? Why, when you saw me all braced up and ready for the complete renunciation of my old beliefs, did you not bid me retain this at least, nay take it from you as a sort of fare, viz. *"to think is something mental"*? But to me is wholly due the credit of getting you to emphasize this declaration in future for your beginners, and carefully to instruct them not to forswear that along with their other principles, with e.g. *"Two and three make five."* Yet I cannot be at all confident that they will manage to follow you. Each man has his own notions and you will find few people to agree with you in that *"ipse dixit"* of yours, as his silent disciples bowed to Pythagoras's opinion. What if some are unwilling? What if some people refuse? if they are recalcitrant? if they remain obstinately attached to their old opinions? what will you do? But not to invoke the aid of your other disciples, I want you to do one thing. When you promise that you will establish by weight of argument that the human soul is not corporeal but wholly spiritual, and if you have proposed as the foundation of your demonstrations, *"to think is a property of the mind, or of a thing that is wholly spiritual and incorporeal,"* will it not look as if your postulate expressed in new words the very statement which was originally the subject of enquiry? As if any person were so stupid, that, believing that *"to think is a property of a thing that is spiritual and incorporeal,"* and knowing at the same time and being conscious that he thought, he could doubt of the existence in him of something spiritual and quite immaterial. (Is there really anyone who needs some person to prompt him to discover that rich vein of thought within himself?) Now, that you may not think that all this is idle assertion on my part, how many people are there, and those serious philosophers, who hold that brutes think and who therefore suppose that thought, while not being an attribute common to all bodies, is an attribute common to extended soul, such as belongs to brutes, and consequently that it is not a property (in the fourth sense) of mind or what is spiritual. What will such philosophers say, pray tell me, when they are asked to set aside this opinion of theirs in order so lightly to assume yours? You yourself, in craving this from us as a postulate, do you ask us to oblige you by conceding this or do you wish us to make a fresh start again? But what is the need for my going on with this discussion? If I have done wrong in going on so far, do you wish me to retrace my steps?

ANNOTATIONS

But what am I? Doubtless some one of the opinions I previously held about myself is true.[1] Here as in countless other places he ascribes a certain opinion to me without the slightest shadow of excuse for doing so.

This was fixed for me from the time when I made my renunciation.[2] Here again he falsely assigns an opinion to me which I do not hold. For I never drew any conclusion from the fact that I had renounced my former belief. On the other hand, I expressed exactly the contrary when I said, "But perhaps it is true that these same things which I supposed were non-existent because they are unknown to me are really not different from the self which I know."[3]

Am I then a mind?[4] It is likewise false that I asked whether I was a mind. For I had not yet explained what I understood by mind. But I enquired whether there existed in me any of the features I was in the practice of attributing to the soul as I had formerly described it. And since I did not find in myself everything which I had referred to it, but thought alone, on that account I did not say that I was a soul, but merely a thinking thing. To this thinking thing I gave the name of mind, or understanding, or reason, and in doing this I had no intention of signifying by the term mind anything more than by the term thinking thing. It was not with that purpose that I exclaimed, "Eureka! Eureka! I have found it"; as he so unfairly and sophistically represents. On the

[1]Cf. p. 248, *sub fin.*
[2]Cf. p. 248.
[3]Cf. Med. II, p. 79.
[4]Cf. above, p. 248.

contrary I added "that the significance of these terms was formerly unknown to me."[1] Thus it cannot be doubted that I meant precisely the same thing by these terms and by the expression "thinking thing."

I was wrong to trust my old beliefs. "Nay," you exclaim. This again is absolutely false. For there I never assumed that my previous beliefs were true. I merely examined them to see if they were true.

I am either body or mind. It is false once more that I ever affirmed this.

It is quite wrong of you to bring up the assertion that you had formerly believed yourself to be something corporeal. What you ought to have believed was that you were something mental. It is false that I bring forward this assertion. My critic may say if he cares that the thing which thinks is better termed body than mind; I shan't gainsay him. But that is a question which he must discuss not with me but with students of language. If, however, he pretends that I have used the term mind to imply anything more than is meant by the term thinking thing, I have my denial ready. As I have again where shortly afterwards he adds: *If you have presupposed the assertion "to think is a property of the mind or of a thing that is wholly spiritual" etc. do you wish me to oblige you by conceding this, or do you wish me to make a fresh start again?* Now I deny that I ever presupposed in any way that the mind was incorporeal. I finally proved this in the sixth Meditation.

But it is very wearisome for me to have to convict my opponent so often of falsification. In future I shall pass it over without notice and shall be a silent spectator right up to the end, while he plays his little game. But surely it is shameful to see a reverend Father so given to the love of quibbling as to make a buffoon of himself, and present himself as captious, dull, and small-witted. Here it is not the Epidicus or Parmeno, the clowns of the ancient comedy, that he tries to imitate, but their modern representative, that very cheap fool who affects to produce laughter by his own *bêtises.*

6. THE ENTRY ATTEMPTED ANEW

"All right," you say, *"so long as you follow closely in my steps."*

Resume then, I implore you; my feet shall not deviate from your tracks a hair's breadth.

"I think," you say.

So do I.

[1]Med. II, p. 79.

"I am," you add, *"so long as I think."*

So it is equally with me.

Your next question is, "But what am I?"

Sagely uttered! For this is what I want to know, and gladly do I say along with you: "But what am I?"

You go on: "Am I what I formerly believed myself to be? What was my previous belief about myself?"

Now don't go on repeating the same words. I have heard them often enough. But, I entreat you, help me. When there is much darkness round my feet I cannot see where to set them.

"Say the words along with me," you reply; *"put your footsteps alongside of mine. What did I formerly believe myself to be?"*

Formerly? Was there ever a former time? Did I formerly believe?

"Wrong!" you reply.

But you, yourself, kindly excuse me, have gone wrong in talking away about "formerly." I renounced all my former beliefs. Even "formerly" has become nothing, is nothing. But what a kind guide you are! You take my hand and lead me!

You say, "I think, I am."

Just so! I think, I am. I have got hold of this securely and this alone. Beyond this one fact there is nothing, has been nothing.

But hurrah! you add; *"what did you formerly believe yourself to be?"*

You want me, I think, to make certain whether I have allotted a fortnight or a whole month to this apprenticeship in renunciation. Really I have given only this brief hour of discussion with you, and with such contention of spirit that the shortness of the time is counterbalanced by the effort required. But I give you a month, a year, if you wish it. Just so! I think, I am. There is nought besides this. I have renounced all.

But you urge me to recollect, to remember.

What is this "recollection"?

True, I now think that formerly I thought. But does the fact that now I think, that formerly I thought, imply that formerly all the time I did think?

Your answer is "Faint heart! you are afraid of a shadow. Pluck up courage. I think."

Poor luckless creature that I am! The darkness gathers round me, and now I am not certain of that "I think," which previously was so clear. I dream I think, I don't think it.

"Nay," you reply, *"he who dreams thinks."*

I see light. To dream is to think, and to think is to dream.

"Not at all," you say. "To think extends more widely than to dream. He who dreams thinks

but he who thinks, does not therefore dream, but thinks in the waking state."

But is that so? Do you dream that or do you think it? What! if you are dreaming when you say that thought is a wider term than dreaming, will it therefore be wider? If you care I shall have no trouble in dreaming that dreaming is wider than thinking. Whence do you have your knowledge that thought is the wider term, if thought does not exist but only dreaming? What will happen if, so often as you thought that you were awake and thinking, you were not awake and thinking, but you dreamed that you were awake and thinking, and consequently the operation is merely the single one of dreaming, which you employ on the one occasion when dreaming that you dream, and on the other, in dreaming that you are awake and thinking. What will you do now? You are silent. Do you want to take my advice? Let us find another ford. This is doubtful and untrustworthy; so much so that I am really surprised that you tried to show me the way across without having made trial of it before. Don't therefore ask me who it was I formerly believed myself to be, but whom I now dream that I formerly dreamed myself to be. This done, I shall reply to you. But lest our discourse be impeded by the use of words proper to people who dream, I shall employ the language of our waking state, provided you remember that "to think" means henceforth merely "to dream" and that nothing more is affirmed in your thoughts than by a dreamer in his dreams. Nay you must designate your method a Method of Dreaming, and this must be the culmination of your art, viz.: He who reasons well dreams. I think this doctrine will go down well, because you proceed as follows.

"What therefore did I formerly believe myself to be?"

Now here is the stone on which I previously stumbled. We must both take care. Wherefore suffer me to ask why you did not premise the statement "I am one of the things that I formerly had believed myself to be," or "I am that which I formerly believed myself to be."

You say there is no need to do so.

Nay, pardon me, there is the greatest need. Otherwise your labour is all in vain in discovering what you formerly believed yourself to be. Indeed, suppose it possible for you not to be what you formerly believed yourself to be, as in Pythagoras's case, but something else. Will it then not be useless for you to ask what you believed yourself formerly to be?

But you say the above statement is one of my old beliefs and has been set aside.

Very true, if indeed everything has been set aside. But what can you do? You must either come to a halt here or make use of it.

"Nay," you say, "we must try again and take another way. So! I am either body or mind. Am I body?"

Pardon me, that is going too far. Whence do you derive that statement "I am either body or mind," now that you have set aside your belief in both body and mind? Nay, what happens if you are neither body nor mind, but soul, or something else? What do I know about it? This is the very question we are investigating, and if I knew the answer, if I were acquainted with it, I should not distress myself so much. Again, I should not like you to think that it was merely the love of trudging around this land of renunciation that brought me here into the midst of its gloom and peril. It is the hope of attaining certainty that alone either attracts me or compels me.

"Let us resume then," you answer. "I am either a body, or something not a body, i.e. incorporeal."

Now you are on another, quite a new track. But are you sure that it is going to lead you aright?

You say it is most trustworthy and entirely necessary.

Why then did you set it aside? Did I not rightly fear that something ought to be retained, and that it was possible you did indulge your incredulity too far? However, so be it. Let this be certain. What next?

"Am I a body?" you go on. "Do I find within myself any of that which I formerly judged to belong to the body?"

But here is another rock of offence. Without any doubt we shall hit against it unless you first grant as a premise this paragon of beliefs "I was right in my former judgment about what pertains to the body"; or "nothing belongs to the body save what I formerly understood to belong to it."

"Wherefore so?" you say.

Precisely because if you omitted anything in your former list of attributes, if your judgment was wrong and, "being human, you repudiate nothing that may well happen to human nature," all your trouble will be superfluous, and you will inevitably be exposed to the dread of being left in the plight of the rustic in the story. For he, on seeing a wolf for the first time and at a great distance, stopped and thus addressed his master, a raw youth whom he was accompanying. "What do I see?" he said. "Without doubt it is an animal; it moves and runs forward. But what sort of animal? Surely one of those that I have seen already. Now what are they? The ox, the horse, the goat and the ass. Is it an ox? No; it doesn't have horns. A horse? No; you could hardly say it has a horse's tail. A goat? But the goat has a beard, this beast none; it isn't a goat. Therefore it must be an ass, since it is neither ox, horse, nor goat." Now don't laugh, but wait for the end of the story. "But come," said his young master, "why don't you make out that it is a horse with as much reason as that it is an ass? See! Is it an ox? No; it doesn't have horns. An ass? Not a bit; I don't see the ears. A goat? No; it has no beard. Then it is a horse." The rustic, somewhat perturbed by this novel analysis, exclaimed: "But it is not an animal at all. Here are the animals I know, the ox, the horse, the goat and the ass. It is not an ox, nor a horse, nor a goat, nor an ass. Therefore" (with great triumph) "it is not an animal, and hence it is non-animal." Here is a stout Philosopher for you, bred not in the Lyceum but in the cow-house! Do you want to err in his company?

"Enough," you say, "I see your point. But the rustic's error lay in thinking (though he did not openly mention it) that he had seen all the animals, or that there was no animal besides those he knew. But what has this to do with the matter we have in hand?"

Well the two cases are as similar as a couple of glasses of milk. Don't pretend. You too keep something suppressed in your mind. Is it not this: "I know everything which has anything to do with or can possibly have anything to do with the body." Or this: "Nothing belongs to the body except what I understood belonged to it formerly"? But if you did not know everything, if you have omitted even one thing; if you have ascribed to the mind anything that really belongs to the body or to something corporeal, e.g. the soul; if you were wrong in separating thought, sense, and imagination from the body or the corporeal soul; if you suspect, I add, that you have erred in one of these points, ought you not to fear the same issue to your argument, and that any conclusion you get may be wrong? Certainly, though you drag me, I shall stick here obstinately and shan't stir a step farther, unless you remove this obstacle.

"Let us go back," you answer, "and try a third avenue of approach. Let us attempt all the entrances, paths, twists and turnings of the method."

Very good, but on the understanding that you will not merely brush by, but remove any doubtful matter that may occur. Come, lead away. I am for complete precision in everything. Proceed.

7. THIRD ATTEMPT TO EFFECT AN ENTRANCE

You say, "I think."

I deny it. You dream that you are thinking.

But you say that this is what you call thinking.

But you are wrong to do so. I call a fig a fig. You are dreaming. This is all you'll get. Go on.

"I am, so long as I think," is your next word.

All right. Since you want to put it so, I shan't object.

But you say this is certain and evident.

I deny it. You merely dream that it is certain and evident.

But you persist, saying that it is at least certain and evident to one who dreams.

I deny it. It merely seems, or appears to be so, it is not really certain.

Against this you urge: "But I don't doubt it. I am conscious of it in myself, and an evil Spirit can't deceive me here, even though he tries hard."

I deny this. You dream that you are conscious in yourself of it, that you don't doubt, and that this is evident. Those two things are very different; viz. "to a dreamer" (and you may add "to one awake" also) "something appears certain and evident," and "to a dreamer" (just as to one who is awake) "something is certain and evident." This is the end of the matter; there is no going beyond it. Hence, let us try another approach, so that we may not waste our lives here dreaming. Though something must be granted; to reap you must sow. But you are quite confident. Proceed. You are getting on.

What you say is: "Whom did I formerly believe myself to be?"

Have you done with that "formerly." There is no road that way. How often have I told you that you were shut off from all your old possessions? You are, so long as you think, and you are certain that you are so long as you think. I enforce the point "so long as you think"; all the past is doubtful and uncertain, the present alone is left you. Yet you persevere. I admire a man whom ill-fortune cannot break.

"There is nothing," you say, "in me who think, who am a thinking thing, nothing, I repeat, belonging to the body or to anything corporeal."

I deny this. Prove it.

You answer: "From the time that I renounced everything, no body, no soul, no mind, in a word, nothing, exists. Therefore if I am, as I am certain that I am, I am not a body nor anything corporeal."

How I admire your warmth and the way you syllogize, referring at each step in the argument to our form of reasoning! Come here, I will show you a quicker way out of these labyrinths, and seeing that you are generous I shall be more so. I deny both your antecedent, your consequent and the necessary connection between the two. Do not be annoyed, pray! My notion is not without warrant. Here are my grounds. I deny the necessary connection, because you might as well prove the opposite, thus "Since I renounced all, neither mind, nor soul, nor body, in a word, nothing exists. Therefore if I am, as I am, I am not a mind." Now here is the flaw, which the sequel will show you plainly. Meanwhile, bethink yourself as to whether it is better to derive the following conclusion henceforth from your antecedent: "Therefore if I am, as I am, I am nothing." Certainly, either the assertion of the antecedent was wrong, or, if it is asserted, it is annulled by the condition brought forward, viz. "If I am." Wherefore I deny that antecedent; "From the time that I renounced all, no body exists, nor soul, nor mind, nor anything else"; and I am quite right in doing so. For while renouncing everything you are either wrong in doing so, or you do not wholly renounce everything; nor can you do the latter, since you yourself who make the renunciation necessarily are. Therefore to make an accurate reply I must say: when you assert Nothing is, no body, no soul, no mind, etc., the alternatives are (1) that you either exclude yourself from that proposition Nothing is, etc., and really mean: Nothing is except myself; which you must necessarily do, in order that your proposition may come into existence and may remain in existence. This is just what the ordinary Logic teaches about such propositions as: "Every proposition written in this book is false"; "I am not telling the truth," with a crowd of similar judgments which always except themselves from the condemnation they pass. Or again (2) according to the other alternative, you include yourself also, and desire to be non-existent while you renounce your old possessions and say: Nothing exists etc. On the former alternative it is impossible to maintain the proposition: "Since I renounced everything, nothing exists etc." For you exist and are something; and necessarily you are either body, or soul, or mind or something else; and so either body or soul or mind or something else exists. On the second alternative you are wrong, and indeed commit a double error. To begin with you attempt the impossible and, though existing, want to cancel your existence; and next you upset that assertion in the consequent when you add: "Therefore if I am, as I am, etc." For how can it come about that you are,

if nothing is? And so long as you affirm that nothing is, how can you affirm that you are? Again if you affirm that you are, don't you destroy the proposition asserted shortly before, viz. "Nothing is etc."? Therefore the antecedent is false, and false also the consequent. But now you renew the conflict.

"While I maintain," you say, "that nothing exists, I am not certain that I am body, soul, mind, or anything else. Nay I am not sure that any other body, soul or mind exists. Therefore, by the law of renunciation which relegates the doubtful to the realm of the false, I shall say and affirm that there is no body, nor soul, nor mind, nor anything else. Therefore if I am, as I am, I am not a body."

That is splendid. But, pray, suffer me to straighten out your statements singly, to weigh them, and balance them. In saying "Nothing is, etc., I am not certain that I am body, soul, mind or anything else." I distinguish the antecedent: "You are not certain that you are determinately a body, determinately a mind, or anything else determinately." Let this antecedent be granted, for it is about this question that you are enquiring. But again we may say you are not certain that you are indeterminately either body, soul, or mind, or anything else; now I deny this antecedent. For you are, and are something and are necessarily either body, or soul, or mind or something else; and you cannot seriously place this in the realm of the doubtful, however much an evil Spirit tempt you to do so. I come now to the consequent: "Therefore by the law of renunciation I shall say that there is no body, no soul, no mind, nor anything else." I make a distinction as to the consequent thus. I shall say: "No body, soul, or mind, or anything else exists determinately." Let the connection between antecedent and consequent be granted. But I may also say: "Neither body, nor soul, nor mind, nor anything else exists indeterminately." Now I deny this consequent. In the same way I draw a distinction as to your ultimate consequent: "Therefore if I am, as I am, I am not a body." Determinately I concede it; indeterminately I deny it. Behold my generosity! I have augmented your statements by adding this triumph of reasoning to their number. But don't despond! Array your line of battle anew! You delight me!

Your next words are: "I know I exist. I ask who that 'I' is whom I know. It is quite certain that the knowledge of this, taken precisely so, does not depend on those things which I do not yet know to exist."

What more? Have you said all you intend to

say? I expected you to state a consequence, as shortly before. Perhaps you feared you would get no better results. This is highly prudent, according to your way of doing things; but I take up the separate points again. You know that you exist. All right. You ask who the you is whom you know. Just so, and I ask the same question along with you, and we have been asking this question for a long time. Knowledge of that which you seek does not depend on those things which you have not yet known to exist. What am I to say? The answer is not yet sufficiently clear; and I don't see quite well where your old dictum comes in. As a matter of fact, if you ask who that you is whom you know, I shall raise the same question too. But why do you ask, if you already know?

You reply: "But I knew that I existed; I don't know who I am."

Excellent! But whence will you discover who that you which exists is, save from what you either knew formerly or some time will know? You will not discover the answer from what you formerly knew. That is teeming with obscurity and has been given up. Therefore your knowledge will come from what you don't yet know, but will know afterwards; and I can't see why you are here so much perturbed.

"I do not yet know," you reply, "that what you mention exists."

Keep up hope; some day you will find out.

But you ask next what you are to do meanwhile.

You will await its discovery, though I shall not allow you to remain long in doubt. I make a distinction as formerly. You do not know who you are determinately and clearly: this I deny. For you know that you are something and necessarily either body or soul or mind or something else. But what then? You will know yourself afterwards clearly and determinately. What will you do now? That single dilemma, Determinately or Indeterminately, will keep you at a standstill a whole century long. Cry for another way, if there is any left. But be daring and don't yet give up the contest. Great and novel enterprises are beset by great and novel difficulties.

You reply that there is one way left, but that if it is blocked by any obstacle or stone of stumbling, your cause is lost. You will retrace your steps and these shores of renunciation will see you wandering thereon no more. You want to know if I wish to explore this route also.

Right, but on the understanding that, since it is the farthest, you may be very sure that it is my last attempt. Go on ahead.

8. THE FOURTH ATTEMPT TO EFFECT AN ENTRANCE— THE PROBLEM GIVEN UP IN DESPAIR

You say, "I am."

I deny it.

You proceed: "I think."

I deny it.

You add: What do you deny?

I deny that you exist, that you think. Well do I know what I did, when I said: "nothing is." It is quite a notable exploit; at one blow I have cut myself adrift from everything. Nothing exists; you do not exist, you do not think.

"But my good sir," you say, "I am certain, I am conscious in myself, this is my consciousness, that I cm, that I think."

Even though you put your hand upon your heart, even though you swear and protest, I shall deny it. Nothing is, you are not, you do not think, you are not conscious in yourself. Here is the obstacle; and I set it before your eyes that you may know it and avoid it. If the proposition, "nothing is," is true, the following also, "you do not exist, you do not think," is necessary. But, as you wish, "Nothing is," is true. Therefore the other, "You do not exist, you do not think," is also true.

"That is being too strict," you contend, you must relax somewhat.

Since you request me to do so, I shall grant your petition, and with great good-will. You are: I allow it. You think: I grant it. You are a thinking thing, you add, "a thinking substance," so much are you given to grandiloquent language. I rejoice, I congratulate you; but no further. Yet you want to go on and you summon up your spirits for the last time.

"I am," you say, "a thinking substance, and know that I, a thinking substance exist, and I have a clear and distinct conception of this thinking substance. Yet I do not know that body exists, nor any of those things which pertain to the concept of corporeal substance. Nay, body does not exist, nor any corporeal thing. I have renounced all that. Therefore the knowledge of the existence of a thinking thing or of an existing thinking thing, does not depend on the knowledge of the existence of body, or of an existing body. Therefore since I exist, and exist as a thinking body, and body does not exist, I am not a body. Therefore I am a mind. These are the things that compel my assent, since there is nothing in them that is not coherent and reasoned to form evident principles according to the laws of Logic."

O swan-like strain! But why didn't you talk like this before? Why did you not clearly and in-

telligibly remove afar off that former renunciation of yours? I have reason to complain of you, seeing you allowed us to wander long here, nay you led me by pathless and impassable places, when you could have brought me to the goal with a single step. I have reason to be wroth and, unless you were my friend, to vent all my spleen upon you, for you have not been so candid and handsome as you used to be; nay you are keeping something entirely to yourself and not going shares in it with me. You are amazed? I shan't detain you long. Here is the source of my complaint. Shortly before, just a few steps back, you asked who that you was whom you knew. Now not only do you know who you are but you have a clear and distinct concept of that. Either you were concealing something, and were pretending ignorance, because you were very cunning; or you have some subterranean code of truth and certainty which you are keeping out of view. Though I prefer, if you point to this hidden source, to be curious rather than cross. Whence, pray tell me, comes that clear and distinct concept of thinking substance? If it is owing to the words employed, to the facts themselves, that it is so clear and evident, I shall ask you again and again to show me that concept, so clear and distinct as it is, if only once, in order that I may fashion myself anew from one glimpse of it, especially since it is practically from it alone that we expect to find out the truth, which is costing us such toil to discover.

"Look," you say, "I knew with certainty that I am, that I think, and that I exist as a thinking substance."

Kindly wait a little till I get myself ready to frame such a difficult concept. I also know and am quite well aware that I exist, that I think and that I, a thinking substance, exist. Proceed now at last, if you please.

"Nay," you say, "the matter is finished. When I thought that I, a thinking substance, existed, I formed a clear and distinct concept of thinking substance."

Goodness, gracious! What a subtle and acute fellow you are! How in a moment you penetrate and traverse everything which is, and everything which is not, which can, and which cannot be! You form a clear and distinct conception of thinking substance, while conceiving clearly and distinctly the existence of thinking substance. Therefore if you know it clearly, as you know it at once (so happy is your talent), that no mountain exists without its valley, will you straightway possess a clear and distinct concept of a mountain without a valley? But, because I am not acquainted with the device by which you achieve this, the new achievement itself does not impress me. Disclose your method, I beg you, and show how it is possible for that concept to be clear and distinct.

Without hesitation you say:—"I clearly and distinctly conceive a thinking substance to exist, and I conceive nothing corporeal, nothing spiritual, nothing else besides, but merely a thinking substance. Therefore that concept of mine of a thinking substance is clear and distinct."

At last I have your answer, and I believe I understand it. That concept of yours is clear because you are quite certain in your knowledge; it is distinct, because you are aware of nothing else. Have I hit the nail on the head? I believe so, for you add:

"That wholly suffices to let me affirm that I, in so far as I know myself, am nothing other than a thinking thing."

Indeed it is quite sufficient; and if I have grasped your meaning clearly, the clear and distinct concept of a thinking substance which you form is due to the fact that it represents to you that a thinking substance exists, no attention being paid to the body, the soul, the mind, or to anything else, but merely to the fact that it exists. Thus you say that you, in so far as you know yourself, are nothing but a thinking substance, but not a body, not a soul, not a mind, nor anything else. Consequently, if you existed precisely to the extent to which you have knowledge of yourself, you would be merely a thinking substance and nothing besides. I fancy you are chuckling and congratulating yourself, and think this unusually long spun out argument of mine is meant to secure delay, to postpone the issue and let me off without attempting to pierce your yet unbroken array. But really I mean something quite different. Do you want me with a single word to shatter all your massed battalions and rend even your reserves, dense and serried as may be their formation? I shall employ not one word but three, and conquer so completely that no survivor will be left to tell the tale.

Here is my first. The argument which reasons from knowledge to existence is not valid. Reflect on this for a fortnight at least, and it will bear fruit. You will have no reason to regret it if you thus cast your eyes on the following table. Thinking substance is that which either understands, or wills, or doubts, or dreams, or imagines, or feels. Thus cognitive acts, like understanding, willing, imagining and feeling, all come under the common notion of thought or perception, or consciousness, and we say that the substance in which they inhere is a thinking thing.

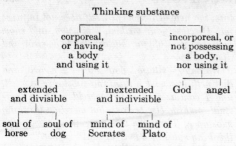

Now for the second. Take those terms—determinately, indeterminately; distinctly, confusedly; explicitly, implicitly. Revolve those too in your mind for a few days. It will be worth your while to apply them one by one, as is proper, to your various pronouncements, to separate and distinguish those opposites from one another. I should not shirk doing this now unless I feared it would prove wearisome. Here is my third objection. The argument that wants too much in its conclusion gets nothing at all. Here then is no time left for meditation. The emergency presses. Come, bethink yourself of your words and see if I come on in the same way. I am a thinking thing, I know that I am a thinking substance, that thinking substance exists and that, nevertheless, I do not yet know that mind exists, nay, no mind exists. Nothing exists, everything has been set aside. Therefore knowledge of the existence of, or of existing thinking substance does not depend on the knowledge of the existence of, or of an existing mind. Therefore since I exist, and exist as a thinking thing, and the mind does not exist, I am not mind; therefore I am body. Well why do you say nothing? Why do you retreat? I have not yet given up all hope. Follow me now. Hurrah! Courage! I bring forward the old formula and method for regulating the reason familiar to all the ancients and (shall I venture?), thoroughly well known to all mankind. Pray bear with me and do not be vexed; I have borne with you. Perhaps that will open a way, as is usual in a situation that is intricate and of which we have despaired. Or certainly, if that does not come off we shall at least, in extricating ourselves, have pointed out the error of your method, if such exists. Here, then, is your matter put in form.

9. THE MATTER SAFELY RECAST IN THE OLD FORM

Nothing which is such that I can doubt whether it exists, actually exists.

Every body is such that I can doubt whether it exists.

Therefore no body actually exists.

Not to raise old issues again, I ask if you do not acknowledge the major premise as your own proposition. The minor must also be yours, if you are to get the conclusion. I resume therefore—

No body actually exists.

Therefore nothing actually existing is a body.

I proceed: Nothing actually existing is a body.

I (I a thinking substance) actually exist.

Therefore I (I a thinking substance) am not a body.

Now your face beams! A new springtime of hope opens in it. My formula favours you, and so does the result which the formula creates. But note my sardonic laughter. Put mind in the place of body and then draw the conclusion with formal correctness, viz. Therefore I (I a thinking substance) am not a mind. Thus—

Nothing which is such that I can doubt whether it actually exists does actually exist.

All mind is such that I can doubt whether it actually exists.

Therefore no mind actually exists.

Nothing actually existing is mind.

I (I a thinking substance) actually exist.

Therefore I (I a thinking substance) am not mind.

What then? The form is correct and valid; it never errs, it never brings a false conclusion unless the premise chance to be false. Therefore, of necessity, any flaw that we judge to exist in the consequent, is not due to the form but to something erroneously stated in the premises. Now really do you think that the assertion to which are due all your subsequent wanderings is properly stated, viz. "Nothing which is such that I can doubt whether it exists or not or is true, actually exists or is true." Is that certain? Are you so familiar with it as to be able to insist upon it confidently and with unembarrassed mind? Tell me, pray, why you deny the statement "I have a body"? Doubtless because it seems to you doubtful. But is this also not doubtful, viz. "I do not have a body"? Is there anyone likely to take as the foundation of his whole science and doctrine, and especially of a doctrine which he wishes to impose on others as the controlling power of their thought, a statement which he would be prudent to deem false? But enough. This is the end at last, the term of our wanderings; I hope for nothing in the future. Therefore, to your question "Whether the renunciation of everything doubtful is a good method of philosophizing," I reply as you expect, frankly and openly, and without mincing matters.

ANNOTATIONS

Up to the present our Reverend Father has been jesting. And because in the sequel he seems to be in earnest and to want to assume a quite different character, I shall in the meantime briefly jot down anything among his jests that has struck me.

These words of his: *Formerly? Was there ever a former time? I dream I think, I don't think it,*[1] and the like are humorous sallies worthy of the character he has assumed. So, too, with the serious question: *Can to think extend more widely than to dream?*[2] and the said argument *About the method of dreaming*, and the consequence that, *He who reasons well dreams.*[3] But I don't think that I ever gave the least provocation for these jibes, because I expressly pointed out when talking of the things I renounced, that I did not affirm that they existed, but that they seemed. Consequently in asking what I had thought myself formerly to be, my question was directed to discover merely what it then seemed to me I had formerly thought. And when I said that I thought, I did not inquire whether I was awake or asleep when I thought. I am surprised that he calls my method a Method of Dreaming when it seems to have roused him into a sufficiently wide awake condition.

Likewise, the reasoning suits his assumed character well enough when, in order that I may discover what I previously thought I was, he wishes me to state the following premiss: *I am some one of the things which I formerly believed myself to be*, or: *I am that which I formerly believed myself to be.*[4] Shortly afterwards, for the purpose of inquiring whether I am a body, he wants me to premise this wonderful proposition: *I was right formerly in my judgment about what pertains to the body*, or: *Nothing belongs to the body save what I formerly understood to belong to it.*[5] For statements which are manifestly contrary to reason, are designed to provoke laughter. It is manifest that I could have asked with quite useful results what I had formerly believed myself to be, and whether I was a body, although I did not know whether I was any of the things that I had formerly believed myself to be, and although my opinion had not been correct, in order that I might examine that very question by the help of what I was then going to perceive for the first time; and, if nothing else, I should at least discover that in that direction no further progress was possible.

My critic again plays his part excellently in his tale about the rustic. But in this there is nothing more ridiculous than the fact that, when he thinks that it is an application of my words, it applies only to his own position. For directly afterwards he finds fault with me for not presupposing this dictum: *I was right formerly in my judgment about what pertains to the body*, or: *Nothing pertains to the body save what I formerly understood to belong to it*. But now he takes this very statement about the omission of which by me he complains, and which is wholly evolved from his own imagination, and criticizes it as though it were mine, likening it to the absurd reasoning of the rustic in his fable. But nowhere, because I presuppose that my former judgment about the nature of body was correct, have I denied that the thing which thinks is a body; it was because I used the term body to signify only a thing of which I had sufficient knowledge, to wit, extended substance, and I recognised that what thinks is distinct from this.

The *jeux d'esprit* which have already appeared rather often and are found here, e.g. you say, "I think." I deny it, you are dreaming,[6] etc. "It is certain," you add, "and evident." I deny it, you are dreaming; it merely seems or appears to be so, it is not really certain,[7] etc., are in this respect at least funny, that if the arguments were intended to be serious, they would be so silly. But lest beginners should chance to go wrong here, and think that to one who doubts whether he is awake or dreaming nothing else can be certain and evident, but that everything must only seem or appear to be, I should like them to recall what was above remarked (at F),[8] viz. that what is clearly perceived, no matter by whom it is perceived, is true and does not merely seem or appear to be true. Yet there are very few who rightly distinguish between that which is really perceived and that which they fancy they perceive, because but few are accustomed to clear and distinct perceptions.

Up to this point our Actor has displayed to us no memorable spectacle of battle; he has merely interposed some slight barriers and after brandishing his weapons there for a time he speedily sounds the retreat and betakes himself to some other part of the field. But here[9] for the first time he begins a mighty con-

---

[1]Cf. p. 250.
[2]Cf. p. 250.
[3]Cf. p. 251.
[4]Cf. p. 251.
[5]Cf. p. 251.

[6]Cf. p. 252.
[7]Cf. p. 252.
[8]Cf. p. 238. F is a section mark in the Latin edition not reproduced in this translation.
[9]Cf. pp. 252–253.

flict with an enemy quite worthy of his stage, viz. with a shade of me, visible indeed to none else, but educed from his own brain. Lest it should not appear sufficiently unreal, he has actually gone to the fountain head of the Non-existent itself in order to derive matter for its composition. But he takes the combat serious-ly; he argues, gets warm, makes truce, calls in Logic to his help, renews the fight, scrutinizes my statements one by one, weighs them, bal-ances them. But fearing to take the blows of his valiant assailant on his shield, he shuns them also with his body. Soon he begins to make distinctions and, creating a diversion by means of his *Determinately and Indeterminate-ly*,[1] he escapes by flight. Really that makes a most entertaining spectacle; especially if the cause of such a mighty quarrel is known. Well, here it is:—He chanced to read in my writings that any true opinions we have before we philosophize seriously are mixed up with so many others that are either false or at least doubtful, that hence in order to separate them from the rest it is best to reject all alike to begin with, or to refuse not to renounce them all, so that it may be possible afterwards more conveniently to distinguish those that were true all the time, or to discover new truths, and to admit nothing but what is true. Now this is just the same as if I had said that in order to prevent there being any rotten apples among those of which our tub or basket is full, we should begin by turning them all out, and then fill up once more either by putting back again those in which there is no flaw or getting similarly sound ones from elsewhere. But my critic, not grasping such a profound specula-tion, or at any rate pretending that he does not grasp it, expresses astonishment especially because I said "Nothing is not to be re-nounced"; and after meditating long and deep-ly on that *Nothing* he has so got it on the brain that, though now his arguments tell against himself, he cannot easily shake himself free of the notion.

After this successful combat, elated with his belief in his victory he assails a new enemy, and once more believes that this is some shade of me, for what he opposes is always of that self-same phantasy. Now however he con-structs it out of new materials, viz. out of the words: *I know that I exist; I ask who I am, etc.*[2] And because he is not so familiar with this semblance of me as with the preceding, he

[1]Cf. p. 253.
[2]Cf. p. 253.

attacks more cautiously and merely skirm-ishes. The first missile he directs against me is: *Why do you ask, if you already know?*[3] But be-cause he imagines that his opponent will ward it off with the reply, *I know that I am, not who I am*,[4] he immediately hurls this more potent weapon: *Whence do you derive the knowledge who you are unless from what you either formerly knew, or some time will know? But not from what you formerly knew; that is teeming with obscurity and has been given up. Therefore your knowledge will come from what you don't yet know but will know afterwards.*[5] Believing that the luckless shade is much put out and almost brought to earth by this blow, he imagines he hears it ex-claim: *I do not yet know that what you mention exists.* Then, changing his wrath to pity he consoles it with these words: *Keep up hope; some day you will find out.*[6] Next he makes the shade reply to this in a querulous and suppli-cating tone with: *What shall I do meanwhile?* But in an imperious voice as becomes a con-queror he cries, "*You will await its discovery.*" Howsoever, being pitiful, he does not allow me to be long in doubt, but flying once more to the side issue: *Determinately, Indeterminately; clearly, confusedly,* and seeing no one following him there secures a lonely triumph. Now cer-tainly all these jests are excellent examples of that fooling which depends upon the unlooked for simulation of stupidity on the part of a man whose looks and garb gave promise of wisdom and seriousness. But, to let this ap-pear more clearly, we ought to consider our Actor friend as a serious and learned man, who, in order to attack our Method of investigating truth, which bids us reject everything as un-certain and, beginning with the knowledge of our own existence, thence proceeds to the examination of our nature, i.e. of that thing which we already know to exist, tries to prove that there is no approach this way to that further knowledge, and employs the following argument: *Since you know only that you exist, but not who you are, you cannot learn this from what you formerly knew, since you have renounced everything; then what you learn must come from what you do not yet know.* But to this even a three years' child could reply that nothing prevents him learning from what he once knew, because though he has set that aside on account of its being doubtful, he may after-

[3]Cf. pp. 253–254.
[4]Cf. p. 254.
[5]Cf. p. 254.
[6]Cf. p. 254.

wards adopt it again, when he has had proof of its truth; and besides, though it were conceded that nothing can be learned from former knowledge, yet at least another way lies perfectly open, viz. that with which he is not yet familiar, but which study and observation will make plain. But here my friend constructs for himself a pretended opponent, who not only admits that the former road is closed, but himself shuts the second with the dictum: *I do not know that the things you mention exist*. This is as if no new knowledge of existence could be acquired and the absence of this precluded all acquaintance with the essential nature of things. But this is surely the stupidest notion possible. Still it contains an allusion to my words, for I wrote that the knowledge I have of a thing which I know to exist cannot depend on the knowledge of what I do not yet know to exist.[1] He, however, ridiculously transfers this, which I enunciated merely about the present, to the future, in the same way as if he were to conclude that because we cannot yet behold those who are not yet born, but will be born this year, we shall never be able to see them. For surely it is highly evident that the knowledge we now possess of a thing which is known as existing, does not depend upon the knowledge of that which is not yet known as existing. For the very reason that if anything is perceived as belonging to something that exists, of necessity it also is perceived to exist. But with the future the case is quite different, because nothing prevents my knowledge of a thing which I know to exist being increased by other facts which I do not yet know to exist, but shall finally learn just when I perceive them to pertain to that thing. My critic however proceeds to say, *Keep up hope; some day you will find out;* and next, *I shan't allow you to remain long in doubt*. Now by these words he bids us expect either that by the way proposed it is impossible to arrive at any further knowledge; or certainly, if he suppose that his opponent has closed that route against him (which, however, would be foolish), that he will open another. But all that he adds is: *You know who you are indeterminately and confusedly, not determinately and clearly*. Now the most natural inference to draw from these words is that there is a way to further knowledge open to us, because by meditation and observation we are able to bring about a change from mere indeterminateness and confusedness in our knowledge to clearness and determinateness.

[1]Cf. Med. ii, p. 79.

Nevertheless he thus concludes, the words *Determinately, indeterminately, furnish a dilemma that will keep us at a standstill a whole century long,*[2] and consequently we must look out for some new route. To me it seems that he could have devised nothing better calculated to simulate an appearance of foolishness and weakness on the part of his own understanding.

You say, "I am,"—I deny it. You proceed: "I think." I deny it, etc. Here he returns once more to do battle with the former shade, and thinking that he has felled it to the ground at the first assault, he boastfully exclaims: *It is quite a notable exploit, at one blow I have cut myself adrift from everything*. But seeing that this shadow takes its origin from his own brain and cannot perish unless he die along with it, even though felled to the ground, it revives. It puts its hand to its heart, and swears that it is, that it exists. My critic, softened by this new style of entreaty, graciously permits it to live, to collect its spirits for the last time and give vent to much futile babble. This he does not refute, but on the contrary gets on friendly terms with it and passes on to other pleasantries.

He begins by scolding it in the following words: *Shortly before, just a few steps back, you asked what you were: Now not only do you know who you are, but you have a clear and distinct concept of that*.[3] Next he asks *to be shown that concept, so clear and distinct as it is, in order that he may fashion himself anew from one glimpse of it*. Then he pretends that it is disclosed to him in the following words: *I certainly know that I am, that I think, that I exist as a thinking substance. The matter is finished*.[4] That this is not adequate he proves by the following example: *you know also that no mountain exists without a valley, therefore you have a clear and distinct concept of a mountain without a valley*.[5] He interprets this in the following way: *That concept of yours is clear because you are quite certain in your knowledge; it is distinct because you are aware of nothing else. —And thus the clear and distinct concept that you form is due to the fact that it represents to you that a thinking substance exists, no attention being paid to the body, the soul, the mind, or to anything else, but merely to the fact that it exists*. Finally he resumes the military frame of mind and imagines he sees these *massed battalions*

[2]Cf. above, p. 254.
[3]Cf. p. 255.
[4]Cf. p. 255.
[5]Cf. p. 255.

and reserves in dense and serried formation, which our new Alexander will shatter with a breath,

As the winds scatter the leaves or tufts of thatch,[1]

and so *no survivor will be left to tell the tale.* With his first breath he utters the following words: *The argument which reasons from knowledge to existence is not valid.*[2] At the same time he flourishes like a standard a table in which he has given a description of thinking substance according to his own pleasure. With his second breath the following comes out: *Determinately, indeterminately. Distinctly, confusedly. Explicitly, implicitly.* In the third place we have: *The argument that wants too much in its conclusion gets nothing at all.* Finally here in his last deliverance: *I know that I exist as a thinking substance, and nevertheless I do not yet know that the mind exists. Therefore the knowledge of my existence does not depend upon my knowledge of existing mind. Therefore since I am, and the mind does not exist, I am not a mind. Therefore I am a body.*[3] On hearing this the shade keeps silence, retreats, gives up hope and allows him to lead it captive in triumph. Here I could point out much that is worthy of undying laughter, but I prefer to spare my Actor-friend's cloth; indeed I believe that it hardly becomes me myself to keep up mirth long about such trifles. Wherefore here I shall note only such matters as perhaps some people might believe I admitted (though they are remote from the truth), if I said nothing at all about them.

First of all I deny that he has any right to complain, alleging that I said I had a clear and distinct concept of myself before I had sufficiently explained how that is attained, seeing that, to use his words, *I had asked who I was just a few steps back.* For between these two points I recounted all the properties of a thing which thinks, viz. intelligence, will, imagination, memory, and feeling, etc., as well as all the other properties popularly remarked which do not belong to its concept, in order that I might distinguish the one set from the other. Now this could not be hoped for except upon the removal of our prejudices. Yet I admit that people who do not divest themselves of their prejudices can with difficulty ever attain to a clear and distinct idea of anything. For it is manifest that those concepts which we pos-

sessed in childhood were not clear and distinct; and that hence, unless they are deposed from their place, they will render obscure and confused any that we subsequently acquire. Therefore when he wishes to be shown *that clear and distinct concept in order that he may fashion himself anew by seeing it,*[4] he is trifling; as also when he introduces me as revealing it to him in the words: *I certainly know that I am,* etc. But when he wishes to refute that trifling account of the matter by the following example: *You also know with certainty that no mountain exists without a valley; therefore you have a clear and distinct concept of a mountain without a valley,* he deceives himself with a fallacy. For from the preceding words he can only conclude: *Therefore you clearly and distinctly perceive that no mountain exists without a valley,* but not: *you have a concept of a mountain without a valley.* For since no such concept exists we do not need to possess it, in order to perceive that there is no mountain without a valley. But, forsooth; he *has such a happy talent,* that he is unable to refute the very futilities he has constructed without employing fresh ones.

When afterwards he says that *I conceive thinking substance, but conceive nothing corporeal, nothing spiritual,* etc. I admit this so far as corporeal substance is concerned, because I had previously explained what I meant by the term body or corporeal; viz. what is extended, or in the concept of which extension is contained. But it is most stupid of him to say what he does in the next words about spiritual substance; and so it is in many other places, where he represents me as saying: *I am a thinking thing, but not body, not soul, not mind,*[5] etc. For I can deny of a thinking thing only those matters in whose concept I find no thought contained; but that this holds with the soul or with the mind I have never maintained in my writings or thought.

Again, when afterwards he says that *he understands my meaning, and that I think my concept is clear because I am quite certain in my knowledge, and that it is distinct because I am aware of nothing else,* he pretends to be very slow of apprehension. For to perceive clearly is one thing, to know with certainty another; for we now know many things with certainty not only by means of faith which is the gift of God, but also because we have perceived them clearly before, and yet we do not at the present

[1]Plautus, *Mil.* I, 1, 17.
[2]Cf. p. 255.
[3]Cf. p. 256.

[4]Cf. p. 255.
[5]Cf. p. 255.

clearly perceive them. Moreover, the knowledge of other things by no means prevents our cognition of any particular thing from being distinct. I have never given the least occasion in my writings for such absurd inferences.

Besides, his dictum: *The argument which reasons from knowledge to existence is not valid*,[1] is plainly false. For although from the fact that we know the essence of any particular thing, it does not follow that it exists; nor from the fact that we think that we know a thing does it follow that that is, if there is a possibility of our being deceived: nevertheless the argument from knowledge to existence is quite valid, because it is impossible to know anything, unless it really is as we know it. We either know it as existent if we perceive it to exist, or as of this or that nature, if only its nature is known to us.

It is likewise false, or at least affirmed by him without the least reason, *that some thinking substance is divisible*,[2] as he has it in that table in which he brings forward the diverse species of thinking substance, as though instructed by an oracle. For we cannot at all understand extension or divisibility on the part of thought, and it is quite absurd to affirm as true with a single word what has neither been revealed by God, nor is grasped by the intellect. Here I cannot conceal my opinion that his doctrine of the divisibility of thinking substance seems to me very dangerous and quite opposed to the Christian religion. For as long as anyone admits it, he will never by force of reasoning acknowledge the real distinctness between the human soul and the body.

The words *Determinately, indeterminately; Distinctly, confusedly; Explicitly, implicitly*, standing alone, as they do here, have no meaning at all. They seem to be merely pretences employed by my Critic when he wishes to persuade his pupils, though he has nothing valuable to say, that he has, nevertheless, much that is valuable in his thought.

Likewise his other dictum: *The argument which wants too much in its conclusion gets nothing at all*, ought not to be admitted without drawing a distinction. For if by the expression *too much* is meant only something in excess of what was sought, as when beneath[3] he objects to the arguments by which I have demonstrated the existence of God, because he thinks that their conclusion contains more than the laws of prudence require, or any mortal demands, his contention is false and absurd; because the more there is in the conclusion, so long as it is rightly inferred, the better is it, and no laws of prudence can ever be opposed to this. But if by the expression *too much* he means not simply something more than was sought, but something incontrovertibly false, then indeed what he says is true. But the Reverend Father makes a great mistake in attempting to foist anything like this on me. For when I wrote: "The knowledge of the things which I know to exist, does not depend on the knowledge of the things which I do not yet know to exist; and yet I know that a thing which thinks exists, and do not as yet know that body exists; therefore the knowledge of a thing which thinks does not depend on the knowledge of the body,"[4] I inferred nothing excessive and nothing incorrect. But when he assumes the statement: *I know that a thinking thing exists, and I do not yet know that mind exists; nay, no mind exists, nothing exists, everything has been renounced*, he assumes something quite nonsensical and false. For I cannot affirm or deny anything of mind, unless I know what I understand by the term *mind;* and I can understand none of the things which that term customarily signifies in which thought is not contained. Thus it is a contradiction for anyone to know that a thinking thing exists and not to know that mind or some part at least of what is signified by the term mind, exists. The words that my critic puts at the end: *Nay, no mind exists, nothing exists, everything has been renounced*, is so absurd as not to deserve any answer. For since subsequently to our renunciation we have acknowledged the existence of a thing which thinks, the acknowledgment of the existence of mind goes along with that (at least in so far as this is the term that stands for a thing which thinks); consequently we have no longer renounced it.

Finally, when he commences his application of formal syllogism to the argument and lauds that as *a method of regulating the reason*[5] opposed to mine, he apparently wishes to prove that I do not favour the syllogistic forms, and that hence the Method I possess is highly irrational. But this is false, as is clear enough from my writings, in which I have nowhere refused to employ syllogisms when the situation demanded such treatment.

Here he brings forward a syllogism constructed out of false premises, which he asserts

---

[1] Cf. p. 255.
[2] Cf. p. 255.
[3] Cf. Reply 4, p. 265.
[4] Cf. Med. ii, p. 79.
[5] Cf. above, p. 256.

to be mine but which I deny time and again. For as to the major: *nothing which is such that we can doubt whether it exists, actually exists*, it is so absurd that I have no fear of his being able to persuade others that I am its author, unless he finds people whom he can at the same time persuade that I am not of sound mind. Nor can I sufficiently admire the sage counsel, the faith, the hope and the confidence with which he has undertaken this. Thus in the first Meditation, in which I was concerned not with the establishment of any truth, but only with the removal of prejudices, after showing that those opinions in which I had been accustomed to place the highest confidence could be considered as doubtful, and that hence I must withhold assent from them no less than from what was openly false, lest I might meet with any impediment in my search for truth, I added these words: "But it is not yet sufficient to have noticed this; I must take care to bear it in mind. For our customary *opinions* keep continually coming back and, almost against my will, seize on my credulity, which is, as it were, enslaved to them by long usage and the law of familiarity. Nor shall I ever get out of the habit of assenting to and trusting them, so long as I assume them to be such as they really are, viz. *in some sense* indeed *doubtful*, as he has already been shown, but none the less very probable, and such that it is much more reasonable to believe them than to deny them. Wherefore I imagine I shall not act amiss if *I change my attitude to its complete contrary* and, deceiving myself, *pretend* for a time that *they are altogether false and imaginary*, until at length I shall as it were equally balance the weight of my respective prejudices, and my judgment will no longer be dominated by bad usage or turned away from the right knowledge of the truth."[1] Out of this passage our Author has chosen the following words, neglecting the others: "*opinions in some sense doubtful*," "*change my attitude to its complete contrary*," and "*pretend that they are in some sense doubtful*." Besides, in place of the word *pretend* he has substituted *affirm, believe, and shall so believe as to affirm as true the contrary of that which is doubtful*. He has tried to make out that this is as it were a dictum or an absolute rule which I always used, not for the purpose of getting rid of prejudices, but for laying the foundation of the most certain and accurate metaphysics. Firstly, nevertheless, he has brought this forward only with hesitation

[1]Cf. Med. i, p. 77.

and surreptitiously, viz. in pars. 2 and 3 of his first Question.[2] Nay, in that third paragraph, after assuming that according to my rule he ought to believe that 2 and 3 do not make 5 he asks *whether he should therefore so believe that, as to persuade himself that it cannot be otherwise.*[3] After several feints and some superfluous talk he introduces me as thus finally replying to this absurdest of all questions: *you will neither affirm nor deny; you will employ neither, and will treat both as false.*[4] Now these words, attributed to me by himself, show clearly that he knew quite well that I did not believe as true the contrary of what is doubtful, and that according to my opinion no one could use that as the major premise of a syllogism from which a certain conclusion is to be expected. For the two things are contradictory, viz. neither to affirm nor deny, *i.e.* to employ neither, and the affirmation and use of one of them as true. But gradually he forgets those things that he had related as being my assertions, and not only affirms the opposite but insists upon it so often, that this forms practically the unique object of his attack throughout the whole of his dissertation; all the twelve errors which, from this point onwards to the end he makes out to have been committed by me, are constructed by him out of this alone.

This forces me to the conclusion that both here where he affirms as my belief this major premise: *nothing which is such that I can doubt whether it exists actually exists*, and in all other passages where he attributes to me anything of the kind, it is clearly proved that, unless I am quite ignorant of the meaning of the verb *to lie*, he is lying without excuse or speaking contrary to his mind and conscience. And although I am very unwilling to use such a discourteous word, yet the defence of the truth which I have undertaken requires this of me, and thus I shall not refuse to call by its proper name what he does not blush to do so openly. And since in the whole of this treatise he does little else than try and persuade the reader of, and enforce upon him, this identical foolish falsehood expressed in an immense variety of ways, I fail to see any other excuse for him than that perhaps he has so often repeated the same thing, that gradually he has persuaded himself that it is true and no longer recognizes it as a fabrication of his own. Next as to the minor premise: *Every body is such that I can*

[2]Cf. pp. 236–237.
[3]Cf. p. 236.
[4]Cf. p. 237.

doubt whether it exists, or[1]: *Every mind is such that I can doubt whether it exists;*[2] if this is understood to apply to any time whatsoever indefinitely, as it must be understood if it is to yield him his conclusion, it is also false and I decline to own it. For immediately after the beginning of the second Meditation, when I said with certainty that there existed a thinking thing, which in popular usage is called *mind*, I could no longer doubt that mind existed. Similarly after the sixth Meditation, in which I ascertained that the body existed, I could no longer doubt its existence. What a colossal intellect our author has! He has with supreme art devised two false premises such that a false conclusion follows from them in good form! But I don't understand why he here ascribes *sardonic laughter* to me, since in his Dissertation I found merely a source of pleasure, not indeed of an intense kind, but quite real and genuine. The reason is that, in criticizing so many things for which I am not responsible but which are fictitiously ascribed to me, he clearly shows that he has left no stone unturned, in order to find something meriting censure in my writings and has found nothing at all.

But certainly it is made sufficiently clear that the humour he has shown up to this time has not been heartfelt, both by the serious onslaught with which he concludes this section, and especially by the succeeding replies, in which he is not only gloomy and severe, but even quite cruel. To account for this we must note various things. To begin with he has no cause for hatred and has found nothing to censure except that single absurdity which with such prudence and insight he foisted on me, and which a little before I could only characterize as being a lie. Yet he thinks that he has now completely convinced the reader that I believe that. (True this cannot be by force of reasoning, since reasons he has none. But, in the first place, he relies on his admirable assurance in affirmation, which, in a man who makes a peculiar profession of piety and Christian charity, is never deemed capable of being exercised in support of a falsehood to so colossal, so shameless an extent. Secondly, he employs a pertinacious and reiterated repetition of the same assertion, and this often brings it about that the custom of hearing what we know to be false produces the habit of believing those things to be true. These two

devices, then, are wont to have more influence than all the weight of argument among the vulgar and all who do not examine things carefully.) So now he haughtily insults the man he has vanquished, and scolds me as a solemn pedagogue might lecture his pupil, and in the following heated replies holds me guilty of sins more in number than the ten commandments. But we must excuse the Reverend Father, as he seems to be no longer master of himself. Just as people who have drunk too much are wont to see two objects instead of one, so he in excess of charitable zeal, finds in a single statement of his own fashioned contrary to his mind and conscience, twelve charges to make against me. These I ought to style nothing but abuse and calumny were I not ashamed here to speak openly and without disguising my words. But, believing that now it is my turn to jest, I shall call them hallucinations merely, and beg the Reader to remember that there is not the least word in his criticisms of me which follow in which he has not been suffering from delusion.

REPLY[3]

Reply 1. *The Method is faulty in its principles. They are both non-existent and infinite. Other systems, in order to evolve the certain from the certain, do indeed posit clear, evident, and innate principles, e.g. The whole is greater than its part; out of nothing, nothing comes, and a great variety of this type, on which they rely when mounting upwards and pressing onwards safely to the truth. But this method proceeds on other lines and in its attempt to get something, not out of something else but out of nothing, cuts off, renounces and forswears its principles one and all; it changes our attitude towards them completely, but lest in its flight it should seem to have no wings to propel it, it assumes new ones, which like Icarus it fixes on with wax, and posits novel principles wholly contrary to our old beliefs. It drops its old prejudices only to adopt new ones; it lays aside certainties in order to assume what is doubtful. Wings it has, but waxen; it soars aloft only to fall. It labours to construct something out of nothing and ends in achieving nothing at all.*

Reply 2. *The Method is faulty in respect of the means it employs. It has none, forsooth, though at the same time it takes away our previous instruments; nor does it bring any to occupy their place. Other systems have logical formulae and syllogisms and sure methods of reasoning, by following which, like Ariadne's clue,*

[1]Cf. p. 256.
[2]Cf. p. 256, §9.
[3]Reply to the Second Question, cf. p. 240.

they find their way out of labyrinths and easily and safely unravel matters that are intricate. But this new method on the contrary disfigures the old formula, while at the same time it grows pale at a new danger, threatened by an evil Spirit of its invention, dreads that it is dreaming, doubts whether it is in a delirium. Offer it a syllogism; it is scared, at the major, whatsoever that may be. "Perhaps," it says, "that Spirit deceives me." The minor? It will grow alarmed and say it is doubtful. "What if I dream? How often have not things appeared certain and clear to a dreamer which, after the dream is over, have turned out to be false?" What finally will the method say as to the conclusion? It will shun all alike as though they were traps and snares. "Do not delirious people, children, and madmen believe that they reason excellently, though wanting anything like sense and judgment? What if the same thing has happened to me? What if that evil Spirit casts dust into my eyes? He is evil, and I do not yet know that God exists and is able to restrain that deceiver." What will you do here? What is to be done, when that method will declare, and obstinately maintain, that the necessity of the conclusion is doubtful, unless you first know with certainty that you are neither dreaming nor crazy, but that God exists, is truthful, and has put that evil Spirit under restraint? What is to be done when the method will repudiate both the matter and the form of this syllogism?—"It is the same thing to say that something is contained in the concept or nature of some matter and to say that it is true of that matter. Yet existence, etc." What about other things of this kind? If you urge them, he will say: "Wait until I know that God exists and till I see that evil Spirit in bonds." But you will reply: "This has at least the advantage that, though it brings forward no syllogisms, it safely avoids all fallacies." That is capital; to prevent the child from having catarrh we shall remove its nose! Could other mothers have a better way of wiping their children's noses? This leaves me therefore just one thing to say, viz. "If you take away all form nothing remains but the formless, the hideous."

Reply 3. The Method has a flaw at the finish, for it attains no certainty. But certainty it cannot attain, while it itself closes against itself all the avenues to truth. You yourself have seen and experienced this in those Ulyssean wanderings in which you have wearied both yourself and me your comrade. You contended that you were a mind, and possessed a mind. But you were not able to prove that at all, and stuck in quagmires and thickets, and indeed did so so often that I can scarcely recall the number of times. Yet it will be advantageous to tell them over again in order to give its proper strength and substance to this reply of mine. Here, then, are the chief heads of the suicidal procedure of the Method, of the way in which it cuts itself off from all hope of attaining to the light of truth. 1. You know not whether you are dreaming or waking, and ought not to give more credence to your thoughts and reasonings (if you really possess any, and do not merely dream that you possess them) than a dreamer puts in his. Hence, everything is doubtful and uncertain and your very conclusions are insecure. I shall not adduce examples; go yourself and review the treasures of your memory and produce anything which is not infected with that taint. I shall congratulate you if you do so. 2. Before I know that God exists to restrain the evil Spirit, I ought to doubt everything and hold everything as altogether suspect. Or certainly, to follow the common philosophy and old method of reasoning, before everything it must be determined whether there are, and what are, these really safe propositions, and we must instruct beginners to keep them in mind. Hence, just as in the former case, all are doubtful and wholly useless for the purpose of investigating the truth. 3. If there is anything that has the least doubt, change completely your attitude towards it and believe it to be false. Nay, believe the opposite and employ it as a principle. Hence I have shut up all avenues to the truth. For what do you hope from this: "I have not a head; there is no body, no mind," and a thousand other such statements? Do not say that your renunciation has not been made in perpetuity, but is like a public vacation which has been instituted for a particular time, a month, or a fortnight, in order that everyone may give the more heed to its observance. For let it be so, let the renunciation be only temporary; yet it is at that time that you are in quest of the truth, it is then that you use, nay misuse, what you renounce, just as though the whole truth depended on that, and consisted in that as in something fixed and stable. "But," you say, "I employ this renunciation in order to make steady pedestal and column, as architects are wont to do. Do they not construct a temporary scaffolding and use it to hoist the column and establish it finally in its place, and then after this has discharged its function admirably break it up and take it away? Why not imitate them?" Imitate away, so far as I am concerned, but look out lest your pedestal and column lean so much upon your temporary scaffolding that they will fall if you remove it. It is this that seems to merit censure in your Method. It repose on false foundations, and it leans upon them so much that if they are removed it itself falls to the ground.

Reply 4. *The Method errs by going too far.* That is to say, it contrives to accomplish more than the laws of prudence require of it, more than any mortal demands. Some people indeed seek for a demonstration of the existence of God and of the immortality of the human mind. But certainly no one has hitherto been found who has not thought that it is enough, if he knows that God exists, and that the world is governed by him, and that the souls of men are spiritual and immortal, with as much certainty as the statement that 2 and 3 make 5, or "I have a head," "I have a body"; and so have made anxiety about seeking for a higher truth superfluous. Besides, just as in the practical life there are assured limits of certainty which quite suffice to allow everyone to conduct himself with prudence and in safety; so in thought and speculation there are definite boundaries, such that he who attains to them is certain. Nay, so certain is he that rightly, when anything else in which others wish to attempt to push farther is either in a desperate case or wholly lost, he prudently and safely falls in with the maxim: "No further, nothing too much." But you say, "the glory is not a common one, viz. that of moving forward the boundaries of knowledge and forcing a passage which no one in the centuries behind us has attempted." Certainly no praise would be too high for you, but to secure it you must effect your journey without coming to grief. Wherefore:

Reply 5. *There is an error of defect.* That is to say, in straining too far it fails altogether. I wish to take you alone as witness, you alone as judge. What have you accomplished with all your magnificent appliances? Of what avail has been that pompous renunciation, so universal and so liberal, that you have not spared yourself anything indeed except the well-worn maxim *I think, I am, I am a thinking thing?* I call it well-worn, nay so familiar even to the common herd, that no one since the beginning of the world has been found to doubt it even in the least degree, much less to demand seriously of himself a proof that he is, exists, thinks, and is a thinking thing. Consequently, no one will give you any thanks, and quite rightly, too, unless perhaps we take into account what I do in virtue of my friendship and singular good-will towards you, in approving of your sustained effort to confer a benefit on the human race, and praising your attempt.

Reply 6. *Your Method commits the common error of which it convicts remaining systems.* Thus it is astonished that all mortals affirm and

assert with such unimpaired confidence: "I have a head, I possess eyes," etc. Yet it is not astonished at itself saying with equal confidence: "I have not a head," etc.

Reply 7. *It has a vice peculiar to itself.* Thus to the belief held with a certain amount of assurance (a sufficient amount) by other men: "I have a head, body exists, mind exists," it with a design peculiar to itself opposes the contrary: "I have not a head, there is no body, no mind," not only as certain but as so certain that it can be taken as the foundation of an accurate Metaphysic. In fact, it rests its weight on this so much that if you remove this prop it falls to the ground.

Reply 8. *Imprudence is one of its errors.* Thus it does not notice that "doubtful" is like a two-edged sword; while avoiding the one edge it is wounded by the other. It is doubtful, according to the method, "whether any body exists"; and since this is doubtful it does away with it and posits the opposite: "there is no body." But imprudently leaning on this, which is itself doubtful, it comes by a wound.

Reply 9. *It errs also wittingly; for with full consciousness and deliberation, and though adequately warned, it blinds itself and voluntarily abandons things that are necessary for an investigation of the truth. It finishes by deluding itself by its own Analysis, not only achieving what it does not intend, but even what it most fears.*

Reply 10. *Sins of commission must be ascribed to it; it returns to its ancient opinions, though that has been forbidden by solemn edict; and contrary to the laws of renunciation, it resumes what it has renounced. It is enough for you to use your memory to be convinced of this.*

Reply 11. *Sins of omission also are to be found in it.* For it is not once merely that it transgresses that principle which it lays down as the basis of our thinking: The greatest care must be taken not to admit anything which we cannot prove to be true. *It barefacedly assumes as quite certain and gives no proof of the statements:* Our senses sometimes deceive us; we all dream; some people go delirious, *and other similar assertions.*

Reply 12. *The Method contains either nothing sound, or nothing new; at most it contains what is superfluous.*

For if it alleges that by its renunciation of the doubtful it means what is called that Metaphysical abstraction by which what is doubtful is considered only as doubtful and our mind is to that extent bidden shun that, (where anything certain is under investigation,) and no more credence is given to the doubtful on that occasion than to what is false; in that case what it says will be sound, but not at all new, nor will that abstraction be new, but old and common to all philosophers up to the last single one.

If by that renunciation of what is doubtful it is meant that it must be set aside in the sense of being supposed and alleged to be false, and if the Method treats the doubtful as false and its opposite as true; what is said will be something new but not at all good, and though that renunciation will be novel, it will be erroneous.

If it alleges that by force and weight of reasoning it achieves the following result with certainty and clearness: "I am a thinking thing and, in so far as a thinking thing, neither mind, soul, nor body, but a thing so much withdrawn from these that I can be comprehended, though these have not yet been grasped, exactly as animal or sentient things can be grasped, without our knowing what neighs, lows, etc., this will be something sound but not new at all. For this is a dictum preached everywhere from all the chairs of philosophy; it is taught in express words by everyone who thinks that certain animated creatures think; and, if thought comprise sense as well, so that everything which feels, sees, and hears, also thinks, all who believe that the brutes feel, i.e. all to the last man, are in agreement.

But if the Method declare that it has proved by valid and well-considered reasons that a thinking thing and substance really exists, but that at the time of its existence the mind, the body, and the soul do not really exist; in this case what it says will be new, but by no means sound, just as if it said that animals could exist without there being lions, foxes, etc.

Another way to interpret this method is to suggest that the author says he thinks, i.e. understands, wills, imagines and feels, and thinks in such a way that he beholds and reviews his own thought by a reflex act. This will imply also that he thinks, or knows, or considers that he thinks (which truly is to be conscious and have consciousness of any activity). And if it is maintained that this is a property of a faculty or thing which has a position superior to matter, and is wholly spiritual, and that it is on this condition that we are mind and spirit; in this case the doctrine will be something not hitherto stated but which ought to have been stated before. I was waiting for this to appear, and when I saw the efforts, futile as they were to produce it, I wanted time and time again to suggest it. To say this would be to say something sound, but nothing new, for we have been told it by our teachers and they by theirs, and one generation by the preced-

ing, in my opinion, beginning with the creation of the race.

If, then, this is the upshot, with what a superfluity of matter will we not be left? What redundancy! What vain repetition! What about those devices for securing glory and prestige? To what purpose this talk about the deception of the senses, the illusion of dreamers, and the freaks of delirium? What an ending for that renunciation which was to be of such austerity that we were to be allowed to retain nothing but a mere scrap? Why those journeys so long and continuous to distant shores, afar from the senses, amidst shades and spectres? Finally, what will they do towards establishing the existence of God, claiming as they do that it cannot stand unless everything in the universe is turned upside down? But what is the reason for interpolating new opinions so often and to such an extent in order to lay aside the old, and then, after dismissing the new, assuming the old once more? Perhaps just as the Good Goddess[1] and Consus[2] and others each had their own peculiar rites, so those new mysteries require new ceremonies! But why has not the method, dropping all circumlocutions, expressed the truth neatly, clearly and briefly in a few words then?—"I think, I have consciousness of thought, therefore I am a mind"?

Finally, there is the interpretation that the method alleges that understanding, willing, imagining, feeling, i.e. thinking, are properties of the mind, in such a way that there are no animals at all except man, that think, imagine, feel, see, and hear etc. This doctrine will be new, but not sound. It will be indeed gratuitous, and thanklessly will it be received unless some chance preserve and rescue it (that is its last refuge), appearing at its own time, like the god in the machine, a marvel for the gaping crowd. But how long have we given up any hope of that happening?

Last reply. Here I think you are fearful for your method, which you love so and which you cherish and treat as your own child. You fear lest, now that I have charged it with many sins, now that it shows flaws and threatens everywhere to collapse, I should deem that it ought to be thrown into the rubbish-heap. But don't be frightened. I am your friend. I shall overcome your apprehension, for I am not mistaken; I shall keep silence and await events. I know you and your keen and clear-sighted mental vision. When you have got some time for meditation, and especially when you have thought over your faith-

[1] *Bona Dea*, the goddess of Chastity and Fertility.

[2] Consus was another ancient Italian divinity

ful Analysis in a secret retreat, you will shake off the dust from it, cleanse it anew, and place before our sight a well trimmed and refined Method. Meanwhile take this, and listen to me while I proceed to reply to your questions. I shall embrace in them many things which in my zeal for brevity I have lightly drawn together, such as, what concerns the mind, the true, the false, and similar topics. But you yourself repeat what had escaped the prudent, and

THIRD QUESTION

WHETHER A METHOD CAN BE DEVISED ANEW

You ask, 3, whether***, (The Reverend Father sent nothing more than this. When the rest were asked for, he replied that he had now no leisure for writing. But we made it a matter of scrupulous observance not to omit the least syllable of what he wrote).

ANNOTATIONS

Whatever may be the nature of my Method of inquiry into truth, I should have deemed it sufficient to have reported this wonderful pronouncement upon it in order to expose its falsity and absurdity, if it had proceeded from an unknown individual. But the person who makes this attack holds a position of such eminence that it will be difficult for anyone to believe that he is either not in his right mind, or is extremely untruthful and slanderous and impudent. Consequently, in order to prevent his excessive authority prevailing against the manifest truth, I ask my readers to remember that above, in what preceded these replies, he has proved nothing or next to nothing against me, but has employed only silly quibbles in order to make out that my opinions were so ridiculous as not to need a reply. I want people to be quite clear about the fact that in these replies he does not indeed try to prove anything, but falsely assumes that everything which he fictitiously ascribes to me has already been proved by him. In order to appreciate the better the equity of his judgment they should remember that previously in his indictment he put things only in a jesting way, but now in his subsequent judgment he is at the extreme of seriousness and severity. Again in the first eleven replies he condemns me without hesitation and with a high hand, but finally in the twelfth he deliberates and distinguishes: *If his is the interpretation, the method contains nothing new; if that, nothing sound etc.* Where-

as, nevertheless, in every one of them he is treating merely of one and the same thing viewed in different ways; and that is nothing but his own fabrication, a fabrication the absurdity and dullness of which I shall here set out by means of a simile.

Everywhere in my writings I made it clear that my procedure was like that of Architects planning houses. In order to construct stable houses where the ground is sandy, and stone or clay or any other durable earthy matter is employed in building, they first dig ditches and throw out of them the sand and whatever else rests on or is mixed with the sand, so that they may rest the foundations on firm soil. For so I, also, at first rejected everything doubtful, as they throw out the sand; then perceiving that it is indubitable that a substance which doubted, *i.e.* which thought, existed, I used this as the rock on which I rested the foundations of my philosophy. But our critic is like a common mason who, wishing to be taken in his town for an expert craftsman, and on that account being very jealous of an Architect who was constructing a chapel there, eagerly sought for opportunities of criticising his art; but who being so poorly educated as not to be able to understand what it was to which the Architect trusted, ventured to assail nothing but the first and most obvious beginnings. Thus he noted that the first step was to dig a trench and remove not only the sand and loose earth, but any timber, stones etc. mixed up with the sand, in order to arrive at a hard stratum and there lay the foundation of the chapel. Besides, he has heard that the Architect, replying to questions about the reason for digging trenches, has said that the surface earth on which we stand is not stable enough for bearing the weight of large edifices; that sand is particularly unstable, because not only does it yield when a heavy weight presses on it, but also because a flow of water often bears it away, thus producing an unexpected collapse of anything resting on it. Finally the Architect has related how when such subsidences occur, as they do from time to time, in mines, the miners are in the habit of ascribing their cause to spectres or evil spirits inhabiting the subterranean places. Our Workman then makes this an opportunity for pretending that the Architect takes their trenching operations to be equivalent to the construction of the chapel. He alleges that the Architect takes either the ditch or the rock uncovered at its base, or if anything is reared above this trench, that at least only if the trench itself meanwhile remain empty, to be all that requires to be done in the construction of the chapel; and he says that the Architect himself is so foolish as to fear lest the earth on which he stands will give way under his feet or that ghosts will make it subside. Perhaps he manages to persuade a few children of this, or others so ignorant of the art of building that it seems to them novel and strange to dig trenches in order to lay the foundations of houses; and who readily believe a man whom they know and whom they believe to be well enough skilled in his trade and honest, touching an Architect whom they do not know and of whom they have heard that he has as yet constructed nothing, but has merely dug trenches. Then he becomes so well pleased with this figment of his that he becomes hopeful of persuading the whole world of its truth. And although the Architect has now had all the trenches previously excavated filled with stones, and has erected his chapel on the top, and employed the hardest building material, and has built most securely and called on everyone to look and see, our Workman nevertheless sticks to his old idea and still hopes to get people one and all to believe his nonsense. To this end he stands daily in the public streets making sport of the Architect to the passing throng. And this is the style of his argument:—

Firstly, he introduces his opponent ordering the digging of trenches and the removing from them not only of sand but also of everything lying among or resting upon the sand, even though it were unhewn boulders, even squared stones; in a word it appears that *everything* must be removed, *nothing* whatsoever left. He lays great stress upon those words, *nothing, everything, even unhewn boulders, even stones.* At the same time he feigns that he wants to learn that art of building from the Architect, and that he would like to descend with him into those trenches. *I beg you to conduct me through them yourself,* he says. *Come express your mind; you have either a comrade or a pupil to whom to show the way. What do you bid me do? Though it is new to me and, since I am not accustomed to its obscurity, to be dreaded, I am quite willing to enter that route. . . . I hear you reply; you bid me do what I see you do, to plant my steps where you put yours. That is certainly an excellent way of commanding and leading me! How well you let me think of you. I am ready.*[1]

[1]Cf. p. 240.

Next pretending that he is in dread of the spectres that lurk in these underground excavations, he tries to provoke the mirth of the spectators by the following words: *But will you substantiate this for me, so that I shall not be in fear, shall have no apprehensions about that evil spirit? Certainly though you may try to strengthen me in any way you please, it is not without extreme fear that I descend into this darkness.*[2] Again, shortly afterwards, he exclaims: *But what have I done? I have been forgetful of what I promised to do. I had committed myself entirely to you at the beginning, had vowed myself your ally and disciple, and here I am hesitating at the very outset, timid and obstinate. Pray forgive me! I have sinned greatly and have merely shown the smallness of my intellectual capacity. It was my duty to have laid aside all fear and to plunge boldly into that subterranean gloom; but I have been unwilling and have resisted.*[3]

In the third place he represents the Architect as showing him the stone or rock in the bottom of the ditch on which he wishes his whole edifice to repose. He greets them with jeers: *Splendid, my good friend! You have found the point that Archimedes wanted to discover; there is no doubt that if you so please you will be able to move the world; look now, it all begins to sway and tremble. But, I beg you (for I have no doubt you wish to prune things down so that there shall be nothing in your science which is not apt, coherent, and necessary), why have you let this stone remain? Did you not order the removal of all stones along with the sand? But perhaps it was by chance that you let this pass: it is so difficult even for an expert to forget altogether the things to which we have been accustomed since childhood, that a slip on the part of a raw hand like me if it chance to occur is hardly likely to be thought ill of,*[4] etc. Further, the Architect having collected some broken stones along with the sand that had been thrown out of the trenches in order to use these materials for building, his critic thus assails him with derision: *Shall I dare, before you push onwards, to ask why you, the man who with such solemn declarations, rejected all broken stones as not being sufficiently stable, want to inspect them again as if you hoped to get something good out of that rubble?*[5] etc. Nay, since everything you rejected a little time ago was weak and threatening to collapse (otherwise why did you set it aside?) hou

[2]A paraphrase of p. 242.
[3]An almost literal reproduction of p. 242.
[4]A paraphrase, p. 244.
[5]Cf. p. 244.

does it come about that the same things are now not weak and on the point of collapse?[1] Again shortly afterwards he says: *Here again suffer me to admire the devices you employ, you who, in order to establish the certain, employ the uncertain; who, in order to bring us into the light, bid us plunge into darkness,*[2] etc. At this point he talks away in a very silly fashion about the designations and duties of Architect and Workman respectively and he contributes nothing to the discussion, except that, by confusing the meaning of the terms, he is less able to distinguish the one from the other.

The fourth episode finds both standing in the bottom of the trench. The Architect thereupon attempts to begin the construction of his wall. But in vain; for at the very outset when he wants to lay a squared stone there at the base, the Workman at once reminds him that he had ordered the removal of all stones, and that it was hence inconsistent with the rules of his art to lay down this one. This reminder, then, prevailing with him like an Archimedian demonstration forces him to desist from work. And next when he begins to use rough stones or bricks, or slaked lime mixed with sand, or any other material, the Workman keeps on inveighing: "You have rejected everything; you have retained nothing," and repeating the words Nothing, Everything etc. as though they were incantations, he succeeds in destroying all the Architect's handiwork. The harangue he made was so like what we find above in paragraphs 5 and 9, that there is no need to report his words here.

The final and fifth scene shows him, when he sees a large enough crowd collected round him, adopting a new tone, and changing his comic jocosity for the severity of tragedy; he wipes the plaster from his face and, with a serious countenance and a censorious voice, enumerates and condemns all the Architect's errors (those forsooth which he supposes he has shown in the previous acts). I shall recount the whole of this judgment of his just as he stated it at the final incident where he acted his pretty play before the crowd; and this I shall do in order to show how my critic has imitated his workman prototype. The latter pretends that the Architect has asked him to pronounce judgment on his art, and he replies in the following way.

In the first place, your Art makes a mistake about the foundations. They are both non-existent

and infinite. Other methods indeed of constructing houses lay very stable foundations, e.g. of squared stones, bricks, rough rock, and countless similar substances, reposing on which the walls mount upwards. But your method proceeds quite otherwise and, in its attempt to get something, not out of something but out of nothing, it tears down, digs up, and casts away every scrap of the old foundations. It changes its attitude completely but, lest in its flight it should seem to have no wings to propel it, like Icarus it assumes new ones and fixes them on with wax. It lays down new foundations entirely the opposite of the old ones; but in so doing it avoids the instability of the previous basis only by incurring a new weakness. It upsets what is firm in order to rely on what is weak; it employs wings, but waxen ones. It rears a mansion to the skies, but only to have it fall. Finally it labours to construct something out of nothing and ends by achieving nothing at all.*[3]

Now the very church alone which the Architect has already built proves that all this is the silliest of nonsense. For it is quite clear that in it the foundations have been most firmly laid, and that the Architect has destroyed nothing which was not worthy of destruction; and that he has never departed from the precepts of others unless he had some better plan; that the building soars to a great height without threatening to fall; finally that he has constructed not out of nothing, but out of the most durable material, not nothing, but a stable and well-built church to the glory of God. But all this together with the other matters in which my critic has suffered from delusions, can be seen clearly enough from the Meditations alone which I published. But there is no reason to impugn the writer's historical knowledge (from whom I took the Workman's words) because he introduced his popular critic as attributing wings to Architecture, as well as much else that seems hardly to be in harmony therewith. For probably this was intentional and it was meant thereby to show how agitated he was when he uttered such things. And certainly all such similes are equally out of place when talking of the Method of inquiring into truth, though my critic nevertheless employs them.

The second reply was: *The Architect's procedure is wrong in respect of the means it employs. It is forsooth possessed of none, though at the same time it removes our previous instruments; and it brings none to occupy their place. Other arts of this kind employ a rule, a level, and*

[1]Cf. p. 245.
[2]A variant, p. 245.
[3]Cf. pp. 263–264.

a plumb line; and employing these to extricate themselves from a labyrinth of difficulties, they manage with ease and exactitude to build together masses of rock however shapeless. But this, on the contrary, disfigures the old shape of buildings, though at the same time it grows pale with a new fear, pretending that subterranean ghosts threaten it, and in terror lest the earth subside and the sands disperse. Set up your column; whatever that be, your art will be apprehensive at the laying of the pedestal and base. "Perhaps," it says, "the ghosts will cast the column down." It will be anxious and say the pillar is weak. What if it is only gypsum and not marble? How often have other things appeared to us to be strong and firm which afterwards, when we came to try them, were found to be easily broken? What then will happen when we come to the crown of the column? Your new method will avoid everything at all times like snares and traps. Have not bad Architects often constructed other buildings which, though they thought them strong, came down of their own accord? What if this style is subject to the same contingency? Suppose the spectres disturb the soil? They are evil. Nor have I known any foundation laid on so firm a rock that the spectres are unable to do anything to overturn it. What will you do here? What, when your art will declare and obstinately maintain that the durability of the crown of the column is doubtful, unless you previously know with certainty, that the column neither consists of fragile material nor rests on the sand, but is based on solid rock, rock which the underground spirits are unable ever to overturn? What, when it will repudiate both the matter and the form of this column? (Here with a jocular audacity he produced a representation of one of these very columns which the Architect had set up in his chapel.) *What about other things of this kind? If you urge them he will say, "Wait till I know that there is a rock beneath me and that no ghosts can ever overturn it." But you will reply, "This has at least the advantage that, though it sets up no new pillars, it safely avoids constructing any wrongly." That is a capital preventive of the child's catarrh etc.,* as above.[1] I will not continue, as the rest is too coarse for repetition. So I ask the reader to compare the present replies with the similar versions of which my critic is the author.

Now this reply like the preceding is convicted of the most impudent falsehood by the existence itself of the chapel in question, since there were in it many strong columns, among them that very one, the picture of which the

[1]Cf. pp. 263, 264.

Workman displayed, making out that the Architect had repudiated it. In the same way my writings definitely settle the fact that I do not cast aspersions on the syllogism and deface its ancient form; I have used it in my writings wherever there was need. Among other syllogistic arguments he has extracted from my works that very one of which he here pretends that I reject both the matter and the form. For it will be found at the end of the reply to the First set of Objections, in Proposition 1, where I prove the existence of God. Moreover I cannot see what is his purpose in making this fabrication, unless perhaps he wishes to hint that everything which I have propounded as true and certain is in conflict with that renunciation of doubtful beliefs with which alone he wishes to identify my Method. Now this is just the same as, and not less childish and silly than, if the Workman were to pretend that the digging out of the trench for the purpose of laying the foundation of houses was the whole of the architect's art, and if he complained that anything the Architect constructed was in disagreement with that excavation.

The third reply was: *Your art has a flaw at the finish, for it ends by constructing nothing stable. But stability it cannot secure, since it itself closes against itself all avenues towards that end. You yourself have seen and experienced this in these Ulyssean wanderings in which you have wearied both yourself and me your companion. You contended that you were an Architect or were possessed of the Architect's art. But you were unable to prove that at all, and stuck in quagmires and thickets, and indeed did so so often that I can scarcely recall the number of times. Yet it will be advantageous to tell them over again now in order to give its proper substance and strength to this reply of mine. Here, then, are the chief heads of the suicidal procedure of your art, of the way in which it cuts itself off from all hope of securing its end. 1. You know not whether beneath the surface there is sand or rock and therefore you ought not to trust to rock more than to sand (if in spite of all you do some time come to have rock beneath you). Hence everything is doubtful and uncertain. I shall not adduce examples. Go yourself and review the treasures of your memory and produce anything which is not infected with that taint. I shall congratulate you if you do so. 2. Before I have found firm soil beneath which I know there is no sand and with no underground spirits troubling it, I ought to reject everything and treat all materials in every way with suspicion. O. certainly to follow the old and common style o.*

building, it must be determined whether there are and what are those materials which really ought not to be rejected, and the diggers ought to be instructed to leave those in the trench. Hence, just as in the former cases, everything is lacking in strength, and quite useless for the construction of buildings. 3. If there is anything in the least liable to be upset, change completely your attitude towards it and believe it to have already fallen, nay believe it ought to be flung out of the trench, and use the empty trench alone as a foundation. Hence I have shut up all the avenues leading to the completion of the building. For what do you hope from this: "There is no earth here, no sand, no stone," and a thousand other such statements? Do not say that this excavation is not to go on for ever but, like a public vacation which has been instituted for a set time, so this also is for a definite period and goes on until the trench is a certain depth corresponding to the depth of the sand at the spot: Let it be so, let the excavation go on for a time only; yet it occurs at the time during which you imagine that you are building, at the time when you employ, nay misemploy the emptiness of the trench in your scheme, just as though the whole of the building art depended on that art and consisted in that as its stable foundation. "But," you say, "I employ it in order to make steady pedestal and column as other Architects are wont to do. Do they not construct a temporary scaffolding and use it to hoist the column?"[1]

Now in this none of the Workman's statements are more ridiculous than what is to be found in our Author's thought. What I have subsequently demonstrated proves that my rejection of doubtful beliefs no more precludes an attainment of knowledge of the truth, than the excavations which the Architect prescribes prevents him from constructing his chapel. Surely otherwise he ought to have noted something false or uncertain in my conclusions. But since he neither does this nor is able to do so, it must be confessed that he is suffering from a quite inexcusable delusion. I have not laboured more to prove that I, or a thinking thing was mind, than my opponent to prove that he *was* an Architect. But our Author with all his toil and effort has certainly not here proved anything except that he has no mind, or at least that his mind is not of good quality. Neither from the fact that metaphysical doubt proceeds so far as to suppose that a man does not know whether he is dreaming or awake, does it follow that he can discover no certainty, any more than that because an Architect,

[1]Cf. pp. 264, 265.

when he begins digging operations, does not yet know whether he is to find rock or clay or sand or anything else beneath the surface, it follows that he will not be able to discover rock there, or that when he has found it he ought not to trust it. Nor from the fact that, before a man knows that God exists, he has an opportunity of doubting everything (viz. everything of which he does not have a clear perception present in his mind, as I have a number of times set forth) does it follow that nothing is of avail in the pursuit of truth, more than it was a consequence of the Architect's getting everything turned out of the trench before firm soil was reached, that there was no rubble or anything else in the trench which he might afterwards deem of use in laying the foundations. It was no stupider a mistake on the part of the Workman to say that the common and ancient style of Architecture forbade their being thrown out of the trench and instructed the diggers to retain them, than it is for our Author both to say that *before everything it must be determined whether there are, and what are, those really safe propositions that are free from doubt* (for how could they be determined by one whom we suppose as yet to know none?), and in the same breath to assert that this is a precept of the common and ancient Philosophy (in which no such precept is found). Nor was it more crass stupidity on the part of the Workman to pretend that the Architect wanted to take an empty ditch as his foundation and that all this building depended upon doing so, than it was manifest raving on the part of my Critic to say that *I employ the opposite of what is doubtful as a principle, that I abuse what I renounce; just as though the whole truth depended on that, and consisted in that as in its stable foundation,* unmindful of the words which he had above reported as mine; *you will neither affirm nor deny, you will treat both as false.* Finally, in comparing the digging of a trench in order to lay a foundation to the setting up of a scaffolding, the Workman did not show his lack of knowledge to any greater extent than our author did in likening the renunciation of doubtful beliefs to this also.

The fourth reply was: *Your art errs by going too far. That is to say, it strives to accomplish more than the laws of prudence require of it, more than any mortal demands. Some people indeed seek to construct durable houses for themselves. But certainly no one has hitherto been found who has not thought it enough for him, if the house in which he lived were as firm as the earth which supports us, so that anxiety about seeking for a still greater strength is superfluous. Besides, just as in walking there are certain conditions relative to the stability of the ground we tread on, which quite suffice to allow everyone to walk on it in safety, so in the building of houses there are certain limiting conditions, such that he who attains to them is certain, etc.,*[1] as above.

Now, though here it is unjust of the Workman to blame the architect, it is with still greater injustice that my critic blames me in the corresponding case. For it is true that in the construction of houses there are certain conditions implying less than absolute firmness of the ground, beyond which it is not worth our while proceeding, and these vary in proportion to the size and mass of the building we are constructing. For it is safe to build the lowlier class of cottages upon sand, the stability of which relative to their burden is as great as that of rock relative to high towers. But it is utterly false that in laying the foundations of a philosophy there are any such limits not reaching so far as full certainty, in which we may prudently and safely acquiesce. For since truth consists in what is indivisible, it is possible that a matter whose complete certainty we do not recognize, however probable it appear, is wholly false. Certainly it would not be prudent philosophising on the part of a man who took as the foundation of his science statements which he knew to be possibly false. Indeed what answer will he make to the sceptics who overpass all the boundaries of doubt? How will he refute them? Oh, he will reckon them among the desperate or the lost! Very fine indeed; but meanwhile to what class will they assign him? Neither must we think that the sect of the Sceptics is long extinct. It flourishes to-day as much as ever, and nearly all who think that they have some ability beyond that of the rest of mankind, finding nothing that satisfies them in the common Philosophy, and seeing no other truth, take refuge in Scepticism. Those people are especially such as demand a proof to be given them of the existence of God and the immortality of the soul. Hence what our author here states constitutes a very bad example, especially as he has a name for great learning. It shows that he thinks there is no possibility of refuting the errors of the Sceptical Atheists; and thus all his efforts result in strengthening and confirming them. Nay, it is true that though no contemporary Sceptics have any doubt when it comes to the

[1] Cf. pp. 264, 265.

practical life about possessing a head and about 2 and 3 making 5, and the like; they say they only employ those statements as truths because they have an appearance of being true, but that they do not believe them with certainty because there are no convincing arguments impelling them to do so. And because to them the existence of God and the immortality of the human mind do not have the same appearance of truth, they think that therefore they ought not to make use of these beliefs even in practical life, unless a proof is first given them with sounder reasoning than any which secures adherence to beliefs that have an appearance of being true. Now since it was those beliefs the truth of which I proved and, at least to my knowledge, no one before me, I think that no greater slander could be devised than that for which our author is responsible when throughout the whole of his Dissertation he continually assigns to me, reiterating the imputation a countless number of times, that single error which constitutes the specialty of Scepticism, viz. excessive doubt. Very liberal is my Critic in recounting the list of my sins. For although he says that *the glory is not a common one, that of moving forward the boundaries of knowledge and forcing a passage which no one in the centuries behind us has attempted,* and though he has no reason for suspecting that I have not done this in the very matter of which he is treating, as I shall show directly, yet he reckons this against me as a sin, saying, *certainly no praise would be too high for you, but to secure it you must effect your journey without coming to grief.* Evidently he wishes his readers to believe that I have come to grief then, or committed some error; yet he does not believe so himself, nor indeed has he any reason to suspect it. For surely if he had been able to devise the least reason for suspecting some straying from the path on my part at any point in the whole of the route by which I conducted the mind from the knowledge of its own existence to the knowledge of the existence of God, and its distinctness from the body, doubtless in a dissertation of such length, such verbosity and such poverty of topics, he would not have failed to mention it! He would have far preferred to do this, rather than change the question, as he always has done whenever the argument required him to treat of that subject, or in such a silly fashion represent me as discussing whether a thinking thing was Mind. Therefore he had no reason for suspecting that I had made any error i what I asserted, and in the Arguments by which I, first of all men, upset the doubt of the Sceptics. He confesses that this is worthy of the highest praise. Yet he has sufficient audacity to censure me on the very same count, and fictitiously ascribes to me that doubt which he might with better right have imputed to any of the rest of mankind who have never refuted that doubt, rather than to me alone. But in his commentary we find

The fifth reply. *There is an error of defect. That is to say, in expending too much effort it completes nothing. I wish to take you alone as witness, you alone as judge. What have you accomplished with all your magnificent appliances? Of what avail has been that pretentious excavation, so universal and so liberal, that you have not spared yourself even the most durable of stones, except this one, this one as to the retention of which you quote the painfully common statement: "The rock which is discovered lower than any sand, is strong and durable." This is a truth, I repeat, so familiar to the common herd,*[1] etc. as above.

Now here I expected to find both the Workman in question and my Critic to prove something. But just as the former's only object was to ask what was the result of the Architect's excavations, except that he had laid bare some rock, and to dissimulate the fact that he had reared his chapel upon this rock; so my Critic asks me merely what I have effected by my rejection of doubtful beliefs other than that I have found this commonplace: *I think I am,* seeing he holds it of no account that from this I have demonstrated the existence of God and many other truths. And he wants to take me alone as witness, witness I suppose of his glaring audacity; just as elsewhere also and in the matter of other fabrications he says *that all to the last man believe them, and that they are doctrines taught from every chair of philosophy;*[2] *that we have been told it by our teachers and they by theirs and so on right up to the creation of the race,* and the like. But we should no more trust these assertions than the oaths of certain men, who are wont to use the more protestations the greater they believe to be the incredibility and falsity of what they want us to believe.

The Workman's next reply, No. 6. *Your art commits the common error of which it convicts remaining systems. Thus it is astonished that all mortals affirm and assert with such unimpaired*

confidence: *"The sand is strong enough on which we stand. This ground we tread on does not move, etc.," yet it is not astonished at itself saying with equal confidence: "We must clear away the sand, etc."*[3]

Now this is no sillier than what our Author in similar circumstances affirms.

Reply 7. *It has a vice peculiar to itself. Thus to the belief held with a certain amount of assurance (a sufficient assurance) by other men, to the effect that the earth on which we stand, sand, stones, etc. are firm enough, it, with a design peculiar to itself, opposes the contrary statement, and takes the trench, forsooth, out of which sand, stones, and the rest have been cast, not only as something strong, but so strong that it can found upon it the solid structure of a chapel. In fact it rests its weight on this so much that if you remove these props the whole falls to the ground.*[4]

Here the illusion is no greater than that which besets our Author, so long as he is forgetful of the words: *You will neither affirm nor deny,* etc.

Reply 8. *Imprudence is one of its errors. Thus it does not notice that the instability of the ground is like a two-edged sword; while avoiding the one edge it is wounded by the other. Sand is not a stable enough soil for it; because it does away with this and posits the opposite, viz. a ditch empty of sand, and imprudently relying on this empty ditch as though it were something firm it comes by a wound.*[5]

Here again we have only to remember the words: *You will neither affirm nor deny.* All this talk about a double-edged sword is more worthy of the sagacity of our Workman than of my Critic.

Reply 9. *It errs also wittingly, for with full consciousness and deliberation, and though adequately warned, it blinds itself and voluntarily abandons those things that are necessary for the building of houses. It finishes by deluding itself with its own rule, not only achieving what it does not intend but even what it most fears.*[6]

But the Architect's success in building his chapel, and the truths I have succeeded in demonstrating, show how much truth there is in the charge against each of us respectively.

Reply 10. *Sins of commission must be ascribed to it. It returns to its ancient opinions, though that has been forbidden by solemn edict and, contrary to its laws about excavation, it resumes what*

[1] Cf. p. 265.
[2] Cf. p. 266.

[3] Cf. p. 265.
[4] Cf. p. 265.
[5] Cf. p. 265.
[6] Cf. p. 265.

it has renounced. It is enough for you to use your memory to be convinced of this.[1]

In his similar accusation our Author is forgetful of the words: *You will neither affirm nor deny.* Otherwise, how could he keep countenance in pretending that that had been forbidden by solemn edict which he previously said had not even been denied?

Reply 11. *Sins of omission also are to be found in it, for it is not once merely that it transgresses that principle which it lays down as a basis: "The greatest care must be taken not to admit anything which we cannot prove to be true." It barefacedly assumes as quite certain and gives no proof of the statements: "Sandy soil is not firm enough on which to build houses," and other similar assertions.*[2]

Here it is clear that our Author, like my Critic in the case of the rejection of doubtful beliefs, was under a delusion, applying to the excavation of a foundation what belongs only to the construction alike of buildings and of a ph losophy. For it is absolutely true that nothing is to be admitted as true, which we cannot prove to be true when it is a question of setting it up or affirming it. But when it is only a case of casting a thing out of a trench or setting aside a belief, it is sufficient to have suspicions about it.

The twelfth reply was: *Your art contains nothing sound or nothing new; at most what is superfluous.*

For (1) *if it alleges that by its excavation of the sand it means that excavation which other architects employ, when they throw out the sand only if they think it not strong enough to bear the weight of buildings; in that case what it says is sound, but not at all new; nor will that method of excavation be new, but old, and common to all architects up to the last single one.*[3]

(2) *If by that digging out of the sand it is meant that the whole of the sand must be thrown away, all removed and none retained, and none of it or its opposite, viz. the vacuity of the place which it formerly filled, must be employed as something firm and stable; that will be something new but not at all good, and though your method of excavation will be novel, it will be spurious.*[4]

(3) *If it alleges that by force and weight of reasoning it achieves the following result with certainty and clearness: "I am an expert in Architecture, and practise it; nevertheless, in so far as I am this, I am neither architect, mason, nor hodman, but something so much withdrawn from these that I can be comprehended though these have not yet been grasped, exactly as animal or sentient thing can be grasped without our knowing what neighs, lows etc.":*[5] *this will be something sound but not new at all. For every crossroad resounds with this tale, and it is taught in express words by everyone who thinks that there are experts in architecture; and if architecture likewise embraces the construction of walls, so that those also are versed in Architecture, who mix lime and sand, who hew stone, and carry up the material in hods, all who think that labourers practice this craft, i.e. all to the last man are in agreement.*[6]

(4) *If it declare that it has proved by valid and well considered reasons that its professor really exists and is a man skilled in Architecture, but that at the time of his existence, no architect really exists, nor any mason, nor hodman; in this case what it says will be new, but by no means sound, just as if it said that animal could exist without there being lions, foxes, etc.*[7]

(5) *Another way to interpret this art is to suggest that the architect builds, i.e. employs the science of architecture in constructing buildings and builds in such a way that he beholds and reviews his own action by a reflex act. This will imply also that he knows or considers that he builds (which truly is to be conscious and to have consciousness of any activity). And if it is maintained that this is a property of architecture, i.e. of an art which holds a place superior to the science of hodmen, and that it is on this condition that he is an architect; in this case the doctrine will be something not hitherto stated, but which ought to have been stated before. I was waiting for this to appear, and when I saw the efforts, futile as they were, to produce it, I wanted time and time again to suggest it. To say this would be to say something sound, but nothing new, for we have been told it by our teachers and they by theirs and, in my opinion, one generation by another beginning with the creation of the race.*[8]

If, then, this is the upshot, with what a superfluity of matter will we not be left! What redundancy! What vain repetition! What about those devices for securing glory and prestige? To what purpose this talk about the instability of the sand, and disturbance of the earth, and spectres, empty figments to terrify us? What an ending for that

[1]Cf. p. 265.
[2]Cf. p. 265.
[3]Cf. p. 265.
[4]Cf. p. 265.

[5]Cf. p. 266.
[6]Cf. p. 266.
[7]Cf. p. 266.
[8]Cf. p. 266.

excavation which was to be so profound that we were to be allowed to retain nothing but a mere scrap! Why those journeys so long and continuous to distant shores, afar from the senses, amidst shades and spectres? Finally what will they do towards securing the stability of your chapel, claiming as they do that it cannot stand unless every thing is turned upside down? But what is the reason for interpolating new materials so often and to such an extent in order to lay aside the old, and then after dismissing the new, resume the old once more? Perhaps just as while we are in a temple or in the presence of sovereign spirits we ought to behave ourselves otherwise than when in taverns or hovels, *so these new mysteries require new ceremonies. But why has not your art, dropping all circumlocutions, expressed the truth neatly, clearly, and briefly in a few words thus: "I build, I have consciousness of this building, therefore I am an Architect"?*

(6) *Finally, there is the interpretation that your art alleges that it constructs houses, that it plans their bedrooms, apartments, porches, doors, windows, pillars and the rest, in the mind beforehand, and arranges them, and next, in order to get them constructed, gives instructions to those who supply the material, to the quarrymen, masons, roof-makers, hodmen and other workmen, and directs their work, and that this is the peculiar function of the Architect in the sense that no other workmen can effect that function. This doctrine will be* new *but not* sound. *It will indeed be gratuitous and thanklessly will it be received, unless some chance preserve and rescue it (that is its last refuge), appearing at its own time, like the god in the machine, a marvel for the gaping crowd. But how long have we given up any hope of that happening?*

Last reply. *Here I think you are fearful for your art, which you love so and which you cherish and treat, pardon me, as your own child. You fear lest, now that I have charged it with so many sins, now that it shows flaws and threatens everywhere to collapse, I should deem that it ought to be thrown into the rubbish-heap. But don't be frightened. I am your friend. I shall overcome your apprehensions, if I am not mistaken; I shall keep silence and await events. I know you and your clear and keen-sighted mental vision. When you have got some time for meditation and specially when you have thought over your faithful rule in a secret retreat, you will shake off the dust from it, cleanse it anew, and place before your sight a well balanced and polished Architecture. Meanwhile take this and listen to me while I proceed to reply to your questions. I shall*

embrace in them many things which, in my zeal for brevity I have lightly drawn together, such as, what concerns the arches, the openings for windows, the columns, the porches, and the like.[1] But here we get the programme of a new comedy.

WHETHER ARCHITECTURE CAN BE ESTABLISHED ANEW

You ask thirdly. When this point was reached, some of his friends seeing that the excessive jealousy and hatred by which he was agitated, had now become quite a disease, prevented him from going about declaiming in the streets any longer, and forthwith carried him to a doctor.

Now I should certainly not venture to imagine any such similar fate for my Critic. I shall here go only so far as to note how accurately he has imitated that Workman in all his actions. It is quite in the same way that he acts the judge, the upright judge forsooth, who takes great and scrupulous care lest he pronounce any rash decision. After condemning me eleven times over on the one count of rejecting the doubtful in order to establish the certain, and as it were digging trenches in order to lay the foundations of my building, he at length on the twelfth occasion comes to the examination of the point to be discussed and says,

1. If I have understood it, as he in reality knows I have understood it, and as is clear from the words, *You will neither affirm nor deny,* etc., which he himself attributed to me: then indeed my doctrine contains something *sound,* but nothing *new.*

2. But if I have understood it in that other way, from which he has extracted the eleven preceding errors, and which he yet knows is quite remote from my meaning, seeing that above in paragraph 3 of his first question he has introduced me as taking an attitude of wonder and mockery towards it and saying: *How could that come into the mind of any sane man?* Then my doctrine, forsooth, contains some *novelty,* but nothing that is *sound.* Now in the history of abuse has there ever been any person, I don't say so impudent, so mendacious, so contemptuous of all truth and verisimilitude, but so impudent and of such short memory, that in an elaborate dissertation to which much thought has been given, he has charged some one with holding an opinion, which in the beginning of the same dissertation, he admitted was held in abhorrence by

[1]Cf. p. 266.

the very man whom he charged with holding it, to such an extent that he believed that no sane man could entertain it?

As to the questions which follow (numbers 3, 4, and 5), both in my Critic's and in the Workman's list of charges, they are quite irrelevant, and were never set forward either by me or by the Architect. It seems very likely that the Workman first devised them, in order that, since he dared not undertake any of the things the architect performed, for fear of showing too evidently his lack of skill, he might nevertheless appear to attack something else besides his policy of excavation. And it appears that my Critic has in this respect followed his methods.

3. For when he says that a thinking thing can be understood, though the mind is not known, nor the soul, nor the body, his philosophy is no better than that of the Workman, when he says that to be skilled in Architecture belongs no more to an architect than to a mason or hodman, and that one so skilled can be understood apart from any of these.

4. Just as, also, it is equally inept to say that a thinking thing exists though the mind does not exist, as to assert that one skilled in architecture can exist though no architect exists (at least if the word mind is taken in the sense in which I, following established usage, announced I understood it). And it is no more contradictory that a thinking thing should exist without a body than a man skilled in architecture should exist without there being masons or hodmen.

5. Likewise, when my Critic says that it is not sufficient that a substance be a thinking one, for it to have a higher position than matter, and be wholly spiritual, such as alone he wishes to call mind, but that in addition it requires by a reflex act to think it thinks or have a consciousness of its own thought, his delusion is as great as that of the Workman when he says that one who is skilled in architecture ought to consider by a reflex act that he possesses that skill before he can be an architect. For although no one as a matter of fact is an architect who has not often reflected or at least been able to reflect that he possesses the skill required in building, yet manifestly he does not require to make that reflection in order to become an architect. Nor is there any more need for that consideration or reflection in order that thinking substance be placed above matter. For the first thought, whatever it be, by which we become aware of anything

does not differ more from the second by which we become aware that we have become aware of that, than this second differs from the third by which we become aware that we have become aware that we have become aware. Again if it be allowed that the first function belongs to a corporeal thing, there is not the least reason why the second should not be so attributed also. Wherefore we must note that our Critic commits a much more dangerous error here than the workman. For he removes the true and highly intelligible differentia between corporeal and incorporeal things, viz. that the former think but the latter do not, and substitutes in its place another which can in no wise be thought essential, viz. that the former reflect that they think, while the latter do not. Thus he does all that he can towards preventing a true understanding of the distinction between the human mind and the body.

6. He is less to be excused in favouring the cause of the brutes and wishing to ascribe thought to them not less than to men, than the Workman in attempting to arrogate to himself and his like a skill in architecture no less than that possessed by the Architect.

Finally, it is in everything sufficiently apparent that both have been alike in thinking not of objections that had any truth or verisimilitude, but merely of such as might be trumped up for the purpose of casting aspersions on an enemy and representing him as quite unskilled and a fool, to those who did not know him or do not take pains to inquire more curiously into the truth of the matter. Indeed he who reports about the Workman, in order to express his mad hatred, relates how he extolled the Architect's excavations as a magnificent contrivance, but scorned the uncovering of the stone which that excavation revealed and the chapel built upon it as matters of no moment. Yet nevertheless out of his friendship and singular good will to him he rendered thanks etc. Likewise at the end he introduces himself as making these wonderful declarations: *If, then, this is the upshot, with what a superfluity of matter will we not be left? What redundancy! What vain repetitions! What about those devices for securing glory and prestige?*[1] etc. And shortly after: *Here I think you are fearful for your art, which you love and cherish so,* etc. Likewise: *But don't be frightened, I am your friend.* All this describes the Workman's malady so graphically that no

[1]Cf. p. 266.

poet could draw a more living picture. But it is surprising that our Author should imitate all the same peculiarities with such enthusiasm that he does not notice what he himself is doing, and does not employ that reflex act of thought by which, according to his recent statement, men are distinguished from the brutes. For he surely would not say that there was too great a display of words in my writings if he considered how many more he employs himself. In what I cannot call his attack, since he uses no arguments to further it, but (to use a somewhat bitter expression since there is none other that so well expresses the truth of the matter) in his revilings, he attacks at large length merely the subject of the doubt of which I treated. Neither would he have talked of *vain repetition* if he had seen how prolix, how redundant, how full of empty loquacity is the whole of his Dissertation, in the end of which, he nevertheless says, he has studied brevity. But since he there says that he is friendly to me, in order that I may deal with him in the friendliest fashion, I shall do as the Workman's friends did who carried him off to the doctor and shall commend him to his Superior.

LETTER TO FATHER DINET

TO THE MOST REVEREND FATHER DINET OF THE SOCIETY OF JESUS, HEAD OF THE PROVINCE OF FRANCE, FROM RENATUS DES CARTES

WHEN recently I indicated to the Reverend Father Mersenne by the letter which I wrote to him, that I would have greatly desired that the Dissertation which I learned the Reverend Father[1] had written concerning me should have been published by him, or else that it should have been sent to me in order that I might have it published with the rest of the Objections that others had sent me; and when I asked that he should try to obtain this either from him, or else, because I judged it a most just request, at least from your Reverence, he replied that he had placed my letter in your Reverence's hands, and that not alone had you favourably received it, but that you had even given many indications of singular sagacity, kindness, and good-will towards me. And this I have very clearly recognised even from the fact that the Dissertation in question was sent me. This not only makes me deeply grateful to you, but it also impels me here to say freely what I think of that Dissertation, and at the same time to ask your advice concerning the plan of my studies.

To tell the truth I no sooner held this Dissertation in my hands, than I rejoiced as though I had in my possession a great treasure; since there is nothing more to be desired than either to protest the certainty of my opinions, as it may haply be if, after distinguished men have examined them, no error is discovered in them, or else that I should be shown my errors in order that I may correct them. And just as in well constituted bodies there is a union and inter-connection of parts so great that no single part employs merely its own strength, but, especially, a sort of common strength belonging to the whole supplements the agency of each member; so, being aware of the intimate connection that ordinarily exists between the various members of your Society, I did not judge, when I received the Dissertation of the Reverend Father,[2] that I received the communication of one individual, but I believed that it was an exact and accurate judgment on my opinions formed by the whole body of your Society.

Nevertheless, after having read it, I was very much taken aback, and I then began to see that I must judge of it in quite another way than I had at first done. For without doubt had the work come from one who was imbued with the same spirit as that which pervades all your Society, more, or certainly not less, kindness, gentleness, and modesty would be observed in it than in the case of those private individuals who have written to me on the same subject; but far from that being so, if you could compare it with their objections to my Meditations, you will not fail to believe that it is the latter which have been composed by men who lead the religious life, convinced that the former is conceived in terms so bitter as to shame any private person and certainly one bound by special vows to practise virtue more than other men. There should also be observed in it a love of God and an ardent zeal for the advancement of His glory; but on the contrary it appears as though the writer impugned all reason and truth, and, by ill-founded authorities and fictions, the principles of which I availed myself in proving the existence of God and the real distinction between the soul of man and the body. There should in addition be observed knowledge, reason, and good sense, but short of desiring to place in the category of knowledge an acquaintance with the Latin tongue such as the riff-raff of Rome had in olden days, I have not observed in his writings any trace of these, any more than I have observed any reasoning which was not either illegitimate or false, nor finally any token of ingenuity of mind, which was not more worthy of an artizan than of a Father of the Society. I do not speak of prudence, or of other virtues which are so preeminent in your Society, and which yet do not appear in this Dissertation, nor is there in it the slightest trace of such shown. But one

[1] The Rev. Father Bourdin.
[2] Bourdin.

might at least expect to remark in it a reverence for truth, probity and candour; on the contrary it is very manifestly seen by the notes I have written,[1] that nothing can be imagined more removed from every appearance of truth than all that he imputes to me in this writing. And further, just as when one portion of our body is so disposed that it is impossible for it to follow the law that is common to the whole body, we infer that it is suffering from some disease peculiar to it, so the Dissertation of the Reverend Father clearly demonstrates to us that he does not enjoy that health which is found in the rest of the body of your Society. As, however, we do not the less esteem the head of a man, or the man in his entirety, because there may possibly be certain evil humours that have flowed against his will and in spite of himself, either into his foot or finger, but rather praise the constancy and virtue with which he does not fail to endure the pains inflicted by his cure: and as no one has ventured to condemn Caius Marius for having varicose veins, and as on the contrary he is often more praised by writers for having courageously suffered one of his legs to be cut, than for having obtained the consulate on seven different occasions and having obtained many victories over his enemies; so, not being ignorant of the pious and paternal affection that you cherish for all that pertains to yourselves, the more unsatisfactory the Dissertation seems to me, the more do I esteem your integrity and prudence in having desired it to be sent to me, and the more do I honour and reverence your whole Society. But inasmuch as the Reverend Father has consented to send me his Dissertation, in case it may seem rash in me to judge that he did not do it of himself, I will explain why I feel impelled to believe this, and so I shall narrate all that has hitherto passed between him and me.

As early as the year 1640 he wrote against me other treatises on Optics which I hear that he read out to his pupils, and he even gave copies to these pupils for purposes of transcription—not perhaps to all, as to that I am ignorant, but certainly to some, and it may be credited that it was to those who were the most cherished and faithful, for on making request of one of them, in whose hands it had been, for a copy, he could not be persuaded to give it. Subsequently he published theses upon that subject, which were for three days sustained in your College of Paris with great dis-

play and extraordinary publicity; while it is true that on this occasion he touched on some other matters, he was chiefly engaged in disputing about my opinions, and obtained many successes at my expense—successes not difficult to achieve over an absentee. I further saw the Attack on me which served as Preface to these Disputations which were read at the beginning, and which the Reverend Father had composed with much toil and study. Here the object was clearly none other than to impugn my opinions; nevertheless the words objected to and laid to my charge were none that I had ever written and thought, and they were all so nonsensical that it was impossible that they should occur to any sane man, any more than those which he attributed to me in his Dissertation. This I explained at the time in the Notes upon it which I sent privately to the author, whom I did not then know as belonging to the Society.

And in the theses it is not only that he condemned my opinions as false, which would be open to any one to do, especially if he had reasons ready to prove his point; but also, with his usual candour, he altered the signification of certain terms. Thus, for example, the angle which in optics is called the refractive, he calls the angle of refraction. The subtlety is much the same as when in his Dissertation he says he understands by body that which thinks, and by soul, that which is extended, and by this artifice certain of my discoveries were expressed in very different language, and brought forward as his own, while me he convicted of having a different and quite foolish opinion about them.

Being warned of this, I at once wrote to the Reverend Rector of the College, and begged that "since my opinions had been judged worthy of public refutation, he would not also judge me unworthy—I who might still be counted amongst his disciples—to see the arguments which had been used to refute them." And I added many other reasons which seemed to me to suffice to cause him to grant me what I asked for, such as, amongst others, that "I much preferred being instructed by those of your Company than by any others whatever, because I excessively honour and respect them both as my masters and as the only instructors of my youth; I have further in the *Discourse on Method*,[2] p. 75, asked all those who may read my writings to take the trouble of making me acquainted with any errors into which they

[1] Cf. Reply to Obj. vi, p. 233.

[2] In this edition, p. 65.

may have seen me slide, telling them that they will ever find me ready to correct them, and that I do not think that any one will be found, above all amongst those who profess a religious life, who would prefer to convict me of error in the presence of others, and in my absence, rather than to show me my faults, and that at least I could not doubt that love to his neighbour would be shown by a person such as I describe."

To this the Reverend Rector made no reply, but the Reverend Father[1] wrote to me that he would send me his treatises in a week, that is, the reasons which he made use of in order to impugn my opinions. A short time thereafter I received letters from certain other Fathers of the Society which promised me in his name the same thing in about six months, perhaps because, as they did not approve of these treatises (for they did not expressly avow that they were aware of anything which he had done against me), they demanded this time in order to correct them. And finally the Reverend Father sent me letters, not only written by his own hand, but also sealed with the seal of the Society, which showed me that it was by the order of his superiors that he wrote; what he said was (1) *That the Reverend Rector, seeing that the communications I had addressed to him concerned him alone, had ordered him to reply to them himself, and to give me his reasons for his action.* (2) *That he had never undertaken, nor would he ever undertake any special attack on my opinions.* (3) *That if he had never responded to the request made in the Method, p. 75, this must be attributed to his ignorance, since he had never read the Method through.* (4) *As regards the Notes which I had made on his opening discourse he had nothing to add to what he had already replied, and would have written if his friends had not counselled him to do otherwise;* that is to say, he had nothing whatever to say on my notes because he has indicated nothing but that he would send me the reasons he had for combating my opinions; and by these words he simply declared that he would never send them to me, because his friends had dissuaded him from doing so.

From all these things it was easy to see that he had burned with the desire of denouncing me and had undertaken that enterprise on his own account and without the consent of the other Fathers of the Society; and consequently that he was actuated by another spirit than that of your Society; and finally that there was

[1]Bourdin.

nothing he desired less than that I should see what he had written against me. Although it seemed to me to be quite unworthy to see a man of his sacred profession, with whom I had never had any controversy, and who was quite unknown to me, so publicly, so openly, and so extraordinarily biassed against me, giving as his excuse simply that he had never read my Discourse on Method, the untruth of which clearly appeared from the fact that he had frequently censured my Analysis, both in his Theses and in that opening discourse, although I nowhere else treated of it at all or even spoke of it under the name Analysis, excepting in that Discourse on Method which he declared he had never read. Yet at the same time, since he promised in the future to abstain from annoying me, I freely overlooked the past.

And I do not wonder in the least that the Reverend Rector had on the first occasion ordered nothing more severe than that he himself should give me his reasons for his proceeding, and thus confess openly that he could not maintain in my presence one of those things that he had arrogantly advanced against me, whether in his Theses or during his Disputations, or in his Treatises; and that he had likewise nothing to reply to the notes I had written on his Attack. But I am certainly much astonished that the Reverend Father has had so great a desire to attack me, that after having seen the little success that this first Attack had happily had, and that, after the time during which he had promised me *to carry on no particular warfare against my opinions*, nothing that was new passed between him and me, or even between me and any one of your members, he yet wrote his Dissertation. For if he does not carry on a *particular warfare* against my opinions, I am altogether ignorant of what combating the opinions of others means, if perchance he does not excuse himself by saying that as a matter of fact he does not impugn my opinions, but those of other insane ones, which calumniously he has ascribed to me; or else that he never thought that his Dissertation would fall into my hands. For it is easy to judge by the style in which it is written, that it has never been purposely designed to be placed in the number of the Objections made against my Meditations; for this is sufficiently clear from the fact that he did not wish me to see his other Treatises (for what could they contain worse than what it contains?); it is finally very manifest by the wonderfully full licence which he gives himself to attribute to me opinions quite different from my own, for he would have shown himself a little more restrained than he is, had he thought that I should have reproached him publicly. For that reason I feel and express my deepest thanks for receiving the Dissertation, certainly not to him, but to the Society and to you.

I should have liked that this opportunity, such as it is, now offered me of thanking you, could be conjoined with concealment of the injuries which he has done me, rather than with some desire to avenge myself, lest I should seem to do this for my own sake; and in fact I should not do so did I not think that it would conduce to your honour and that of your Society, and lead to the discovery of very useful truths. But, as the Reverend Father teaches mathematics in your College of Paris, which may be called one of the most celebrated in the whole world, and as the mathematical is the faculty in which I am said principally to be engaged, so, just as there is no person in all your Society whose authority can more efficaciously impugn my opinions than his, there is similarly no one whose errors in this matter could more easily be attributed to you all, were I to pass them over in silence. For many people would persuade themselves that he alone from out of all your Body, had been selected to judge of my opinions, and thus that on the above question as much regard ought to be paid to him alone as to you all, and in this matter that the same judgment should be passed on you as on him.

And further, though the advice which he has followed in this matter is very well suited to impede, or temporarily retard, the knowledge of the truth, it is not sufficient to suppress it altogether, and you would certainly receive no honour if it came to be discovered. For he made no effort to refute my opinions by reasoning, but contented himself with setting forth as mine, other opinions of a very inappropriate and pointless description, conceived in terms sufficiently like mine, and simply mocking them as unworthy of being refuted. By this artifice he would easily have turned away all those who do not know me, or who have never seen my writings, from reading them; and he would perhaps by this means have prevented a yet further examination by those who having seen them do not sufficiently understand them as yet, that is to say, the most part of those who have seen them: for, as a matter of fact, they would never have doubted that a man of his profession, and especially one

belonging to your Society, would have dared confidently to set forth opinions as mine, which were not mine, and to mock at them.

And to this end it would have helped greatly that his Dissertation had not been seen by all, but had merely been communicated privately to certain of his friends; for by this means it would have been easy for him to arrange that it would be seen by none of those who could have recognized his fictions; and the others would have placed so much the more credence in him, inasmuch as they would be persuaded that he would not have desired to bring it to light in case of its prejudicing my reputation, and that he was rendering to me the service of a friend. And yet there would have been no danger of its not being read by a sufficient number of persons; for if he had only been able to persuade the friends of your Society, in your College of Paris, as he hoped to do, this their opinion would have easily passed on to all the other members of your Society who are scattered all over the world; and from them it would have passed to almost all other men, who had placed their trust in the authority of your Society. And if that had happened, I should not have been much surprised, for since each of you is incessantly occupied with his own particular studies, it is impossible that all can examine all the new books which are every day in great numbers published; I fancy, however, that you would refer a book to the judgment of whoever of your Society was the first to read it, and follow his judgment in deciding whether the others would read the work, or abstain from so doing. It seems to me that this has already been proved in respect of the Treatise which I published on Meteors; for seeing it treats of a section of philosophy which is therein explained more accurately, if I am not mistaken, and more probably, than it is by any of the authors who have written upon it before me, I do not see that there is any reason why these philosophers, who year by year teach Meteors in your College, should not deal with it, if it be not that possibly by believing the wrongful judgments made upon me by the Reverend Father, they have never read it.

But as long as he never did anything but attack those writings of mine which deal with physics or mathematics, I did not concern myself greatly. But seeing that in this Dissertation he undertook to destroy, not by reasoning, but by abuse, the principles of Metaphysics of which I availed myself in demonstrating the existence of God and the real distinction between the soul of man and the body, I judged the knowledge of these truths to be so important, that I believed no sensible man could object if I undertook to defend what I have written with all my strength. And it will not be difficult to accomplish this, for, since he has not objected to anything in me but that I carried doubt much too far, it is not necessary in order to show how unjust he is in blaming me for this, that I should here mention all the places in my Meditations in which I have diligently, and, if I mistake not, more accurately than any other who has written on the subject, successfully refuted that doubt; but it is sufficient that I should here make known to you what I have expressly written in the beginning of my reply to the third Objection; for I set forth no reasons for doubt with the object of persuading others thereto, but on the contrary for the purpose of refuting them; in this matter I clearly followed the example of doctors who "describe the illness in regard to which they wish to teach the cure." And tell me, pray, who has been so audacious and impudent as to blame Hippocrates or Galen for having shown the causes which engender illness, and who has concluded therefrom that they neither of them taught anything but the Method of falling ill?

Certainly those who know that the Reverend Father has had this audacity, would have difficulty in persuading themselves that in this matter he acted on his own account and following his own counsel, if I did not myself bear witness and make known, how it came about that his previous writings against me had not been approved by your Society, and his last Dissertation has been sent to me at your request. And as this could not be more conveniently done than in this letter, I think that it is not out of place that I cause it to be printed with the Annotations which I have made on his *Dissertation*.

And in order that I might myself derive some profit therefrom, I would like here to say something to you of the Philosophy on which I am engaged, and which, if nothing prevents me, I mean to bring to light in one or two years.[1] Having in the year 1637 published some specimens of this Philosophy, I did all in my power to protect myself from the ill-will which I well saw, unworthy as I was, would be drawn upon me; this was the reason why I did not wish to put my name to them; not as perhaps has appeared to some, because I had not con-

[1] i.e. *The Principles of Philosophy*, published in 1644.

fidence in the truth of the reasons contained in them, and was in any degree ashamed of having written them; it was for the same reason that I declared expressly in my *Discourse on Method* that it appeared to me that I should in nowise consent to my philosophy being published during my life. And I should still be of the same mind if, as I hoped, as reason seemed to promise me, this had freed me from at least some measure of ill-will. But the result was quite otherwise. For such has been the lot of my writings, that although they could not have been understood by many, yet because they were comprehended by some, and indeed by persons who were very intellectual and learned, who deigned to examine them with more care than others, many truths which had not hitherto been discovered were there recognised as being present, and the fame of this becoming bruited abroad, made many persons likewise believe that I knew somewhat as certain and incontrovertible in Philosophy, which was not subject to dispute. This finally caused the greater part not only of those who, being outside the Schools, were at liberty to philosophize as they liked, but even the greater part of those who teach, more especially of the younger teachers, who place their trust more on strength of intellect than on a false reputation for knowledge, and, in a word, all those who love truth, to beg me to bring my philosophy to the light of day. But as to the others, that is to say those who prefer to appear learned rather than to be such, and who already imagine themselves to have acquired some renown amongst the learned just because they are able to dispute with acrimony in all the controversies of the Schools, since they feared that if the truth came to be discovered all these controversies would cease, and by the same means all their teaching would come into contempt; and further having some idea that if I published my philosophy the truth might be discovered; they have not indeed dared to declare openly that they did not desire that it should be published, but they have betrayed a great animosity towards me. And it has been very easy for me to distinguish the one from the others. For those who wish to see my philosophy published recollected very well that I had intended not to publish it during my life, and many even complained of me that I preferred to leave it to our successors rather than to give it to my contemporaries; however, all men of intelligence who knew the reason of it, and who saw that it was not due to want of will on my part to serve the public, did not for all that like me the less. But as for those who apprehended that it might never see the light, they have never recollected the facts of the case, or at least they have not wished to believe them, but on the contrary they supposed that I had merely promised its publication: hence, according to these I was called *the famous promiser* and compared to those who for many years boasted that they were going to publish books, to which they had never even put pen. This likewise causes the Reverend Father to say that *I had been expected to publish for so long that now we must despair of publication altogether;* this is truly absurd, as if one could expect something of a man not yet old, which no one has been able to accomplish during centuries. And it not also bears evidence of imprudence, since in thinking to blame me, he yet confesses that I am such that a few years have sufficed to make the delay of a work on my part seem long which I should not expect him to finish within a thousand years supposing we both could live so long. Men of this type, in the full belief that I had resolved to publish this philosophy which gave them so much apprehension, as soon as it was in a state of readiness, commenced to decry by calumnies, concealed as well as open and public, not only the opinions expounded in the writings which I had already published, but principally also this to them still unknown philosophy, with the idea either of preventing me from printing it, or of destroying it so soon as it came to light and so to speak strangling it in its cradle. At first I did nothing but laugh at the vanity of all their efforts, and the more vehemently I found them attacking my writings, the higher in my opinion did they rate me. But when I saw that their number increased from day to day, and, as generally happens, that there were many more who lost no occasion of seeking to injure me than there were of those who were desirous of giving me their support, I dreaded that they might by their secret practices acquire some power, and more disturb my leisure, if I remained constant in my design of not printing my philosophy, than were I to oppose them openly; and by producing the whole of that which they do fear I shall see to it that they have nothing to fear. I have resolved to give to the public all the small amount of my Meditations on Philosophy, and to work to the utmost of my power to bring it to pass that if they are found to be true, my opinions may be generally accepted. This will cause

their not being prepared in the same order and style as I have formerly adopted with the greater part of them in the Treatise whose argument I expounded in the Discourse on Method, but I shall make use of a mode of writing more suited to the usages of the Schools, in treating each question in short articles, so that each one may depend for its proof only on those that precede, and thus all may together form but one single body. And by this means I hope that the truth of all things as to which there is disputation in philosophy will be so clearly seen that all those who desire to seek it will find it very easily in my writings.

In fact all young people seek truth when first they apply themselves to the study of philosophy. All others also, of whatever age, seek it when they meditate alone by themselves on the matters of Philosophy, and examine them for their own use. Even the princes and magistrates and all those who establish academies or colleges, and who furnish great sums for the teaching of Philosophy in them, are quite unanimous in desiring that as far as possible, only true Philosophy shall be taught. And if it be permitted by princes that dubious and controversial questions shall be agitated, it is not in order that those who are their subjects shall by this custom of disputation and controversy learn to become more contentious, more refractory, and more opinionative, and thus less obedient to their superiors and more likely to become seditious, but merely in order that, by such disputes, they may be convinced of the truth; or if a long experience has persuaded them that it is rarely discovered by such means, they are yet so jealous of it, that they believe that the small amount of hope there is of finding it should not be neglected. For there has never been a people so savage or barbarous, or one which shrinks so much from the right use of the reason which pertains to man alone, as to desire opinions to be taught in its midst contrary to the known truth. And there is no doubt that we ought to prefer truth to all the opinions opposed to it, however deep-rooted and common they may be; and that all those who teach others should be obliged to seek it with all their might and when they have found it to teach it.

But perhaps it may not be thought that it will be found in the new Philosophy which I promise. For it is not likely that I alone should have seen more clearly than thousands of the most intelligent of men who have accepted the opinions commonly received in the Schools;

and roads frequently followed and known are always more reliable than new and unknown ones, and this is particularly true of our theology, as to which the experience of many years has shown us that it agrees with the old and ordinary philosophy very well, and this is uncertain with regard to a new one. And it is for that reason that some maintain that we must early prevent its publication and demolish it, in case, by attracting to itself by the charm of novelty a multitude of ignorant persons, it may gradually increase, and strengthen itself through time, or eise trouble the peace and quietude of the Schools or Academies, or even bring new heresies into the Church.

I reply to this that, in truth, I make claim to nothing, nor do I profess to see more than other men; but this perhaps has been of use to me, namely, that, not trusting very much to my own genius, I followed only the simplest and easiest roads. For we must not be astonished if anyone makes more progress in following these paths than others, endowed with much greater talent, make over the rough and impenetrable roads which they follow.

I further add that I do not desire that my simple word should be accepted regarding the truth of what I promise, but that judgment should be made on the writings which I have already published. For I did not there make trial of one question or two, but explained more than a thousand which had not so far been expounded by any one before; and although hitherto many had looked at my writings askance, and endeavoured in all sorts of ways to refute them, no one that I know of has yet been able to find them not true. If an enumeration is made of all the questions that have during all the centuries through which the other philosophies have flourished, been through their means solved, we shall find them neither so numerous nor so celebrated as those of mine. But further, I state boldly that the solution of no one question has ever been given by the aid of the principles of the philosophy of the Peripatetics, that I myself cannot demonstrate to be false and illegitimate. And to prove this, let any one set before me, not all, for I do not consider that they are worth the trouble of employing much time upon, but some of the most striking questions, and I promise that I shall stand by what I have said. I simply make it known here in order to remove all matter of dispute, that in speaking of the particular principles of the Peripatetic philosophy, I do not except questions the solution

of which are derived either entirely from the experience common to all men, or from the consideration of figures and movements proper to mathematicians, or finally from the notions of Metaphysics which are commonly received, and which seem to have been admitted by me just as much as are the preceding, as appears from my Meditations.

I go further and say what may seem to be a paradox, viz. that there is nothing in all this philosophy in so far as it is termed Peripatetic and different from others, that is not new; and that on the other hand there is nothing in mine that is not old. For, as regards principles, I accept those alone which have been generally accepted by all Philosophers, and which for that reason are the most ancient of all; and that which I finally deduce from them appears to be, as I clearly show, so contained and implied in these principles, that it would seem that it is likewise very ancient, since nature herself has engraved it upon our minds. But, on the other hand, the principles of the ordinary philosophy, at least at the time at which they were invented by Aristotle or by others, were new, nor should they be esteemed to be better now than they then were; and nothing has been as yet deduced from them which is not contested, and which, according to the custom of the Schools, is not subject to change at the hands of individual Philosophers, and hence which is not entirely new, since it is every day made afresh.

As to Theology, as one truth can never be contrary to another truth, it would be a kind of impiety to fear that the truths discovered in philosophy were contrary to those of the true Faith. And I even assert that our religion teaches us nothing which could not be as easily or even more easily, explained in accordance with my principles, than with those commonly received. And it seems to me that I have already given a sufficiently full proof of that at the end of my Reply to the Fourth Objections, in respect of a question in which we usually have the greatest trouble in making Philosophy accord with Theology. And I am still ready to do the same in regard to other questions, were there need; and even likewise to show that there are many things in the ordinary Philosophy which are not really in accordance with these that in Theology are certain, although this is usually dissimulated by those who support that philosophy, or through long habit of acceptance of them, the fact is not perceived.

We must not likewise fear that my opinions

may increase too much by attracting to them a multitude ignorant and greedy for novelty. On the contrary, since experience shows that those who approve of them are the more cultivated, whom not novelty but truth attracts, they cannot make headway too quickly.

We must not either apprehend that it may disturb the peace of the Schools; but on the other hand, since all the Philosophers embroil themselves in so many controversies that they can never be in a greater warfare than they now are, there is no better method for establishing peace amongst them, and refuting the heresies which day by day revive their controversies, than by obliging them to receive the opinions which, like mine, are proved to be true. For the clear conception that we have of them, will remove all matter of doubt and disputation.

And from all this we see clearly that there is in truth no reason why some men should be so anxious to turn away others from a knowledge of my opinions, except that holding them to be evident and certain they are afraid that they should stand in the way of that reputation for learning that they themselves have acquired through the knowledge of other less probable reasoning. So that this very envy that they bear, is no small proof of the truth and certainty of my philosophy. But lest perhaps I may seem to be boasting falsely of the envy in which I am held, with nothing to call in evidence but the Dissertation of the Reverend Father, I shall tell you here what has happened not long since in one of the most recent Academies of these Provinces.

A certain Doctor of Medicine[1]—a man of most subtle and perceptive mind, and of the number of those who, although they are well taught in the philosophy of the Schools, yet because they disbelieve it and are open minded, are not on that account very proud, nor imagine themselves to be wise in the way in which others do, who are so to speak drunken with knowledge—read my *Dioptric* and *Meteors* so soon as they saw the light, and at once judged that they contained within them the principles of a Philosophy more true than any other. And having diligently collated them and deduced others from them, he was so skilful and diligent as in a few months to compose an entire treatise on Physiology which, when shown to a few of his own friends, gave them such pleasure that they made application to

the magistracy and obtained for him a professoriate of medicine which was then vacant, and which he had hitherto not tried to procure. In this way, having become professor, he judged that it was his duty to make it his business mainly to teach those things which had procured him the office; and that so much the more that he believed them to be true, and held the contrary to be false. But as it came to pass that by this means he attracted to himself a large number of auditors who deserted the other classes, certain of his colleagues, seeing that he was preferred to them, commenced to be envious and frequently brought complaints against him to the magistracy, requesting that he should be forbidden to teach the new doctrine. And yet for three years they could obtain nothing against him excepting that he was exhorted to teach the elements of the ordinary Philosophy and Medicine along with his own principles, so that by this means he should put it in the power of his audience to read the works of others. For the magistracy being prudent saw very clearly that if these new opinions were true, it should not prevent their being published; if, on the other hand, they were false, there was no need to prohibit them, because in a short while they would collapse of themselves. But seeing that on the contrary they grew from day to day, and that they were followed out for the most part by men of highest merit and distinction, rather than by the more humble and youthful who were more easily turned aside by the authority or advice of the envious, the magistrates gave a new employment to this doctor, which was indeed to explain on certain days of the week certain extra lessons on Problems of Physics—both those suggested by Aristotle and by others—thus giving to him a better occasion for the treatment of all portions of Physics than he could have had in merely dealing with his own subject of Medicine. And his other colleagues would have thereafter remained quiet and given place to the truth, if it had not been that one, the Rector of the Academy,[2] resolved to use all the machinery in his power to oust him. And in order that you may know something of these my adversaries I shall in a few words sketch his character.

This one is termed a theologian, an orator, and a controversialist; and he has acquired great repute amongst the populace from the fact that declaring now against the Roman

---

[1]Henricus Regius or Henry de Roy, of Utrecht, at one time an ardent adherent of Descartes.

[2]Gisbertus Voetius, Rector of the University of Utrecht 1641–1642.

church, now against others which are different from his own, and now against the powers that be, he betrays an ardent and indomitable zeal for religion, and occasionally also mingles in his discourse words of a scurrilous kind which gains the ears of the commonalty; but since every day he brings out many little books which, however, deserve to be read by none, and further cites various authors who yet more frequently tell against him than in his favour, and whom he probably knows only by their table of contents; and as he speaks very boldly, but also with very little skill, of all the sciences, as though he were very learned in them, he passes for being very wise before the ignorant. But those persons who have greater understanding, who know how he has always shown himself ready to quarrel with anybody, and how frequently in disputes he has brought forward abuse rather than reasons, and basely retreated after being vanquished, if they are of a religion different from his, openly jeer at and disdain him; and some have even so controverted him publicly that it would seem that nothing further remained to be said against him; and if they are of the same religion, although they excuse and support him as much as they can, they yet do not in their hearts approve of him.

After this individual had been Rector for some time, it came to pass that when my medical friend was presiding at the defence of certain theses by some of his pupils, they were not given an opportunity to reply to the arguments brought before them, but were disturbed all the time by students stamping their feet. I do not say that this stamping was instigated by this theologian through his friends, for as to this I have no knowledge, but certainly it was not done previously; and I heard afterwards from some who are worthy of credence, and who were present, that it could not have been excited through the fault of the President or his respondents, since these noises always began before they had explained their views. And yet the report was spread abroad that the new philosophy was badly defended, in order to make everyone conclude that it was not worthy of being publicly taught.

It happened also that as there were frequently disputes under the presidency of this physician, and as the theses were filled with questions of a very various and disconnected kind, arranged in accordance with the fancy of those who supported them, and not at all in a careful way, someone placed in his theses the

assertion *that the union of soul and body produced not a unity which was an entity on its own account, but one which was accidental*, meaning by an *accidental entity* whatever is composed of two substances altogether different, without at the same time denying the substantial unity by which the mind is joined to the body, nor the natural aptitude or inclination that every individual part has for this union. This we see from the fact that they had added immediately afterwards: *that these substances were termed incomplete by reason of the compound which resulted from their union;* so that nothing remained to reply to either of these propositions, excepting perhaps that they were not expressed after the manner of the Schools.

This seemed indeed to the Theologian and Rector to give a sufficient opportunity for attacking my medical friend on every side, and in order to remove him by this means from his chair if the matter succeeded as he hoped, even in spite of the magistracy. And it was of no avail to the Physician that as soon as he knew that the Rector did not approve of this thesis, he went to see him and the other theological professors, and having explained to them his meaning, assured them that he had no intention of writing anything contrary to their theology, and his. For a few days later the Rector caused these theses to be published to which I am assured he intended to preface this title: *Corollaries propounded for the instruction of students by the authority of the sacred faculty of Theology;* and added *that the opinion of Taurellus, whom the theologians of Heidelberg termed the Atheist Physician, and that of the foolish young Gorlaeus who says that man is an entity by accident, is in very many ways at variance with Physics, Metaphysics, Philosophy of Spirit and Theology &c.* So that after having made all the other theological professors and preachers in the place sign these (if they really signed them, for of that I am not informed), he might depute certain of his colleagues who were to tell the magistracy that the physician had been condemned for heresy by an ecclesiastical council and placed in the company of Taurellus and Gorlaeus, authors whom he might possibly never have read, and who for my part are absolutely unknown to me; and that thus the magistrate could not with the popular goodwill have him longer occupying the chair. But as these theses were still in the press, they fell by chance into the hands of certain of the magistrates who, having called to them the Theologian, admonished him of his duty and charged him at least to alter the title and not thus publicly abuse the authority of the Faculty of Theology by resting his calumnies upon it.

Notwithstanding this, he went on with the publication of the theses, and, in imitation of the Reverend Father,[1] supported them in disputation for three days. And because they would have had too little matter in them had he not treated of any thing but this verbal question: *whether or not a composition formed of two substances should be called an entity by accident*, he added to this certain others, the principal of which was *concerning the substantial forms of material things*, all of which had been denied by the Physician with the exception of the reasonable soul; he, however, on the contrary, tried to maintain and defend them by every reason in his power, as being the palladium of the Peripatetic School. And in order that you may not here think that it is without cause that I interest myself in the disputes of others, in addition to the fact that in his theses my name was mentioned, as was frequently done by the physician in his, he also mentioned me by name in the course of his disputation, and demanded of his opponent—a man whom I had never seen—if it were not I who suggested to him his arguments; and availing himself of an odious comparison, he added that those who were dissatisfied with the ordinary method of philosophising expected of me another, as the Jews expected their Elias, to lead them into all truth.

When he had thus triumphed for three days, the Physician, who saw very clearly that if he were silent many would imagine him to be vanquished, and if, on the other hand, he defended himself by public disputations, people would not cease as formerly to prevent his being heard, formed the resolution to reply in writing to the theses of the Theologian, in which writing he should refute by good and solid reasons all that had been said against him or his opinions in these theses; but at the same time he should treat their author so gently and respectfully as to try to conciliate, or at least not to exasperate him, inflamed as he was against him. And in truth his reply was such that many of those who read it, believed it to contain nothing of which the Theologian could complain, unless it were, perhaps, that he termed him a man of piety and desirous of opposing every sort of malevolence.

But although he had not been maligned by word of mouth, he yet held that the Doctor

[1]Bourdin.

had done him a great injury, because he had got the better of him by reasoning, and indeed by reasons that clearly showed him to be a calumniator and ignorant of the matter in hand. And to remedy this evil, he thought he could do no better than make use of his power, and in his own town secure the prohibition of the circulation of a reply which was so odious to him. He may possibly have heard the assertion some people have made about Aristotle, namely, that when he had no good arguments wherewith to refute the opinions of the philosophers who preceded him, he attributed to them others which were quite absurd, that is to say those given in his writings, and, in order to prevent those who came after him from discovering his imposture, he caused all their books to be diligently sought out and burned. Attempting as a faithful Peripatetic to imitate this, our Theologian assembled the Senate of his Academy, and complained of the libel which had been made upon him by one of his colleagues, and said that he must suppress it and at the same time exterminate all this philosophy which disturbed the peace of the Academy. The most assented to this statement. Three of their number were deputed to go to the magistracy and they made to him the same complaints. The magistracy, in order to satisfy them, caused a few copies to be taken from the publisher's shop, which caused the rest to be more greedily sought after, and read with more interest. But as no one found anything therein of which the Theologian could justly complain, excepting the strength of reasoning which he could not evade, he was made the laughing-stock of all.

He yet gave himself no rest, and assembled his Senatus Academicus every day, in order to acquaint the members with particulars of this infamy. He had a great task in hand: he had to show what were the reasons that he desired the reply of the Physician and all his philosophy to be condemned, and he had none to give. Still a judgment finally appeared which was in the name of the Senatus Academicus, but which should be rather attributed to the Rector alone; for as in all the assemblages which he convoked he took his seat in the capacity of judge and at the same time as the most strenuous of accusers, while the Physician was neither heard in his defence nor even summoned, who can doubt that he would easily have drawn the greater part of his colleagues on the side that he desired, and that the large number of votes that he had on his part would have prevailed over the small number of the others? This was evidenced principally by the fact that amongst them there were certain ones who had the same, and even more reason for wishing ill to the physician; and that others who were peaceable men, knowing the ill-temper of their Rector, did not willingly contradict him. And there was this that was remarkable, that not one of them desired to be nominated as approving of this judgment, and there was even one, neither a friend of the Physician nor ever known to me,[1] who, not desiring to participate in the infamy which he foresaw would fall one day on this action, expressly desired that his name be given as not approving of it.

I shall however here append a copy of this judgment, both because possibly your Reverence may not be sorry to know what passes in these parts between men of letters, and also, so far as I can—when in some years the fragile leaflets on which it is printed have all been dispersed—in order to prevent certain calumniators from making use of their authority by causing it to be believed that the judgment contained reasons sufficiently valid to bring about the condemnation of my philosophy. I shall only omit the name of the University, in case that which occurred through the imprudence of a turbulent Rector just a day or two ago, and which another may perhaps change tomorrow, might disgrace it amongst strangers.

JUDGMENT PUBLISHED UNDER THE NAME OF THE SENATUS ACADEMICUS OF ***[2]

*The Professors of the Academy of *** not having been able to see without grave regret the pamphlet which was published in the month of February, 1642, with the title,* Reply about the notes to the Theological-Philosophical Corollary &c., *and having recognized that it tended only to the ruin and shame of the University, and that it could only excite sinister suspicions in the minds of others, judged it proper to certify to one and all whom it may concern.*

FIRST, *that they do not approve of this proceeding whereby a colleague publishes books or pamphlets against another of his number, especially pamphlets in which he is expressly named; and this merely on the occasion of certain theses or corollaries which have been printed anony-*

mously, regarding matters of controversy in the University.

FURTHER, *that they do not approve of this mode of vindicating a new and assumed philosophy in the said book; especially since it constantly made use of insolent language, opprobrious to those who here or elsewhere teach a philosophy contrary to the above, and uphold the ordinary philosophy which is everywhere received in the Academies as that which is more true. For example, when the author of the before mentioned pamphlet says:*

Page 6. For it is a long time since I perceived that the great progress my auditors made in a short time under me, has caused some people to be jealous.

Page 7. The terms of which the others usually avail themselves in order to resolve difficulties, never fully satisfy those who have more clear-sighted intelligence, however little, but merely fill their minds with mist and darkness.

In the same place. From me men learn much more easily and quickly to understand the true meaning of a difficulty than is commonly done from others; this is proved by the experience of many of my followers who have made an honourable appearance in public disputes, without having given more than some months of their time to study under me. Nor have I any doubt that anyone with any mind at all will allow that there is nothing to demur to in all this, but on the contrary that all is worthy of praise.

Page 9. These miserable entities (i.e. the substantial forms and real qualities) are clearly not of any use at all, unless to blind the eyes of those who study, and bring it to pass that in place of this learned ignorance that you so commend, another and haughty sort of ignorance will be obtruded.

Page 15. On the other hand from the beliefs of those who assert the existence of substantial forms, it is easy to fall into the views of those who hold that the soul is corporeal and mortal.

Page 20. It may be asked whether this mode of philosophising which is in the habit of reducing everything to one active principle, i.e. the substantial form, is not merely worthy of being rated as that of a Choræbus.[3]

Page 25. From this it clearly follows that it is not those who deny substantial forms, but rather those who maintain them, that may by

---

[1] Cyprianus Regneri, professor of Law.

[2] According to Adams and Tannery, Descartes here substituted asterisks for Ultrajectini, and in the line below for Ultrajectinae, i.e. of Utrecht (Ultrajectum).

[3] A foolish man who tries to count the waves (Suidas).

good reasoning be driven to such a point that they are made to appear atheists or brutes.

Page 39. Because the reasons that have thus far been established by others for the least important of propositions, are for the most part absolutely sterile and untrue, nor do they satisfy a mind which is seeking for truth.

THIRDLY. *That they reject this new philosophy, firstly because it is contrary to the ancient, which has hitherto with good reason been taught in all the Academies of the world, and that it subverts the fundamental principles on which it rests; secondly, because it turns away the young from the study of the old and true Philosophy, and prevents them from arriving at the fulness of erudition, because, being once imbued with the principles of this so-called philosophy, they are no longer capable of understanding the terms made use of by authors in their books, or those used by professors in their lectures and disputes; and finally because not only do many false and absurd opinions follow from this philosophy, but an imprudent youth can deduce from it certain opinions which are opposed to the other disciplines and faculties, and above all to the orthodox Theology.*

That for these reasons they express the judgment that all who teach Philosophy in this University shall henceforward abstain from the purpose and design of teaching the new philosophy, contenting themselves with that modicum of liberty which is practised here after the example of other most celebrated academies, without for all that destroying the foundations of the old and accepted philosophy, and labouring with all their power in every way to preserve the good name and tranquillity of the University. Given this 16th day of March, 1642.

And it is a matter worthy of remark that this judgment was published some time after it had been a subject of derision that the Rector had preferred to suppress the Doctor's book rather than reply to it. Hence it cannot be doubted that, if not all the reasons possible, at least all those that he could invent, in order to excuse his action, are expressed here. Let us then, if you please, run through them all.

First it is asserted, that the Physician's book *tends to hurt and disgrace the Academy, and to excite evil principles in the minds of others.* I cannot interpret this otherwise than that from it we might find occasion to suspect, or rather to be assured, that the Rector of the University was imprudent in opposing the manifest truth, as well as malicious, in that having been conquered by reason, he yet tried to conquer

by his authority. But this shame and ignominy has waned because he is Rector no longer;[1] and the University suffers less dishonour in still having such a one as a professor, than it is honoured in still having the Physician, provided always that she does not render herself unworthy of him.

It is said secondly *that it is unseemly that a colleague should publish books against another colleague especially one in which he is expressly named.* But on this account the Rector himself, who in this judgment was prosecutor and presiding judge, should be the only one guilty, and the only one to be condemned. For before this, without being provoked to do so, he had caused to be published against his colleague two little books in the form of theses, and had even tried to rest them on the authority of the Sacred Faculty of Theology, in order to assail an innocent man and overthrow him by calumny. And it is absurd for him to excuse himself by the fact that he had not named him, because he quoted the same words that this doctor formerly printed, and so designated him that no one could doubt who was being indicted. But the Doctor, on the contrary, replied so moderately, and spoke of his name with such praise, that it might have been believed that it was not against him, but as a friend that he wrote to him, and as a person whose name was even held in honour; and this was really what would have been thought by the world, if the Theologian had availed himself of arguments, however little probable they might be, wherewith to refute the Physician. But what is more unjust than to see a Rector accuse one of his colleagues of having injured another, for the sole reason that he brought forward reasons so manifest and true to purge himself of the accusation of heresy and atheism which he had made against him, that by this means he prevented his being assailed on all sides?

And certainly the Theologian does not approve this manner of *defending the new and assumed philosophy* of which the Physician avails himself in the pamphlet annexed, *since it contains insolent language designed to bring into opprobrium those who teach the ordinary philosophy which is everywhere received as that which is more true.* But this very moderate man does not observe that he reprehends in another the insolence of his words, as to which I am nevertheless assured that no one could

[1] Voetius' tenure of office ceased on March 16, 1642.

see the slightest indication, if he merely studies those passages here cited, which have most likely been picked purposely in the book of the Physician, as being the most insolent and the best suited to raise up ill-will. Above all is this so if it be likewise observed that there is nothing more usual in the Schools of Philosophy than to see each one say without any disguise or reserve, that which he thinks, and hence that all the opinions of others are false, and that his alone are true; for the custom philosophers contract in their disputations insensibly habituates them to this liberty, which may seem somewhat rude to those whose lives are more urbane and polished. So the greater part of the expressions which are here cited as having been used in a kind of ill-will against all those who in all places profess Philosophy, should not be understood as being said except of our Theologian, as is made manifest from the book of the Physician; and he spoke in the plural number and third person in order to offend him the less. And, finally, as he has made the comparison with Choræbus, and spoken of atheists and beasts, etc., that has not been done spontaneously by the Physician, but subsequently to having had thrown at him those injurious opprobrious terms by the Theologian, the opprobrium of which he could not repel but by showing by good and evident reasoning that they were totally inapplicable to him, but that they did apply to his adversary. What can you do with a headstrong man like this who arrogates to himself the liberty of calumniating others by calling them atheists and beasts, and who yet cannot endure being refuted by convincing reasoning? But I hasten to matters which concern me more.

He alleges three reasons by which he condemns my new philosophy. The first is that it is *opposed to the ancient*. I do not repeat here what I have said above, that my philosophy is of all others the most ancient, or that there is nothing in the ordinary philosophy which is contrary to it, which is not new. But I only ask whether it is credible that a man is likely to understand a philosophy which he condemns, who is so stupid (or if you wish it, so malicious) as to have desired to bring it under the suspicion of being magical, because it regards figures. I further ask what is the object of the disputations which take place in the Schools. Doubtless, it will be said, by their means to discover the truth. For if it were once discovered, the disputations would grow less frequent, as we see in regard to Geometry,

as to which there is usually no dispute. But if this evident truth so long looked for and expected, was at length set before us by an angel, would it not also be rejected for the sole reason that it would seem novel to those accustomed to the disputations of the Schools? But it will possibly be said that the principles which are overturned by the philosophy we assume are not disputed. But why does he thus suffer them to be so easily overturned? And is not their uncertainty sufficiently shown from the fact that nothing has as yet been built up upon them which is certain and assured?

The other reason is *that youth, once imbued with the principles of this so-called Philosophy, is no longer capable of understanding the terminology which is in use by authors in their books.* As though it were a necessity that philosophy, which is only instituted for the knowledge of the truth, should teach certain terms of which it itself has no need! Why does he not condemn grammar and rhetoric, because it is rather their function to treat of words, while yet they are so much opposed to the teaching of those scholastic terms that they reject them as barbarous? Were he therefore to complain that *by them youth is turned away from the study of the true Philosophy, and prevented from reaching the fulness of erudition*, there would be no reason for laughing at him more than when he says the same of our philosophy; for it is not from it, but from the writings of those who make use of these terms that we should expect their explanation.

The third and last reason has two parts, the one of which is manifestly absurd, and the other insulting and false. For what is there so true or so clear as that it is not easy *for imprudent youth to deduce many false and absurd ideas from it?* But to say that anything follows from my philosophy *which clashes with the orthodox Theology*, is clearly false and insulting. And I do not desire to take exception to this statement in that I do not hold his theology to be orthodox: I have never despised anyone for not being of the same sentiments as myself, more especially regarding matters of belief; for I know that faith is a gift of God. Quite otherwise, I even cherish and honour many theologians and preachers who profess the same religion as he. But I have frequently protested that I did not desire to mix myself up with any theological controversies; as inasmuch as I only treat in my philosophy of things clearly known by the light of nature. They cannot be contrary to the Theology of anyone, unless this Theology is manifestly opposed to the light of reason, which I know no one will allow of the Theology professed by himself.

For the rest, in case it is believed that it is without foundation that I assert that the Theologian could not refute any of the reasons used by the physician, I shall here bring forward two or three examples to confirm the statement. For there are already two or three little books which have been published on this subject, not in truth by the Theologian, but for him, and by persons who, if they had contained anything that was good, would very gladly have attributed to him the credit, nor would he in covering himself as he does with their name, have permitted that these foolish things should have been said, had he had better to say.

The first of these booklets was published under the title of theses by his son, who was a professor in the same university.[1] And in it, having done no more than repeat the futile argument which his father had used to establish the substantial forms or add others yet more inane; and having made no mention at all of the reasoning of the Physician, by which he had already refuted all these arguments, nothing can be concluded but that its author did not understand them, or at least that he was not quick at learning.

The other booklet which comprehends two, appeared under the name of that student who had replied in the seditious dispute which lasted three days under the presidency of the Rector.[2] The title of it is *Prodromus, or a thorough examination of the principles of the orthodox Philosophy*, etc. And it is true that in this booklet all the reasons are placed which could thus far have been collated by its author or by its authors, to refute those of the Physician; for a second part was for the first time added, or a new *Prodromus*, so that nothing might be omitted of all that which came into the mind of the author while the first was being printed. But yet we shall see that in these two booklets not even the slightest of the reasons brought forward by the Doctor has been, I shall not say thoroughly, but even with probability, refuted. And it would thus appear that the author has had no other design in composing this great volume of pure ineptitudes, and entitling it *Prodromus* in order to make it anticipate another, unless it be to prevent anyone

from condescending to reply to it; and by this means to triumph before an ignorant populace, which thinks that books are better the larger they are, and that the loudest and longest talkers, are always adjudged the victors.

But for one who does not look for the good graces of the populace, and who has no other end in view but to give contentment to the honourable and cultured and satisfy his own conscience in defending so far as is possible the truth, I hope to make the futile subtleties and all the other things which our adversaries are accustomed to employ, so open and clear that nobody may be able to use them in future except a man who does not blush at being known by everyone as a calumniator, and as one who does not love truth. And to speak the truth, it has so far served not a little to hold in check the more conscientious, that from the beginning I have asked all who find anything to object to in my writings, to do me the honour of telling me of it, and at the same time I promised that I should not fail to reply to them; for they have seen very clearly that they could say nothing of me before the world with which they had not beforehand made me acquainted, without putting themselves under suspicion of being thought to be calumniators. But it has nevertheless come to pass that many have disregarded this request, and have even secretly censured my writings, even though they found nothing in them that they could convict of falsity, and even sometimes it happened that they had never read them: some indeed have gone so far as to compose entire books, not with a view of publishing them, but what I think much worse, with the view of privately reading them to credulous persons;[3] and they have partially filled them with false reasoning covered with a veil of much ambiguous language, and partially with reasoning which was true, but with which they combated only opinions which have been falsely attributed to me. Now, however, I beg and exhort them all to bring their writings to light. For experience has taught me that this will be better than if they were to address these questions to me, as I asked them to do before, so that, if I did not judge them to be worthy of reply, they should not have reason to complain that I had disdained them, or be able to boast falsely that I could not reply to them. And I should even desire this in order that others whose writings

[1]Paul Voet.
[2]Lambert Waterlaet.

[3]Descartes here refers to Gassendi, cf. pp. 166 sqq. above.

I might publish may be prevented from imagining that I did them an injury by joining my replies to their writings, because (as someone said to me lately about his own case) they would by this means be deprived of the fruit in which they might be able to take pleasure if they had published them themselves, which would cause them to be read everywhere for some months and thus have the possibility of occupying and influencing the minds of many persons, before I had time to reply. I do not desire to grudge them that fruit; nay, I do not promise to reply to them, unless I find that their reasons are such that I fear that they cannot be resolved as they pass from point to point by the readers. For as to those cavillings and revilings, and all the other things said outside the real subject, I shall believe that they are more for me than against me. For this reason I do not think that anyone would employ them in such a cause except he who desires to obtain evidence of more than he can prove by reasons, and who shall show in this matter that he has not sought the truth but is desirous of impugning it and therefore is not a man of probity and honour.

I do not indeed doubt that many good and pious men might hold my opinions in suspicion, both because they see that many reject them, and also because they are supposed to be new, and because few people have so far understood them. And it might even be difficult to find any company in which, if one came to deliberate on my opinions, many more would not be met with who would judge that they should be rejected, than who ventured to approve of them. For reason and prudence dictate that having to give our opinion on something not quite known to us, we should frequently judge of it in accordance with what happens in similar cases: and it has so many times happened that men have introduced new opinions into philosophy which have afterwards been recognized to be no better, but even much more dangerous than those commonly received, that it would not be without reason, if those who do not as yet sufficiently clearly perceive mine, when asked, judge that they should reject them. And so, true as they are, I should yet believe myself to have reason to apprehend that in accordance with the example of the Senate of that Academy of which I have spoken to you above, they might be condemned by all your Society, and generally by all assemblies of those who profess to teach, had I not promised myself that through your goodness

and prudence you would take me under your protection. But as you are the head of a Society[1] which can read my essays more easily than many others, the greater part of them being written in French, I do not doubt that you alone can do much in this matter. And I do not ask more of your bounty, than that you will be good enough to examine them yourself, or if greater business prevents your doing that, that you will not hand over the duty to the Reverend Father[2] alone, but to others more qualified than he; and as in the judgments of the law courts, when two or three witnesses worthy of credence say that they have seen something, they are believed rather than a multitude of other men, who, carried away perhaps by simple conjectures, imagine the contrary,—so I beg you to give credence only to those who shall declare that they understand perfectly those things on which they pass judgment; and the last boon I ask is that if you have certain reasons whereby you judge that I should change my plan of procedure, you will not feel it a burden to tell me of them.

Further, in this small number of Meditations which I published, all the principles of the philosophy which I am preparing are contained; and in the Dioptric and Meteors I have deduced from these principles many particular things which show what is my manner of reasoning; and that is why, although I am not yet setting forth all that philosophy, I yet consider that what I have already given forth, suffices to make known what it will be. Nor do I think that I am without good reason for having preferred to publish first some of my essays, rather than to give my system in its entirety before it was expected. For to speak frankly, although I do not doubt of the truth of it, yet because I know that the truth itself may very easily be condemned by many persons of good understanding, through being impugned by a few envious ones under the plea of novelty, I am not entirely certain that it is desired by all men, nor do I wish to constrain them to receive it. That is why I have given long warning to everyone that I am preparing it; many individuals wait for and expect it; one school alone has judged that it must reject it; but because I know that it only did so on the solicitation of its Rector, turbulent and

[1] Père Dinet as Provincial administered the Province of Paris, as it was denominated by the Society of Jesus.
[2] Père Bourdin.

foolish as he is, it has not much influence with me. But if perchance some others did not desire it, and had juster reasons for not desiring it, then I do not doubt that their opinions ought to be preferred to those of private individuals. And I even declare sincerely that I should never knowingly do anything contrary to the dictates of prudence, or the wishes of powers that be. And as I do not doubt that the side on which your Society will range itself ought to preponderate over the other, it would be to me the greatest boon if you would tell me your decision and that of your Society; so that as in other things of life I have always honoured and respected you above all others, I now undertake nothing in this affair which I think can be of some importance without having your approval. Farewell.

CONTENTS

Geometry

GEOMETRY

FIRST BOOK

PROBLEMS THE CONSTRUCTION OF WHICH REQUIRES ONLY STRAIGHT LINES AND CIRCLES

ANY PROBLEM in geometry can easily be reduced to such terms that a knowledge of the lengths of certain straight lines is sufficient for its construction. Just as arithmetic consists of only four or five operations, namely, addition, subtraction, multiplication, division and the extraction of roots, which may be considered a kind of division, so in geometry, to find required lines it is merely necessary to add or subtract other lines; or else, taking one line which I shall call unity in order to relate it as closely as possible to numbers, and which can in general be chosen arbitrarily, and having given two other lines, to find a fourth line which shall be to one of the given lines as the other is to unity (which is the same as multiplication); or, again, to find a fourth line which is to one of the given lines as unity is to the other (which is equivalent to division); or, finally, to find one, two, or several mean proportionals between unity and some other line (which is the same as extracting the square root, cube root, etc., of the given line). And I shall not hesitate to introduce these arithmetical terms into geometry, for the sake of greater clearness.

For example, let AB be taken as unity, and let it be required to multiply BD by BC. I have only to join the points A and C, and draw DE parallel to CA; then BE is the product of BD and BC.

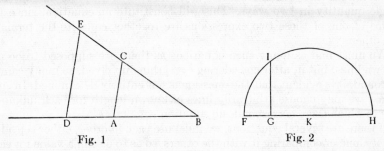

Fig. 1   Fig. 2

If it be required to divide BE by BD, I join E and D, and draw AC parallel to DE; then BC is the result of the division.

If the square root of GH is desired, I add, along the same straight line, FG equal to unity; then, bisecting FH at K, I describe the circle FIH about K as a center, and draw from G a perpendicular and extend it to I, and GI is the required root. I do not speak here of cube root, or other roots, since I shall speak more conveniently of them later.

Often it is not necessary thus to draw the lines on paper, but it is sufficient to designate each by a single letter. Thus, to add the lines BD and GH, I call one a and the other b, and write $a+b$. Then $a-b$ will indicate that b is subtracted from a; ab that a is multiplied by b; $\frac{a}{b}$ that a is divided by b; aa or a^2 that a is multiplied by itself; a^3 that this result is multiplied by a, and so on, indefinitely. Again, if I wish to extract the square root of a^2+b^2, I write $\sqrt{a^2+b^2}$; if I wish to extract the cube root of $a^3-b^3+ab^2$, I write $\sqrt[3]{a^3-b^3+ab^2}$, and similarly for other roots. Here it must be observed that by a^2, b^3, and similar expressions, I ordinarily mean only simple lines, which, however, I name squares, cubes, etc., so that I may make use of the terms employed in algebra.

It should also be noted that all parts of a single line should always be expressed by the same number of dimensions, provided unity is not determined by the conditions of the problem. Thus, a^3 contains as many dimensions as ab^2 or b^3, these being the component parts of the line which I have called $\sqrt[3]{a^3-b^3+ab^2}$. It is not, however, the same thing when unity is determined, because unity can always be understood, even where there are too many or too few dimensions: thus, if it be required to extract the cube root of a^2b^2-b, we must consider the quantity a^2b^2 divided once by unity, and the quantity b multiplied twice by unity.

Finally, so that we may be sure to remember the names of these lines, a separate list should always be made as often as names are assigned or changed. For example, we may write, AB$=1$, that is AB is equal to 1; GH$=a$, BD$=b$, and so on.

If, then, we wish to solve any problem, we first suppose the solution already effected, and give names to all the lines that seem needful for its construction,—to those that are unknown as well as to those that are known. Then, making no distinction between known and unknown lines, we must unravel the difficulty in any way that shows most naturally the relations between these lines, until we find it possible to express a single quantity in two ways. This will constitute an equation, since the terms of one of these two expressions are together equal to the terms of the other.

We must find as many such equations as there are supposed to be unknown lines; but if, after considering everything involved, so many cannot be found, it is evident that the question is not entirely determined. In such a case we may choose arbitrarily lines of known length for each unknown line to which there corresponds no equation.

If there are several equations, we must use each in order, either considering it alone or comparing it with the others, so as to obtain a value for each of the unknown lines; and so we must combine them until there remains a single unknown line which is equal to some known line, or whose square, cube, fourth power, fifth power, sixth power, etc., is equal to the sum or difference of two or more quantities, one of which is known, while the others consist of mean proportionals between unity and this square, or cube, or fourth power, etc., multiplied by other known lines. I may express this as follows:

$$z = b,$$
$$\text{or } z^2 = -az + b^2,$$
$$\text{or } z^3 = az^2 + b^2z - c^3,$$
$$\text{or } z^4 = az^3 - c^3z + d^4, \text{ etc.}$$

That is, z, which I take for the unknown quantity, is equal to b; or, the square of z is equal to the square of b diminished by a multiplied by z; or, the cube of z is equal to a multiplied by the square of z, plus the square of b multiplied by z, diminished by the cube of c; and similarly for the others.

Thus, all the unknown quantities can be expressed in terms of a single quantity, whenever the problem can be constructed by means of circles and straight lines, or by conic sections, or even by some other curve of degree not greater than the third or fourth.

But I shall not stop to explain this in more detail, because I should deprive you of the pleasure of mastering it yourself, as well as of the advantage of training your mind by working over it, which is in my opinion the principal benefit to be derived from this science. Because, I find nothing here so difficult that it cannot be worked out by any one at all familiar with ordinary geometry and with algebra, who will consider carefully all that is set forth in this treatise.

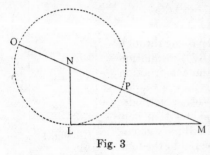

Fig. 3

I shall therefore content myself with the statement that if the student, in solving these equations, does not fail to make use of division wherever possible, he will surely reach the simplest terms to which the problem can be reduced.

And if it can be solved by ordinary geometry, that is, by the use of straight lines and circles on a plane surface, when the last equation shall have been entirely solved there will remain at most only the square of an unknown quantity, equal to the product of its root by some known quantity, increased or diminished by some other quantity also known. Then this root or unknown line can easily be found. For example, if I have $z^2 = az + b^2$, I construct a right triangle NLM with one side LM, equal to b, the square root of the known quantity b^2, and the other side, LN, equal to $\frac{1}{2}a$, that is, to half the other known quantity which was multiplied by z, which I supposed to be the unknown line. Then prolonging MN, the hypotenuse of this triangle, to O, so that NO is equal to NL, the whole line OM is the required line z. This is expressed in the following way:

$$z = \frac{1}{2}a + \sqrt{\frac{1}{4}a^2 + b^2}.$$

But if I have $y^2 = -ay + b^2$, where y is the quantity whose value is de-

sired, I construct the same right triangle NLM, and on the hypotenuse MN
lay off NP equal to NL, and the remainder PM is y, the desired root. Thus
I have

$$y = -\tfrac{1}{2}a + \sqrt{\tfrac{1}{4}a^2 + b^2}.$$

In the same way, if I had

$$x^4 = -ax^2 + b^2,$$

PM would be x^2 and I should have

$$x = \sqrt{-\tfrac{1}{2}a + \sqrt{\tfrac{1}{4}a^2 + b^2}},$$

and so for other cases.

Finally, if I have $z^2 = az - b^2$, I make NL equal to $\tfrac{1}{2}a$ and LM equal to b
as before; then, instead of joining the points M and N, I draw MQR parallel to LN, and with N as a center describe a circle through L cutting
MQR in the points Q and R; then z, the line sought, is
either MQ or MR, for in this case it can be expressed
in two ways, namely:

$$z = \tfrac{1}{2}a + \sqrt{\tfrac{1}{4}a^2 - b^2},$$

and

$$z = \tfrac{1}{2}a - \sqrt{\tfrac{1}{4}a^2 - b^2}.$$

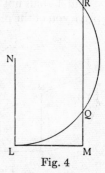

Fig. 4

And if the circle described about N and passing through
L neither cuts nor touches the line MQR, the equation
has no root, so that we may say that the construction
of the problem is impossible.

These same roots can be found by many other methods;
I have given these very simple ones to show that it is
possible to construct all the problems of ordinary geometry by doing no more than the little covered in the four
figures that I have explained. This is one thing which I believe the ancient mathematicians did not observe, for otherwise they would not have
put so much labor into writing so many books in which the very sequence
of the propositions shows that they did not have a sure method of finding
all, but rather gathered together those propositions on which they had happened by accident.

This is also evident from what Pappus has done in the beginning of his
seventh book, where, after devoting considerable space to an enumeration
of the books on geometry written by his predecessors, he finally refers to a
question which he says that neither Euclid nor Apollonius nor any one else
had been able to solve completely; and these are his words:

Quem autem dicit (Apollonius) in tertio libro locum ad tres, & quatuor lineas
ab Euclide perfectum non esse, neque ipse perficere poterat, neque aliquis alius;
sed neque paululum quid addere iis, quæ Euclides scripsit, per ea tantum co-
nica, quæ usque ad Euclidis tempora præmonstrata sunt, &c.[1]

[1]Moreover, he (Apollonius) says that the problem of the locus related to three or
four lines was not entirely solved by Euclid, and that neither he himself, nor any one
else has been able to solve it completely, nor were they able to add anything at
all to those things which Euclid had written, by means of the conic sections only
which had been demonstrated before Euclid.

A little farther on, he states the question as follows:

At locus ad tres, & quatuor lineas, in quo (Apollonius) magnifice se jactat, & ostentat, nulla habita gratia ei, qui prius scripserat, est hujusmodi. Si positione datis tribus rectis lineis ab uno & eodem puncto, ad tres lineas in datis angulis rectæ lineæ ducantur, & data sit proportio rectanguli contenti duabus ductis ad quadratum reliquæ: punctum contingit positione datum solidum locum, hoc est unam ex tribus conicis sectionibus. Et si ad quatuor rectas lineas positione datas in datis angulis lineæ ducantur; & rectanguli duabus ductis contenti ad contentum duabus reliquis proportio data sit; similiter punctum datum coni sectionem positione continget. Si quidem igitur ad duas tantum locus planus ostensus est. Quod si ad plures quam quatuor, punctum continget locos non adhuc cognitos, sed lineas tantum dictas; quales autem sint, vel quam habeant proprietatem, non constat: earum unam, neque primam, & quæ manifestissima videtur, composuerunt ostendentes utilem esse. Propositiones autem ipsarum hæ sunt.

Si ab aliquo puncto ad positione datas rectas lineas quinque ducantur rectæ lineae in datis angulis, & data sit proportio solidi parallelepipedi rectanguli, quod tribus ductis lineis continetur ad solidum parallelepipedum rectangulum, quod continetur reliquis duabus, & data quapiam linea, punctum positione datam lineam continget. Si autem ad sex, & data sit proportio solidi tribus lineis contenti ad solidum, quod tribus reliquis continetur; rursus punctum continget positione datam lineam. Quod si ad plures quam sex, non adhuc habent dicere, an data sit proportio cujuspiam contenti quatuor lineis ad id quod reliquis continetur, quoniam non est aliquid contentum pluribus quam tribus dimensionibus.[1]

Here I beg you to observe in passing that the considerations that forced ancient writers to use arithmetical terms in geometry, thus making it impossible for them to proceed beyond a point where they could see clearly

[1] The problem of the locus related to three or four lines, about which he (Apollonius) boasts so proudly, giving no credit to the writer who has preceded him, is of this nature: If three straight lines are given in position, and if straight lines be drawn from one and the same point, making given angles with the three given lines; and if there be given the ratio of the rectangle contained by two of the lines so drawn to the square of the other, the point lies on a solid locus given in position, namely, one of the three conic sections.

Again, if lines be drawn making given angles with four straight lines given in position, and if the rectangle of two of the lines so drawn bears a given ratio to the rectangle of the other two; then, in like manner, the point lies on a conic section given in position. It has been shown that to only two lines there corresponds a plane locus. But if there be given more than four lines, the point generates loci not known up to the present time, but merely called 'lines.' It is not clear what they are, or what their properties. One of them, not the first but the most manifest, has been examined, and this has proved to be helpful. These, however, are the propositions concerning them.

If from any point straight lines be drawn making given angles with five straight lines given in position, and if the solid rectangular parallelepiped contained by three of the lines so drawn bears a given ratio to the solid rectangular parallelepiped contained by the other two and any given line whatever, the point lies on a 'line' given in position. Again, if there be six lines, and if the solid contained by three of the lines bears a given ratio to the solid contained by the other three lines, the point also lies on a 'line' given in position. But if there be more than six lines, we cannot say whether a ratio of something contained by four lines is given to that which is contained by the rest, since there is no figure of more than three dimensions.

the relation between the two subjects, caused much obscurity and embarrassment, in their attempts at explanation.

Pappus proceeds as follows:

Acquiescunt autem his, qui paulo ante talia interpretati sunt; neque unum aliquo pacto comprehensibile significantes quod his continetur. Licebit autem per conjunctas proportiones hæc, & dicere & demonstrare universe in dictis proportionibus, atque his in hunc modum. Si ab aliquo puncto ad positione datas rectas lineas ducantur rectæ lineæ in datis angulis, & data sit proportio conjuncta ex ea, quam habet una ductarum ad unam, & altera ad alteram, & alia ad aliam, & reliqua ad datam lineam, si sint septem; si vero octo, & reliqua ad reliquam: punctum continget positione datas lineas. Et similiter quotcumque sint impares vel pares multitudine, cum hæc, ut dixi, loco ad quatuor lineas respondeant, nullum igitur posuerunt ita ut linea nota sit, &c.[1]

The question, then, the solution of which was begun by Euclid and carried farther by Apollonius, but was completed by no one, is this:

Having three, four or more lines given in position, it is first required to find a point from which as many other lines may be drawn, each making a given angle with one of the given lines, so that the rectangle of two of the lines so drawn shall bear a given ratio to the square of the third (if there be only three); or to the rectangle of the other two (if there be four), or again, that the parallelepiped constructed upon three shall bear a given ratio to that upon the other two and any given line (if there be five), or to the parallelepiped upon the other three (if there be six); or (if there be seven) that the product obtained by multiplying four of them together shall bear a given ratio to the product of the other three, or (if there be eight) that the product of four of them shall bear a given ratio to the product of the other four. Thus the question admits of extension to any number of lines.

Then, since there is always an infinite number of different points satisfying these requirements, it is also required to discover and trace the curve containing all such points. Pappus says that when there are only three or four lines given, this line is one of the three conic sections, but he does not undertake to determine, describe, or explain the nature of the line required when the question involves a greater number of lines. He only adds that the ancients recognized one of them which they had shown to be useful, and which seemed the simplest, and yet was not the most important. This led me to try to find out whether, by my own method, I could go as far as they had gone.

[1]For in this are agreed those who formerly interpreted these things (that the dimensions of a figure cannot exceed three) in that they maintain that a figure that is contained by these lines is not comprehensible in any way. This is permissible, however, both to say and to demonstrate generally by this kind of proportion, and in this manner: If from any point straight lines be drawn making given angles with straight lines given in position; and if there be given a ratio compounded of them, that is the ratio that one of the lines drawn has to one, the second has to a second, the third to a third, and so on to the given line if there be seven lines, or, if there be eight lines, of the last to a last, the point lies on the lines that are given in position. And similarly, whatever may be the odd or even number, since these, as I have said, correspond in position to the four lines: therefore they have not set forth any method so that a line may be known.

First, I discovered that if the question be proposed for only three, four, or five lines, the required points can be found by elementary geometry, that is, by the use of the ruler and compasses only, and the application of those principles that I have already explained, except in the case of five parallel lines. In this case, and in the cases where there are six, seven, eight, or nine given lines, the required points can always be found by means of the geometry of solid loci, that is, by using some one of the three conic sections. Here, again, there is an exception in the case of nine parallel lines. For this and the cases of ten, eleven, twelve, or thirteen given lines, the required points may be found by means of a curve of degree next higher than that of the conic sections. Again, the case of thirteen parallel lines must be excluded, for which, as well as for the cases of fourteen, fifteen, sixteen, and seventeen lines, a curve of degree next higher than the preceding must be used; and so on indefinitely.

Next, I have found that when only three or four lines are given, the required points lie not only all on one of the conic sections but sometimes on the circumference of a circle, or even on a straight line.

When there are five, six, seven, or eight lines, the required points lie on a curve of degree next higher than the conic sections, and it is impossible to imagine such a curve that may not satisfy the conditions of the problem; but the required points may possibly lie on a conic section, a circle, or a straight line. If there are nine, ten, eleven, or twelve lines, the required curve is only one degree higher than the preceding, but any such curve may meet the requirements, and so on to infinity.

Finally, the first and simplest curve after the conic sections is the one generated by the intersection of a parabola with a straight line in a way to be described presently.

I believe that I have in this way completely accomplished what Pappus tells us the ancients sought to do, and I will try to give the demonstration in a few words, for I am already wearied by so much writing.

Let AB, AD, EF, GH, $\cdots$ be any number of straight lines given in position, and let it be required to find a point C, from which straight lines CB, CD, CF, CH, $\cdots$ can be drawn, making given angles CBA, CDA, CFE, CHG, $\cdots$ respectively, with the given lines, and such that the product of certain of them is equal to the product of the rest, or at least such that these two products shall have a given ratio, for this condition does not make the problem any more difficult.

First, I suppose the thing done, and since so many lines are confusing, I may simplify matters by considering one of the given lines and one of those to be drawn (as, for example, AB and BC) as the principal lines, to which I shall try to refer all the others. Call the segment of the line AB between A and B, x, and call BC, y. Produce all the other given lines to meet these two (also produced if necessary) provided none is parallel to either of the principal lines. Thus, in the figure, the given lines cut AB in the points A, E, G, and cut BC in the points R, S, T.

Now, since all the angles of the triangle ARB are known, the ratio between the sides AB and BR is known. If we let $AB:BR = z:b$, since $AB = x$, we have $RB = \dfrac{bx}{z}$; and since B lies between C and R, we have $CR = y + \dfrac{bx}{z}$.

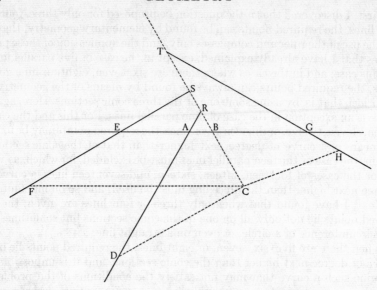

Fig. 5

(When R lies between C and B, CR is equal to $y - \dfrac{bx}{z}$, and when C lies be-

tween B and R, CR is equal to $-y + \dfrac{bx}{z}$.) Again, the three angles of the

triangle DRC are known, and therefore the ratio between the sides CR

and CD is determined. Calling this ratio $z:c$, since $CR = y + \dfrac{bx}{z}$, we have

$CD = \dfrac{cy}{z} + \dfrac{bcx}{z^2}$. Then, since the lines AB, AD, and EF are given in position,

the distance from A to E is known. If we call this distance k, then $EB = k + x$;
although $EB = k - x$ when B lies between E and A, and $E = -k + x$ when E
lies between A and B. Now the angles of the triangle ESB being given, the

ratio of BE to BS is known. We may call this ratio $z:d$. Then $BS = \dfrac{dk + dx}{z}$

and $CS = \dfrac{zy + dk + dx}{z}$. When S lies between B and C we have $CS = \dfrac{zy - dk - dx}{z}$,

and when C lies between B and S we have $CS = \dfrac{-zy + dk + dx}{z}$. The angles

of the triangle FSC are known, and hence, also the ratio of CS to CF,

or $z:e$. Therefore, $CF = \dfrac{ezy + dek + dex}{z^2}$. Likewise, AG or l is given, and

$BG = l - x$. Also, in triangle BGT, the ratio of BG to BT, or $z:f$, is known.

Therefore, $BT = \dfrac{fl - fx}{z}$ and $CT = \dfrac{zy + fl - fx}{z}$. In triangle TCH, the ratio of

TC to CH, or $z:g$, is known, whence $CH = \dfrac{gzy + fgl - fgx}{z}$.

And thus you see that, no matter how many lines are given in position, the length of any such line through C making given angles with these lines can always be expressed by three terms, one of which consists of the unknown quantity y multiplied or divided by some known quantity; another consisting of the unknown quantity x multiplied or divided by some other known quantity; and the third consisting of a known quantity. An exception must be made in the case where the given lines are parallel either to AB (when the term containing x vanishes), or to CB (when the term containing y vanishes). This case is too simple to require further explanation. The signs of the terms may be either $+$ or $-$ in every conceivable combination.

You also see that in the product of any number of these lines the degree of any term containing x or y will not be greater than the number of lines (expressed by means of x and y) whose product is found. Thus, no term will be of degree higher than the second if two lines be multiplied together, nor of degree higher than the third, if there be three lines, and so on to infinity.

Furthermore, to determine the point C, but one condition is needed, namely, that the product of a certain number of lines shall be equal to, or (what is quite as simple), shall bear a given ratio to the product of certain other lines. Since this condition can be expressed by a single equation in two unknown quantities, we may give any value we please to either x or y and find the value of the other from this equation. It is obvious that when not more than five lines are given, the quantity x, which is not used to express the first of the lines, can never be of degree higher than the second.

Assigning a value to y, we have $x^2 = \pm ax \pm b^2$, and therefore x can be found with ruler and compasses, by a method already explained. If then we should take successively an infinite number of different values for the line y, we should obtain an infinite number of values for the line x, and therefore an infinity of different points, such as C, by means of which the required curve could be drawn.

This method can be used when the problem concerns six or more lines, if some of them are parallel to either AB or BC, in which case either x or y will be of only the second degree in the equation, so that the point C can be found with ruler and compasses.

On the other hand, if the given lines are all parallel even though a question should be proposed involving only five lines, the point C cannot be found in this way. For, since the quantity x does not occur at all in the equation, it is no longer allowable to give a known value to y. It is then necessary to find the value of y. And since the term in y will now be of the third degree, its value can be found only by finding the root of a cubic equation, which cannot in general be done without the use of one of the conic sections.

And furthermore, if not more than nine lines are given, not all of them being parallel, the equation can always be so expressed as to be of degree not higher than the fourth. Such equations can always be solved by means of the conic sections in a way that I shall presently explain.

Again, if there are not more than thirteen lines, an equation of degree not higher than the sixth can be employed, which admits of solution by means of a curve just one degree higher than the conic sections by a method to be explained presently.

This completes the first part of what I have to demonstrate here, but it is necessary, before passing to the second part, to make some general statements concerning the nature of curved lines.

SECOND BOOK

ON THE NATURE OF CURVED LINES

THE ANCIENTS were familiar with the fact that the problems of geometry may be divided into three classes, namely, plane, solid, and linear problems. This is equivalent to saying that some problems require only circles and straight lines for their construction, while others require a conic section and still others require more complex curves. I am surprised, however, that they did not go further, and distinguish between different degrees of these more complex curves, nor do I see why they called the latter mechanical, rather then geometrical.

If we say that they are called mechanical because some sort of instrument has to be used to describe them, then we must, to be consistent, reject circles and straight lines, since these cannot be described on paper without the use of compasses and a ruler, which may also be termed instruments. It is not because the other instruments, being more complicated than the ruler and compasses, are therefore less accurate, for if this were so they would have to be excluded from mechanics, in which accuracy of construction is even more important than in geometry. In the latter, exactness of reasoning alone is sought, and this can surely be as thorough with reference to such lines as to simpler ones. I cannot believe, either, that it was because they did not wish to make more than two postulates, namely, (1) a straight line can be drawn between any two points, and (2) about a given center a circle can be described passing through a given point. In their treatment of the conic sections they did not hesitate to introduce the assumption that any given cone can be cut by a given plane. Now to treat all the curves which I mean to introduce here, only one additional assumption is necessary, namely, two or more lines can be moved, one upon the other, determining by their intersection other curves. This seems to me in no way more difficult.

It is true that the conic sections were never freely received into ancient geometry, and I do not care to undertake to change names confirmed by usage; nevertheless, it seems very clear to me that if we make the usual assumption that geometry is precise and exact, while mechanics is not; and if we think of geometry as the science which furnishes a general knowledge of the measurement of all bodies, then we have no more right to exclude the more complex curves than the simpler ones, provided they can be conceived of as described by a continuous motion or by several successive motions, each motion being completely determined by those which precede; for in this way an exact knowledge of the magnitude of each is always obtainable.

Probably the real explanation of the refusal of ancient geometers to accept curves more complex than the conic sections lies in the fact that the first curves to which their attention was attracted happened to be the spiral, the quadratrix, and similar curves, which really do belong only to mechanics, and are not among those curves that I think should be included here, since they must be conceived of as described by two separate movements whose relation does not admit of exact determination. Yet they afterwards examined the conchoid, the cissoid, and a few others which should be accepted; but not knowing much about their properties they took no more account of these than of the others. Again, it may have been that, knowing as they did only a little about the conic sections, and being still ignorant of many of the possibilities of the ruler and compasses, they dared not yet attack a matter of still greater difficulty. I hope that hereafter those who are clever enough to make use of the geometric methods herein suggested will find no great difficulty in applying them to plane or solid problems. I therefore think it proper to suggest to such a more extended line of investigation which will furnish abundant opportunities for practice.

Consider the lines AB, AD, AF, and so forth, which we may suppose to be described by means of the instrument YZ. This instrument consists of several rulers hinged together in such a way that YZ being placed along the line AN the angle XYZ can be increased or decreased in size, and when its sides are together the points B, C, D, E, F, G, H, all coincide with A; but as the size of the angle is increased, the ruler BC, fastened at right angles to XY at the point B, pushes toward Z the ruler CD which slides along YZ always at right angles. In like manner, CD pushes DE which slides along

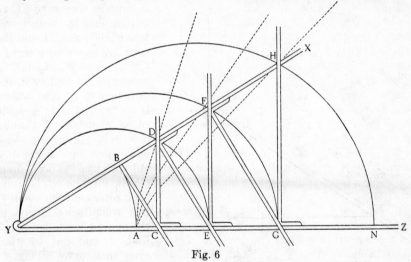

Fig. 6

YX always parallel to BC; DE pushes EF; EF pushes FG; FG pushes GH, and so on. Thus we may imagine an infinity of rulers, each pushing another, half of them making equal angles with YX and the rest with YZ.

Now as the angle XYZ is increased the point B describes the curve AB, which is a circle; while the intersections of the other rulers, namely, the points D, F, H describe other curves, AD, AF, AH, of which the latter are more complex than the first, and this more complex than the circle. Nevertheless, I see no reason why the description of the first cannot be conceived as clearly and distinctly as that of the circle, or at least as that of the conic sections; or why that of the second, third, or any other that can be thus described, cannot be as clearly conceived of as the first; and therefore I see no reason why they should not be used in the same way in the solution of geometric problems.

I could give here several other ways of tracing and conceiving a series of curved lines, each curve more complex than any preceding one, but I think the best way to group together all such curves and then classify them in order, is by recognizing the fact that all points of those curves which we may call "geometric," that is, those which admit of precise and exact measurement, must bear a definite relation to all points of a straight line, and that this relation must be expressed by means of a single equation. If this equation contains no term of higher degree than the rectangle of two unknown quantities, or the square of one, the curve belongs to the first and simplest class, which contains only the circle, the parabola, the hyperbola, and the ellipse; but when the equation contains one or more terms of the third or fourth degree in one or both of the two unknown quantities (for it requires two unknown quantities to express the relation between two points) the curve belongs to the second class; and if the equation contains a term of the fifth or sixth degree in either or both of the unknown quantities the curve belongs to the third class, and so on indefinitely.

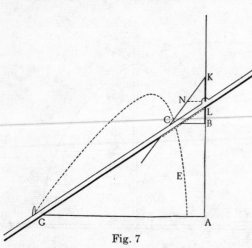

Fig. 7

Suppose the curve EC to be described by the intersection of the ruler GL and the rectilinear plane figure CNKL, whose side KN is produced indefinitely in the direction of C, and which, being moved in the same plane in such a way that its side KL always coincides with some part of the line BA (produced in both directions), imparts to the ruler GL a rotary motion about G (the ruler being hinged to the figure CNKL at L). If I wish to find out to what class this curve belongs, I choose a straight line, as AB, to which to refer all its points, and in AB I choose a point A at which to begin the investigation. I say "choose this and that," because we are free to choose what we will, for, while it is necessary to use care in the choice in order to make the equation as short and simple as possible, yet no matter what line I should take instead of AB the curve would always prove to be of the same class, a fact easily demonstrated.

Then I take on the curve an arbitrary point, as C, at which we will suppose the instrument applied to describe the curve. Then I draw through C the line CB parallel to GA. Since CB and BA are unknown and indeterminate quantities, I shall call one of them y and the other x. To the relation between these quantities I must consider also the known quantities which determine the description of the curve, as GA, which I shall call a; KL, which I shall call b; and NL parallel to GA, which I shall call c. Then I say that as NL is to LK, or as c is to b, so CB, or y, is to BK, which is therefore equal to $\frac{b}{c}y$. Then BL is equal to $\frac{b}{c}y-b$, and AL is equal to $x+\frac{b}{c}y-b$. Moreover, as CB is to LB, that is, as y is to $\frac{b}{c}y-b$, so AG or a is to LA or $x+\frac{b}{c}y-b$. Multiplying the second by the third, we get $\frac{ab}{c}y-ab$ equal to

$$xy+\frac{b}{c}y^2-by,$$

which is obtained by multiplying the first by the last. Therefore, the required equation is

$$y^2=cy-\frac{cx}{b}y+ay-ac.$$

From this equation we see that the curve EC belongs to the first class, it being, in fact, a hyperbola.

If in the instrument used to describe the curve we substitute for the rectilinear figure CNK this hyperbola or some other curve of the first class lying in the plane CNKL, the intersection of this curve with the ruler GL will describe, instead of the hyperbola EC, another curve, which will be of the second class.

Thus, if CNK be a circle having its center at L, we shall describe the first conchoid of the ancients, while if we use a parabola having KB as axis we shall describe the curve which, as I have already said, is the first and simplest of the curves required in the problem of Pappus, that is, the one which furnishes the solution when five lines are given in position.

If, instead of one of these curves of the first class, there be used a curve of the second class lying in the plane CNKL, a curve of the third class will be described; while if one of the third class be used, one of the fourth class will be obtained, and so on to infinity. These statements are easily proved by actual calculation.

Thus, no matter how we conceive a curve to be described, provided it be one of those which I have called geometric, it is always possible to find in this manner an equation determining all its points. Now I shall place curves whose equations are of the fourth degree in the same class with those whose equations are of the third degree; and those whose equations are of the sixth degree in the same class with those whose equations are of the fifth degree, and similarly for the rest. This classification is based upon the fact that there is a general rule for reducing to a cubic any equation of the fourth degree, and to an equation of the fifth degree any equation of the sixth degree, so that the latter in each case need not be considered any more complex than the former.

It should be observed, however, with regard to the curves of any one class, that while many of them are equally complex so that they may be employed to determine the same points and construct the same problems, yet there are certain simpler ones whose usefulness is more limited. Thus, among the curves of the first class, besides the ellipse, the hyperbola, and the parabola, which are equally complex, there is also found the circle, which is evidently a simpler curve; while among those of the second class we find the common conchoid, which is described by means of the circle, and some others which, though less complicated than many curves of the same class, cannot be placed in the first class.

Having now made a general classification of curves, it is easy for me to demonstrate the solution which I have already given of the problem of Pappus. For, first, I have shown that when there are only three or four lines the equation which serves to determine the required points is of the second degree. It follows that the curve containing these points must belong to the first class, since such an equation expresses the relation between all points of curves of Class I and all points of a fixed straight line. When there are not more than eight given lines the equation is at most a biquadratic, and therefore the resulting curve belongs to Class II or Class I. When there are not more than twelve given lines, the equation is of the sixth degree or lower, and therefore the required curve belongs to Class III or a lower class, and so on for other cases.

Now, since each of the given lines may have any conceivable position, and since any change in the position of a line produces a corresponding change in the values of the known quantities as well as in the signs $+$ and $-$ of the equation, it is clear that there is no curve of Class I that may not furnish a solution of this problem when it relates to four lines, and that there is no curve of Class II that may not furnish a solution when the problem relates to eight lines, none of Class III when it relates to twelve lines, etc. It follows that there is no geometric curve whose equation can be obtained that may not be used for some number of lines.

It is now necessary to determine more particularly and to give the method of finding the curve required in each case, for only three or four given lines. This investigation will show that Class I contains only the circle and the three conic sections.

Consider again the four lines AB, AD, EF, and GH, given before, and let it be required to find the locus generated by a point C, such that, if four lines CB, CD, CF, and CH be drawn through it making given angles with the given lines, the product of CB and CF is equal to the product of CD and CH. This is equivalent to saying that if

$$\text{CB} = y,$$

$$\text{CD} = \frac{czy + bcx}{z^2},$$

$$\text{CF} = \frac{ezy + dek + dex}{z^2},$$

and

$$\text{CH} = \frac{gzy + fgl - fgx}{z^2}.$$

then the equation is

$$y^2 = \frac{(cfglz - dekz^2)y - (dez^2 + cfgz - bcgz)xy + bcfglx - bcfgx^2}{ez^3 - cgz^2}.$$

It is here assumed that ez is greater than cg; otherwise the signs $+$ and $-$ must all be changed. If y is zero or less than nothing in this equation, the point C being supposed to lie within the angle DAG, then C must be supposed to lie within one of the angles DAE, EAR, or RAG, and the signs must be changed to produce this result. If for each of these four positions y is equal to zero, then the problem admits of no solution in the case proposed.

Let us suppose the solution possible, and to shorten the work let us write

$2m$ instead of $\dfrac{cflgz-dekz^2}{ez^3-cgz^2}$, and $\dfrac{2n}{z}$ instead of $\dfrac{dez^2+cfgz-bcgz}{ez^3-cgz^2}$. Then we have

$$y^2 = 2my - \frac{2n}{z}xy + \frac{bcfglx - bcfgx^2}{ez^3 - cgz^2},$$

of which the root is

$$y = m - \frac{nx}{z} + \sqrt{m^2 - \frac{2mnx}{z} + \frac{n^2x^2}{z^2} + \frac{bcfglx - bcfgx^2}{ez^3 - cgz^2}}.$$

Again, for the sake of brevity, put $-\dfrac{2mn}{z} + \dfrac{bcfgl}{ez^3 - cgz^2}$ equal to o, and

$\dfrac{n^2}{z^2} - \dfrac{bcfg}{ez^3 - cgz^2}$ equal to $\dfrac{p}{m}$; for these quantities being given, we can represent them in any way we please. Then we have

$$y = m - \frac{n}{z}x + \sqrt{m^2 + ox + \frac{p}{m}x^2}.$$

This must give the length of the line BC, leaving AB or x undetermined. Since the problem relates to only three or four lines, it is obvious that we shall always have such terms, although some of them may vanish and the signs may all vary.

After this, I make KI equal and parallel to BA, and cutting off on BC a

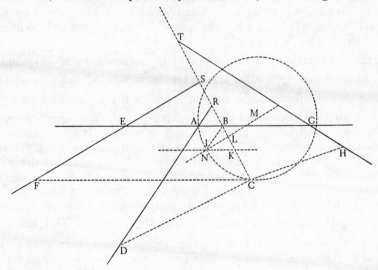

Fig. 8

segment BK equal to m (since the expression for BC contains $+m$; if this were $-m$, I should have drawn IK on the other side of AB, while if m were zero, I would not have drawn IK at all). Then I draw IL so that $IK:KL$ $=z:n$; that is, so that if IK is equal to x, KL is equal to $\frac{n}{z}x$. In the same way I know the ratio of KL to IL, which I may call $n:a$, so that if KL is equal to $\frac{n}{z}x$, IL is equal to $\frac{a}{z}x$. I take the point K between L and C, since the equation contains $-\frac{n}{z}x$; if this were $+\frac{n}{z}x$, I should take L between K and C; while if $\frac{n}{z}x$ were equal to zero, I should not draw IL.

This being done, there remains the expression

$$LC = \sqrt{m^2 + ox + \frac{p}{m}x^2},$$

from which to construct LC. It is clear that if this were zero the point C would lie on the straight line IL; that if it were a perfect square, that is if m^2 and $\frac{p}{m}x^2$ were both $+$ and o^2 was equal to $4pm$, or if m^2 and ox, or ox and $\frac{p}{m}x^2$, were zero, then the point C would lie on another straight line, whose position could be determined as easily as that of IL.

If none of these exceptional cases occur, the point C always lies on one of the three conic sections, or on a circle having its diameter in the line IL and having LC a line applied in order to this diameter, or, on the other hand, having LC parallel to a diameter and IL applied in order.

In particular, if the term $\frac{p}{m}x^2$ is zero, the conic section is a parabola; if it is preceded by a plus sign, it is a hyperbola; and, finally, if it is preceded by a minus sign, it is an ellipse. An exception occurs when a^2m is equal to pz^2 and the angle ILC is a right angle, in which case we get a circle instead of an ellipse.

If the conic section is a parabola, its latus rectum is equal to $\frac{oz}{a}$ and its axis always lies along the line IL. To find its vertex, N, make IN equal to $\frac{am^2}{oz}$, so that the point I lies between L and N if m^2 is positive and ox is positive; and L lies between I and N if m^2 is positive and ox negative; and N lies between I and L if m^2 is negative and ox positive. It is impossible that m^2 should be negative when the terms are arranged as above. Finally, if m^2 is equal to zero, the points N and I must coincide. It is thus easy to determine this parabola, according to the first problem of the first book of Apollonius.

If, however, the required locus is a circle, an ellipse, or a hyperbola, the point M, the center of the figure, must first be found. This will always lie on the line IL and may be found by taking IM equal to $\frac{aom}{2pz}$. If o is equal to zero, M coincides with I. If the required locus is a circle or an ellipse, M and L must lie on the same side of I when the term ox is positive and on opposite sides when ox is negative. On the other hand, in the case of the

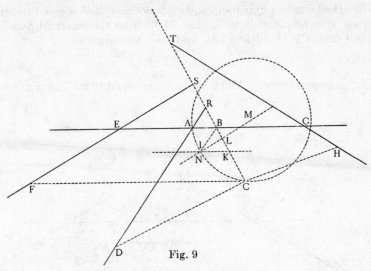

Fig. 9

hyperbola, M and L lie on the same side of I when ox is negative and on opposite sides when ox is positive.

The latus rectum of the figure must be

$$\sqrt{\frac{o^2z^2}{a^2} + \frac{4mpz^2}{a^2}}$$

if m^2 is positive and the locus is a circle or an ellipse, or if m^2 is negative and the locus is a hyperbola. It must be

$$\sqrt{\frac{o^2z^2}{a^2} - \frac{4mpz^2}{a^2}}$$

if the required locus is a circle or an ellipse and m^2 is negative, or if it is an hyperbola and o^2 is greater than $4mp$, m^2 being positive.

But if m^2 is equal to zero, the latus rectum is $\frac{oz}{a}$; and if oz is equal to zero, it is

$$\sqrt{\frac{4mpz^2}{a^2}}.$$

For the corresponding diameter a line must be found which bears the ratio $\frac{a^2m}{pz^2}$ to the latus rectum; that is, if the latus rectum is

$$\sqrt{\frac{o^2z^2}{a^2} + \frac{4mpz^2}{a^2}}$$

the diameter is

$$\sqrt{\frac{a^2o^2m^2}{p^2z^2} + \frac{4a^2m^3}{pz^2}}.$$

In every case, the diameter of the section lies along IM, and LC is one of its lines applied in order. It is thus evident that, by making MN equal to half the diameter and taking N and L on the same side of M, the point N will be the vertex of this diameter. It is then a simple matter to determine the curve, according to the second and third problems of the first book of Apollonius.

When the locus is a hyperbola and m^2 is positive, if o^2 is equal to zero or less than $4pm$ we must draw the line MOP from the center M parallel to LC, and draw CP parallel to LM, and take MO equal to

$$\sqrt{m^2 - \frac{o^2m}{4p}} \, ;$$

while if ox is equal to zero, MO must be taken equal to m. Then considering

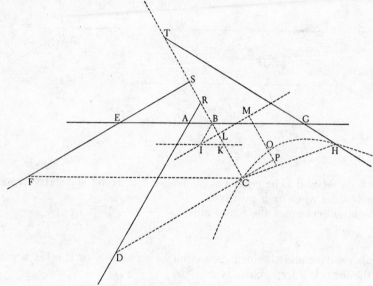

Fig. 10

O as the vertex of this hyperbola, the diameter being OP and the line applied in order being CP, its latus rectum is

$$\sqrt{\frac{4a^4m^4}{p^2z^4} - \frac{a^4o^2m^3}{p^3z^4}}$$

and its diameter is

$$\sqrt{4m^2 - \frac{o^2m}{p}} \, .$$

An exception must be made when ox is equal to zero, in which case the latus rectum is $\dfrac{2a^2m^2}{pz^2}$ and the diameter is $2m$. From these data the curve can be determined in accordance with the third problem of the first book of Apollonius.

The demonstrations of the above statements are all very simple, for, forming the product of the quantities given above as latus rectum, diameter, and segment of the diameter NL or OP, by the methods of Theorems 11, 12, and 13 of the first book of Apollonius, the result will contain exactly the terms which express the square of the line CP or CL, which is an ordinate of this diameter.

In this case take IM or $\dfrac{aom}{2pz}$ from NM or from its equal

$$\frac{am}{2pz}\sqrt{o^2+4mp}.$$

To the remainder IN add IL or $\frac{a}{z}x$, and we have

$$\mathrm{NL}=\frac{a}{z}x-\frac{aom}{2pz}+\frac{am}{2pz}\sqrt{o^2+4mp}.$$

Multiplying this by

$$\frac{z}{a}\sqrt{o^2+4mp},$$

the latus rectum of the curve, we get

$$x\sqrt{o^2+4mp}-\frac{om}{2p}\sqrt{o^2+4mp}+\frac{mo^2}{2p}+\overline{2}m^2$$

for the rectangle, from which is to be subtracted a rectangle which is to the

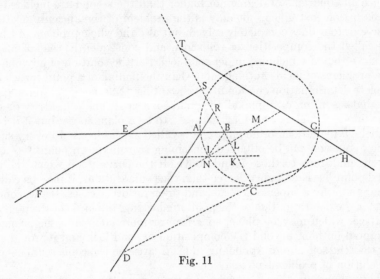

Fig. 11

square of NL as the latus rectum is to the diameter. The square of NL is

$$\frac{a^2}{2^2}x^2-\frac{a^2om}{pz^2}x+\frac{a^2m}{pz^2}x\sqrt{o^2+4mp}+\frac{a^2o^2m^2}{2p^2z^2}+\frac{a^2m^3}{pz^2}-\frac{a^2om^2}{2p^2z^2}\sqrt{o^2+4mp}.$$

Divide this by a^2m and multiply the quotient by pz^2, since these terms express the ratio between the diameter and the latus rectum. The result is

$$\frac{p}{m}x^2-ox+x\sqrt{o^2+4mp}+\frac{o^2m}{2p}-\frac{om}{2p}\sqrt{o^2+4mp}+m^2.$$

This quantity being subtracted from the rectangle previously obtained, we get

$$\overline{\mathrm{CL}}^2=m^2+ox-\frac{p}{m}x^2.$$

It follows that CL is an ordinate of an ellipse or circle applied to NL, the segment of the axis.

Suppose all the given quantities expressed numerically, as EA$=3$, AG$=5$, AB$=$BR, BS$=\frac12$BE, GB$=$BT, CD$=\frac32$CR, CF$=2$CS, CH$=\frac23$CT, the angle ABR$=60°$; and let CB$\cdot$CF$=$CD$\cdot$CH. All these quantities must be known if the problem is to be entirely determined. Now let AB$=x$, and CB$=y$. By the method given above we shall obtain

$$y^2 = 2y - xy + 5x - x^2;$$
$$y = 1 - \tfrac{1}{2}x + \sqrt{1 + 4x - \tfrac{3}{4}x^2};$$

whence BK must be equal to 1, and KL must be equal to one-half KI; and since the angle IKL=angle ABR=60° and angle KIL (which is one-half angle KIB, or one-half angle IKL) is 30°, the angle ILK is a right angle. Since IK=AB$=x$, KL$=\tfrac{1}{2}x$, IL$=x\sqrt{\tfrac{3}{4}}$, and the quantity represented by z above is 1, we have $a = \sqrt{\tfrac{3}{4}}$, $m = 1$, $o = 4$, $p = \tfrac{3}{4}$, whence IM$=\sqrt{\tfrac{16}{3}}$, NM$=\sqrt{\tfrac{19}{3}}$; and since a^2m (which is $\tfrac{3}{4}$) is equal to pz^2, and the angle ILC is a right angle, it follows that the curve NC is a circle. A similar treatment of any of the other cases offers no difficulty.

Since all equations of degree not higher than the second are included in the discussion just given, not only is the problem of the ancients relating to three or four lines completely solved, but also the whole problem of what they called the composition of solid loci, and consequently that of plane loci, since they are included under solid loci. For the solution of any one of these problems of loci is nothing more than the finding of a point for whose complete determination one condition is wanting, the other conditions being such that (as in this example) all the points of a single line will satisfy them. If the line is straight or circular, it is said to be a plane locus; but if it is a parabola, a hyperbola, or an ellipse, it is called a solid locus. In every such case an equation can be obtained containing two unknown quantities and entirely analogous to those found above. If the curve upon which the required point lies is of higher degree than the conic sections, it may be called in the same way a supersolid locus, and so on for other cases. If two conditions for the determination of the point are lacking, the locus of the point is a surface, which may be plane, spherical, or more complex. The ancients attempted nothing beyond the composition of solid loci, and it would appear that the sole aim of Apollonius in his treatise on the conic sections was the solution of problems of solid loci.

I have shown, further, that what I have termed the first class of curves contains no others besides the circle, the parabola, the hyperbola, and the ellipse. This is what I undertook to prove.

If the problem of the ancients be proposed concerning five lines, all parallel, the required point will evidently always lie on a straight line. Suppose it be proposed concerning five lines with the following conditions:

(1) Four of these lines parallel and the fifth perpendicular to each of the others;

(2) The lines drawn from the required point to meet the given lines at right angles;

(3) The parallelepiped composed of the three lines drawn to meet three of the parallel lines must be equal to that composed of three lines, namely, the one drawn to meet the fourth parallel, the one drawn to meet the perpendicular, and a certain given line.

This is, with the exception of the preceding one, the simplest possible case. The point required will lie on a curve generated by the motion of a parabola in the following way:

Let the required lines be AB, IH, ED, GF, and GA, and let it be required to find the point C, such that if CB, CF, CD, CH, and CM be drawn perpendicular respectively to the given lines, the parallelepiped of the three lines CF, CD, and CH shall be equal to that of the other two, CB and CM, and a third line AI. Let $CB=y$, $CM=x$, AI or AE or $GE=a$; whence if C lies between AB and DE, we have $CF=2a-y$, $CD=a-y$, and $CH=y+a$. Multiplying these three together we get $y^3-2ay^2-a^2y+2a^3$ equal to the product of the other three, namely to axy.

I shall consider next the curve CEG, which I imagine to be described by the intersection of the parabola CKN (which is made to move so that its axis KL always lies along the straight line AB) with the ruler GL (which rotates about the point G in such a way that it constantly lies in the plane of the parabola and passes through the point L). I take KL equal to a and let the principal parameter, that is, the parameter corresponding to the axis of the given parabola, be also equal to a, and let $GA=2a$, CB or $MA=y$, CM or $AB=x$. Since the triangles GMC and CBL are similar, GM (or $2a-y$) is to MC (or x) as CB (or y) is to BL, which is therefore equal to $\dfrac{xy}{2a-y}$. Since KL is a, BK is $a-\dfrac{xy}{2a-y}$ or $\dfrac{2a^2-ay-xy}{2a-y}$. Finally, since this same BK is a segment of the axis of the parabola, BK is to BC (its ordinate) as BC is to a (the latus rectum), whence we get $y^3-2ay^2-a^2y+2a^3=axy$, and therefore C is the required point.

The point C can be taken on any part of the curve CEG or of its adjunct cEGc, which is described in the same way as the former, except that the vertex of the parabola is turned in the opposite direction; or it may lie on their counterparts NIo and nIO, which are generated by the intersection of the line GL with the other branch of the parabola KN.

Again, suppose that the given parallel lines AB, IH, ED, and GF are not equally distant from one another and are not perpendicular to GA, and that the lines through C are oblique to the given lines. In this case the point C will not always lie on a curve of just the same nature. This may even occur when no two of the given lines are parallel.

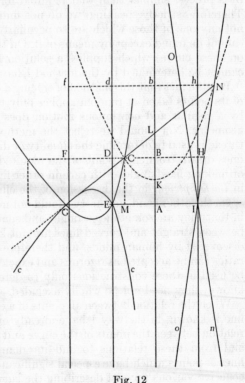

Fig. 12

Next, suppose that we have four parallel lines, and a fifth line cutting them, such that the parallelepiped of three lines drawn through the point C (one to the cutting line and two to two of the parallel lines) is equal to the parallelepiped of two lines drawn through C to meet the other two parallels respectively and another given line. In this case the required point lies on a curve of different nature, namely, a curve such that, all the ordinates to its axis being equal to the ordinates of a conic section, the segments of the axis between the vertex and the ordinates bear the same ratio to a certain given line that this line bears to the segments of the axis of the conic section having equal ordinates.

I cannot say that this curve is less simple than the preceding; indeed, I have always thought the former should be considered first, since its description and the determination of its equation are somewhat easier.

I shall not stop to consider in detail the curves corresponding to the other cases, for I have not undertaken to give a complete discussion of the subject; and having explained the method of determining an infinite number of points lying on any curve, I think I have furnished a way to describe them.

It is worthy of note that there is a great difference between this method in which the curve is traced by finding several points upon it, and that used for the spiral and similar curves. In the latter not any point of the required curve may be found at pleasure, but only such points as can be determined by a process simpler than that required for the composition of the curve. Therefore, strictly speaking, we do not find any one of its points, that is, not any one of those which are so peculiarly points of this curve that they cannot be found except by means of it. On the other hand, there is no point on these curves which supplies a solution for the proposed problem that cannot be determined by the method I have given.

But the fact that this method of tracing a curve by determining a number of its points taken at random applies only to curves that can be generated by a regular and continuous motion does not justify its exclusion from geometry. Nor should we reject the method in which a string or loop of thread is used to determine the equality or difference of two or more straight lines drawn from each point of the required curve to certain other points, or making fixed angles with certain other lines. We have used this method in *La Dioptrique* in the discussion of the ellipse and the hyperbola.

On the other hand, geometry should not include lines that are like strings, in that they are sometimes straight and sometimes curved, since the ratios between straight and curved lines are not known, and I believe cannot be discovered by human minds, and therefore no conclusion based upon such ratios can be accepted as rigorous and exact. Nevertheless, since strings can be used in these constructions only to determine lines whose lengths are known, they need not be wholly excluded.

When the relation between all points of a curve and all points of a straight line is known, in the way I have already explained, it is easy to find the relation between the points of the curve and all other given points and lines; and from these relations to find its diameters, axes, center and other lines or points which have especial significance for this curve, and thence to conceive various ways of describing the curve, and to choose the easiest.

By this method alone it is then possible to find out all that can be determined about the magnitude of their areas, and there is no need for further explanation from me.

Finally, all other properties of curves depend only on the angles which these curves make with other lines. But the angle formed by two intersecting curves can be as easily measured as the angle between two straight lines, provided that a straight line can be drawn making right angles with one of these curves at its point of intersection with the other. This is my reason for believing that I shall have given here a sufficient introduction to the study of curves when I have given a general method of drawing a straight line making right angles with a curve at an arbitrarily chosen point upon it. And I dare say that this is not only the most useful and most general problem in geometry that I know, but even that I have ever desired to know.

Let CE be the given curve, and let it be required to draw through C a straight line making right angles with CE. Suppose the problem solved, and let the required line be CP. Produce CP to meet the straight line GA, to whose points the points of CE are to be related. Then, let MA or CB $=y$; and CM or BA $=x$. An equation must be found expressing the relation between x and y. I let PC $=s$, PA $=v$, whence PM $=v-y$. Since PMC is a right triangle, we see that s^2, the square of the hypotenuse, is equal to $x^2+v^2-2vy+y^2$, the sum of the squares of the two sides. That is to say, $x=\sqrt{s^2-v^2+2vy-y^2}$ or $y=v+\sqrt{s^2-x^2}$. By means of these last two equations, I can eliminate one of the two quantities x and y from the equation expressing the relation between the points of the curve CE and those of the straight line GA. If x is to be eliminated, this may easily be done by replacing x wherever it occurs by $\sqrt{s^2-v^2+2vy-y^2}$, x^2 by the square of this expression, x^3 by its cube, etc., while if y is to be eliminated, y must be replaced by $v+\sqrt{s^2-x^2}$, and y^2, y^3, $\cdots$ by the square of this expression, its cube, and so on. The result will be an equation in only one unknown quantity, x or y.

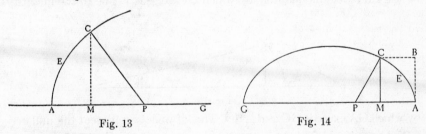

Fig. 13   Fig. 14

For example, if CE is an ellipse, MA the segment of its axis of which CM is an ordinate, r its latus rectum, and q its transverse axis, then by Theorem 13, Book I, of Apollonius, we have $x^2=ry-\dfrac{r}{q}y^2$. Eliminating x^2 the resulting equation is

$$s^2-v^2+2vy-y^2=ry-\frac{r}{q}y^2, \quad \text{or} \quad y^2+\frac{qry-2qvy+qv^2-qs^2}{q-r}=0.$$

In this case it is better to consider the whole as constituting a single expression than as consisting of two equal parts.

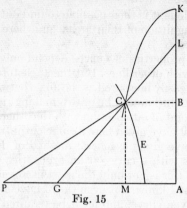

Fig. 15

If CE be the curve generated by the motion of a parabola (see pages 306, 307) already discussed, and if we represent GA by b, KL by c, and the parameter of the axis KL of the parabola by d, the equation expressing the relation between x and y is $y^3 - by^2 - cdy + bcd + dxy = 0$. Eliminating x, we have
$$y^3 - by^2 - cdy + bcd + dy \sqrt{s^2 - v^2 + 2vy - y^2} = 0.$$
Arranging the terms according to the powers of y by squaring, this becomes
$$y^6 - 2by^5 + (b^2 - 2cd + d^2)y^4 + (4bcd - 2d^2v)y^3$$
$$+ (c^2d^2 - d^2s^2 + d^2v^2 - 2b^2cd)y^2 - 2bc^2d^2y + b^2c^2d^2 = 0,$$
and so for the other cases. If the points of the curve are not related to those of a straight line in the way explained, but are related in some other way, such an equation can always be found.

Let CE be a curve which is so related to the points F, G, and A, that a straight line drawn from any point on it, as C, to F exceeds the line FA by a quantity which bears a given ratio to the excess of GA over the line drawn from the point C to G. Let GA $= b$, AF $= c$, and taking an arbitrary point C on the curve let the quantity by which CF exceeds FA be to the quantity

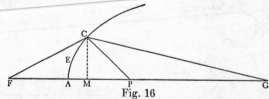

Fig. 16

by which GA exceeds GC as d is to e. Then if we let z represent the undetermined quantity, FC $= c + z$ and GC $= b - \dfrac{e}{d}z$. Let MA $= y$, GM $= b - y$, and FM $= c + y$. Since CMG is a right triangle, taking the square of GM from the square of GC we have left the square of CM, or $\dfrac{e^2}{d^2}z^2 - \dfrac{2be}{d}z + 2by - y^2$. Again, taking the square of FM from the square of FC we have the square of CM expressed in another way, namely: $z^2 + 2cz - 2cy - y^2$. These two expressions being equal they will yield the value of y or MA, which is
$$\frac{d^2z^2 + 2cd^2z - e^2z^2 + 2bdez}{2bd^2 + 2cd^2}.$$

Substituting this value for y in the expression for the square of CM, we have

$$\overline{\text{CM}}^2 = \frac{bd^2z^2 + ce^2z^2 + 2bcd^2z - 2bcdez}{bd^2 + cd^2} - y^2.$$

If now we suppose the line PC to meet the curve at right angles at C, and let PC $= s$ and PA $= v$ as before, PM is equal to $v - y$; and since PCM is a right triangle, we have $s^2 - v^2 + 2vy - y^2$ for the square of CM. Substituting for y its value, and equating the values of the square of CM, we have

$$z^2 + \frac{2bcd^2z - 2bcdez - 2cd^2vz - 2bdevz - bd^2s^2 + bd^2v^2 - cd^2s^2 + cd^2v^2}{bd^2 + ce^2 + e^2v - d^2v} = 0$$

for the required equation.

Such an equation having been found it is to be used, not to determine x, y, or z, which are known, since the point C is given, but to find v or s, which determine the required point P. With this in view, observe that if the point P fulfills the required conditions, the circle about P as center and passing through the point C will touch but not cut the curve CE; but if this point P be ever so little nearer to, or farther from, A than it should be, this circle must cut the curve not only at C but also in another point. Now if this circle cuts CE, the equation involving x and y as unknown quantities (supposing PA and PC known) must have two unequal roots. Suppose, for example that the circle cuts the curve in the points C and E. Draw EQ parallel to CM. Then x and y may be used to represent EQ and QA respectively in just the same way as they were used to represent CM and MA; since PE is equal to PC (being radii of the same circle), if we seek EQ and QA (supposing PE and PA given) we shall get the same equation that we should obtain by seeking CM and MA (supposing PC and PA given). It follows that the value of x, or y, or any other such quantity, will be two-fold in this equation, that is, the equation will have two unequal roots. If the value of x be required, one of these roots will be CM and the other EQ; while if y be required, one root will be MA and the other QA. It is true that if E is not on the same side of the curve as C, only one of these will be a true root, the other being drawn in the opposite direction, or less than nothing. The nearer together the points C and E are taken, however, the less difference there is between the roots; and when the points coincide, the roots are exactly equal, that is to say, the circle through C will touch the curve CE at the point C without cutting it.

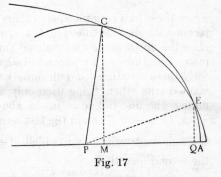

Fig. 17

Furthermore, it is to be observed that when an equation has two equal roots, its left-hand member must be similar in form to the expression obtained by multiplying by itself the difference between the unknown quantity and a known quantity equal to it; and then, if the resulting expression is not of as high a degree as the original equation, multiplying it by another expression which will make it of the same degree. This last step makes the two expressions correspond term by term.

For example, I say that the first equation found in the present discussion, namely

$$y^2 + \frac{qry - 2qvy + qv^2 - qs^2}{q - r},$$

must be of the same form as the expression obtained by making $e = y$ and multiplying $y - e$ by itself, that is, as $y^2 - 2ey + e^2$. We may then compare the two expressions term by term, thus: Since the first term, y^2, is the same in each, the second term, $\dfrac{qry - 2qvy}{q - r}$, of the first is equal to $-2ey$, the second term of the second; whence, solving for v, or PA, we have $v = e - \dfrac{r}{q}e + \tfrac{1}{2}r$; or, since we have assumed e equal to y, $v = y - \dfrac{r}{q}y + \tfrac{1}{2}r$. In the same way,

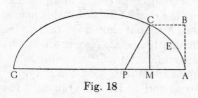

Fig. 18

we can find s from the third term, $e^2 = \dfrac{qv^2 - qs^2}{q - r}$; but since v completely determines P, which is all that is required, it is not necessary to go further.

In the same way, the second equation found above, namely,

$$y^6 - 2by^5 + (b^2 - 2cd + d^2)y^4 + (4bcd - 2d^2v)y^3$$
$$+ (c^2d^2 - 2b^2cd + d^2v^2 - d^2s^2)y^2 - 2bc^2d^2y + b^2c^2d^2,$$

must have the same form as the expression obtained by multiplying

$$y^2 - 2ey + e^2 \text{ by } y^4 + fy^3 + g^2y^2 + h^3y + k^4,$$

that is, as

$$y^6 + (f - 2e)y^5 + (g^2 - 2ef + e^2)y^4 + (h^3 - 2eg^2 + e^2f)y^3$$
$$+ (k^4 - 2eh^3 + e^2g^2)y^2 + (e^2h^3 - 2ek^4)y + e^2k^4.$$

From these two equations, six others may be obtained, which serve to determine the six quantities f, g, h, k, v, and s. It is easily seen that to whatever class the given curve may belong, this method will always furnish just as many equations as we necessarily have unknown quantities. In order to solve these equations, and ultimately to find v, which is the only value really wanted (the others being used only as means of finding v), we first determine f, the first unknown in the above expression, from the second term. Thus, $f = 2e - 2b$. Then in the last terms we can find k, the last unknown in the same expression, from which $k^4 = \dfrac{b^2c^2d^2}{e^2}$. From the third term we get the second quantity

$$g^2 = 3e^2 - 4be - 2cd + b^2 + d^2.$$

From the next to the last term we get h, the next to the last quantity, which is

$$h^3 = \frac{2b^2c^2d^2}{e^3} - \frac{2bc^2d^2}{e^2}.$$

In the same way we should proceed in this order, until the last quantity is found.

Then from the corresponding term (here the fourth) we may find v, and we have

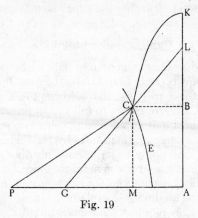

Fig. 19

$$v = \frac{2e^3}{d^2} - \frac{3be^2}{d^2} + \frac{b^2e}{d^2} - \frac{2ce}{d} + e + \frac{2bc}{d} + \frac{bc^2}{e^2} - \frac{b^2c^2}{e^3};$$

or putting y for its equal e, we get

$$v = \frac{2y^3}{d^2} - \frac{3by^2}{d^2} + \frac{b^2y}{d^2} - \frac{2cy}{d} + y + \frac{2bc}{d} + \frac{bc^2}{y^2} - \frac{b^2c^2}{y^3},$$

for the length of AP.

Again, the third equation, namely,

$$z^2 + \frac{2bcd^2z - 2bcdez - 2cd^2vz - 2bdevz - bd^2s^2 + bd^2v^2 - cd^2s^2 + cd^2v^2}{bd^2 + ce^2 + e^2v - d^2v},$$

is of the same form as $z^2 - 2fz + f^2$ where $f = z$, so that $-2f$ or $-2z$ must be equal to

$$\frac{2bcd^2 - 2bcde - 2cd^2v - 2bdev}{bd^2 + ce^2 + e^2v - d^2v},$$

whence

$$v = \frac{bcd^2 - bcde + bd^2z + ce^2z}{cd^2 + bde - e^2z + d^2z}.$$

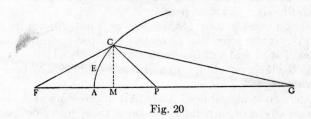

Fig. 20

Therefore, if we take AP equal to the above value of v, all the terms of which are known, and join the point P thus determined to C, this line will cut the curve CE at right angles, which was required. I see no reason why this solu-

tion should not apply to every curve to which the methods of geometry are
applicable.

It should be observed regarding the expression taken arbitrarily to raise
the original product to the required degree, as we just now took

$$y^4+fy^3+g^2y^2+h^3y+k^4,$$

that the signs $+$ and $-$ may be chosen at will, without producing different
values of v or AP. This is easily found to be the case, but if I should stop to
demonstrate every theorem I use, it would require a much larger volume
than I wish to write. I desire rather to tell you in passing that this method,
of which you have here an example, of supposing two equations to be of the
same form in order to compare them term by term and so to obtain several
equations from one, will apply to an infinity of other problems and is not
the least important feature of my general method.

I shall not give the constructions for the required tangents and normals
in connection with the method just explained, since it is always easy to find
them, although it often requires some ingenuity to get short and simple
methods of construction.

Given, for example, CD, the first conchoid of the ancients. Let A be its
pole and BH the ruler, so that the segments of all straight lines, as CE
and DB, converging toward A and
included between the curve CD and
the straight line BH, are equal. Let
it be required to find a line CG
normal to the curve at the point C.
In trying to find the point on BH
through which CG must pass (according to the method just explained), we would involve ourselves
in a calculation as long as, or longer
than any of those just given, and yet
the resulting construction would be
very simple. For we need only take
CF on CA equal to CH, the perpendicular to BH; then through F draw
FG parallel to BA and equal to EA, thus determining the point G, through
which the required line CG must pass.

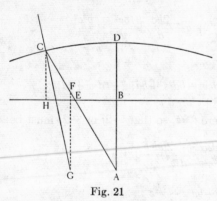

Fig. 21

To show that a consideration of these curves is not without its use, and
that they have diverse properties of no less importance than those of the
conic sections, I shall add a discussion of certain ovals which you will find
very useful in the theory of catoptrics and dioptrics. They may be described
in the following way:

Drawing the two straight lines FA and AR intersecting at A under any
angle, I choose arbitrarily a point F on one of them (more or less distant
from A according as the oval is to be large or small). With F as center I
describe a circle cutting FA at a point a little beyond A, as at the point 5.
I then draw the straight line 56 cutting AR at 6, so that A6 is less than A5,
and so that A6 is to A5 in any given ratio, as, for example, that which

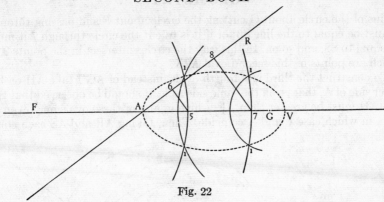

Fig. 22

measures the refraction, if the oval is to be used for dioptrics. This being done, I take an arbitrary point G in the line FA on the same side as the point 5, so that AF is to GA in any given ratio. Next, along the line A6 I lay off RA equal to GA, and with G as center and a radius equal to R6 I describe a circle. This circle will cut the first one in two points 1, 1, through which the first of the required ovals must pass.

Next, with F as center I describe a circle which cuts FA as little nearer to, or farther from, A than the point 5, as, for example, at the point 7. I then draw 78 parallel to 56, and with G as center and a radius equal to R8 I describe another circle. This circle will cut the one through 7 in the points 1, 1, which are points of the same oval. We can thus find as many points as may be desired, by drawing lines parallel to 78 and describing circles with F and G as centers.

In the construction of the second oval the only difference is that instead of AR we must take AS on the other side of A, equal to AG, and that the

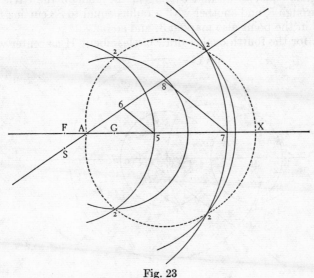

Fig. 23

radius of the circle about G cutting the circle about F and passing through 5 must be equal to the line S6; or if it is to cut the circle through 7 it must be equal to S8, and so on. In this way the circles intersect in the points 2, 2, which are points of this second oval A2X.

To construct the third and fourth ovals, instead of AG I take AH on the other side of A, that is, on the same side as F. It should be observed that this line AH must be greater than AF, which in any of these ovals may even be zero, in which case F and A coincide. Then, taking AR and AS each equal

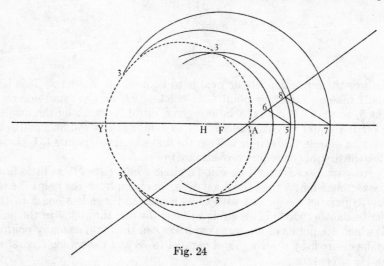

Fig. 24

to AH, to describe the third oval, A3Y, I draw a circle about H as center with a radius equal to S6 and cutting in the point 3 the circle about F passing through 5, and another with a radius equal to S8 cutting the circle through 7 in the point also marked 3, and so on.

Finally, for the fourth oval, I draw circles about H as center with radii

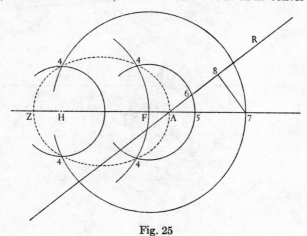

Fig. 25

equal to R6, R8, and so on, and cutting the other circles in the points marked 4.

There are many other ways of describing these same ovals. For example, the first one, AV (provided we assume FA and AG equal) might be traced as follows:

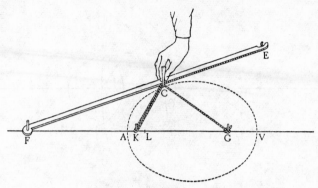

Fig. 26

Divide the line FG at L so that FL : LG = A5 : A6, that is, in the ratio corresponding to the index of refraction. Then bisecting AL at K, turn a ruler FE about the point F, pressing with the finger at C the cord EC, which, being attached at E to the end of the ruler, passes from C to K and then back to C and from C to G, where its other end is fastened. Thus the entire length of the cord is composed of GA+AL+FE−AF, and the point C will describe the first oval in a way similar to that in which the ellipse and hyperbola are described in *La Dioptrique*. But I cannot give any further attention to this subject.

Although these ovals seem to be of almost the same nature, they nevertheless belong to four different classes, each containing an infinity of subclasses, each of which in turn contains as many different kinds as does the class of ellipses or of hyperbolas; the sub-classes depending upon the value of the ratio of A5 to A6. Then, as the ratio of AF to AG, or of AF to AH changes, the ovals of each sub-class change in kind, and the length of AG or AH determines the size of the oval.

If A5 is equal to A6, the ovals of the first and third classes become straight lines; while among those of the second class we have all possible hyperbolas, and among those of the fourth all possible ellipses.

In the case of each oval it is necessary further to consider two portions having different properties. In the first oval the portion toward A (see Fig. 27) causes rays passing through the air from F to converge towards G upon meeting the convex surface 1A1 of a lens whose index of refraction, according to dioptrics, determines such ratios as that of A5 to A6, by means of which the oval is described.

But the portion toward V causes all rays coming from G to converge toward F when they strike the concave surface of a mirror of the shape of 1V1 and of such material that it diminishes the velocity of these rays in the

ratio of A5 to A6, for it is proved in dioptrics that in this case the angles of
reflection will be unequal as well as the angles of refraction, and can be
measured in the same way.

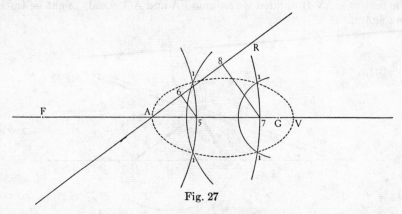

Fig. 27

Now consider the second oval. Here, too, the portion 2A2 (see Fig. 23)
serves for reflections of which the angles may be assumed unequal. For if
the surface of a mirror of the same material as in the case of the first oval be
of this form, it will reflect all rays from G, making them seem to come from
F. Observe, too, that if the line AG is considerably greater than AF, such a
mirror will be convex in the center (toward A) and concave at each end; for
such a curve would be heart-shaped rather than oval. The other part, X2,
is useful for refracting lenses; rays which pass through the air toward F are
refracted by a lens whose surface has this form.

The third oval is of use only for refraction, and causes rays traveling
through the air toward F to move through the glass toward H, after they
have passed through the surface whose form is A3Y3, which is convex
throughout except toward A, where it is slightly concave, so that this curve
is also heart-shaped. The difference between the two parts of this oval is
that the one part is nearer F and farther from H, while the other is nearer H
and farther from F.

Similarly, the last of these ovals is useful only in the case of reflection.
Its effect is to make all rays coming from H and meeting the concave surface
of a mirror of the same material as those previously discussed, and of the
form A4Z4, converge towards F after reflection.

The points F, G and H may be called the "burning points" of these ovals,
to correspond to those of the ellipse and hyperbola, and they are so named
in dioptrics.

I have not mentioned several other kinds of reflection and refraction that
are effected by these ovals; for being merely reverse or opposite effects they
are easily deduced.

I must not, however, fail to prove the statements already made. For this
purpose, take any point C on the first part of the first oval, and draw the
straight line CP normal to the curve at C. This can be done by the method
given above, as follows:

Let AG $=b$, AF $=c$, FC $=c+z$. Suppose the ratio of d to e, which I always take here to measure the refractive power of the lens under consideration, to represent the ratio of A5 to A6 or similar lines used to describe the oval. Then

$$GC = b - \frac{e}{d}z,$$

whence

$$AP = \frac{bcd^2 - bcde + bd^2z + ce^2z}{bde + cd^2 + d^2z - e^2z}.$$

From P draw PQ perpendicular to FC, and PN perpendicular to GC. Now if PQ:PN $=d:e$, that is, if PQ:PN is equal to the same ratio as that between

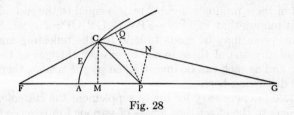

Fig. 28

the lines which measure the refraction of the convex glass AC, then a ray passing from F to C must be refracted toward G upon entering the glass. This follows at once from dioptrics.

Now let us determine by calculation if it be true that PQ: PN $=d:e$. The right triangles PQF and CMF are similar, whence it follows that CF:CM $=$ FP:PQ, and $\dfrac{FP \cdot CM}{CF} =$ PQ. Again, the right triangles PNG and CMG are similar, and therefore $\dfrac{GP \cdot CM}{CG} =$ PN. Now since the multiplication or division of two terms of a ratio by the same number does not alter the ratio, if $\dfrac{FP \cdot CM}{CF} : \dfrac{GP \cdot CM}{CG} = d:e$, then, dividing each term of the first ratio by CM and multiplying each by both CF and CG, we have FP·CG:GP·CF $=d:e$. Now by construction,

$$FP = c + \frac{bcd^2 - bcde + bd^2z + ce^2z}{cd^2 + bde - e^2z + d^2z},$$

or

$$FP = \frac{bcd^2 + c^2d^2 + bd^2z + cd^2z}{cd^2 + bde - e^2z + d^2z},$$

and

$$CG = b - \frac{e}{d}z.$$

Then

$$FP \cdot CG = \frac{b^2cd^2 + bc^2d^2 + b^2d^2z + bcd^2z - bcdez - c^2dez - bdez^2 - cdez^2}{cd^2 + bde - e^2z + d^2z}.$$

Then

$$GP = b - \frac{bcd^2 - bcde + bd^2z + ce^2z}{cd^2 + bde - e^2z + d^2z};$$

or

$$GP = \frac{b^2de + bcde - be^2z - ce^2z}{cd^2 + bde - e^2z + d^2z};$$

and $CF = c + z$. So that

$$GP \cdot CF = \frac{b^2cde + bc^2de + b^2dez + bcdez - bce^2z - c^2e^2z - be^2z^2 - ce^2z^2}{cd^2 + bde - e^2z + d^2z}.$$

The first of these products divided by d is equal to the second divided by e, whence it follows that $PQ : PN = FP \cdot CG : GP \cdot CF = d : e$, which was to be proved. This proof may be made to hold for the reflecting and refracting properties of any one of these ovals, by proper changes of the signs plus and minus; and as each can be investigated by the reader, there is no need for further discussion here.

It now becomes necessary for me to supplement the statements made in my *Dioptrique* to the effect that lenses of various forms serve equally well to cause rays coming from the same point and passing through them to converge to another point; and that among such lenses those which are convex on one side and concave on the other are more powerful burning-glasses than those which are convex on both sides; while, on the other hand, the latter make the better telescopes. I shall describe and explain only those which I believe to have the greatest practical value, taking into consideration the difficulties of cutting. To complete the theory of the subject, I shall now have to describe again the form of lens which has one side of any desired degree of convexity or concavity, and which makes all the rays that are parallel or that come from a single point converge after passing through it; and also the form of lens having the same effect but being equally convex on both sides, or such that the convexity of one of its surfaces bears a given ratio to that of the other.

In the first place, let G, Y, C, and F be given points, such that rays coming from G or parallel to GA converge at F after passing through a concave lens. Let Y be the center of the inner surface of this lens and C its edge, and let the chord CMC be given, and also the altitude of the arc CYC. First we must determine which of these ovals can be used for a lens that will cause rays passing through it in the direction of H (a point as yet undetermined) to converge toward F after leaving it.

There is no change in the direction of rays by means of reflection or refraction which cannot be effected by at least one of these ovals; and it is easily seen that this particular result can be obtained by using either part of the third oval, marked 3A3 or 3Y3, or the part of the second oval marked 2X2 (see Figs. 23, 24). Since the same method applied to each of these, we may in each case take Y as the vertex, C as a point on the curve, and F as one of the foci. It then remains to determine H, the other focus. This may be found by considering that the difference between FY and FC is to the difference between HY and HC as d is to e; that is, as the longer of the lines measuring the refractive power of the lens is to the shorter, as is evident from the manner of describing the ovals.

Since the lines FY and FC are given, we know their difference; and then, since the ratio of the two differences is known, we know the difference between HY and HC.

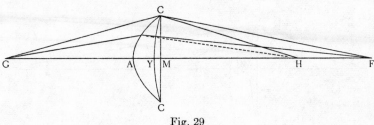

Fig. 29

Again, since YM is known, we know the difference between MH and HC, and therefore CM. It remains to find MH, the side of the right triangle CMH. The other side of this triangle, CM, is known, and also the difference between the hypotenuse, CH and the required side, MH. We can therefore easily determine MH as follows:

Let $k = \mathrm{CH} - \mathrm{MH}$ and $n = \mathrm{CM}$; then $\dfrac{n^2}{2k} - \tfrac{1}{2}k = \mathrm{MH}$, which determines the position of the point H.

If HY is greater than HF, the curve CY must be the first part of the third class of oval, which has already been designated by 3A3.

But suppose that HY is less than FY. This includes two cases: In the first, HY exceeds HF by such an amount that the ratio of their difference to the whole line FY is greater than the ratio of e, the smaller of the two lines that represent the refractive power, to d, the larger; that is, if $\mathrm{HF} = c$, and $\mathrm{HY} = c + h$, then dh is greater than $2ce + eh$. In this case CY must be the second part 3Y3 of the same oval of the third class.

In the second case dh is less than or equal to $2ce + eh$, and CY is the second part 2X2 of the oval of the second class.

Finally, if the points H and F coincide, $\mathrm{FY} = \mathrm{FC}$ and the curve YC is a circle.

It is also necessary to determine CAC, the other surface of the lens. If we suppose the rays falling on it to be parallel, this will be an ellipse having H as one of its foci, and the form is easily determined. If, however, we suppose the rays to come from the point G, the lens must have the form of the first part of an oval of the first class, the two foci of which are G and H, and which passes through the point C. The point A is seen to be its vertex from the fact that the excess of GC over GA is to the excess of HA over HC as d is to e. For if k represents the difference between CH and HM, and x represents AM, then $x - k$ will represent the difference between AH and CH; and if g represents the difference between GC and GM, which are given, $g+x$ will represent the difference between GC and GA; and since $g+x:x-k=d:e$, we have $ge+ex=dx-dk$, or $AM=x=\dfrac{ge+dk}{d-e}$, which enables us to determine the required point A.

Again, suppose that only the points G, C, and F are given, together with the ratio of AM to YM; and let it be required to determine the form of the lens ACY which causes all the rays coming from the point G to converge to F.

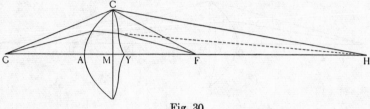

Fig. 30

In this case, we can use two ovals, AC and CY, with foci G and H, and F and H respectively. To determine these, let us suppose first that H, the focus common to both, is known. Then AM is determined by the three points, G, C, and H in the way just now explained; that is if k represents the difference between CH and HM, and g the difference between GC and GM, and if AC be the first part of the oval of the first class, we have

$$AM=\frac{ge+dk}{d-e}.$$

We may then find MY by means of the three points F, C, and H. If CY is the first part of an oval of the third class and we take y for MY and f for the difference between CF and FM, we have the difference between CF and FY equal to $f+y$; then let the difference between CH and HM equal k, and the difference between CH and HY equal $k+y$. Now $k+y:f+y=e:d$, since the oval is of the third class, whence $MY=\dfrac{fe-dk}{d-e}$. Therefore, $AM+MY=AY=\dfrac{ge+fe}{d-e}$, whence it follows that on whichever side the point H may lie, the ratio of the line AY to the excess of GC+CF over GF is always equal to the ratio of e, the smaller of the two lines representing the refractive power of the glass, to $d-e$, the difference of these two lines, which gives a very interesting theorem.

The line AY being found, it must be divided in the proper ratio into AM and MY, and since M is known the points A and Y, and finally the point H, may be found by the preceding problem. We must first find whether the line AM thus found is greater than, equal to, or less than $\dfrac{ge}{d-e}$. If it is greater, AC must be the first part of one of the third class, as they have been considered here. If it is smaller, CY must be the first part of an oval of the first class and AC the first part of one of the third class. Finally, if AM is equal to $\dfrac{ge}{d-e}$, the curves AC and CY must both be hyperbolas.

These two problems can be extended to an infinity of other cases which I will not stop to deduce, since they have no practical value in dioptrics.

I might go farther and show how, if one surface of a lens is given and is neither entirely plane nor composed of conic sections or circles, the other surface can be so determined as to transmit all the rays from a given point to another point, also given. This is no more difficult than the problems I have just explained; indeed, it is much easier since the way is now open; I prefer, however, to leave this for others to work out, to the end that they may appreciate the more highly the discovery of those things here demonstrated, through having themselves to meet some difficulties.

In all this discussion I have considered only curves that can be described upon a plane surface, but my remarks can easily be made to apply to all those curves which can be conceived of as generated by the regular movement of the points of a body in three-dimensional space. This can be done by dropping perpendiculars from each point of the curve under consideration upon two planes intersecting at right angles, for the ends of these perpendiculars will describe two other curves, one in each of the two planes, all points of which may be determined in the way already explained, and all of which may be related to those of a straight line common to the two planes; and by means of these the points of the three-dimensional curve will be entirely determined.

We can even draw a straight line at right angles to this curve at a given point, simply by drawing a straight line in each plane normal to the curve lying in that plane at the foot of the perpendicular drawn from the given point of the three-dimensional curve to that plane and then drawing two other planes, each passing through one of the straight lines and perpendicular to the plane containing it; the intersection of these two planes will be the required normal.

And so I think I have omitted nothing essential to an understanding of curved lines.

THIRD BOOK

ON THE CONSTRUCTION OF SOLID AND SUPERSOLID PROBLEMS

WHILE it is true that every curve which can be described by a continuous motion should be recognized in geometry, this does not mean that we should use at random the first one that we meet in the construction of a given problem. We should always choose with care the simplest curve that can be used in the solution of a problem, but it should be noted that the simplest means not merely the one most easily described, nor the one that leads to the easiest demonstration or construction of the problem, but rather the one of the simplest class that can be used to determine the required quantity.

For example, there is, I believe, no easier method of finding any number of mean proportionals, nor one whose demonstration is clearer, than the one which employs the curves described by the instrument XYZ, previously explained. Thus, if two mean proportionals between YA and YE be re-

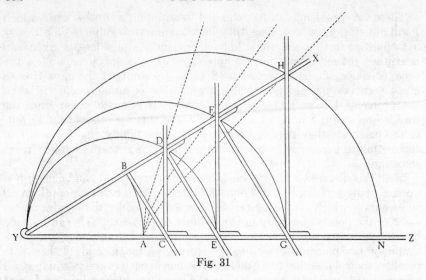

Fig. 31

quired, it is only necessary to describe a circle upon YE as diameter, cutting the curve AD in D, and YD is then one of the required mean proportionals. The demonstration becomes obvious as soon as the instrument is applied to YD, since YA (or YB) is to YC as YC is to YD as YD is to YE.

Similarly, to find four mean proportionals between YA and YG, or six between YA and YN, it is only necessary to draw the circle YFG, which determines by its intersection with AF the line YF, one of the four mean proportionals; or the circle YHN, which determines by its intersection with AH the line YH, one of the six mean proportionals, and so on.

But the curve AD is of the second class, while it is possible to find two mean proportionals by the use of the conic sections, which are curves of the first class. Again, four or six mean proportionals can be found by curves of lower classes than AF and AH respectively. It would therefore be a geometric error to use these curves. On the other hand, it would be a blunder to try vainly to construct a problem by means of a class of lines simpler than its nature allows.

Before giving the rules for the avoidance of both these errors, some general statements must be made concerning the nature of equations. An equation consists of several terms, some known and some unknown, some of which are together equal to the rest; or rather, all of which taken together are equal to nothing; for this is often the best form to consider.

Every equation can have as many distinct roots (values of the unknown quantity) as the number of dimensions of the unknown quantity in the equation. Suppose, for example, $x=2$ or $x-2=0$, and again, $x=3$, or $x-3=0$. Multiplying together the two equations $x-2=0$ and $x-3=0$, we have $x^2-5x+6=0$, or $x^2=5x-6$. This is an equation in which x has the value 2 and at the same time x has the value 3. If we next make $x-4=0$

and multiply this by $x^2-5x+6=0$, we have $x^3-9x^2+26x-24=0$ another equation, in which x, having three dimensions, has also three values, namely 2, 3, and 4.

It often happens, however, that some of the roots are false or less than nothing. Thus, if we suppose x to represent the defect of a quantity 5, we have $x+5=0$ which, multiplied by $x^3-9x^2+26x-24=0$, yields $x^4-4x^3-19x^2+106x-120=0$, an equation having four roots, namely three true roots, 2, 3, and 4, and one false root, 5.

It is evident from the above that the sum of an equation having several roots is always divisible by a binomial consisting of the unknown quantity diminished by the value of one of the true roots, or plus the value of one of the false roots. In this way, the degree of an equation can be lowered.

On the other hand, if the sum of the terms of an equation is not divisible by a binomial consisting of the unknown quantity plus or minus some other quantity, then this latter quantity is not a root of the equation. Thus the above equation $x^4-4x^3-19x^2+106x-120=0$ is divisible by $x-2$, $x-3$, $x-4$ and $x+5$, but is not divisible by x plus or minus any other quantity. Therefore the equation can have only the four roots, 2, 3, 4, and 5. We can determine also the number of true and false roots that any equation can have, as follows: An equation can have as many true roots as it contains changes of sign, from $+$ to $-$ or from $-$ to $+$; and as many false roots as the number of times two $+$ signs or two $-$ signs are found in succession.

Thus, in the last equation, since $+x^4$ is followed by $-4x^3$, giving a change of sign from $+$ to $-$, and $-19x^2$ is followed by $+106x$, and $+106x$ by -120, giving two more changes, we know there are three true roots; and since $-4x^3$ is followed by $-19x^2$ there is one false root.

It is also easy to transform an equation so that all the roots that were false shall become true roots, and all those that were true shall become false. This is done by changing the signs of the second, fourth, sixth, and all even terms, leaving unchanged the signs of the first, third, fifth, and other odd terms. Thus, if instead of

$$+x^4-4x^3-19x^2+106x-120=0$$

we write

$$+x^4+4x^3-19x^2-106x-120=0$$

we get an equation having one true root, 5, and three false roots, 2, 3, and 4.

If the roots of an equation are unknown and it be desired to increase or diminish each of these roots by some known number, we must substitute for the unknown quantity throughout the equation, another quantity greater or less by the given number. Thus, if it be desired to increase by 3 the value of each root of the equation

$$x^4+4x^3-19x^2-106x-120=0$$

put y in the place of x, and let y exceed x by 3, so that $y-3=x$. Then for x^2 put the square of $y-3$, or y^2-6y+9; for x^3 put its cube, $y^3-9y^2+27y-27$; and for x^4 put its fourth power, or

$$y^4-12y^3+54y^2-108y+81.$$

Substituting these values in the above equation, and combining, we have

$$y^4 - 12y^3 + 54y^2 - 108y + 81$$
$$+ 4y^3 - 36y^2 + 108y - 108$$
$$- 19y^2 + 114y - 171$$
$$- 106y + 318$$
$$- 120$$
$$\overline{y^4 - 8y^3 - y^2 + 8y = 0,}$$

or

$$y^3 - 8y^2 - y + 8 = 0,$$

whose true root is now 8 instead of 5, since it has been increased by 3. If, on the other hand, it is desired to diminish by 3 the roots of the same equation, we must put $y+3=x$ and $y^2+6y+9=x^2$, and so on, so that instead of $x^4 + 4x^3 - 19x^2 - 106x - 120 = 0$, we have

$$y^4 + 12y^3 + 54y^2 + 108y + 81$$
$$+ 4y^3 + 36y^2 + 108y + 108$$
$$- 19y^2 - 114y - 171$$
$$- 106y - 318$$
$$- 120$$
$$\overline{y^4 + 16y^3 + 71y^2 - 4y - 420 = 0.}$$

It should be observed that increasing the true roots of an equation diminishes the false roots by the same amount; and, on the contrary, diminishing the true roots increases the false roots; while diminishing either a true or a false root by a quantity equal to it makes the root zero; and diminishing it by a quantity greater than the root renders a true root false or a false root true. Thus by increasing the true root 5 by 3, we diminish each of the false roots, so that the root previously 4 is now only 1, the root previously 3 is zero, and the root previously 2 is now a true root, equal to 1, since $-2+3 = +1$. This explains why the equation $y^3 - 8y^2 - y + 8 = 0$ has only three roots, two of them, 1 and 8, being true roots, and the third, also 1, being false; while the other equation $y^4 - 16y^3 + 71y^2 - 4y - 420 = 0$ has only one true root, 2, since $+5-3 = +2$, and three false roots, 5, 6, and 7.

Now this method of transforming the roots of an equation without determining their values yields two results which will prove useful: First, we can always remove the second term of an equation by diminishing its true roots by the known quantity of the second term divided by the number of dimensions of the first term, if these two terms have opposite signs; or, if they have like signs, by increasing the roots by the same quantity. Thus, to remove the second term of the equation $y^4 + 16y^3 + 71y^2 - 4y - 420 = 0$ I divide 16 by 4 (the exponent of y in y^4), the quotient being 4. I then make $z - 4 = y$ and write

$$z^4 - 16z^3 + 96z^2 - 256z + 256$$
$$+ 16z^3 - 192z^2 + 768z - 1024$$
$$+ 71z^2 - 568z + 1136$$
$$- 4z + 16$$
$$- 420$$
$$\overline{z^4 \qquad - 25z^2 - 60z - 36 = 0.}$$

The true root of this equation which was 2 is now 6, since it has been increased by 4, and the false roots, 5, 6, and 7, are only 1, 2, and 3, since each has been diminished by 4. Similarly, to remove the second terms of $x^4 - 2ax^3 + (2a^2 - c^2)x^2 - 2a^3x + a^4 = 0$; since $2a \div 4 = \frac{1}{2}a$ we must put $z + \frac{1}{2}a = x$ and write

$$z^4 + 2az^3 + \tfrac{3}{2}a^2z^2 + \tfrac{1}{2}a^3z + \tfrac{1}{16}a^4$$
$$- 2az^3 - 3a^2z^2 - \tfrac{3}{2}a^3z - \tfrac{1}{4}a^4$$
$$+ 2a^2z^2 + 2a^3z + \tfrac{1}{2}a^4$$
$$- c^2z^2 - ac^2z - \tfrac{1}{4}a^2c^2$$
$$- 2a^3z - a^4$$
$$+ a^4$$
$$\overline{z^4 + (\tfrac{1}{2}a^2 - c^2)z^2 - (a^3 + ac^2)z + \tfrac{5}{16}a^4 - \tfrac{1}{4}a^2c^2 = 0.}$$

Having found the value of z, that of x is found by adding $\frac{1}{2}a$. Second, by increasing the roots by a quantity greater than any of the false roots we make all the roots true. When this is done, there will be no two consecutive $+$ or $-$ terms; and further, the known quantity of the third term will be greater than the square of half that of the second term. This can be done even when the false roots are unknown, since approximate values can always be obtained for them and the roots can then be increased by a quantity as large as, or larger than, is required. Thus, given,

$$x^6 + nx^5 - 6n^2x^4 + 36n^3x^3 - 216n^4x^2 + 1296n^5x - 7776n^6 = 0,$$

make $y - 6n = x$ and we have,

$$\begin{array}{l|l|l|l|l|l}
y^6 - 36n & y^5 + 540n^2 & y^4 - 4320n^3 & y^3 + 19440n^4 & y^2 - 46656n^5 & y + 46656n^6 \\
\;\; + \;\; n & \;\;\; - 30n^2 & \;\;\; + 360n^3 & \;\;\; - 2160n^4 & \;\;\; + 6480n^5 & \;\;\; - 7776n^6 \\
 & \;\;\; - 6n^2 & \;\;\; + 144n^3 & \;\;\; - 1296n^4 & \;\;\; + 5184n^5 & \;\;\; - 7776n^6 \\
 & & \;\;\; + 36n^3 & \;\;\; - 648n^4 & \;\;\; + 3888n^5 & \;\;\; - 7776n^6 \\
 & & & \;\;\; - 216n^4 & \;\;\; + 2592n^5 & \;\;\; - 7776n^6 \\
 & & & & \;\;\; + 1296n^5 & \;\;\; - 7776n^6 \\
 & & & & & \;\;\; - 7776n^6
\end{array}$$

$$\overline{y^6 - 35ny^5 + 504n^2y^4 - 3780n^3y^3 + 15120n^4y^2 - 27216n^5y = 0.}$$

Now it is evident that $504n^2$, the known quantity of the third term, is larger than $(\tfrac{35}{2}n)^2$; that is, than the square of half that of the second term; and there is no case for which the true roots need be increased by a quantity larger in proportion to those given than for this one.

If it is undesirable to have the last term zero, as in this case, the roots must be increased just a little more, yet not too little, for the purpose. Similarly if it is desired to raise the degree of an equation, and also to have all its terms present, as if instead of $x^5 - b = 0$, we wish an equation of the sixth degree with no term zero, first, for $x^5 - b = 0$ write $x^6 - bx = 0$, and letting $y - a = x$, we have

$$y^6 - 6ay^5 + 15a^2y^4 - 20a^3y^3 + 15a^4y^2 - (6a^5 + b)y + a^6 + ab = 0.$$

It is evident that, however small the quantity a, every term of this equation must be present.

We can also multiply or divide all the roots of an equation by a given quantity, without first determining their values. To do this, suppose the unknown quantity when multiplied or divided by the given number to be equal to a second unknown quantity. Then multiply or divide the known quantity of the second term by the given quantity, that in the third term by the square of the given quantity, that in the fourth term by its cube, and so on, to the end.

This device is useful in changing fractional terms of an equation to whole numbers, and often in rationalizing the terms. Thus, given $x^3 - \sqrt{3}x^2 + \frac{26}{27}x - \frac{8}{27\sqrt{3}} = 0$, let there be required another equation in which all the terms are expressed in rational numbers. Let $y = \sqrt{3}$ and multiply the second term by $\sqrt{3}$, the third by 3, and the last by $3\sqrt{3}$. The resulting equation is $y^3 - 3y^2 + \frac{26}{9}y - \frac{8}{9} = 0$. Next let it be required to replace this equation by another in which the known quantities are expressed only by whole numbers. Let $z = 3y$. Multiplying 3 by 3, $\frac{26}{9}$ by 9, and $\frac{8}{9}$ by 27, we have

$$z^3 - 9z^2 + 26z - 24 = 0.$$

The roots of this equation are 2, 3, and 4; and hence the roots of the preceding equation are $\frac{2}{3}$, 1 and $\frac{4}{3}$, and those of the first equation are

$$\tfrac{2}{9}\sqrt{3}, \ \tfrac{1}{3}\sqrt{3}, \ \text{and} \ \tfrac{4}{9}\sqrt{3}.$$

This method can also be used to make the known quantity of any term equal to a given quantity. Thus, given the equation

$$x^3 - b^2x + c^3 = 0,$$

let it be required to write an equation in which the coefficient of the third term, namely b^2, shall be replaced by $3a^2$. Let

$$y = x\sqrt{\frac{3a^2}{b^2}}$$

and we have

$$y^3 - 3a^2y + \frac{3a^3c^3}{b^3}\sqrt{3} = 0.$$

Neither the true nor the false roots are always real; sometimes they are imaginary; that is, while we can always conceive of as many roots for each equation as I have already assigned, yet there is not always a definite quantity corresponding to each root so conceived of. Thus, while we may conceive of the equation $x^3 - 6x^2 + 13x - 10 = 0$ as having three roots, yet there is only one real root, 2, while the other two, however we may increase, diminish, or multiply them in accordance with the rules just laid down, remain always imaginary.

When the construction of a problem involves the solution of an equation in which the unknown quantity has three dimensions, the following steps must be taken:

First, if the equation contains some fractional coefficients, change them to whole numbers by the method explained above; if it contains surds, change them as far as possible into rational numbers, either by multiplication or by one of several other methods easy enough to find. Second, by examining in order all the factors of the last term, determine whether the left member of the equation is divisible by a binomial consisting of the unknown quantity plus or minus any one of these factors. If it is, the problem is plane, that is, it can be constructed by means of the ruler and compasses; for either the known quantity of the binomial is the required root or else, having divided the left member of the equation by the binomial, the quotient is of the second degree, and from this quotient the root can be found as explained in the first book.

Given, for example, $y^6 - 8y^4 - 124y^2 - 64 = 0$: the last term, 64, is divisible by 1, 2, 4, 8, 16, 32, and 64; therefore, we must find whether the left member is divisible by y^2-1, y^2+1, y^2-2, y^2+2, y^2-4, and so on. We shall find that it is divisible by $y^2 - 16$ as follows:

$$
\begin{array}{l}
+y^6 - 8y^4 - 124y^2 - 64 = 0 \\
\underline{-y^6 - 8y^4 - 4y^2}\ \\
0 - 16y^4 - 128y^2 \ \Big)\!-16 \\
\underline{-16\ -\ 16} \\
+\ \ y^4 + 8y^2 + 4 = 0.
\end{array}
$$

Beginning with the last term, I divide -64 by -16 which gives $+4$; write this in the quotient; multiply $+4$ by $+y^2$ which gives $+4y^2$, and write in the dividend $-4y^2$ (for the opposite sign from that obtained by the multiplication must always be used). Adding $-124y^2$ and $-4y^2$ I have $-128y^2$. Dividing this by -16 I have $+8y^2$ in the quotient, and multiplying by y^2 I have $-8y^4$ to be added to the corresponding term, $-8y^4$, in the dividend. This gives $-16y^4$ which divided by -16 yields $+y^4$ in the quotient and $-y^6$ to be added to $+y^6$ which gives zero, and shows that the division is finished.

If, however, there is a remainder, or if any modified term is not exactly divisible by 16, then it is clear that the binomial is not a divisor.

Similarly, given

$$
\begin{array}{l}
y^6 + \ a^2\Big\} y^4 - a^4 \Big\} y^2 - \ a^6 \ \ \Big\} \\
-2c^2\Big\}+c^4\Big\}-2a^4c^2 \Big\} = 0, \\
-\ a^2c^4\Big\}
\end{array}
$$

the last term is divisible by a, a^2, a^2+c^2, a^3+ac^2, and so on, but only two of these need be considered, namely a^2 and a^2+c^2. The others give a term in the quotient of lower or higher degree than the known quantity of the next to the last term, and thus render the division impossible. Note that I am here considering y^6 as of the third degree, since there are no terms in y^5, y^3, or y. Trying the binomial

$$y^2 - a^2 - c^2 = 0$$

we find that the division can be performed as follows:

$$
\begin{array}{l}
+y^6 + \ a^2 \Big\} y^4 - a^4 \ \ \Big\} y^2 - \ \ a^6 \ \ \Big\} \\
\underline{-y^6 - 2c^2}\Big\}+c^4\ \ \Big\}-2a^4c^2 \Big\} = 0 \\
0 - 2a^2 \Big\} \underline{y^4 - a^4 \ \ \ }\Big\} y^2 - \ a^2c^4 \Big\} \\
+\ c^2 \Big\}-a^2c^2 \Big\}\underline{-a^2-c^2} \\
\underline{-a^2-c^2 \ \ -a^2-c^2} \\
+y^4 +2a^2 \Big\} y^2 + a^4 \ \ \Big\} \\
-\ c^2 \Big\}+a^2c^2 \Big\} = 0.
\end{array}
$$

This shows that a^2+c^2 is the required root, which can easily be proved by multiplication.

But when no binomial divisor of the proposed equation can be found, it is certain that the problem depending upon it is solid, and it is then as great a mistake to try to construct it by using only circles and straight lines as it is to use the conic sections to construct a problem requiring only circles; for any evidence of ignorance may be termed a mistake.

Again, given an equation in which the unknown quantity has four dimensions. After removing any surds or fractions, see if a binomial having one term a factor of the last term of the expression will divide the left member. If such a binomial can be found, either the known quantity of the binomial is the required root, or, after the division is performed, the resulting equation, which is of only three dimensions, must be treated in the same way. If no such binomial can be found, we must increase or diminish the roots so as to remove the second term, in the way already explained, and then reduce it to another of the third degree, in the following manner: Instead of

$$x^4 \pm px^2 \pm qx \pm r = 0$$

write

$$y^6 \pm 2py^4 + (p^2 \pm 4r)y^2 - q^2 = 0.$$

For the ambiguous sign put $+2p$ in the second expression if $+p$ occurs in the first; but if $-p$ occurs in the first, write $-2p$ in the second; and on the contrary, put $-4r$ if $+r$, and $+4r$ if $-r$ occurs; but whether the first expression contains $+q$ or $-q$ we always write $-q^2$ and $+p^2$ in the second, provided that x^4 and y^6 have the sign $+$; otherwise, we write $+q^2$ and $-p^2$. For example, given

$$x^4 - 4x^2 - 8x + 35 = 0$$

replace it by

$$y^6 - 8y^4 - 124y^2 - 64 = 0.$$

For since $p = -4$, we replace $2py^4$ by $-8y^4$; and since $r = 35$, we replace $(p^2 - 4r)y^2$ by $(16 - 140)y^2$ or $-124y^2$; and since $q = 8$, we replace $-q^2$ by -64.

Similarly, instead of

$$x^4 - 17x^2 - 20x - 6 = 0$$

we must write

$$y^6 - 34y^4 + 313y^2 - 400 = 0,$$

for 34 is twice 17, and 313 is the square of 17 increased by four times 6, and 400 is the square of 20.

In the same way, instead of

$$+z^4 + (\tfrac{1}{2}a^2 - c^2)z^2 - (a^3 + ac^2)z - \tfrac{5}{16}a^4 - \tfrac{1}{4}a^2c^2 = 0,$$

we must write

$$y^6 + (a^2 - 2c^2)y^4 + (c^4 - a^4)y^2 - a^6 - 2a^4c^2 - a^2c^4 = 0;$$

for

$$p = \tfrac{1}{2}a^2 - c^2, \quad p^2 = \tfrac{1}{4}a^4 - a^2c^2 + c^4, \quad 4r = -\tfrac{5}{4}a^4 + a^2c^2.$$

And finally,

$$-q^2 = -a^6 - 2a^4c^2 - a^2c^4.$$

When the equation has been reduced to three dimensions, the value of y^2 is found by the method already explained. If this cannot be done it is useless to pursue the question further, for it follows inevitably that the problem is solid. If, however, the value of y^2 can be found, we can by means of it separate the preceding equation into two others, each of the second degree, whose roots will be the same as those of the original equation. Instead of $+x^4 \pm px^2 \pm qx \pm r = 0$, write the two equations

$$+x^2 - yx + \tfrac{1}{2}y^2 \pm \tfrac{1}{2}p \pm \frac{q}{2y} = 0$$

and

$$+x^2 + yx + \tfrac{1}{2}y^2 \pm \tfrac{1}{2}p \pm \frac{q}{2y} = 0.$$

For the ambiguous signs write $+\tfrac{1}{2}p$ in each new equation, when p has a positive sign, and $-\tfrac{1}{2}p$ when p has a negative sign, but write $+\frac{q}{2y}$ when we have $-yx$, and $-\frac{q}{2y}$ when we have $+yx$, provided q has a positive sign, and the opposite when q has a negative sign. It is then easy to determine all the roots of the proposed equation, and consequently to construct the problem of which it contains the solution, by the exclusive use of circles and straight lines. For example, writing $y^6 - 34y^4 + 313y^2 - 400 = 0$ instead of $x^4 - 17x^2 - 20x - 6 = 0$, we find that $y^2 = 16$; then, instead of the original equation

$$+x^4 - 17x^2 - 20x - 6 = 0$$

write the two equations $+x^2 - 4x - 3 = 0$ and $+x^2 + 4x + 2 = 0$. For, $y = 4$, $\tfrac{1}{2}y^2 = 8$, $p = 17$, $q = 20$, and therefore

$$+\tfrac{1}{2}y^2 - \tfrac{1}{2}p - \frac{q}{2y} = -3$$

and

$$+\tfrac{1}{2}y^2 - \tfrac{1}{2}p + \frac{q}{2y} = +2.$$

Obtaining the roots of these two equations, we get the same results as if we had obtained the roots of the equation containing x^4, namely, one true root, $\sqrt{7}+2$, and three false ones, $\sqrt{7}-2$, $2+\sqrt{2}$, and $2-\sqrt{2}$. Again, given $x^4 - 4x^2 - 8x + 35 = 0$, we have $y^6 - 8y^4 - 124y^2 - 64 = 0$, and since the root of the latter equation is 16, we must write $x^2 - 4x + 5 = 0$ and $x^2 + 4x + 7 = 0$. For in this case,

$$+\tfrac{1}{2}y^2 - \tfrac{1}{2}p - \frac{q}{2y} = 5$$

and

$$+\tfrac{1}{2}y^2 - \tfrac{1}{2}p + \frac{q}{2y} = 7.$$

Now these two equations have no roots either true or false, whence we know that the four roots of the original equation are imaginary; and that the problem whose solution depends upon this equation is plane, but that its construction is impossible, because the given quantities cannot be united.

Similarly, given

$$z^4+(\tfrac{1}{2}a^2-c^2)z^2-(a^3+ac^2)z+\tfrac{5}{16}a^4-\tfrac{1}{4}a^2c^2=0,$$

since we have found $y^2=a^2+c^2$, we must write

and

$$z^2-\sqrt{a^2+c^2}z+\tfrac{3}{4}a^2-\tfrac{1}{2}a\sqrt{a^2+c^2}=0,$$

$$z^2+\sqrt{a^2+c^2}z+\tfrac{3}{4}a^2+\tfrac{1}{2}a\sqrt{a^2+c^2}=0.$$

For $y=\sqrt{a^2+c^2}$ and $+\tfrac{1}{2}y^2+\tfrac{1}{2}p=\tfrac{3}{4}a^2$, and $\dfrac{q}{2y}=\tfrac{1}{2}a\sqrt{a^2+c^2}$; then we have

or

$$z=\tfrac{1}{2}\sqrt{a^2+c^2}+\sqrt{-\tfrac{1}{2}a^2+\tfrac{1}{4}c^2+\tfrac{1}{2}a\sqrt{a^2+c^2}}$$

$$z=\tfrac{1}{2}\sqrt{a^2+c^2}-\sqrt{-\tfrac{1}{2}a^2+\tfrac{1}{4}c^2+\tfrac{1}{2}a\sqrt{a^2+c^2}}.$$

Now we already have $z+\tfrac{1}{2}a=x$, and therefore x, the quantity in the search for which we have performed all these operations, is

$$+\tfrac{1}{2}a+\sqrt{\tfrac{1}{4}a^2+\tfrac{1}{4}c^2}-\sqrt{\tfrac{1}{4}c^2-\tfrac{1}{2}a^2+\tfrac{1}{2}a\sqrt{a^2+c^2}}.$$

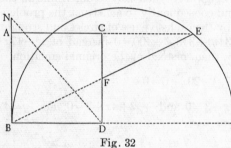

Fig. 32

To emphasize the value of this rule, I shall apply it to a problem. Given the square AD and the line BN, to prolong the side AC to E, so that EF, laid off from E on EB, shall be equal to NB.

Pappus showed that if BD is produced to G, so that DG = DN, and a circle is described on BG as diameter, the required point E will be the intersection of the straight line AC (produced) with the circumference of this circle.

Those not familiar with this construction would not be likely to discover it, and if they applied the method suggested here they would never think of taking DG for the unknown quantity rather than CF or FD, since either of these would much more easily lead to an equation. They would thus get an equation which could not easily be solved without the rule which I have just explained.

For, putting a for BD or CD, c for EF and x for DF, we have CF $=a-x$, and, since CF is to FE as FD is to BF, we have

$$a-x:c=x:\text{BF},$$

whence BF $=\dfrac{cx}{a-x}$. Now, in the right triangle BDF whose sides are x and a, x^2+a^2, the sum of their squares, is equal to the square of the hypotenuse, which is $\dfrac{c^2x^2}{x^2-2ax+a^2}$. Multiplying both sides by

$$x^2-2ax+a^2,$$

we get the equation,

$$x^4 - 2ax^3 + 2a^2x^2 - 2a^3x + a^4 = c^2x^2,$$

or

$$x^4 - 2ax^3 + (2a^2 - c^2)x^2 - 2a^3x + a^4 = 0,$$

and by the preceding rule we know that its root, which is the length of the line DF, is

$$\tfrac{1}{2}a + \sqrt{\tfrac{1}{4}a^2 + \tfrac{1}{4}c^2} - \sqrt{\tfrac{1}{4}c^2 - \tfrac{1}{2}a^2 + \tfrac{1}{2}a\sqrt{a^2 + c^2}}.$$

If, on the other hand, we consider BF, CE, or BE as the unknown quantity, we obtain an equation of the fourth degree, but much easier to solve, and quite simply obtained.

Again, if DG were used, the equation would be much more difficult to obtain, but its solution would be very simple. I state this simply to warn you that, when the proposed problem is not solid, if one method of attack yields a very complicated equation, a much simpler one can usually be found by some other method.

I might add several different rules for the solution of cubic and biquadratic equations but they would be superfluous, since the construction of any plane problem can be found by means of those already given.

I could also add rules for equations of the fifth, sixth, and higher degrees, but I prefer to consider them all together and to state the following general rule:

First, try to put the given equation into the form of an equation of the same degree obtained by multiplying together two others, each of a lower degree. If, after all possible ways of doing this have been tried, none has been successful, then it is certain that the given equation cannot be reduced to a simpler one; and, consequently, if it is of the third or fourth degree, the problem depending upon it is solid; if of the fifth or sixth, the problem is one degree more complex, and so on. I have also omitted here the demonstration of most of my statements, because they seem to me so easy that if you take the trouble to examine them systematically the demonstrations will present themselves to you and it will be of much more value to you to learn them in that way than by reading them.

Now, when it is clear that the proposed problem is solid, whether the equation upon which its solution depends is of the fourth degree or only of the third, its roots can always be found by any one of the three conic sections, or even by some part of one of them, however small, together with only circles and straight lines. I shall content myself with giving here a general rule for finding them all by means of a parabola, since that is in some respects the simplest of these curves.

First, remove the second term of the proposed equation, if this is not already zero, thus reducing it to the form $z^3 = \pm apz \pm a^2q$, if the given equation is of the third degree, or $z^4 = \pm apz^2 \pm a^2qz \pm a^3r$, if it is of the fourth degree. By choosing a as the unit, the former may be written $z^3 = \pm pz \pm q$ and the latter $z^4 = \pm pz^2 \pm qz \pm r$. Suppose that the parabola FAG is already described; let ACDKL be its axis, a, or 1 which equals 2AC, its latus rectum (C being within the parabola), and A its vertex. Lay off CD equal to $\frac{1}{2}p$ so that the points D and A lie on the same side of C if the equation contains $+p$ and on opposite sides if it contains $-p$. Then at the point D (or, if $p = 0$, at C), erect DE perpendicular to CD, so that DE is equal to $\frac{1}{2}q$, and about E as center, with AE as radius, describe the circle FG, if the given equation is a cubic, that is, if r is zero.

If the equation contains $+r$, on one side of AE produced, lay off AR equal to r, and on the other side lay off AS equal to the latus rectum of the parabola, that is, to 1, and describe a circle on RS as diameter. Then if AH is drawn perpendicular to AE it will

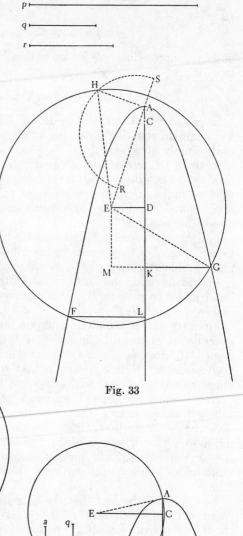

Fig. 33

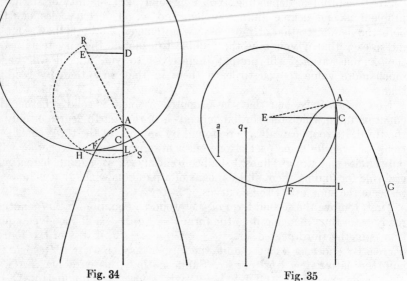

Fig. 34

Fig. 35

meet the circle RHS in the point H, through which the other circle FHG
must pass.

If the equation contains $-r$, construct a circle upon AE as diameter and
in it inscribe AI, a line equal to AH; then the first circle must pass through
the point I.

Now the circle FG can cut or touch the parabola in 1, 2, 3, or 4 points;
and if perpendiculars are drawn from these points upon the axis they will

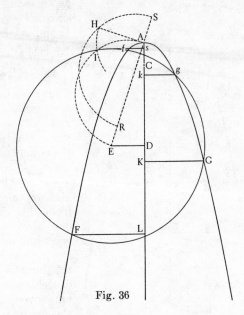

Fig. 36

represent all the roots of the equation, both true and false. If the quantity
q is positive, the true roots will be those perpendiculars, such as FL, on the
same side of the parabola, as E, the center of the circle; while the others, as
GK, will be the false roots. On the other hand, if q is negative, the true roots
will be those on the opposite side, and the false or negative roots will be
those on the same side as E, the center of the circle. If the circle neither cuts
nor touches the parabola at any point, it is an indication that the equation
has neither a true nor a false root, but that all the roots are imaginary.

This rule is evidently as general and complete as could possibly be desired. Its demonstration is also very easy. If the line GK thus constructed
be represented by z, then AK is z^2, since by the nature of the parabola, GK
is the mean proportional between AK and the latus rectum, which is 1.
Then if AC or $\frac{1}{2}$, and CD or $\frac{1}{2}p$, be subtracted from AK, the remainder is
DK or EM, which is equal to $z^2-\frac{1}{2}p-\frac{1}{2}$ of which the square is

$$z^4-pz^2-z^2+\tfrac{1}{4}p^2+\tfrac{1}{2}p+\tfrac{1}{4}.$$

And since DE $=$ KM $=\frac{1}{2}q$, the whole line GM $=z+\frac{1}{2}q$, and the square of GM
equals $z^2+qz+\frac{1}{4}q^2$. Adding these two squares we have

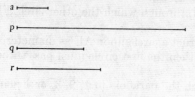

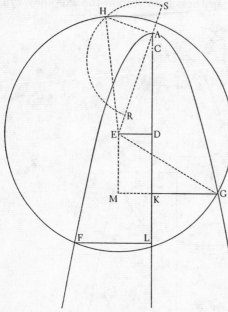

Fig. 37

$z^4 - pz^2 + qz + \frac{1}{4}q^2 + \frac{1}{4}p^2 + \frac{1}{2}p + \frac{1}{4}$

for the square of GE, since GE is the hypotenuse of the right triangle EMG.

But GE is the radius of the circle FG and can therefore be expressed in another way. For since ED $= \frac{1}{2}q$, and AD $= \frac{1}{2}p + \frac{1}{2}$, and ADE is a right angle, we have

$$EA = \sqrt{\frac{1}{4}q^2 + \frac{1}{4}p^2 + \frac{1}{2}p + \frac{1}{4}}.$$

Then, since HA is the mean proportional between AS or 1 and AR or r, HA $= \sqrt{r}$; and since EAH is a right angle, the square of HE or of EG is

$$\frac{1}{4}q^2 + \frac{1}{4}p^2 + \frac{1}{2}p + \frac{1}{4} + r,$$

and we can form an equation from this expression and the one already obtained. This equation will be of the form $z^4 = pz^2 - qz + r$, and therefore the line GK, or z, is the root of this equation, which was to be proved. If you will apply this method in all the other cases, with the proper changes of sign, you will be convinced of its usefulness, without my writing anything further about it.

Let us apply it to the problem of finding two mean proportionals between the lines a and q. It is evident that if we represent one of the mean proportionals by z, then

$a : z = z : \dfrac{z^2}{a} = \dfrac{z^2}{a} : \dfrac{z^3}{a^2}$. Thus we have

an equation between q and $\dfrac{z^3}{a^2}$, namely, $z^3 = a^2q$.

Describe the parabola FAG with its axis along AC, and with AC equal to $\frac{1}{2}a$, that is, to half the latus rectum. Then erect CE equal to $\frac{1}{2}q$ and perpendicular to AC at C, and describe the circle AF about E as

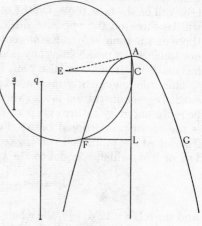

Fig. 38

center, passing through A. Then FL and LA are the required mean proportionals.

Again, let it be required to divide the angle NOP, or rather, the circular arc NQTP, into three equal parts. Let NO = 1 be the radius of the circle, NP = q be the chord subtending the given arc, and NQ = z be the chord subtending one-third of that arc; then the equation is $z^3 = 3z - q$. For, drawing NQ, OQ and OT, and drawing QS parallel to TO, it is obvious that NO is to NQ as NQ is to QR as QR is to RS. Since NO = 1 and NQ = z, then QR = z^2 and RS = z^3; and since NP or q lacks only RS or z^3 of being three times NQ or z, we have $q = 3z - z^3$ or $z^3 = 3z - q$.

Describe the parabola FAG so that CA, one-half its latus rectum, shall be equal to $\frac{1}{2}$; take CD = $\frac{3}{2}$ and the perpendicular DE = $\frac{1}{2}q$; then describe the

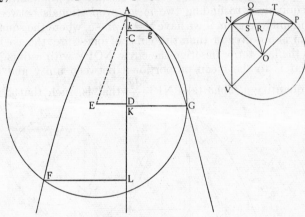

Fig. 39

circle FAgG about E as center, passing through A. This circle cuts the parabola in three points, F, g, and G, besides the vertex, A. This shows that the given equation has three roots, namely, the two true roots, GK and gk, and one false root, FL. The smaller of the two roots, gk, must be taken as the length of the required line NQ, for the other root, GK, is equal to NV, the chord subtended by one-third the arc NVP, which, together with the arc NQP constitutes the circle; and the false root, FL, is equal to the sum of QN and NV, as may easily be shown.

It is unnecessary for me to give other examples here, for all problems that are only solid can be reduced to such forms as not to require this rule for their construction except when they involve the finding of two mean proportionals or the trisection of an angle. This will be obvious if it is noted that the most difficult of these problems can be expressed by equations of the third or fourth degree; that all equations of the fourth degree can be reduced to quadratic equations by means of other equations not exceeding the third degree; and finally, that the second terms of these equations can be removed; so that every such equation can be reduced to one of the following forms:

$$z^3 = -pz + q \qquad\qquad z^3 = +pz + q \qquad\qquad z^3 = +pz - q.$$

Now, if we have $z^3 = -pz+q$, the rule, attributed by Cardan to one Scipio Ferreus, gives us the root

$$\sqrt[3]{\tfrac{1}{2}q+\sqrt{\tfrac{1}{4}q^2+\tfrac{1}{27}p^3}}-\sqrt[3]{-\tfrac{1}{2}q+\sqrt{\tfrac{1}{4}q^2+\tfrac{1}{27}p^3}}.$$

Similarly, when we have $z^3 = +pz+q$ where the square of half the last term is greater than the cube of one-third the coefficient of the next to the last term, the corresponding rule gives us the root

$$\sqrt[3]{\tfrac{1}{2}q+\sqrt{\tfrac{1}{4}q^2-\tfrac{1}{27}p^3}}+\sqrt[3]{\tfrac{1}{2}q-\sqrt{\tfrac{1}{4}q^2-\tfrac{1}{27}p^3}}.$$

It is now clear that all problems of which the equations can be reduced to either of these two forms can be constructed without the use of the conic sections except to extract the cube roots of certain known quantities, which process is equivalent to finding two mean proportionals between such a quantity and unity. Again, if we have $z^3 = +pz+q$, where the square of half the last term is not greater than the cube of one-third the coefficient of the next to the last term, describe the circle NQPV with radius NO equal to $\sqrt{\tfrac{1}{3}p}$, that is to the mean proportional between unity and one-third the known quantity p. Then take $NP = \dfrac{3q}{p}$, that is, such that NP is to q,

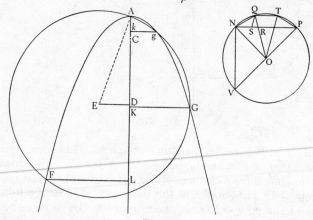

Fig. 40

the other known quantity, as 1 is to $\tfrac{1}{3}p$, and inscribe NP in the circle. Divide each of the two arcs NQP and NVP into three equal parts, and the required root is the sum of NQ, the chord subtending one-third the first arc, and NV, the chord subtending one-third of the second arc.

Finally, suppose that we have $z^3 = pz-q$. Construct the circle NQPV whose radius NO is equal to $\sqrt{\tfrac{1}{3}p}$, and let NP, equal to $\dfrac{3q}{p}$, be inscribed in this circle; then NQ, the chord of one-third the arc NQP, will be the first of the required roots, and NV, the chord of one-third the other arc, will be the second.

An exception must be made in the case in which the square of half the last term is greater than the cube of one-third the coefficient of the next to the last term; for then the line NP cannot be inscribed in the circle, since it is longer than the diameter. In this case, the two roots that were true are merely imaginary, and the only real root is the one previously false, which according to Cardan's rule is

$$\sqrt[3]{\tfrac{1}{2}q+\sqrt{\tfrac{1}{4}q^2-\tfrac{1}{27}p^3}} + \sqrt[3]{\tfrac{1}{2}q- \sqrt{\tfrac{1}{4}q^2-\tfrac{1}{27}p^3}}.$$

Furthermore, it should be remarked that this method of expressing the roots by means of the relations which they bear to the sides of certain cubes whose contents only are known is in no respect clearer or simpler than the method of expressing them by means of the relations which they bear to the chords of certain arcs (or portions of circles), when arcs three times as long are known. And the roots of the cubic equations which cannot be solved by Cardan's method can be expressed as clearly as any others, or more clearly than the others, by the method given here.

For example, grant that we may consider a root of the equation $z^3 = -qz+p$ known, because we know that it is the sum of two lines of which one is the side of a cube whose volume is $\tfrac{1}{2}q$ increased by the side of a square whose area is $\tfrac{1}{4}q^2-\tfrac{1}{27}p^3$, and the other is the side of another cube whose volume is the difference between $\tfrac{1}{2}q$ and the side of a square whose area is $\tfrac{1}{4}q^2-\tfrac{1}{27}p^3$. This is as much knowledge of the roots as is furnished by Cardan's method. There is no doubt that the value of the root of the equation $z^3 = +qz-p$ is quite as well known and as clearly conceived when it is considered as the length of a chord inscribed in a circle of radius $\sqrt{\tfrac{1}{3}p}$ and subtending an arc that is one-third the arc subtended by a chord of length $\dfrac{3q}{p}$.

Indeed, these terms are much less complicated than the others, and they might be made even more concise by the use of some particular symbol to express such chords, just as the symbol $\sqrt[3]{}$ is used to represent the side of a cube.

By methods similar to those already explained, we can express the roots of any biquadratic equation, and there seems to me nothing further to be desired in the matter; for by their very nature these roots cannot be expressed in simpler terms, nor can they be determined by any construction that is at the same time easier and more general.

It is true that I have not yet stated my grounds for daring to declare a thing possible or impossible, but if it is remembered that in the method I use all problems which present themselves to geometers reduce to a single type, namely, to the question of finding the values of the roots of an equation, it will be clear that a list can be made of all the ways of finding the roots, and that it will then be easy to prove our method the simplest and most general. Solid problems in particular cannot, as I have already said, be constructed without the use of a curve more complex than the circle. This follows at once from the fact that they all reduce to two constructions, namely, to one in which two mean proportionals are to be found between two given lines, and one in which two points are to be found which divide a given arc into three equal parts. Inasmuch as the curvature of a circle depends only upon a simple relation between the center and all points on the circumference, the circle can only be used to determine a single point between two extremes, as, for example, to find one mean proportional between two given lines or to bisect a given arc; while, on the other hand, since the curvature of the conic sections always depends upon two different things, it can be used to determine two different points.

For a similar reason, it is impossible that any problem of degree more complex than the solid, involving the finding of four mean proportionals or the division of an angle into five equal parts, can be constructed by the use of one of the conic sections.

I therefore believe that I shall have accomplished all that is possible when I have given a general rule for constructing problems by means of the curve described by the intersection of a parabola and a straight line, as previously explained; for I am convinced that there is nothing of a simpler nature that will serve this purpose. You have seen, too, that this curve directly follows the conic sections in that question to which the ancients devoted so much attention, and whose solution presents in order all the curves that should be received into geometry.

When quantities required for the construction of these problems are to be found, you already know how an equation can always be formed that is of no higher degree than the fifth or sixth. You also know how by increasing the roots of this equation we can make them all true, and at the same time

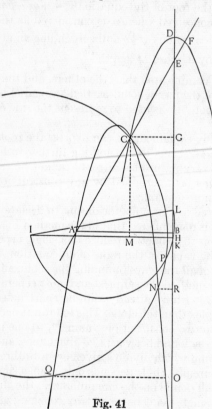

have the coefficient of the third term greater than the square of half that of the second term. Also, if it is not higher than the fifth degree it can always be changed into an equation of the sixth degree in which every term is present.

Now to overcome all these difficulties by means of a single rule, I shall consider all these directions applied and the equation thereby reduced to the form: $y^6 - py^5 + qy^4 - ry^3 + sy^2 - ty + u = 0$ in which q is greater than the square of $\frac{1}{2}p$.

Produce BK indefinitely in both directions, and at B draw AB perpendicular to BK and equal to $\frac{1}{2}p$. In a separate plane describe the parabola CDF whose principal parameter is

$$\sqrt{\frac{t}{\sqrt{u}} + q - \frac{1}{4}p^2}$$

which we shall represent by n.

Now place the plane containing the parabola on that contain-

Fig. 41

ing the lines AB and BK, in such a way that the axis DE of the parabola falls along the line BK. Take a point E such that $DE = \dfrac{2\sqrt{u}}{pn}$ and place a ruler so as to connect this point E and the point A of the lower plane. Hold the ruler so that it always connects these points, and slide the parabola up or down, keeping its axis always along BK. Then the point C, the intersection of the parabola and the ruler, will describe the curve ACN, which is to be used in the construction of the proposed problem.

Having thus described the curve, take a point L in the line BK on the concave side of the parabola, and such that $BL = DE = \dfrac{2\sqrt{u}}{pn}$; then lay off on BK, toward B, LH equal to $\dfrac{t}{2n\sqrt{u}}$, and from H draw HI perpendicular to LH and on the same side as the curve ACN. Take HI equal to

$$\frac{r}{2n^2} + \frac{\sqrt{u}}{n^2} + \frac{pt}{4n^2\sqrt{u}}$$

which we may, for the sake of brevity, set equal to $\dfrac{m}{n^2}$. Join L and I, and describe the circle LPI on LI as diameter; then inscribe in this circle the line LP equal to $\sqrt{\dfrac{s+p\sqrt{u}}{n^2}}$. Finally, describe the circle PCN about I as center and passing through P. This circle will cut or touch the curve ACN in as many points as the equation has roots; and hence the perpendiculars CG, NR, QO, and so on, dropped from these points upon BK, will be the required roots. This rule never fails, nor does it admit of any exceptions.

For, if the quantity s were so large in proportion to the others, p, q, r, t, u, that the line LP was greater than the diameter of the circle LI, so that LP could not be inscribed in it, every root of the proposed equation would be imaginary; and the same would be true if the circle IP were so small that it did not cut the curve ACN at any point. The circle IP will in general cut the curve ACN in six different points, so that the equation can have six distinct roots. But if it cuts it in fewer points, this indicates that some of the roots are equal or else imaginary.

If, however, this method of tracing the curve ACN by the translation of a parabola seems to you awkward, there are many other ways of describing it. We might take AB and BL as before, and BK equal to the latus rectum of the parabola, and describe the semi-circle KST with its center in BK and cutting AB in some point S. Then from the point T where it ends, take TV toward K equal to BL and join S and V. Draw AC through A parallel to SV, and draw SC through S parallel to BK; then C, the intersection of AC and SC, will be one point of the required curve. In this way we can find as many points of the curve as may be desired.

The demonstration of all this is very simple. Place the ruler AE and the parabola FD so that both pass through the point C. This can always be done, since C lies on the curve ACN which is described by the intersection of the parabola and the ruler. If we let $CG = y$, GD will equal $\dfrac{y^2}{n}$, since the

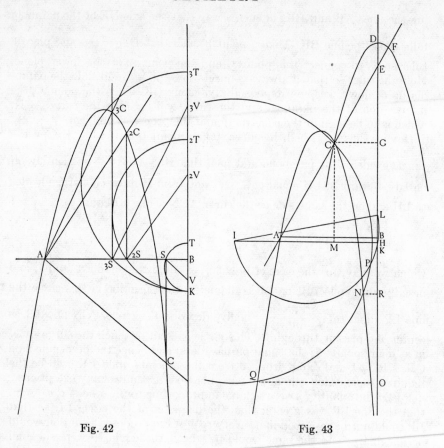

Fig. 42   Fig. 43

latus rectum n is to CG as CG is to GD. Then $DE = \dfrac{2\sqrt{u}}{pn}$, and subtracting

DE from GD we have $GE = \dfrac{y^2}{n} - \dfrac{2\sqrt{u}}{pn}$. Since AB is to BE as CG is to GE,

and AB is equal to $\tfrac{1}{2}p$, therefore $BE = \dfrac{py}{2n} - \dfrac{\sqrt{u}}{ny}$. Now let C be a point on

the curve generated by the intersection of the line SC, which is parallel to
BK, and AC, which is parallel to SV. Let $SB = CG = y$, and $BK = n$, the

latus rectum of the parabola. Then $BT = \dfrac{y^2}{n}$, for KB is to BS as BS is to BT,

and since $TV = BL = \dfrac{2\sqrt{u}}{pn}$ we have $BV = \dfrac{y^2}{n} - \dfrac{2\sqrt{u}}{pn}$. Also, SB is to BV as AB

is to BE, whence $BE = \dfrac{py}{2n} - \dfrac{\sqrt{u}}{ny}$ as before. It is evident, therefore, that one

and the same curve is described by these two methods.

Furthermore, $BL = DE$, and therefore $DL = BE$; also $LH = \dfrac{t}{2n\sqrt{u}}$ and

$$DL = \frac{py}{2n} - \frac{\sqrt{u}}{ny};$$

therefore,
$$DH = LH + DL = \frac{py}{2n} - \frac{\sqrt{u}}{ny} + \frac{t}{2n\sqrt{u}}.$$

Also, since $GD = \dfrac{y^2}{n}$,

$$GH = DH - GD = \frac{py}{2n} - \frac{\sqrt{u}}{ny} + \frac{t}{2n\sqrt{u}} - \frac{y^2}{n}$$

which may be written

$$GH = \frac{-y^3 + \frac{1}{2}py^2 + \dfrac{ty}{2\sqrt{u}} - \sqrt{u}}{n\ y}$$

and the square of GH is equal to

$$\frac{y^6 - py^5 + \left(\frac{1}{4}p^2 - \dfrac{t}{\sqrt{u}}\right)y^4 + \left(2\sqrt{u} + \dfrac{pt}{2\sqrt{u}}\right)y^3 + \left(\dfrac{t^2}{4u} - p\sqrt{u}\right)y^2 - ty + u}{n^2y^2}.$$

Whatever point of the curve is taken as C, whether toward N or toward Q, it will always be possible to express the square of the segment of BH between the point H and the foot of the perpendicular from C to BH in these same terms connected by these same signs.

Again,
$$IH = \frac{m}{n^2}, \quad LH = \frac{t}{2n\sqrt{u}},$$
whence
$$IL = \sqrt{\frac{m^2}{n^4} + \frac{t^2}{4n^2u}},$$

since the angle IHL is a right angle; and since

$$LP = \sqrt{\frac{s}{n^2} + \frac{p\sqrt{u}}{n^2}}$$

and the angle IPL is a right angle,

$$IC = IP = \sqrt{\frac{m^2}{n^4} + \frac{t^2}{4n^2u} - \frac{s}{n^2} - \frac{p\sqrt{u}}{n^2}}.$$

Now draw CM perpendicular to IH, and

$$IM = HI - HM = HI - CG = \frac{m}{n^2} - y;$$

whence the square of IM is $\dfrac{m^2}{n^4} - \dfrac{2my}{n^2} + y^2$.

Taking this from the square of IC there remains the square of CM, or

$$\frac{t^2}{4n^2u} - \frac{s}{n^2} - \frac{p\sqrt{u}}{n^2} + \frac{2my}{n^2} - y^2,$$

and this is equal to the square of GH, previously found. This may be written

$$\frac{-n^2y^4+2my^3-p\sqrt{u}\,y^2-sy^2+\dfrac{t^2}{4u}y^2}{n^2y^2}.$$

Now, putting

$$\frac{t}{\sqrt{u}}y^4+qy^4-\tfrac{1}{4}p^2y^4$$

for n^2y^4, and

$$ry^3+2\sqrt{u}\,y^3+\frac{pt}{2\sqrt{u}}y^3$$

for $2my^3$, and multiplying both members by n^2y^2, we have

$$y^6-py^5+\left(\tfrac{1}{4}p^2-\frac{t}{\sqrt{u}}\right)y^4+\left(2\sqrt{u}+\frac{pt}{2\sqrt{u}}\right)y^3+\left(\frac{t^2}{4u}-p\sqrt{u}\right)y^2-ty+u$$

equals

$$\left(\tfrac{1}{4}p^2-q-\frac{t}{\sqrt{u}}\right)y^4+\left(r+2\sqrt{u}+\frac{pt}{2\sqrt{u}}\right)y^3+\left(\frac{t^2}{4u}-s-p\sqrt{u}\right)y^2,$$

or

$$y^6-py^5+qy^4-ry^3+sy^2-ty+u=0,$$

whence it appears that the lines CG, NR, QO, etc., are the roots of this equation.

If then it be desired to find four mean proportionals between the lines a and b, if we let x be the first, the equation is $x^5-a^4b=0$, or $x^6-a^4bx=0$. Let $y-a=x$, and we get

$$y^6-6ay^5+15a^2y^4-20a^3y^3+15a^4y^2-(6a^5+a^4b)y+a^6+a^5b=0.$$

Therefore, we must take $AB=3a$, and BK, the latus rectum of the parabola, must be

$$\sqrt{\frac{6a^3+a^2b}{\sqrt{a^2+ab}}+6a^2}$$

which I shall call n, and DE or BL will be

$$\frac{2a}{3n}\sqrt{a^2+ab}.$$

Then, having described the curve ACN, we must have

$$LH=\frac{6a^3+a^2b}{2n\sqrt{a^2+ab}}$$

and

$$HI=\frac{10a^3}{n^2}+\frac{a^2}{n^2}\sqrt{a^2+ab}+\frac{18a^4+3a^3b}{2n^2\sqrt{a^2+ab}},$$

and

$$LP=\frac{a}{n}\sqrt{15a^2+6a\sqrt{a^2+ab}}.$$

For the circle about I as center will pass through the point P thus found, and cut the curve in the two points C and N. If we draw the perpendiculars NR and CG, and subtract NR, the smaller, from CG, the greater, the remainder will be x, the first of the four required mean proportionals.

This method applies as well to the division of an angle into five equal parts, the inscription of a regular polygon of eleven or thirteen sides in a circle, and an infinity of other problems. It should be remarked, however, that in many of these problems it may happen that the circle cuts the parabola of the second class so obliquely that it is hard to determine the exact point of intersection. In such cases this construction is not of practical value. The difficulty could easily be overcome by forming other rules analogous to these, which might be done in a thousand different ways.

But it is not my purpose to write a large book. I am trying rather to include much in a few words, as will perhaps be inferred from what I have done, if it is considered that, while reducing to a single construction all the problems of one class, I have at the same time given a method of transforming them into an infinity of others, and thus of solving each in an infinite number of ways; that, furthermore, having constructed all plane problems by the cutting of a circle by a straight line, and all solid problems by the cutting of a circle by a parabola; and, finally, all that are but one degree more complex by cutting a circle by a curve but one degree higher than the parabola, it is only necessary to follow the same general method to construct all problems, more and more complex, ad infinitum; for in the case of a mathematical progression, whenever the first two or three terms are given, it is easy to find the rest.

I hope that posterity will judge me kindly, not only as to the things which I have explained, but also as to those which I have intentionally omitted so as to leave to others the pleasure of discovery.

SPINOZA

BIOGRAPHICAL NOTE
BENEDICT DE SPINOZA, 1632–1677

BENEDICT (BARUCH) DE SPINOZA was born in Amsterdam on the 24th of November, 1632, the son of a Jewish family which had emigrated from Portugal in the last decade of the sixteenth century to have the benefit of Dutch religious toleration. His father seems to have been of some prominence in the local Jewish community, and young Baruch was presumably educated in the Jewish schools. Whatever may be the value of the various reports as to the course of his education, there can be no doubt that he early acquired unorthodox opinions, for in July, 1656, after some controversy, the details of which are far from clear, he was solemnly excommunicated by the Jewish authorities for "abominable heresies which he practises and teaches." Cut off from his own people, his parents dead, Spinoza was thrown on his own resources.

The next four years Spinoza spent in or near Amsterdam, associating with members of the Collegiant, Mennonite, and Remonstrant sects, and devoting himself to the study of Latin, Greek, and other "humane sciences." Probably it was also during these years that he acquired or at least perfected the trade of lens-grinder, which provided him with a means of support throughout the rest of his life. Leaving Amsterdam in 1660, he retired to Rijnsburg, a small village near Leyden and headquarters of the Collegiant group, where, according to his first biographer, "removed from all the obstacles which he could only overcome by flight, he devoted himself entirely to philosophy."

During his three years at Rijnsburg Spinoza wrote the *Short Treatise on God, Man and his Well-Being*, the *Treatise on the Improvement of the Understanding*, *Descartes' Principles of Philosophy Geometrically Demonstrated* with appended *Metaphysical Thoughts*, and seems to have begun work on what eventually became the *Ethics*. The exposition of Descartes' *Principles* was undertaken for the instruction of a group of students, who had formed a sort of philosophical club in Amsterdam, and it was far from representing Spinoza's own views, as, indeed, the preface to the published work stated. Spinoza allowed it to be published, however, hoping that "perhaps on this occasion there will be found some who hold the first places in my country, who will desire to see the other things which I have written and which I acknowledge as my own, and they will make it their business that I should be able to publish them without any risk of trouble."

His reputation was already growing. He had been visited by and was corresponding with Henry Oldenburg, one of the first two secretaries of the Royal Society of London, and through him with Robert Boyle; through the years he became acquainted with numerous other prominent personages of both the political and intellectual worlds, among them Christian Huygens. Possibly in order to be closer to some of these friends, he moved to Voorburg, near The Hague, in 1663. Although the publication of his version of Descartes aroused considerable interest, it did not produce the consequences he had desired, since publication of his other works did not follow. While continuing to work on the *Ethics*, he began, in 1665, the composition of the *Theological-Political Treatise*, which was published anonymously in 1670. Spinoza was moved to write this book partly by a desire to assert "the liberty of philosophizing and of saying what we think," which "cannot be destroyed unless the peace and piety of the state is therewith also destroyed."

Condemnations of the *Treatise* immediately flew thick and fast, and in many Spinoza's name was mentioned. In the disorders consequent upon the French invasion of 1672, Jan de Witt, former Grand Pensionary of Holland and powerful friend and protector of Spinoza, was murdered by an angry mob. Spinoza, whose *Theological-Political Treatise* had been denounced as "forged in hell by a renegade Jew and the devil, and issued with the knowledge of Mr. Jan de Witt," was so aroused by this event that he was with difficulty restrained from public denunciation of the murderers. The Prince of Condé, commanding the French Army at Utrecht, invited Spinoza to visit him, and Spinoza went, but with what motives this visit was requested or why paid is far from certain. In any case the effort was wasted, for Condé had been called away, and Spinoza returned to The Hague, where he found himself an object of popular suspicion. The same year, 1673, he was offered a professorship at the University of Heidelberg, but he gracefully declined, declaring that he held back, "not in the hope of some better fortune, but from love of tranquillity, which I believe I can obtain in some measure by refraining from public lectures."

The remainder of his life was spent quietly at The Hague, where he had settled in 1670. He completed his *Ethics* and sought to publish it, but was discouraged by the complaints aroused by the mere rumor of its being on the press. Subsequently he began his *Political Treatise*, which remained unfinished, and planned a Hebrew grammar. In 1676, already seriously ill with the consumption which was to kill him, he received a visit from Leibnitz, with whom he had already corresponded on problems of optics, and they conversed "often and at great length." Four months later, on a quiet Sunday afternoon in February, 1677, while the "people of the house" were at church, he died in the presence of an Amsterdam physician-friend. His funeral was "attended by many illustrious personages and followed by six coaches." He was forty-four. He left a small library, his clothes, a little furniture, some finished lenses (which "sold pretty dear"), and his manuscripts, which were published the same year by his friends.

CONTENTS

ETHICS

FIRST PART

OF GOD

DEFINITIONS

1. BY CAUSE of itself, I understand that, whose essence involves existence; or that, whose nature cannot be conceived unless existing.

2. That thing is called finite in its own kind (*in suo genere*) which can be limited by another thing of the same nature. For example, a body is called finite, because we always conceive another which is greater. So a thought is limited by another thought; but a body is not limited by a thought, nor a thought by a body.

3. By substance, I understand that which is in itself and is conceived through itself; in other words, that, the conception of which does not need the conception of another thing from which it must be formed.

4. By attribute, I understand that which the intellect perceives of substance, as if constituting its essence.[1]

5. By mode, I understand the affections of substance, or that which is in another thing through which also it is conceived.

6. By God, I understand Being absolutely infinite, that is to say, substance consisting of infinite attributes, each one of which expresses eternal and infinite essence.

Explanation. I say absolutely infinite but not infinite in its own kind (*in suo genere*); for of whatever is infinite only in its own kind (*in suo genere*), we can deny infinite attributes; but to the essence of that which is absolutely infinite pertains whatever expresses essence and involves no negation.

7. That thing is called free which exists from the necessity of its own nature alone, and is determined to action by itself alone. That thing, on the other hand, is called necessary, or rather compelled, which by another is determined to existence and action in a fixed and prescribed manner.

[1]See Part I, Prop. 19.

8. By eternity, I understand existence itself, so far as it is conceived necessarily to follow from the definition alone of the eternal thing.

Explanation. For such existence, like the essence of the thing, is conceived as an eternal truth. It cannot therefore be explained by duration or time, even if the duration be conceived without beginning or end.

AXIOMS

1. Everything which is, is either in itself or in another.

2. That which cannot be conceived through another must be conceived through itself.

3. From a given determinate cause an effect necessarily follows; and, on the other hand, if no determinate cause be given, it is impossible that an effect can follow.

4. The knowledge (cognitio) of an effect depends upon and involves the knowledge of the cause.

5. Those things which have nothing mutually in common with one another cannot through one another be mutually understood, that is to say, the conception of the one does not involve the conception of the other.

6. A true idea must agree with that of which it is the idea (*cum suo ideato*).

7. The essence of that thing which can be conceived as not existing does not involve existence.

PROP. 1. *Substance is by its nature prior to its affections.*

Demonst. This is evident from Defs. 3 and 5.

PROP. 2. *Two substances having different attributes have nothing in common with one another.*

Demonst. This is also evident from Def. 3. For each substance must be in itself and must be conceived through itself, that is to say, the conception of one does not involve the conception of the other. Q.E.D.

PROP. 3. *If two things have nothing in common with one another, one cannot be the cause of the other.*

Demonst. If they have nothing mutually in common with one another, they cannot (Ax. 5) through one another be mutually understood, and therefore (Ax. 4) one cannot be the cause of the other. Q.E.D.

PROP. 4. *Two or more distinct things are distinguished from one another, either by the difference of the attributes of the substances, or by the difference of their affections.*

Demonst. Everything which is, is either in itself or in another (Ax. 1), that is to say (Defs. 3 and 5), outside the intellect there is nothing but substances and their affections. There is nothing therefore outside the intellect by which a number of things can be distinguished one from another, but substances or (which is the same thing by Def. 4) their attributes and their affections. Q.E.D.

PROP. 5. *In nature there cannot be two or more substances of the same nature or attribute.*

Demonst. If there were two or more distinct substances, they must be distinguished one from the other by difference of attributes or difference of affections (Prop. 4). If they are distinguished only by difference of attributes, it will be granted that there is but one substance of the same attribute. But if they are distinguished by difference of affections, since substance is prior by nature to its affections (Prop. 1), the affections therefore being placed on one side, and the substance being considered in itself, or, in other words (Def. 3 and Ax. 6), truly considered, it cannot be conceived as distinguished from another substance, that is to say (Prop. 4), there cannot be two or more substances, but only one possessing the same nature or attribute. Q.E.D.

PROP. 6. *One substance cannot be produced by another substance.*

Demonst. There cannot in nature be two substances of the same attribute (Prop. 5), that is to say (Prop. 2), two which have anything in common with one another. And therefore (Prop. 3) one cannot be the cause of the other, that is to say, one cannot be produced by the other. Q.E.D.

Corol. Hence it follows that there is nothing by which substance can be produced, for in nature there is nothing but substances and their affections (as is evident from Ax. 1 and Defs. 3 and 5). But substance cannot be produced by substance (Prop. 6). Therefore absolutely there is nothing by which substance can be produced. Q.E.D.

Another Demonst. This corollary is demonstrated more easily by the *reductio ad absurdum*. For if there were anything by which substance could be produced, the knowledge of substance would be dependent upon the knowledge of its cause (Ax. 4), and therefore (Def. 3) it would not be substance.

PROP. 7. *It pertains to the nature of substance to exist.*

Demonst. There is nothing by which substance can be produced (Corol. Prop. 6). It will therefore be the cause of itself, that is to say (Def. 1), its essence necessarily involves existence, or in other words it pertains to its nature to exist. Q.E.D.

PROP. 8. *Every substance is necessarily infinite.*

Demonst. Substance which has only one attribute cannot exist except as one substance (Prop. 5), and to the nature of this one substance it pertains to exist (Prop. 7). It must therefore from its nature exist as finite or infinite. But it cannot exist as finite substance, for (Def. 2) it must (if finite) be limited by another substance of the same nature, which also must necessarily exist (Prop. 7), and therefore would be two substances of the same attribute, which is absurd (Prop. 5). It exists therefore as infinite substance. Q.E.D.

Schol. 1. Since finiteness is in truth partly negation, and infinitude absolute affirmation of existence of some kind, it follows from Prop 7 alone that all substance must be infinite.

Schol. 2. I fully expect that those who judge things confusedly, and who have not been accustomed to cognise things through their first causes, will find it difficult to comprehend the demonstration of the 7th Proposition, since they do not distinguish between the modifications of substances and substance themselves, and are ignorant of the manner in which things are produced. Hence it comes to pass that they erroneously ascribe to substances a beginning like that which they see belongs to natural things; for those who are ignorant of the true causes of things confoun every thing, and without any mental repugnance represent trees speaking like men, or imagine that men are made out of stones as well as begotten from seed, and that all forms can be changed the one into the other. So also those who confound human nature with the divine, readily attribute to God human affects,[1] especially so long as they are ignorant of the manner in which affects are produced in the mind. But if men would attend to the nature of substance, they could not entertain a single doubt of the truth of Proposition 7; indeed this proposition would be considered by all to be axiomatic, and reckoned amongst common notions. For by "substance" would be understood that which is in itself and is conceived through itself, or, in other words, that, the knowledge of which does not need the knowledge of another thing. But by "modifications" would be understood those things which are in another thing—those things, the conception of which is formed from the conception of the thing in which they are. Hence we can have true ideas of non-existent modifications, since although they may not actually exist outside the intellect, their essence nevertheless is so comprehended in something else, that they may be conceived through it. But the truth of substances is not outside the intellect unless in the substances themselves, because they are conceived through themselves. If any one, therefore, were to say that he possessed a clear and distinct, that is to say, a true idea of substance, and that he nevertheless doubted whether such a substance exists, he would forsooth be in the same position as if he were to say that he had a true idea and nevertheless doubted whether or not it was false (as is evident to any one who pays a little attention). Similarly if any one were to affirm that substance is created, he would affirm at the same time that a false idea had become true, and this is a greater absurdity than can be conceived. It is therefore necessary to admit that the existence of substance, like its essence, is an eternal truth. Hence a demonstration (which I have thought worth while to append) by a different method is possible, showing that there are not two substances possessing the same nature. But in order to prove this methodically it is to be noted: 1. That the true definition of any one thing neither involves nor expresses anything except the nature of the thing defined. From which it follows, 2. That a definition does not involve or

express any certain number of individuals, since it expresses nothing but the nature of the thing defined. For example, the definition of a triangle expresses nothing but the simple nature of a triangle, and not any certain number of triangles. 3. It is to be observed that of every existing thing there is some certain cause by reason of which it exists. 4. Finally, it is to be observed that this cause, by reason of which a thing exists, must either be contained in the nature itself and definition of the existing thing (simply because it pertains to the nature of the thing to exist), or it must exist outside the thing. This being granted, it follows that if a certain number of individuals exist in nature, there must necessarily be a cause why those individuals, and neither more nor fewer, exist. If, for example, there are twenty men in existence (whom, for the sake of greater clearness, I suppose existing at the same time, and that no others existed before them), it will not be sufficient, in order that we may give a reason why twenty men exist, to give a cause for human nature generally; but it will be necessary, in addition, to give a reason why neither more nor fewer than twenty exist, since, as we have already observed under the third head, there must necessarily be a cause why each exists. But this cause (as we have shown under the second and third heads) cannot be contained in human nature itself, since the true definition of a man does not involve the number twenty, and therefore (by the fourth head) the cause why these twenty men exist, and consequently the cause why each exists, must necessarily lie outside each one; and therefore we must conclude generally that whenever it is possible for several individuals of the same nature to exist, there must necessarily be an external cause for their existence.

Since now it pertains to the nature of substance to exist (as we have shown in this scholium), its definition must involve necessary existence, and consequently from its definition alone its existence must be concluded. But from its definition (as we have already shown under the second and third heads) the existence of more substances than one cannot be deduced. It follows, therefore, from this definition necessarily that there cannot be two substances possessing the same nature.

PROP 9. *The more reality or being a thing possesses, the more attributes belong to it.*

Demonst. This is evident from Def. 4.

[1] See Part I, Def. III.

PROP 10. *Each attribute of a substance must be conceived through itself.*

Demonst. For an attribute is that which the intellect perceives of substance, as if constituting its essence (Def. 4), and therefore (Def. 3) it must be conceived through itself. Q.E.D.

Schol. From this it is apparent that although two attributes may be conceived as really distinct—that is to say, one without the assistance of the other—we cannot nevertheless thence conclude that they constitute two beings or two different substances; for this is the nature of substance, that each of its attributes is conceived through itself, since all the attributes which substance possesses were always in it together, nor could one be produced by another; but each expresses the reality or being of substance. It is very far from being absurd, therefore, to ascribe to one substance a number of attributes, since nothing in nature is clearer than that each being must be conceived under some attribute, and the more reality or being it has, the more attributes it possesses expressing necessity or eternity and infinity. Nothing consequently is clearer than that Being absolutely infinite is necessarily defined, as we have shown (Def. 6), as Being which consists of infinite attributes, each one of which expresses a certain essence, eternal and infinite. But if any one now asks by what sign, therefore, we may distinguish between substances, let him read the following propositions, which show that in nature only one substance exists, and that it is absolutely infinite. For this reason that sign would be sought for in vain.

PROP. 11. *God, or substance consisting of infinite attributes, each one of which expresses eternal and infinite essence, necessarily exists.*

Demonst. If this be denied, conceive, if it be possible, that God does not exist. Then it follows (Ax. 7) that His essence does not involve existence. But this (Prop. 7) is absurd. Therefore God necessarily exists. Q.E.D.

Another proof. For the existence or non-existence of everything there must be a reason or cause. For example, if a triangle exists, there must be a reason or cause why it exists; and if it does not exist, there must be a reason or cause which hinders its existence or which negates it. But this reason or cause must either be contained in the nature of the thing or lie outside it. For example, the nature of the thing itself shows the reason why a square

circle does not exist, the reason being that a square circle involves a contradiction. And the reason, on the other hand, why substance exists follows from its nature alone, which involves existence (see Prop. 7). But the reason why a circle or triangle exists or does not exist is not drawn from their nature, but from the order of corporeal nature generally; for from that it must follow, either that a triangle necessarily exists, or that it is impossible for it to exist. But this is self-evident. Therefore it follows that if there be no cause nor reason which hinders a thing from existing, it exists necessarily. If, therefore, there be no reason nor cause which hinders God from existing, or which negates His existence, we must conclude absolutely that He necessarily exists. But if there be such a reason or cause, it must be either in the nature itself of God or must lie outside it, that is to say, in another substance of another nature. For if the reason lay in a substance of the same nature, the existence of God would be by this very fact admitted. But substance possessing another nature could have nothing in common with God (Prop. 2), and therefore could not give Him existence nor negate it. Since, therefore, the reason or cause which could negate the divine existence cannot be outside the divine nature, it will necessarily, supposing that the divine nature does not exist, be in His Nature itself, which would therefore involve a contradiction. But to affirm this of the Being absolutely infinite and consummately perfect is absurd. Therefore neither in God nor outside God is there any cause or reason which can negate His existence, and therefore God necessarily exists. Q.E.D.

Another proof. Inability to exist is impotence, and, on the other hand, ability to exist is power, as is self-evident. If, therefore, there is nothing which necessarily exists excepting things finite, it follows that things finite are more powerful than the absolutely infinite Being, and this (as is self-evident) is absurd; therefore either nothing exists or Being absolutely infinite also necessarily exists. But we ourselves exist, either in ourselves or in something else which necessarily exists (Ax. 1 and Prop. 7). Therefore the Being absolutely infinite, that is to say (Def. 6), God, necessarily exists. Q.E.D.

Schol. In this last demonstration I wished to prove the existence of God *a posteriori*, in order that the demonstration might be the more easily understood, and not because the existence of God does not follow *a priori* from the same grounds. For since ability to exist is power, it follows that the more reality belongs to the nature of anything, the greater is the power for existence it derives from itself; and it also follows, therefore, that the Being absolutely infinite, or God, has from Himself an absolutely infinite power of existence, and that He therefore necessarily exists. Many persons, nevertheless, will perhaps not be able easily to see the force of this demonstration, because they have been accustomed to contemplate those things alone which flow from external causes, and they see also that those things which are quickly produced from these causes, that is to say, which easily exist, easily perish, whilst, on the other hand, they adjudge those things to be more difficult to produce, that is to say, not so easy to bring into existence, to which they conceive more properties pertain. In order that these prejudices may be removed, I do not need here to show in what respect this saying, "What is quickly made quickly perishes," is true, nor to inquire whether, looking at the whole of nature, all things are or are not equally easy. But this only it will be sufficient for me to observe, that I do not speak of things which are produced by external causes, but that I speak of substances alone which (Prop. 6) can be produced by no external cause. For whatever perfection or reality those things may have which are produced by external causes, whether they consist of many parts or of few, they owe it all to the virtue of an external cause, and therefore their existence springs from the perfection of an external cause alone and not from their own. On the other hand, whatever perfection substance has is due to no external cause. Therefore its existence must follow from its nature alone, and is therefore nothing else than its essence. Perfection consequently does not prevent the existence of a thing, but establishes it; imperfection, on the other hand, prevents existence, and so of no existence can we be more sure than of the existence of the Being absolutely infinite or perfect, that is to say, God. For since His essence shuts out all imperfection and involves absolute perfection, for this very reason all cause of doubt concerning His existence is taken away, and the highest certainty concerning it is given,—a truth which I trust will be evident to any one who bestows only moderate attention.

PROP. 12. *No attribute of substance can be truly conceived from which it follows that substance can be divided.*

Demonst. For the parts into which substance thus conceived would be divided will or will not retain the nature of substance. If they retain it, then (Prop. 8) each part will be infinite, and (Prop. 6) the cause of itself, and will consist of an attribute differing from that of any other part (Prop. 5), so that from one substance more substances could be formed, which (Prop. 6) is absurd. Moreover the parts (Prop. 2) would have nothing in common with their whole, and the whole (Def. 4 and Prop. 10) could be, and could be conceived without its parts, which no one will doubt to be an absurdity. But if the second case be supposed, namely, that the parts will not retain the nature of substance, then, since the whole substance might be divided into equal parts, it would lose the nature of substance and cease to be, which (Prop. 7) is absurd.

PROP. 13. *Substance absolutely infinite is indivisible.*

Demonst. For if it were divisible, the parts into which it would be divided will or will not retain the nature of substance absolutely infinite. If they retain it, there will be a plurality of substances possessing the same nature, which (Prop. 5) is absurd. If the second case be supposed, then (as above), substance absolutely infinite can cease to be, which (Prop. 11) is also absurd.

Corol. Hence it follows that no substance, and consequently no bodily substance in so far as it is substance, is divisible.

Schol. That substance is indivisible is more easily to be understood from this consideration alone, that the nature of substance cannot be conceived unless as infinite, and that by a part of substance nothing else can be understood than finite substance, which (Prop. 8) involves a manifest contradiction.

PROP. 14. *Besides God, no substance can be nor can be conceived.*

Demonst. Since God is Being absolutely infinite, of whom no attribute can be denied which expresses the essence of substance (Def. 6), and since He necessarily exists (Prop. 11), it follows that if there were any substance besides God, it would have to be explained by some attribute of God, and thus two substances would exist possessing the same attribute, which (Prop. 5) is absurd; and therefore there cannot be any substance excepting God, and consequently none other can be conceived. For if any other could be conceived, it would necessarily be conceived as existing, and this (by the first part of this demonstration) is absurd. Therefore besides God no substance can be, nor can be conceived. Q.E.D.

Corol. 1. Hence it follows with the greatest clearness, firstly, that God is one, that is to say (Def. 6), in nature there is but one substance, and it is absolutely infinite, as (Schol. Prop. 10) we have already intimated.

Corol. 2. It follows, secondly, that the thing extended (*rem extensam*) and the thing thinking (*rem cogitantem*) are either attributes of God or (Ax. 1) affections of the attributes of God.

PROP. 15. *Whatever is, is in God, and nothing can either be or be conceived without God.*

Demonst. Besides God there is no substance, nor can any be conceived (Prop. 14), that is to say (Def. 3), nothing which is in itself and is conceived through itself. But modes (Def. 5) can neither be nor be conceived without substance; therefore in the divine nature only can they be, and through it alone can they be conceived. But besides substances and modes nothing is assumed (Ax. 1). Therefore nothing can be or be conceived without God. Q.E.D.

Schol. There are those who imagine God to be like a man, composed of body and soul and subject to passions; but it is clear enough from what has already been demonstrated how far off men who believe this are from the true knowledge of God. But these I dismiss, for all men who have in any way looked into the divine nature deny that God is corporeal. That He cannot be so they conclusively prove by showing that by "body" we understand a certain quantity possessing length, breadth, and depth, limited by some fixed form; and that to attribute these to God, a being absolutely infinite, is the greatest absurdity. But yet at the same time, from other arguments by which they endeavour to confirm their proof, they clearly show that they remove altogether from the divine nature substance itself corporeal or extended, affirming that it was created by God By what divine power, however, it could have been created they are altogether ignorant, so that it is clear they do not understand what they themselves say. But I have demonstrated, at least in my own opinion, with sufficient clearness (see Corol. Prop. 6 and Schol. 2, Prop. 8), that no substance can be produced or created by another being (*ab alio*). Moreover (Prop. 14), we have shown that besides God no substance can be nor can be conceived;

and hence we have concluded that extended substance is one of the infinite attributes of God. But for the sake of a fuller explanation, I will refute my adversaries' arguments, which, taken altogether, come to this. First, that corporeal substance, in so far as it is substance, consists, as they suppose, of parts, and therefore they deny that it can be infinite, and consequently that it can pertain to God. This they

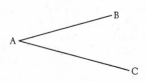

illustrate by many examples, one or two of which I will adduce. If corporeal substance, they say, be infinite, let us conceive it to be divided into two parts; each part, therefore, will be either finite or infinite. If each part be finite, then the infinite is composed of two finite parts, which is absurd. If each part be infinite, there is then an infinite twice as great as another infinite, which is also absurd. Again, if infinite quantity be measured by equal parts of a foot each, it must contain an infinite number of such parts, and similarly if it be measured by equal parts of an inch each; and therefore one infinite number will be twelve times greater than another infinite number. Lastly, if from one point of any infinite quantity it be imagined that two lines, AB, AC, which at first are at a certain and determinate distance from one another, be infinitely extended, it is plain that the distance between B and C will be continually increased, and at length from being determinate will be indeterminable. Since therefore these absurdities follow, as they think, from supposing quantity to be infinite, they conclude that corporeal substance must be finite, and consequently cannot pertain to the essence of God. A second argument is assumed from the absolute perfection of God. For God, they say, since He is a being absolutely perfect, cannot suffer; but corporeal substance, since it is divisible, can suffer it follows, therefore, that it does not pertain to God's essence. These are the arguments which I find in authors, by which they endeavour to show that corporeal substance is unworthy of the divine nature, and cannot pertain to it But any one who will properly attend will discover that I have already answered these arguments, since the sole foundation of them is th pposition that bodily substance consists of arts, a supposition which (Prop. 12 and orol. Prop. 13) I have shown to be absurd. Moreover, if any one will rightly consider the matter, he will see that all these absurdities (supposing that they are all absurdities, a point which I will now take for granted), from which these authors attempt to draw the conclusion that substance extended is finite, do not by any means follow from the supposition that quantity is infinite, but from the supposition that infinite quantity is measurable, and that it is made up of finite parts. Therefore, from the absurdities to which this leads nothing can be concluded, excepting that infinite quantity is not measurable, and that it cannot be composed of finite parts. But this is what we have already demonstrated (Prop. 12, c.), and the shaft therefore which is aimed at us turns against those who cast it. If, therefore, from these absurdities any one should attempt to conclude that substance extended must be finite, he would, forsooth, be in the position of the man who supposes a circle to have the properties of a square, and then concludes that it has no centre, such that all the lines drawn from it to the circumference are equal. For corporeal substance, which cannot be conceived except as infinite, one and indivisible (Props. 8, 5, and 12), is conceived by those against whom I argue to be composed of finite parts, and to be multiplex and divisible, in order that they may prove it finite. Just in the same way others, after they have imagined a line to consist of points, know how to discover many arguments, by which they show that a line cannot be divided *ad infinitum;* and indeed it is not less absurd to suppose that corporeal substance is composed of bodies or parts than to suppose that a body is composed of surfaces, surfaces of lines, and that lines, finally, are composed of points. Every one who knows that clear reason is infallible ought to admit this, and especially those who deny that a vacuum can exist. For if corporeal substance could be so divided that its parts could be really distinct, why could not one part be annihilated, the rest remaining, as before, connected with one another? And why must all be so fitted together that there can be no vacuum? For of things which are really distinct the one from the other, one can be and remain in its own position without the other. Since, therefore, it is supposed that there is no vacuum in nature (about which I will speak at an-

other time), but that all the parts must be united, so that no vacuum can exist, it follows that they cannot be really separated; that is to say, that corporeal substance, in so far as it is substance, cannot be divided. If, nevertheless, any one should now ask why there is a natural tendency to consider quantity as capable of division, I reply that quantity is conceived by us in two ways: either abstractly or superficially; that is to say, as we imagine it, or else as substance, in which way it is conceived by the intellect alone. If, therefore, we regard quantity (as we do very often and easily) as it exists in the imagination, we find it to be finite, divisible, and composed of parts; but if we regard it as it exists in the intellect, and conceive it in so far as it is substance, which is very difficult, then, as we have already sufficiently demonstrated, we find it to be infinite, one, and indivisible. This will be plain enough to all who know how to distinguish between the imagination and the intellect, and more especially if we remember that matter is everywhere the same, and that, except in so far as we regard it as affected in different ways, parts are not distinguished in it; that is to say, they are distinguished with regard to mode, but not with regard to reality. For example, we conceive water as being divided, in so far as it is water, and that its parts are separated from one another; but in so far as it is corporeal substance we cannot thus conceive it, for as such it is neither separated nor divided. Moreover, water, in so far as it is water, is originated and destroyed; but in so far as it is substance, it is neither originated nor destroyed. By this reasoning I think that I have also answered the second argument, since that too is based upon the assumption that matter, considered as substance, is divisible and composed of parts. And even if what I have urged were not true, I do not know why matter should be unworthy of the divine nature, since (Prop. 14) outside God no substance can exist from which the divine nature could suffer. All things, I say, are in God, and everything which takes place takes place by the laws alone of the infinite nature of God, and follows (as I shall presently show) from the necessity of His essence. Therefore in no way whatever can it be asserted that God suffers from anything, or that substance extended, even if it be supposed divisible, is unworthy of the divine nature, provided only it be allowed that it is eternal and infinite. But enough on this point for the present.

Prop. 16. *From the necessity of the divine nature infinite numbers of things in infinite ways (that is to say, all things which can be conceived by the infinite intellect) must follow.*

Demonst. This proposition must be plain to every one who considers that from the given definition of anything a number of properties necessarily following from it (that is to say, following from the essence of the thing itself) are inferred by the intellect, and just in proportion as the definition of the thing expresses a greater reality, that is to say, just in porportion as the essence of the thing defined involves a greater reality, will more properties be inferred. But the divine nature possesses absolutely infinite attributes (Def. 6), each one of which expresses infinite essence in its own kind (*in suo genere*), and therefore, from the necessity of the divine nature, infinite numbers of things in infinite ways (that is to say, all things which can be conceived by the infinite intellect) must necessarily follow. Q.E.D.

Corol. 1. Hence it follows that God is the efficient cause of all things which can fall under the infinite intellect.

Corol. 2. It follows, secondly, that God is cause through Himself, and not through that which is contingent (*per accidens*).

Corol. 3. It follows, thirdly, that God is absolutely the first cause.

Prop. 17. *God acts from the laws of His own nature only, and is compelled by no one.*

Demonst. We have just shown (Prop. 16) that from the necessity, or (which is the same thing) from the laws only of the divine nature, infinite numbers of things absolutely follow; and we have demonstrated (Prop. 15) that nothing can be, nor can be conceived, without God, but that all things are in God. Therefore, outside Himself, there can be nothing by which He may be determined or compelled to act; and therefore He acts from the laws of His own nature only, and is compelled by no one. Q.E.D.

Corol. 1. Hence it follows, firstly, that there is no cause, either external to God or within Him, which can excite Him to act except the perfection of His own nature.

Corol. 2 It follows, secondly, that God alone is a free cause; for God alone exists from the necessity alone of His own nature (Prop. 11, and Corol. 1, Prop. 14), and acts from the necessity alone of His own nature (Prop. 17). Therefore (Def. 7) He alone is a free cause. Q.E.D.

Schol. There are some who think that Go is a free cause because He can, as they thin bring about that those things which we hav said follow from His nature—that is to say those things which are in His power—shoul not be, or should not be produced by Him. Bu this is simply saying that God could brin about that it should not follow from the n ture of a triangle that its three angles shoul be equal to two right angles, or that from given cause an effect should not follow, whic is absurd. But I shall show farther on, withou the help of this proposition, that neither inte lect nor will pertain to the nature of God.

I know, indeed, that there are many wh think themselves able to demonstrate that i tellect of the highest order and freedom of wi both pertain to the nature of God, for they sa that they know nothing more perfect which the can attribute to Him than that which is th chief perfection in ourselves. But althoug they conceive God as actually possessing th highest intellect, they nevertheless do not b lieve that He can bring about that all thos things should exist which are actually in H intellect, for they think that by such a suppo sition they would destroy His power. If H had created, they say, all things which are i His intellect, He could have created nothin more, and this, they believe, does not accor with God's omnipotence so then they prefer t consider God as indifferent to all things, an creating nothing excepting that which He ha decreed to create by a certain absolute wil But I think that I have shown with sufficien clearness (Prop. 16) that from the suprem power of God, or from His infinite nature, in finite things in infinite ways, that is to say, a things, have necessarily flowed, or continuall follow by the same necessity, in the same wa as it follows from the nature of a triangle, from eternity and to eternity, that its three angle are equal to two right angles. The omnipo tence of God has therefore been actual from eternity, and in the same actuality will remai to eternity. In this way the omnipotence o God, in my opinion, is far more firmly estab lished. My adversaries, indeed (if I may b permitted to speak plainly), seem to deny th omnipotence of God, inasmuch as they ar forced to admit that He has in His mind a infinite number of things which might be cre ated, but which, nevertheless, He will never b able to create, for if He were to create al things which He has in His mind, He would according to them, exhaust His omnipotenc and make Himself imperfect. Therefore, in order to make a perfect God, they are compelled to make Him incapable of doing all those things to which His power extends, and anything more absurd than this, or more opposed to God's omnipotence, I do not think can be imagined. Moreover—to say a word, too, here about the intellect and will which we commonly attribute to God—if intellect and will pertain to His eternal essence, these attributes cannot be understood in the sense in which men generally use them, for the intellect and will which could constitute His essence would have to differ entirely from our intellect and will, and could resemble ours in nothing except in name. There could be no further likeness than that between the celestial constellation of the Dog and the animal which barks. This I will demonstrate as follows. If intellect pertains to the divine nature, it cannot, like our intellect, follow the things which are its object (as many suppose), nor can it be simultaneous in its nature with them, since God is prior to all things in casuality (Corol. 1, Prop. 16); but, on the contrary, the truth and formal essence of things is what it is, because as such it exists objectively in God's intellect. Therefore the intellect of God, in so far as it is conceived to constitute His essence, is in truth the cause of things, both of their essence and of their existence,—a truth which seems to have been understood by those who have maintained that God's intellect, will, and power are one and the same thing. Since, therefore, God's intellect is the sole cause of things, both of their essence and of their existence (as we have already shown), it must necessarily differ from them with regard both to its essence and existence; for an effect differs from its cause precisely in that which it has from its cause. For example, one man is the cause of the existence but not of the essence of another, for the essence is an eternal truth; and therefore with regard to essence the two men may exactly resemble one another, but with regard to existence they must differ. Consequently if the existence of one should perish, that of the other will not therefore perish; but if the essence of one could be destroyed and become false, the essence of the other would be likewise destroyed. Therefore a thing which is the cause both of the essence and of the existence of any effect must differ from that effect both with regard to its essence and with regard to its existence. But the intellect of God is the cause both of the essence and existence of our intellect;

therefore the intellect of God, so far as it is conceived to constitute the divine essence, differs from our intellect both with regard to its essence and its existence, nor can it coincide with our intellect in anything except the name, which is what we essayed to prove. The same demonstration may be applied to the will, as anyone may easily see for himself.

PROP. 18. *God is the immanent, and not the transitive cause of all things.*
Demonst. All things which are, are in God and must be conceived through Him (Prop. 15), and therefore (Corol. 1, Prop. 16) He is the cause of the things which are in Himself. This is the first thing which was to be proved. Moreover, outside God there can be no substance (Prop. 14), that is to say (Def. 3), outside Him nothing can exist which is in itself. This was the second thing to be proved. God, therefore, is the immanent, but not the transitive cause of all things.   Q.E.D.

PROP. 19. *God is eternal, or, in other words, all His attributes are eternal.*
Demonst. For God (Def. 6) is substance, which (Prop. 11) necessarily exists, that is to say (Prop. 7), a substance to whose nature it pertains to exist, or (which is the same thing) a substance from the definition of which it follows that it exists, and therefore (Def. 8) He is eternal. Again, by the attributes of God is to be understood that which (Def. 4) expresses the essence of the divine substance, that is to say, that which pertains to substance. It is this, I say, which the attributes themselves must involve. But eternity pertains to the nature of substance (Prop. 7). Therefore each of the attributes must involve eternity, and therefore all are eternal.   Q.E.D.
Schol. This proposition is as clear as possible, too, from the manner in which (Prop. 11) I have demonstrated the existence of God. From that demonstration I say it is plain that the existence of God, like His essence, is an eternal truth. Moreover (Prop. 19 of the "Principles of the Cartesian Philosophy"), I have demonstrated by another method the eternity of God, and there is no need to repeat the demonstration here.

PROP. 20. *The existence of God and His essence are one and the same thing.*
God (Prop. 19) and all His attributes are eternal, that is to say (Def. 8), each one of His attributes expresses existence. The same attri-

butes of God, therefore, which (Def. 4) manifest the eternal essence of God, at the same time manifest His eternal existence; that is to say, the very same thing which constitutes the essence of God constitutes at the same time His existence, and therefore His existence and His essence are one and the same thing. Q.E.D.

Corol. 1. Hence it follows, 1. That the existence of God, like His essence, is an eternal truth.

Corol. 2. It follows, 2. That God is immutable, or (which is the same thing) all His attributes are immutable; for if they were changed as regards their existence, they must be changed also as regards their essence (Prop. 20); that is to say (as is self-evident), from being true, they would become false, which is absurd.

PROP. 21. *All things which follow from the absolute nature of any attribute of God must for ever exist, and must be infinite; that is to say, through that same attribute they are eternal and infinite.*

Demonst. Conceive, if possible (supposing that the truth of the proposition is denied), that in some attribute of God something which is finite and has a determinate existence or duration follows from the absolute nature of that attribute; for example, an idea of God in thought. But thought, since it is admitted to be an attribute of God, is necessarily (Prop. 11) in its nature infinite. But so far as it has the idea of God it is by supposition finite. But (Def. 2) it cannot be conceived as finite unless it be determined by thought itself. But it cannot be determined by thought itself so far as it constitutes the idea of God, for so far by supposition it is finite. Therefore it must be determined by thought so far as it does not constitute the idea of God, but which, nevertheless (Prop. 11), necessarily exists. Thought, therefore, exists which does not form the idea of God, and therefore from its nature, in so far as it is absolute thought, the idea of God does not necessarily follow (for it is conceived as forming and as not forming the idea of God), which is contrary to the hypothesis. Therefore, if an idea of God in thought, or anything else in any attribute of God, follow from the necessity of the absolute nature of that attribute (for the demonstration being universal will apply in every case), that thing must necessarily be infinite, which was the first thing to be proved.

Again, that which thus follows from the necessity of the nature of any attribute cannot have a determinate duration. For, if the truth of this be denied, let it be supposed that in some attribute of God a thing exists which follows from the necessity of the nature of the attribute—for example, an idea of God in thought—and let it be supposed that at some time it has either not existed or will not exist. But since thought is supposed to be an attribute of God, it must exist both necessarily and unchangeably (Prop. 11, and Corol. 2, Prop. 20). Therefore, beyond the limits of the duration of the idea of God (for it is supposed that at some time it has either not existed or will not exist), thought must exist without the idea of God; but this is contrary to hypothesis, for the supposition is that thought being given, the idea of God necessarily follows. Therefore neither an idea of God in thought, nor anything else which necessarily follows from the absolute nature of any attribute of God, can have a determinate duration, but through the same attribute is eternal; which was the second thing to be proved. Observe that what we have affirmed here is true of everything which in any attribute of God necessarily follows from the absolute nature of God.

PROP. 22. *Whatever follows from any attribute of God, in so far as it is modified by a modification which through the same attribute exists necessarily and infinitely, must also exist necessarily and infinitely.*

Demonst. This proposition is demonstrated in the same manner as the preceding proposition.

PROP. 23. *Every mode which exists necessarily and infinitely must necessarily follow either from the absolute nature of some attribute of God, or from some attribute modified by a modification which exists necessarily and infinitely.*

Demonst. Mode is that which is in something else through which it must be conceived (Def. 5), that is to say (Prop. 15), it is in God alone and through God alone can be conceived. If a mode, therefore, be conceived to exist necessarily and to be infinite, its necessary existence and infinitude must be concluded from some attribute of God or perceived through it, in so far as it is conceived to express infinitude and necessity of existence, that is to say (Def. 8), eternity, or in other words (Def. 6 and Prop. 19), in so far as it is considered absolutely. A mode, therefore, which exists necessarily and infinitely must follow from th absolute nature of some attribute of God, either immediately (Prop. 21), or mediately through some modification following from His absolute nature, that is to say (Prop. 22), a modification which necessarily and infinitely exists. Q.E.D.

PROP. 24. *The essence of things produced by God does not involve existence.*

This is evident from the first Definition; for that thing whose nature (considered, that is to say, in itself) involves existence, is the cause of itself and exists from the necessity of its own nature alone.

Corol. Hence it follows that God is not only the cause of the commencement of the existence of things, but also of their continuance in existence, or, in other words (to use scholastic phraseology), God is the *causa essendi rerum.* For if we consider the essence of things, whether existing or non-existing, we discover that it neither involves existence nor duration, and therefore the essence of existing things cannot be the cause of their existence nor of their duration, but God only is the cause, to whose nature alone existence pertains (Corol. 1, Prop. 14).

PROP. 25. *God is not only the efficient cause of the existence of things, but also of their essence.*

Demonst. Suppose that God is not the cause of the essence of things; then (Ax. 4) the essence of things can be conceived without God which (Prop. 15) is absurd. Therefore God is the cause of the essence of things. Q.E.D.

Schol. This proposition more clearly follows from Prop. 16. For from this proposition it follows that, from the existence of the divine nature, both the essence of things and their existence must necessarily be concluded, or, in a word, in the same sense in which God is said to be the cause of Himself He must be called the cause of all things. This will appear still more clearly from the following corollary.

Corol. Individual things are nothing but affections or modes of God's attributes, expressing those attributes in a certain and determinate manner. This is evident from Prop. 15 and Def. 5.

PROP. 26. *A thing which has been determined to any action was necessarily so determined by God, and that which has not been thus determined by God cannot determine itself to action.*

Demonst. That by which things are said to be determined to any action is necessarily

something positive (as is self-evident); and therefore God, from the necessity of His nature, is the efficient cause both of its essence and of its existence (Props. 25 and 16), which was the first thing to be proved. From this also the second part of the proposition follows most clearly. For if a thing which has not been determined by God could determine itself, the first part of the proposition would be false, and to suppose this possible is an absurdity, as we have shown.

PROP. 27. *A thing which has been determined by God to any action cannot render itself indeterminate.*

Demonst. This proposition is evident from the third Axiom.

PROP. 28. *An individual thing, or a thing which is finite and which has a determinate existence, cannot exist nor be determined to action unless it be determined to existence and action by another cause which is also finite and has a determinate existence; and again, this cause cannot exist nor be determined to action unless by another cause which is also finite and determined to existence and action, and so on ad infinitum.*

Demonst. Whatever is determined to existence and action is thus determined by God (Prop. 26 and Corol. Prop. 24). But that which is finite and which has a determinate existence could not be produced by the absolute nature of any attribute of God, for whatever follows from the absolute nature of any attribute of God is infinite and eternal (Prop. 21). The finite and determinate must therefore follow from God, or from some attribute of God, in so far as the latter is considered to be affected by some mode, for besides substance and modes nothing exists (Ax. 1, and Defs. 3 and 5), and modes (Corol. Prop. 25) are nothing but affections of God's attributes. But the finite and determinate could not follow from God, or from any one of His attributes, so far as that attribute is affected with a modification which is eternal and infinite (Prop. 22). It must, therefore, follow or be determined to existence and action by God, or by some attribute of God, in so far as the attribute is modified by a modification which is finite, and which has a determinate existence. This was the first thing to be proved. Again, this cause or this mode (by the same reasoning by which we have already demonstrated the first part of this proposition) must be determined by another cause, which is also finite, and which has a determinate existence, and this last cause (by the same reasoning) must, in its turn, be determined by another cause, and so on continually (by the same reasoning) *ad infinitum*.

Schol. Since certain things must have been immediately produced by God, that is to say, those which necessarily follow from His absolute nature; these primary products being the mediating cause for those things which, nevertheless, without God can neither be nor can be conceived; it follows, firstly, that of things immediately produced by God He is the proximate cause absolutely, and not in their own kind (*in suo genere*), as we say; for effects of God can neither be nor be conceived without their cause (Prop. 15, and Corol. Prop. 24).

It follows, secondly, that God cannot be properly called the remote cause of individual things, unless for the sake of distinguishing them from the things which He has immediately produced, or rather which follow from His absolute nature. For by a remote cause we understand that which is in no way joined to its effect. But all things which are, are in God, and so depend upon Him that without Him they can neither be nor be conceived.

PROP. 29. *In nature there is nothing contingent, but all things are determined from the necessity of the divine nature to exist and act in a certain manner.*

Demonst. Whatever is, is in God (Prop. 15); but God cannot be called a contingent thing, for (Prop. 11) He exists necessarily and not contingently. Moreover, the modes of the divine nature have followed from it necessarily and not contingently (Prop. 16), and that, too, whether it be considered absolutely (Prop. 21), or as determined to action in a certain manner (Prop. 27). But God is the cause of these modes, not only in so far as they simply exist (Corol. Prop. 24), but also (Prop. 26) in so far as they are considered as determined to any action. And if they are not determined by God (by the same proposition), it is an impossibility and not a contingency that they should determine themselves; and, on the other hand (Prop. 27), if they are determined by God, it is an impossibility and not a contingency that they should render themselves indeterminate. Wherefore all things are determined from a necessity of the divine nature, not only to exist, but to exist and act in a certain manner, and there is nothing contingent. Q.E.D.

Schol. Before I go any farther, I wish here to explain, or rather to recall to recollection, what we mean by *natura naturans* and what by *natura naturata.* For, from what has gone before, I think it is plain that by *natura naturans* we are to understand that which is in itself and is conceived through itself, or those attributes of substance which express eternal and infinite essence, that is to say (Corol. 1, Prop. 14, and Corol. 2, Prop. 17), God in so far as He is considered as a free cause. But by *natura naturata* I understand everything which follows from the necessity of the nature of God, or of any one of God's attributes, that is to say, all the modes of God's attributes in so far as they are considered as things which are in God, and which without God can neither be nor can be conceived.

PROP. 30. *The actual intellect, whether finite or infinite, must comprehend the attributes of God and the affections of God, and nothing else.*

Demonst. A true idea must agree with that of which it is the idea (Ax. 6), that is to say (as is self-evident), that which is objectively contained in the intellect must necessarily exist in nature. But in nature (Corol. 1, Prop. 14) only one substance exists, namely, God, and no affections (Prop. 15) excepting those which are in God, and which (by the same proposition) can neither be nor be conceived without God. Therefore the actual intellect, whether finite or infinite, must comprehend the attributes of God and the affections of God, and nothing else. Q.E.D.

PROP. 31. *The actual intellect, whether it be finite or infinite, together with the will, desire, love, &c., must be referred to the* natura naturata *and not to the* natura naturans.

Demonst. For by the intellect (as is self-evident) we do not understand absolute thought, but only a certain mode of thought, which mode differs from other modes, such as desire, love, &c., and therefore (Def. 5) must be conceived through absolute thought, that is to say (Prop. 15 and Def. 6), it must be conceived through some attribute of God which expresses the eternal and infinite essence of thought in such a manner that without that attribute it can neither be nor can be conceived. Therefore (Schol. Prop. 29) the actual intellect, &c., must be referred to the *natura naturata* and not to the *natura naturans*, in the same manner as all other modes of thought. Q.E.D.

Schol. I do not here speak of the *actual* intellect because I admit that any intellect *potentially* exists, but because I wish, in order that there may be no confusion, to speak of nothing excepting of that which we perceive with the utmost clearness, that is to say, the understanding itself, which we perceive as clearly as we perceive anything. For we can understand nothing through the intellect which does not lead to a more perfect knowledge of the understanding.

PROP. 32. *The will cannot be called a free cause, but can only be called necessary.*

Demonst. The will is only a certain mode of thought, like the intellect, and therefore (Prop. 28) no volition can exist or be determined to action unless it be determined by another cause, and this again by another, and so on *ad infinitum.* And if the will be supposed infinite, it must be determined to existence and action by God, not in so far as He is substance absolutely infinite, but in so far as He possesses an attribute which expresses the infinite and eternal essence of thought (Prop. 23). In whatever way, therefore, the will be conceived, whether as finite or infinite, it requires a cause by which it may be determined to existence and action, and therefore (Def. 7) it cannot be called a free cause but only necessary or compelled. Q.E.D.

Corol. 1. Hence it follows, firstly, that God does not act from freedom of the will.

Corol. 2. It follows, secondly, that will and intellect are related to the nature of God as motion and rest, and absolutely as all natural things, which (Prop. 29) must be determined by God to existence and action in a certain manner. For the will, like all other things, needs a cause by which it may be determined to existence and action in a certain manner, and although from a given will or intellect infinite things may follow, God cannot on this account be said to act from freedom of will, any more than He can be said to act from freedom of motion and rest by reason of the things which follow from motion and rest (for from motion and rest infinite numbers of things follow). Therefore, will does not appertain to the nature of God more than other natural things, but is related to it as motion and rest and all other things are related to it; these all following, as we have shown, from the necessity of the divine nature, and being determined to existence and action in a certain manner.

PROP. 33. *Things could have been produced by God in no other manner and in no other order than that in which they have been produced.*

Demonst. All things have necessarily followed from the given nature of God (Prop. 16), and from the necessity of His nature have been determined to existence and action in a certain manner (Prop. 29). If, therefore, things could have been of another nature, or could have been determined in another manner to action, so that the order of nature would have been different, the nature of God might then be different to that which it now is, and hence (Prop. 11) that different nature would necessarily exist, and there might consequently be two or more Gods, which (Corol. 1, Prop. 14) is absurd. Therefore, things could be produced by God in no other manner and in no other order than that in which they have been produced. Q.E.D.

Schol. 1. Since I have thus shown, with greater clearness than that of noonday light, that in things there is absolutely nothing by virtue of which they can be called contingent, I wish now to explain in a few words what is to be understood by *contingent*, but firstly, what is to be understood by *necessary* and *impossible*. A thing is called necessary either in reference to its essence or its cause. For the existence of a thing necessarily follows either from the essence and definition of the thing itself, or from a given efficient cause. In the same way a thing is said to be impossible either because the essence of the thing itself or its definition involves a contradiction, or because no external cause exists determinate to the production of such a thing. But a thing cannot be called contingent unless with reference to a deficiency in our knowledge. For if we do not know that the essence of a thing involves a contradiction, or if we actually know that it involves no contradiction, and nevertheless we can affirm nothing with certainty about its existence because the order of causes is concealed from us, that thing can never appear to us either as necessary or impossible, and therefore we call it either contingent or possible.

Schol. 2. From what has gone before it clearly follows that things have been produced by God in the highest degree of perfection, since they have necessarily followed from the existence of a most perfect nature. Nor does this doctrine accuse God of any imperfection, but, on the contrary, His perfection has compelled us to affirm it. Indeed, from its contrary would clearly follow, as I have shown above, that God is not absolutely perfect, since if things had been produced in any other fashion another nature would have had to be assigned to Him, different from that which the consideration of the most perfect Being compels us to assign to Him. I do not doubt that many will reject this opinion as ridiculous, nor will they care to apply themselves to its consideration, and this from no other reason than that they have been in the habit of assigning to God another liberty widely different from that absolute will which (Def. 7) we have taught. On the other hand, I do not doubt, if they were willing to study the matter and properly to consider the series of our demonstrations, that they would altogether reject this liberty which they now assign to God, not only as of no value, but as a great obstacle to knowledge. Neither is there any need that I should here repeat those things which are said in the scholium to Prop. 17. But for the sake of those who differ from me, I will here show that although it be granted that will pertains to God's essence, it follows nevertheless from His perfection that things could be created in no other mode or order by Him. This it will be easy to show if we first consider that which my opponents themselves admit, that it depends upon the decree and will of God alone that each thing should be what it is, for otherwise God would not be the cause of all things. It is also admitted that all God's decrees were decreed by God Himself from all eternity, for otherwise imperfection and inconstancy would be proved against Him. But since in eternity there is no *when* nor *before* nor *after*, it follows from the perfection of God alone that He neither can decree nor could ever have decreed anything else than that which He has decreed; that is to say, God has not existed before His decrees, and can never exist without them. But it is said that although it be supposed that God had made the nature of things different from that which it is, or that from eternity He had decreed something else about nature and her order, it would not thence follow that any imperfection exists in God. But if this be said, it must at the same time be allowed that God can change His decrees. For if God had decreed something about nature and her order other than that which He has decreed—that is to say, if He had willed and conceived something else about nature—He would necessarily have had an intellect and a will different from those which He now has. And if it be allowed to assign to God another intellect and another will without any change of His essence and of His perfections, what is the reason why He cannot now change His decrees about creation

and nevertheless remain equally perfect? For His intellect and will regarding created things and their order remain the same in relationship to His essence and perfection in whatever manner His intellect and will are conceived. Moreover, all the philosophers whom I have seen admit that there is no such thing as an intellect existing potentially in God, but only an intellect existing actually. But since His intellect and His will are not distinguishable from His essence, as all admit, it follows from this also that if God had had another intellect actually and another will, His essence would have been necessarily different, and hence, as I showed at the beginning, if things had been produced by God in a manner different from that in which they now exist, God's intellect and will, that is to say, His essence (as has been granted), must have been different, which is absurd.

Since, therefore, things could have been produced by God in no other manner or order, this being a truth which follows from His absolute perfection, there is no sound reasoning which can persuade us to believe that God was unwilling to create all things which are in His intellect with the same perfection as that in which they exist in His intellect. But we shall be told that there is no perfection nor imperfection in things, but that that which is in them by reason of which they are perfect or imperfect and are said to be good or evil depends upon the will of God alone, and therefore if God had willed He could have effected that that which is now perfection should have been the extreme of imperfection, and *vice versa*. But what else would this be than openly to affirm that God, who necessarily understands what He wills, is able by His will to understand things in a manner different from that in which He understands them, which, as I have just shown, is a great absurdity? I can therefore turn the argument on my opponents in this way. All things depend upon the power of God. In order that things may be differently constituted, it would be necessary that God's will should be differently constituted; but God's will cannot be other than it is, as we have lately most clearly deduced from His perfection. Things therefore cannot be differently constituted. I confess that this opinion, which subjects all things to a certain indifferent God's will, and affirms that all things depend upon God's good pleasure, is at a less distance from the truth than the opinion of those who affirm that God does everything for

e sake of the Good. For these seem to place
mething outside of God which is independent
 Him, to which He looks while He is at work
 to a model, or at which He aims as if at a
ertain mark. This is indeed nothing else than
 subject God to fate, the most absurd thing
hich can be affirmed of Him whom we have
own to be the first and only free cause of the
ssence of all things as well as of their existnce. Therefore it is not worth while that I
ould waste time in refuting this absurdity.

ROP. 34. *The power of God is His essence
self.*

Demonst. From the necessity alone of the
ssence of God it follows that God is the cause
f Himself (Prop. 11), and (Prop. 16 and its
orol.) the cause of all things. Therefore the
ower of God, by which He Himself and all
hings are and act, is His essence itself. Q.E.D.

ROP. 35. *Whatever we conceive to be in God's
ower necessarily exists.*

Demonst. For whatever is in God's power
ust (Prop. 34) be so comprehended in His
ssence that it necessarily follows from it, and
onsequently exists necessarily. Q.E.D.

ROP. 36. *Nothing exists from whose nature an
ffect does not follow.*

Demonst. Whatever exists expresses the na-
ure or the essence of God in a certain and de-
erminate manner (Corol. Prop. 25); that is to
ay (Prop. 34), whatever exists expresses the
ower of God, which is the cause of all things,
n a certain and determinate manner, and
herefore (Prop. 16) some effect must follow
rom it.

APPENDIX

I have now explained the nature of God and
ts properties. I have shown that He neces-
arily exists; that He is one God; that from
he necessity alone of His own nature He is
nd acts; that He is, and in what way He is,
he free cause of all things; that all things are
n Him, and so depend upon Him that without
Him they can neither be nor can be conceived;
nd, finally, that all things have been prede-
ermined by Him, not indeed from freedom of
vill or from absolute good pleasure, but from
His absolute nature or infinite power.

Moreover, wherever an opportunity was af-
orded, I have endeavoured to remove prej-
dices which might hinder the perception of
he truth of what I have demonstrated; but

because not a few still remain which have been
and are now sufficient to prove a very great
hindrance to the comprehension of the connection of things in the manner in which I have
explained it, I have thought it worth while to
call them up to be examined by reason. But all
these prejudices which I here undertake to
point out depend upon this solely: that it is
commonly supposed that all things in nature,
like men, work to some end; and indeed it is
thought to be certain that God Himself directs
all things to some sure end, for it is said that
God has made all things for man, and man
that he may worship God. This, therefore, I
will first investigate by inquiring, firstly, why
so many rest in this prejudice, and why all are
so naturally inclined to embrace it? I shall
then show its falsity, and, finally, the manner
in which there have arisen from it prejudices
concerning *good* and *evil, merit* and *sin, praise*
and *blame, order* and *disorder, beauty* and *deformity,* and so forth. This, however, is not the
place to deduce these things from the nature
of the human mind. It will be sufficient if I
here take as an axiom that which no one ought
to dispute, namely, that man is born ignorant
of the causes of things, and that he has a desire,
of which he is conscious, to seek that which is
profitable to him. From this it follows, firstly,
that he thinks himself free because he is conscious of his wishes and appetites, whilst at
the same time he is ignorant of the causes by
which he is led to wish and desire, not dreaming what they are; and, secondly, it follows
that man does everything for an end, namely,
for that which is profitable to him, which is
what he seeks. Hence it happens that he attempts to discover merely the final causes of
that which has happened; and when he has
heard them he is satisfied, because there is no
longer any cause for further uncertainty. But
if he cannot hear from another what these
final causes are, nothing remains but to turn
to himself and reflect upon the ends which
usually determine him to the like actions, and
thus by his own mind he necessarily judges
that of another. Moreover, since he discovers,
both within and without himself, a multitude
of means which contribute not a little to the
attainment of what is profitable to himself—
for example, the eyes, which are useful for
seeing, the teeth for mastication, plants and
animals for nourishment, the sun for giving
light, the sea for feeding fish, &c.—it comes to
pass that all natural objects are considered as
means for obtaining what is profitable. These

too being evidently discovered and not created by man, hence he has a cause for believing that some other person exists, who has prepared them for man's use. For having considered them as means it was impossible to believe that they had created themselves, and so he was obliged to infer from the means which he was in the habit of providing for himself that some ruler or rulers of nature exist, endowed with human liberty, who have taken care of all things for him, and have made all things for his use. Since he never heard anything about the mind of these rulers, he was compelled to judge of it from his own, and hence he affirmed that the gods direct everything for his advantage, in order that he may be bound to them and hold them in the highest honour. This is the reason why each man has devised for himself, out of his own brain, a different mode of worshipping God, so that God might love him above others, and direct all nature to the service of his blind cupidity and insatiable avarice.

Thus has this prejudice been turned into a superstition and has driven deep roots into the mind—a prejudice which was the reason why every one has so eagerly tried to discover and explain the final causes of things. The attempt, however, to show that nature does nothing in vain (that is to say, nothing which is not profitable to man), seems to end in showing that nature, the gods, and man are alike mad.

Do but see, I pray, to what all this has led. Amidst so much in nature that is beneficial, not a few things must have been observed which are injurious, such as storms, earthquakes, diseases, and it was affirmed that these things happened either because the gods were angry because of wrongs which had been inflicted on them by man, or because of sins committed in the method of worshipping them; and although experience daily contradicted this, and showed by an infinity of examples that both the beneficial and the injurious were indiscriminately bestowed on the pious and the impious, the inveterate prejudices on this point have not therefore been abandoned. For it was much easier for a man to place these things aside with others of the use of which he was ignorant, and thus retain his present and inborn state of ignorance, than to destroy the whole superstructure and think out a new one. Hence it was looked upon as indisputable that the judgments of the gods far surpass our comprehension; and this opinion alone would have been sufficient to keep the human race in

darkness to all eternity, if mathematics, whic does not deal with ends, but with the essence and properties of forms, had not placed befor us another rule of truth. In addition to math ematics, other causes also might be assigned which it is superfluous here to enumerate tending to make men reflect upon these un versal prejudices, and leading them to a tru knowledge of things.

I have thus sufficiently explained what promised in the first place to explain. Ther will now be no need of many words to show that nature has set no end before herself, an that all final causes are nothing but huma fictions. For I believe that this is sufficientl evident both from the foundations and cause of this prejudice, and from Prop. 16 and Coro Prop. 32, as well as from all those proposition in which I have shown that all things are be gotten by a certain eternal necessity of natur and in absolute perfection. Thus much, never theless, I will add, that this doctrine concern ing an end altogether overturns nature. Fo that which is in truth the cause it considers a the effect, and *vice versa*. Again, that which i first in nature it puts last; and, finally, tha which is supreme and most perfect it make the most imperfect. For (passing by the firs two assertions as self-evident) it is plain fron Props. 21, 22, and 23, that that effect is th most perfect which is immediately produce by God, and in proportion as intermediat causes are necessary for the production of thing is it imperfect. But if things which ar immediately produced by God were made i order that He might obtain the end He had i view, then the last things for the sake of whic the first exist, must be the most perfect of all Again, this doctrine does away with God' perfection. For if God works to obtain an end He necessarily seeks something of which h stands in need. And although theologians and metaphysicians distinguish between the en of want and the end of assimilation (*finem in degentiæ et finem assimilationis*), they confes that God has done all things for His own sake and not for the sake of the things to be created because before the creation they can assig nothing excepting God for the sake of whic God could do anything; and therefore the are necessarily compelled to admit that Goc stood in need of and desired those things fo which He determined to prepare means. This is self-evident. Nor is it here to be overlooked that the adherents of this doctrine, who have found a pleasure in displaying their ingenuity in assigning the ends of things, have introduced a new species of argument, not the *reductio ad impossibile*, but the *reductio ad ignorantiam*, to prove their position, which shows that it had no other method of defence left. For, by way of example, if a stone has fallen from some roof on somebody's head and killed him, they will demonstrate in this manner that the stone has fallen in order to kill the man. For if it did not fall for that purpose by the will of God, how could so many circumstances concur through chance (and a number often simultaneously do concur)? You will answer, perhaps, that the event happened because the wind blew and the man was passing that way. But, they will urge, why did the wind blow at that time, and why did the man pass that way precisely at the same moment? If you again reply that the wind rose then because the sea on the preceding day began to be stormy, the weather hitherto having been calm, and that the man had been invited by a friend, they will urge again—because there is no end of questioning—But why was the sea agitated? why was the man invited at that time? And so they will not cease from asking the causes of causes, until at last you fly to the will of God, the refuge for ignorance.

So, also, when they behold the structure of the human body, they are amazed; and because they are ignorant of the causes of such art, they conclude that the body was made not by mechanical but by a supernatural or divine art, and has been formed in such a way so that the one part may not injure the other. Hence it happens that the man who endeavours to find out the true causes of miracles, and who desires as a wise man to understand nature, and not to gape at it like a fool, is generally considered and proclaimed to be a heretic and impious by those whom the vulgar worship as the interpreters both of nature and the gods. For these know that if ignorance be removed, amazed stupidity, the sole ground on which they rely in arguing or in defending their authority, is taken away also. But these things I leave and pass on to that which I determined to do in the third place.

After man has persuaded himself that all things which exist are made for him, he must in everything adjudge that to be of the greatest importance which is most useful to him, and he must esteem that to be of surpassing worth by which he is most beneficially affected. In this way he is compelled to form those notions by which he explains nature; such, for instance,

as *good, evil, order, confusion, heat, cold, beauty,* and *deformity,* &c.; and because he supposes himself to be free, notions like those of *praise* and *blame, sin* and *merit,* have arisen. These latter I shall hereafter explain when I have treated of human nature; the former I will here briefly unfold.

It is to be observed that man has given the name *good* to everything which leads to health and the worship of God; on the contrary, everything which does not lead thereto he calls *evil.* But because those who do not understand nature affirm nothing about things themselves, but only imagine them, and take the imagination to be understanding, they therefore, ignorant of things and their nature, firmly believe an *order* to be in things: for when things are so placed that, if they are represented to us through the senses, we can easily imagine them, and consequently easily remember them, we call them well arranged; but if they are not placed so that we can imagine and remember them, we call them badly arranged or *confused.* Moreover, since those things are more especially pleasing to us which we can easily imagine, men therefore prefer order to confusion, as if order were something in nature apart from our own imagination; and they say that God has created everything in order, and in this manner they ignorantly attribute imagination to God, unless they mean perhaps that God, out of consideration for the human imagination, has disposed things in the manner in which they can most easily be imagined. No hesitation either seems to be caused by the fact that an infinite number of things are discovered which far surpass our imagination, and very many which confound it through its weakness. But enough of this. The other notions which I have mentioned are nothing but modes in which the imagination is affected in different ways, and nevertheless they are regarded by the ignorant as being specially attributes of things, because, as we have remarked, men consider all things as made for themselves, and call the nature of a thing good, evil, sound, putrid, or corrupt, just as they are affected by it. For example, if the motion by which the nerves are affected by means of objects represented to the eye conduces to well-being, the objects by which it is caused are called *beautiful;* while those exciting a contrary motion are called *deformed.* Those things, too, which stimulate the senses through the nostrils are called sweet-smelling or thinking; those which act through the taste are called sweet or bitter, full-flavoured or insipid; those which act through the touch, hard or soft, heavy or light; those, lastly, which act through the ears are said to make a noise, sound, or harmony, the last having caused men to lose their senses to such a degree that they have believed that God even is delighted with it. Indeed, philosophers may be found who have persuaded themselves that the celestial motions beget a harmony. All these things sufficiently show that every one judges things by the constitution of his brain, or rather accepts the affections of his imagination in the place of things. It is not, therefore, to be wondered at, as we may observe in passing, that all those controversies which we see have arisen amongst men, so that at last scepticism has been the result. For although human bodies agree in many things, they differ in more, and therefore that which to one person is good will appear to another evil, that which to one is well arranged to another is confused, that which pleases one will displease another, and so on in other cases which I pass by both because we cannot notice them at length here, and because they are within the experience of every one. For every one has heard the expressions: So many heads, so many ways of thinking; Every one is satisfied with his own way of thinking; Differences of brains are not less common than differences of taste;—all which maxims show that men decide upon matters according to the constitution of their brains, and imagine rather than understand things. If men understood things, they would, as mathematics prove, at least be all alike convinced if they were not all alike attracted. We see, therefore, that all those methods by which

the common people are in the habit of explaining nature are only different sorts of imaginations, and do not reveal the nature of anything in itself, but only the constitution of the imagination; and because they have names as if they were entities existing apart from the imagination, I call them entities not of the reason but of the imagination. All argument, therefore, urged against us based upon such notions can be easily refuted. Many people, for instance, are accustomed to argue thus:— If all things have followed from the necessity of the most perfect nature of God, how is it that so many imperfections have arisen in nature—corruption, for instance, of things till they stink; deformity, exciting disgust; confusion, evil, crime, &c.? But, as I have just observed, all this is easily answered. For the perfection of things is to be judged by their nature and power alone; nor are they more or less perfect because they delight or offend the human senses, or because they are beneficial or prejudicial to human nature. But to those who ask why God has not created all men in such a manner that they might be controlled by the dictates of reason alone, I give but this answer: Because to Him material was not wanting for the creation of everything, from the highest down to the very lowest grade of perfection; or, to speak more properly, because the laws of His nature were so ample that they sufficed for the production of everything which can be conceived by an infinite intellect, as I have demonstrated in Prop. 16.

These are the prejudices which I undertook to notice here. If any others of a similar character remain, they can easily be rectified with a little thought by any one.

SECOND PART

OF THE NATURE AND ORIGIN
OF THE MIND

I PASS on now to explain those things which must necessarily follow from the essence of God or the Being eternal and infinite; not indeed to explain all these things, for we have demonstrated (Prop. 16, pt. 1) that an infinitude of things must follow in an infinite number of ways,—but to consider those things only which may conduct us as it were by the hand to a knowledge of the human mind and its highest happiness.

DEFINITIONS

1. By body, I understand a mode which expresses in a certain and determinate manner the essence of God in so far as He is considered as the thing extended. (See Corol. Prop. 25, pt. 1.)

2. I say that to the essence of anything pertains that, which being given, the thing itself is necessarily posited, and being taken away, the thing is necessarily taken; or, in other words, that, without which the thing can neither be nor be conceived, and which in its turn cannot be nor be conceived without the thing.

3. By idea, I understand a conception of the mind which the mind forms because it is a thinking thing.

Explanation.—I use the word conception rather than perception because the name perception seems to indicate that the mind is passive in its relation to the object. But the word conception seems to express the action of the mind.

4. By adequate idea, I understand an idea which, in so far as it is considered in itself, without reference to the object, has all the properties or internal signs (*denominationes intrinsecas*) of a true idea.

Explanation.—I say internal, so as to exclude that which is external, the agreement, namely, of the idea with its object.

5. Duration is the indefinite continuation of existence.

Explanation.—I call it indefinite because it cannot be determined by the nature itself of the existing thing nor by the efficient cause, which necessarily posits the existence of the thing but does not take it away.

6. By reality and perfection I understand the same thing.

7. By individual things I understand things which are finite and which have a determinate existence; and if a number of individuals so unite in one action that they are all simultaneously the cause of one effect, I consider them all, so far, as a one individual thing.

AXIOMS

1. The essence of man does not involve necessary existence; that is to say, the existence as well as the non-existence of this or that man may or may not follow from the order of nature.

2. Man thinks.

3. Modes of thought, such as love, desire, or the affections of the mind, by whatever name they may be called, do not exist, unless in the same individual the idea exist of a thing loved, desired, &c. But the idea may exist although no other mode of thinking exist.

4. We perceive that a certain body is affected in many ways.

5. No individual things are felt or perceived by us excepting bodies and modes of thought.

The postulates will be found after Proposition 13.

PROP. 1.   *Thought is an attribute of God, or God is a thinking thing.*

Demonst.   Individual thoughts, or this and that thought, are modes which express the nature of God in a certain and determinate manner (Corol. Prop. 25, pt. 1). God therefore possesses an attribute (Def. 5, pt. 1), the conception of which is involved in all individual thoughts, and through which they are conceived. Thought, therefore, is one of the infinite attributes of God which expresses the eternal and infinite essence of God (Def. 6, pt. 1), or, in other words, God is a thinking thing.   Q.E.D.

Schol. This proposition is plain from the fact that we can conceive an infinite thinking Being. For the more things a thinking being can think, the more reality or perfection we conceive it to possess, and therefore the being which can think an infinitude of things in infinite ways is necessarily infinite by his power of thinking. Since, therefore, we can conceive an infinite Being by attending to thought alone, thought is necessarily one of the infinite attributes of God (Defs. 4 and 6, pt. 1), which is the proposition we wished to prove.

PROP. 2.   *Extension is an attribute of God, or God is an extended thing.*

Demonst. The demonstration of this proposition is of the same character as that of the last.

PROP. 3.   *In God there necessarily exists the idea of His essence, and of all things which necessarily follow from His essence.*

Demonst. For God (Prop. 1, pt. 2) can think an infinitude of things in infinite ways, or (which is the same thing, by Prop. 16, pt. 1) can form an idea of His essence and of all the things which necessarily follow from it. But everything which is in the power of God is necessary (Prop. 35, pt. 1), and therefore this idea necessarily exists, and (Prop. 15, pt. 1) it cannot exist unless in God.

Schol. The common people understand by God's power His free will and right over all existing things, which are therefore commonly looked upon as contingent; for they say that God has the power of destroying everything and reducing it to nothing. They very frequently, too, compare God's power with the power of kings. That there is any similarity between the two we have disproved in the first and second Corollaries of Prop. 32, pt. 1, and in Prop. 16, pt. 1, we have shown that God does everything with that necessity with which He understands Himself; that is to say, as it follows from the necessity of the divine nature that God understands Himself (a truth admitted by all, so by the same necessity it follows that God does an infinitude of things in infinite ways. Moreover, in Prop. 34, pt. 1, we have shown that the power of God is nothing but the active essence of God, and therefore it is as impossible for us to conceive that God does not act as that He does not exist. If it pleased me to go farther, I could show besides that the power which the common people ascribe to God is not only a human power

(which shows that they look upon God as a man, or as being like a man), but that it also involves a weakness. But I do not care to talk so much upon the same subject. Again and again I ask the reader to consider and reconsider what is said upon this subject in the first part, from Prop. 16 to the end. For it is not possible for any one properly to understand the things which I wish to prove unless he takes great care not to confound the power of God with the human power and right of kings.

PROP. 4.   *The idea of God, from which infinite numbers of things follow in infinite ways, can be one only.*

Demonst. The infinite intellect comprehends nothing but the attributes of God and His affections (Prop. 30, pt. 1). But God is one (Corol. 1, Prop. 14, pt. 1). Therefore the idea of God, from which infinite numbers of things follow in infinite ways, can be only one. Q.E.D.

PROP. 5.   *The formal Being of ideas recognises God for its cause in so far only as He is considered as a thinking thing, and not in so far as He is manifested by any other attribute; that is to say, the ideas both of God's attributes and of individual things do not recognise as their efficient cause the objects of the ideas or the things which are perceived, but God Himself in so far as He is a thinking thing.*

Demonst. This is plain, from Prop. 3, pt. 2; for we there demonstrated that God can form an idea of His own essence, and of all things which necessarily follow from it, solely because He is a thinking thing, and not because He is the object of His idea. Therefore the formal Being of ideas recognises God as its cause in so far as He is a thinking thing. But the proposition can be proved in another way. The formal Being of ideas is a mode of thought (as is self-evident); that is to say, (Corol. Prop. 25, pt. 1), a mode which expresses in a certain manner the nature of God in so far as He is a thinking thing. It is a mode, therefore (Prop. 10, pt. 1) that involves the conception of no other attribute of God, and consequently is the effect (Ax. 4, pt. 1) of no other attribute except that of thought; therefore the formal Being of ideas, &c.   Q.E.D.

PROP. 6.   *The modes of any attribute have God for a cause only in so far as He is considered under that attribute of which they are modes, and not in so far as He is considered under any other attribute.*

Demonst. Each attribute is conceived by itself and without any other (Prop. 10, pt. 1). Therefore the modes of any attribute involve the conception of that attribute and of no other, and therefore (Ax. 4, pt. 1) have God for a cause in so far as He is considered under that attribute of which they are modes, and not so far as He is considered under any other attribute. Q.E.D.

Corol. Hence it follows that the formal Being of things which are not modes of thought does not follow from the divine nature because of His prior knowledge of these things, but, as we have shown, just as ideas follow from the attribute of thought, in the same manner and with the same necessity the objects of ideas follow and are concluded from their attributes.

PROP. 7. *The order and connection of ideas is the same as the order and connection of things.*

This is evident from Ax. 4, pt. 1. For the idea of anything caused depends upon a knowledge of the cause of which the thing caused is the effect.

Corol. Hence it follows that God's power of thinking is equal to His actual power of acting; that is to say, whatever follows *formally* from the infinite nature of God, follows from the idea of God [idea Dei], in the same order and in the same connection *objectively* in God.

Schol. Before we go any farther, we must here recall to our memory what we have already demonstrated, that everything which can be perceived by the infinite intellect as constituting the essence of substance pertains entirely to the one sole substance only, and consequently that substance thinking and substance extended are one and the same substance, which is now comprehended under this attribute and now under that. Thus, also, a mode of extension and the idea of that mode are one and the same thing expressed in two different ways—a truth which some of the Hebrews appear to have seen as if through a cloud, since they say that God, the intellect of God, and the things which are the objects of that intellect are one and the same thing. For example, the circle existing in nature and the idea that is in God of an existing circle are one and the same thing, which is manifested through different attributes; and, therefore, whether we think of nature under the attribute of extension, or under the attribute of thought, or under any other attribute whatever, we shall discover one and the same order, or one and the same connection of causes; that is to

say, in every case the same sequence of things. Nor have I had any other reason for saying that God is the cause of the idea, for example, of the circle in so far only as He is a thinking thing, and of the circle itself in so far as He is an extended thing, but this, that the formal Being of the idea of a circle can only be perceived through another mode of thought, as its proximate cause, and this again must be perceived through another, and so on *ad infinitum*. So that when things are considered as modes of thought, we must explain the order of the whole of nature or the connection of causes by the attribute of thought alone, and when things are considered as modes of extension, the order of the whole of nature must be explained through the attribute of extension alone, and so with other attributes. Therefore God is in truth the cause of things as they are in themselves in so far as He consists of infinite attributes, nor for the present can I explain the matter more clearly.

PROP. 8. *The ideas of non-existent individual things or modes are comprehended in the infinite idea of God, in the same way that the formal essences of individual things or modes are contained in the attributes of God.*

Demonst. This proposition is evident from the preceding proposition, but it is to be understood more clearly from the preceding scholium.

Corol. Hence it follows that when individual things do not exist unless in so far as they are comprehended in the attributes of God, their objective Being or ideas do not exist unless in so far as the infinite idea of God exists; and when individual things are said to exist, not only in so far as they are included in God's attributes, but in so far as they are said to have duration, their ideas involve the existence through which they are said to have duration.

Schol. If any one desires an instance in order that what I have said may be more fully understood, I cannot give one which will adequately explain what I have been saying, since an exact parallel does not exist: nevertheless, I will endeavour to give as good an illustration as can be found.

The circle, for example, possesses this property, that the rectangles contained by the segments of all straight lines cutting one another in the same circle are equal; therefore in a circle there is contained an infinite number of rectangles equal to one another, but none of them can be said to exist unless in so far as the circle exists, nor can the idea of any one of these rectangles be said to exist unless in so far as it is comprehended in the idea of the circle. Out of this infinite number of rectangles, let two only, E and D, be conceived to exist. The ideas of these two rectangles do not now exist

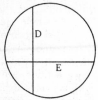

merely in so far as they are comprehended in the idea of the circle, but because they involve the existence of their rectangles, and it is this which distinguishes them from the other ideas of the other rectangles.

PROP. 9.   *The idea of an individual thing actually existing has God for a cause, not in so far as He is infinite, but in so far as He is considered to be affected by another idea of an individual thing actually existing, of which idea also He is the cause in so far as He is affected by a third, and so on* ad infinitum.

Demonst.   The idea of any individual thing actually existing is an individual mode of thought, and is distinct from other modes of thought (Corol. and Schol. Prop. 8, pt. 2), and therefore (Prop. 6, pt. 2) has God for a cause in so far only as He is a thinking thing; not indeed as a thinking thing absolutely (Prop. 28, pt. 1), but in so far as He is considered as affected by another mode of thought. Again, He is the cause of this latter mode of thought in so far as He is considered as affected by another, and so on *ad infinitum*. But the order and connection of ideas (Prop. 7, pt. 2) is the same as the order and connection of causes; therefore every individual idea has for its cause another idea, that is to say, God in so far as He is affected by another idea; while of this second idea God is again the cause in the same way, and so on *ad infinitum*.   Q.E.D.

Corol.   A knowledge of everything which happens in the individual object of any idea exists in God in so far only as He possesses the idea of that object.

Demonst.   The idea of everything which happens in the object of any idea exists in God (Prop. 3, pt. 2), not in so far as He is infinite, but in so far as He is considered as affected by another idea of an individual thing (Prop. 9, pt. 2); but (Prop. 7, pt. 2) the order and connection of ideas is the same as the order and

connection of things, and therefore the knowledge of that which happens in any individual object will exist in God in so far only as He has the idea of that object.

PROP. 10.   *The Being of substance does not pertain to the essence of man, or, in other words, substance does not constitute the form of man.*

Demonst.   The Being of substance involves necessary existence (Prop. 7, pt. 1). If, therefore, the Being of substance pertained to the essence of man, the existence of man would necessarily follow from the existence of substance (Def. 2, pt. 2), and consequently he would necessarily exist, which (Ax. 1, pt. 2) is an absurdity. Therefore the Being of substance does not pertain, &c.   Q.E.D.

Schol.   This proposition may be demonstrated from Prop. 5, pt. 1, which proves that there are not two substances of the same nature. For since it is possible for more men than one to exist, therefore that which constitutes the form of man is not the Being of substance. This proposition is evident also from the other properties of substance; as, for example, that it is by its nature infinite, immutable, indivisible, &c., as any one may easily see.

Corol.   Hence it follows that the essence of man consists of certain modifications of the attributes of God; for the Being of substance does not pertain to the essence of man (Prop. 10, pt. 2). It is therefore something (Prop. 15, pt. 1) which is in God, and which without God can neither be nor be conceived, or (Corol. Prop. 25, pt. 1) an affection or mode which expresses the nature of God in a certain and determinate manner.

Schol.   Every one must admit that without God nothing can be nor be conceived; for every one admits that God is the sole cause both of the essence and of the existence of all things; that is to say, God is not only the cause of things, to use a common expression, *secundum fieri*, but also *secundum esse*. But many people say that that pertains to the essence of a thing without which the thing can neither be nor can be conceived, and they therefore believe either that the nature of God belongs to the essence of created things, or that created things can be or can be conceived without God; or, which is more probable, there is no consistency in their thought. I believe that the cause of this confusion is that they have not observed a proper order of philosophic study. For although the divine nature ought to be studied first, because it is first in the order of knowledge and in the order of things, they think it last; while, on the other hand, those things which are called objects of the senses are believed to stand before everything else. Hence it has come to pass that there was nothing of which men thought less than the divine nature while they have been studying natural objects, and when they afterwards applied themselves to think about God, there was nothing of which they could think less than those prior fictions upon which they had built their knowledge of natural things, for these fictions could in no way help to the knowledge of the divine nature. It is no wonder, therefore, if we find them continually contradicting themselves. But this I pass by. For my only purpose was to give a reason why I did not say that that pertains to the essence of a thing without which the thing can neither be nor can be conceived; and my reason is, that individual things cannot be nor be conceived without God, and yet God does not pertain to their essence. I have rather, therefore, said that the essence of a thing is necessarily that which being given, the thing is posited, and being taken away, the thing is taken away, or that without which the thing can neither be nor be conceived, and which in its turn cannot be nor be conceived without the thing.

PROP. 11. *The first thing which forms the actual Being of the human mind is nothing else than the idea of an individual thing actually existing.*

Demonst. The essence of man is formed (Corol. Prop. 10, pt. 2) by certain modes of the attributes of God, that is to say (Ax. 2, pt. 2), modes of thought, the idea of all of them being prior by nature to the modes of thought themselves (Ax. 3, pt. 2); and if this idea exists, other modes (which also have an idea in nature prior to them) must exist in the same individual likewise (Ax. 3, pt. 2). Therefore an idea is the first thing which forms the Being of the human mind. But it is not the idea of a nonexistent thing, for then the idea itself (Corol. Prop. 8, pt. 2) could not be said to exist. It will, therefore, be the idea of something actually existing. Neither will it be the idea of an infinite thing, for an infinite thing must always necessarily exist (Props. 21 and 22, pt. 1), and this (Ax. 1, pt. 2) is absurd. Therefore the first thing which forms the actual Being of the human mind is the idea of an individual thing actually existing. Q.E.D.

Corol. Hence it follows that the human mind is a part of the infinite intellect of God, and therefore, when we say that the human mind

perceives this or that thing, we say nothing else than that God has this or that idea; not indeed in so far as He is infinite, but in so far as He is manifested through the nature of the human mind, or in so far as He forms the essence of the human mind; and when we say that God has this or that idea, not merely in so far as He forms the nature of the human mind, but in so far as He has at the same time with the human mind the idea also of another thing, then we say that the human mind perceives the thing partially or inadequately.

Schol. At this point many of my readers will no doubt stick fast, and will think of many things which will cause delay; and I therefore beg of them to advance slowly, step by step, with me, and not to pronounce judgment until they shall have read everything which I have to say.

PROP. 12. *Whatever happens in the object of the idea constituting the human mind must be perceived by the human mind; or, in other words, an idea of that thing will necessarily exist in the human mind. That is to say, if the object of the idea constituting the human mind be a body, nothing can happen in that body which is not perceived by the mind.*

Demonst. The knowledge of everything which happens in the object of any idea necessarily exists in God (Corol. Prop. 9, pt. 2), in so far as He is considered as affected with the idea of that object; that is to say (Prop. 11, pt. 2), in so far as He forms the mind of any being. The knowledge, therefore, necessarily exists in God of everything which happens in the object of the idea constituting the human mind; that is to say, it exists in Him in so far as He forms the nature of the human mind; or, in other words (Corol. Prop. 11, pt. 2), the knowledge of this thing will necessarily be in the mind, or the mind perceives it. Q.E.D.

Schol. This proposition is plainly deducible and more easily to be understood from Schol. Prop. 7, pt. 2, to which the reader is referred.

PROP. 13. *The object of the idea constituting the human mind is a body, or a certain mode of extension actually existing, and nothing else.*

Demonst. For if the body were not the object of the human mind, the ideas of the affections of the body would not be in God (Corol. Prop. 9, pt. 2) in so far as He has formed our mind, but would be in Him in so far as He has formed the mind of another thing; that is to say (Corol. Prop. 11, pt. 2), the ideas of the affections of the body would not be in our mind. But (Ax. 4, pt. 2) we have ideas of the affections of a body; therefore the object of the idea constituting the human mind is a body, and that too (Prop. 11, pt. 2) actually existing. Again, if there were also any other object of the mind besides a body, since nothing exists from which some effect does not follow (Prop. 36, pt. 1), the idea of some effect produced by this object would necessarily exist in our mind (Prop. 11, pt. 2). But (Ax. 5, pt. 2) there is no such idea, and therefore the object of our mind is a body existing, and nothing else.   Q.E.D.

Corol. Hence it follows that man is composed of mind and body, and that the human body exists as we perceive it.

Schol. Hence we see not only that the human mind is united to the body, but also what is to be understood by the union of the mind and body. But no one can understand it adequately or distinctly without knowing adequately beforehand the nature of our body; for those things which we have proved hitherto are altogether general, nor do they refer more to man than to other individuals, all of which are animate, although in different degrees. For of everything there necessarily exists in God an idea of which He is the cause, in the same way as the idea of the human body exists in Him; and therefore everything that we have said of the idea of the human body is necessarily true of the idea of any other thing. We cannot, however, deny that ideas, like objects themselves, differ from one another, and that one is more excellent and contains more reality than another, just as the object of one idea is more excellent and contains more reality than another. Therefore, in order to determine the difference between the human mind and other things and its superiority over them, we must first know, as we have said, the nature of its object, that is to say, the nature of the human body. I am not able to explain it here, nor is such an explanation necessary for what I wish to demonstrate.

This much, nevertheless, I will say generally, that in proportion as one body is better adapted than another to do or suffer many things, in the same proportion will the mind at the same time be better adapted to perceive many things, and the more the actions of a body depend upon itself alone, and the less other bodies co-operate with it in action, the better adapted will the mind be for distinctly understanding. We can thus determine the superiority of one mind to another; we can also see

the reason why we have only a very confused knowledge of our body, together with many other things which I shall deduce in what follows. For this reason I have thought it worth while more accurately to explain and demonstrate the truths just mentioned, to which end it is necessary for me to say beforehand a few words upon the nature of bodies.

AXIOM 1.   All bodies are either in a state of motion or rest.

AXIOM 2.   Every body moves, sometimes slowly, sometimes quickly.

LEMMA 1.   *Bodies are distinguished from one another in respect of motion and rest, quickness and slowness, and not in respect of substance.*

Demonst. I suppose the first part of this proposition to be self-evident. But it is plain that bodies are not distinguished in respect of substance, both from Prop. 5, pt. 1, and Prop. 8, pt. 1, and still more plainly from what I have said in the scholium to Prop. 15, pt. 1.

LEMMA 2.   *All bodies agree in some respects.*

Demonst. For all bodies agree in this, that they involve the conception of one and the same attribute (Def. 1, pt. 2). They have, moreover, this in common, that they are capable generally of motion and of rest, and of motion at one time quicker and at another slower.

LEMMA 3.   *A body in motion or at rest must be determined to motion or rest by another body, which was also determined to motion or rest by another, and that in its turn by another, and so on ad infinitum.*

Demonst. Bodies (Def. 1, pt. 2) are individual things, which (Lem. 1) are distinguished from one another in respect of motion and rest, and therefore (Prop. 28, pt. 1) each one must necessarily be determined to motion or rest by another individual thing; that is to say (Prop. 6, pt. 1), by another body which (Ax. 1) is also either in motion or at rest. But this body, by the same reasoning, could not be in motion or at rest unless it had been determined to motion or rest by another body, and this again, by the same reasoning, must have been determined by a third, and so on *ad infinitum*.   Q.E.D.

Corol. Hence it follows that a body in motion will continue in motion until it be determined to a state of rest by another body, and that a body at rest will continue at rest until it be determined to a state of motion by another body. This indeed is self-evident. For if I suppose that a body, A, for example, is at rest, if I pay no regard to other bodies in motion, I can say nothing about the body A except that it is at rest. If it should afterwards happen that the body A should move, its motion could not certainly be a result of its former rest, for from its rest nothing could follow than that the body A should remain at rest. If, on the other hand, A be supposed to be in motion, so long as we regard A alone, the only thing we can affirm about it is that it moves. If it should afterwards happen that A should be at rest, the rest could not certainly be a result of the former motion, for from its motion nothing could follow but that A should move; the rest must therefore be a result of something which was not in A, that is to say, of an external cause by which it was determined to rest.

• Axiom 1.　All the modes by which one body is affected by another follow from the nature of the body affected, and at the same time from the nature of the affecting body, so that one and the same body may be moved in different ways according to the diversity of the nature of the moving bodies, and, on the other hand, different bodies may be moved in different ways by one and the same body.

Axiom 2.　When a body in motion strikes against another which is at rest and immovable, it is reflected, in order that it may continue its motion, and the angle of the line of reflected motion with the plane of the body at rest against which it struck will be equal to the angle which the line of the motion of incidence makes with the same plane.

Thus much for simplest bodies which are distinguished from one another by motion and rest, speed and slowness alone; let us now advance to composite bodies.

Def.　When a number of bodies of the same or of different magnitudes are pressed together by others, so that they lie one upon the other, or if they are in motion with the same or with different degrees of speed, so that they communicate their motion to one another in a certain fixed proportion, these bodies are said to be mutually united, and taken altogether they are said to compose one body or individual, which is distinguished from other bodies by this union of bodies.

Axiom 3.　Whether it is easy or difficult to force the parts composing an individual to change their situation, and consequently whether it is easy or difficult for the individual to change its shape, depends upon whether the parts of the individual or of the compound body lie with less, or whether they lie with greater surfaces upon one another. Hence bodies whose parts lie upon each other with greater surfaces I will call hard; those soft, whose parts lie on one another with smaller surfaces; and those fluid, whose parts move amongst each other.

Lemma 4.　*If a certain number of bodies be separated from the body or individual which is composed of a number of bodies, and if their place be supplied by the same number of other bodies of the same nature, the individual will retain the nature which it had before without any change of form.*

Demonst.　Bodies are not distinguished in respect of substance (Lem. 1); but that which makes the form of an individual is the union of bodies (by the preceding definition). This form, however (by hypothesis), is retained, although there may be a continuous change of the bodies. The individual, therefore, will retain its nature, with regard both to substance and to mode, as before.

Lemma 5.　*If the parts composing an individual become greater or less proportionately, so that they preserve towards one another the same kind of motion and rest, the individual will also retain the nature which it had before without any change of form.*

Demonst.　The demonstration is of the same kind as that immediately preceding.

Lemma 6.　*If any number of bodies composing an individual are compelled to divert into one direction the motion they previously had in another, but are nevertheless able to continue and reciprocally communicate their motions in the same manner as before, the individual will then retain its nature without any change of form.*

Demonst.　This is self-evident, for the individual is supposed to retain everything which, according to the definition, constitutes its form.

Lemma 7.　*The individual thus composed will, moreover, retain its nature whether it move as a whole or be at rest, or whether it move in this or that direction, provided that each part retain its own motion and communicate it as before to the rest.*

Demonst. The proof is evident from the definition preceding Lemma 4.

Schol. We thus see in what manner a composite individual can be affected in many ways and yet retain its nature. Up to this point we have conceived an individual to be composed merely of bodies which are distinguished from one another solely by motion and rest, speed and slowness, that is to say, to be composed of the most simple bodies. If we now consider an individual of another kind, composed of many individuals of diverse natures, we shall discover that it may be affected in many other ways, its nature nevertheless being preserved. For since each of its parts is composed of a number of bodies, each part (by the preceding Lemma), without any change of its nature, can move more slowly or more quickly, and consequently can communicate its motion more quickly or more slowly to the rest. If we now imagine a third kind of individual composed of those of the second kind, we shall discover that it can be affected in many other ways without any change of form. Thus, if we advance *ad infinitum,* we may easily conceive the whole of nature to be one individual, whose parts, that is to say, all bodies, differ in infinite ways without any change of the whole individual. If it had been my object to consider specially the question of a body, I should have had to explain and demonstrate these things more fully. But, as I have already said, I have another end in view, and I have noticed them only because I can easily deduce from them those things which I have proposed to demonstrate.

Postulate 1. The human body is composed of a number of individuals of diverse nature, each of which is composite to a high degree.

Postulate 2. Of the individuals of which the human body is composed, some are fluid, some soft, and some hard.

Postulate 3. The individuals composing the human body, and consequently the human body itself, are affected by external bodies in many ways.

Postulate 4. The human body needs for its preservation many other bodies by which it is, as it were, continually regenerated.

Postulate 5. When a fluid part of the human body is determined by an external body, so that it often strikes upon another which is soft, the fluid part changes the plane of the soft part, and leaves upon it, as it were, some traces of the impelling external body.

Postulate 6. The human body can move and arrange external bodies in many ways.

PROP. 14. *The human mind is adapted to the perception of many things, and its aptitude increases in proportion to the number of ways in which its body can be disposed.*

Demonst. The human body is affected (Post. 3 and 6) in many ways by external bodies, and is so disposed as to affect external bodies in many ways. But the human mind must perceive (Prop. 12, pt. 2) everything which happens in the human body. The human mind is therefore adapted, &c. Q.E.D.

PROP. 15. *The idea which constitutes the formal Being of the human mind is not simple, but is composed of a number of ideas.*

Demonst. The idea which constitutes the formal Being of the human mind is the idea of a body (Prop. 13, pt. 2) which (Post. 1) is composed of a number of individuals composite to a high degree. But an idea of each individual composing the body must necessarily exist in God (Corol. Prop. 8, pt. 2); therefore (Prop. 7, pt. 2) the idea of the human body is composed of these several ideas of the component parts. Q.E.D.

PROP. 16. *The idea of every way in which the human body is affected by external bodies must involve the nature of the human body, and at the same time the nature of the external body.*

Demonst. All the ways in which any body is affected follow at the same time from the nature of the affected body, and from the nature of the affecting body (Ax. 1, following Corol. Lem. 3); therefore the idea of these affections (Ax. 4, pt. 1) necessarily involves the nature of each body, and therefore the idea of each way in which the human body is affected by an external body involves the nature of the human body and of the external body. Q.E.D.

Corol. 1. Hence it follows, in the first place, that the human mind perceives the nature of many bodies together with that of its own body.

Corol. 2. It follows, secondly, that the ideas we have of external bodies indicate the constitution of our own body rather than the nature of external bodies. This I have explained in the Appendix of the First Part by many examples.

PROP. 17. *If the human body be affected in a way which involves the nature of any external body, the human mind will contemplate that external body as actually existing or as present, until the human body be affected by an affect which excludes the existence or presence of the external body.*

Demonst. This is evident. For so long as the human body is thus affected, so long will the human mind (Prop. 12, pt. 2) contemplate this affection of the external body, that is to say (Prop. 16, pt. 2), it will have an idea of a mode actually existing which involves the nature of the external body, that is to say, an idea which does not exclude the existence or presence of the nature of the external body, but posits it; and therefore the mind (Corol. 1, Prop. 16, pt. 2) will contemplate the external body as actually existing, &c. Q.E.D.

Corol. The mind is able to contemplate external things by which the human body was once affected as if they were present, although they are not present and do not exist.

Demonst. When external bodies so determine the fluid parts of the human body that they often strike upon the softer parts, the fluid parts change the plane of the soft parts (Post. 5); and thence it happens that the fluid parts are reflected from the new planes in a direction different from that in which they used to be reflected (Ax. 2, following Corol. Lem. 3), and that also afterwards when they strike against these new planes by their own spontaneous motion, they are reflected in the same way as when they were impelled towards those planes by external bodies. Consequently those fluid bodies produce an affection in the human body while they keep up this reflex motion similar to that produced by the presence of an external body. The mind, therefore (Prop. 12, pt. 2), will think as before, that is to say, it will again contemplate the external body as present (Prop. 17, pt. 2). This will happen as often as the fluid parts of the human body strike against those planes by their own spontaneous motion. Therefore, although the external bodies by which the human body was once affected do not exist the mind will perceive them as if they were present so often as this action is repeated in the body.

Schol. We see, therefore, how it is possible for us to contemplate things which do not exist as if they were actually present. This may indeed be produced by other causes, but I am satisfied with having here shown one cause through which I could explain it, just as if I had explained it through the true cause. I do not think however, that I am far from the

truth, since no postulate which I have assumed contains anything which is not confirmed by an experience that we cannot mistrust after we have proved the existence of the human body as we perceive it (Corol. following Prop. 13, pt. 2). Moreover (Corol. Prop. 17, pt. 2, and Corol. 2, Prop. 16, pt. 2), we clearly see what is the difference between the idea, for example, of Peter, which constitutes the essence of the mind itself of Peter, and the idea of Peter himself which is in another man; for example, in Paul. For the former directly manifests the essence of the body of Peter himself, nor does it involve existence unless so long as Peter exists; the latter, on the other hand, indicates rather the constitution of the body of Paul than the nature of Peter; and therefore so long as Paul's body exists with that constitution, so long will Paul's mind contemplate Peter as present, although he does not exist. But in order that we may retain the customary phraseology, we will give to those affections of the human body, the ideas of which represent to us external bodies as if they were present, the name of *images of things*, although they do not actually reproduce the forms of the things. When the mind contemplates bodies in this way, we will say that it imagines. Here I wish it to be observed, in order that I may begin to show what *error* is, that these imaginations of the mind, regarded by themselves, contain no error, and that the mind is not in error because it imagines, but only in so far as it is considered as wanting in an idea which excludes the existence of those things which it imagines as present. For if the mind, when it imagines non-existent things to be present, could at the same time know that those things did not really exist, it would think its power of imagination to be a virtue of its nature and not a defect, especially if this faculty of imagining depended upon its own nature alone, that is to say (Def. 7, pt. 1), if this faculty of the mind were free.

PROP. 18. *If the human body has at any time been simultaneously affected by two or more bodies, whenever the mind afterwards imagines one of them, it will also remember the others.*

Demonst. The mind imagines a body (Corol. Prop. 17, pt. 2) because the human body is affected and disposed by the impressions of an external body, just as it was affected when certain of its parts received an impulse from the external body itself. But by hypothesis, the body was at that time disposed in such a manner that the mind imagined two bodies at once; therefore it will imagine two at once now, and whenever it imagines one, it will immediately recollect the other.　Q.E.D.

Schol. We clearly understand by this what memory is. It is nothing else than a certain concatenation of ideas, involving the nature of things which are outside the human body, a concatenation which corresponds in the mind to the order and concatenation of the affections of the human body. I say, firstly, that it is a concatenation of those ideas only which involve the nature of things which are outside the human body, and not of those ideas which explain the nature of those things, for there are in truth (Prop. 16, pt. 2) ideas of the affections of the human body, which involve its nature as well as the nature of external bodies. I say, in the second place, that this concatenation takes place according to the order and concatenation of the affections of the human body, that I may distinguish it from the concatenation of ideas which takes place according to the order of the intellect, and enables the mind to perceive things through their first causes, and is the same in all men. Hence we can clearly understand how it is that the mind from the thought of one thing at once turns to the thought of another thing which is not in any way like the first. For example, from the thought of the word *pomum* a Roman immediately turned to the thought of the fruit, which has no resemblance to the articulate sound *pomum*, nor anything in common with it, excepting this, that the body of that man was often affected by the thing and the sound; that is to say, he often heard the word *pomum* when he saw the fruit. In this manner each person will turn from one thought to another according to the manner in which the habit of each has arranged the images of things in the body. The soldier, for instance, if he sees the footsteps of a horse in the sand, will immediately turn from the thought of a horse to the thought of a horseman, and so to the thought of war. The countryman, on the other hand, from the thought of a horse will turn to the thought of his plough, his field, &c.; and thus each person will turn from one thought to this or that thought, according to the manner in which he has been accustomed to connect and bind together the images of things in his mind.

PROP. 19.　*The human mind does not know the human body itself, nor does it know that the body*

exists, *except through ideas of affections by which the body is affected.*

Demonst. The human mind is the idea itself or the knowledge of the human body (Prop. 13, pt. 2). This knowledge (Prop. 9, pt. 2) is in God in so far as He is considered as affected by another idea of an individual thing. But because (Post. 4) the human body needs a number of bodies by which it is, as it were, continually regenerated, and because the order and connection of ideas is the same as the order and connection of causes (Prop. 7, pt. 2), this idea will be in God in so far as He is considered as affected by the ideas of a multitude of individual things.

God, therefore, has the idea of the human body or knows the human body in so far as He is affected by a multitude of other ideas, and not in so far as He forms the nature of the human mind; that is to say (Corol. 11, pt. 2), the human mind does not know the human body. But the ideas of the affections of the body are in God in so far as He forms the nature of the human mind; that is to say (Prop. 12, pt. 2), the human mind perceives these affections, and consequently (Prop. 16, pt. 2) the human body itself actually existing (Prop. 17, pt. 2). The human mind, therefore, perceives the human body, &c.　Q.E.D.

PROP. 20.　*There exists in God the idea or knowledge of the human mind, which follows in Him, and is related to Him in the same way as the idea or knowledge of the human body.*

Demonst. Thought is an attribute of God (Prop. 1, pt. 2), and therefore there must necessarily exist in God an idea of Himself (Prop. 3, pt. 2), together with an idea of all His affections, and consequently (Prop. 11, pt. 2) an idea of the human mind. Moreover, this idea or knowledge of the mind does not exist in God in so far as He is infinite, but in so far as He is affected by another idea of an individual thing (Prop. 9, pt. 2). But the order and connection of ideas is the same as the order and connection of causes (Prop. 7, pt. 2). This idea or knowledge of the mind, therefore, follows in God, and is related to God in the same manner as the idea or knowledge of the body.　Q.E.D.

PROP. 21.　*This idea of the mind is united to the mind in the same way as the mind itself is united to the body.*

Demonst. We have shown that the mind is united to the body because the body is the object of the mind (Props. 12 and 13, pt. 2), therefore, by the same reasoning, the idea of the mind must be united with its object, the mind itself, in the same way as the mind itself is united to the body.   Q.E.D.

Schol. This proposition is to be understood much more clearly from what has been said in the scholium to Prop. 7, pt. 2, for we have here shown that the idea of the body and the body, that is to say (Prop. 13, pt. 2), the mind and the body, are one and the same individual, which at one time is considered under the attribute of thought, and at another under that of extension: the idea of the mind, therefore, and the mind itself are one and the same thing, which is considered under one and the same attribute, that of thought. It follows, I say, that the idea of the mind and the mind itself exist in God from the same necessity and from the same power of thought. For, indeed, the idea of the mind, that is to say, the idea of the idea, is nothing but the form of the idea in so far as this is considered as a mode of thought and without relation to the object, just as a person who knows anything, by that very fact knows that he knows, and knows that he knows that he knows, and so *ad infinitum*. But more on this subject afterwards.

PROP. 22. *The human mind not only perceives the affections of the body, but also the ideas of these affections.*

Demonst. The ideas of the ideas of affections follow in God and are related to God in the same way as the ideas themselves of affections. This is demonstrated like Prop. 20, pt. 2. But the ideas of the affections of the body are in the human mind (Prop. 12, pt. 2), that is to say, in God (Corol. Prop. 11, pt. 2), in so far as He constitutes the essence of the human mind; therefore, the ideas of these ideas will be in God in so far as He has the knowledge or idea of the human mind; that is to say (Prop. 21, pt. 2), they will be in the human mind itself, which, therefore, not only perceives the affections of the body, but also the ideas of these affections.   Q.E.D.

PROP. 23. *The mind does not know itself except in so far as it perceives the ideas of the affections of the body.*

Demonst. The idea or knowledge of the mind (Prop. 20, pt. 2) follows in God and is related to God in the same way as the idea or knowledge of the body. But since (Prop. 19, pt. 2) the human mind does not know the human body itself, that is to say (Corol. Prop.

11, pt. 2), since the knowledge of the human body is not related to God in so far as He constitutes the nature of the human mind, therefore the knowledge of the mind is not related to God in so far as He constitutes the essence of the human mind; and therefore (Corol. Prop. 11, pt. 2) the human mind so far does not know itself. Moreover, the ideas of the affections by which the body is affected involve the nature of the human body itself (Prop. 16, pt. 2), that is to say (Prop. 13, pt. 2), they agree with the nature of the mind; therefore a knowledge of these ideas will necessarily involve a knowledge of the mind. But (Prop. 22, pt. 2) the knowledge of these ideas is in the human mind itself, and therefore the human mind so far only has a knowledge of itself.   Q.E.D.

PROP. 24. *The human mind does not involve an adequate knowledge of the parts composing the human body.*

Demonst. The parts composing the human body pertain to the essence of the body itself only in so far as they communicate their motions to one another by some certain method (see Def. following Corol. Lem. 3), and not in so far as they can be considered as individuals without relation to the human body. For the parts of the human body are individuals (Post. 1), composite to a high degree, parts of which (Lem. 4) can be separated from the human body and communicate their motions (Ax. 1, following Lem. 3) to other bodies in another way, although the nature and form of the human body itself is closely preserved. Therefore (Prop. 3, pt. 2) the idea or knowledge of each part will be in God in so far as He is considered as affected (Prop. 9, pt. 2) by another idea of an individual thing, which individual thing is prior to the part itself in the order of nature (Prop. 7, pt. 2). The same thing may be said of each part of the individual itself composing the human body, and therefore the knowledge of each part composing the human body exists in God in so far as He is affected by a number of ideas of things, and not in so far as He has the idea of the human body only; that is to say (Prop. 13, pt. 2), the idea which constitutes the nature of the human mind; and therefore (Corol. Prop. 11, pt. 2) the human mind does not involve an adequate knowledge of the parts composing the human body.   Q.E.D.

PROP. 25. *The idea of each affection of the human body does not involve an adequate knowledge of an external body.*

Demonst. We have shown that the idea of an affection of the human body involves the nature of an external body so far as (Prop. 16, pt. 2) the external body determines the human body in some certain manner. But in so far as the external body is an individual which is not related to the human body, its idea or knowledge is in God (Prop. 9, pt. 2) in so far as He is considered as affected by the idea of another thing, which idea (Prop. 7, pt. 2) is prior by nature to the external body itself. Therefore the adequate knowledge of an external body is not in God in so far as He has the idea of the affection of the human body, or, in other words, the idea of the affection of the human body does not involve an adequate knowledge of an external body. Q.E.D.

PROP. 26. *The human mind perceives no external body as actually existing, unless through the ideas of the affections of its body.*

Demonst. If the human body is in no way affected by any external body, then (Prop. 7, pt. 2) the idea of the human body, that is to say (Prop. 13, pt. 2), the human mind, is not affected in any way by the idea of the existence of that body, nor does it in any way perceive the existence of that external body. But in so far as the human body is affected in any way by any external body, so far (Prop. 16, pt. 2, with its Corol.) does it perceive the external body. Q.E.D.

Corol. In so far as the human mind imagines an external body, so far it has not an adequate knowledge of it.

Demonst. When the human mind through the ideas of the affections of its body contemplates external bodies, we say that it then imagines (Schol. Prop. 17, pt. 2), nor can the mind (Prop. 26, pt. 2) in any other way imagine external bodies as actually existing. Therefore (Prop. 25, pt. 2) in so far as the mind imagines external bodies it does not possess an adequate knowledge of them. Q.E.D.

PROP. 27. *The idea of any affection of the human body does not involve an adequate knowledge of the human body itself.*

Demonst. Every idea of any affection of the human body involves the nature of the human body in so far as the human body itself is considered as affected in a certain manner (Prop. 16, pt. 2). But in so far as the human body is an individual which can be affected in a multitude of other ways, its idea, &c. (See Demonst. Prop. 25, pt. 2.)

PROP. 28. *The ideas of the affections of the human body, in so far as they are related only to the human mind, are not clear and distinct, but confused.*

Demonst. The ideas of the affections of the human body involve the nature both of external bodies and of the human body itself (Prop. 16, pt. 2), and must involve the nature not only of the human body, but of its parts, for the affections are ways (Post. 3) in which the parts of the human body, and consequently the whole body, is affected. But (Props. 24 and 25, pt. 2) an adequate knowledge of external bodies and of the parts composing the human body does not exist in God in so far as He is considered as affected by the human mind, but in so far as He is affected by other ideas. These ideas of affections, therefore, in so far as they are related to the human mind alone, are like conclusions without premises, that is to say, as is self-evident, they are confused ideas. Q.E.D.

Schol. The idea which forms the nature of the mind is demonstrated in the same way not to be clear and distinct when considered in itself. So also with the idea of the human mind, and the ideas of the ideas of the affections of the human body, in so far as they are related to the mind alone, as every one may easily see.

PROP. 29. *The idea of the idea of any affection of the human body does not involve an adequate knowledge of the human mind.*

Demonst. The idea of an affection of the human body (Prop. 27, pt. 2) does not involve an adequate knowledge of the body itself, or, in other words, does not adequately express its nature, that is to say (Prop. 13, pt. 2), it does not correspond adequately with the nature of the human mind, and therefore (Ax. 6, pt. 1) the idea of this idea does not adequately express the nature of the human mind, nor involve an adequate knowledge of it. Q.E.D.

Corol. From this it is evident that the human mind, when it perceives things in the common order of nature, has no adequate knowledge of itself nor of its own body, nor of external bodies, but only a confused and mutilated knowledge; for the mind does not know itself unless in so far as it perceives the ideas of the affections of the body (Prop. 23, pt. 2). Moreover (Prop. 19, pt. 2), it does not perceive its body unless through those same ideas of the affections by means of which alone (Prop. 26, pt. 2) it perceives external bodies. Therefore in so far as it possesses these ideas it possesses an adequate knowledge neither of itself (Prop. 29, pt. 2), nor of its body (Prop. 27, pt. 2), nor of external bodies (Prop. 25, pt. 2), but merely (Prop. 28, pt. 2, together with the scholium) a mutilated and confused knowledge. Q.E.D.

Schol. I say expressly that the mind has no adequate knowledge of itself, nor of its body, nor of external bodies, but only a confused knowledge, as often as it perceives things in the common order of nature, that is to say, as often as it is determined to the contemplation of this or that *externally*—namely, by a chance coincidence, and not as often as it is determined *internally*—for the reason that it contemplates[1] several things at once, and is determined to understand in what they differ, agree, or oppose one another; for whenever it is internally disposed in this or in any other way, it then contemplates things clearly and distinctly, as I shall show presently.

PROP. 30. *About the duration of our body we can have but a very inadequate knowledge.*

Demonst. The duration of our body does not depend upon its essence (Ax. 1, pt. 2), nor upon the absolute nature of God (Prop. 21, pt. 1), but (Prop. 28, pt. 1) the body is determined to existence and action by causes which also are determined by others to existence and action in a certain and determinate manner, whilst these, again, are determined by others, and so on *ad infinitum*. The duration, therefore, of our body depends upon the common order of nature and the constitution of things. But an adequate knowledge of the way in which things are constituted, exists in God in so far as He possesses the ideas of all things, and not in so far as He possesses only the idea of the human body (Corol. Prop. 9, pt. 2). Therefore the knowledge of the duration of our body is altogether inadequate in God, in so far as He is only considered as constituting the nature of the human mind, that is to say (Corol. Prop. 11, pt. 2), this knowledge in our mind is altogether inadequate. Q.E.D.

PROP. 31. *About the duration of individual things which are outside us we can have but a very inadequate knowledge.*

Demonst. Each individual thing, like the human body, must be determined to existence and action by another individual thing in a certain and determinate manner, and this again by another, and so on *ad infinitum* (Prop.

[1] In this latter case.—TR.

28, pt. 1). But we have demonstrated in the preceding proposition, from this common property of individual things, that we have but a very inadequate knowledge of the duration of our own body; therefore the same conclusion is to be drawn about the duration of individual things, that is to say, that we can have but a very inadequate knowledge of it. Q.E.D.

Corol. Hence it follows that all individual things are contingent and corruptible, for we can have no adequate knowledge concerning their duration (Prop. 31, pt. 2), and this is what is to be understood by us as their contingency and capability of corruption (Schol. 1, Prop. 33, pt. 1); for (Prop. 29, pt. 1) there is no other contingency but this.

PROP. 32. *All ideas, in so far as they are related to God, are true.*

Demonst. All the ideas which are in God always agree with those things of which they are the ideas (Corol. Prop. 7, pt. 2), and therefore (Ax. 6, pt. 1) they are all true. Q.E.D.

PROP. 33. *In ideas there is nothing positive on account of which they are called false.*

Demonst. If the contrary be asserted, conceive, if it be possible, a positive mode of thought which shall constitute the form or error of falsity. This mode of thought cannot be in God (Prop. 32, pt. 2), but outside God it can neither be nor be conceived (Prop. 15, pt. 1), and therefore in ideas there is nothing positive on account of which they are called false. Q.E.D.

PROP. 34. *Every idea which in us is absolute, that is to say, adequate and perfect, is true.*

Demonst. When we say that an adequate and perfect idea is in us, we say nothing else than (Corol. Prop. 11, pt. 2) that an adequate and perfect idea exists in God in so far as He constitutes the essence of the human mind, and consequently (Prop. 32, pt. 2) we say nothing else than that this idea is true. Q.E.D.

PROP. 35. *Falsity consists in the privation of knowledge, which inadequate, that is to say, mutilated and confused ideas involve.*

Demonst. There is nothing positive in ideas which can constitute a form of falsity (Prop. 33, pt. 2). But falsity cannot consist in absolute privation (for we say that minds and not bodies err and are mistaken); nor can it consist in absolute ignorance, for to be ignorant and to be in error are different. Falsehood, therefore, consists in the privation of knowledge which is involved by inadequate knowledge of things or by inadequate and confused ideas. Q.E.D.

Schol. In the scholium of Prop. 17, pt. 2, I have explained how error consists in the privation of knowledge; but for the sake of fuller explanation, I will give an example. For instance, men are deceived because they think themselves free, and the sole reason for thinking so is that they are conscious of their own actions, and ignorant of the causes by which those actions are determined. Their idea of liberty therefore is this—that they know no cause for their own actions; for as to saying that their actions depend upon their will, these are words to which no idea is attached. What the will is, and in what manner it moves the body, every one is ignorant, for those who pretend otherwise, and devise seats and dwelling-places of the soul, usually excite our laughter or disgust. Just in the same manner, when we look at the sun, we imagine his distance from us to be about 200 feet; the error not consisting solely in the imagination, but arising from our not knowing what the true distance is when we imagine, and what the causes of our imagination. For although we may afterwards know that the sun is more than 600 diameters of the earth distant from us, we still imagine it near us, since we imagine it to be so near, not because we are ignorant of its true distance, but because an affection of our body involves the essence of the sun, in so far as our body itself is affected by it.

PROP. 36. *Inadequate and confused ideas follow by the same necessity as adequate or clear and distinct ideas.*

Demonst. All ideas are in God (Prop. 15, pt. 1), and in so far as they are related to God are true (Prop. 32, pt. 2) and (Corol. Prop. 7, pt. 2) adequate. No ideas, therefore, are inadequate or confused unless in so far as they are related to the individual mind of some person (see Props. 24 and 28, pt. 2). All ideas, therefore, both adequate and inadequate, follow by the same necessity (Corol. Prop. 6, pt. 2).

PROP. 37. *That which is common to everything (see Lemma 2), and which is equally in the part and in the whole, forms the essence of no individual thing.*

Demonst. For if this be denied, let that which is common be conceived, if possible, to constitute the essence of some individual thing, —the essence, for example, of B. Without B, therefore (Def. 2, pt. 2), that which is common can neither be nor be conceived. But this is contrary to the hypothesis. Therefore that which is common does not pertain to the essence of B, nor does it form the essence of any other individual thing.

PROP. 38. *Those things which are common to everything, and which are equally in the part and in the whole, can only be adequately conceived.*

Demonst. Let there be something A, which is common to all bodies, and which is equally in the part of each body and in the whole. I say that A can only be adequately conceived. For the idea of A (Corol. Prop. 7, pt. 2) will necessarily be adequate in God, both in so far as He has the idea of the human body and in so far as He has the idea of its affections, which (Props. 16, 25, and 27, pt. 2) involve the nature of the human body, and partly also the nature of external bodies; that is to say (Props. 12 and 13, pt. 2), this idea will necessarily be adequate in God in so far as He constitutes the human mind, or in so far as He has ideas which are in the human mind. The mind, therefore (Corol. Prop. 11, pt. 2), necessarily perceives A adequately, both in so far as it perceives itself or its own or any external body; nor can A be conceived in any other manner. Q.E.D.

Corol. Hence it follows that some ideas or notions exist which are common to all men, for (Lem. 2) all bodies agree in some things, which (Prop. 38, pt. 2) must be adequately, that is to say, clearly and distinctly, perceived by all.

PROP. 39. *There will exist in the human mind an adequate idea of that which is common and proper to the human body, and to any external bodies by which the human body is generally affected—of that which equally in the part of each of these external bodies and in the whole is common and proper.*

Demonst. Let A be something which is common and proper to the human body and certain external bodies; let it exist equally in the human body and in those external bodies, and let it exist equally in the part of each external body and in the whole. An adequate idea of A itself will exist in God (Corol. Prop. 7, pt. 2), both in so far as He has the idea of the human body and in so far as He has the idea of the given external bodies. Let it be supposed that the human body is affected by an external body through that which it has in common with the external body, that is to say, by A. The idea of this affection will involve the property of A (Prop. 16, pt. 2), and therefore (Corol. Prop. 7, pt. 2) the idea of this affection, in so far as it involves the property of A, will exist adequately in God in so far as He is affected by the idea of the human body, that is to say (Prop. 13, pt. 2), in so far as He constitutes the nature of the human mind. Therefore (Corol. Prop. 11, pt. 2) this idea is also adequate in the human mind. Q.E.D.

Corol. Hence it follows that the more things the body has in common with other bodies, the more things will the mind be adapted to perceive.

PROP. 40. *Those ideas are also adequate which follow in the mind from ideas which are adequate in it.*

Demonst. This is evident. For when we say that an idea follows in the human mind from ideas which are adequate in it, we do but say (Corol. Prop. 11, pt. 2) that in the divine intellect itself an idea exists of which God is the cause, not in so far as He is infinite, nor in so far as He is affected by the ideas of a multitude of individual things, but in so far only as He constitutes the essence of the human mind.

Schol. 1. I have thus explained the origin of those notions which are called common, and which are the foundations of our reasoning; but of some axioms or notions other causes exist which it would be advantageous to explain by our method, for we should thus be able to distinguish those notions which are more useful than others, and those which are scarcely of any use; those which are common; those which are clear and distinct only to those persons who do not suffer from prejudice; and, finally, those which are ill-founded. Moreover, it would be manifest whence these notions which are called *second*, and consequently the axioms founded upon them, have taken their origin, and other things, too, would be explained which I have thought about these matters at different times. Since, however, I have set apart this subject for another treatise, and because I do not wish to create disgust with excessive prolixity, I have determined to pass by this matter here. But not to omit anything which is necessary for us to know, I will briefly give the causes from which terms called *Transcendental*, such as *Being, Thing, Something*, have taken their origin. These terms have arisen because the human body, inasmuch as it is limited, can form distinctly in

itself a certain number only of images at once. (For the explanation of the word *image*, see Schol. Prop. 17, pt. 2.) If this number be exceeded, the images will become confused; and if the number of images which the body is able to form distinctly be greatly exceeded, they will all run one into another. Since this is so, it is clear (Corol. Prop. 17, and Prop. 18, pt. 2) that in proportion to the number of images which can be formed at the same time in the body will be the number of bodies which the human mind can imagine at the same time. If the images in the body, therefore, are all confused, the mind will confusedly imagine all the bodies without distinguishing the one from the other, and will include them all, as it were, under one attribute, that of being or thing. The same confusion may also be caused by lack of uniform force in the images and from other analogous causes, which there is no need to discuss here, the consideration of one cause being sufficient for the purpose we have in view. For it all comes to this, that these terms signify ideas in the highest degree confused. It is in this way that those notions have arisen which are called *Universal*, such as, *Man, Horse, Dog*, &c.; that is to say, so many images of men, for instance, are formed in the human body at once, that they exceed the power of the imagination, not entirely, but to such a degree that the mind has no power to imagine the determinate number of men and the small differences of each, such as colour and size, &c. It will therefore distinctly imagine that only in which all of them agree in so far as the body is affected by them, for by that the body was chiefly affected, that is to say, by each individual, and this it will express by the name *man*, covering thereby an infinite number of individuals; to imagine a determinate number of individuals being out of its power. But we must observe that these notions are not formed by all persons in the same way, but that they vary in each case according to the thing by which the body is more frequently affected, and which the mind more easily imagines or recollects. For example, those who have more frequently looked with admiration upon the stature of men, by the name *man* will understand an animal of erect stature, while those who have been in the habit of fixing their thoughts on something else, will form another common image of men, describing man, for instance, as an animal capable of laughter, a biped without feathers, a rational animal, and so on; each person forming universal images of things according to the temperament of his own body. It is not therefore to be wondered at that so many controversies have arisen amongst those philosophers who have endeavoured to explain natural objects by the images of things alone.

Schol. 2.   From what has been already said, it clearly appears that we perceive many things and form universal ideas:

1. From individual things, represented by the senses to us in a mutilated and confused manner, and without order to the intellect (Corol. Prop. 29, pt. 2). These perceptions I have therefore been in the habit of calling knowledge from vague experience.

2. From signs; as, for example, when we hear or read certain words, we recollect things and form certain ideas of them similar to them, through which ideas we imagine things (Schol. Prop. 18, pt. 2). These two ways of looking at things I shall hereafter call knowledge of the first kind, opinion or imagination.

3. From our possessing common notions and adequate ideas of the properties of things (Corol. Prop. 38, Prop. 39, with Corol. and Prop. 40, pt. 2). This I shall call reason and knowledge of the second kind.

Besides these two kinds of knowledge, there is a third, as I shall hereafter show, which we shall call intuitive science. This kind of knowing advances from an adequate idea of the formal essence of certain attributes of God to the adequate knowledge of the essence of things. All this I will explain by one example. Let there be three numbers given through which it is required to discover a fourth which shall be to the third as the second is to the first. A merchant does not hesitate to multiply the second and third together and divide the product by the first, either because he has not yet forgotten the things which he heard without any demonstration from his schoolmaster, or because he has seen the truth of the rule with the more simple numbers, or because from the 19th Prop. in the 7th book of Euclid he understands the common property of all proportionals.

But with the simplest numbers there is no need of all this. If the numbers 1, 2, 3, for instance, be given, every one can see that the fourth proportional is 6 much more clearly than by any demonstration, because from the ratio in which we see by one intuition that the first stands to the second we conclude the fourth.

PROP. 41.   *Knowledge of the first kind alone is the cause of falsity; knowledge of the second and third orders is necessarily true.*

Demonst.   To knowledge of the first kind we have said, in the preceding scholium, that all those ideas belong which are inadequate and confused, and, therefore (Prop. 35, pt. 2), this knowledge alone is the cause of falsity. Moreover, to knowledge of the second and third kind we have said that those ideas belong which are adequate, and therefore this knowledge (Prop. 34, pt. 2) is necessarily true.

PROP. 42.   *It is the knowledge of the second and third, and not that of the first kind, which teaches us to distinguish the true from the false.*

Demonst.   This proposition is self-evident. For he who knows how to distinguish between the true and the false must have an adequate idea of the true and the false, that is to say (Schol. 2, Prop. 40, pt. 2), he must know the true and the false by the second or third kind of knowledge.

PROP. 43.   *He who has a true idea knows at the same time that he has a true idea, nor can he doubt the truth of the thing.*

Demonst.   A true idea in us is that which in God is adequate, in so far as He is manifested by the nature of the human mind (Corol. Prop. 11, pt. 2). Let us suppose, therefore, that there exists in God, in so far as He is manifested by the nature of the human mind, an adequate idea, A. Of this idea there must necessarily exist in God an idea, which is related to Him in the same way as the idea A (Prop. 20, pt. 2, the demonstration of which is universal). But the idea A is supposed to be related to God in so far as He is manifested by the nature of the human mind. The idea of the idea A must therefore be related to God in the same manner, that is to say (Corol. Prop. 11, pt. 2), this adequate idea of the idea A will exist in the mind itself which has the adequate idea A. He therefore who has an adequate idea, that is to say (Prop. 34, pt. 2), he who knows a thing truly, must at the same time have an adequate idea or a true knowledge of his knowledge, that is to say (as is self-evident) he must be certain.   Q.E.D.

Schol.   In the scholium to Prop. 21, pt. 2, I have explained what is the idea of an idea, but it is to be observed that the preceding proposition is evident by itself. For no one who has a true idea is ignorant that a true idea involves the highest certitude; to have a true idea sig nifying just this, to know a thing perfectly or as well as possible. No one, in fact, can doubt this, unless he supposes an idea to be something dumb, like a picture on a tablet, instead of being a mode of thought, that is to say, intelligence itself. Moreover, I ask who can know that he understands a thing unless he first of all understands that thing? that is to say, who can know that he is certain of anything unless he is first of all certain of that thing? Then, again, what can be clearer or more certain than a true idea as the standard of truth? Just as light reveals both itself and the darkness, so truth is the standard of itself and of the false. I consider what has been said to be a sufficient answer to the objection that if a true idea is distinguished from a false idea only in so far as it is said to agree with that of which it is the idea, the true idea therefore has no reality nor perfection above the false idea (since they are distinguished by an external sign alone), and consequently the man who has true ideas will have no greater reality or perfection than he who has false ideas only. I consider, too, that I have already replied to those who inquire why men have false ideas, and how a man can certainly know that he has ideas which agree with those things of which they are the ideas. For with regard to the difference between a true and a false idea, it is evident from Prop. 35, pt. 2, that the former is related to the latter as being is to non-being. The causes of falsity, too, I have most clearly shown in Props. 19–35, including the scholium to the last. From what has there been said, the nature of the difference between a man who has true ideas and one who has only false ideas is clear. With regard to the last-mentioned point—how a man can know that he has an idea which agrees with that of which it is the idea—I have shown almost more times than enough that he knows it simply because he has an idea which agrees with that of which it is the idea, that is to say, because truth is its own standard. We must remember, besides, that our mind, in so far as it truly perceives things, is a part of the infinite intellect of God (Corol. Prop. 11, pt. 2), and therefore it must be that the clear and distinct ideas of the mind are as true as those of God.

Prop. 44. *It is not of the nature of reason to consider things as contingent but as necessary.*

Demonst. It is in the nature of reason to perceive things truly (Prop. 41, pt. 2), that is to say (Ax. 6, pt. 1), as they are in themselves, that is to say (Prop. 29, pt. 1), not as contingent but as necessary. Q.E.D.

Corol. 1. Hence it follows that it is through the imagination alone that we look upon things as contingent both with reference to the past and the future.

Schol. How this happens I will explain in a few words. We have shown above (Prop. 17, pt. 2, with Corol.) that unless causes occur preventing the present existence of things, the mind always imagines them present before it, even if they do not exist. Again (Prop. 18, pt. 2), we have shown that if the human body has once been simultaneously affected by two external bodies, whenever the mind afterwards imagines one it will immediately remember the other; that is to say, it will look upon both as present before it, unless causes occur which prevent the present existence of the things. No one doubts, too, that we imagine time because we imagine some bodies to move with a velocity less, or greater than, or equal to that of others. Let us therefore suppose a boy who yesterday, for the first time, in the morning saw Peter, at midday Paul, in the evening Simeon, and to-day in the morning again sees Peter. It is plain from Prop. 18, pt. 2, that as soon as he sees the morning light he will imagine the sun passing through the same part of the sky as on the day preceding; that is to say, he will imagine the whole day, and at the same time Peter will be connected in his imagination with the morning, Paul with midday, and Simeon with the evening. In the morning, therefore, the existence of Paul and Simeon will be imagined in relation to future time, while in the evening, if the boy should see Simeon, he will refer Peter and Paul to the past, since they will be connected with the past in his imagination. This process will be constant in proportion to the regularity with which he sees Peter, Paul, and Simeon in this order. If it should by some means happen that on some other evening, in the place of Simeon, he should see James, on the following morning he will connect in his imagination with the evening at one time Simeon and at another James, but not both together. For he is supposed to have seen one and then the other in the evening, but not both together. His imagination will therefore fluctuate, and he will connect with a future evening first one and then the other; that is to say, he will consider neither as certain, but both as a contingency in the future.

This fluctuation of the imagination will take

place in the same way if the imagination is dealing with things which we contemplate in the same way with reference to past or present time, and consequently we imagine things related to time past, present, or future as contingent.

Corol. 2. It is of the nature of reason to perceive things under a certain form of eternity.

Demonst. It is of the nature of reason to consider things as necessary and not as contingent (Prop. 44, pt. 2). This necessity of things it perceives truly (Prop. 41, pt. 2); that is to say (Ax. 6, pt. 1), as it is in itself. But (Prop. 16, pt. 1) this necessity of things is the necessity itself of the eternal nature of God. Therefore it is of the nature of reason to consider things under this form of eternity. Moreover, the foundations of reason are notions which explain those things which are common to all (Prop. 38, pt. 2), and these things explain the essence of no individual thing (Prop. 37, pt. 2), and must therefore be conceived without any relation to time, but under a certain form of eternity. Q.E.D.

PROP. 45. *Every idea of any body or actually existing individual thing necessarily involves the eternal and infinite essence of God.*

Demonst. The idea of an individual thing actually existing necessarily involves both the essence and existence of the thing itself (Corol. Prop. 8, pt. 2). But individual things (Prop. 15, pt. 1) cannot be conceived without God, and since (Prop. 6, pt. 2) God is their cause in so far as He is considered under that attribute of which they are modes, their ideas (Ax. 4, pt. 1) must necessarily involve the conception of that attribute, or, in other words (Def. 6, pt. 1), must involve the eternal and infinite essence of God. Q.E.D.

Schol. By existence is to be understood here not duration, that is, existence considered in the abstract, as if it were a certain kind of quantity, but I speak of the nature itself of the existence which is assigned to individual things, because from the eternal necessity of the nature of God infinite numbers of things follow in infinite ways (Prop. 16, pt. 1). I repeat, that I speak of the existence itself of individual things in so far as they are in God. For although each individual thing is determined by another individual thing to existence in a certain way, the force nevertheless by which each thing perseveres in its existence follows from the eternal necessity of the nature of God (see Corol. Prop. 24, pt. 1).

PROP. 46. *The knowledge of the eternal and infinite essence of God which each idea involves is adequate and perfect.*

Demonst. The demonstration of the preceding proposition is universal, and whether a thing be considered as a part or as a whole, its idea, whether it be of a part or whole, will involve the eternal and infinite essence of God (Prop. 45, pt. 2). Therefore that which gives a knowledge of the eternal and infinite essence of God is common to all, and is equally in the part and in the whole. This knowledge therefore (Prop. 38, pt. 2) will be adequate. Q.E.D.

PROP. 47. *The human mind possesses an adequate knowledge of the eternal and infinite essence of God.*

Demonst. The human mind possesses ideas (Prop. 22, pt. 2) by which (Prop. 23, pt. 2) it perceives itself and its own body (Prop. 19, pt. 2), together with (Corol. 1, Prop. 16, and Prop. 17, pt. 2) external bodies, as actually existing. Therefore (Props. 45 and 46, pt. 2) it possesses an adequate knowledge of the eternal and infinite essence of God. Q.E.D.

Schol. Hence we see that the infinite essence and the eternity of God are known to all; and since all things are in God and are conceived through Him, it follows that we can deduce from this knowledge many things which we can know adequately, and that we can thus form that third sort of knowledge mentioned in Schol. 2, Prop. 40, pt. 2, of whose excellence and value the Fifth Part will be the place to speak. The reason why we do not possess a knowledge of God as distinct as that which we have of common notions is, that we cannot imagine God as we can bodies; and because we have attached the name God to the images of things which we are in the habit of seeing, an error we can hardly avoid, inasmuch as we are continually affected by external bodies. Many errors, of a truth, consist merely in the application of the wrong names to things. For if a man says that the lines which are drawn from the centre of the circle to the circumference are not equal, he understands by the circle, at all events for the time, something else than mathematicians understand by it. So when men make errors in calculation, the numbers which are in their minds are not those which are upon the paper. As far as their mind is concerned there is no error, although it seems as if there were, because we think that the numbers in their minds are those which are upon the paper. If we did not think so, we hould not believe them to be in error. For example, when I lately heard a man complaining that his court had flown into one of his neighbour's fowls, I understood what he meant, and therefore did not imagine him to be in error. This is the source from which so many controversies arise—that men either do not properly explain their own thoughts, or do not properly interpret those of other people; for, in truth, when they most contradict one another, they either think the same things or something different, so that those things which they suppose to be errors and absurdities in another person are not so.

PROP. 48. *In the mind there is no absolute or free will, but the mind is determined to this or that volition by a cause, which is also determined by another cause, and this again by another, and so on* ad infinitum.

Demonst. The mind is a certain and determinate mode of thought (Prop. 11, pt. 2), and therefore (Corol. 2, Prop. 17, pt. 1) it cannot be the free cause of its own actions, or have an absolute faculty of willing or not willing, but must be determined to this or that volition (Prop. 28, pt. 1) by a cause which is also determined by another cause, and this again by another, and so on *ad infinitum.* Q.E.D.

Schol. In the same manner it is demonstrated that in the mind there exists no absolute faculty of understanding, desiring, loving, &c. These and the like faculties, therefore, are either altogether fictitious, or else are nothing but metaphysical or universal entities, which we are in the habit of forming from individual cases. The intellect and will, therefore, are related to this or that idea or volition as rockiness is related to this or that rock, or as man is related to Peter or Paul. The reason why men imagine themselves to be free we have explained in the Appendix to the First Part. Before, however, I advance any farther, I must observe that by the will I understand a faculty of affirming or denying, but not a desire; a faculty, I say, by which the mind affirms or denies that which is true or false, and not a desire by which the mind seeks a thing or turns away from it. But now that we have demonstrated that these faculties are universal notions which are not distinguishable from the individual notions from which they are formed, we must now inquire whether the volitions themselves are anything more than the ideas of things. We must inquire, I say, whether in the mind there exists any other affirmation or

negation than that which the idea involves in so far as it is an idea. For this purpose see the following proposition, together with Def. 3, pt. 2, so that thought may not fall into pictures. For by ideas I do not understand the images which are formed at the back of the eye, or, if you please, in the middle of the brain, but rather the conceptions of thought.

PROP. 49. *In the mind there is no volition or affirmation and negation excepting that which the idea, in so far as it is an idea, involves.*

Demonst. In the mind there exists (Prop. 48, pt. 2) no absolute faculty of willing or not willing. Only individual volitions exist, that is to say, this and that affirmation and this and that negation. Let us conceive therefore, any individual volition, that is, any mode of thought, by which the mind affirms that the three angles of a triangle are equal to two right angles. This affirmation involves the conception or idea of the triangle, that is to say, without it the affirmation cannot be conceived. For to say that A must involve the conception B, is the same as saying that A cannot be conceived without B. Moreover, without the idea of the triangle this affirmation (Ax. 3, pt. 2) cannot be, and it can therefore neither be nor be conceived without that idea. But this idea of the triangle must involve this same affirmation that its three angles are equal to two right angles. Therefore also, *vice versa*, this idea of the triangle without this affirmation can neither be nor be conceived. Therefore (Def. 2, pt. 2) this affirmation pertains to the essence of the idea of the triangle, nor is it anything else besides this. Whatever too we have said of this volition (since it has been taken arbitrarily) applies to all other volitions, that is to say, they are nothing but ideas. Q.E.D.

Corol. The will and the intellect are one and the same.

Demonst. The will and the intellect are nothing but the individual volitions and ideas themselves (Prop. 48, pt. 2, and its Schol.) But the individual volition and idea (Prop. 49, pt. 2) are one and the same. Therefore the will and the intellect are one and the same. Q.E.D.

Schol. I have thus removed what is commonly thought to be the cause of error. It has been proved above that falsity consists solely in the privation which mutilated and confused ideas involve. A false idea, therefore, in so far as it is false, does not involve certitude. Consequently, when we say that a man assents to what is false and does not doubt it, we do not say that he is certain, but merely that he does not doubt, that is to say, that he assents to what is false, because there are no causes sufficient to make his imagination waver (Schol. Prop. 44, pt. 2). Although, therefore, a man may be supposed to adhere to what is false, we shall never on that account say that he is certain. For by certitude we understand something positive (Prop. 43, pt. 2, with the Schol.), and not the privation of doubt; but by the privation of certitude we understand falsity. If the preceding proposition, however, is to be more clearly comprehended, a word or two must be added; it yet remains also that I should answer the objections which may be brought against our doctrine, and finally, in order to remove all scruples, I have thought it worth while to indicate some of its advantages. I say some, as the principal advantages will be better understood when we come to the Fifth Part. I begin, therefore, with the first, and I warn my readers carefully to distinguish between an idea or conception of the mind and the images of things formed by our imagination. Secondly, it is necessary that we should distinguish between ideas and the words by which things are signified. For it is because these three things, images, words, and ideas, are by many people either altogether confounded or not distinguished with sufficient accuracy and care that such ignorance exists about this doctrine of the will, so necessary to be known both for the purposes of speculation and for the wise government of life. Those who think that ideas consist of images, which are formed in us by meeting with external bodies, persuade themselves that those ideas of things of which we can form no similar image are not ideas, but mere fancies constructed by the free power of the will. They look upon ideas, therefore, as dumb pictures on a tablet, and being prepossessed with this prejudice, they do not see that an idea, in so far as it is an idea, involves affirmation or negation. Again, those who confound words with the idea, or with the affirmation itself which the idea involves, think that they can will contrary to their perception, because they affirm or deny something in words alone contrary to their perception. It will be easy for us, however, to divest ourselves of these prejudices if we attend to the nature of thought, which in no way involves the conception of extension, and by doing this we clearly see that an idea, since it is a mode of thought, is not an image of anything, nor does it consist of words. For the essence of

words and images is formed of bodily motion alone, which involve in no way whatever the conception of thought.

Let thus much suffice under this head. I pass on now to the objections to which I have already alluded.

The first is, that it is supposed to be certain that the will extends itself more widely than the intellect, and is therefore different from it. The reason why men suppose that the will extends itself more widely than the intellect is because they say they have discovered that they do not need a larger faculty of assent—that is to say, of affirmation—and denial than that which they now have for the purpose of assenting to an infinite number of other things which we do not perceive, but that they do need a greater faculty for understanding them. The will, therefore, is distinguished from the intellect, the latter being finite, the former infinite. The second objection which can be made is that there is nothing which experience seems to teach more clearly than the possibility of suspending our judgment, so as not to assent to the things we perceive; and we are strengthened in this opinion because no one is said to be deceived in so far as he perceives a thing, but only in so far as he assents to it or dissents from it. For example, a man who imagines a winged horse does not therefore admit the existence of a winged horse; that is to say, he is not necessarily deceived, unless he grants at the same time that a winged horse exists. Experience, therefore, seems to show nothing more plainly than that the will or faculty of assent is free, and different from the faculty of the intellect.

Thirdly, it may be objected that one affirmation does not seem to contain more reality than another; that is to say, it does not appear that we need a greater power for affirming a thing to be true which is true than for affirming a thing to be true which is false. Nevertheless, we observe that one idea contains more reality or perfection than another, for as some objects are nobler than others, in the same proportion are their ideas more perfect. It appears indisputable, therefore, that there is a difference between the will and the intellect.

Fourthly, it may be objected that if a man does not act from freedom of the will, what would he do if he were in a state of equilibrium, like the ass of Buridanus? Would he not perish from hunger and thirst? and if this is granted, do we not seem to conceive him as a statue of a man or as an ass? If I deny that he would thus perish, he will consequently determine himself and possess the power of going where he likes and doing what he likes.

There may be other objections besides these, but as I am not bound to discuss what every one may dream, I shall therefore make it my business to answer as briefly as possible those only which I have mentioned. In reply to the first objection, I grant that the will extends itself more widely than the intellect, if by the intellect we understand only clear and distinct ideas; but I deny that the will extends itself more widely than the perceptions or the faculty of conception; nor, indeed, do I see why the faculty of will should be said to be infinite any more than the faculty of feeling; for as by the same faculty of will we can affirm an infinite number of things (one after the other, for we cannot affirm an infinite number of things at once), so also by the same faculty of feeling we can feel or perceive (one after another) an infinite number of bodies. If it be said that there are an infinite number of things which we cannot perceive, I reply that such things as these we can reach by no thought, and consequently by no faculty of will. But it is said that if God wished us to perceive those things, it would be necessary for Him to give us a larger faculty of perception, but not a larger faculty of will than He has already given us, which is the same thing as saying that if God wished us to understand an infinite number of other beings, it would be necessary for Him to give us a greater intellect, but not a more universal idea of being (in order to embrace that infinite number of beings), than He has given us. For we have shown that the will is a Universal, or the idea by which we explain all individual volitions, that is to say, that which is common to them all. It is not to be wondered at, therefore, that those who believe this common or universal idea of all the volitions to be a faculty should say that it extends itself infinitely beyond the limits of the intellect. For the universal is predicated of one or of many, or of an infinite number of individuals.

The second objection I answer by denying that we have free power of suspending judgment. For when we say that a person suspends judgment, we only say in other words that he sees that he does not perceive the thing adequately. The suspension of the judgment, therefore, is in truth a perception and not free will. In order that this may be clearly understood, let us take the case of a boy who imagines a horse and perceives nothing else. Since this imagination involves the existence of the horse (Corol. Prop. 17, pt. 2), and the boy does not perceive anything which negates its existence, he will necessarily contemplate it as present, nor will he be able to doubt its existence although he may not be certain of it. This is a thing which we daily experience in dreams, nor do I believe that there is any one who thinks that he has the free power during dreams of suspending his judgment upon those things which he dreams, and of causing himself not to dream those things which he dreams that he sees; and yet in dreams it nevertheless happens that we suspend our judgment, for we dream that we dream.

I grant, it is true, that no man is deceived in so far as he perceives; that is to say, I grant that mental images considered in themselves involve no error (Schol. Prop. 17, pt. 2); but I deny that a man in so far as he perceives affirms nothing. For what else is it to perceive a winged horse than to affirm of the horse that it has wings? For if the mind perceived nothing else but this winged horse, it would regard it as present, nor would it have any reason for doubting its existence, nor any power of refusing assent to it, unless the image of the winged horse be joined to an idea which negates its existence, or the mind perceives that the idea of the winged horse which it has is inadequate. In either of the two latter cases it will necessarily deny or doubt the existence of the horse.

With regard to the third objection, what has been said will perhaps be a sufficient answer,— namely, that the will is something universal, which is predicated of all ideas, and that it signifies that only which is common to them all, that is to say, affirmation. Its adequate essence, therefore, in so far as it is thus considered in the abstract, must be in every idea, and in this sense only must it be the same in all; but not in so far as it is considered as constituting the essence of an idea, for so far, the individual affirmations differ just as the ideas differ. For example, the affirmation which the idea of a circle involves differs from that which the idea of a triangle involves, just as the idea of a circle differs from the idea of a triangle. Again, I absolutely deny that we need a power of thinking in order to affirm that to be true which is true, equal to that which we need in order to affirm that to be true which is false. For these two affirmations, if we look to the mind, are related to one another as being and non-being, for there is nothing positive in ideas which constitutes a form of falsity (Prop. 35, pt. 2, with its Schol., and Schol. to Prop. 47, pt. 2).

Here therefore particularly is it to be observed how easily we are deceived when we confuse universals with individuals, and the entities of reason and abstractions with realities.

With regard to the fourth objection, I say that I entirely grant that if a man were placed in such a state of equilibrium he would perish of hunger and thirst, supposing he perceived nothing but hunger and thirst, and the food and drink which were equidistant from him. If you ask me whether such a man would not be thought an ass rather than a man, I reply that I do not know; nor do I know what ought to be thought of a man who hangs himself, or of children, fools, and madmen.

It remains for me now to show what service to our own lives a knowledge of this doctrine is. This we shall easily understand from the remarks which follow.

Notice:

1. It is of service in so far as it teaches us that we do everything by the will of God alone, and that we are partakers of the divine nature in proportion as our actions become more and more perfect and we more and more understand God. This doctrine, therefore, besides giving repose in every way to the soul, has also this advantage, that it teaches us in what our highest happiness or blessedness consists, namely, in the knowledge of God alone, by which we are drawn to do those things only which love and piety persuade. Hence we clearly see how greatly those stray from the true estimation of virtue who expect to be distinguished by God with the highest regards for virtue and the noblest actions as if for the completest servitude, just as if virtue itself and the service of God were not happiness itself and the highest liberty.

2. It is of service to us in so far as it teaches us how we ought to behave with regard to the things of fortune, or those which are not in our power, that is to say, which do not follow from our own nature; for it teaches us with equal mind to wait for and bear each form of fortune, because we know that all things follow from the eternal decree of God, according to that same necessity by which it follows from the essence of a triangle that its three angles are equal to two right angles.

3. This doctrine contributes to the welfare of our social existence, since it teaches us to hate no one, to despise no one, to mock no one, to be angry with no one, and to envy no one. It teaches every one, moreover, to be content with his own, and to be helpful to his neighbour, not from any womanish pity, from partiality, or superstition, but by the guidance of reason alone, according to the demand of time and circumstance, as I shall show in the Third Part.

4. This doctrine contributes not a little to the advantage of common society, in so far as it teaches us by what means citizens are to be governed and led; not in order that they may be slaves, but that they may freely do those things which are best.

Thus I have discharged the obligation laid upon me in this scholium, and with it I make an end of the Second Part, in which I think that I have explained the nature of the human mind and its properties at sufficient length, and, considering the difficulties of the subject, with sufficient clearness. I think, too, that certain truths have been established, from which much that is noble, most useful, and necessary to be known can be deduced, as we shall partly see from what follows.

THIRD PART

ON THE ORIGIN AND NATURE OF THE AFFECTS

MOST persons who have written about the affects and man's conduct of life seem to discuss, not the natural things which follow the common laws of nature, but things which are outside her. They seem indeed to consider man in nature as a kingdom within a kingdom. For they believe that man disturbs rather than follows her order; that he has an absolute power over his own actions; and that he is altogether self-determined. They then proceed to attribute the cause of human weakness and changeableness, not to the common power of nature, but to some vice of human nature, which they therefore bewail, laugh at, mock, or, as is more generally the case, detest; whilst he who knows how to revile most eloquently or subtilly the weakness of the mind is looked upon as divine. It is true that very eminent men have not been wanting, to whose labour and industry we confess ourselves much indebted, who have written many excellent things about the right conduct of life, and who have given to mortals counsels full of prudence, but no one so far as I know has determined the nature and strength of the affects, and what the mind is able to do towards controlling them. I remember, indeed, that the celebrated Descartes, although he believed that the mind is absolute master over its own actions, tried nevertheless to explain by their first causes human affects, and at the same time to show the way by which the mind could obtain absolute power over them; but in my opinion he has shown nothing but the acuteness of his great intellect, as I shall make evident in the proper place, for I wish to return to those who prefer to detest and scoff at human affects and actions than understand them. To such as these it will doubtless seem a marvellous thing for me to endeavour to treat by a geometrical method the vices and follies of men, and to desire by a sure method to demonstrate those things which these people cry out against as being opposed to reason, or as being vanities, absurdities, and monstrosities. The following is my reason for so doing. Nothing happens in nature which can be attributed to any vice of nature, for she is always the same and everywhere one. Her virtue is the same, and her power of acting; that is to say, her laws and rules, according to which all things are and are changed from form to form, are everywhere and always the same; so that there must also be one and the same method of understanding the nature of all things whatsoever, that is to say, by the universal laws and rules of nature. The affects, therefore, of hatred, anger, envy, considered in themselves, follow from the same necessity and virtue of nature as other individual things; they have therefore certain causes through which they are to be understood, and certain properties which are just as worthy of being known as the properties of any other thing in the contemplation alone of which we delight. I shall, therefore, pursue the same method in considering the nature and strength of the affects and the power of the mind over them which I pursued in our previous discussion of God and the mind, and I shall consider human actions and appetites just as if I were considering lines, planes, or bodies.

DEF. 1. I call that an adequate cause whose effect can be clearly and distinctly perceived by means of the cause. I call that an inadequate or partial cause whose effect cannot be understood by means of the cause alone.

DEF. 2. I say that we act when anything is done, either within us or without us, of which we are the adequate cause, that is to say (by the preceding Def.), when from our nature anything follows, either within us or without us, which by that nature alone can be clearly and distinctly understood. On the other hand, I say that we suffer when anything is done within us, or when anything follows from our nature, of which we are not the cause excepting partially.

DEF. 3. By affect I understand the affections of the body, by which the power of acting of the body itself is increased, diminished, helped, or hindered, together with the ideas of these affections.

If, therefore, we can be the adequate cause of any of these affections, I understand the affect to be an action, otherwise it is a passion.

Postulate 1.   The human body can be affected in many ways by which its power of acting is increased or diminished, and also in other ways which make its power of acting neither greater nor less.

This postulate or axiom is based upon Post. 1 and Lems. 5 and 7, following Prop. 13, pt. 2.

Postulate 2.   The human body is capable of suffering many changes, and, nevertheless, can retain the impressions or traces of objects (Post. 5, pt. 2), and consequently the same images of things. (For the definition of images see Schol. Prop. 17, pt. 2.)

PROP. 1.   *Our mind acts at times and at times suffers: in so far as it has adequate ideas, it necessarily acts; and in so far as it has inadequate ideas, it necessarily suffers.*

Demonst.   In every human mind some ideas are adequate, and others mutilated and confused (Schol. Prop. 40, pt. 2). But the ideas which in any mind are adequate are adequate in God in so far as He forms the essence of that mind (Corol. Prop. 11, pt. 2), while those again which are inadequate in the mind are also adequate in God (by the same Corol.), not in so far as He contains the essence of that mind only, but in so far as He contains the ideas of other things at the same time in Himself. Again, from any given idea some effect must necessarily follow (Prop. 36, pt. 1), of which God is the adequate cause (Def. 1, pt. 3), not in so far as He is infinite, but in so far as He is considered as affected with the given idea (Prop. 9, pt. 2). But of that effect of which God is the cause, in so far as He is affected by an idea which is adequate in any mind, that same mind is the adequate cause (Corol. Prop. 11, pt. 2). Our mind, therefore (Def. 2, pt. 3), in so far as it has adequate ideas, necessarily at times acts, which is the first thing we had to prove. Again, if there be anything which necessarily follows from an idea which is adequate in God, not in so far as He contains within Himself the mind of one man only, but also, together with this, the ideas of other things, then the mind of that man (Corol. Prop. 11, pt. 2) is not the adequate cause of that thing, but is only its partial cause, and therefore (Def. 2, pt. 3), in so far as the mind has inadequate ideas, it necessarily at times suffers. This was the second thing to be proved. Therefore our mind, &c.   Q.E.D.

Corol.   Hence it follows that the mind is subject to passions in proportion to the number of inadequate ideas which it has, and that it acts in proportion to the number of adequate ideas which it has.

PROP. 2.   *The body cannot determine the mind to thought, neither can the mind determine the body to motion nor rest, nor to anything else, if there be anything else.*

Demonst.   All modes of thought have God for a cause in so far as He is a thinking thing, and not in so far as He is manifested by any other attribute (Prop. 6, pt. 2). That which determines the mind to thought, therefore, is a mode of thought and not of extension, that is to say (Def. 1, pt. 2), it is not the body. This is the first thing which was to be proved. Again, the motion and rest of the body must be derived from some other body, which has also been determined to motion or rest by another, and, absolutely, whatever arises in the body must arise from God, in so far as He is considered as affected by some mode of extension, and not in so far as He is considered as affected by any mode of thought (Prop. 6, pt. 2), that is to say, whatever arises in the body cannot arise from the mind, which is a mode of thought (Prop. 11, pt. 2). This is the second thing which was to be proved. Therefore, the body cannot determine, &c.   Q.E.D.

Schol.   This proposition will be better understood from what has been said in the scholium of Prop. 7, pt. 2, that is to say, that the mind and the body are one and the same thing, conceived at one time under the attribute of thought, and at another under that of extension. For this reason, the order or concatenation of things is one, whether nature be conceived under this or under that attribute, and consequently the order of the actions and passions of our body is coincident in nature with the order of the actions and passions of the mind. This is also plain from the manner in which we have demonstrated Prop. 12, pt. 2.

Although these things are so, and no ground for doubting remains, I scarcely believe, nevertheless, that, without a proof derived from experience, men will be induced calmly to weigh what has been said, so firmly are they persuaded that, solely at the bidding of the mind, the body moves or rests, and does a number of things which depend upon the will of the mind alone, and upon the power of thought. For what the body can do no one has hitherto determined, that is to say, experience has taught no one hitherto what the body, without being determined by the mind, can do and what it cannot do from the laws of nature alone, in so far as nature is considered merely as corporeal. For no one as yet has understood the structure of the body so accurately as to be able to explain all its functions, not to mention the fact that many things are observed in brutes which far surpass human sagacity, and that sleep-walkers in their sleep do very many things which they dare not do when awake; all this showing that the body itself can do many things from the laws of its own nature alone at which the mind belonging to that body is amazed. Again, nobody knows by what means or by what method the mind moves the body, nor how many degrees of motion it can communicate to the body, nor with what speed it can move the body. So that it follows that when men say that this or that action of the body springs from the mind which has command over the body, they do not know what they say, and they do nothing but confess with pretentious words that they know nothing about the cause of the action, and see nothing in it to wonder at. But they will say, that whether they know or do not know by what means the mind moves the body, it is nevertheless in their experience that if the mind were not fit for thinking the body would be inert. They say, again, it is in their experience that the mind alone has power both to speak and be silent, and to do many other things which they therefore think to be dependent on a decree of the mind. But with regard to the first assertion, I ask them if experience does not also teach that if the body be sluggish the mind at the same time is not fit for thinking? When the body is asleep, the mind slumbers with it, and has not the power to think, as it has when the body is awake. Again, I believe that all have discovered that the mind is not always equally fitted for thinking about the same subject, but in proportion to the fitness of the body for this or that image to be excited in it will the mind be better fitted to contemplate this or that object. But my opponents will say, that from the laws of nature alone, in so far as it is considered to be corporeal merely, it cannot be that the causes of architecture, painting, and things of this sort, which are the results of human art alone, could be deduced, and that the human body, unless it were determined and guided by the mind, would not be able to build a temple. I have already shown, however, that they do not know what the body can do, nor what can

be deduced from the consideration of its nature alone, and that they find that many things are done merely by the laws of nature which they would never have believed to be possible without the direction of the mind, as, for example, those things which sleep-walkers do in their sleep, and at which they themselves are astonished when they wake. I adduce also here the structure itself of the human body, which so greatly surpasses in workmanship all those things which are constructed by human art, not to mention what I have already proved, that an infinitude of things follows from nature under whatever attribute it may be considered.

With regard to the second point, I should say that human affairs would be much more happily conducted if it were equally in the power of men to be silent and to speak; but experience shows over and over again that there is nothing which men have less power over than the tongue, and that there is nothing which they are less able to do than to govern their appetites, so that many persons believe that we do those things only with freedom which we seek indifferently; as the desire for such things can easily be lessened by the recollection of another thing which we frequently call to mind; it being impossible, on the other hand, to do those things with freedom which we seek with such ardour that the recollection of another thing is unable to mitigate it. But if, however, we had not found out that we do many things which we afterwards repent, and that when agitated by conflicting affects we see that which is better and follow that which is worse, nothing would hinder us from believing that we do everything with freedom. Thus the infant believes that it is by free will that it seeks the breast; the angry boy believes that by free will he wishes vengeance; the timid man thinks it is with free will he seeks flight; the drunkard believes that by a free command of his mind he speaks the things which when sober he wishes he had left unsaid. Thus the madman, the chatterer, the boy, and others of the same kind, all believe that they speak by a free command of the mind, whilst, in truth, they have no power to restrain the impulse which they have to speak, so that experience itself, no less than reason, clearly teaches that men believe themselves to be free simply because they are conscious of their own actions, knowing nothing of the causes by which they are determined: it teaches, too, that the decrees of the mind are nothing but the appetites themselves, which differ, therefore, according to the different temper of the body. For every man determines all things from his affect; those who are agitated by contrary affects do not know what they want, whilst those who are agitated by no affect are easily driven hither and thither. All this plainly shows that the decree of the mind, the appetite, and determination of the body are coincident in nature, or rather that they are one and the same thing, which, when it is considered under the attribute of thought and manifested by that, is called a decree, and when it is considered under the attribute of extension and is deduced from the laws of motion and rest, is called a determination. This, however, will be better understood as we go on, for there is another thing which I wish to be observed here—that we cannot by a mental decree do a thing unless we recollect it. We cannot speak a word, for instance, unless we recollect it. But it is not in the free power of the mind either to recollect a thing or to forget it. It is believed, therefore, that the power of the mind extends only thus far—that from a mental decree we can speak or be silent about a thing only when we recollect it. But when we dream that we speak, we believe that we do so from a free decree of the mind; and yet we do not speak, or, if we do, it is the result of a spontaneous motion of the body. We dream, again, that we are concealing things, and that we do this by virtue of a decree of the mind like that by which, when awake, we are silent about things we know. We dream, again, that, from a decree of the mind, we do some things which we should not dare to do when awake. And I should like to know, therefore, whether there are two kinds of decrees in the mind—one belonging to dreams and the other free. If this be too great nonsense, we must necessarily grant that this decree of the mind, which is believed to be free, is not distinguishable from the imagination or memory, and is nothing but the affirmation which the idea necessarily involves in so far as it is an idea (Prop. 49, pt. 2). These decrees of the mind, therefore, arise in the mind by the same necessity as the ideas of things actually existing. Consequently, those who believe that they speak, or are silent, or do anything else from a free decree of the mind, dream with their eyes open.

PROP. 3. *The actions of the mind arise from adequate ideas alone, but the passions depend upon those alone which are inadequate.*

Demonst. The first thing which constitutes the essence of the mind is nothing but the idea of an actually existing body (Props. 11 and 13, pt. 2). This idea is composed of a number of others (Prop. 15, pt. 2), some of which are adequate and others inadequate (Corol. Prop. 38, pt. 2, and Corol. Prop. 29, pt. 2). Everything therefore, of which the mind is the proximate cause, and which follows from the nature of the mind, through which it must be understood, must necessarily follow from an adequate or from an inadequate idea. But in so far as the mind (Prop. 1, pt. 3) has inadequate ideas, so far it necessarily suffers; therefore the actions of the mind follow from adequate ideas alone, and the mind therefore suffers only because it has inadequate ideas.

Schol. We see, therefore, that the passions are not related to the mind, unless in so far as it possesses something which involves negation; in other words, unless in so far as it is considered as a part of nature, which by itself and without the other parts cannot be clearly and distinctly perceived. In the same way I could show that passions are related to individual things, just as they are related to the mind, and that they cannot be perceived in any other way; but my purpose is to treat of the human mind alone.

PROP. 4. *A thing cannot be destroyed except by an external cause.*

Demonst. This proposition is self-evident for the definition of any given thing affirm and does not deny the existence of the thing that is to say, it posits the essence of the thing and does not negate it. So long, therefore, a we attend only to the thing itself, and not t external causes, we shall discover nothing in which can destroy it. Q.E.D.

PROP. 5. *In so far as one thing is able to destro another are they of contrary natures; that is t say, they cannot exist in the same subject.*

Demonst. If it were possible for them t come together, or to coexist in the same subject, there would then be something in the subject able to destroy it, which (Prop. 4, pt. is absurd. Therefore, in so far, &c. Q.E.D.

PROP. 6. *Each thing, in so far as it is in itse endeavours to persevere in its being.*

Demonst. Individual things are modes which the attributes of God are expressed in certain and determinate manner (Corol. Pro 25, pt. 1); that is to say (Prop. 34, pt. 1), th are things which express in a certain and determinate manner the power of God, by which He is and acts. A thing, too, has nothing in itself through which it can be destroyed, or which can negate its existence (Prop. 4, pt. 3), but, on the contrary, it is opposed to everything which could negate its existence (Prop. 5, pt. 3). Therefore, in so far as it can and is in itself, it endeavours to persevere in its own being. Q.E.D.

PROP. 7. *The effort by which each thing endeavours to persevere in its own being is nothing but the actual essence of the thing itself.*

Demonst. From the given essence of anything certain things necessarily follow (Prop. 36, pt. 1); nor are things able to do anything else than what necessarily follows from their determinate nature (Prop. 29, pt. 1). Therefore, the power of a thing, or the effort by means of which it does or endeavours to do anything, either by itself or with others—that is to say (Prop. 6, pt. 3), the power or effort by which it endeavours to persevere in its being—is nothing but the given or actual essence of the thing itself. Q.E.D.

PROP. 8. *The effort by which each thing endeavours to persevere in its own being does not involve finite but indefinite time.*

Demonst. If it involved a limited time, which would determine the duration of the thing, then from that power alone by which the thing exists it would follow that, after that limited time, it could not exist but must be destroyed. But this (Prop. 4, pt. 3) is absurd. The effort, therefore, by which a thing exists does not involve definite time, but, on the contrary (Prop. ?, pt. 3), if the thing be destroyed by no external cause, by the same power by which it now exists it will always continue to exist, and this effort, therefore, by which it endeavours to persevere, &c. Q.E.D.

PROP. 9. *The mind, both in so far as it has clear and distinct ideas, and in so far as it has confused ideas, endeavours to persevere in its being for an indefinite time, and is conscious of this effort.*

Demonst. The essence of the mind is composed of adequate and inadequate ideas (as we have shown in Prop. 3, pt. 3), and therefore (Prop. 7, pt. 3), both in so far as it has the former and in so far as it has the latter, it endeavours to persevere in its being, and endeavours to persevere in it for an indefinite time (Prop.

8, pt. 3). But since the mind (Prop. 23, pt. 2), through the ideas of the affections of the body, is necessarily conscious of itself, it is therefore conscious (Prop. 7, pt. 3) of its effort.

Schol. This effort, when it is related to the mind alone, is called *will*, but when it is related at the same time both to the mind and the body, is called *appetite*, which is therefore nothing but the very essence of man, from the nature of which necessarily follow those things which promote his preservation, and thus he is determined to do those things. Hence there is no difference between appetite and desire, unless in this particular, that desire is generally related to men in so far as they are conscious of their appetites, and it may therefore be defined as appetite of which we are conscious. From what has been said it is plain, therefore, that we neither strive for, wish, seek, nor desire anything because we think it to be good, but, on the contrary, we adjudge a thing to be good because we strive for, wish, seek, or desire it.

PROP. 10. *There can be no idea in the mind which excludes the existence of the body, for such an idea is contrary to the mind.*

Demonst. There can be nothing in our body which is able to destroy it (Prop. 5, pt. 3), and there cannot be, therefore, in God an idea of any such thing in so far as He has the idea of the body (Corol. Prop. 9, pt. 2); that is to say (Props. 11 and 13, pt. 2), no idea of any such thing can exist in our mind, but, on the contrary, since (Props. 11 and 13, pt. 2) the first thing which constitutes the essence of the mind is the idea of a body actually existing, the first and chief thing belonging to our mind is the effort (Prop. 7, pt. 3) to affirm the existence of our body, and therefore the idea which denies the existence of our body is contrary to our mind. Q.E.D.

PROP. 11. *If anything increases, diminishes, helps, or limits our body's power of action, the idea of that thing increases, diminishes, helps, or limits our mind's power of thought.*

Demonst. This proposition is evident from Prop. 7, pt. 2, and also from Prop. 14, pt. 2.

Schol. We thus see that the mind can suffer great changes, and can pass now to a greater and now to a lesser perfection; these passions explaining to us the affects of joy and sorrow. By *joy*, therefore, in what follows, I shall understand the passion by which the mind passes to a greater perfection; by *sorrow*, on the other hand, the passion by which it passes to a less perfection. The affect of joy, related at the same time both to the mind and the body, I call *pleasurable excitement (titillatio)* or *cheerfulness;* that of sorrow I call *pain* or *melancholy.* It is, however, to be observed that pleasurable excitement and pain are related to a man when one of his parts is affected more than the others; cheerfulness and melancholy, on the other hand, when all parts are equally affected. What the nature of desire is I have explained in the scholium of Prop. 9, pt. 3; and besides these three—joy, sorrow, and desire— I know of no other primary affect, the others springing from these, as I shall show in what follows. But before I advance any farther, I should like to explain more fully Prop. 10, pt. 3, so that we may more clearly understand in what manner one idea is contrary to another.

In the scholium of Prop. 17, pt. 2, we have shown that the idea which forms the essence of the mind involves the existence of the body so long as the body exists. Again, from Corol. Prop. 8, pt. 2, and its scholium, it follows that the present existence of our mind depends solely upon this—that the mind involves the actual existence of the body. Finally, we have shown that the power of the mind by which it imagines and remembers things also depends upon this—that it involves the actual existence of the body (Props. 17 and 18, pt. 2, with the Schol.) From these things it follows, that the present existence of the mind and its power of imagination are negated as soon as the mind ceases to affirm the present existence of the body. But the cause by which the mind ceases to affirm this existence of the body cannot be the mind itself (Prop. 4, pt. 2), nor can it be the body's ceasing to be; for (Prop. 6, pt. 2) the mind does not affirm the existence of the body because the body began to exist, and therefore, by the same reasoning, it does not cease to affirm the existence of the body because the body ceases to be, but (Prop. 17, pt. 2) because of another idea excluding the present existence of our body, and consequently of our mind, and contrary, therefore, to the idea which forms the essence of our mind.

PROP. 12. *The mind endeavours as much as possible to imagine those things which increase or assist the body's power of acting.*

Demonst. The human mind will contemplate any external body as present so long as the human body is affected in a way which involves the nature of that external body (Prop. 17, pt. 2), and consequently (Prop. 7, pt. 2) as long as the human mind contemplates any external body as present, that is to say (Schol. Prop. 17, pt. 2), imagines it, so long is the human body affected in a way which involves the nature of that external body. Consequently as long as the mind imagines those things which increase or assist our body's power of action, so long is the body affected in a way which increases or assists that power (Post. 1, pt. 3), and consequently (Prop. 11, pt. 3) so long the mind's power of thought is increased or assisted; therefore (Props. 6 and 9, pt. 3) the mind endeavours as much as possible to imagine those things.   Q.E.D.

PROP. 13. *Whenever the mind imagines those things which lessen or limit the body's power of action, it endeavours as much as possible to recollect what excludes the existence of these things.*

Demonst. So long as the mind imagines anything of this sort, the power of the body and of the mind is lessened or limited (as we have shown in the preceding proposition). Nevertheless the mind will continue to imagine these things until it imagines some other thing which will exclude their present existence (Prop. 17, pt. 2); that is to say, as we have just shown, the power of the mind and of the body is diminished or limited until the mind imagines something which excludes the existence of these things. This, therefore (Prop. 9, pt. 3), the mind will endeavour to imagine or recollect as much as possible.   Q.E.D.

Corol. Hence it follows that the mind is averse to imagine those things which lessen or hinder its power and that of the body.

Schol. From what has been said we can clearly see what love is and what hatred is. *Love* is nothing but joy accompanied with the idea of an external cause, and *hatred* is nothing but sorrow with the accompanying idea of an external cause. We see too that he who loves a thing necessarily endeavours to keep it before him and to preserve it, and, on the other hand, he who hates a thing necessarily endeavours to remove and destroy it. But we shall speak at greater length upon these points in what follows.

PROP. 14. *If the mind at any time has been simultaneously affected by two affects, whenever it is afterwards affected by one of them, it will also be affected by the other.*

Demonst. If the human body has at any time been simultaneously affected by two bodies, whenever the mind afterwards imagines one of them, it will immediately remember the other (Prop. 18, pt. 2). But the imaginations of the mind indicate rather the affects of our body than the nature of external bodies (Corol. 2, Prop. 16, pt. 2), and therefore if the body, and consequently the mind (Def. 3, pt. 3), has been at any time, &c. 1   Q.E.D.

Prop. 15. *Anything may be accidentally the cause of joy, sorrow, or desire.*

Demonst. Let the mind be supposed to be affected at the same time by two affects, its power of action not being increased or diminished by one, while it is increased or diminished by the other (Post 1, pt. 3). From the preceding proposition it is plain that when the mind is afterwards affected by the first affect through its true cause, which (by hypothesis) of itself neither increases nor diminishes the mind's power of thinking, it will at the same time be affected by the other affect, which does increase or diminish that power, that is to say (Schol. Prop. 11, pt. 3), it will be affected with joy or sorrow; and thus the thing itself will be the cause of joy or of sorrow, not of itself, but accidentally. In the same way it can easily be shown that the same thing may accidentally be the cause of desire.   Q.E.D.

Corol. The fact that we have contemplated a thing with an affect of joy or sorrow, of which it is not the efficient cause, is a sufficient reason for being able to love or hate it.

Demonst. For this fact alone is a sufficient reason (Prop. 14, pt. 3) for its coming to pass that the mind in imagining the thing afterwards is affected with the affect of joy or sorrow, that is to say (Prop. 11, pt. 3), that the power of the mind and of the body is increased or diminished, &c., and, consequently (Prop. 2, pt. 3), that the mind desires to imagine the thing or (Corol. Prop. 13, pt. 3) is averse to doing so, that is to say (Schol. Prop. 13, pt. 3), that the mind loves the thing or hates it.

Schol. We now understand why we love or hate certain things from no cause which is known to us, but merely from sympathy or antipathy, as they say. To this class, too, as we shall show in the following propositions, are to be referred those objects which affect us with joy or sorrow solely because they are somewhat like objects which usually affect us with those affects. I know indeed that the writers who first introduced the words "Sympathy" and "Antipathy" desired thereby to signify certain hidden qualities of things, but

nevertheless I believe that we shall be permitted to understand by those names qualities which are plain and well known.

Prop. 16. *If we imagine a certain thing to possess something which resembles an object which usually affects the mind with joy or sorrow, although the quality in which the thing resembles the object is not the efficient cause of these affects, we shall nevertheless, by virtue of the resemblance alone, love or hate the thing.*

Demonst. The quality in which the thing resembles the object we have contemplated in the object itself (by hypothesis) with the affect of joy or sorrow, and since (Prop. 14, pt. 3), whenever the mind is affected by the image of this quality, it is also affected by the former or latter affect, the thing which is perceived by us to possess this quality will be (Prop. 15, pt. 3) accidentally the cause of joy or sorrow. Therefore (by the preceding Corol.), although the quality in which the thing resembles the object is not the efficient cause of these affects, we shall nevertheless love the thing or hate it.

Prop. 17. *If we imagine that a thing that usually affects us with the affect of sorrow has any resemblance to an object which usually affects us equally with a great affect of joy, we shall at the same time hate the thing and love it.*

Demonst. This thing (by hypothesis) is of itself the cause of sorrow, and (Schol. Prop. 13, pt. 3) in so far as we imagine it with this affect we hate it; but in so far as we imagine it to resemble an object which usually affects us equally with a great affect of joy do we love it with an equally great effort of joy (Prop. 16, pt. 3), and so we shall both hate it and love it at the same time.   Q.E.D.

Schol. This state of mind, which arises from two contrary affects, is called *vacillation of the mind.* It is related to affect as doubt is related to the imagination (Schol. Prop. 44, pt. 2). Nor do vacillation and doubt differ from one another except as greater and less. It is to be observed that in the preceding proposition I have deduced these vacillations of the mind from causes which occasion the one affect directly and the other contingently. This I have done because the affects could thus be more easily deduced from what preceded, and not because I deny that these vacillations often originate from the object itself which is the efficient cause of both affects. For the human body (Post. 1, pt. 2) is composed of a number of individuals of different natures, and therefore (Ax. 1, after Lem. 3, following Prop. 13, pt. 2) it can be affected by one and the same body in very many and in different ways. On the other hand, the same object can be affected in a number of different ways, and consequently can affect the same part of the body in different ways. It is easy, therefore, to see how one and the same object may be the cause of many and contrary affects.

PROP. 18. *A man is affected by the image of a past or future thing with the same affect of joy or sorrow as that with which he is affected by the image of a present thing.*

Demonst. As long as a man is affected by the image of anything, he will contemplate the thing as present although it does not exist (Prop. 17, pt. 2, with Corol.), nor does he imagine it as past or future, unless in so far as its image is connected with that of past or future time (Schol. Prop. 44, pt. 2) Therefore the image of the thing considered in itself alone is the same whether it be related to future, past, or present time; that is to say (Corol. 2, Prop. 16, pt. 2), the state of the body or the affect is the same whether the image be that of a past, present, or future thing. The affect, therefore, of joy and sorrow is the same whether the image be that of a past, present, or future thing. Q.E.D.

Schol. 1. I call a thing here past or future in so far as we have been or shall be affected by it; for example, in so far as we have seen a thing or are about to see it, in so far as it has strengthened us or will strengthen us; has injured or will injure us. For in so far as we thus imagine it do we affirm its existence; that is to say, the body is affected by no affect which excludes the existence of the thing, and therefore (Prop. 17, pt. 2) the body is affected by the image of the thing in the same way as if the thing itself were present. But because it generally happens that those who possess much experience hesitate when they think of a thing as past or future, and doubt greatly concerning its issue (Schol. Prop. 44, pt. 2), therefore the affects which spring from such images of things are not so constant, but are generally disturbed by the images of other things, until men become more sure of the issue.

Schol. 2. From what has now been said we understand the nature of Hope, Fear, Confidence, Despair, Gladness, Remorse. *Hope* is nothing but unsteady joy, arising from the image of a future or past thing about whose issue we are in doubt. *Fear*, on the other hand,

is an unsteady sorrow, arising from the image of a doubtful thing. If the doubt be removed from these affects, then hope and fear become *Confidence* and *Despair*, that is to say, joy or sorrow, arising from the image of a thing for which we have hoped or which we have feared. *Gladness*, again, is joy arising from the image of a past thing whose issues we have doubted. *Remorse* is the sorrow which is opposed to gladness.

PROP. 19. *He who imagines that what he loves is destroyed will sorrow, but if he imagines that it is preserved he will rejoice.*

Demonst. The mind endeavours as much as it can to imagine those things which increase or assist the body's power of action (Prop. 12, pt 3), that is to say (Schol. Prop. 13, pt. 3), to imagine those things which it loves. But the imagination is assisted by those things which posit the existence of the object and is restrained by those which exclude its existence (Prop. 17, pt. 2). Therefore the images of things which posit the existence of the beloved object assist the mind's effort to imagine it that is to say (Schol. Prop. 11, pt. 3), they affect the mind with joy; whilst those, on the other hand, which exclude the existence of the beloved object restrain that same effort of the mind, that is to say (Schol. Prop. 11, pt. 3) they affect the mind with sorrow. He, therefore, who imagines that what he loves is destroyed, &c. Q.E.D.

PROP. 20. *He who imagines that what he hates is destroyed will rejoice.*

Demonst. The mind (Prop. 13, pt. 3) endeavours to imagine those things which exclude the existence of whatever lessens or limits its body's power of action; that is to say (Schol. Prop. 13, pt. 3), it endeavours to imagine those things which exclude the existence of what it hates, and therefore the image of the thing which excludes the existence of what the mind hates assists this endeavour of the mind, that is to say (Schol. Prop. 11, pt. 3), affects the mind with joy. He, therefore, who imagines that what he hates is destroyed will rejoice. Q.E.D.

PROP. 21. *He who imagines that what he loves is affected with joy or sorrow will also be affected with joy or sorrow, and these affects will be greater or less in the lover as they are greater or less in the thing loved.*

Demonst. The images of things (Prop.

pt. 3) which posit the existence of the beloved object assist the effort of the mind to imagine it; but joy posits the existence of the thing which rejoices, and the greater the joy the more is existence posited, for (Schol. Prop. 11, pt. 3) joy is the transition to a greater perfection. The image, therefore, in the lover of the joy of the beloved object assists the effort of his mind to imagine the object, that is to say (Schol. Prop. 11, pt. 3), affects the lover with joy proportionate to the joy of the object he loves. This was the first thing to be proved. Again, in so far as anything is affected with sorrow, so far is it destroyed, and the destruction is greater as the sorrow with which it is affected is greater (Schol. Prop. 11, pt. 3). Therefore (Prop. 19, pt. 3) he who imagines that what he loves is affected with sorrow will also be affected with sorrow, and it will be greater as this affect shall have been greater in the object beloved.

Prop. 22. *If we imagine that a person affects with joy a thing which we love, we shall be affected with love towards him. If, on the contrary, we imagine that he affects it with sorrow, we shall also be affected with hatred towards him.*

Demonst. He who affects with joy or sorrow the thing we love affects us also with joy or sorrow whenever we imagine the beloved object so affected (Prop. 21, pt. 3). But this joy or sorrow is supposed to exist in us accompanied with the idea of an external cause; therefore (Schol. Prop. 13, pt. 3) if we imagine that a person affects with joy or sorrow a thing which we love, we shall be affected with love or hatred towards him. Q.E.D.

Schol. Prop. 21 explains to us what *commiseration* is, which we may define as sorrow which springs from another's loss. By what name the joy is to be called which springs from another's good I do not know. Love toward the person who has done good to another we shall call *favour* (*favor*), whilst hatred towards him who has done evil to another we shall call *indignation* (*indignatio*). It is to be observed, too, that we not only feel pity for the object which we have loved, as we showed in Prop. 21, but also for that to which we have been attached by no affect; provided only we adjudge it to be like ourselves (as I shall show hereafter), and so we shall regard with favour him who has done any good to the object which is like us, and, on the contrary, be indignant with him who has done it any harm.

Prop. 23. *He who imagines that what he hates is affected with sorrow will rejoice; if, on the other hand, he imagines it to be affected with joy he will be sad; and these affects will be greater or less in him in proportion as their contraries are greater or less in the object he hates.*

Demonst. In so far as the hated thing is affected with sorrow is it destroyed, and the destruction is greater as the sorrow is greater (Schol. Prop. 11, pt. 3). He, therefore (Prop. 20, pt. 3), who imagines that the thing which he hates is affected with sorrow will on the contrary be affected with joy, and the joy will be the greater in proportion as he imagines the hated thing to be affected with a greater sorrow. This was the first thing to be proved. Again, joy posits the existence of the thing which rejoices (Schol. Prop. 11, pt. 3), and it does so the more in proportion as the joy is conceived to be greater. If a person, therefore, imagines that he whom he hates is affected with joy, this idea (Prop. 13, pt. 3) will restrain the effort of the mind of him who hates, that is to say (Schol. Prop. 11, pt. 3), he will be affected with sorrow. Q.E.D.

Schol. This joy can hardly be solid and free from any mental conflict. For, as I shall show directly in Prop. 27, in so far as we imagine that what is like ourselves is affected with sorrow, we must be sad; and, on the contrary, if we imagine it to be affected with joy, we rejoice. Here, however, we are considering merely hatred.

Prop. 24. *If we imagine that a person affects with joy a thing which we hate, we are therefore affected with hatred towards him. On the other hand, if we imagine that he affects it with sorrow, we are therefore affected with love towards him.*

Demonst. This proposition is proved in the same manner as Prop. 22, pt. 3, which see.

Schol. These and the like affects of hatred are related to *envy*, which is therefore nothing but hatred in so far as it is considered to dispose a man so that he rejoices over the evil and is saddened by the good which befalls another.

Prop. 25. *We endeavour to affirm everything, both concerning ourselves and concerning the beloved object which we imagine will affect us or the object with joy, and, on the contrary, we endeavour to deny everything that will affect either it or ourselves with sorrow.*

Demonst. Everything which we imagine as affecting the beloved object with joy or sorrow affects us also with joy or sorrow (Prop. 21, pt. 3). But the mind (Prop. 12, pt. 3) endeavours as much as it can to imagine those things which affect us with joy, that is to say (Prop. 17, pt. 2 and its Corol.), it endeavours to consider them as present. On the contrary (Prop. 13, pt. 3), it endeavours to exclude the existence of what affects us with sorrow: therefore we endeavour to affirm everything both concerning ourselves and concerning the beloved object which we imagine will affect us or it with joy, &c. Q.E.D.

PROP. 26. *If we hate a thing, we endeavour to affirm concerning it everything which we imagine will affect it with sorrow, and, on the other hand, to deny everything concerning it which we imagine will affect it with joy.*

Demonst. This proposition follows from Prop. 23, as the preceding proposition follows from Prop. 21.

Schol. We see from this how easily it may happen, that a man should think too much of himself or of the beloved object, and, on the contrary, should think too little of what he hates. When a man thinks too much of himself, this imagination is called *pride*, and is a kind of delirium, because he dreams with his eyes open, that he is able to do all those things to which he attains in imagination alone, regarding them therefore as realities, and rejoicing in them so long as he cannot imagine anything to exclude their existence and limit his power of action. Pride, therefore, is that joy which arises from a man's thinking too much of himself. The joy which arises from thinking too much of another is called overestimation, and that which arises from thinking too little of another is called contempt.

PROP. 27. *Although we may not have been moved towards a thing by any affect, yet if it is like ourselves, whenever we imagine it to be affected by any affect we are therefore affected by the same.*

Demonst. The images of things are affections of the human body, and the ideas of these affections represent to us external bodies as if they were present (Schol. Prop. 17, pt. 2), that is to say (Prop. 16, pt. 2), these ideas involve both the nature of our own body and at the same time the present nature of the external body. If, therefore, the nature of the external body be like that of our body, then the idea of the external body which we imagine will involve an affection of our body like that of the external body. Therefore, if we imagine any

one who is like ourselves to be affected with any affect, this imagination will express an affection of our body like that affect, and therefore we shall be affected with a similar affect ourselves, because we imagine something like us to be affected with the same. If, on the other hand, we hate a thing which is like ourselves, we shall so far (Prop. 23, pt. 3) be affected with an affect contrary and not similar to that with which it is affected. Q.E.D.

Schol. This imitation of affects, when it is connected with sorrow, is called *commiseration* (see Schol. Prop. 22, pt. 3), and where it is connected with desire is called *emulation*, which is nothing else than the desire which is engendered in us for anything, because we imagine that other persons, who are like ourselves, possess the same desire.

Corol. 1. If we imagine that a person to whom we have been moved by no affect, affects with joy a thing which is like us, we shall therefore be affected with love towards him. If, on the other hand, we imagine that he affects it with sorrow, we shall be affected with hatred towards him.

Demonst. This Corol. follows from the preceding proposition, just as Prop. 22, pt. 3, follows from Prop. 21, pt. 3.

Corol. 2. If we pity a thing, the fact that its misery affects us with sorrow will not make us hate it.

Demonst. If we could hate the thing for this reason, we should then (Prop. 23, pt. 3) rejoice over its sorrow, which is contrary to the hypothesis.

Corol. 3. If we pity a thing, we shall endeavour as much as possible to free it from its misery.

Demonst. That which affects with sorrow the thing that we pity, affects us likewise with the same sorrow (Prop. 27, pt. 3), and we shall, therefore, endeavour to devise every means by which we may take away or destroy the existence of the cause of the sorrow (Prop. 13, pt. 3); that is to say (Schol. Prop. 9. pt. 3), we shall seek to destroy it, or shall be determined thereto, and therefore we shall endeavour to free from its misery the thing we pity.

Schol. This will or desire of doing good, arising from our pity for the object which we want to benefit, is called *benevolence*, which is, therefore, simply the desire which arises from commiseration. With regard to the love or hatred towards the person who had done good or evil to the thing we imagine to be like ourselves, see Schol. Prop. 22, pt. 3.

PROP. 28. *We endeavour to bring into existence everything which we imagine conduces to joy, and to remove or destroy everything opposed to it, or which we imagine conduces to sorrow.*

Demonst. We endeavour to imagine as much as possible all those things which we think conduce to joy (Prop. 12, pt. 3), that is to say (Prop. 17, pt. 2), we strive as much as possible to perceive them as present or actually existing. But the mind's effort or power in thinking is equal to and correspondent with the body's effort or power in acting, as clearly follows from Corol. Prop. 7, pt. 2, and Corol. Prop. 11, pt. 2, and therefore absolutely whatever conduces to joy we endeavour to make exist, that is to say (Schol. Prop. 9, pt. 3), we seek after it and aim at it. This is the first thing which was to be proved. Again, if we imagine that a thing which we believe causes us sorrow, that is to say (Schol. Prop. 13, pt. 3). which we hate is destroyed, we shall rejoice (Prop. 20, pt. 3), and therefore (by the first part of this demonstration) we shall endeavour to destroy it, or (Prop. 13, pt. 3) to remove it from us, so that we may not perceive it as present. This is the second thing which was to be proved. We endeavour, therefore, to bring into existence, &c. Q.E.D.

PROP. 29. *We shall endeavour to do everything which we imagine men[1] will look upon with joy, and, on the contrary, we shall be averse to doing anything to which we imagine men are averse.*

Demonst. If we imagine men to love or hate a thing, we shall therefore love or hate it (Prop. 27, pt. 3); that is to say (Schol. Prop. 13, pt. 3), we shall therefore rejoice or be sad at the presence of the thing, and therefore (Prop. 28, pt. 3) everything which we imagine that men love or look upon with joy, we shall endeavour to do, &c. Q.E.D.

Schol. This effort to do some things and omit doing others, solely because we wish to please men, is called *ambition*, especially if our desire to please the common people is so strong that our actions or omissions to act are accompanied with injury to ourselves or to others. Otherwise this endeavour is usually called *humanity*. Again, the joy with which we imagine another person's action, the purpose of which is to delight us, I call *praise*, and the sorrow with which we turn away from an action of a contrary kind I call *blame*.

[1]Both here and in what follows I understand by the word *men*, men to whom we are moved by no affect.—SPINOZA.

PROP. 30. *If a person has done anything which he imagines will affect others with joy, he also will be affected with joy, accompanied with an idea of himself as its cause; that is to say, he will look upon himself with joy. If, on the other hand, he has done anything which he imagines will affect others with sorrow, he will look upon himself with sorrow.*

Demonst. He who imagines that he affects others with joy or sorrow will necessarily be affected with joy or sorrow (Prop. 27, pt. 3). But since man is conscious of himself (Props. 19 and 23, pt. 2) by means of the affections by which he is determined to act; therefore he who has done anything which he imagines will affect others with joy will be affected with joy accompanied with a consciousness of himself as its cause; that is to say, he will look upon himself with joy, and, on the other hand, &c. Q.E.D.

Schol. Since love (Schol. Prop. 13, pt. 3) is joy attended with the idea of an external cause, and hatred is sorrow attended with the idea of an external cause, the joy and sorrow spoken of in this proposition will be a kind of love and hatred. But because love and hatred are related to external objects, we will therefore give a different name to the affects which are the subject of this proposition, and we will call this kind of joy which is attended with the idea of an external cause *self-exaltation*, and the sorrow opposed to it we will call *shame*. The reader is to understand that this is the case in which joy or sorrow arises because the man believes that he is praised or blamed, otherwise I shall call this joy accompanied with the idea of an external cause *contentment with one's-self*, and the sorrow opposed to it *repentance*. Again, since (Corol. Prop. 17, pt. 2) it may happen that the joy with which a person imagines that he affects other people is only imaginary, and since (Prop. 25, pt. 3) every one endeavours to imagine concerning himself what he supposes will affect himself with joy, it may easily happen that the self-exalted man becomes proud, and imagines that he is pleasing everybody when he is offensive to everybody.

PROP. 31. *If we imagine that a person loves, desires, or hates a thing which we ourselves love, desire, or hate, we shall on that account love, desire, or hate the thing more steadily. If, on the other hand, we imagine that he is averse to the thing we love or loves the thing to which we are averse, we shall then suffer vacillation of mind.*

Demonst. If we imagine that another person loves a thing, on that very account we shall love it (Prop. 27, pt. 3). But we are supposed to love it independently of this, and a new cause for our love is therefore added, by which it is strengthened, and consequently the object we love will be loved by us on this account the more steadily. Again, if we imagine that a person is averse to a thing, on that very account we shall be averse to it (Prop. 27, pt. 3); but if we suppose that we at the same time love it, we shall both love the thing and be averse to it, that is to say (Schol. Prop. 17, pt. 3), we shall suffer vacillation of mind. Q.E.D.

Corol. It follows from this proposition and from Prop. 28, pt. 3, that every one endeavours as much as possible to make others love what he loves, and to hate what he hates. Hence the poet says—

Speremus pariter, pariter metuamus amantes;
Ferreus est, si quis, quod sinit alter, amat.[1]

This effort to make every one approve what we love or hate is in truth ambition (Schol. Prop. 29, pt. 3), and so we see that each person by nature desires that other persons should live according to his way of thinking; but if every one does this, then all are a hindrance to one another, and if every one wishes to be praised or beloved by the rest, then they all hate one another.

PROP. 32. *If we imagine that a person enjoys a thing which only one can possess, we do all we can to prevent his possessing it.*

Demonst. If we imagine that a person enjoys a thing, that will be a sufficient reason (Prop. 27, pt. 3, with Corol. 1) for making us love the thing and desiring to enjoy it. But (by hypothesis) we imagine that his enjoyment of the thing is an obstacle to our joy, and therefore (Prop. 28, pt. 3) we endeavour to prevent his possessing it. Q.E.D.

Schol. We see, therefore, that the nature of man is generally constituted so as to pity those who are in adversity and envy those who are in prosperity, and (Prop. 32, pt. 3) he envies with a hatred which is the greater in proportion as he loves what he imagines another possesses. We see also that from the same property of human nature from which it follows that men pity one another it also follows that they are envious and ambitious. If we will consult experience, we shall find that she teaches the same doctrine, especially if we consider the

[1]Ovid, *Amor.* ii. 19: Spinoza has, however, transposed the lines.—TR.

first years of our life. For we find that children, because their body is, as it were, continually in equilibrium, laugh and cry merely because they see others do the same; whatever else they see others do they immediately wish to imitate; everything which they think is pleasing to other people they want. And the reason is, as we have said, that the images of things are the affections themselves of the human body, or the ways in which it is affected by external causes and disposed to this or that action.

PROP. 33. *If we love a thing which is like ourselves, we endeavour as much as possible to make it love us in return.*

Demonst. We endeavour as much as possible to imagine before everything else the thing we love (Prop. 12, pt. 3). If, therefore, it be like ourselves, we shall endeavour to affect it with joy before everything else (Prop. 29, pt. 3); that is to say, we shall endeavour as much as possible to cause the beloved object to be affected with joy attended with the idea of ourselves, or, in other words (Schol. Prop. 13, pt. 3), we try to make it love us in return. Q.E.D.

PROP. 34. *The greater the affect with which we imagine that a beloved object is affected towards us, the greater will be our self-exaltation.*

Demonst. We endeavour as much as possible to make a beloved object love us in return (Prop. 33, pt. 3), that is to say (Schol. Prop. 13, pt. 3), to cause it to be affected with joy attended with the idea of ourselves. In proportion, therefore, as we imagine the beloved object to be affected with a joy of which we are the cause, will our endeavour be assisted, that is to say (Prop. 11, pt. 3 with Schol.), will be the greatness of the joy with which we are affected. But since we rejoice because we have affected with joy another person like ourselves, we shall look upon ourselves with joy (Prop. 30, pt. 3); and therefore the greater the affect with which we imagine that the beloved object is affected towards us, the greater will be the joy with which we shall look upon ourselves, that is to say (Schol. Prop. 30, pt. 3), the greater will be our self-exaltation. Q.E.D.

PROP. 35. *If I imagine that an object beloved by me is united to another person by the same, or by a closer bond of friendship than that by which I myself alone held the object, I shall be affected with hatred towards the beloved object itself, and shall envy that other person.*

Demonst. The greater the love with which a person imagines a beloved object to be affected towards him, the greater will be his self-exaltation (Prop. 34, pt. 3), that is to say (Schol. rop. 30, pt. 3), the more will he rejoice. Therefore (Prop. 28, pt. 3) he will endeavour as much as he can to imagine the beloved object united to him as closely as possible, and his effort or desire is strengthened if he imagines that another person desires for himself the same object (Prop. 31, pt. 3). But this effort or desire is supposed to be checked by the image of the beloved object itself attended by the image of the person whom it connects with itself. Therefore (Schol. Prop. 11, pt. 3) the lover on this account will be affected with sorrow attended with the idea of the beloved object as its cause together with the image of another person; that is to say (Schol. Prop. 13, pt. 3), he will be affected with hatred towards the beloved object and at the same time towards this other person (Corol. Prop. 15, pt. 3), whom he will envy (Prop. 23, pt. 3) as being delighted with it. Q.E.D.

Schol. This hatred towards a beloved object when joined with envy is called Jealousy, which is therefore nothing but a vacillation of the mind springing from the love and hatred both felt together, and attended with the idea of another person whom we envy. Moreover, his hatred towards the beloved object will be greater in proportion to the joy with which the jealous man has been usually affected from the mutual affection between him and his beloved, and also in proportion to the affect with which he had been affected towards the person who is imagined to unite to himself the beloved object. For if he has hated him, he will for that very reason hate the beloved object (Prop. 24, pt. 3), because he imagines it to affect with joy that which he hates, and also (Corol. Prop. 15, pt. 3) because he is compelled to connect the image of the beloved object with the image of him whom he hates. This feeling is generally excited when the love is love towards a woman. The man who imagines that the woman he loves prostitutes herself to another is not merely troubled because his appetite is restrained, but he turns away from her because he is obliged to connect the image of a beloved object with the privy parts and with what is excremental in another man; and in addition to this, the jealous person is not received with the same favour which the beloved object formerly bestowed on him,—a new cause of sorrow to the lover, as I shall show.

PROP. 36. *He who recollects a thing with which he has once been delighted, desires to possess it with every condition which existed when he was first delighted with it.*

Demonst. Whatever a man has seen together with an object which has delighted him will be (Prop. 15, pt. 3) contingently a cause of joy, and therefore (Prop. 28, pt. 3) he will desire to possess it all, together with the object which has delighted him, that is to say, he will desire to possess the object with every condition which existed when he was first delighted with it. Q.E.D.

Corol. If, therefore, the lover discovers that one of these conditions be wanting, he will be sad.

Demonst. For in so far as he discovers that any one condition is wanting does he imagine something which excludes the existence of the object. But since (Prop. 36, pt. 3) he desires the object or condition from love, he will therefore be sad (Prop. 19, pt. 3) in so far as he imagines that condition to be wanting. Q.E.D.

Schol. This sorrow, in so far as it is related to the absence of what we love, is called *longing.*

PROP. 37. *The desire which springs from sorrow or joy, from hatred or love, is greater in proportion as the affect is greater.*

Demonst. Sorrow lessens or limits a man's power of action (Schol. Prop. 11, pt. 3), that is to say (Prop. 7, pt. 3), it lessens or limits the effort by which a man endeavours to persevere in his own being, and therefore (Prop. 5, pt. 3) it is opposed to this effort; consequently, if a man be affected with sorrow, the first thing he attempts is to remove that sorrow; but (by the definition of sorrow) the greater it is, the greater is the human power of action to which it must be opposed, and so much the greater, therefore, will be the power of action with which the man will endeavour to remove it: that is to say (Schol. Prop. 9, pt. 3), with the greater eagerness or desire will he struggle to remove it. Again, since joy (Schol. Prop. 11, pt. 3) increases or assists a man's power of action, it is easily demonstrated, by the same method, that there is nothing which a man who is affected with joy desires more than to preserve it, and his desire is in proportion to his joy. Again, since hatred and love are themselves affects either of joy or sorrow, it follows in the same manner that the effort, desire, or eagerness which arises from hatred or love will be greater in proportion to the hatred or love. Q.E.D.

PROP. 38. *If a man has begun to hate a beloved thing, so that his love to it is altogether destroyed, he will for this very reason hate it more than he would have done if he had never loved it, and his hatred will be in greater proportion to his previous love.*

Demonst. If a man begins to hate a thing which he loves, a constraint is put upon more appetites than if he had never loved it. For love is joy (Schol. Prop. 13, pt. 3), which a man endeavours to preserve as much as possible (Prop. 28, pt. 3),both by looking on the beloved object as present (Schol. Prop. 13, pt. 3), and by affecting it with joy as much as possible (Prop. 21, pt. 3); this effort (Prop. 37, pt. 3) to preserve the joy of love being the greater in proportion as his love is greater, and so also is the effort to bring the beloved object to love him in return (Prop. 33, pt. 3). But these efforts are restrained by the hatred towards the beloved object (Corol. Prop. 13, and Prop. 23, pt. 3); therefore the lover (Schol. Prop. 11, pt. 3) for this reason also will be affected with sorrow, and that the more as the love had been greater; that is to say, in addition to the sorrow which was the cause of the hatred there is another produced by his having loved the object, and consequently he will contemplate with a greater affect of sorrow the beloved object; that is to say (Schol. Prop. 13, pt. 3), he will hate it more than he would have done if he had not loved it, and his hatred will be in proportion to his previous love. Q.E.D.

PROP. 39. *If a man hates another, he will endeavour to do him evil, unless he fears a greater evil will therefrom arise to himself; and, on the other hand, he who loves another will endeavour to do him good by the same rule.*

Demonst. To hate a person (Schol. Prop. 13, pt. 3) is to imagine him as a cause of sorrow, and therefore (Prop. 28, pt. 3) he who hates another will endeavour to remove or destroy him. But if he fears lest a greater grief, or, which is the same thing, a greater evil, should fall upon himself, and one which he thinks he can avoid by refraining from inflicting the evil he meditated, he will desire not to do it (Prop. 28, pt. 3); and this desire will be stronger than the former with which he was possessed of inflicting the evil, and will prevail over it (Prop. 37, pt. 3). This is the first part of the proposition. The second is demonstrated in the same way. Therefore if a man hates another, &c. Q.E.D.

Schol. By *good*, I understand here every kind of joy and everything that conduces to it;

chiefly, however, anything that satisfies longing, whatever that thing may be. By *evil*, I understand every kind of sorrow, and chiefly whatever thwarts longing. For we have shown above (Schol. Prop. 9, pt. 3) that we do not desire a thing because we adjudge it to be good, but, on the contrary, we call it good because we desire it, and consequently everything to which we are averse we call evil. Each person, therefore, according to his affect judges or estimates what is good and what is evil, what is better and what is worse, and what is the best and what is the worst. Thus the covetous man thinks plenty of money to be the best thing and poverty the worst. The ambitious man desires nothing like glory, and on the other hand dreads nothing like shame. To the envious person, again, nothing is more pleasant than the misfortune of another, and nothing more disagreeable than the prosperity of another. And so each person according to his affect judges a thing to be good or evil, useful or useless. We notice, moreover, that this affect, by which a man is so disposed as not to will the thing he wills, and to will that which he does not will, is called *fear*, which may therefore be defined as that *apprehension* which leads a man to avoid an evil in the future by incurring a lesser evil (Prop. 28, pt. 3). If the evil feared is shame, then the fear is called *modesty*. If the desire of avoiding the future is restrained by the fear of another evil, so that the man does not know what he most wishes, then this apprehension is called *consternation*, especially if both the evils feared are very great.

PROP. 40. *If we imagine that we are hated by another without having given him any cause for it, we shall hate him in return.*

Demonst. If we imagine that another person is affected with hatred, on that account we shall also be affected with it (Prop. 27, pt. 3); that is to say, we shall be affected with sorrow (Schol. Prop. 13, pt. 3), accompanied with the idea of an external cause. But (by hypothesis) we imagine no cause for this sorrow excepting the person himself who hates us, and therefore, because we imagine ourselves hated by another, we shall be affected with sorrow accompanied with the idea of him who hates us; that is to say (Schol. Prop. 13, pt. 3), we shall hate him. Q.E.D.

Schol. If we imagine that we have given just cause for the hatred, we shall then (Prop. 30, pt. 3, with its Schol.) be affected with shame. This, however (Prop. 25, pt. 3), rarely happens.

This reciprocity of hatred may also arise
om the fact that hatred is followed by an
tempt to bring evil upon him who is hated
'rop. 39, pt. 3). If, therefore, we imagine that
e are hated by any one else, we shall imagine
m as the cause of some evil or sorrow, and
us we shall be affected with sorrow or appre-
nsion accompanied with the idea of the per-
n who hates us as a cause; that is to say,
e shall hate him in return, as we have said
ove.

Corol. 1. If we imagine that the person we
ve is affected with hatred towards us, we
all be agitated at the same time both with
ve and hatred. For in so far as we imagine
at we are hated are we determined (Prop.
, pt. 3) to hate him in return. But (by hy-
thesis) we love him notwithstanding, and
erefore we shall be agitated both by love and
tred.

Corol. 2. If we imagine that an evil has been
ought upon us through the hatred of some
rson towards whom we have hitherto been
oved by no affect, we shall immediately en-
avour to return that evil upon him.

Demonst. If we imagine that another per-
n is affected with hatred towards us, we shall
ate him in return (Prop. 40, pt. 3), and (Prop.
, pt. 3) we shall endeavour to devise and
'rop. 39, pt. 3) bring upon him everything
hich can affect him with sorrow. But (by hy-
thesis) the first thing of this kind we imagine
the evil brought upon ourselves, and there-
re we shall immediately endeavour to bring
at upon him.   q.e.d.

Schol. The attempt to bring evil on those
e hate is called *anger*, and the attempt to re-
rn the evil inflicted on ourselves is called
ngeance.

ROP. 41. *If we imagine that we are beloved by a
erson without having given any cause for the
ve (which may be the case by Corol. Prop. 15,
t. 3, and by Prop. 16, pt. 3), we shall love him
n return.*

Demonst. This proposition is demonstrated
the same way as the preceding, to the scho-
um of which the reader is also referred.

Schol. If we imagine that we have given just
ause for love, we shall pride ourselves upon it
Prop. 30, pt. 3, with its Schol.). This frequent-
occurs (Prop. 25, pt. 3), and we have said
hat the contrary takes place when we believe
hat we are hated by another person (Schol.
rop. 40, pt. 3). This reciprocal love, and con-
equently (Prop. 39, pt. 3) this attempt to do

good to the person who loves us, and who (by
the same Prop. 39, pt. 3) endeavours to do
good to us, is called *thankfulness* or *gratitude*,
and from this we can see how much readier
men are to revenge themselves than to return
a benefit.

Corol. If we imagine that we are loved by a
person we hate, we shall at the same time be
agitated both by love and hatred. This is demonstrated in the same way as the preceding
proposition.

Schol. If the hatred prevail, we shall endeavour to bring evil upon the person by whom
we are loved. This affect is called Cruelty,
especially if it is believed that the person who
loves has not given any ordinary reason for
hatred.

PROP. 42. *If, moved by love or hope of self-
exaltation, we have conferred a favour upon another person, we shall be sad if we see that the
favour is received with ingratitude.*

Demonst. If we love a thing which is of the
same nature as ourselves, we endeavour as
much as possible to cause it to love us in return
(Prop. 33, pt. 3). If we confer a favour, therefore, upon any one because of our love towards
him, we do it with a desire by which we are
possessed that we may be loved in return; that
is to say (Prop. 34, pt. 3), from the hope of
self-exaltation, or (Schol. Prop. 30, pt. 3) of
joy, and we shall consequently (Prop. 12, pt.
3) endeavour as much as possible to imagine
this cause of self-exaltation, or to contemplate
it as actually existing. But (by hypothesis) we
imagine something else which excludes the existence of that cause, and, therefore (Prop. 19,
pt. 3), this will make us sad.   q.e.d.

PROP. 43. *Hatred is increased through return of
hatred, but may be destroyed by love.*

Demonst. If we imagine that the person we
hate is affected with hatred towards us, a new
hatred is thereby produced (Prop. 40, pt. 3),
the old hatred still remaining (by hypothesis).
If, on the other hand, we imagine him to be
affected with love towards us, in so far as we
imagine it (Prop. 30, pt. 3) shall we look upon
ourselves with joy, and endeavour (Prop. 29,
pt. 3) to please him; that is to say (Prop. 41,
pt. 3), in so far shall we endeavour not to hate
him nor to affect him with sorrow. This effort
(Prop. 37, pt. 3) will be greater or less as the
affect from which it arises is greater or less,
and, therefore, should it be greater than that
which springs from hatred, and by which

(Prop. 26, pt. 3) we endeavour to affect with sorrow the object we hate, then it will prevail and banish hatred from the mind. Q.E.D.

PROP. 44. *Hatred which is altogether overcome by love passes into love, and the love is therefore greater than if hatred had not preceded it.*

Demonst. The demonstration is of the same kind as that of Prop. 38, pt. 3. For if we begin to love a thing which we hated, or upon which we were in the habit of looking with sorrow, we shall rejoice for the very reason that we love, and to this joy which love involves (see its definition in the Schol. of Prop. 13, pt. 3) a new joy is added, which springs from the fact that the effort to remove the sorrow which hatred involves (Prop. 37, pt. 3) is so much assisted, there being also present before us as the cause of our joy the idea of the person whom we hated.

Schol. Notwithstanding the truth of this proposition, no one will try to hate a thing or will wish to be affected with sorrow in order that he may rejoice the more; that is to say, no one will desire to inflict loss on himself in the hope of recovering the loss, or to become ill in the hope of getting well, inasmuch as every one will always try to preserve his being and to remove sorrow from himself as much as possible. Moreover, if it can be imagined that it is possible for us to desire to hate a person in order that we may love him afterwards the more, we must always desire to continue the hatred. For the love will be the greater as the hatred has been greater, and therefore we shall always desire the hatred to be more and more increased. Upon the same principle we shall desire that our sickness may continue and increase in order that we may afterwards enjoy the greater pleasure when we get well, and therefore we shall always desire sickness, which (Prop. 6, pt. 3) is absurd.

PROP. 45. *If we imagine that any one like ourselves is affected with hatred towards an object like ourselves which we love, we shall hate him.*

Demonst. The beloved object hates him who hates it (Prop. 40, pt. 3), and therefore we who love it, who imagine that any one hates it, imagine also that it is affected with hatred; that is to say, with sorrow (Schol. Prop. 13, pt. 3), and consequently (Prop. 21, pt. 3) we are sad, our sadness being accompanied with the idea of the person, as the cause thereof, who hates the beloved object; that is to say (Schol. Prop. 13, pt. 3), we shall hate him. Q.E.D.

PROP. 46. *If we have been affected with joy or sorrow by any one who belongs to a class or nation different from our own, and if our joy or sorrow is accompanied with the idea of this person as its cause, under the common name of his class or nation, we shall not love or hate him merely, but the whole of the class or nation to which he belongs.*

Demonst. This proposition is demonstrated in the same way as Prop. 16, pt. 3.

PROP. 47. *The joy which arises from our imagining that what we hate has been destroyed or has been injured is not unaccompanied with some sorrow.*

Demonst. This is evident from Prop. 27, pt. 3; for in so far as we imagine an object like ourselves affected with sorrow shall we be sad.

Schol. This proposition may also be demonstrated from Corol. Prop. 17, pt. 2. For as often as we recollect the object, although it does not actually exist, we contemplate it as present, and the body is affected in the same way as if it were present. Therefore, so long as the memory of the object remains, we are so determined as to contemplate it with sorrow, and this determination, while the image of the object abides, is restrained by the recollection of those things which exclude the existence of the object, but is not altogether removed. Therefore we rejoice only so far as the determination is restrained, and hence it happens that the joy which springs from the misfortune of the object we hate is renewed as often as we recollect the object. For, as we have already shown, whenever its image is excited, inasmuch as this involves the existence of the object, we are so determined as to contemplate it with the same sorrow with which we were accustomed to contemplate it when it really existed. But because we have connected with this image other images which exclude its existence, the determination to sorrow is immediately restrained, and we rejoice anew; and this happens as often as this repetition takes place. This is the reason why we rejoice as often as we call to mind any evil that is past, and why we like to tell tales about the dangers we have escaped, since whenever we imagine any danger, we contemplate it as if it were about to be, and are so determined as to fear it—a determination which is again restrained by the idea of freedom, which we connected with the idea of the danger when we were freed from it, and this idea of freedom again makes us fear less, so that we again rejoice.

PROP. 48. *Love and hatred towards any object, for example, towards Peter, are destroyed if the joy and the sorrow which they respectively involve be joined to the idea of another cause; and they are respectively diminished in proportion as we imagine that Peter has not been their sole cause.*

Demonst. This is plain from the very definition of love and hatred (see Schol. Prop. 13, pt. 3), joy being called love to Peter and sorrow being called hatred to him, solely because he is considered to be the cause of this or that affect. Whenever, therefore, we can no longer consider him either partially or entirely its cause, the affect towards him ceases or is diminished. Q.E.D.

PROP. 49. *For the same reason, love or hatred towards an object we imagine to be free must be greater than towards an object which is under necessity.*

Demonst. An object which we imagine to be free must (Def. 7, pt. 1) be perceived through itself and without others. If, therefore, we imagine it to be the cause of joy or sorrow, we shall for that reason alone love or hate it (Schol. Prop. 13, pt. 3), and that too with the greatest love or the greatest hatred which can spring from the given affect (Prop. 48, pt. 3). But if we imagine that the object which is the cause of that effect is necessary, then (by the same Def. 7, pt. 1) we shall imagine it as the cause of that affect, not alone, but together with other causes, and so (Prop. 48, pt. 3) our love or hatred towards it will be less. Q.E.D.

Schol. Hence it follows that our hatred or love towards one another is greater than towards other things, because we think we are free. We must take into account also the imitation of affects which we have discussed in Props. 27, 34, 40, and 43, pt. 3.

PROP. 50. *Anything may be accidentally the cause either of hope or fear.*

This proposition is demonstrated in the same way as Prop. 15, pt. 3, which see, together with Schol. 2, Prop. 18, pt. 3.

Schol. Things which are accidentally the causes either of hope or fear are called good or evil omens. In so far as the omens are the cause of hope and fear (by the Def. of hope and fear in Schol. 2, Prop. 18, pt. 3) are they the cause of joy or of sorrow, and consequently (Corol. Prop. 15, pt. 3) so far do we love them or hate them, and (Prop. 28, pt. 3) endeavour to use them as means to obtain those things for which we hope, or to remove them as obstacles or

causes of fear. It follows, too, from Prop. 25, pt. 3, that our natural constitution is such that we easily believe the things we hope for, and believe with difficulty those we fear, and that we think too much of the former and too little of the latter. Thus have superstitions arisen, by which men are everywhere disquieted. I do not consider it worth while to go any farther, and to explain here all those vacillations of mind which arise from hope and fear, since it follows from the definition alone of these affects that hope cannot exist without fear, nor fear without hope (as we shall explain more at length in the proper place). Besides, in so far as we hope for a thing or fear it, we love it or hate it, and therefore everything which has been said about hatred and love can easily be applied to hope and fear.

PROP. 51. *Different men may be affected by one and the same object in different ways, and the same man may be affected by one and the same object in different ways at different times.*

Demonst. The human body (Post. 3, pt. 2) is affected by external bodies in a number of ways. Two men, therefore, may be affected in different ways at the same time, and, therefore (Ax. 1, after Lemma 3, following Prop. 13, pt. 2), they can be affected by one and the same object in different ways. Again (Post. 3, pt. 2), the human body may be affected now in this and now in that way, and consequently (by the axiom just quoted) it may be affected by one and the same object in different ways at different times. Q.E.D.

Schol. We thus see that it is possible for one man to love a thing and for another man to hate it; for this man to fear what this man does not fear, and for the same man to love what before he hated, and to dare to do what before he feared. Again, since each judges according to his own affect what is good and what is evil, what is better and what is worse (Schol. Prop. 39, pt. 3), it follows that men may change in their judgment as they do in their affects,[1] and hence it comes to pass that when we compare men, we distinguish them solely by the difference in their affects, calling some brave, others timid, and others by other names. For example, I shall call a man *brave* who despises an evil which I usually fear, and if, besides this, I consider the fact that his desire of doing evil to a person whom he hates or doing good to

[1]That this may be the case, although the human mind is part of the divine intellect, we have shown in Corol. Prop. 11, pt. 2.—SPINOZA.

one whom he loves is not restrained by that fear of evil by which I am usually restrained, I call him *audacious*. On the other hand, the man who fears an evil which I usually despise will appear *timid*, and if, besides this, I consider that his desire is restrained by the fear of an evil which has no power to restrain me, I call him *pusillanimous;* and in this way everybody will pass judgment. Finally, from this nature of man and the inconstancy of his judgment, in consequence of which he often judges things from mere effect, and the things which he believes contribute to his joy or his sorrow, and which, therefore, he endeavours to bring to pass or remove (Prop. 28, pt. 3), are often only imaginary—to say nothing about what we have demonstrated in the Second Part of this book about the uncertainty of things—it is easy to see that a man may often be himself the cause of his sorrow or his joy, or of being affected with sorrow or joy accompanied with the idea of himself as its cause, so that we can easily understand what repentance and what self-approval are. Repentance is sorrow accompanied with the idea of one's self as the cause, and self-approval is joy accompanied with the idea of one's self as the cause; and these affects are very intense because men believe themselves free (Prop. 49, pt. 3).

Prop. 52. *An object which we have seen before together with other objects, or which we imagine possesses nothing which is not common to it with many other objects, we shall not contemplate so long as that which we imagine possesses something peculiar.*

Demonst. Whenever we imagine an object which we have seen with others, we immediately call these to mind (Prop. 18, pt. 2, with Schol.), and thus from the contemplation of one object we immediately fall to contemplating another. This also is our way with an object which we imagine to possess nothing except what is common to a number of other objects. For this is the same thing as supposing that we contemplate nothing in it which we have not seen before with other objects. On the other hand, if we suppose ourselves to imagine in an object something peculiar which we have never seen before, it is the same as saying that the mind, while it contemplates that object, holds nothing else in itself to the contemplation of which it can pass, turning away from the contemplation of the object, and therefore it is determined to the contemplation solely of the object. Therefore an object, &c. Q.E.D.

Schol. This affection of the mind or imagination of a particular thing, in so far as it alone occupies the mind, is called *astonishment*, and if it is excited by an object we dread, we call it *consternation*, because astonishment at the evil so fixes us in the contemplation of itself, that we cannot think of anything else by which we might avoid the evil. On the other hand, if the objects at which we are astonished are human wisdom, industry, or anything of this kind, inasmuch as we consider that their possessor is by so much superior to ourselves, the astonishment goes by the name of *veneration;* whilst, if the objects are human anger, envy, or anything of this sort, it goes by the name of *horror*. Again, if we are astonished at the wisdom of industry of a man we love, then our love on that account (Prop. 12, pt. 3) will be greater, and this love, united to astonishment or veneration, we call *devotion*. In the same manner it is possible to conceive of hatred, hope, confidence, and other affects being joined to astonishment, so that more affects may be deduced than are indicated by the words in common use. From this we see that names have been invented for affects from common usage, rather than from accurate knowledge of them.

To astonishment is opposed contempt, which is usually caused, nevertheless, by our being determined to astonishment, love, or fear towards an object either because we see that another person is astonished at, loves or fears this same object, or because at first sight it appears like other objects, at which we are astonished or which we love or fear (Prop. 15 with Corol. pt. 3, and Prop. 27, pt. 3). But if the presence of the object or a more careful contemplation of it should compel us to deny that there exists in it any cause for astonishment, love, fear, &c., then from its presence itself, the mind remains determined to think rather of those things which are not in it than of those which are in it, although from the presence of an object the mind is accustomed to think chiefly about what is in the object. We may also observe that as devotion springs from astonishment at a thing we love, so *derision* springs from the contempt of a thing we hate or fear, whilst *scorn* arises from the contempt of folly, as veneration arises from astonishment at wisdom. We may also conceive of love, hope, glory, and other affects being joined to contempt, and thus deduce other affects which also we are not in the habit of distinguishing by separate words.

Prop. 53. *When the mind contemplates itself and its own power of acting it rejoices, and it rejoices in proportion to the distinctness with which it imagines itself and its power of action.*

Demonst. Man has no knowledge of himself except through the affections of his own body and their ideas (Props. 19 and 23, pt. 2); whenever, therefore, it happens that the mind is able to contemplate itself, it is thereby supposed to pass to a greater perfection, that is to say (Schol. Prop. 11, pt. 3), it is supposed to be affected with joy, and the joy is greater in proportion to the distinctness with which it imagines itself and its power of action. Q.E.D.

Corol. The more a man imagines that he is praised by other men, the more is this joy strengthened; for the more a man imagines that he is praised by others, the more does he imagine that he affects others with joy accompanied by the idea of himself as a cause (Schol. Prop. 29, pt. 3), and therefore (Prop. 27, pt. 3) he is affected with greater joy accompanied with the idea of himself. Q.E.D.

Prop. 54. *The mind endeavours to imagine those things only which posit its power of acting.*

Demonst. The effort or power of the mind is the essence of the mind itself (Prop. 7, pt. 3), but the essence of the mind, as is self-evident, affirms only that which the mind is and is able to do, and does not affirm that which the mind is not and cannot do, and therefore the mind endeavours to imagine those things only which affirm or posit its power of acting. Q.E.D.

Prop. 55. *When the mind imagines its own weakness it necessarily sorrows.*

Demonst. The essence of the mind affirms only that which the mind is and is able to do, or, in other words, it is the nature of the mind to imagine those things only which posit its power of acting (Prop. 54, pt. 3). If we say, therefore, that the mind, while it contemplates itself, imagines its own weakness, we are merely saying in other words that the effort of the mind to imagine something which posits its power of acting is restrained, that is to say (Schol. Prop. 11, pt. 3), the mind is sad. Q.E.D.

Corol. This sorrow is strengthened in proportion as the mind imagines that it is blamed by others. This is demonstrated in the same way as Corol. Prop. 53, pt. 3.

Schol. This sorrow, accompanied with the idea of our own weakness, is called *humility*, and the joy which arises from contemplating ourselves is called *self-love* or *self-approval*. Inasmuch as this joy recurs as often as a man contemplates his own virtues or his own power of acting, it comes to pass that every one loves to tell of his own deeds, and to display the powers both of his body and mind; and that for this reason men become an annoyance to one another. It also follows that men are naturally envious (Schol. Prop. 24, and Schol. Prop. 32, pt. 3), that is to say, they rejoice over the weaknesses of their equals and sorrow over their strength. For whenever a person imagines his own actions he is affected with joy (Prop. 53, pt. 3), and his joy is the greater in proportion as he imagines that his actions express more perfection, and he imagines them more distinctly; that is to say (by what has been said in Schol. 1, Prop. 40, pt. 2), in proportion as he is able to distinguish them from others, and to contemplate them as individual objects. A man's joy in contemplating himself will therefore be greatest when he contemplates something in himself which he denies of other people. For if he refers that which he affirms of himself to the universal idea of man or of animal nature, he will not so much rejoice; on the other hand, he will be sad if he imagines that his own actions when compared with those of other people are weaker than theirs, and this sorrow he will endeavour to remove (Prop. 28, pt. 3), either by misinterpreting the actions of his equals, or giving as great a lustre as possible to his own. It appears, therefore, that men are by nature inclined to hatred and envy, and we must add that their education assists them in this propensity, for parents are accustomed to excite their children to follow virtue by the stimulus of honour and envy alone. But an objection perhaps may be raised that we not unfrequently venerate men and admire their virtues. In order to remove this objection I will add the following corollary.

Corol. No one envies the virtue of a person who is not his equal.

Demonst. Envy is nothing but hatred (Schol. Prop. 24, pt. 3), that is to say (Schol. Prop. 13, pt. 3), sorrow, or, in other words (Schol. Prop. 11, pt. 3), an affection by which the effort of a man or his power of action is restrained. But (Schol. Prop. 9, pt. 3) a man neither endeavours to do nor desires anything excepting what can follow from his given nature, therefore a man will not desire to affirm of himself any power of action, or which is the same thing, any virtue which is peculiar to another nature and foreign to his own. His desire, therefore, cannot be restrained, that is to say (Schol. Prop. 11, pt. 3), he cannot feel any sorrow because he contemplates a virtue in another person altogether unlike himself, and consequently he cannot envy that person, but will only envy one who is his own equal, and who is supposed to possess the same nature.

Schol. Since, therefore, we have said in Schol. Prop. 52, pt. 3, that we venerate a man because we are astonished at his wisdom and bravery, &c., this happens because (as is evident from the proposition itself) we imagine that he specially possesses these virtues, and that they are not common to our nature. We therefore envy them no more than we envy trees their height or lions their bravery.

PROP. 56. *Of joy, sorrow, and desire, and consequently of every effort which either, like vacillation of mind, is compounded of these, or, like love, hatred, hope, and fear, is derived from them, there are just as many kinds as there are kinds of objects by which we are affected.*

Demonst. Joy and sorrow, and consequently the affects which are compounded of these or derived from them, are passions (Schol. Prop. 11, pt. 3). But (Prop. 1, pt. 3) we necessarily suffer in so far as we have inadequate ideas, and (Prop. 3, pt. 3) only in so far as we have them; that is to say (see Schol. Prop. 40, pt. 2), we necessarily suffer only in so far as we imagine, or (see Prop. 17, pt. 2, with its Schol.) in so far as we are affected with an effect which involves the nature of our body and that of an external body. The nature, therefore, of each passion must necessarily be explained in such a manner, that the nature of the object by which we are affected is expressed. The joy, for example, which springs from an object A. involves the nature of that object A., and the joy which springs from B. involves the nature of that object B., and therefore these two affects of joy are of a different nature. In like manner the affect of sorrow which arises from one object is of a different kind from that which arises from another cause, and the same thing is to be understood of love, hatred, hope, fear, vacillation of mind, &c.; so that there are necessarily just as many kinds of joy, sorrow, love, hatred, &c., as there are kinds of objects by which we are affected. But desire is the essence itself or nature of a person in so far as this nature is conceived from its given constitution as determined towards any action (Schol. Prop. 9, pt. 3), and therefore as a person is affected by external causes with this or

that kind of joy, sorrow, love, hatred, &c., that is to say, as his nature is constituted in this or that way, so must his desire vary and the nature of one desire differ from that of another, just as the affects from which each desire arises differ. There are as many kinds of desires, therefore, as there are kinds of joy, sorrow, love, &c., and, consequently (as we have just shown), as there are kinds of objects by which we are affected. Q.E.D.

Schol. Amongst the different kinds of affects, which (by the preceding Prop.) must be very great in number, the most remarkable are *voluptuousness, drunkenness, lust, avarice,* and *ambition,* which are nothing but notions of love or desire, which explain the nature of this or that affect through the objects to which they are related. For by *voluptuousness, drunkenness, lust, avarice,* and *ambition* we understand nothing but an immoderate love or desire for good living, for drinking, for women, for riches, and for glory. It is to be observed that these affects, in so far as we distinguish them by the object alone to which they are related, have no contraries. For *temperance, sobriety,* and *chastity,* which we are in the habit of opposing to voluptuousness, drunkenness, and lust, are not affects nor passions: but merely indicate the power of the mind which restrains these affects.

The remaining kinds of affects I cannot explain here (for they are as numerous as are the varieties of objects), nor, if I could explain them, is it necessary to do so. For it is sufficient for the purpose we have in view, the determination, namely, of the strength of the affects and the mind's power over them, to have a general definition of each kind of affect. It is sufficient for us, I say, to understand the common properties of the mind and the affects, so that we may determine what and how great is the power of the mind to govern and constrain the affects. Although, therefore, there is a great difference between this or that affect of love, of hatred, or of desire—for example, between the love towards children and the love towards a wife—it is not worth while for us to take cognisance of these differences, or to investigate the nature and origin of the affects any further.

PROP. 57. *The affect of one person differs from the corresponding affect of another as much as the essence of the one person differs from that of the other.*

Demonst. This proposition is evident from

Ax. 1, following Lem. 3, after Schol. Prop. 13, pt. 2. Nevertheless, we will demonstrate it from the definitions of the three primitive affects. All affects are related to desire, joy, or sorrow, as the definitions show which we have given of those affects. But desire is the very nature or essence of a person (Schol. Prop. 9, pt. 3), and therefore the desire of one person differs from the desire of another as much as the nature or essence of the one differs from that of the other. Again, joy and sorrow are passions by which the power of a person or his effort to persevere in his own being is increased or diminished, helped, or limited (Prop. 11, pt. 3, with its Schol.). But by the effort to persevere in his own being, in so far as it is related at the same time to the mind and the body, we understand appetite and desire (Schol. Prop. 9, pt. 3), and therefore joy and sorrow are desire or appetite in so far as the latter is increased, diminished, helped, or limited by external causes; that is to say (Schol. Prop. 9, pt. 3), they are the nature itself of each person.

The joy or sorrow of one person therefore differs from the joy or sorrow of another as much as the nature or essence of one person differs from that of the other, and consequently the affect of one person differs from the corresponding affect of another, &c. Q.E.D.

Schol. Hence it follows that the affects of animals which are called irrational (for after we have learnt the origin of the mind we can in no way doubt that brutes feel) differ from human affects as much as the nature of a brute differs from that of a man. Both the man and the horse, for example, are swayed by the lust to propagate, but the horse is swayed by equine lust and the man by that which is human. The lusts and appetites of insects, fishes, and birds must vary in the same way; and so, although each individual lives contented with its own nature and delights in it, nevertheless the life with which it is contented and its joy are nothing but the idea or soul of that individual, and so the joy of one differs in character from the joy of the other as much as the essence of the one differs from the essence of the other. Finally, it follows from the preceding proposition that the joy by which the drunkard is enslaved is altogether different from the joy which is the portion of the philosopher,—a thing I wished just to hint in passing. So much, therefore, for the affects which are related to man in so far as he suffers. It remains that I should say a few words about those things which are related to him in so far as he acts.

PROP. 58. *Besides the joys and sorrows which are passions, there are other affects of joy and sorrow which are related to us in so far as we act.*

Demonst. When the mind conceives itself and its own power of acting, it is rejoiced (Prop. 53, pt. 3). But the mind necessarily contemplates itself whenever it conceives a true or adequate idea (Prop. 43, pt. 2); and as (Schol. 2, Prop. 40, pt. 2) it does conceive some adequate ideas, it is rejoiced in so far as it conceives them, or, in other words (Prop. 1, pt. 3), in so far as it acts. Again, the mind, both in so far as it has clear and distinct ideas and in so far as it has confused ideas, endeavours to persevere in its own being (Prop. 9, pt. 3). But by this effort we understand desire (Schol. Prop. 9, pt. 3), and therefore desire also is related to us in so far as we think; that is to say (Prop. 1, pt. 3), in so far as we act. Q.E.D.

PROP. 59. *Amongst all the affects which are related to the mind in so far as it acts, there are none which are not related to joy or desire.*

Demonst. All the affects are related to desire, joy, or sorrow, as the definitions we have given of them show. By sorrow, however, we understand that the mind's power of acting is lessened or limited (Prop. 11, pt. 3, and its Schol.), and therefore, in so far as the mind suffers sorrow is its power of thinking, that is to say (Prop. 1, pt. 3), its power of acting, lessened or limited. Therefore no affects of sorrow can be related to the mind in so far as it acts, but only affects of joy and desire, which (by the preceding Prop.) are also so far related to the mind. Q.E.D.

Schol. All the actions which follow from the affects which are related to the mind in so far as it thinks I ascribe to *fortitude*, which I divide into *strength of mind* (*animositas*) and *generosity*. By *strength of mind*, I mean the desire by which each person endeavours from the dictates of reason alone to preserve his own being. By *generosity*, I mean the desire by which from the dictates of reason alone each person endeavours to help other people and to join them to him in friendship. Those actions, therefore, which have for their aim the advantage only of the doer I ascribe to strength of mind, whilst those which aim at the advantage of others I ascribe to generosity. Temperance, however, sobriety, and presence of mind in danger, are a species of strength of mind, while moderation and mercy are a species of generosity.

I have now, I think, explained the principal affects and vacillations of the mind which are compounded of the three primary affects, desire, joy and sorrow, and have set them forth through their first causes. From what has been said it is plain that we are disturbed by external causes in a number of ways, and that, like the waves of the sea agitated by contrary winds, we fluctuate in our ignorance of our future and destiny. I have said, however, that I have only explained the principal mental complications, and not all which may exist. For by the same method which we have pursued above it would be easy to show that love unites itself to repentance, scorn, shame, &c.; but I think it has already been made clear to all that the affects can be combined in so many ways, and that so many variations can arise, that no limits can be assigned to their number. It is sufficient for my purpose to have enumerated only those which are of consequence; the rest, of which I have taken no notice, being more curious than important. There is one constantly recurring characteristic of love which I have yet to notice, and that is, that while we are enjoying the thing which we desired, the body acquires from that fruition a new disposition by which it is otherwise determined, and the images of other things are excited in it, and the mind begins to imagine and to desire other things. For example, when we imagine anything which usually delights our taste, we desire to enjoy it by eating it. But whilst we enjoy it the stomach becomes full, and the constitution of the body becomes altered. If, therefore, the body being now otherwise disposed, the image of the food, in consequence of its being present, and therefore also the effort or desire to eat it, become more intense, then this new disposition of the body will oppose this effort or desire, and consequently the presence of the food which we desired will become hateful to us, and this hatefulness is what we call loathing or disgust. As for the external affections of the body which are observed in the affects, such as trembling, paleness, sobbing, laughter, and the like, I have neglected to notice them, because they belong to the body alone without any relationship to the mind. A few things remain to be said about the definitions of the affects, and I will therefore here repeat the definitions in order, appending to them what is necessary to be observed in each.

THE AFFECTS. DEF. 1. *Desire* is the essence itself of man in so far as it is conceived as determined to any action by any one of his affections.

Explanation. We have said above, in the Schol. of Prop. 9, pt. 3, that desire is appetite which is self-conscious, and that appetite is the essence itself of man in so far as it is determined to such acts as contribute to his preservation. But in the same scholium I have taken care to remark that in truth I cannot recognise any difference between human appetite and desire. For whether a man be conscious of his appetite or not, it remains one and the same appetite, and so, lest I might appear to be guilty of tautology, I have not explained desire by appetite, but have tried to give such a definition of desire as would include all the efforts of human nature to which we give the name of appetite, desire, will, or impulse. For I might have said that desire is the essence itself of man in so far as it is considered as determined to any action; but from this definition it would not follow (Prop. 23, pt. 2) that the mind could be conscious of its desire or appetite, and therefore, in order that I might include the cause of this consciousness, it was necessary (by the same proposition) to add the words, *in so far as it is conceived as determined to any action by any one of his affections.* For by an affection of the human essence we understand any constitution of that essence, whether it be innate, whether it be conceived through the attribute of thought alone or of extension alone, or whether it be related to both. By the word "desire," therefore, I understand all the efforts, impulses, appetites, and volitions of a man, which vary according to his changing disposition, and not unfrequently are so opposed to one another that he is drawn hither and thither, and knows not whither he ought to turn.

2. *Joy* is man's passage from a less to a greater perfection.

3. *Sorrow* is man's passage from a greater to a less perfection.

Explanation. I say passage, for joy is not perfection itself. If a man were born with the perfection to which he passes, he would possess it without the affect of joy; a truth which will appear the more clearly from the affect of sorrow, which is the opposite to joy. For that sorrow consists in the passage to a less perfection, but not in the less perfection itself, no one can deny, since in so far as a man shares any perfection he cannot be sad. Nor can we say that sorrow consists in the privation of a greater perfection, for privation is nothing. But the affect of sorrow is a reality, and it therefore must be the reality of the passage to a lesser perfection, or the reality by which man's power of acting is diminished or limited (Schol. Prop. 11, pt. 3). As for the definitions of cheerfulness, pleasurable excitement, melancholy, and grief, I pass these by, because they are related rather to the body than to the mind, and are merely different kinds of joy or of sorrow.

4. *Astonishment* is the imagination of an object in which the mind remains fixed because this particular imagination has no connection with others.

Explanation. In the Schol. of Prop. 18, pt. 2, we have shown that that which causes the mind from the contemplation of one thing immediately to pass to the thought of another is that the images of these things are connected one with the other, and are so arranged that the one follows the others; a process which cannot be conceived when the image of the thing is new, for the mind will be held in the contemplation of the same object until other causes determine it to think of other things. The imagination, therefore, considered in itself, of a new object is of the same character as other imaginations; and for this reason I do not class astonishment among the affects, nor do I see any reason why I should do it, since this abstraction of the mind arises from no positive cause by which it is abstracted from other things, but merely from the absence of any cause by which from the contemplation of one thing the mind is determined to think other things. I acknowledge, therefore (as I have shown in Schol. Prop. 11, pt. 3), only three primitive or primary affects, those of joy, sorrow, and desire; and the only reason which has induced me to speak of astonishment is, that it has been the custom to give other names to certain affects derived from the three primitives whenever these affects are related to objects at which we are astonished. This same reason also induces me to add the definition of contempt.

5. *Contempt* is the imagination of an object which so little touches the mind that the mind is moved by the presence of the object to imagine those qualities which are not in it rather than those which are in it. (See Schol. Prop. 52, pt. 3.)

The definitions of veneration and scorn I pass by here, because they give a name, so far as I know, to none of the affects.

6. *Love* is joy with the accompanying idea of an external cause.

Explanation. This definition explains with sufficient clearness the essence of love; that which is given by some authors, who define love to be the will of the lover to unite himself to the beloved object, expressing not the essence of love but one of its properties, and in as much as these authors have not seen with sufficient clearness what is the essence of love, they could not have a distinct conception of its properties, and consequently their definition has by everybody been thought very obscure. I must observe, however, when I say that it is a property in a lover to will a union with the beloved object, that I do not understand by a will a consent or deliberation or a free decree of the mind (for that this is a fiction we have demonstrated in Prop. 48, pt. 2), nor even a desire of the lover to unite himself with the beloved object when it is absent, nor a desire to continue in its presence when it is present, for love can be conceived without either one or the other of these desires; but by will I understand the satisfaction that the beloved object produces in the lover by its presence, by virtue of which the joy of the lover is strengthened, or at any rate supported.

7. *Hatred* is sorrow with the accompanying idea of an external cause.

Explanation. What is to be observed here will easily be seen from what has been said in the explanation of the preceding definitions. (See, moreover, Schol. Prop. 13, pt. 3.)

8. *Inclination* (*propensio*) is joy with the accompanying idea of some object of being accidentally the cause of the joy.

9. *Aversion* is sorrow with the accompanying idea of some object which is accidentally the cause of the sorrow. (See Schol. Prop. 15, pt. 3.)

10. *Devotion* is love towards an object which astonishes us.

Explanation. That astonishment arises from the novelty of the object we have shown in Prop. 52, pt. 3. If, therefore, it should happen that we often imagine the object at which we are astonished, we shall cease to be astonished at it, and hence we see that the affect of devotion easily degenerates into simple love.

11. *Derision* is joy arising from the imagination that something we despise is present in an object we hate.

Explanation. In so far as we despise a thing we deny its existence (Schol. Prop. 52, pt. 3), and so far (Prop. 20, pt. 3) do we rejoice. But inasmuch as we suppose that a man hates what he ridicules, it follows that this joy is not solid. (See Schol. Prop. 47, pt. 3.)

12. *Hope* is a joy not constant, arising from the idea of something future or past, about the issue of which we sometimes doubt.

13. *Fear* is a sorrow not constant, arising from the idea of something future or past, about the issue of which we sometimes doubt. (See Schol. 2, Prop. 18, pt. 3.)

Explanation. From these definitions it follows that there is no hope without fear nor fear without hope, for the person who wavers in hope and doubts concerning the issue of anything is supposed to imagine something which may exclude its existence, and so far, therefore, to be sad (Prop. 19, pt. 3), and consequently while he wavers in hope, to fear lest his wishes should not be accomplished. So also the person who fears, that is to say, who doubts whether what he hates will not come to pass, imagines something which excludes the existence of what he hates, and therefore (Prop. 20, pt. 3) is rejoiced, and consequently so far hopes that it will not happen.

14. *Confidence* is joy arising from the idea of a past or future object from which cause for doubting is removed.

15. *Despair* is sorrow arising from the idea of a past or future object from which cause for doubting is removed.

Explanation. Confidence, therefore, springs from hope and despair from fear, whenever the reason for doubting the issue is taken away; a case which occurs either because we imagine a thing past or future to be present and contemplate it as present, or because we imagine other things which exclude the existence of those which made us to doubt.

For although we can never be sure about the issue of individual objects (Corol. Prop. 31, pt. 2), it may nevertheless happen that we do not doubt it. For elsewhere we have shown (Schol. Prop. 49, pt. 2) that it is one thing not to doubt and another to possess certitude, and so it may happen that from the image of an object either past or future we are affected with the same affect of joy or sorrow as that by which we should be affected from the image of an object present, as we have demonstrated in Prop. 18, pt. 3, to which, together with the scholium, the reader is referred.

16. *Gladness* (*gaudium*) is joy with the accompanying idea of something past, which, unhoped for, has happened.

17. *Remorse* is sorrow with the accompanying idea of something past, which, unhoped for, has happened.

18. *Commiseration* is sorrow with the accompanying idea of evil which has happened to some one whom we imagine like ourselves (Schol. Prop. 22, and Schol. Prop. 27, pt. 3).

Explanation. Between commiseration and compassion there seems to be no difference, excepting perhaps that commiseration refers rather to an individual affect and compassion to it as a habit.

19. *Favour* is love towards those who have benefited others.

20. *Indignation* is hatred towards those who have injured others.

Explanation. I am aware that these names in common bear a different meaning. But my object is not to explain the meaning of words but the nature of things, and to indicate them by words whose customary meaning shall not be altogether opposed to the meaning which I desire to bestow upon them. I consider it sufficient to have said this once for all. As far as the cause of these affects is concerned, see Corol. 1, Prop. 27, pt. 3, and Schol. Prop. 22, pt. 3.

21. *Over-estimation* consists in thinking too highly of another person in consequence of our love for him.

22. *Contempt* consists in thinking too little of another person in consequence of our hatred for him.

Explanation. Over-estimation and contempt are therefore respectively effects or properties of love or hatred, and so over-estimation may be defined as love in so far as it affects a man so that he thinks too much of the beloved object; and, on the contrary, contempt may be defined as hatred in so far as it affects a man so that he thinks too little of the object he hates. (See Schol. Prop. 26, pt. 3.)

23. *Envy* is hatred in so far as it affects a man so that he is sad at the good fortune of another person and is glad when any evil happens to him.

Explanation. To envy is generally opposed compassion (*misericordia*), which may therefore be defined as follows, notwithstanding the usual signification of the word:—

24. *Compassion* is love in so far as it affects a man so that he is glad at the prosperity of another person and is sad when any evil happens to him.

Explanation. With regard to the other properties of envy, see Schol. Prop. 24, and Schol. Prop. 32, pt. 3. These are affects of joy and sorrow which are attended by the idea of an external object as their cause, either of itself or accidentally. I pass now to consider other affects which are attended by the idea of something within us as the cause.

25. *Self-satisfaction* is the joy which is produced by contemplating ourselves and our own power of action.

26. *Humility* is the sorrow which is produced by contemplating our impotence or helplessness.

Self-satisfaction is opposed to humility in so far as we understand by the former the joy which arises from contemplating our power of action, but in so far as we understand by it joy attended with the idea of something done, which we believe has been done by a free decree of our mind, it is opposed to repentance which we may thus define:—

27. *Repentance* is sorrow accompanied with the idea of something done which we believe has been done by a free decree of our mind.

Explanation. We have shown what are the causes of these affects in Schol. Prop. 51, pt. 3, Props. 53 and 54, pt. 3, and Prop. 55, pt. 3, together with its Schol. With regard to a free decree of the mind, see Schol. Prop. 35, pt. 2. Here, however, I must observe, that it is not to be wondered at that sorrow should always follow all those actions which are from custom called wicked, and that joy should follow those which are called good. But that this is chiefly the effect of education will be evident from what we have before said. Parents, by reprobating what are called bad actions, and frequently blaming their children whenever they commit them, while they persuade them to what are called good actions, and praise their children when they perform them, have caused the emotions of sorrow to connect themselves with the former, and those of joy with the latter. Experience proves this, for custom and religion are not the same everywhere; but, on the contrary, things which are sacred to some are profane to others, and what are honourable with some are disgraceful with others. Education alone, therefore, will determine whether a man will repent of any deed or boast of it.

28. *Pride* is thinking too much of ourselves, through self-love.

Explanation. Pride differs, therefore, from over-estimation, inasmuch as the latter is related to an external object, but pride to the man himself who thinks of himself too highly. As over-estimation, therefore, is an effect or property of love, so pride is an effect or property of self-love, and it may therefore be defined as love of ourselves or self-satisfaction, in so far as it affects us so that we think too highly of ourselves. (See Schol. Prop. 26, pt. 3.)

To this affect a contrary does not exist, for no one, through hatred of himself, thinks too little of himself; indeed, we may say that no one thinks too little of himself, in so far as he imagines himself unable to do this or that thing. For whatever he imagines that he cannot do, that thing he necessarily imagines, and by his imagination is so disposed that he is actually incapable of doing what he imagines he cannot do. So long, therefore, as he imagines himself unable to do this or that thing, so long is he not determined to do it, and consequently so long it is impossible for him to do it. If, however, we pay attention to what depends upon opinion alone, we shall be able to conceive it possible for a man to think too little of himself, for it may happen that while he sorrowfully contemplates his own weakness he will imagine himself despised by everybody, although nothing could be further from their thoughts than to despise him. A man may also think too little of himself if in the present he denies something of himself in relation to a future time of which he is not sure; for example, when he denies that he can conceive of nothing with certitude, and that he can desire and do nothing which is not wicked and base. We may also say that a man thinks too little of himself when we see that, from an excess of fear or shame, he does not dare to do what others who are his equals dare to do. This affect, to which I will give the name of Despondency, may therefore be opposed to pride; for as self-satisfaction springs from pride, so despondency springs from humility, and it may therefore be defined thus:—

29. *Despondency* is thinking too little of ourselves through sorrow.

Explanation. We are, nevertheless, often in the habit of opposing humility to pride, but only when we attend to their effects rather than to their nature. For we are accustomed to call a man proud who boasts too much (Schol. Prop. 30, pt. 3), who talks about nothing but his own virtues and other people's vices, who wishes to be preferred to everybody else, and who marches along with that stateliness and pomp which belong to others whose position is far above his. On the other hand, we call a man humble who often blushes, who confesses his own faults and talks about the virtues of others, who yields to every one, who walks with bended head, and who neglects to adorn himself. These affects, humility and despondency, are very rare, for human nature, considered in itself, struggles against them as much as it can (Props. 13 and 54, pt. 3), and hence those who have the most credit for being abject and humble are generally the most ambitious and envious.

30. *Self-exaltation* is joy with the accompanying idea of some action we have done, which we imagine people praise.

31. *Shame* is sorrow, with the accompanying idea of some action which we imagine people blame.

Explanation. With regard to these affects see Schol. Prop. 30, pt. 3. A difference, however, is here to be observed between shame and modesty. Shame is sorrow which follows a deed of which we are ashamed. Modesty is the dread or fear of shame, which keeps a man from committing any disgraceful act. To modesty is usually opposed impudence, which indeed is not an affect, as I shall show in the proper place; but the names of affects, as I have already said, are matters rather of custom than indications of the nature of the affects. I have thus discharged the task which I set myself of explaining the affects of joy and sorrow. I will advance now to those which I ascribe to desire.

32. *Regret* is the desire or longing to possess something, the affect being strengthened by the memory of the object itself, and at the same time being restrained by the memory of other things which exclude the existence of the desired object.

Explanation. Whenever we recollect a thing, as we have often said, we are thereby necessarily disposed to contemplate it with the same affect as if it were present before us. But this disposition or effort, while we are awake, is generally restrained by the images of things which exclude the existence of the thing which we recollect. Whenever, therefore, we recollect a thing which affects us with any kind of joy, we thereby endeavour to contemplate it with the same affect of joy as if it were present,—an attempt which is, however, immediately restrained by the memory of that which excludes the existence of the thing. Regret, therefore, is really a sorrow which is opposed to the joy which arises from the absence of what we hate. (See Schol. Prop. 47, pt. 3.) But because the name *regret* seems to connect this affect with desire, I therefore ascribe it to desire.

33. *Emulation* is the desire which is begotten in us of a thing because we imagine that other persons have the same desire.

Explanation. He who seeks flight because others seek it, he who fears because he sees others fear, or even he who withdraws his hand and moves his body as if his hand were burning because he sees that another person has burnt his hand, such as these, I say, although they may indeed imitate the affect of another, are not said to emulate it; not because we have recognised one cause for emulation and another for imitation, but because it has been the custom to call that man only emulous who imitates what we think noble, useful, or pleasant. With regard to the cause of emulation, see also Prop. 27, pt. 3, with the Schol. For the reason why envy is generally connected with this affect, see Prop. 32, pt. 3, with its Schol.

34. *Thankfulness* or *gratitude* is the desire or endeavour of love with which we strive to do good to others who, from a similar affect of love, have done good to us (Prop. 39, with Schol. Prop. 41, pt. 3).

35. *Benevolence* is the desire to do good to those whom we pity (Schol. Prop. 27, pt. 3).

36. *Anger* is the desire by which we are impelled, through hatred, to injure those whom we hate (Prop. 39, pt. 3).

37. *Vengeance* is the desire which, springing from mutual hatred, urges us to injure those who, from a similar affect, have injured us (Corol. 2, Prop. 40, pt. 3, with Schol.).

38. *Cruelty* or *ferocity* is the desire by which a man is impelled to injure any one whom we love or pity.

Explanation. To cruelty is opposed mercy, which is not a passion, but a power of the mind by which a man restrains anger and vengeance.

39. *Fear* is the desire of avoiding the greater of two dreaded evils by the less (Schol. Prop. 39, pt. 3).

40. *Audacity* is the desire by which we are impelled to do something which is accompanied with a danger which our equals fear to meet.

41. A person is said to be *pusillanimous* whose desire is restrained by the fear of a danger which his equals dare to meet.

Explanation. Pusillanimity, therefore, is nothing but the dread of some evil which most persons do not usually fear, and therefore I do not ascribe it to the affects of desire. I wished, notwithstanding, to explain it here, because in so far as we attend to desire, pusillanimity is the true opposite of the affect of audacity.

42. *Consternation* is affirmed of the man whose desire of avoiding evil is restrained by astonishment at the evil which he fears.

Explanation. Consternation is therefore a kind of pusillanimity. But because consternation springs from a double fear, it may be more aptly defined as that dread which holds a man stupefied or vacillating, so that he cannot remove an evil. I say *stupefied*, in so far as we understand his desire of removing the evil to be restrained by his astonishment. I say also *vacillating*, in so far as we conceive the same desire to be restrained by the fear of another evil which equally tortures him, so that he does not know which of the two evils to avoid. See Schol. Prop. 39, and Schol. Prop. 52, pt. 3. With regard to pusillanimity and audacity, see Schol. Prop. 51, pt. 3.

43. *Courtesy* or *moderation* is the desire of doing those things which please men and omitting those which displease them.

44. *Ambition* is the immoderate desire of glory.

Explanation. Ambition is a desire which increases and strengthens all the affects (Props. 27 and 31, pt. 3), and that is the reason why it can hardly be kept under control. For so long as a man is possessed by any desire, he is necessarily at the same time possessed by this. *Every noble man*, says Cicero, *is led by glory, and even the philosophers who write books about despising glory place their names on the title-page.*[1]

45. *Luxuriousness* is the immoderate desire or love of good living.

46. *Drunkenness* is the immoderate desire and love of drinking.

47. *Avarice* is the immoderate desire and love of riches.

48. *Lust* is the immoderate desire and love of sexual intercourse.

Explanation. This desire of sexual intercourse is usually called lust, whether it be held within bounds or not. I may add that the five last-mentioned affects (as we have shown in Schol. Prop. 56, pt. 3) have no contraries, for moderation is a kind of ambition (see Schol. Prop. 29, pt. 3), and I have already observed that temperance, sobriety, and chastity show a power and not a passion of the mind. Even supposing that an avaricious, ambitious, or timid man refrains from an excess of eating, drinking, or sexual intercourse, avarice, ambition, and fear are not therefore the opposites of voluptuousness, drunkenness, or lust. For the avaricious man generally desires to swallow as much meat and drink as he can, provided only it belong to another person. The am-

[1] Pro Archia.

bitious man, too, if he hopes he can keep it a secret, will restrain himself in nothing, and if he lives amongst drunkards and libertines, will be more inclined to their vices just because he is ambitious. The timid man, too, does what he does not will; and although, in order to avoid death, he may throw his riches into the sea, he remains avaricious; nor does the lascivious man cease to be lascivious because he is sorry that he cannot gratify his desire. Absolutely, therefore, these affects have reference not so much to the acts themselves of eating and drinking as to the appetite and love itself. Consequently nothing can be opposed to these affects but nobility of soul and strength of mind, as we shall see afterwards.

The definitions of jealousy and the other vacillations of the mind I pass over in silence, both because they are compounded of the affects which we have already defined, and also because many of them have no names,—a fact which shows that, for the purposes of life, it is sufficient to know these combinations generally. Moreover, it follows from the definitions of the affects which we have explained that they all arise from desire, joy, or sorrow, or rather that there are none but these three, which pass under names varying as their relations and external signs vary. If, therefore, we attend to these primitive affects and to what has been said above about the nature of the mind, we shall be able here to define the affects in so far as they are related to the mind alone.

General definition of the affects. Affect, which is called *animi pathema*, is a confused idea by which the mind affirms of its body, or any part of it, a greater or less power of existence than before; and this increase of power being given, the mind itself is determined to one particular thought rather than to another.

Explanation. I say, in the first place, that an affect or passion of the mind *is a confused idea.* For we have shown (Prop. 3, pt. 3) that the mind suffers only in so far as it has inadequate or confused ideas. I say again, *by which the mind affirms of its body, or any part of it, a greater or less power of existence than before.* For all ideas which we possess of bodies indicate the actual constitution of our body rather than the nature of the external body (Corol. 2, Prop. 16, pt. 2); but this idea, which constitutes the form of an affect, must indicate or express the constitution of the body, or of some part of it; which constitution the body or any part of it possesses from the fact that its power of action or force of existence is increased or diminished, helped or limited. But it is to be observed, that when I say *a greater or less power of existence than before*, I do not mean that the mind compares the present with the past constitution of the body, but that the idea which constitutes the form of affect affirms something of the body which actually involves more or less reality than before. Moreover, since the essence of the mind (Props. 11 and 13, pt. 2) consists in its affirmation of the actual existence of its body, and since we understand by perfection the essence itself of the thing, it follows that the mind passes to a greater or less perfection when it is able to affirm of its body, or some part of it, something which in-

volves a greater or less reality than before. When, therefore, I have said that the mind's power of thought is increased or diminished, I have wished to be understood as meaning nothing else than that the mind has formed an idea of its body, or some part of its body, which expresses more or less reality than it had hitherto affirmed of the body. For the value of ideas and the actual power of thought are measured by the value of the object. Finally, I added, *which being given, the mind itself is determined to one particular thought rather than to another*, that I might also express the nature of desire in addition to that of joy and sorrow, which is explained by the first part of the definition.

FOURTH PART

OF HUMAN BONDAGE OR OF THE STRENGTH OF THE AFFECTS

PREFACE

THE impotence of man to govern or restrain the affects I call bondage, for a man who is under their control is not his own master, but is mastered by fortune, in whose power he is, so that he is often forced to follow the worse, although he sees the better before him. I propose in this part to demonstrate why this is, and also to show what of good and evil the affects possess. But before I begin I should like to say a few words about perfection and imperfection, and about good and evil. If a man has proposed to do a thing and has accomplished it, he calls it perfect, and not only he, but every one else who has really known or has believed that he has known the mind and intention of the author of that work will call it perfect too. For example, having seen some work (which I suppose to be as yet not finished), if we know that the intention of the author of that work is to build a house, we shall call the house imperfect; while, on the other hand, we shall call it perfect as soon as we see the work has been brought to the end which the author had determined for it. But if we see any work such as we have never seen before, and if we do not know the mind of the workman, we shall then not be able to say whether the work is perfect or imperfect. This

seems to have been the first signification of these words; but afterwards men began to form universal ideas, to think out for themselves types of houses, buildings, castles, and to prefer some types of things to others; and so it happened that each person called a thing perfect which seemed to agree with the universal idea which he had formed of that thing, and, on the other hand, he called a thing imperfect which seemed to agree less with his typical conception, although, according to the intention of the workman, it had been entirely completed. This appears to be the only reason why the words *perfect* and *imperfect* are commonly applied to natural objects which are not made with human hands; for men are in the habit of forming, both of natural as well as of artificial objects, universal ideas which they regard as types of things, and which they think nature has in view, setting them before herself as types too; it being the common opinion that she does nothing except for the sake of some end. When, therefore, men see something done by nature which does not altogether answer to that typal conception which they have of the thing, they think that nature herself has failed or committed an error, and that she has left the thing imperfect. Thus we see that the custom of applying the words *perfect* and *imperfect* to natural objects has arisen rather from prejudice than from true knowledge of them. For we have shown in the Appendix to the First Part of this work that nature does nothing for the sake of an end, for that eternal and infinite Being whom we call God or Nature acts by the same necessity by which He exists; for we have shown that He acts by the same necessity of nature as that by which He exists (Prop. 16, pt. 1). The reason or cause, therefore, why God or nature acts and the reason why He exists are one and the same. Since, therefore, He exists for no end, He acts for no end; and since He has no principle or end of existence, He has no principle or end of action. A final cause, as it is called, is nothing, therefore, but human desire, in so far as this is considered as the principle or primary cause of anything. For example, when we say that the having a house to live in was the final cause of this or that house, we merely mean that a man, because he imagined the advantages of a domestic life, desired to build a house. Therefore, having a house to live in, in so far as it is considered as a final cause, is merely this particular desire, which is really an efficient cause, and is considered as primary, because men are usually ignorant of the causes of their desires; for, as I have often said, we are conscious of our actions and desires, but ignorant of the causes by which we are determined to desire anything. As for the vulgar opinion that nature sometimes fails or commits an error, or produces imperfect things, I class it amongst those fictions mentioned in the Appendix to the First Part.

Perfection, therefore, and imperfection are really only modes of thought; that is to say, notions which we are in the habit of forming from the comparison with one another of individuals of the same species or genus, and this is the reason why I have said, in Def. 6, pt. 2, that by reality and perfection I understand the same thing; for we are in the habit of referring all individuals in nature to one genus, which is called the most general; that is to say, to the notion of being, which embraces absolutely all the individual objects in nature. In so far, therefore, as we refer the individual objects in nature to this genus, and compare them one with another, and discover that some possess more being or reality than others, in so far do we call some more perfect than others; and in so far as we assign to the latter anything which, like limitation, termination, impotence, &c., involves negation, shall we call them imperfect, because they do not affect our

minds so strongly as those we call perfect, but not because anything which really belongs to them is wanting, or because nature has committed an error. For nothing belongs to the nature of anything excepting that which follows from the necessity of the nature of the efficient cause, and whatever follows from the necessity of the nature of the efficient cause necessarily happens.

With regard to good and evil, these terms indicate nothing positive in things considered in themselves, nor are they anything else than modes of thought, or notions which we form from the comparison of one thing with another. For one and the same thing may at the same time be both good and evil or indifferent. Music, for example, is good to a melancholy person, bad to one mourning, while to a deaf man it is neither good nor bad. But although things are so, we must retain these words. For since we desire to form for ourselves an idea of man upon which we may look as a model of human nature, it will be of service to us to retain these expressions in the sense I have mentioned. By *good*, therefore, I understand in the following pages everything which we are certain is a means by which we may approach nearer and nearer to the model of human nature we set before us. By *evil*, on the contrary, I understand everything which we are certain hinders us from reaching that model. Again, I shall call men more or less perfect or imperfect in so far as they approach more or less nearly to this same model. For it is to be carefully observed, that when I say that an individual passes from a less to a greater perfection and *vice versa*, I do not understand that from one essence or form he is changed into another (for a horse, for instance, would be as much destroyed if it were changed into a man as if it were changed into an insect), but rather we conceive that his power of action, in so far as it is understood by his own nature, is increased or diminished. Finally, by perfection generally, I understand as I have said, reality; that is to say, the essence of any object in so far as it exists and acts in a certain manner, no regard being paid to its duration. For no individual thing can be said to be more perfect because for a longer time it has persevered in existence; inasmuch as the duration of things cannot be determined by their essence, the essence of things involving no fixed or determined period of existence; any object, whether it be more or less perfect, always being able to persevere in existence with the same force as that with which it commenced existence. All things, therefore, are equal in this respect.

DEFINITIONS

1. By good, I understand that which we certainly know is useful to us.

2. By evil, on the contrary, I understand that which we certainly know hinders us from possessing anything that is good.

With regard to these two definitions, see the close of the preceding preface.

3. I call individual things contingent in so far as we discover nothing, whilst we attend to their essence alone, which necessarily posits their existence or which necessarily excludes it.

4. I call these individual things possible, in so far as we are ignorant, whilst we attend to the causes from which they must be produced, whether these causes are determined to the production of these things. In Schol. 1, Prop. 33, pt. 1, I made no difference between possible and contingent, because there was no occasion there to distinguish them accurately.

5. By contrary affects, I understand in the following pages those which, although they may be of the same kind, draw a man in different directions; such as voluptuousness and avarice, which are both a species of love, and are not contrary to one another by nature, but only by accident.

6. What I understand by affect towards a thing future, present, and past, I have explained in Schol. 1 and 2, Prop. 18, pt. 3, to which the reader is referred.

Here, however, it is to be observed that it is the same with time as it is with place; for as beyond a certain limit we can form no distinct imagination of distance—that is to say, as we usually imagine all objects to be equally distant from us, and as if they were on the same plane, if their distance from us exceeds 200 feet, or if their distance from the position we occupy is greater than we can distinctly imagine—so we imagine all objects to be equally distant from the present time, and refer them as if to one moment, if the period to which their existence belongs is separated from the present by a longer interval than we can usually imagine distinctly.

7. By end for the sake of which we do anything, I understand appetite.

8. By virtue and power, I understand the same thing; that is to say (Prop. 7, pt. 3),

virtue, in so far as it is related to man, is the essence itself or nature of the man in so far as it has the power of affecting certain things which can be understood through the laws of its nature alone.

AXIOM

There is no individual thing in nature which is not surpassed in strength and power by some other thing, but any individual thing being given, another and a stronger is also given, by which the former can be destroyed.

PROP. 1. *Nothing positive contained in a false idea is removed by the presence of the true in so far as it is true.*

Demonst. Falsity consists in nothing but the privation of knowledge which inadequate ideas involve (Prop. 35, pt. 2), nor do they possess anything positive on account of which they are called false (Prop. 33, pt. 2); on the contrary, in so far as they are related to God, they are true (Prop. 32, pt. 2). If, therefore, anything positive contained in a false idea were removed by the presence of the true in so far as it is true, a true idea would be removed by itself, which (Prop. 4, pt. 3) is absurd. Nothing positive, therefore, &c. Q.E.D.

Schol. This proposition can be understood more clearly from Corol. 2, Prop. 16, pt. 2. For an imagination is an idea which indicates the present constitution of the human body rather than the nature of an external body, not indeed distinctly but confusedly, so that the mind is said to err. For example, when we look at the sun, we imagine his distance from us to be about 200 feet, and in this we are deceived so long as we remain in ignorance of the true distance. When this is known, the error is removed, but not the imagination, that is to say, the idea of the sun which manifests his nature in so far only as the body is affected by him; so that although we know his true distance, we nevertheless imagine him close to us. For, as we have shown in Schol. Prop. 35, pt 2, it is not because we are ignorant of the sun's true distance that we imagine him to be so close to us, but because the mind conceives the magnitude of the sun just in so far as the body is affected by him. So when the rays of the sun falling upon a surface of water are reflected to our eyes, we imagine him to be in the water although his true place is known to us. So with the other imaginations by which the mind is deceived; whether they indicate the natura constitution of the body or an increase or diminution in its power of action, they are not opposed to the truth, nor do they disappear with the presence of the truth. We know that when we groundlessly fear any evil, the fear vanishes when we hear correct intelligence; but we also know, on the other hand, that when we fear an evil which will actually come upon us, the fear vanishes when we hear false intelligence, so that the imaginations do not disappear with the presence of the truth, in so far as it is true, but because other imaginations arise which are stronger, and which exclude the present existence of the objects we imagine, as we have shown in Prop. 17, pt. 2.

Prop. 2. *We suffer in so far as we are a part of nature, which part cannot be conceived by itself nor without the other parts.*

Demonst. We are said to suffer when anything occurs in us of which we are only the partial cause (Def. 2, pt. 3), that is to say (Def. 1, pt. 3), anything which cannot be deduced from the laws of our own nature alone; we suffer, therefore, in so far as we are a part of nature, which part cannot be conceived by itself nor without the other parts. Q.E.D.

Prop. 3. *The force by which man perseveres in existence is limited, and infinitely surpassed by the power of external causes.*

Demonst. This is evident from the Axiom, pt. 4. For any man being given, there is given something else—for example, A—more powerful than he is, and A being given, there is again given something, B, more powerful than A, and so on *ad infinitum*. Hence the power of man is limited by the power of some other object, and is infinitely surpassed by the power of external causes. Q.E.D.

Prop. 4. *It is impossible that a man should not be a part of nature, and that he should suffer no changes but those which can be understood through his own nature alone, and of which he is the adequate cause.*

Demonst. The power by which individual things and consequently man preserve their being is the actual power of God or nature (Corol. Prop. 24, pt. 1), not in so far as it is infinite, but in so far as it can be manifested by the actual essence of man (Prop. 7, pt. 3). The power therefore of man, in so far as it is manifested by his actual essence, is part of the infinite power of God or nature, that is to say (Prop. 34, pt. 1), part of His essence. This was

the first thing to be proved. Again, if it were possible that man could suffer no changes but those which can be understood through his nature alone, it would follow (Props. 4 and 6, pt. 3) that he could not perish, but that he would exist for ever necessarily; and this necessary existence must result from a cause whose power is either finite or infinite, that is to say, either from the power of man alone, which would be able to place at a distance from himself all other changes which could take their origin from external causes, or it must result from the infinite power of nature by which all individual things would be so directed that man could suffer no changes but those tending to his preservation. But the first case (by the preceding proposition, whose demonstration is universal and capable of application to all individual objects) is absurd; therefore if it were possible for a man to suffer no changes but those which could be understood through his own nature alone, and consequently (as we have shown) that he should always necessarily exist, this must follow from the infinite power of God; and therefore (Prop. 16, pt. 1) from the necessity of the divine nature, in so far as it is considered as affected by the idea of any one man, the whole order of nature, in so far as it is conceived under the attributes of thought and extension, would have to be deduced. From this it would follow (Prop. 21, pt. 1) that man would be infinite, which (by the first part of this demonstration) is an absurdity. It is impossible, therefore, that a man can suffer no changes but those of which he is the adequate cause. Q.E.D.

Corol. Hence it follows that a man is necessarily always subject to passions, and that he follows and obeys the common order of nature, accommodating himself to it as far as the nature of things requires.

Prop. 5. *The force and increase of any passion and its perseverance in existence are not limited by the power by which we endeavour to persevere in existence, but by the power of an external cause compared with our own power.*

Demonst. The essence of a passion cannot be explained by our essence alone (Defs. 1 and 2, pt. 3); that is to say (Prop. 7, pt. 3), the power of a passion cannot be limited by the power by which we endeavour to persevere in our being, but (as has been shown in Prop. 16, pt. 2) must necessarily be limited by the power of an external cause compared with our own power. Q.E.D.

PROP. 6. *The other actions or power of a man may be so far surpassed by force of some passion or affect, that the affect may obstinately cling to him.*

Demonst. The force and increase of any passion and its perseverance in existence are limited by the power of an external cause compared with our own power (Prop. 5, pt. 4), and therefore (Prop. 3, pt. 4) may surpass the power of man. Q.E.D.

PROP. 7. *An affect cannot be restrained nor removed unless by an opposed and stronger affect.*

Demonst. An affect, in so far as it is related to the mind, is an idea by which the mind affirms a greater or lesser power of existence for its body than the body possessed before (by the general definition of affects at the end of Third Part). Whenever, therefore, the mind is agitated by any affect, the body is at the same time affected with an affection by which its power of action is increased or diminished. Again, this affection of the body (Prop. 5, pt. 4) receives from its own cause a power to persevere in its own being, a power, therefore, which cannot be restrained nor removed unless by a bodily cause (Prop. 6, pt. 2) affecting the body with an affection contrary to the first (Prop. 5, pt. 3), and stronger than it (Ax. 1, pt. 4). Thus the mind (Prop. 12, pt. 2) is affected by the idea of an affection stronger than the former and contrary to it; that is to say (by the general definition of the affects), it will be affected with an affect stronger than the former and contrary to it, and this stronger affect will exclude the existence of the other or remove it. Thus an affect cannot be restrained nor removed unless by an opposed and stronger affect. Q.E.D.

Corol. An affect, in so far as it is related to the mind, cannot be restrained nor removed unless by the idea of a bodily affection opposed to that which we suffer and stronger than it. For the affect which we suffer cannot be restrained nor removed unless by an opposed and stronger affect (Prop. 7, pt. 4); that is to say (by the general definition of the affects), it cannot be removed unless by the idea of a bodily affection stronger than that which affects us, and opposed to it.

PROP. 8. *Knowledge of good or evil is nothing but an affect of joy or sorrow in so far as we are conscious of it.*

Demonst. We call a thing good which con-tributes to the preservation of our being, and we call a thing evil if it is an obstacle to the preservation of our being (Defs. 1 and 2, pt. 4); that is to say (Prop. 7, pt. 3), a thing is called by us good or evil as it increases or diminishes, helps or restrains, our power of action. In so far, therefore (Defs. of *joy* and *sorrow* in Schol. Prop. 11, pt. 3), as we perceive that any object affects us with joy or sorrow do we call it good or evil, and therefore the knowledge of good or evil is nothing but an idea of joy or sorrow which necessarily follows from the affect itself of joy or sorrow (Prop. 22, pt. 2). But this idea is united to the affect in the same way as the mind is united to the body (Prop. 21, pt. 2), or, in other words (as we have shown in the Schol. to Prop. 21, pt. 2), this idea is not actually distinguished from the affect itself; that is to say (by the general definition of the affects), it is not actually distinguished from the idea of the affection of the body unless in conception alone. This knowledge, therefore, of good and evil is nothing but the affect itself of joy and sorrow in so far as we are conscious of it. Q.E.D.

PROP. 9. *If we imagine the cause of an affect to be actually present with us, that affect will be stronger than if we imagined the cause not to be present.*

Demonst. The imagination is an idea by which the mind contemplates an object as present (see the definition of the imagination in Schol. Prop. 17, pt. 2), an idea which nevertheless indicates the constitution of the human body rather than the nature of the external object (Corol. 2, Prop. 16, pt. 2). Imagination, therefore (by the general definition of the affects), is an affect in so far as it indicates the constitution of the body. But the imagination (Prop. 17, pt. 2) increases in intensity in proportion as we imagine nothing which excludes the present existence of the external object. If, therefore, we imagine the cause of an affect to be actually present with us, that affect will be intenser or stronger than if we imagined the cause not to be present. Q.E.D.

Schol. When I said (in Prop. 18, pt. 3) that we are affected by the image of an object in the future or the past with the same affect with which we should be affected if the object we imagined were actually present, I was careful to warn the reader that this was true in so far only as we attend to the image alone of the object itself, for the image is of the same nature whether we have imagined the object or not;

but I have not denied that the image becomes weaker when we contemplate as present other objects which exclude the present existence of the future object. This exception I neglected to make, because I had determined to treat in this part of my work of the strength of the affects.

Corol. The image of a past or future object, that is to say, of an object which we contemplate in relation to the past or future to the exclusion of the present, other things being equal, is weaker than the image of a present object, and consequently the affect towards a future or past object, other things being equal, is weaker then than the affect towards a present object.

PROP. 10. *We are affected with regard to a future object which we imagine will soon be present more powerfully than if we imagine that the time at which it will exist is further removed from the present, and the memory of an object which we imagine has but just passed away also affects us more powerfully than if we imagine the object to have passed away some time ago.*

Demonst. In so far as we imagine that an object will quickly be present or has not long since passed away, do we imagine something which excludes the presence of the object less than if we imagine that the time of its existence is at a great distance from the present, either in the future or the past (as is self-evident), and therefore (Prop. 9, pt. 4) so far shall we be affected more strongly with regard to it. Q.E.D.

Schol. From the observations which we made upon Def. 6, pt. 4, it follows that all objects which are separated from the present time by a longer interval than our imagination has any power to determine affect us equally slightly, although we know them to be separated from one another by a large space of time.

PROP. 11. *The affect towards an object which we imagine as necessary, other things being equal, is stronger than that towards an object that is possible, contingent, or not necessary.*

Demonst. In so far as we imagine any object to be necessary do we affirm its existence, and, on the other hand, we deny its existence in so far as we imagine it to be not necessary (Schol. 1, Prop. 33, pt. 1), and therefore (Prop. 9, pt. 4) the affect towards a necessary object, other things being equal, is stronger than that which we feel towards one that is not necessary.

PROP. 12. *The affect towards an object which we know does not exist in the present, and which we imagine as possible, other things being equal, is stronger than the affect towards a contingent object.*

Demonst. In so far as we imagine an object as contingent, we are not affected by the image of any other object which posits the existence of the first (Def. 3, pt. 4), but, on the contrary (by hypothesis), we imagine some things which exclude its present existence. But in so far as we imagine any object in the future to be possible do we imagine some things which posit its existence (Def. 4, pt. 4), that is to say (Schol. 2, Prop. 18, pt. 3), things which foster hope or fear, and therefore the affect towards a possible object is stronger, &c. Q.E.D.

Corol. The affect towards an object which we know does not exist in the present, and which we imagine as contingent, is much weaker than if we imagined that the object were present to us.

Demonst. The affect towards an object which we imagine to exist in the present is stronger than if we imagined it as future (Corol. Prop. 9, pt. 4), and is much stronger if we imagine the future to be at a great distance from the present time (Prop. 10, pt. 4). The affect, therefore, towards an object which we imagine will not exist for a long time is so much feebler than if we imagined it as present, and nevertheless (Prop. 12, pt. 4) is stronger than if we imagined it as contingent; and therefore the affect towards a contingent object is much feebler than if we imagined the object to be present to us. Q.E.D.

PROP. 13. *The affect towards a contingent object which we know does not exist in the present, other things being equal, is much weaker than the affect towards a past object.*

Demonst. In so far as we imagine an object as contingent, we are affected with no image of any other object which posits the existence of the first (Def. 3, pt. 4). On the contrary, we imagine (by hypothesis) certain things which exclude its present existence. But in so far as we imagine it in relationship to past time are we supposed to imagine something which brings it back to the memory or which excites its image (Prop. 18, pt. 2, with the Schol.), and therefore so far causes us to contemplate it as present (Corol. Prop. 17, pt. 2). Therefore (Prop. 9, pt. 4), the affect towards a contingent object which we know does not exist in the present, other things being equal, will be weaker than the affect towards a past object. Q.E.D.

PROP. 14. *No affect can be restrained by the true knowledge of good and evil in so far as it is true, but only in so far as it is considered as an affect.*

Demonst. An affect is an idea by which the mind affirms a greater or less power of existence for the body than it possessed before (by the general definition of the affects); and therefore (Prop. 1, pt. 4) this idea has nothing positive which can be removed by the presence of the truth, and consequently the true knowledge of good and evil, in so far as it is true, can restrain no affect. But in so far as it is an affect (see Prop. 8, pt. 4) will it restrain any other affect, provided that the latter be the weaker of the two (Prop. 7, pt. 4). Q.E.D.

PROP. 15. *Desire which arises from a true knowledge of good and evil can be extinguished or restrained by many other desires which take their origin from the affects by which we are agitated.*

Demonst. From the true knowledge of good and evil, in so far as this (Prop. 8, pt. 4) is an affect, necessarily arises desire (Def. 1 of the affects, pt. 3), which is greater in proportion as the affect from which it springs is greater (Prop. 37, pt. 3). But this desire (by hypothesis), because it springs from our understanding something truly, follows therefore in us in so far as we act (Prop. 1, pt. 3), and therefore must be understood through our essence alone (Def. 2, pt. 3), and consequently its strength and increase must be limited by human power alone (Prop. 7, pt. 3). But the desires which spring from the affects by which we are agitated are greater as the affects themselves are greater, and therefore their strength and increase (Prop. 5, pt. 4) must be limited by the power of external causes, a power which, if it be compared with our own, indefinitely surpasses it (Prop. 3, pt. 4). The desires, therefore, which take their origin from such affects as these may be much stronger than that which takes its origin from a true knowledge of good and evil, and the former (Prop. 7, pt. 4) may be able to restrain and extinguish the latter. Q.E.D.

PROP. 16. *The desire which springs from a knowledge of good and evil can be easily extinguished or restrained, in so far as this knowledge is connected with the future, by the desire of things which in the present are sweet.*

Demonst. The affect towards an object which we imagine as future is weaker than towards that which we imagine as present (Corol. Prop. 9, pt. 4). But the desire which springs from a true knowledge of good and evil, even although the knowledge be of objects which are good at the present time, may be extinguished or restrained by any casual desire (Prop. 15, pt. 4, the demonstration of this proposition being universal), and therefore the desire which springs from a knowledge of good and evil, in so far as this knowledge is connected with the future, can be easily restrained or extinguished. Q.E.D.

PROP. 17. *The desire which springs from a true knowledge of good and evil can be still more easily restrained, in so far as this knowledge is connected with objects which are contingent, by the desire of objects which are present.*

Demonst. This proposition is demonstrated in the same way as the preceding proposition from Corol. Prop. 12, pt. 4.

Schol. In these propositions I consider that I have explained why men are more strongly influenced by an opinion than by true reason, and why the true knowledge of good and evil causes disturbance in the mind, and often gives way to every kind of lust, whence the saying of the poet, *"Video meliora proboque, deteriora sequor."* The same thought appears to have been in the mind of the Preacher when he said, *"He that increaseth knowledge increaseth sorrow."* I say these things not because I would be understood to conclude, therefore, that it is better to be ignorant than to be wise, or that the wise man in governing his passions is nothing better than the fool, but I say them because it is necessary for us to know both the strength and weakness of our nature, so that we may determine what reason can do and what it cannot do in governing our affects. This, moreover, let it be remembered, is the Part in which I meant to treat of human weakness alone, all consideration of the power of reason over the passions being reserved for a future portion of the book.

PROP. 18. *The desire which springs from joy, other things being equal, is stronger than that which springs from sorrow.*

Demonst. Desire is the very essence of man (Def. 1 of the Affects, pt. 3), that is to say (Prop. 7, pt. 3), the effort by which a man strives to persevere in his being. The desire, therefore, which springs from joy, by that very affect of joy (by the definition of joy in Schol. Prop. 11, pt. 3) is assisted or increased, while that which springs from sorrow, by that very affect of sorrow (by the same Schol.) is lessened or restrained, and so the force of the desire which springs from joy must be limited by human power, together with the power of an external cause, while that which springs from sorrow must be limited by human power alone. The latter is, therefore, weaker than the former. Q.E.D.

Schol. I have thus briefly explained the causes of human impotence and want of stability, and why men do not obey the dictates of reason. It remains for me now to show what it is which reason prescribes to us, which affects agree with the rules of human reason, and which, on the contrary, are opposed to these rules. Before, however, I begin to demonstrate these things by our full geometrical method, I should like briefly to set forth here these dictates of reason, in order that what I have in my mind about them may be easily comprehended by all. Since reason demands nothing which is opposed to nature, it demands, therefore, that every person should love himself, should seek his own profit,—what is truly profitable to him,—should desire everything that really leads man to greater perfection, and absolutely that every one should endeavour, as far as in him lies, to preserve his own being. This is all true as necessarily as that the whole is greater than its part (Prop. 6, pt. 3). Again, since virtue (Def. 8, pt. 4) means nothing but acting according to the laws of our own nature, and since no one endeavours to preserve his being (Prop. 7, pt. 3) except in accordance with the laws of his own nature, it follows: *Firstly,* That the foundation of virtue is that endeavour itself to preserve our own being, and that happiness consists in this—that a man can preserve his own being. *Secondly,* It follows that virtue is to be desired for its own sake, nor is there anything more excellent or more useful to us than virtue, for the sake of which virtue ought to be desired. *Thirdly,* It follows that all persons who kill themselves are impotent in mind, and have been thoroughly overcome by external causes opposed to their nature. Again, from Post. 4, pt. 2, it follows that we can never free ourselves from the need of something outside us for the preservation of our being, and that we can never live in such a manner as to have no intercourse with objects which are outside us. Indeed, so far as the mind is concerned, our intellect would be less perfect if the mind were alone, and understood nothing but itself. There

are many things, therefore, outside us which are useful to us, and which, therefore, are to be sought. Of all these, none more excellent can be discovered than those which exactly agree with our nature. If, for example, two individuals of exactly the same nature are joined together, they make up a single individual, doubly stronger than each alone. Nothing, therefore, is more useful to man than man. Men can desire, I say, nothing more excellent for the preservation of their being than that all should so agree at every point that the minds and bodies of all should form, as it were, one mind and one body; that all should together endeavour as much as possible to preserve their being, and that all should together seek the common good of all. From this it follows that men who are governed by reason,—that is to say, men who, under the guidance of reason, seek their own profit,—desire nothing for themselves which they do not desire for other men, and that, therefore, they are just, faithful, and honourable.

These are those dictates of reason which I purposed briefly to set forth before commencing their demonstration by a fuller method, in order that, if possible, I might win the attention of those who believe that this principle,— that every one is bound to seek his own profit, —is the foundation of impiety, and not of virtue and piety. Having now briefly shown that this belief of theirs is the contrary of the truth, I proceed, by the same method as that which we have hitherto pursued, to demonstrate what I have said.

PROP. 19. *According to the laws of his own nature each person necessarily desires that which he considers to be good, and avoids that which he considers to be evil.*

Demonst. The knowledge of good and evil (Prop. 8, pt. 4), is the affect itself of joy or sorrow, in so far as we are conscious of it, and, therefore (Prop. 28, pt. 3), each person necessarily desires that which he considers to be good, and avoids that which he considers to be evil. But this desire is nothing but the essence itself or nature of man (Def. of appetite in Schol. Prop. 9, pt. 3, and Def. 1 of the Affects, pt. 3). Therefore, according to the laws of his own nature alone, he necessarily desires or avoids, &c. Q.E.D.

PROP. 20. *The more each person strives and is able to seek his own profit, that is to say, to preserve his being, the more virtue does he possess;*

on the other hand, in so far as each person neglects his own profit, that is to say, neglects to preserve his own being, is he impotent.

Demonst. Virtue is human power itself, which is limited by the essence alone of man (Def. 8, pt. 4), that is to say (Prop. 7, pt. 3), which is limited by the effort alone by which man endeavours to persevere in his being. The more, therefore, each person strives and is able to preserve his being, the more virtue does he possess, and consequently (Props. 4 and 6, pt. 3), in proportion as he neglects to preserve his being is he impotent.

Schol. No one, therefore, unless defeated by external causes and those which are contrary to his nature, neglects to seek his own profit or preserve his being. No one, I say, refuses food or kills himself from a necessity of his nature, but only when forced by external causes. The compulsion may be exercised in many ways. A man kills himself under compulsion by another when that other turns the right hand, with which the man had by chance laid hold of a sword, and compels him to direct the sword against his own heart; or the command of a tyrant may compel a man, as it did Seneca, to open his own veins, that is to say, he may desire to avoid a greater evil by a less. External and hidden causes also may so dispose his imagination and may so affect his body as to cause it to put on another nature contrary to that which it had at first, and one whose idea cannot exist in the mind (Prop. 10, pt. 3); but a very little reflection will show that it is as impossible that a man, from the necessity of his nature, should endeavour not to exist, or to be changed into some other form, as it is that something should be begotten from nothing.

Prop. 21. *No one can desire to be happy, to act well and live well, who does not at the same time desire to be, to act, and to live, that is to say, actually to exist.*

Demonst. The demonstration of this proposition, or rather the proposition itself, is self-evident, and is also evident from the definition of desire. For desire (Def. 1 of the Affects, pt. 3), whether it be desire of living or acting happily or well, is the very essence of man, that is to say (Prop. 7, pt. 3), the endeavour by which every one strives to preserve his own being. No one, therefore, can desire, &c.   Q.E.D.

Prop. 22. *No virtue can be conceived prior to this (the endeavour, namely, after self-preservation).*

Demonst. The endeavour after self-preservation is the essence itself of a thing (Prop. 7, pt. 3). If, therefore, any virtue could be conceived prior to this of self-preservation, the essence itself of the thing would be conceived (Def. 8, pt. 4) as prior to itself, which (as is self-evident) is absurd. No virtue, therefore, &c.   Q.E.D.

Corol. The endeavour after self-preservation is the primary and only foundation of virtue. For prior to this principle no other can be conceived (Prop. 22, pt. 4), and without it (Prop. 21, pt. 4) no virtue can be conceived.

Prop. 23. *A man cannot be absolutely said to act in conformity with virtue, in so far as he is determined to any action because he has inadequate ideas, but only in so far as he is determined because he understands.*

Demonst. In so far as a man is determined to action because he has inadequate ideas (Prop. 1, pt. 3), he suffers, that is to say (Defs. 1 and 2, pt. 3), he does something which through his essence alone cannot be perceived, that is to say (Def. 8, pt. 4), which does not follow from his virtue. But in so far as he is determined to any action because he understands, he acts (Prop. 1, pt. 3), that is to say (Def. 2, pt. 3), he does something which is perceived through his essence alone, or (Def. 8, pt. 4) which adequately follows from his virtue.   Q.E.D.

Prop. 24. *To act absolutely in conformity with virtue is, in us, nothing but acting, living, and preserving our being (these three things have the same meaning) as reason directs, from the ground of seeking our own profit.*

Demonst. To act absolutely in conformity with virtue is nothing (Def. 8, pt. 4) but acting according to the laws of our own proper nature. But only in so far as we understand do we act (Prop. 3, pt. 3). Therefore, to act in conformity with virtue is nothing but acting, living, and preserving our being as reason directs, and doing so (Corol. Prop. 22, pt. 4) from the ground of seeking our own profit.

Prop. 25. *No one endeavours to preserve his own being for the sake of another object.*

Demonst. The effort by which any object strives to persevere in its own being is limited solely by the essence of the object itself (Prop 7, pt. 3), and from this given essence alone it necessarily follows (and not from the essence of any other object) (Prop. 6, pt. 3) that each

ject strives to preserve its being. This prop-
sition is also evident from Corol. Prop. 22,
t. 4. For if a man endeavoured to preserve his
eing for the sake of any other object, this
oject would then become the primary foun-
ation of virtue (as is self-evident), which (by
e Corol. just quoted) is an absurdity. No
ne, therefore, endeavours to preserve his
eing, &c. Q.E.D.

ROP. 26. *All efforts which we make through
ason are nothing but efforts to understand, and
e mind, in so far as it uses reason, adjudges
othing as profitable to itself excepting that which
nduces to understanding.*

Demonst. The endeavour after self-preser-
ation is nothing but the essence of the object
self (Prop. 7, pt. 3), which, in so far as it
xists, is conceived to have power to persevere
 existence (Prop. 6, pt. 3), and to do those
ings which necessarily follow from its given
ature. (See the definition of desire in Schol.
rop. 9, pt. 3). But the essence of reason is
othing but our mind, in so far as it clearly
nd distinctly understands. (See definition of
lear and distinct understanding in Schol. 2,
rop. 40, pt. 2.) Therefore (Prop. 40, pt. 2),
ll efforts which we make through reason are
othing else than efforts to understand. Again,
nce this effort of the mind, by which the
ind, in so far as it reasons endeavours to pre-
erve its being, is nothing but the effort to
nderstand (by the first part of this demon-
tration), it follows (Corol. Prop. 22, pt. 4),
hat this effort to understand is the primary
nd sole foundation of virtue, and that (Prop.
5, pt. 4) we do not endeavour to understand
hings for the sake of any end, but, on the
ontrary, the mind, in so far as it reasons, can
onceive nothing as being good for itself except
hat which conduces to understanding (Def. 1,
t. 4). Q.E.D.

ROP. 27. *We do not know that anything is cer-
ainly good or evil excepting that which actually
onduces to understanding, or which can prevent
s from understanding.*

Demonst. The mind, in so far as it reasons,
esires nothing but to understand, nor does it
djudge anything to be profitable to itself ex-
epting what conduces to understanding (Prop.
6, pt. 4). But the mind (Props. 41 and 43, pt.
, with the Schol.) possesses no certitude, un-
ess in so far as it possesses adequate ideas, or
which by Schol. Prop. 40, pt. 2, is the same
hing) in so far as it reasons. We do not know,

therefore, that anything is certainly good,
excepting that which actually conduces to
understanding, and, on the other hand, we
do not know that anything is evil excepting that which can hinder us from understanding. Q.E.D.

PROP. 28. *The highest good of the mind is the
knowledge of God, and the highest virtue of the
mind is to know God.*

Demonst. The highest thing which the mind
can understand is God, that is to say (Def. 6,
pt. 1), Being absolutely infinite, and without
whom (Prop. 15, pt. 1) nothing can be nor can
be conceived, and therefore (Props. 26 and 27,
pt. 4) that which is chiefly profitable to the
mind, or (Def. 1, pt. 4) which is the highest
good of the mind, is the knowledge of God.
Again, the mind acts only in so far as it understands (Props. 1 and 3, pt. 3), and only in so
far (Prop. 23, pt. 4) can it be absolutely said
to act in conformity with virtue. To understand, therefore, is the absolute virtue of the
mind. But the highest thing which the mind can
understand is God (as we have already demonstrated), and therefore the highest virtue of the
mind is to understand or know God. Q.E.D.

PROP. 29. *No individual object whose nature
is altogether different from our own can either
help or restrain our power of acting, and absolutely nothing can be to us either good or evil
unless it possesses something in common with
ourselves.*

Demonst. The power of an individual object,
and consequently (Corol. Prop. 10, pt. 2) that
of man, by which he exists and acts, is determined only by another individual object (Prop.
28, pt. 1), whose nature (Prop. 6, pt. 2) must
be understood through the same attribute as
that by means of which human nature is conceived. Our power of acting, therefore, in whatever way it may be conceived, can be determined, and consequently helped or restrained,
by the power of another individual object possessing something in common with us, and
cannot be thus determined by the power of an
object whose nature is altogether different
from ours. Inasmuch, therefore, as a thing is
called good or evil because it is the cause of
joy or sorrow (Prop. 8, pt. 4), that is to say
(Schol. Prop. 11, pt. 3), because it increases or
diminishes, helps or restrains, our power of
action; an object, whose nature is altogether
different from our own, cannot be either good
or evil to us. Q.E.D.

PROP. 30. *Nothing can be evil through that which it possesses in common with our nature, but in so far as a thing is evil to us is it contrary to us.*

Demonst. We call that thing evil which is the cause of sorrow (Prop. 8, pt. 4), that is to say (by the definition of sorrow in Schol. Prop. 11, pt. 3), which lessens or restrains our power of action. If, therefore, any object were evil to us through that which it possesses in common with us, it could lessen or restrain what it possesses in common with us, which (Prop. 4, pt. 3) is absurd. Nothing, therefore, through that which it possesses in common with us can be evil to us, but, on the contrary, in so far as it is evil, that is to say (as we have already shown), in so far as it can lessen or restrain our power of action (Prop. 5, pt. 3), is it contrary to us. Q.E.D.

PROP. 31. *In so far as an object agrees with our nature is it necessarily good.*

Demonst. In so far as any object agrees with our nature (Prop. 30, pt. 4) it cannot be evil. It must, therefore, necessarily be either good or indifferent. If it be supposed as indifferent, that is to say, as neither good nor evil, nothing (Ax. 3, pt. 1, and Def. 1, pt. 4) will follow from its nature which conduces to the preservation of our nature, that is to say (by hypothesis), which conduces to its own preservation. But this (Prop. 6, pt. 3) is absurd, and, therefore, in so far as the object agrees with our nature, it will necessarily be good. Q.E.D.

Corol. Hence it follows that the more an object agrees with our own nature, the more profitable it is to us, that is to say, the better it is for us, and, conversely, the more profitable an object is to us, the more does it agree with our own nature. For in so far as it does not agree with our nature it will necessarily be either diverse from our nature or contrary to it. If diverse, it can (Prop. 29, pt. 4) be neither good nor evil, but if contrary, it will therefore be contrary also to that which agrees with our own nature, that is to say (Prop. 31, pt. 4), contrary to the good, or, in other words, it will be evil. Nothing, therefore, can be good except in so far as it agrees with our nature, and therefore the more an object agrees with our nature the more profitable it will be, and *vice versa.* Q.E.D.

PROP. 32. *In so far as men are subject to passions, they cannot be said to agree in nature.*

Demonst. Things which are said to agree in nature are understood to agree in power (Prop. 7, pt. 3), and not in impotence or negation, and consequently (Schol. Prop. 3, pt. 3), not in passion, and therefore men, in so far as they are subject to passion, cannot be said to agree in nature. Q.E.D.

Schol. This proposition is self-evident, for he who says that black and white agree solely in the fact that neither of them is red, absolutely affirms that black and white agree in nothing. So also if we say that a stone and a man agree solely in this, that they are both finite or impotent, or do not exist from the necessity of their nature, or are both to an indefinite extent dominated by external causes, we affirm that a stone and a man agree in nothing, for things which agree in negation only, or in that which they have not, really agree in nothing.

PROP. 33. *Men may differ in nature from one another in so far as they are agitated by affects which are passions, and in so far also as one and the same man is agitated by passions is he changeable and inconstant.*

Demonst. The nature or essence of the affects cannot be explained through our essence or nature alone (Defs. 1 and 2, pt. 3), but must be determined by the power, that is to say (Prop. 7, pt. 3), the nature of external causes compared with our own nature. Hence it follows that there are as many kinds of each affect as there are kinds of objects by which we are affected (Prop. 56, pt. 3); that men are affected in different ways by one and the same object (Prop. 51, pt. 3), and so far differ in nature; and, finally, that one and the same man (Prop. 51, pt. 3) is affected in different ways towards the same object, and so far is changeable and inconstant. Q.E.D.

PROP. 34. *In so far as men are agitated by affects which are passions can they be contrary to one another.*

Demonst. A man, Peter, for example, may be a cause of sorrow to Paul, because he possesses something resembling that which Paul hates (Prop. 16, pt. 3), or because he alone possesses something which Paul himself also loves (Prop. 32, pt. 3, with its Schol.), or for other reasons (the chief of which are mentioned in Schol. Prop. 55, pt. 3). Hence it will come to pass (Def. 7 of the affects) that Paul hates Peter, and, consequently, it will easily happen (Prop. 40, pt. 3, with its Schol.) that Peter in turn hates Paul, and that they endeavour (Prop. 39, pt. 3) to injure one another, or, in other words (Prop. 30, pt. 4), that they are contrary to one another. But the affect of sorrow is always a passion (Prop. 59, pt. 3), and therefore men, in so far as they are agitated by affects which are passions, can be contrary to one another.　Q.E.D.

Schol. I have said that Paul hates Peter because he imagines that Peter possesses something which he himself loves, from which at first sight it appears to follow, that because they both love the same thing, and consequently agree in nature with one another, they are, therefore, injurious to one another; and if this be true, Props. 30 and 31, pt. 4, would be false. But if we will examine the matter impartially, we shall see that all these things are quite in accord. For Peter and Paul are not injurious to one another in so far as they agree in nature, that is to say, in so far as they both love the same object, but in so far as they differ from one another. For in so far as they both love the same object is the love of each strengthened (Prop. 31, pt. 3), that is to say (Def. 6 of the affects), so far is the joy of both increased. It is far from true, therefore, that in so far as they love the same object and agree in nature they are injurious to one another. They are injurious to one another, on the contrary, as I have said, solely because they are supposed to differ in nature. For we suppose Peter to have an idea of a beloved object which he now possesses, and Paul, on the other hand, to have an idea of a beloved object which he has lost. The former, therefore, is affected with joy, and the latter, on the contrary, with sorrow, and so far they are contrary to one another. In this manner we can easily show that the other causes of hatred depend solely on the fact that men differ by nature and not on anything in which they agree.

Prop. 35. *So far as men live in conformity with the guidance of reason, in so far only do they always necessarily agree in nature.*

Demonst. In so far as men are agitated by affects which are passions can they differ in nature (Prop. 33, pt. 4) and be contrary to one another (Prop. 34, pt. 4). But men are said to act only in so far as they live according to the guidance of reason (Prop. 3, pt. 3), and therefore, whatever follows from human nature, in so far as it is determined by reason (Def. 2, pt. 3), must be understood through human nature alone as through its proximate cause. But because every one, according to the laws of his

own nature, desires that which he adjudges to be good, and endeavours to remove that which he adjudges to be evil (Prop. 19, pt. 4), and because that which from the dictates of reason we judge to be good or evil is necessarily good or evil (Prop. 41, pt. 2), it follows that men, only in so far as they live according to the guidance of reason, necessarily do those things which are good to human nature, and consequently to each man, that is to say (Corol. Prop. 31, pt. 4), which agree with the nature of each man, and therefore also men necessarily always agree with one another in so far as they live according to the guidance of reason.　Q.E.D.

Corol. 1. There is no single thing in nature which is more profitable to man than a man who lives according to the guidance of reason. For that is most profitable to man which most agrees with his own nature (Corol. Prop. 31, pt. 4), that is to say, man (as is self-evident). But a man acts absolutely from the laws of his own nature when he lives according to the guidance of reason (Def. 2, pt. 3), and so far only does he always necessarily agree with the nature of another man (Prop. 35, pt. 4); therefore there is no single thing more profitable to a man than man, &c.　Q.E.D.

Corol. 2. When each man seeks most that which is profitable to himself, then are men most profitable to one another; for the more each man seeks his own profit and endeavours to preserve himself, the more virtue does he possess (Prop. 20, pt. 4), or, in other words (Def. 8, pt. 4), the more power does he possess to act according to the laws of his own nature, that is to say (Prop. 3, pt. 3), to live according to the guidance of reason. But men most agree in nature when they live according to the guidance of reason (Prop. 35, pt. 4), therefore (by the previous Corol.) men will be most profitable to one another when each man seeks most what is profitable to himself.　Q.E.D.

Schol. To what we have just demonstrated daily experience itself testifies by so many and such striking proofs, that it is in almost everybody's mouth that man is a God to man. It is very seldom indeed that men live according to the guidance of reason; on the contrary, it so happens that they are generally envious and injurious to one another. But, nevertheless, they are scarcely ever able to lead a solitary life, so that to most men the definition of man that he is a social animal entirely commends itself, and indeed it is the case that far more advantages than disadvantages arise from the common society of men. Let satirists therefore scoff at human affairs as much as they please, let theologians denounce them, and let the melancholy praise as much as they can a life rude and without refinement, despising men and admiring the brutes, men will nevertheless find out that by mutual help they can much more easily procure the things they need, and that it is only by their united strength they can avoid the dangers which everywhere threaten them, to say nothing about its being far nobler and worthier of our knowledge to meditate upon the doings of men than upon those of brutes. But more of this elsewhere.

PROP. 36.   *The highest good of those who follow after virtue is common to all, and all may equally enjoy it.*

Demonst.   To act in conformity with virtue is to act according to the guidance of reason (Prop. 24, pt. 4), and every effort which we make through reason is an effort to understand (Prop. 26, pt. 4), and therefore (Prop. 28, pt. 4) the highest good of those who follow after virtue is to know God, that is to say (Prop. 47, pt. 2, with its Schol.), it is a good which is common to all men, and can be equally possessed by all men in so far as they are of the same nature.   Q.E.D.

Schol.   If anybody asks, What if the highest good of those who follow after virtue were not common to all? would it not thence follow (as above, see Prop. 34, pt. 4) that men who live according to the guidance of reason, that is to say (Prop. 35, pt. 4), men in so far as they agree in nature, would be contrary to one another? We reply that it arises from no accident, but from the nature itself of reason, that the highest good of man is common to all, inasmuch as it is deduced from the human essence itself, in so far as it is determined by reason, and also because man could not be nor be conceived if he had not the power of rejoicing in this highest good. For it pertains (Prop. 47, pt. 2) to the essence of the human mind to have an adequate knowledge of the eternal and infinite essence of God.

PROP. 37.   *The good which every one who follows after virtue seeks for himself he will desire for other men; and his desire on their behalf will be greater in proportion as he has a greater knowledge of God.*

Demonst.   Men are most profitable to man in so far as they live according to the guidance of reason (Corol. 1, Prop. 35, pt. 4), and therefore (Prop. 19, pt. 4), according to the guid-

ance of reason, we necessarily endeavour to cause men to live according to the guidance of reason. But the good which each person seeks who lives according to the dictates of reason, that is to say (Prop. 24, pt. 4), who follows after virtue, is to understand (Prop. 26, pt. 4), and therefore the good which each person seeks who follows after virtue he will also desire for other men. Again, desire, in so far as it is related to the mind, is the essence itself of the mind (Def. 1 of the Affects). But the essence of the mind consists in knowledge (Prop. 11, pt. 2), which involves the knowledge of God (Prop. 47, pt. 2), and without this knowledge the essence of the mind can neither be nor be conceived (Prop. 15, pt. 1); and therefore the greater the knowledge of God which the essence of the mind involves, the greater will be the desire with which he who follows after virtue will desire for another the good which he seeks for himself.   Q.E.D.

Another Demonstration.   The good which a man seeks for himself and which he loves he will love more unchangeably if he sees that others love it (Prop. 31, pt. 3), and therefore (Corol. Prop. 31, pt. 3) he will endeavour to make others love it; and because this good (Prop. 36, pt. 4) is common to all and all can rejoice in it, he will endeavour (by the same reasoning) to cause all to rejoice in it, and (Prop. 37, pt. 3) he will do so the more, the more he rejoices in this good himself.   Q.E.D.

Schol. 1.   He who strives from an affect alone to make others love what he himself loves, and to make others live according to his way of thinking, acts from mere impulse, and is therefore hateful, especially to those who have other tastes and who therefore also desire, and by the same impulse strive to make others live according to their way of thinking.

Again, since the highest good which men seek from an affect is often such that only one person can possess it, it follows that persons who love are not consistent with themselves, and, whilst they delight to recount the praises of the beloved object, fear lest they should be believed. But he who endeavours to lead others by reason does not act from impulse, but with humanity and kindness, and is always consistent with himself.

Everything which we desire and do, of which we are the cause in so far as we possess an idea of God, or in so far as we know God, I refer to *Religion.* The desire of doing well which is born in us, because we live according to the guidance of reason, I call *Piety.* The desire to join others in friendship to himself, with which a man living according to the guidance of reason is possessed, I call *Honour*. I call that thing *Honourable* which men who live according to the guidance of reason praise; and that thing, on the contrary, I call *Base* which sets itself against the formation of friendship. Moreover, I have also shown what are the foundations of a State.

The difference also between true virtue and impotence may, from what has already been said, be easily seen to be this—that true virtue consists in living according to the guidance of reason alone; and that impotence therefore consists in this alone—that a man allows himself to be led by things which are outside himself, and by them to be determined to such actions as the common constitution of external things demands, and not to such as his own nature considered in itself alone demands. These are the things which I promised in Schol. Prop. 18, pt. 4, I would demonstrate. From them we see that the law against killing animals is based upon an empty superstition and womanish tenderness, rather than upon sound reason. A proper regard, indeed, to one's own profit teaches us to unite in friendship with men, and not with brutes, nor with things whose nature is different from human nature. It teaches us, too, that the same right which they have over us we have over them. Indeed, since the right of any person is limited by his virtue or power, men possess a far greater right over brutes than brutes possess over men. I by no means deny that brutes feel, but I do deny that on this account it is unlawful for us to consult our own profit by using them for our own pleasure and treating them as is most convenient for us, inasmuch as they do not agree in nature with us, and their affects are different from our own (Schol. Prop. 57, pt. 3).

It now remains that I should explain what are Justice, Injustice, Crime, and, finally, Merit. With regard to these, see the following scholium.

Schol. 2. In the Appendix to the First Part I promised I would explain what are praise and blame, merit and crime, justice and injustice. I have already shown what is the meaning of praise and blame in Schol. Prop. 29, pt. 3, and this will be a fitting place for the explanation of the rest. A few words must, however, first be said about the natural and civil state of man.

It is by the highest right of nature that each person exists, and consequently it is by the

highest right of nature that each person does those things which follow from the necessity of his nature; and therefore it is by the highest right of nature that each person judges what is good and what is evil, consults his own advantage as he thinks best (Props. 19 and 20, pt. 4), avenges himself (Corol. 2, Prop. 40, pt. 3), and endeavours to preserve what he loves and to destroy what he hates (Prop. 28, pt. 3). If men lived according to the guidance of reason, every one would enjoy this right without injuring any one else (Corol. 1, Prop. 35, pt. 4). But because men are subject to affects (Corol. Prop. 4, pt. 4), which far surpass human power or virtue (Prop. 6, pt. 4), they are often drawn in different directions (Prop. 33, pt. 4), and are contrary to one another (Prop. 34, pt. 4), although they need one another's help (Schol. Prop. 35, pt. 4).

In order, then, that men may be able to live in harmony and be a help to one another, it is necessary for them to cede their natural right, and beget confidence one in the other that they will do nothing by which one can injure the other. In what manner this can be done, so that men who are necessarily subject to affects (Corol. Prop. 4, pt. 4), and are uncertain and changeable (Prop. 33, pt. 4), can beget confidence one in the other and have faith in one another, is evident from Prop. 7, pt. 4, and Prop. 39, pt. 3. It is there shown that no affect can be restrained unless by a stronger and contrary affect, and that every one abstains from doing an injury through fear of a greater injury. By this law, therefore, can society be strengthened, if only it claims for itself the right which every individual possesses of avenging himself and deciding what is good and what is evil, and provided, therefore, that it possess the power of prescribing a common rule of life, of promulgating laws and supporting them, not by reason, which cannot restrain the affects (Schol. Prop. 17, pt. 4), but by penalties.

This society, firmly established by law and with a power of self-preservation, is called a *State*, and those who are protected by its right are called *Citizens*. We can now easily see that in the natural state there is nothing which by universal consent is good or evil, since every one in a natural state consults only his own profit; deciding according to his own way of thinking what is good and what is evil with reference only to his own profit, and is not bound by any law to obey any one but himself. Hence in a natural state sin cannot be conceived, but only in a civil state, where it is decided by universal consent what is good and what is evil, and where every one is bound to obey the State. *Sin*, therefore, is nothing but disobedience, which is punished by the law of the State alone; obedience, on the other hand, being regarded as a *merit* in a citizen, because on account of it he is considered worthy to enjoy the privileges of the State. Again, in a natural state no one by common consent is the owner of anything, nor is there anything in nature which can be said to be the rightful property of this and not of that man, but all things belong to all, so that in a natural state it is impossible to conceive a desire of rendering to each man his own or taking from another that which is his; that is to say, in a natural state there is nothing which can be called just or unjust, but only in a civil state, in which it is decided by universal consent what is one person's and what is another's. Justice and injustice, therefore, sin and merit, are external notions, and not attributes, which manifest the nature of the mind. But enough of these matters.

PROP. 38. *That which so disposes the human body that it can be affected in many ways, or which renders it capable of affecting external bodies in many ways, is profitable to man, and is more profitable in proportion as by its means the body becomes better fitted to be affected in many ways, and to affect other bodies; on the other hand, that thing is injurious which renders the body less fitted to affect or be affected.*

Demonst. In proportion as the body is rendered more fitted for this is the mind rendered more capable of perception (Prop. 14, pt. 2), and, therefore, whatever disposes the body in this way, and renders it fitted for this, is necessarily good or profitable (Props. 26 and 27, pt. 4), and is more profitable in proportion to its power of rendering the body more fitted for this, while, on the contrary (by Prop. 14, pt. 2, conversely, and Props. 26 and 27, pt. 4), it is injurious if it renders the body less fitted for this. Q.E.D.

PROP. 39. *Whatever is effective to preserve the proportion of motion and rest which the parts of the human body bear to each other is good, and, on the contrary, that is evil which causes the parts of the human body to have a different proportion of motion and rest to each other.*

Demonst. The human body needs for its preservation very many other bodies (Post.

4, pt. 2). But what constitutes the form of the human body is this, that its parts communicate their motions to one another in a certain fixed proportion (Def. preceding Lem. 4, following Prop. 13, pt. 2). Whatever, therefore, is effective to preserve the proportion of motion and rest which the parts of the human body bear to each other, preserves the form of the human body, and, consequently (Posts. 3 and 6, pt. 2), is effective to enable the body to be affected in many ways, and to affect external bodies in many ways, and, therefore (Prop. 38, pt. 4), is good. Again, whatever causes the parts of the human body to get a different proportion of motion and rest (by the definition just quoted), causes the human body to assume another form, that is to say (as is self-evident, and as we observed at the end of the preface to this part), causes the human body to be destroyed, rendering it consequently incapable of being affected in many ways, and is, therefore (Prop. 38, pt. 4), bad. Q.E.D.

Schol. In what degree these things may injure or profit the mind will be explained in the Fifth Part. Here I observe merely that I understand the body to die when its parts are so disposed as to acquire a different proportion of motion and rest to each other. For I dare not deny that the human body, though the circulation of the blood and the other things by means of which it is thought to live be preserved, may, nevertheless, be changed into another nature altogether different from its own. No reason compels me to affirm that the body never dies unless it is changed into a corpse. Experience, indeed, seems to teach the contrary. It happens sometimes that a man undergoes such changes that he cannot very well be said to be the same man, as was the case with a certain Spanish poet of whom have heard, who was seized with an illness and although he recovered, remained, nevertheless, so oblivious of his past life that he did not believe the tales and tragedies he had composed were his own, and he might, indeed have been taken for a grown-up child if he had also forgotten his native tongue. But if this seems incredible, what shall we say of children? The man of mature years believes the nature of children to be so different from his own that it would be impossible to persuade him he had ever been a child, if he did not conjecture regarding himself from what he sees of others. But in order to avoid giving to the superstitious matter for new questions, I prefer

fer to go no farther in the discussion of these matters.

Prop. 40. *Whatever conduces to the universal fellowship of men, that is to say, whatever causes men to live in harmony with one another, is profitable, and, on the contrary, whatever brings discord into the State is evil.*

Demonst. For whatever causes men to live in harmony with one another causes them to live according to the guidance of reason (Prop. 35, pt. 4), and, therefore (Props. 26 and 27, pt. 4), is good, and (by the same reasoning) those things are evil which excite discord. Q.E.D.

Prop. 41. *Joy is not directly evil, but good; sorrow, on the other hand, is directly evil.*

Demonst. Joy (Prop. 11, pt. 3, with its Schol.) is an affect by which the body's power of action is increased or assisted. Sorrow, on the other hand, is an affect by which the body's power of action is lessened or restrained, and, therefore (Prop. 38, pt. 4), joy is directly good. Q.E.D.

Prop. 42. *Cheerfulness can never be excessive, but is always good; melancholy, on the contrary, is always evil.*

Demonst. Cheerfulness (see its definition in Schol. Prop. 11, pt. 3) is joy, which, in so far as it is related to the body, consists in this, that all the parts of the body are equally affected, that is to say (Prop. 11, pt. 3), the body's power of action is increased or assisted, so that all the parts acquire the same proportion of motion and rest to each other. Cheerfulness, therefore (Prop. 39, pt. 4), is always good, and can never be excessive. But melancholy (see its definition in Schol. Prop. 11, pt. 3) is sorrow, which, in so far as it is related to the body, consists in this, that the body's power of action is absolutely lessened or restrained, and melancholy, therefore (Prop. 38, pt. 4), is always evil. Q.E.D.

Prop. 43. *Pleasurable excitement may be excessive and an evil, and pain may be good in so far as pleasurable excitement or joy is evil.*

Demonst. Pleasurable excitement is joy, which, in so far as it is related to the body, consists in this, that one or some of the parts of the body are affected more than others (see Def. in Schol. Prop. 11, pt. 3). The power of this affect may, therefore, be so great as to overcome the other actions of the body (Prop.

6, pt. 4); it may cling obstinately to the body; it may impede the body in such a manner as to render it less capable of being affected in many ways, and therefore (Prop. 38, pt. 4) may be evil. Again, pain, which, on the contrary, is sorrow, considered in itself alone cannot be good (Prop. 41, pt. 4). But because its power and increase is limited by the power of an external cause compared with our own power (Prop. 5, pt. 4), we can therefore conceive infinite degrees of strength of this affect, and infinite kinds of it (Prop. 3, pt. 4), and we can therefore conceive it to be such that it can restrain an excess of pleasurable excitement, and so far (by the first part of this proposition) preventing the body from becoming less capable. So far, therefore, will pain be good. Q.E.D.

Prop. 44. *Love and desire may be excessive.*

Demonst. Love is joy (Def. 6 of the Affects) with the accompanying idea of an external cause. Pleasurable excitement, therefore (Schol. Prop. 11, pt. 3), with the accompanying idea of an external cause, is love, and therefore love (Prop. 43, pt. 4) may be excessive. Again, desire is greater as the affect from which it springs is greater (Prop. 37, pt. 3). Inasmuch, therefore, as an affect (Prop. 6, pt. 4) may overpower the other actions of a man, so also the desire which springs from this affect may also overpower the other desires, and may therefore exist in the same excess which we have shown (in the preceding proposition) that pleasurable excitement possesses. Q.E.D.

Schol. Cheerfulness, which I have affirmed to be good, is more easily imagined than observed; for the affects by which we are daily agitated are generally related to some part of the body which is affected more than the others, and therefore it is that the affects exist for the most part in excess, and so hold the mind down to the contemplation of one object alone, that it can think about nothing else; and although men are subject to a number of affects, and therefore few are found who are always under the control of one and the same affect, there are not wanting those to whom one and the same affect obstinately clings. We see men sometimes so affected by one object, that although it is not present, they believe it to be before them; and if this happens to a man who is not asleep, we say that he is delirious or mad. Nor are those believed to be less mad who are inflamed by love, dreaming about nothing but a mistress or harlot day and night, for they excite our laughter. But the avaricious man who thinks of nothing else but gain or money, and the ambitious man who thinks of nothing but glory, inasmuch as they do harm, and are, therefore, thought worthy of hatred, are not believed to be mad. In truth, however, avarice, ambition, lust, &c., are a kind of madness, although they are not reckoned amongst diseases.

PROP. 45.   *Hatred can never be good.*

Demonst.   The man whom we hate we endeavour to destroy (Prop. 39, pt. 3), that is to say (Prop. 37, pt. 4), we endeavour to do something which is evil. Therefore hatred, &c.   Q.E.D.

Schol.   It is to be observed that here and in the following propositions I understand by hatred, hatred towards men only.

Corol. 1.   Envy, mockery, contempt, anger, revenge, and the other affects which are related to hatred or arise from it, are evil. This is also evident from Prop. 39, pt. 3, and Prop. 37, pt. 4.

Corol. 2.   Everything which we desire because we are affected by hatred is base and unjust in the State. This is also evident from Prop. 39, pt. 3, and from the definition in Schol. Prop. 37, pt. 4, of what is base and unjust.

Schol.   I make a great distinction between mockery (which I have said in Corol. 1 of this Prop. is bad) and laughter; for laughter and merriment are nothing but joy, and therefore, provided they are not excessive, are in themselves good (Prop. 41, pt. 4). Nothing but a gloomy and sad superstition forbids enjoyment. For why is it more seemly to extinguish hunger and thirst than to drive away melancholy? My reasons and my conclusions are these:—No God and no human being, except an envious one, is delighted by my impotence or my trouble, or esteems as any virtue in us tears, sighs, fears, and other things of this kind, which are signs of mental impotence; on the contrary, the greater the joy with which we are affected, the greater the perfection to which we pass thereby, that is to say, the more do we necessarily partake of the divine nature. To make use of things, therefore, and to delight in them as much as possible (provided we do not disgust ourselves with them, which is not delighting in them), is the part of a wise man. It is the part of a wise man, I say, to refresh and invigorate himself with moderate and pleasant eating and drinking, with sweet scents and the beauty of green plants, with

ornament, with music, with sports, with the theatre, and with all things of this kind which one man can enjoy without hurting another. For the human body is composed of a great number of parts of diverse nature, which constantly need new and varied nourishment, in order that the whole of the body may be equally fit for everything which can follow from its nature, and consequently that the mind may be equally fit to understand many things at once. This mode of living best of all agrees both with our principles and with common practice; therefore this mode of living is the best of all, and is to be universally commended. There is no need, therefore, to enter more at length into the subject.

PROP. 46.   *He who lives according to the guidance of reason strives as much as possible to repay the hatred, anger, or contempt of others towards himself with love or generosity.*

Demonst.   All affects of hatred are evil (Corol. 1, Prop. 45, pt. 4), and, therefore, the man who lives according to the guidance of reason will strive as much as possible to keep himself from being agitated by the affects of hatred (Prop. 19, pt. 4), and, consequently (Prop. 37, pt. 4), will strive to keep others from being subject to the same affects. But hatred is increased by reciprocal hatred, and, on the other hand, can be extinguished by love (Prop. 43, pt. 3), so that hatred passes into love (Prop. 44, pt. 3). Therefore he who lives according to the guidance of reason will strive to repay the hatred of another, &c., with love, that is to say, with generosity (see definition of generosity in Schol. Prop. 59, pt. 3).   Q.E.D.

Schol.   He who wishes to avenge injuries by hating in return does indeed live miserably. But he who, on the contrary, strives to drive out hatred by love, fights joyfully and confidently, with equal ease resisting one man or a number of men, and needing scarcely any assistance from fortune. Those whom he conquers yield gladly, not from defect of strength, but from an increase of it. These truths, however, all follow so plainly from the definitions alone of love and the intellect. that there is no need to demonstrate them singly.

PROP. 47.   *The affects of hope and fear cannot be good of themselves.*

Demonst.   The affects of hope and fear cannot exist without sorrow; for fear (Def. 13 of the Affects) is sorrow, and hope (see the explanation of Defs. 12 and 13 of the Affects) cannot exist without fear. Therefore (Prop. 41, pt. 4) these affects cannot be good of themselves, but only in so far as they are able to restrain the excesses of joy (Prop. 43, pt. 4). Q.E.D.

Schol. We may here add that these affects indicate want of knowledge and impotence of mind, and, for the same reason, confidence, despair, gladness, and remorse are signs of weakness of mind. For although confidence and gladness are affects of joy, they nevertheless suppose that sorrow has preceded them, namely, hope or fear. In proportion, therefore, as we endeavour to live according to the guidance of reason, shall we strive as much as possible to depend less on hope, to liberate ourselves from fear, to rule fortune, and to direct our actions by the sure counsels of reason.

Prop. 48. *The affects of over-estimation and contempt are always evil.*

Demonst. These affects (Defs. 21 and 22 of the Affects) are opposed to reason, and therefore (Props. 26 and 27, pt. 4) are evil. Q.E.D.

Prop. 49. *Over-estimation easily renders the man who is over-estimated proud.*

Demonst. If we see that a person, through love, thinks too much of us, we shall easily glorify ourselves (Schol. 41, pt. 3), or, in other words, be affected with joy (Def. 30 of the Affects), and easily believe the good which we hear others affirm of us (Prop. 25, pt. 3), and consequently, through self-love, we shall think too much of ourselves, that is to say (Def. 28 of the Affects), we shall easily grow proud. Q.E.D.

Prop. 50. *Pity in a man who lives according to the guidance of reason is in itself evil and unprofitable.*

Demonst. Pity (Def. 18 of the Affects) is sorrow, and therefore (Prop. 41, pt. 4) is in itself evil. The good, however, which issues from pity, namely, that we endeavour to free from misery the man we pity (Corol. 3, Prop. 27, pt. 3), we desire to do from the dictate of reason alone (Prop. 37, pt. 4); nor can we do anything except by the dictate of reason alone, which we are sure is good (Prop. 27, pt. 4). Pity, therefore, in a man who lives according to the guidance of reason is in itself bad and unprofitable. Q.E.D.

Corol. Hence it follows that a man who lives according to the dictates of reason endeavours as much as possible to prevent himself from being touched by pity.

Schol. The man who has properly understood that everything follows from the necessity of the divine nature, and comes to pass according to the eternal laws and rules of nature, will in truth discover nothing which is worthy of hatred, laughter, or contempt, nor will he pity any one, but, so far as human virtue is able, he will endeavour to *do well*, as we say, and to *rejoice*. We must add also, that a man who is easily touched by the affect of pity, and is moved by the misery or tears of another, often does something of which he afterward repents, both because from an affect we do nothing which we certainly know to be good, and also because we are so easily deceived by false tears. But this I say expressly of the man who lives according to the guidance of reason. For he who is moved neither by reason nor pity to be of any service to others is properly called inhuman; for (Prop. 27, pt. 3) he seems to be unlike a man.

Prop. 51. *Favour is not opposed to reason, but agrees with it, and may arise from it.*

Demonst. Favour is love towards him who does good to another (Def. 19 of the Affects), and therefore can be related to the mind in so far as it is said to act (Prop. 59, pt. 3), that is to say (Prop. 3, pt. 3), in so far as it understands, and therefore favour agrees with reason. Q.E.D.

Another Demonstration. If we live according to the guidance of reason, we shall desire for others the good which we seek for ourselves (Prop. 37, pt. 4). Therefore if we see one person do good to another, our endeavour to do good is assisted, that is to say (Schol. Prop. 11, pt. 3), we shall rejoice, and our joy (by hypothesis) will be accompanied with the idea of the person who does good to the other, that is to say (Def. 19 of the Affects), we shall favour him. Q.E.D.

Schol. Indignation, as it is defined by us (Def. 20 of the Affects), is necessarily evil (Prop. 45, pt. 4); but it is to be observed that when the supreme authority, constrained by the desire of preserving peace, punishes a citizen who injures another, I do not say that it is indignant with the citizen, since it is not excited by hatred to destroy him, but punishes him from motives of piety.

Prop. 52. *Self-satisfaction may arise from reason, and the self-satisfaction alone which arises from reason is the highest which can exist.*

Demonst. Self-satisfaction is the joy which arises from a man's contemplating himself and his power of action (Def. 25 of the Affects). But man's true power of action or his virtue is reason itself (Prop. 3, pt. 3), which he contemplates clearly and distinctly (Props. 40 and 43, pt. 2). Self-satisfaction therefore arises from reason. Again, man, when he contemplates himself, perceives nothing clearly and distinctly or adequately, excepting those things which follow from his power of action (Def. 2, pt. 3), that is to say (Prop. 3, pt. 3), those things which follow from his power of understanding; and therefore from this contemplation alone the highest satisfaction which can exist arises. Q.E.D.

Schol. Self-satisfaction is indeed the highest thing for which we can hope, for (as we have shown in Prop. 25, pt. 4) no one endeavours to preserve his being for the sake of any end. Again, because this self-satisfaction is more and more nourished and strengthened by praise (Corol. Prop. 53, pt. 3), and, on the contrary (Corol. Prop. 55, pt. 3), more and more disturbed by blame, therefore we are principally led by glory, and can scarcely endure life with disgrace.

PROP. 53. *Humility is not a virtue, that is to say, it does not spring from reason.*

Demonst. Humility is sorrow, which springs from this, that a man contemplates his own weakness (Def. 26 of the Affects). But in so far as a man knows himself by true reason is he supposed to understand his essence, that is to say (Prop. 7, pt. 3), his power. If, therefore, while contemplating himself, he perceives any impotence of his, this is not due to his understanding himself, but, as we have shown (Prop. 55, pt. 3), to the fact that his power of action is restrained. But if we suppose that he forms a conception of his own impotence because he understands something to be more powerful than himself, by the knowledge of which he limits his own power of action, in this case we simply conceive that he understands himself distinctly (Prop. 26, pt. 4), and his power of action is increased. Humility or sorrow, therefore, which arises because a man contemplates his own impotence, does not spring from true contemplation or reason, and is not a virtue, but a passion. Q.E.D.

PROP. 54. *Repentance is not a virtue, that is to say, it does not spring from reason; on the contrary, the man who repents of what he has done is doubly wretched or impotent.*

Demonst. The first part of this proposition is demonstrated in the same manner as the preceding proposition. The second part follows from the definition alone of this affect (Def. 27 of the Affects). For, in the first place, we allow ourselves to be overcome by a depraved desire, and, in the second place, by sorrow.

Schol. Inasmuch as men seldom live as reason dictates, therefore these two affects, humility and repentance, together with hope and fear, are productive of more profit than disadvantage, and therefore, since men must sin, it is better that they should sin in this way. For if men impotent in mind were all equally proud, were ashamed of nothing, and feared nothing, by what bonds could they be united or constrained? The multitude becomes a thing to be feared if it has nothing to fear. It is not to be wondered at, therefore, that the prophets, thinking rather of the good of the community than of a few, should have commended so greatly humility, repentance, and reverence. Indeed, those who are subject to these affects can be led much more easily than others, so that, at last, they come to live according to the guidance of reason, that is to say, become free men, and enjoy the life of the blessed.

PROP. 55. *The greatest pride or the greatest despondency is the greatest ignorance of one's self.*

Demonst. This is evident from Defs. 28 and 29 of the Affects.

PROP. 56. *The greatest pride or despondency indicates the greatest impotence of mind.*

Demonst. The primary foundation of virtue is the preservation of our being (Corol. Prop. 22, pt. 4) according to the guidance of reason (Prop. 24, pt. 4). The man, therefore, who is ignorant of himself is ignorant of the foundation of all the virtues, and consequently is ignorant of all the virtues. Again, to act in conformity with virtue is nothing but acting according to the guidance of reason (Prop. 24, pt. 4), and he who acts according to the guidance of reason must necessarily know that he acts according to the guidance of reason (Prop. 43, pt. 2). He, therefore, who is ignorant of himself, and consequently (as we have just shown) altogether ignorant of all the virtues, cannot in any way act in conformity with virtue, that is to say (Def. 8, pt. 4), is altogether impotent in mind. Therefore (Prop. 55, pt. 4), the greatest pride or despondency indicates the greatest impotence of mind. Q.E.D.

Corol. Hence follows, with the utmost clear

ness, that the proud and the desponding are above all others subject to affects.

Schol. Despondency, nevertheless, can be corrected more easily than pride, since the former is an affect of sorrow, while the latter is an affect of joy, and is, therefore (Prop. 18, pt. 4), stronger than the former.

PROP. 57. *The proud man loves the presence of parasites or flatterers, and hates that of the noble-minded.*

Demonst. Pride is joy arising from a man's having too high an opinion of himself (Defs. 28 and 6 of the Affects). This opinion a proud man will endeavour, as much as he can, to cherish (Schol. Prop. 13, pt. 3), and, therefore, will love the presence of parasites or flatterers (the definitions of these people are omitted, because they are too well known), and will shun that of the noble-minded who think of him as is right. Q.E.D.

Schol. It would take too much time to enumerate here all the evils of pride, for the proud are subject to all affects, but to none are they less subject than to those of love and pity. It is necessary, however, to observe here that a man is also called proud if he thinks too little of other people, and so, in this sense, pride is to be defined as joy which arises from the false opinion that we are superior to other people, while despondency, the contrary to this pride, would be defined as sorrow arising from the false opinion that we are inferior to other people. This being understood, it is easy to see that the proud man is necessarily envious (Schol. Prop. 55, pt. 3), and that he hates those above all others who are the most praised on account of their virtues. It follows, too, that his hatred of them is not easily overcome by love or kindness (Schol. Prop. 41, pt. 3), and that he is delighted by the presence of those only who humour his weakness, and from a fool make him a madman. Although despondency is contrary to pride, the despondent man is closely akin to the proud man. For since the sorrow of the despondent man arises from his judging his own impotence by the power or virtue of others, his sorrow will be mitigated, that is to say, he will rejoice, if his imagination be occupied in contemplating the vices of others. Hence the proverb—It is a consolation to the wretched to have had companions in their misfortunes. On the other hand, the more the despondent man believes himself to be below other people, the more will he sorrow; and this is the reason why none are

more prone to envy than the despondent; and why they, above all others, try to observe men's actions with a view to finding fault with them rather than correcting them, so that at last they praise nothing but despondency and glory in it; but in such a manner, however, as always to seem despondent.

These things follow from this affect as necessarily as it follows from the nature of a triangle that its three angles are equal to two right angles. It is true, indeed, that I have said that I call these and the like affects evil, in so far as I attend to human profit alone; but the laws of nature have regard to the common order of nature of which man is a part—a remark I desired to make in passing, lest it should be thought that I talk about the vices and absurdities of men rather than attempt to demonstrate the nature and properties of things. As I said in the Preface to the Third Part, I consider human affects and their properties precisely as I consider other natural objects; and, indeed, the affects of man, if they do not show his power, show, at least, the power and workmanship of nature, no less than many other things which we admire and delight to contemplate. I proceed, however, to notice those things connected with the affects which are productive either of profit or loss to man.

PROP. 58. *Self-exaltation is not opposed to reason, but may spring from it.*

Demonst. This is plain from Def. 30 of the Affects, and also from the definition of honour in Schol. 1, Prop. 37, pt. 4.

Schol. What is called vainglory is self-satisfaction, nourished by nothing but the good opinion of the multitude, so that when that is withdrawn, the satisfaction, that is to say (Schol. Prop. 52, pt. 4), the chief good which every one loves, ceases. For this reason those who glory in the good opinion of the multitude anxiously and with daily care strive, labour, and struggle to preserve their fame. For the multitude is changeable and fickle, so that fame, if it be not preserved, soon passes away. As every one, moreover, is desirous to catch the praises of the people, one person will readily destroy the fame of another; and, consequently, as the object of contention is what is commonly thought to be the highest good, a great desire arises on the part of every one to keep down his fellows by every possible means, and he who at last comes off conqueror boasts more because he has injured another person than because he has profited himself. This glory of self-satisfaction, therefore, is indeed vain, for it is really no glory. What is worthy of notice with regard to shame may easily be gathered from what has been said about compassion and repentance. I will only add that pity, like shame, although it is not a virtue, is nevertheless good, in so far as it shows that a desire of living uprightly is present in the man who is possessed with shame, just as pain is called good in so far as it shows that the injured part has not yet putrefied. A man, therefore, who is ashamed of what he has done, although he is sorrowful, is nevertheless more perfect than the shameless man who has no desire of living uprightly. These are the things which I undertook to establish with regard to the affects of joy and sorrow. With reference to the desires, these are good or evil as they spring from good or evil affects. All of them, however, in so far as they are begotten in us of affects which are passions, are blind (as may easily be inferred from what has been said in Schol. Prop. 44, pt. 4), nor would they be of any use if men could be easily persuaded to live according to the dictates of reason alone, as I shall show in a few words.

PROP. 59. *To all actions to which we are determined by an affect which is a passion we may, without the affect, be determined by reason.*

Demonst. To act according to reason is nothing (Prop. 3, and Def. 2, pt. 3) but to do those things which follow from the necessity of our nature considered in itself alone. But sorrow is evil so far as it lessens or restrains this power of action (Prop. 41, pt. 4); therefore we can be determined by this affect to no action which we could not perform if we were led by reason. Again, joy is evil so far only as it hinders our fitness for action (Props. 41 and 43, pt. 4); and therefore also we can so far be determined to no action which we could not do if we were led by reason. Finally, in so far as joy is good, so far it agrees with reason (for it consists in this, that a man's power of action is increased or assisted), and it is not a passion unless in so far as man's power of action is not increased sufficiently for him to conceive adequately himself and his actions (Prop. 3, pt. 3, with its Schol.). If, therefore, a man affected with joy were led to such perfection as to conceive adequately himself and his actions, he would be fitted—better even than before—for the performance of those actions to which he is now determined by the affects which are pas-

sions. But all the affects are related to joy, sorrow, or desire (see the explanation of Def. 4 of the Affects), and desire (Def. 1 of the Affects) is nothing but the endeavour itself to act; therefore to all actions to which we are determined by an affect which is a passion we may without the affect be determined by reason alone. Q.E.D.

Another Demonstration. Any action is called evil in so far as it arises from our being affected with hatred or some evil affect (Corol. 1, Prop. 45, pt. 4). But no action considered in itself alone is either good or evil (as we have already shown in the preface to this part), but one and the same action is sometimes good and sometimes evil. Therefore we may be led by reason (Prop. 19, pt. 4) to that same action which is sometimes evil, or which arises from some evil affect. Q.E.D.

Schol. This can be explained more clearly by an example. The action of striking, for instance, in so far as it is considered physically, and we attend only to the fact that a man raises his arm, closes his hand, and forcibly moves the whole arm downwards, is a virtue which is conceived from the structure of the human body. If, therefore, a man agitated by anger or hatred is led to close the fist or move the arm, this comes to pass, as we have shown in the Second Part, because one and the same action can be joined to different images of things, and therefore we may be led to one and the same action as well by the images of things which we conceive confusedly as by those which we conceive clearly and distinctly. If it appears, therefore, that every desire which arises from an affect which is a passion would be of no use if men could be led by reason. We shall now see why a desire which arises from an affect which is a passion is called blind.

PROP. 60. *The desire which arises from joy or sorrow, which is related to one or to some, but not to all, the parts of the body, has no regard to the profit of the whole man.*

Demonst. Let it be supposed that a part of the body—A, for example—is so strengthened by the force of some external cause that it prevails over the others (Prop. 6, pt. 4). It will not endeavour, therefore, to lose its strength in order that the remaining parts of the body may perform their functions, for in that case it would have a force or power of losing its strength, which (Prop. 6, pt. 3) is absurd. It will endeavour, therefore, and consequently (Props. 7 and 12, pt. 3) the mind also will endeavour, to preserve this same state; and so the desire which arises from such an affect of joy has no regard to the whole man. If, on the other hand, it be supposed that the part A is restrained so that the other parts prevail, it can be demonstrated in the same way that the desire which springs from sorrow has no regard to the whole man.

Schol. Since, therefore, joy is most frequently related to one part of the body (Schol. Prop. 44, pt. 4), we generally desire to preserve our being without reference to our health as a whole; and, moreover, the desires by which we are chiefly controlled (Corol. Prop. 9, pt. 4) have regard to the present only, and not to the future.

PROP. 61. *A desire which springs from reason can never be in excess.*

Demonst. Desire (Def. 1 of the Affects), absolutely considered, is the very essence of man, in so far as he is conceived as determined in any way whatever to any action, and therefore the desire which springs from reason, that is to say (Prop. 3, pt. 3), which is begotten in us in so far as we act, is the very essence or nature of man in so far as it is conceived as determined to actions which are adequately conceived by the essence of man alone (Def. 2, pt. 3). If, therefore, this desire could be in excess, it would be possible for human nature, considered in itself alone, to exceed itself, or, in other words, more would be possible to it than is possible, which is a manifest contradiction, and therefore this desire can never be in excess. Q.E.D.

PROP. 62. *In so far as the conception of an object is formed by the mind according to the dictate of reason, the mind is equally affected, whether the idea be that of something future, past, or present.*

Demonst. Everything which the mind, under the guidance of reason, conceives, it conceives under the same form of eternity or necessity (Corol. 2, Prop. 44, pt. 2), and it is affected with the same certainty (Prop. 43, pt. 2, and its Schol.). Therefore, whether the idea be one of a future, past, or present object, the mind conceives the object with the same necessity, and is affected with the same certainty; and whether the idea be that of a future, past, or present object, it will nevertheless be equally true (Prop. 41, pt. 2), that is to say (Def. 4, pt. 2), it will always have the same properties of an adequate idea. There-

fore, in so far as the conception of an object is formed by the mind according to the dictates of reason, the mind will be affected in the same way whether the idea be that of something future, past, or present. Q.E.D.

Schol. If it were possible for us to possess an adequate knowledge concerning the duration of things, and to determine by reason the periods of their existence, we should contemplate with the same affect objects future and present, and the good which the mind conceived to be future, it would seek just as it would seek the present good. Consequently it would necessarily neglect the present good for the sake of a greater future good, and would, as we shall presently show, be very little disposed to seek a good which was present, but which would be a cause of any future evil. But it is not possible for us to have any other than a very inadequate knowledge of the duration of things (Prop. 31, pt. 2), and we determine (Schol. Prop. 44, pt. 2) the periods of the existence of objects by the imagination alone, which is not affected by the image of a present object in the same way as it is by that of future object. Hence it comes to pass that the true knowledge of good and evil which we possess is only abstract or universal, and the judgment we pass upon the order of things and the connection of causes, so that we may determine what is good for us in the present and what is evil, is rather imaginary than real. It is not, therefore, to be wondered at if the desire which arises from a knowledge of good and evil, in so far as this knowledge has regard to the future, is capable of being easily restrained by the desire of objects which are sweet to us at the present moment. (See Prop. 16, pt. 4).

PROP. 63. *He who is led by fear, and does what is good in order that he may avoid what is evil, is not led by reason.*

Demonst. All the affects which are related to the mind, in so far as it acts, that is to say (Prop. 3, pt. 3), which are related to reason, are no other than affects of joy and desire (Prop. 59, pt. 3); and therefore (Def. 13 of the Affects), he who is led by fear and does good through fear of evil is not led by reason. Q.E.D.

Schol. The superstitious, who know better how to rail at vice than to teach virtue, and who study not to lead man by reason, but to hold him in through fear, in order that he may shun evil rather than love virtue, aim at nothing more than that others should be as miserable as themselves, and, therefore, it is not to be wondered at if they generally become annoying and hateful to men.

Corol. By the desire which springs from reason we follow good directly and avoid evil indirectly.

Demonst. For the desire which springs from reason cannot spring from sorrow, but only from an affect of joy, which is not a passion (Prop. 59, pt. 3), that is to say, from joy which cannot be in excess (Prop. 61, pt. 4). This desire springs, therefore (Prop. 8, pt. 4), from the knowledge of good, and not from the knowledge of evil, and therefore, according to the guidance of reason, we seek what is good directly, and so far only do we shun what is evil. Q.E.D.

Schol. This corollary is explained by the example of a sick man and a healthy man. The sick man, through fear of death, eats what he dislikes; the healthy man takes a pleasure in his food, and so enjoys life more than if he feared death and directly desired to avoid it. So also the judge who condemns a guilty man to death, not from hatred or anger, but solely from love for the public welfare, is led by reason alone.

PROP. 64. *The knowledge of evil is inadequate knowledge.*

Demonst. The knowledge of evil (Prop. 8, pt. 4) is sorrow itself, in so far as we are conscious of it. But sorrow is the passage to a less perfection (Def. 3 of the Affects), and it cannot, therefore, be understood through the essence itself of man (Props. 6 and 7, pt. 3). It is, therefore (Def. 2, pt. 3), a passion which (Prop. 3, pt. 3) depends upon inadequate ideas, and consequently (Prop. 29, pt. 2) the knowledge of sorrow, that is to say, the knowledge of evil, is inadequate. Q.E.D.

Corol. Hence it follows that if the human mind had none but adequate ideas, it would form no notion of evil.

PROP. 65. *According to the guidance of reason, of two things which are good, we shall follow the greater good, and of two evils, we shall follow the less.*

Demonst. The good which hinders us from enjoying a greater good is really an evil, for good and evil (as we have shown in the preface to this part) are affirmed of things in so far as we compare them with one another. By the same reasoning a less evil is really a good, and therefore (Corol. Prop. 63, pt. 4), according to the guidance of reason, we shall seek or follow the greater good only and the lesser evil. Q.E.D.

Corol. According to the guidance of reason, we shall follow a lesser evil for the sake of a greater good, and a lesser good which is the cause of a greater evil we shall neglect. For the evil which we here call less is really a good, and the good, on the other hand, is evil; and therefore (Corol. Prop. 63, pt. 4) we shall seek the former and neglect the latter. Q.E.D.

PROP. 66. *According to the guidance of reason, we shall seek the greater future good before that which is less and present, and we shall seek also the less and present evil before that which is greater and future.*

Demonst. If it were possible for the mind to have an adequate knowledge of a future object, it would be affected by the same affect towards the future object as towards a present object (Prop. 62, pt. 4). Therefore, in so far as we attend to reason itself, as we are supposing in this proposition that we do, it is the same thing whether the greater good or evil be supposed to be future or present, and therefore (Prop. 65, pt. 4) we shall seek the greater future good before that which is less and present, &c. Q.E.D.

Corol. According to the guidance of reason, we shall seek the lesser present evil which is the cause of the greater future good, and the lesser present good which is the cause of a greater future evil we shall neglect. This corollary is connected with the foregoing proposition in the same way as Corol. Prop. 65 is connected with Prop. 65.

Schol. If what has been said here be compared with what has been demonstrated about the strength of the passions in the first eighteen Props. pt. 4, and in Schol. Prop. 18, pt. 4, it will easily be seen in what consists the difference between a man who is led by affect or opinion alone and one who is led by reason. The former, whether he wills it or not, does those things of which he is entirely ignorant, but the latter does the will of no one but himself, and does those things only which he knows are of greatest importance in life, and which he therefore desires above all things. I call the former, therefore, a slave, and the latter free.

I will add here a few words concerning the character of the free man and his manner of life.

PROP. 67. *A free man thinks of nothing less than of death, and his wisdom is not a meditation upon death but upon life.*

Demonst. A free man, that is to say, a man who lives according to the dictates of reason alone, is not led by the fear of death (Prop. 63, pt. 4), but directly desires the good (Corol. Prop. 63, pt. 4); that is to say (Prop. 24, pt. 4), desires to act, to live, and to preserve his being in accordance with the principle of seeking his own profit. He thinks, therefore, of nothing less than of death, and his wisdom is a meditation upon life. Q.E.D.

PROP. 68. *If men were born free, they would form no conception of good and evil so long as they were free.*

Demonst. I have said that that man is free who is led by reason alone. He, therefore, who is born free and remains free has no other than adequate ideas, and therefore has no conception of evil (Corol. Prop. 64, pt. 4), and consequently (as good and evil are correlative) no conception of good. Q.E.D.

Schol. It is clear from Prop. 4, pt. 4, that the hypothesis of this proposition is false, and cannot be conceived unless in so far as we regard human nature alone, or rather God, not in so far as He is infinite, but in so far only as He is the cause of man's existence. This (together with the other things we have before demonstrated) appears to have been what was meant by Moses in that history of the first man. In that history no other power of God is conceived excepting that by which He created man; that is to say, the power with which He considered nothing but the advantage of man. Therefore we are told that God forbad free man to eat of the tree of knowledge of good and evil, and warned him that as soon as he ate of it he would immediately dread death rather than desire to live. Afterwards we are told that when man found a wife who agreed entirely with his nature, he saw that there could be nothing in nature which could be more profitable to him than his wife. But when he came to believe that the brutes were like himself, he immediately began to imitate their affects (Prop. 27, pt. 3), and to lose his liberty, which the Patriarchs afterwards recovered, being led by the spirit of Christ, that is to say, by the idea of God, which alone can make a man free, and cause him to desire for other men the good he desires for himself, as (Prop. 37, pt. 4) we have already demonstrated.

PROP. 69. *The virtue of a free man is seen to be as great in avoiding danger as in overcoming it.*

Demonst. An affect cannot be restrained or removed unless a contrary and stronger affect restrains it (Prop. 7, pt. 4); but blind audacity and fear are affects which may be conceived as being equally great (Props. 5 and 3, pt. 4). The virtue or strength of mind, therefore (for the definition of this, see Schol. Prop. 59, pt. 3), which is required to restrain audacity must be equally great with that which is required to restrain fear; that is to say (Defs. 40 and 41 of the Affects), a free man avoids danger by the same virtue of the mind as that by which he seeks to overcome it. Q.E.D.

Corol. Flight at the proper time, just as well as fighting, is to be reckoned, therefore, as showing strength of mind in a man who is free; that is to say, a free man chooses flight by the same strength or presence of mind as that by which he chooses battle.

Schol. What strength of mind is, or what I understand by it, I have explained in Schol. Prop. 59, pt. 3. By danger, I understand anything which may be the cause of sorrow, hatred, discord, or any other evil like them.

PROP. 70. *The free man who lives amongst those who are ignorant strives as much as possible to avoid their favours.*

Demonst. Every one, according to his own disposition, judges what is good (Schol. Prop. 39, pt. 3). The ignorant man, therefore, who has conferred a favour on another person, will value it according to his own way of thinking, and he will be sad if a less value seems to be placed upon it by the person who has received it (Prop. 42, pt. 3). But a free man strives to unite other men with himself by friendship (Prop. 37, pt. 4), and not to return to them favours which they, according to their affects, may consider to be equal to those which they have bestowed. He desires rather to govern himself and others by the free decisions of reason, and to do those things only which he has discovered to be of the first importance. A free man, therefore, in order that he may not be hated by the ignorant nor yet yield to their appetites, but only to reason, will endeavour as much as possible to avoid their favours. Q.E.D.

Schol. I say *as much as possible.* For although men are ignorant, they are nevertheless men, who, when we are in straits, are able to afford us human assistance—the best assistance which man can receive. It is often necessary, therefore, to receive a favour from the ignorant, and to thank them for it according to their taste; and besides this, care must be used, even in declining favours, not to seem either to despise the givers or through avarice to dread a return, so that we may not, while striving to escape their hatred, by that very act incur their displeasure. In avoiding favours, therefore, we must be guided by a consideration of what is profitable and honourable.

PROP. 71. *None but those who are free are very grateful to one another.*

Demonst. None but those who are free are very profitable to one another, or are united by the closest bond of friendship (Prop. 35, pt. 4, and Corol. 1), or with an equal zeal of love strive to do good to one another (Prop. 37, pt. 4), and therefore (Def. 34 of the Affects) none but those who are free are very grateful to one another. Q.E.D.

Schol. The gratitude to one another of men who are led by blind desire is generally a matter of business or a snare rather than gratitude. Ingratitude, it is to be observed, is not an affect. It is nevertheless base, because it is generally a sign that a man is too much affected by hatred, anger, pride, or avarice. For he who through stupidity does not know how to return a gift is not ungrateful; and much less is he ungrateful who is not moved by the gifts of a harlot to serve her lust, nor by those of a thief to conceal his thefts, nor by any other gifts of a similar kind. On the contrary, a man shows that he possesses a steadfast mind if he does not suffer himself to be enticed by any gifts to his own or to common ruin.

PROP. 72. *A free man never acts deceitfully, but always honourably.*

Demonst. If a free man did anything deceitfully, in so far as he is free, he would do it at the bidding of reason (for so far only do we call him free); and therefore to act deceitfully would be a virtue (Prop. 24, pt. 4), and consequently (by the same proposition) it would be more advantageous to every one, for the preservation of his being, to act deceitfully; that is to say (as is self-evident), it would be more advantageous to men to agree only in words and to be opposed in reality, which (Corol. Prop. 31, pt. 4) is absurd. A free man, therefore, &c. Q.E.D.

Schol. If it be asked whether, if a man by breach of faith could escape from the danger of instant death, reason does not counsel him, for the preservation of his being, to break faith; I reply in the same way, that if reason gives such counsel, she gives it to all men, and reason therefore generally counsels men to make no agreements for uniting their strength and possessing laws in common except deceitfully, that is to say, to have in reality no common laws, which is absurd.

PROP. 73. *A man who is guided by reason is freer in a State where he lives according to the common laws than he is in solitude, where he obeys himself alone.*

Demonst. A man who is guided by reason is not led to obey by fear (Prop. 63, pt. 4), but in so far as he endeavours to preserve his being in accordance with the bidding of reason, that is to say (Schol. Prop. 66, pt. 4), in so far as he endeavours to live in freedom, does he desire to have regard for the common life and the common profit (Prop. 37, pt. 4), and consequently (as we have shown in Schol. 2, Prop. 37, pt. 4) he desires to live according to the common laws of the State. A man, therefore, who is guided by reason desires, in order that he may live more freely, to maintain the common rights of the State. Q.E.D.

Schol. These, and the like things which we have demonstrated concerning the true liberty of man, are related to fortitude, that is to say (Schol. Prop. 59, pt. 3), to strength of mind and generosity. Nor do I think it worth while to demonstrate here, one by one, all the properties of fortitude, and still less to show how its possessor can hate no one, be angry with no one, can neither envy, be indignant with, nor despise anybody, and can least of all be proud. For all this, together with truths of a like kind which have to do with the true life and religion, are easily deduced from Props. 37 and 46, pt. 4, which show that hatred is to be overcome by love, and that every one who is guided by reason desires for others the good which he seeks for himself. In addition, we must remember what we have already observed in Schol. Prop. 50, pt. 4, and in other places, that the brave man will consider above everything that all things follow from the necessity of the divine nature; and that, consequently, whatever he thinks injurious and evil, and, moreover whatever seems to be impious, dreadful, unjust, or wicked, arises from this, that he conceives things in a disturbed, mutilated, and confused fashion. For this reason, his chief effort is to conceive things as they are in themselves, and to remove the hindrances to true knowledge, such as hatred, anger, envy, derision, pride, and others of this kind which we have before noticed; and so he endeavours, as we have said, as much as possible to do well and rejoice. How far human virtue reaches in the attainment of these things, and what it can do, I shall show in the following part.

APPENDIX

My observations in this part concerning the true method of life have not been arranged so that they could be seen at a glance, but have been demonstrated here and there according as I could more easily deduce one from another. I have determined, therefore, here to collect them, and reduce them under principal heads.

I

All our efforts or desires follow from the necessity of our nature in such a manner that they can be understood either through it alone as their proximate cause, or in so far as we are a part of nature, which part cannot be adequately conceived through itself and without the other individuals.

II

The desires which follow from our nature in such a manner that they can be understood through it alone, are those which are related to the mind, in so far as it is conceived to consist of adequate ideas. The remaining desires are not related to the mind, unless in so far as it conceives things inadequately, whose power and increase cannot be determined by human power, but by the power of objects which are without us. The first kind of desires, therefore, are properly called actions, but the latter passions; for the first always indicate our power, and the latter, on the contrary, indicate our impotence and imperfect knowledge.

III

Our actions, that is to say, those desires which are determined by man's power or reason, are always good; the others may be good as well as evil.

IV

It is therefore most profitable to us in life to make perfect the intellect or reason as far as possible, and in this one thing consists the highest happiness or blessedness of man; for blessedness is nothing but the peace of mind which springs from the intuitive knowledge of God, and to perfect the intellect is nothing but to understand God, together with the attributes and actions of God, which flow from the necessity of His nature. The final aim, therefore, of a man who is guided by reason, that is to say, the chief desire by which he strives to govern all his other desires, is that by which he is led adequately to conceive himself and all things which can be conceived by his intelligence.

V

There is no rational life therefore, without intelligence, and things are good only in so far as they assist man to enjoy that life of the mind which is determined by intelligence. Those things alone, on the other hand, we call evil which hinder man from perfecting his reason and enjoying a rational life.

VI

But because all those things of which man is the efficient cause are necessarily good, it follows that no evil can happen to man except from external causes, that is to say, except in so far as he is a part of the whole of nature, whose laws human nature is compelled to obey—compelled also to accommodate himself to this whole of nature in almost an infinite number of ways.

VII

It is impossible that a man should not be a part of nature and follow her common order; but if he be placed amongst individuals who agree with his nature, his power of action will by that very fact be assisted and supported. But if, on the contrary, he be placed amongst individuals who do not in the least agree with his nature, he will scarcely be able without great change on his part to accommodate himself to them.

VIII

Anything that exists in nature which we judge to be evil or able to hinder us from existing and enjoying a rational life, we are allowed to remove from us in that way which seems the safest; and whatever, on the other hand, we judge to be good or to be profitable for the preservation of our being or the enjoyment of a rational life, we are permitted to take for our use and use in any way we may think proper; and absolutely, every one is allowed by the highest right of nature to do that which he believes contributes to his own profit.

IX

Nothing, therefore, can agree better with the nature of any object than other individuals of the same kind, and so (see § 7) there is nothing more profitable to man for the preservation of his being and the enjoyment of a rational life than a man who is guided by reason. Again, since there is no single thing we know which is more excellent than a man who is guided by reason, it follows that there is nothing by which a person can better show how much skill and talent he possesses than by so educating men that at last they will live under the direct authority of reason.

X

In so far as men are carried away by envy or any affect of hatred towards one another, so far are they contrary to one another, and consequently so much the more are they to be feared, as they have more power than other individuals of nature.

XI

Minds, nevertheless, are not conquered by arms, but by love and generosity.

XII

Above all things is it profitable to men to form communities and to unite themselves to one another by bonds which may make all of them as one man; and absolutely, it is profitable for them to do whatever may tend to strengthen their friendships.

XIII

But to accomplish this skill and watchfulness are required; for men are changeable (those being very few who live according to the laws of reason), and nevertheless generally envious and more inclined to vengeance than pity. To bear with each, therefore, according to his disposition and to refrain from imitating his affects requires a singular power of mind. But those, on the contrary, who know how to revile men, to denounce vices rather than teach virtues, and not to strengthen men's minds but to weaken them, are injurious both to themselves and others, so that many of them through an excess of impatience and a false zeal for religion prefer living with brutes rather than amongst men; just as boys or youths, unable to endure with equanimity the rebukes of their parents, fly to the army, choosing the discomforts of war and the rule of a tyrant rather than the comforts of home and the admonitions of a father, suffering all kinds of burdens to be imposed upon them in order that they may revenge themselves upon their parents.

XIV

Although, therefore, men generally determine everything by their pleasure, many more advantages than disadvantages arise from their common union. It is better, therefore, to endure with equanimity the injuries inflicted by them, and to apply our minds to those things which subserve concord and the establishment of friendship.

XV

The things which beget concord are those which are related to justice, integrity, and honour; for besides that which is unjust and injurious, men take ill also anything which is esteemed base, or that any one should despise the received customs of the State. But in order to win love, those things are chiefly necessary which have reference to religion and piety. (See Schols. 1 and 2, Prop. 37, Schol. Prop. 46, and Schol. Prop. 73, pt. 4.)

XVI

Concord, moreover, is often produced by fear, but it is without good faith. It is to be observed, too, that fear arises from impotence of mind, and therefore is of no service to reason; nor is pity, although it seems to present an appearance of piety.

XVII

Men also are conquered by liberality, especially those who have not the means wherewith to procure what is necessary for the support of life. But to assist every one who is needy far surpasses the strength or profit of a private person, for the wealth of a private person is altogether insufficient to supply such wants. Besides, the power of any one man is too limited for him to be able to unite every one with himself in friendship. The care, therefore, of the poor is incumbent on the whole of society and concerns only the general profit.

XVIII

In the receipt of benefits and in returning thanks, care altogether different must be taken—concerning which see Schol. Prop. 70, and Schol. Prop. 71, pt. 4.

XIX

The love of a harlot, that is to say, the lust ' sexual intercourse, which arises from mere ternal form, and absolutely all love which cognises any other cause than the freedom ' the mind, easily passes into hatred, unless, hich is worse, it becomes a species of delir- m, and thereby discord is cherished rather an concord (Corol. Prop. 31, pt. 3).

XX

With regard to marriage, it is plain that it is accordance with reason, if the desire of con- ection is engendered not merely by external rm, but by a love of begetting children and isely educating them; and if, in addition, the ve both of the husband and wife has for its ause not external form merely, but chiefly berty of mind.

XXI

Flattery, too, produces concord, but only by eans of the disgraceful crime of slavery or erfidy; for there are none who are more taken y flattery than the proud, who wish to be first nd are not so.

XXII

There is a false appearance of piety and re- igion in dejection; and although dejection is he opposite of pride, the humble dejected an is very near akin to the proud (Schol. ?rop. 57, pt. 4).

XXIII

Shame also contributes to concord, but only with regard to those matters which cannot be oncealed. Shame, too, inasmuch as it is a kind of sorrow, does not belong to the service of reason.

XXIV

The remaining affects of sorrow which have man for their object are directly opposed to justice, integrity, honour, piety, and religion; and although indignation may seem to present an appearance of equity, yet there is no law where it is allowed to every one to judge the deeds of another, and to vindicate his own or another's right.

XXV

Affability, that is to say, the desire of pleas- ing men, which is determined by reason, is re- lated to piety (Schol. Prop. 37, pt. 4). But if affability arise from an affect, it is ambition or desire, by which men, generally under a false pretence of piety, excite discords and sedi- tions. For he who desires to assist other people, either by advice or by deed, in order that they may together enjoy the highest good, will strive, above all things, to win their love, and not to draw them into admiration, so that a doctrine may be named after him, nor abso- lutely to give any occasion for envy. In com- mon conversation, too, he will avoid referring to the vices of men, and will take care only sparingly to speak of human impotence, while he will talk largely of human virtue or power, and of the way by which it may be made per- fect, so that men being moved not by fear or aversion, but solely by the affect of joy, may endeavour as much as they can to live under the rule of reason.

XXVI

Excepting man, we know no individual thing in nature in whose mind we can take pleasure, nor anything which we can unite with our- selves by friendship or any kind of intercourse, and therefore regard to our own profit does not demand that we should preserve anything which exists in nature excepting men, but teaches us to preserve it or destroy it in ac- cordance with its varied uses, or to adapt it to our own service in any way whatever.

XXVII

The profit which we derive from objects without us, over and above the experience and knowledge which we obtain because we ob- serve them and change them from their exist- ing forms into others, is chiefly the preserva- tion of the body, and for this reason those ob- jects are the most profitable to us which can feed and nourish the body, so that all its parts are able properly to perform their functions. For the more capable the body is of being af- fected in many ways, and affecting external bodies in many ways, the more capable of thinking is the mind (Props. 38 and 39, pt. 4). But there seem to be very few things in nature of this kind, and it is consequently necessary for the requisite nourishment of the body to use many different kinds of food; for the hu- man body is composed of a great number of parts of different nature, which need constant and varied food in order that the whole of the body may be equally adapted for all those things which can follow from its nature, and consequently that the mind also may be equally adapted to conceive many things.

XXVIII

The strength of one man would scarcely suffice to obtain these things if men did not mutually assist one another. As money has presented us with an abstract of everything, it has come to pass that its image above every other usually occupies the mind of the multitude, because they can imagine hardly any kind of joy without the accompanying idea of money as its cause.

XXIX

This, however, is a vice only in those who seek money not from poverty or necessity, but because they have learnt the arts of gain, by which they keep up a grand appearance. As for the body itself, they feed it in accordance with custom, but sparingly, because they believe that they lose so much of their goods as they spend upon the preservation of their body. Those, however, who know the true use of money, and regulate the measure of wealth according to their needs, live contented with few things.

XXX

Since, therefore, those things are good which help the parts of the body to perform their functions, and since joy consists in this, that the power of man, in so far as he is made up of mind and body, is helped or increased, it follows that all those things which bring joy are good. But inasmuch as things do not work to this end—that they may affect us with joy—nor is their power of action guided in accordance with our profit, and finally, since joy is generally related chiefly to some one part of the body, it follows that generally the affects of joy (unless reason and watchfulness be present), and consequently the desires which are begotten from them, are excessive. It is to be added, that an affect causes us to put that thing first which is sweet to us in the present, and that we are not able to judge the future

with an equal affect of the mind (Schol. Prop. 44, and Schol. Prop. 60, pt. 4).

XXXI

Superstition, on the contrary, seems to affirm that what brings sorrow is good, and, on the contrary, that what brings joy is evil. But as we have already said (Schol. Prop. 45, pt. 4), no one excepting an envious man is delighted at my impotence or disadvantage, for the greater the joy with which we are affected the greater the perfection to which we pass, and consequently the more do we participate in the divine nature; nor can joy ever be evil which is controlled by a true consideration for our own profit. On the other hand, the man who is led by fear, and does what is good that he may avoid what is evil, is not guided by reason.

XXXII

But human power is very limited, and is infinitely surpassed by the power of external causes, so that we do not possess an absolute power to adapt to our service the things which are without us. Nevertheless we shall bear with equanimity those things which happen to us contrary to what a consideration of our own profit demands, if we are conscious that we have performed our duty, that the power we have could not reach so far as to enable us to avoid those things, and that we are a part of the whole of nature, whose order we follow. If we clearly and distinctly understand this, the part of us which is determined by intelligence, that is to say, the better part of us, will be entirely satisfied therewith, and in that satisfaction will endeavour to persevere; for, in so far as we understand, we cannot desire anything excepting what is necessary, nor, absolutely, can we be satisfied with anything but the truth. Therefore in so far as we understand these things properly will the efforts of the better part of us agree with the order of the whole of nature.

FIFTH PART

OF THE POWER OF THE INTELLECT, OR OF HUMAN LIBERTY

PREFACE

I pass at length to the other part of Ethic which concerns the method or way which leads to liberty. In this part, therefore, I shall treat of the power of reason, showing how much reason itself can control the affects, and then what is freedom of mind or blessedness. Thence we shall see how much stronger the wise man is than the ignorant. In what manner and in what way the intellect should be rendered perfect, and with what art the body is to be cared for in order that it may properly perform its functions, I have nothing to do with here; for all former belongs to logic, the latter to medicine. I shall occupy myself here, as I have said, solely with the power of the mind or of reason, first of all showing the extent and nature of the authority which it has over the affects in restraining them and governing them; for that we have not absolute authority over them we have already demonstrated. The Stoics indeed thought that the affects depend absolutely on our will, and that we are absolutely masters over them; but they were driven, by the contradiction of experience, though not by their own principles, to confess that not a little practice and study are required in order to restrain and govern the affects. This, one of them attempted to illustrate, if I remember rightly, by the example of two dogs, one of a domestic and the other of a hunting breed; for he was able by habit to make the house-dog hunt, and the hunting dog, on the contrary, to desist from running after hares. To the Stoical opinion Descartes much inclines. He affirms that the soul or mind is united specially to a certain part of the brain called the pineal gland, which the mind by the mere exercise of the will is able to move in different ways, and by whose help the mind perceives all the movements which are excited in the body and external objects. This gland he affirms is suspended in the middle of the brain in such a manner that it can be moved by the least motion of the animal spirits. Again, he affirms

that any variation in the manner in which the animal spirits impinge upon this gland is followed by a variation in the manner in which it is suspended in the middle of the brain, and moreover that the number of different impressions on the gland is the same as that of the different external objects which propel the animal spirits towards it. Hence it comes to pass that if the gland, by the will of the soul moving it in different directions, be afterwards suspended in this or that way in which it had once been suspended by the spirits agitated in this or that way, then the gland itself will propel and determine the animal spirits themselves in the same way as that in which they had before been repelled by a similar suspension of the gland. Moreover, he affirmed that each volition of the mind is united in nature to a certain motion of the gland. For example, if a person wishes to behold a remote object, this volition will cause the pupil of the eye to dilate, but if he thinks merely of the dilation of the pupil, to have that volition will profit him nothing, because nature has not connected a motion of the gland which serves to impel the animal spirits towards the optic nerve in a way suitable for dilation or contraction of the pupil with the volition of dilation or contraction, but only with the volition of beholding objects afar off or close at hand. Finally, he maintained that although each motion of this gland appears to be connected by nature from the commencement of our life with an individual thought, these motions can nevertheless be connected by habit with other thoughts, a proposition which he attempts to demonstrate in his "Passions of the Soul," art. 50, pt. 1.

From this he concludes that there is no mind so feeble that it cannot, when properly directed, acquire absolute power over its passions; for passions, as defined by him, are "perceptions, or sensations, or emotions of the soul which are related to it specially, and which (N.B.) are produced, preserved, and strengthened by some motion of the spirits." (See the "Passions of the Soul," art. 27, pt. 1.)

But since it is possible to join to a certain volition any motion of the gland, and consequently of the spirits, and since the determination of the will depends solely on our power, we shall be able to acquire absolute mastery over our passions provided only we determine our will by fixed and firm decisions by which we desire to direct our actions and bind with these decisions the movements of the passions we wish to have. So far as I can gather from his own words, this is the opinion of that distinguished man, and I could scarcely have believed it possible for one so great to have put it forward if it had been less subtle. I can hardly wonder enough that a philosopher who firmly resolved to make no deduction except from self-evident principles, and to affirm nothing but what he clearly and distinctly perceived, and who blamed all the schoolmen because they desired to explain obscure matters by occult qualities, should accept a hypothesis more occult than any occult quality. What does he understand, I ask, by the union of the mind and body? What clear and distinct conception has he of thought intimately connected with a certain small portion of matter? I wish that he had explained this union by its proximate cause. But he conceived the mind to be so distinct from the body that he was able to assign no single cause of this union, nor of the mind itself, but was obliged to have recourse to the cause of the whole universe, that is to say, to God. Again, I should like to know how many degrees of motion the mind can give to that pineal gland, and with how great a power the mind can hold it suspended. For I do not understand whether this gland is acted on by the mind more slowly or more quickly than by the animal spirits, and whether the movements of the passions, which we have so closely bound with firm decisions, might not be separated from them again by bodily causes, from which it would follow that although the mind had firmly determined to meet danger, and had joined to this decision the motion of boldness, the sight of the danger might cause the gland to be suspended in such a manner that the mind could think of nothing but flight. Indeed, since there is no relation between the will and motion, so there is no comparison between the power or strength of the body and that of the mind, and consequently the strength of the body can never be determined by the strength of the mind. It is to be remembered also that this gland is not found to be so situated in the middle of the brain that it can be driven about

so easily and in so many ways, and that all the nerves are not extended to the cavities of the brain. Lastly, I omit all that Descartes asserts concerning the will and the freedom of the will, since I have shown over and over again that it is false. Therefore, inasmuch as the power of the mind, as I have shown above, is determined by intelligence alone, we shall determine by the knowledge of the mind alone the remedies against the affects—remedies which every one, I believe, has experienced, although there may not have been any accurate observation or distinct perception of them, and from this knowledge of the mind alone shall we deduce everything which relates to its blessedness.

AXIOMS

1. If two contrary actions be excited in the same subject, a change must necessarily take place in both, or in one alone, until they cease to be contrary.

2. The power of an affect is limited by the power of its cause, in so far as the essence of the affect is manifested or limited by the essence of the cause itself.

This axiom is evident from Prop. 7, pt. 3.

PROP. 1. *As thoughts and the ideas of things are arranged and connected in the mind, exactly so are the affections of the body or the images of things arranged and connected in the body.*

Demonst. The order and connection of ideas is the same (Prop. 7, pt. 2) as the order and connection of things, and *vice versa*, the order and connection of things is the same (Corol. Props. 6 and 7, pt. 2) as the order and connection of ideas. Therefore, as the order and connection of ideas in the mind is according to the order and connection of the affections of the body (Prop. 18, pt. 2), it follows, *vice versa* (Prop. 2, pt. 3), that the order and connection of the affections of the body is according to the order and connection in the mind of the thoughts and ideas of things. Q.E.D.

PROP. 2. *If we detach an emotion of the mind or affect from the thought of an external cause and connect it with other thoughts, then the love or hatred towards the external cause and the fluctuations of the mind which arise from these affects will be destroyed.*

Demonst. That which constitutes the form of love or hatred is joy or sorrow, accompanied with the idea of an external cause (Defs. 6 and 7 of the Affects). If this idea therefore be taken away, the form of love or hatred is also re-

oved, and therefore these affects and any
hers which arise from them are destroyed.
E.D.

PROP. 3. *An affect which is a passion ceases to
be a passion as soon as we form a clear and dis-
nct idea of it.*

Demonst. An affect which is a passion is a
onfused idea (by the general definition of the
ffects). If, therefore, we form a clear and dis-
nct idea of this affect, the idea will not be
istinguished—except by reason—from this
ffect, in so far as the affect is related to the
ind alone (Prop. 21, pt. 2, with its Schol.),
nd therefore (Prop. 3, pt. 3) the affect will
ease to be a passion. Q.E.D.

Corol. In proportion, then, as we know an
ffect better is it more within our control, and
he less does the mind suffer from it.

PROP. 4. *There is no affection of the body of
which we cannot form some clear and distinct
conception.*

Demonst. Those things which are common
o all cannot be otherwise than adequately
onceived (Prop. 38, pt. 2), and therefore
(Prop. 12, and Lem. 2, following Schol. Prop.
13, pt. 2) there is no affection of the body of
which we cannot form some clear and distinct
conception. Q.E.D.

Corol. Hence it follows that there is no af-
ect of which we cannot form some clear and
distinct conception. For an affect is an idea of
an affection of the body (by the general definition of the Affects), and this idea therefore
(Prop. 4, pt. 5) must involve some clear and
distinct conception.

Schol. Since nothing exists from which some
effect does not follow (Prop. 36, pt. 1), and
since we understand clearly and distinctly
everything which follows from an idea which
is adequate in us (Prop. 40, pt. 2), it is a necessary consequence that every one has the
power, partly at least, if not absolutely, of
understanding clearly and distinctly himself
and his affects, and consequently of bringing
it to pass that he suffers less from them. We
have therefore mainly to strive to acquire a
clear and distinct knowledge as far as possible
of each affect, so that the mind may be led to
pass from the affect to think those things
which it perceives clearly and distinctly, and
with which it is entirely satisfied, and to strive
also that the affect may be separated from the
thought of an external cause and connected
with true thoughts. Thus not only love, hatred,

&c., will be destroyed (Prop. 2, pt. 5), but also
the appetites or desires to which the affect
gives rise cannot be excessive (Prop. 61, pt. 4).
For it is above everything to be observed that
the appetite by which a man is said to act is
one and the same appetite as that by which he
is said to suffer. For example, we have shown
that human nature is so constituted that every
one desires that other people should live according to his way of thinking (Schol. Prop.
31, pt. 3), a desire which in a man who is not
guided by reason is a passion which is called
ambition, and is not very different from pride;
while, on the other hand, in a man who lives
according to the dictates of reason it is an
action or virtue which is called piety (Schol. 1,
Prop. 37, pt. 4, and Demonst. 2 of the same
Prop.). In the same manner, all the appetites
or desires are passions only in so far as they
arise from inadequate ideas, and are classed
among the virtues whenever they are excited
or begotten by adequate ideas; for all the desires by which we are determined to any action
may arise either from adequate or inadequate
ideas (Prop. 59, pt. 4). To return, therefore, to
the point from which we set out: there is no
remedy within our power which can be conceived more excellent for the affects than that
which consists in a true knowledge of them,
since the mind possesses no other power than
that of thinking and forming adequate ideas,
as we have shown above (Prop. 3, pt. 3).

PROP. 5. *An affect towards an object which we
do not imagine as necessary, possible, or contingent, but which we simply imagine, is, other
things being equal, the greatest of all.*

Demonst. The affect towards an object which
we imagine to be free is greater than towards
one which is necessary (Prop. 49, pt. 3), and
consequently still greater than towards one
which we imagine as possible or contingent
(Prop. 11, pt. 4). But to imagine an object as
free can be nothing else than to imagine it
simply, while we know not the causes by which
it was determined to action. (See Schol. Prop.
35, pt. 2.) An affect, therefore, towards an
object which we simply imagine is, other
things being equal, greater than towards one
which we imagine as necessary, possible,
or contingent, and consequently greatest of
all. Q.E.D.

PROP. 6. *In so far as the mind understands all
things as necessary, so far has it greater power
over the affects, or suffers less from them.*

Demonst. The mind understands all things to be necessary (Prop. 29, pt. 1), and determined by an infinite chain of causes to existence and action (Prop. 28, pt. 1), and therefore (Prop. 5, pt. 5) so far enables itself to suffer less from the affects which arise from these things, and (Prop. 48, pt. 3) to be less affected towards them. Q.E.D.

Schol. The more this knowledge that things are necessary is applied to individual things which we imagine more distinctly and more vividly, the greater is this power of the mind over the affects,—a fact to which experience also testifies. For we see that sorrow for the loss of anything good is diminished if the person who has lost it considers that it could not by any possibility have been preserved. So also we see that nobody pities an infant because it does not know how to speak, walk, or reason, and lives so many years not conscious, as it were, of itself; but if a number of human beings were born adult, and only a few here and there were born infants, every one would pity the infants, because we should then consider infancy not as a thing natural and necessary, but as a defect or fault of nature. Many other facts of a similar kind we might observe.

Prop. 7. *The affects which spring from reason or which are excited by it are, if time be taken into account, more powerful than those which are related to individual objects which we contemplate as absent.*

Demonst. We do not contemplate an object as absent by reason of the affect by which we imagine it, but by reason of the fact that the body is affected with another affect, which excludes the existence of that object (Prop. 17, pt. 2). The affect, therefore, which is related to an object which we contemplate as absent, is not of such a nature as to overcome the other actions and power of man (concerning these things see Prop. 6, pt. 4), but, on the contrary, is of such a nature that it can in some way be restrained by those affections which exclude the existence of its external cause (Prop. 9, pt. 4). But the affect which arises from reason is necessarily related to the common properties of things (see the definition of reason in Schol. 2, Prop. 40, pt. 2), which we always contemplate as present (for nothing can exist which excludes their present existence), and which we always imagine in the same way (Prop. 38, pt. 2). This affect, therefore, always remains the same, and consequently (Ax. 1, pt. 5), the affects which are contrary to it, and which are

not maintained by their external cause, mus more and more accommodate themselves to : until they are no longer contrary to it. So fa therefore, the affect which springs from reaso is the stronger. Q.E.D.

Prop. 8. *The greater the number of the cause which simultaneously concur to excite any affec the greater it will be.*

Demonst. A number of simultaneous cause can do more than if they were fewer (Prop 7, pt. 3), and therefore (Prop. 5, pt. 4) th greater the number of the simultaneou causes by which an affect is excited, the great er it is. Q.E.D.

Schol. This proposition is also evident from Ax. 2, pt. 5.

Prop. 9. *If we are affected by an affect which i related to many and different causes, which th mind contemplates at the same time with the af fect itself, we are less injured, suffer less from it and are less affected therefore towards each caus than if we were affected by another affect equall; great which is related to one cause only or t; fewer causes.*

Demonst. An affect is bad or injurious only in so far as it hinders the mind from thinking (Props. 26 and 27, pt. 4), and therefore that affect by which the mind is determined to the contemplation of a number of objects at the same time is less injurious than another affect equally great which holds the mind in the contemplation of one object alone or of a few objects, so that it cannot think of others. This is the first thing we had to prove. Again, since the essence of the mind, that is to say (Prop. 7, pt. 3), its power, consists in thought alone (Prop. 11, pt. 2), the mind suffers less through an affect by which it is determined to the contemplation of a number of objects at the same time than through an affect equally great which holds it occupied in the contemplation of one object alone or of a few objects. This is the second thing we had to prove. Finally, this affect (Prop. 48, pt. 3), in so far as it is related to a number of external causes, is therefore less towards each. Q.E.D.

Prop. 10. *So long as we are not agitated by affects which are contrary to our nature do we possess the power of arranging and connecting the affections of the body according to the order of the intellect.*

Demonst. The affects which are contrary to our nature, that is to say (Prop. 30, pt. 4), which are evil, are evil so far as they hinder the mind from understanding (Prop. 27, pt. 4). So long, therefore, as we are not agitated by affects which are contrary to our nature, so long the power of the mind by which it endeavours to understand things (Prop. 26, pt. 4) is not hindered, and therefore so long does it possess the power of forming clear and distinct ideas, and of deducing them the one from the other (see Schol. 2, Prop. 40, and Schol. Prop. 47, pt. 2). So long, consequently (Prop. 1, pt. 5), do we possess the power of arranging and connecting the affections of the body according to the order of the intellect. Q.E.D.

Schol. Through this power of properly arranging and connecting the affections of the body we can prevent ourselves from being easily affected by evil affects. For (Prop. 7, pt. 5) a greater power is required to restrain affects which are arranged and connected according to the order of the intellect than is required to restrain those which are uncertain and unsettled. The best thing, therefore, we can do, so long as we lack a perfect knowledge of our affects, is to conceive a right rule of life, or sure maxims (*dogmata*) of life,—to commit these latter to memory, and constantly to apply them to the particular cases which frequently meet us in life, so that our imagination may be widely affected by them, and they may always be ready to hand. For example, amongst the maxims of life we have placed this (see Prop. 46, pt. 4, with its Schol.), that hatred is to be conquered by love or generosity, and is not to be met with hatred in return. But in order that we may always have this prescript of reason in readiness whenever it will be of service, we must think over and often meditate upon the common injuries inflicted by men, and consider how and in what way they may best be repelled by generosity; for thus we shall connect the image of injury with the imagination of this maxim, and (Prop. 18, pt. 2) it will be at hand whenever an injury is offered to us. If we also continually have regard to our own true profit, and the good which follows from mutual friendship and common fellowship, and remember that the highest peace of mind arises from a right rule of life (Prop. 52, pt. 4), and also that man, like other things, acts according to the necessity of nature, then the injury or the hatred which usually arises from that necessity will occupy but the least part of the imagination, and will be easily overcome: or supposing that the anger which generally arises from the greatest injuries is

not so easily overcome, it will nevertheless be overcome, although not without fluctuation of mind, in a far shorter space of time than would have been necessary if we had not possessed those maxims on which we had thus meditated beforehand. This is evident from Props. 6, 7, and 8, pt. 5.

Concerning strength of mind, we must reflect in the same way for the purpose of getting rid of fear, that is to say, we must often enumerate and imagine the common dangers of life, and think upon the manner in which they can best be avoided and overcome by presence of mind and courage. It is to be observed, however, that in the ordering of our thoughts and images we must always look (Corol. Prop. 63, pt. 4, and Prop. 59, pt. 3) to those qualities which in each thing are good, so that we may be determined to action always by an affect of joy.

For example, if a man sees that he pursues glory too eagerly, let him think on its proper use, for what end it is to be followed, and by what means it can be obtained; but let him not think upon its abuse and vanity, and on the inconstancy of men and things of this sort, about which no one thinks unless through disease of mind; for with such thoughts do those who are ambitious greatly torment themselves when they despair of obtaining the honours for which they are striving; and while they vomit forth rage, wish to be thought wise. Indeed it is certain that those covet glory the most who are loudest in declaiming against its abuse and the vanity of the world. Nor is this a peculiarity of the ambitious, but is common to all to whom fortune is adverse and who are impotent in mind; for we see that a poor and avaricious man is never weary of speaking about the abuse of money and the vices of the rich, thereby achieving nothing save to torment himself and show to others that he is unable to bear with equanimity not only his own poverty but also the wealth of others. So also a man who has not been well received by his mistress thinks of nothing but the fickleness of women, their faithlessness, and their other oft-proclaimed failings,—all of which he forgets as soon as he is taken into favour by his mistress again. He, therefore, who desires to govern his affects and appetites from a love of liberty alone will strive as much as he can to know virtues and their causes, and to fill his mind with that joy which springs from a true knowledge of them. Least of all will he desire to contemplate the vices of men and disparage men, or to delight in a false show of liberty. He who will diligently observe these things (and they are not difficult), and will continue to practise them, will assuredly in a short space of time be able for the most part to direct his actions in accordance with the command of reason.

PROP. 11.   *The greater the number of objects to which an image is related, the more constant is it, or the more frequently does it present itself, and the more does it occupy the mind.*

Demonst.   The greater the number of objects to which an image or affect is related, the greater is the number of causes by which it can be excited and cherished. All these causes the mind contemplates simultaneously by means of the affect (by hypothesis), and therefore the more constant is the affect, or the more frequently does it present itself, and the more does it occupy the mind (Prop. 8, pt. 5). Q.E.D.

PROP. 12.   *The images of things are more easily connected with those images which are related to things which we clearly and distinctly understand than with any others.*

Demonst.   Things which we clearly and distinctly understand are either the common properties of things or what are deduced from them (see the definition of reason in Schol. 2, Prop. 40, pt. 2), and consequently (Prop. 11, pt. 5) are more frequently excited in us; and therefore it is easier for us to contemplate other things together with these which we clearly and distinctly understand than with any others, and consequently (Prop. 18, pt. 2), it is easier to connect things with these which we clearly and distinctly understand than with any others.

PROP. 13.   *The greater the number of other things with which any image is connected, the more frequently does it present itself.*

Demonst.   For the greater the number of other things with which an image is connected, the greater is the number of causes (Prop. 18, pt. 2) by which it may be excited. Q.E.D.

PROP. 14.   *The mind can cause all the affections of the body or the images of things to be related to the idea of God (ideam Dei).*

Demonst.   There is no affection of the body of which the mind cannot form some clear and distinct conception (Prop. 4, pt. 5), and therefore (Prop. 15, pt. 1) it can cause all the affections of the body to be related to the idea of God. Q.E.D.

PROP. 15.   *He who clearly and distinctly understands himself and his affects loves God, and loves Him better the better he understands himself and his affects.*

Demonst.   He who clearly and distinctly understands himself and his affects rejoices (Prop. 53, pt. 3), and his joy is attended with the idea of God (Prop. 14, pt. 5), therefore (Def. 6 of the Affects) he loves God, and (by the same reasoning) loves Him better the better he understands himself and his affects. Q.E.D.

PROP. 16.   *This love to God above everything else ought to occupy the mind.*

Demonst.   For this love is connected with all the affections of the body (Prop. 14, pt. 5), by all of which it is cherished (Prop. 15, pt. 5), and therefore (Prop. 11, pt. 5) above everything else ought to occupy the mind. Q.E.D.

PROP. 17.   *God is free from passions, nor is He affected with any affect of joy or sorrow.*

Demonst.   All ideas, in so far as they are related to God, are true (Prop. 32, pt. 2); that is to say (Def. 4, pt. 2), are adequate, and therefore (by the general definition of the Affects) God is free from passions. Again, God can neither pass to a greater nor to a less perfection (Corol. 2, Prop. 20, pt. 1), and therefore (Defs. 2 and 3 of the Affects) He cannot be affected with any affect of joy or sorrow. Q.E.D.

Corol.   Properly speaking, God loves no one and hates no one; for God (Prop. 17, pt. 5) is not affected with any affect of joy or sorrow, and consequently (Defs. 6 and 7 of the Affects) He neither loves nor hates any one.

PROP. 18.   *No one can hate God.*

Demonst.   The idea of God which is in us is adequate and perfect (Props. 46 and 47, pt. 2), and therefore in so far as we contemplate God do we act (Prop. 3, pt. 3), and consequently (Prop. 59, pt. 3) no sorrow can exist with the accompanying idea of God; that is to say (Def. 7 of the Affects), no one can hate God. Q.E.D.

Corol.   Love to God cannot be turned into hatred.

Schol.   But some may object, that if we understand God to be the cause of all things, we do for that very reason consider Him to be the cause of sorrow. But I reply, that in so far as we understand the causes of sorrow, it ceases to be a passion (Prop. 3, pt. 5), that is to say (Prop. 59, pt. 3), it ceases to be sorrow; and therefore in so far as we understand God to be the cause of sorrow do we rejoice.

PROP. 19. *He who loves God cannot strive that God should love him in return.*

Demonst. If a man were to strive after this, he would desire (Corol. Prop. 17, pt. 5) that God, whom he loves, should not be God, and consequently (Prop. 19, pt. 3) he would desire to be sad, which (Prop. 28, pt. 3) is absurd. Therefore he who loves God, &c. Q.E.D.

PROP. 20. *This love to God cannot be defiled either by the affect of envy or jealousy, but is the more strengthened the more people we imagine to be connected with God by the same bond of love.*

Demonst. This love to God is the highest good which we can seek according to the dictate of reason (Prop. 28, pt. 4); is common to all men (Prop. 36, pt. 4); and we desire that all may enjoy it (Prop. 37, pt. 4). It cannot, therefore (Def. 23 of the Affects), be sullied by the affect of envy, nor (Prop. 18, pt. 5, and Def. of Jealousy in Schol. Prop. 35, pt. 3) by that of jealousy, but, on the contrary (Prop. 31, pt. 3), it must be the more strengthened the more people we imagine to rejoice in it. Q.E.D.

Schol. It is possible to show in the same manner that there is no affect directly contrary to this love and able to destroy it, and so we may conclude that this love to God is the most constant of all the affects, and that, in so far as it is related to the body, it cannot be destroyed unless with the body itself. What its nature is, in so far as it is related to the mind alone, we shall see hereafter.

I have, in what has preceded, included all the remedies for the affects, that is to say, everything which the mind, considered in itself alone, can do against them. It appears therefrom that the power of the mind over the affects consists—

1. In the knowledge itself of the affects. (See Schol. Prop. 4, pt. 5.)

2. In the separation by the mind of the affects from the thought of an external cause, which we imagine confusedly. (See Prop. 2, pt. 5, and Schol. Prop. 4, pt. 5.)

3. In duration, in which the affections which are related to objects we understand surpass those related to objects conceived in a mutilated or confused manner. (Prop. 7, pt. 5.)

4. In the multitude of causes by which the affections which are related to the common properties of things or to God are nourished. (Props. 9 and 11, pt. 5.)

5. In the order in which the mind can arrange its affects and connect them one with the other. (Schol. Prop. 10, pt. 5, and see also Props. 12, 13, and 14, pt. 5.)

But that this power of the mind over the affects may be better understood, it is to be carefully observed that we call the affects great when we compare the affect of one man with that of another, and see that one man is agitated more than another by the same affect, or when we compare the affects of one and the same man with one another, and discover that he is affected or moved more by one affect than by another.

For (Prop. 5, pt. 4) the power of any affect is limited by the power of the external cause as compared with our own power. But the power of the mind is limited solely by knowledge, whilst impotence or passion is estimated solely by privation of knowledge, or, in other words, by that through which ideas are called inadequate; and it therefore follows that that mind suffers the most whose largest part consists of inadequate ideas, so that it is distinguished rather by what it suffers than by what it does, while, on the contrary, that mind acts the most whose largest part consists of adequate ideas, so that although it may possess as many inadequate ideas as the first, it is nevertheless distinguished rather by those which belong to human virtue than by those which are a sign of human impotence. Again, it is to be observed that our sorrows and misfortunes mainly proceed from too much love towards an object which is subject to many changes, and which we can never possess. For no one is troubled or anxious about any object he does not love, neither do wrongs, suspicions, hatreds, &c., arise except from love towards objects of which no one can be truly the possessor.

From all this we easily conceive what is the power which clear and distinct knowledge, and especially that third kind of knowledge (see Schol. Prop. 47, pt. 2) whose foundation is the knowledge itself of God, possesses over the affects; the power, namely, by which it is able, in so far as they are passions, if not actually to destroy them (see Prop. 3, pt. 5, with the Schol. to Prop. 4, pt. 5), at least to make them constitute the smallest part of the mind (see Prop. 14, pt. 5). Moreover, it begets a love towards an immutable and eternal object (see Prop. 15, pt. 5) of which we are really partakers (see Prop. 45, pt. 2); a love which therefore cannot be vitiated by the defects which are in common love, but which can always become greater and greater (Prop. 15, pt. 5), occupy the largest part of the mind (Prop. 16, pt. 5), and thoroughly affect it.

I have now concluded all that I had to say relating to this present life. For any one who will attend to what has been urged in this scholium, and to the definition of the mind and its affects, and to Props. 1 and 3, pt. 3, will easily be able to see the truth of what I said in the beginning of the scholium, that in these few words all the remedies for the affects are comprehended. It is time, therefore, that I should now pass to the consideration of those matters which appertain to the duration of the mind without relation to the body.

PROP. 21. *The mind can imagine nothing, nor can it recollect anything that is past, except while the body exists.*

Demonst. The mind does not express the actual existence of its body, nor does it conceive as actual the affections of the body, except while the body exists (Corol. Prop. 8, pt. 2), and consequently (Prop. 26, pt. 2) it conceives no body as actually existing except while its own body exists. It can therefore imagine nothing (see the definition of Imagination in Schol. Prop. 17, pt. 2), nor can it recollect anything that is past, except while the body exists (see the definition of Memory in Schol. Prop. 18, pt. 2). Q.E.D.

PROP. 22. *In God, nevertheless, there necessarily exists an idea which expresses the essence of this or that human body under the form of eternity.*

Demonst. God is not only the cause of the existence of this or that human body, but also of its essence (Prop. 25, pt. 1), which therefore must necessarily be conceived through the essence of God itself (Ax. 4, pt. 1) and by a certain eternal necessity (Prop. 16, pt. 1). This conception, moreover, must necessarily exist in God (Prop. 3, pt. 2). Q.E.D.

PROP. 23. *The human mind cannot be absolutely destroyed with the body, but something of it remains which is eternal.*

Demonst. In God there necessarily exists a conception or idea which expresses the essence of the human body (Prop. 22, pt. 5). This conception or idea is therefore necessarily something which pertains to the essence of the human mind (Prop. 13, pt. 2). But we ascribe to the human mind no duration which can be limited by time, unless in so far as it expresses the actual existence of the body, which is manifested through duration, and which can be

limited by time, that is to say (Corol. Prop. 8, pt. 2), we cannot ascribe duration to the mind except while the body exists.

But nevertheless, since this something is that which is conceived by a certain eternal necessity through the essence itself of God (Prop. 22, pt. 5), this something which pertains to the essence of the mind will necessarily be eternal. Q.E.D.

Schol. This idea which expresses the essence of the body under the form of eternity is, as we have said, a certain mode of thought which pertains to the essence of the mind and is necessarily eternal. It is impossible, nevertheless, that we should recollect that we existed before the body, because there are no traces of any such existence in the body, and also because eternity cannot be defined by time, or have any relationship to it. Nevertheless we feel and know by experience that we are eternal. For the mind is no less sensible of those things which it conceives through intelligence than of those which it remembers, for demonstrations are the eyes of the mind by which it sees and observes things.

Although, therefore, we do not recollect that we existed before the body, we feel that our mind, in so far as it involves the essence of the body under the form of eternity, is eternal, and that this existence of the mind cannot be limited by time nor manifested through duration. Only in so far, therefore, as it involves the actual existence of the body can the mind be said to possess duration, and its existence be limited by a fixed time, and so far only has it the power of determining the existence of things in time, and of conceiving them under the form of duration.

PROP. 24. *The more we understand individual objects, the more we understand God.*

Demonst. This is evident from Corol. Prop. 25, pt. 1.

PROP. 25. *The highest effort of the mind and its highest virtue is to understand things by the third kind of knowledge.*

Demonst. The third kind of knowledge proceeds from an adequate idea of certain attributes of God to an adequate knowledge of the essence of things (see its definition in Schol. 2, Prop. 40, pt. 2); and the more we understand things in this manner (Prop. 24, pt. 5), the more we understand God; and therefore (Prop. 28, pt. 4) the highest virtue of the mind, that is to say (Def. 8, pt. 4), the power or nature of the mind, or (Prop. 7, pt. 3) its highest effort, is to understand things by the third kind of knowledge. Q.E.D.

PROP. 26. *The better the mind is adapted to understand things by the third kind of knowledge, the more it desires to understand them by this kind of knowledge.*

Demonst. This is evident; for in so far as we conceive the mind to be adapted to understand things by this kind of knowledge, do we conceive it to be determined to understand things by this kind of knowledge, and consequently (Def. 1 of the Affects) the better the mind is adapted to this way of understanding things, the more it desires it. Q.E.D.

PROP. 27. *From this third kind of knowledge arises the highest possible peace of mind.*

Demonst. The highest virtue of the mind is to know God (Prop. 28, pt. 4), or to understand things by the third kind of knowledge (Prop. 25, pt. 5). This virtue is greater the more the mind knows things by this kind of knowledge (Prop. 24, pt. 5), and therefore he who knows things by this kind of knowledge passes to the highest human perfection, and consequently (Def. 2 of the Affects) is affected with the highest joy, which is accompanied with the idea of himself and his own virtue (Prop. 43, pt. 2); and therefore (Def. 25 of the Affects) from this kind of knowledge arises the highest possible peace of mind. Q.E.D.

PROP. 28. *The effort or the desire to know things by the third kind of knowledge cannot arise from the first kind, but may arise from the second kind of knowledge.*

Demonst. This proposition is self-evident; for everything that we clearly and distinctly understand, we understand either through itself or through something which is conceived through itself; or, in other words, ideas which are clear and distinct in us, or which are related to the third kind of knowledge (Schol. 2, Prop. 40, pt. 2), cannot follow from mutilated and confused ideas, which (by the same scholium) are related to the first kind of knowledge, but from adequate ideas, that is to say (by the same scholium), from the second and third kinds of knowledge. Therefore (Def. 1 of the Affects) the desire of knowing things by the third kind of knowledge cannot arise from the first kind, but may arise from the second. Q.E.D.

PROP. 29. *Everything which the mind understands under the form of eternity, it understands not because it conceives the present actual existence of the body, but because it conceives the essence of the body under the form of eternity.*

Demonst. In so far as the mind conceives the present existence of its body does it conceive duration which can be determined in time, and so far only has it the power of conceiving things in relation to time (Prop. 21, pt. 5, and Prop. 26, pt. 2). But eternity cannot be manifested through duration (Def. 8, pt. 1), and its explanation; therefore the mind so far has not the power of conceiving things under the form of eternity; but because it is the nature of reason to conceive things under the form of eternity (Corol. 2, Prop. 44, pt. 2), and because it also pertains to the nature of the mind to conceive the essence of the body under the form of eternity (Prop. 23, pt. 5), and excepting these two things nothing else pertains to the nature of the mind (Prop. 13, pt. 2), therefore this power of conceiving things under the form of eternity does not pertain to the mind except in so far as it conceives the essence of the body under the form of eternity. Q.E.D.

Schol. Things are conceived by us as actual in two ways; either in so far as we conceive them to exist with relation to a fixed time and place, or in so far as we conceive them to be contained in God, and to follow from the necessity of the divine nature. But those things which are conceived in this second way as true or real we conceive under the form of eternity, and their ideas involve the eternal and infinite essence of God, as we have shown in Prop. 45, pt. 2, to the scholium of which proposition the reader is also referred.

PROP. 30. *Our mind, in so far as it knows itself and the body under the form of eternity, necessarily has a knowledge of God, and knows that it is in God and is conceived through Him.*

Demonst. Eternity is the very essence of God, in so far as that essence involves necessary existence (Def. 8, pt. 1). To conceive things therefore under the form of eternity, is to conceive them in so far as they are conceived through the essence of God as actually existing things, or in so far as through the essence of God they involve existence. Therefore our mind, in so far as it conceives itself and its body under the form of eternity, necessarily has a knowledge of God, and knows, &c. Q.E.D.

PROP. 31. *The third kind of knowledge depends upon the mind as its formal cause, in so far as the mind itself is eternal.*

Demonst. The mind conceives nothing under the form of eternity, unless in so far as it conceives the essence of its body under the form of eternity (Prop. 29, pt. 5), that is to say (Props. 21 and 23, pt. 5), unless in so far as it is eternal. Therefore (Prop. 30, pt. 5) in so far as the mind is eternal it has a knowledge of God, which is necessarily adequate (Prop. 46, pt. 2), and therefore in so far as it is eternal it is fitted to know all those things which can follow from this knowledge of God (Prop. 40, pt. 2), that is to say it is fitted to know things by the third kind of knowledge (see the definition of this kind of knowledge in Schol. 2, Prop. 40, pt. 2), of which (Def. 1, pt. 3), in so far as the mind is eternal, it is the adequate or formal cause. Q.E.D.

Schol. As each person therefore becomes stronger in this kind of knowledge, the more is he conscious of himself and of God; that is to say, the more perfect and the happier he is, a truth which will still more clearly appear from what follows. Here, however, it is to be observed, that although we are now certain that the mind is eternal in so far as it conceives things under the form of eternity, yet, in order that what we wish to prove may be more easily explained and better understood, we shall consider the mind, as we have hitherto done, as if it had just begun to be, and had just begun to understand things under the form of eternity. This we can do without any risk of error, provided only we are careful to conclude nothing except from clear premises.

PROP. 32. *We delight in whatever we understand by the third kind of knowledge, and our delight is accompanied with the idea of God as its cause.*

Demonst. From this kind of knowledge arises the highest possible peace of mind, that is to say (Def. 25 of the Affects), the highest joy, attended moreover with the idea of one's self (Prop. 27, pt. 5), and consequently (Prop. 30, pt. 5) attended with the idea of God as its cause. Q.E.D.

Corol. From the third kind of knowledge necessarily springs the intellectual love of God. —For from this kind of knowledge arises (Prop. 32, pt. 5) joy attended with the idea of God as its cause, that is to say (Def. 6 of the Affects), the love of God, not in so far as we imagine Him as present (Prop. 29, pt. 5), but in so far as we understand that He is eternal; and that is what I call the intellectual love of God.

PROP. 33. *The intellectual love of God which arises from the third kind of knowledge is eternal.*

Demonst. The third kind of knowledge (Prop. 31, pt. 5, and Ax. 3, pt. 1) is eternal, and therefore (by the same axiom) the love which springs from it is necessarily eternal. Q.E.D.

Schol. Although this love to God has no beginning (Prop. 33, pt. 5), it nevertheless has all the perfections of love, just as if it had originated;—as we supposed in the corollary of Prop. 32, pt. 5. Nor is there here any difference, excepting that the mind has eternally possessed these same perfections which we imagined as now accruing to it, and has possessed them with the accompanying idea of God as the eternal cause. And if joy consist in the passage to a greater perfection, blessedness must indeed consist in this, that the mind is endowed with perfection itself.

PROP. 34. *The mind is subject to affects which are related to passions only so long as the body exists.*

Demonst. An imagination is an idea by which the mind contemplates any object as present (see its definition in Schol. Prop. 17, pt. 2). This idea nevertheless indicates the present constitution of the human body rather than the nature of the external object (Corol. 2, Prop. 16, pt. 2). An affect, therefore (by the general definition of the Affects), is an imagination in so far as it indicates the present constitution of the body, and therefore (Prop. 21, pt. 5) the mind, only so long as the body exists, is subject to affects which are related to passions. Q.E.D.

Corol. Hence it follows that no love except intellectual love is eternal.

Schol. If we look at the common opinion of men, we shall see that they are indeed conscious of the eternity of their minds, but they confound it with duration, and attribute it to imagination or memory, which they believe remain after death.

PROP. 35. *God loves Himself with an infinite intellectual love.*

God is absolutely infinite (Def. 6, pt. 1) that is to say (Def. 6, pt. 2), the nature of God delights in infinite perfection accompanied (Prop. 3, pt. 2) with the idea of Himself, that is to say (Prop. 11, and Def. 1, pt. 1), with the idea of Himself as cause, and this is what, in Corol. Prop. 32, pt. 5, we have called intellectual love.

Prop. 36. *The intellectual love of the mind towards God is the very love with which He loves Himself, not in so far as He is infinite, but in so far as He can be manifested through the essence of the human mind, considered under the form of eternity; that is to say, the intellectual love of the mind towards God is part of the infinite love with which God loves Himself.*

Demonst. This love of the mind must be related to the actions of the mind (Corol. Prop. 32, pt. 5, and Prop. 3, pt. 3), and it is therefore an action by which the mind contemplates itself; and which is accompanied with the idea of God as cause (Prop. 32, pt. 5, with the Corol.); that is to say (Corol. Prop. 25, pt. 1, and Corol. Prop. 11, pt. 2), it is an action by which God, in so far as He can be manifested through the human mind, contemplates Himself, the action being accompanied with the idea of Himself; and therefore (Prop. 35, pt. 5), this love of the mind is part of the infinite love with which God loves Himself. Q.E.D.

Corol. Hence it follows that God, in so far as He loves Himself, loves men, and consequently that the love of God towards men and the intellectual love of the mind towards God are one and the same thing.

Schol. Hence we clearly understand that our salvation, or blessedness, or liberty consists in a constant and eternal love towards God, or in the love of God towards men. This love or blessedness is called Glory in the sacred writings, and not without reason. For whether it be related to God or to the mind, it may properly be called repose of mind, which (Defs. 25 and 30 of the Affects) is, in truth, not distinguished from glory. For in so far as it is related to God, it is (Prop. 35, pt. 5) joy (granting that it is allowable to use this word), accompanied with the idea of Himself, and it is the same thing when it is related to the mind (Prop. 27, pt. 5). Again, since the essence of our mind consists in knowledge alone, whose beginning and foundation is God (Prop. 15, pt. 1, and Schol. Prop. 47, pt. 2), it is clear to us in what manner and by what method our mind, with regard both to essence and existence, follows from the divine nature, and continually depends upon God. I thought it worth while for me to notice this here, in order that I might show, by this example, what that knowledge of individual objects which I have called intuitive or of the third kind (Schol. 2, Prop. 40, pt. 2) is able to do, and how much more potent it is than the universal knowledge, which I have called knowledge of the

second kind. For although I have shown generally in the First Part that all things, and consequently also the human mind, depend upon God both with regard to existence and essence, yet that demonstration, although legitimate, and placed beyond the possibility of a doubt, does not, nevertheless, so affect our mind as a proof from the essence itself of any individual object which we say depends upon God.

Prop. 37. *There is nothing in nature which is contrary to this intellectual love, or which can negate it.*

This intellectual love necessarily follows from the nature of the mind, in so far as it is considered, through the nature of God, as an eternal truth (Props. 33 and 29, pt. 5). If there were anything, therefore, contrary to this love, it would be contrary to the truth, and consequently whatever might be able to negate this love would be able to make the true false, which (as is self-evident) is absurd. There exists, therefore, nothing in nature, &c. Q.E.D.

Schol. The axiom of the Fourth Part refers only to individual objects, in so far as they are considered in relation to a fixed time and place. This, I believe, no one can doubt.

Prop. 38. *The more objects the mind understands by the second and third kinds of knowledge, the less it suffers from those affects which are evil, and the less it fears death.*

Demonst. The essence of the mind consists in knowledge (Prop. 11, pt. 2). The more things, therefore, the mind knows by the second and third kinds of knowledge, the greater is that part which abides (Props. 29 and 23, pt. 5), and consequently (Prop. 37, pt. 5) the greater is that part which is not touched by affects which are contrary to our nature, that is to say (Prop. 30, pt. 4), which are evil. The more things, therefore, the mind understands by the second and third kinds of knowledge, the greater is that part which remains unharmed, and the less consequently does it suffer from the affects.

Schol. We are thus enabled to understand that which I touched upon in Schol. Prop. 39, pt. 4, and which I promised to explain in this part, namely, that death is by so much the less injurious to us as the clear and distinct knowledge of the mind is greater, and consequently as the mind loves God more. Again, since (Prop. 27, pt. 5) from the third kind of knowledge there arises the highest possible peace, it follows that it is possible for the human mind to be of such a nature that that part of it which we have shown perishes with its body (Prop. 21, pt. 5), in comparison with the part of it which remains, is of no consequence. But more fully upon this subject presently.

PROP. 39.   *He who possesses a body fit for many things possesses a mind of which the greater part is eternal.*

Demonst.   He who possesses a body fitted for doing many things is least of all agitated by those affects which are evil (Prop. 38, pt. 4), that is to say (Prop. 30, pt. 4), by affects which are contrary to our nature, and therefore (Prop. 10, pt. 5) he possesses the power of arranging and connecting the affections of the body according to the order of the intellect, and consequently (Prop. 14, pt. 5) of causing all the affections of the body to be related to the idea of God (Prop. 15, pt. 5); in consequence of which he is affected with a love to God, which (Prop. 16, pt. 5) must occupy or form the greatest part of his mind, and therefore (Prop. 33, pt. 5) he possesses a mind of which the greatest part is eternal.

Schol.   Inasmuch as human bodies are fit for many things, we cannot doubt the possibility of their possessing such a nature that they may be related to minds which have a large knowledge of themselves and of God, and whose greatest or principal part is eternal, so that they scarcely fear death. To understand this more clearly, it is to be here considered that we live in constant change, and that according as we change for the better or the worse we are called happy or unhappy. For he who passes from infancy or childhood to death is called unhappy, and, on the other hand, we consider ourselves happy if we can pass through the whole period of life with a sound mind in a sound body. Moreover he who, like an infant or child, possesses a body fit for very few things, and almost altogether dependent on external causes, has a mind which, considered in itself alone, is almost entirely unconscious of itself, of God, and of objects. On the other hand, he who possesses a body fit for many things possesses a mind which, considered in itself alone, is largely conscious of itself, of God, and of objects. In this life, therefore, it is our chief endeavour to change the body of infancy, so far as its nature permits and is conducive thereto, into another body which is fitted for many things, and which is related to a mind conscious as much as possible of itself,

of God, and of objects; so that everything which is related to its memory or imagination in comparison with the intellect is scarcely of any moment, as I have already said in the scholium of the preceding proposition.

PROP. 40.   *The more perfection a thing possesses the more it acts and the less it suffers, and conversely the more it acts the more perfect it is.*

Demonst.   The more perfect a thing is, the more reality it possesses (Def. 6, pt. 2), and consequently (Prop. 3, pt. 3, with the Schol.) the more it acts and the less it suffers. Inversely also it may be demonstrated in the same way that the more a thing acts the more perfect it is.   Q.E.D.

Corol.   Hence it follows that that part of the mind which abides, whether great or small, is more perfect than the other part. For the part of the mind which is eternal (Props. 23 and 29 pt. 5) is the intellect, through which alone we are said to act (Prop. 3, pt. 3), but that part which, as we have shown, perishes, is the imagination itself (Prop. 21, pt. 5), through which alone we are said to suffer (Prop. 3, pt. 3, and the general definition of the affects). Therefore (Prop. 40, pt. 5) that part which abides, whether great or small, is more perfect than the latter.   Q.E.D.

Schol.   These are the things I proposed to prove concerning the mind, in so far as it is considered without relation to the existence of the body, and from these, taken together with Prop. 21, pt. 1, and other propositions, it is evident that our mind, in so far as it understands, is an eternal mode of thought, which is determined by another eternal mode of thought, and this again by another, and so on *ad infinitum*, so that all taken together form the eternal and infinite intellect of God.

PROP. 41.   *Even if we did not know that our mind is eternal, we should still consider as of primary importance Piety and Religion, and absolutely everything which in the Fourth Part we have shown to be related to strength of mind and generosity.*

Demonst.   The primary and sole foundation of virtue or of the proper conduct of life (by Corol. Prop. 22, and Prop. 24, pt. 4) is to seek our own profit. But in order to determine what reason prescribes as profitable, we had no regard to the eternity of the mind, which we did not recognise till we came to the Fifth Part. Therefore, although we were at that time ignorant that the mind is eternal, we considered as of primary importance those things which we have shown are related to strength of mind and generosity; and therefore, even if we were now ignorant of the eternity of the mind, we should consider those commands of reason as of primary importance. Q.E.D.

Schol. The creed of the multitude seems to be different from this; for most persons seem to believe that they are free in so far as it is allowed them to obey their lusts, and that they give up a portion of their rights, in so far as they are bound to live according to the commands of divine law. Piety, therefore, and religion, and absolutely all those things that are related to greatness of soul, they believe to be burdens which they hope to be able to lay aside after death; hoping also to receive some reward for their bondage, that is to say, for their piety and religion. It is not merely this hope, however, but also and chiefly fear of dreadful punishments after death, by which they are induced to live according to the commands of divine law, that is to say, as far as their feebleness and impotent mind will permit; and if this hope and fear were not present to them, but if they, on the contrary, believed that minds perish with the body, and that there is no prolongation of life for miserable creatures exhausted with the burden of their piety, they would return to ways of their own liking; they would prefer to let everything be controlled by their own passions, and to obey fortune rather than themselves.

This seems to me as absurd as if a man, because he does not believe that he will be able to feed his body with good food to all eternity, should desire to satiate himself with poisonous and deadly drugs; or as if, because he sees that the mind is not eternal or immortal, he should therefore prefer to be mad and to live without reason,—absurdities so great that they scarcely deserve to be repeated.

PROP. 42. *Blessedness is not the reward of virtue, but is virtue itself; nor do we delight in blessedness because we restrain our lusts; but, on the contrary, because we delight in it, therefore are we able to restrain them.*

Demonst. Blessedness consists in love towards God (Prop. 36, pt. 5, and its Schol.), which arises from the third kind of knowledge (Corol. Prop. 32, pt. 5), and this love, therefore (Props. 59 and 3, pt. 3), must be related to the mind in so far as it acts. Blessedness, therefore (Def. 8, pt. 4), is virtue itself, which was the first thing to be proved. Again, the more the mind delights in this divine love or blessedness, the more it understands (Prop. 32, pt. 5), that is to say (Corol. Prop. 3, pt. 5), the greater is the power it has over its affects, and (Prop. 38, pt. 5) the less it suffers from affects which are evil. Therefore, it is because the mind delights in this divine love or blessedness that it possesses the power of restraining the lusts; and because the power of man to restrain the affects is in the intellect alone, no one, therefore, delights in blessedness because he has restrained his affects, but, on the contrary, the power of restraining his lusts springs from blessedness itself. Q.E.D.

Schol. I have finished everything I wished to explain concerning the power of the mind over the affects and concerning its liberty. From what has been said we see what is the strength of the wise man, and how much he surpasses the ignorant who is driven forward by lust alone. For the ignorant man is not only agitated by external causes in many ways, and never enjoys true peace of soul, but lives also ignorant, as it were, both of God and of things, and as soon as he ceases to suffer ceases also to be. On the other hand, the wise man, in so far as he is considered as such, is scarcely ever moved in his mind, but, being conscious by a certain eternal necessity of himself, of God, and of things, never ceases to be, and always enjoys true peace of soul. If the way which, as I have shown, leads hither seem very difficult, it can nevertheless be found. It must indeed be difficult since it is so seldom discovered; for if salvation lay ready to hand and could be discovered without great labour, how could it be possible that it should be neglected almost by everybody? But all noble things are as difficult as they are rare.

THE GREAT IDEAS, Volumes 2 and 3

·····················

ANGEL

ANIMAL

ARISTOCRACY

ART

ASTRONOMY

BEAUTY

BEING

CAUSE

CHANCE

CHANGE

CITIZEN

CONSTITUTION

COURAGE

CUSTOM AND
  CONVENTION

DEFINITION

DEMOCRACY

DESIRE

DIALECTIC

DUTY

EDUCATION

ELEMENT

EMOTION

ETERNITY

EVOLUTION

EXPERIENCE

FAMILY

FATE

FORM

GOD

GOOD AND EVIL

GOVERNMENT

HABIT

HAPPINESS

HISTORY

HONOR

HYPOTHESIS

IDEA

IMMORTALITY

INDUCTION

INFINITY

JUDGMENT

JUSTICE

KNOWLEDGE

LABOR

LANGUAGE

LAW

LIBERTY

LIFE AND DEATH

LOGIC

LOVE

MAN

MATHEMATICS